The Ethical Life

The Ethical Life

Fundamental Readings in Ethics and Moral Problems

Sixth Edition

RUSS SHAFER-LANDAU
University of Wisconsin-Madison

OXFORD
UNIVERSITY PRESS

Oxford University Press is a department of the University of Oxford.
It furthers the University's objective of excellence in research, scholarship,
and education by publishing worldwide. Oxford is a registered trade mark
of Oxford University Press in the UK and in certain other countries.

Published in the United States of America by Oxford University Press
198 Madison Avenue, New York, NY 10016, United States of America.

For titles covered by Section 112 of the US Higher Education Opportunity
Act, please visit www.oup.com/us/he for the latest information about
pricing and alternate formats.

CIP data is on file at the Library of Congress.
Library of Congress Control Number: 2023935119
ISBN 9780197697627

Printed by Quad/Graphics, Inc., Mexico

CONTENTS

PART IV Moral Problems

PREFACE

B rief yet thorough, *The Ethical Life: Fundamental Readings in Ethics and Moral Problems* is a collection of original writings in ethics. Its four parts—The Good Life, Normative Ethics, Metaethics, and Moral Problems—serve to introduce readers to each of the major branches of moral philosophy, with readings that have been carefully selected for their engaging style and their accessibility. This book can be usefully read on its own, and is an ideal way to acquaint students with the major themes of moral philosophy through a large selection of primary source material.

Changes to the Sixth Edition

This edition of *The Ethical Life* contains twelve new selections and two new sections. The changes all appear in Parts III and IV. Part III now includes a piece, commissioned from Diane Jeske, on the pros and cons of cultural relativism. Part IV now includes a new section on sex and gender, with pieces by Christin Scarlett Milloy, Kathleen Stock, and Sophie-Grace Chappell, and another new section on genetic engineering, with pieces by Michael Sandel and Julian Savulescu. A selection by Jason Brennan now rounds out the Poverty and Hunger section; an article commissioned from Javier Hidalgo is a new entry in the Immigration section; one from Nick Zangwill appears in the section on Animals; by popular demand, Michael Huemer's article on the drug laws returns to the section on Drugs. Finally, the section on The Legacy of Racism now includes an article on reparations by Chandran Kukathas and Peggy McIntosh's classic piece on white privilege.

Input from students, instructors and reviewers, plus a mandate to keep the book to the length of previous editions, has also led to having to say goodbye to several pieces from the last edition, many of which are personal favorites of mine. With some sadness, the following articles have been deleted for this edition: Gilbert Harman, "Ethics and Observation"; Mary Midgley, "Trying Out One's New Sword"; Michael Huemer, "Is There a Right to Immigrate?"; Peter Carruthers, "Against the Moral Standing of Animals"; Elizabeth Anderson, "The Future of Racial Integration"; Douglas Husak, "In Favor of Drug Legalization."

Digital Resources and Oxford Learning Link

Oxford University Press offers a variety of digital solutions that:

- Engage your students in the required reading
- Make assigned content available on the first day of class
- Provide the required resources available at the lowest cost possible

Inclusive Access

Your institution may already have an Inclusive Access (IA) program in place in which students pay for their course materials through their course registration. You can log in to the program here: https://pages.oup.com/he/us/oup-inclusiveaccess.

Through IA, rather than relying on individual student purchases, digital products are delivered directly to an entire class of students through their LMS (Learning Management System) at the most affordable price, increasing the use of our products.

Our partnerships with major higher education bookstore retailers and e-learning delivery leaders make it possible for students to easily and quickly access affordable content on the first day of class.

With Inclusive Access, you can:

- Provide students with course material on **Day One**
- Make course material **more affordable**—students **save as much as 70%**
- **Increase engagement** with immersive, engaging digital content
- **Enjoy academic freedom**—virtually any content can be adopted for use in Inclusive Access
- **Improve student success and retention** with analytical tools and insights

How Does It Work?

All students are given access to digital course materials on day one of classes through your school's Learning Management System. For more information, please visit https://pages.oup.com/he/us/oup-inclusiveaccess.

Direct to Student purchasing:

Now available! Students can purchase their course materials directly from OUP at the lowest retail price available. Please visit https://global.oup.com/ushe/?cc=us&lang=en. Search for the book in use by author name or book title.

E-book solutions for students:

OUP partners with the largest e-book providers so that students have access to course content anytime, anywhere.

Oxford University Press philosophy titles are available through major publishing e-book vendors:

Perusall

Perusall is a collaborative reading and learning platform that prepares students for class. The platform incorporates a unique e-book reader with social annotation tools that motivate students to actively participate in their learning, come to class prepared, and become more engaged with the course content you assign. For instructors, Perusall will help you teach more effectively, understand student misconceptions prior to class, introduce active learning strategies, and save time. Find out more at perusall.com.

RedShelf

As one of the nation's leading edtech companies, RedShelf has helped thousands of colleges, businesses, and publishers transition effortlessly from traditional print to more affordable, efficient digital textbooks and learning content.

Offering a vast catalog of titles on our award-winning eReader, plus an end-to-end Content Delivery System to streamline every step in the distribution process, RedShelf is a premier e-book partner.

Award-Winning eReader

All of the digital books are delivered on the award-winning RedShelf eReader, packed with built-in study tools including highlighting, definitions, text-to-speech, flashcards, note-sharing, and more. Please visit https://www.about.redshelf.com/home.

VitalSource

VitalSource is a leading authority in digital course materials, e-Textbooks, and student savings. Bookshelf® by VitalSource is the world's leading eReader, preferred by thousands of institutions and millions of students in 240+ countries and territories for reading, studying and succeeding. Partnering with publishers and institutions since 1994, VitalSource has the most extensive academic digital content catalog available and are at the forefront in setting privacy and security standards to protect learners around the world.

Features include: online/offline access, text to speech tool, study tools (such as highlighting, flashcard creation, notes, etc.). Please go to: https://www.vitalsource.com/

Oxford Learning Link

Oxford Learning Link delivers a wealth of engaging digital learning tools and resources to help both instructors and students get the most of their Oxford University Press title. Students can access self-study resources and instructors can view instructor resources at **https://learninglink.oup.com/access/shafer-landau-el6e**

Enhanced E-book

Included in Oxford Learning Link, Oxford's Enhanced e-books combine high-quality text content with a rich assortment of integrated multimedia and practice questions to deliver a more engaging and interactive learning experience.

The Enhanced e-book version of *The Ethical Life* is available via Red-Shelf, VitalSource, Perusall, and other leading higher education e-book vendors.

Oxford Learning Link for *The Ethical Life* includes the following resources.

Instructor Resources

- **Test Bank**—over 150 test questions in multiple choice, short answer, and essay formats
- **Instructor's Manual**—includes learning objectives, chapter outlines, lecture suggestions, class activity suggestions, issues for discussion, video resources, and Internet resources
- **Lecture PowerPoints**—presentations for course instruction, enabling instructors and/or lecturers to spend less time preparing class materials and more time with students

Student Resources

- **Enhanced e-book**—contains section-level practice quizzes, topical videos, and chapter summaries
- **Chapter Quizzes**—assignable multiple-choice questions to evaluate chapter comprehension
- **Video Quizzes**—short assessments capturing students' understanding and application of key concepts
- **Learning Objectives and Key Concepts**—to guide study and reinforce reading comprehension
- **Web Activities**—for thematic chapters and country profiles, suggested activities to familiarize students with today's major comparative politics sources and databases

Acknowledgments

It has been a lot of fun putting this book together, but it hasn't always been an easy thing to do. By far the most difficult aspect of the project was the winnowing. Ethics is so large a field, with so much that is provocative and interesting within it, yet books must have their page limits, and those limits often forced me to leave a prized piece behind. It has been a real challenge to offer a representative sampling of subject matter and viewpoints within a book of this size. To the extent that I have met with any success, it is owing in large part to the helpful suggestions and kind critical advice I have received from the following philosophers: Kristofer Arca at Miami Dade College, Ben Almassi at College of Lake County, Fidel Arnecillo at CSU-San Bernardino, Ralph Baergen at Idaho State University, Jeffrey Brand-Ballard at George Washington University, Patrick Martin Breen at the College of Staten Island, Adam Briggle at University of North Texas, David Burris at Arizona Western College, Tom Carson at Loyola University Chicago, Charles Comer at Harrisburg Area Community College, Christian Coons at Bowling Green State University, Richard DeGeorge at the University of Kansas, Neil Delaney at the University of Notre Dame, David Detmer at Purdue University Calumet, Tyler Doggett at the University of Vermont, Robert M. Farley at Hillsborough Community College, Douglas Fishel at Metropolitan Community College, Andrew Fitz-Gibbon at SUNY Cortland, Amber George at Le Moyne College, Deke Gould at Syracuse University, Christopher Grau at Clemson University, Craig Hanks at Texas State University, Ataollah Hashemi at Saint Louis University, Richard Haynes at the University of Florida, Darren Hibbs at Nova Southeastern University, Kelly Heuer at Georgetown University, Richard Hine at the University of Connecticut, John Holder at Pensacola State, John Huss at the University of Akron, Clark Hutton at Volunteer State Community College, Henry Imler at Moberly Area Community College, Phil Jenkins at Marywood University, Carla Johnson at St. Cloud State University, Keith Korcz at the University of Louisiana at Lafayette, Jacob Krch at University of Wisconsin-Madison, Mark LeBar at Ohio University, Richard Lee at the University of Arkansas, Hilde Lindeman at Michigan State University, Patrick Linden at NYU Polytechnic, Jessica Logue at the University of Portland, Sarah Lublink at Florida Southwestern State College, Eugene Marshall at Wellesley College, Michael McKenna at Florida State University, Brian Merrill at Brigham Young University-Idaho, John Messerly at Shoreline Community College, Christian Miller at Wake Forest University, Richard Momeyer at Miami University of Ohio, Michelle Moon at CSU-Channel Islands, Jennifer Morton at CUNY, Mark Murphy at Georgetown University, Nathan Nobis at Morehouse College, Aleksandr Pjevalica at University of Texas-El Paso, David Pereplyotchik at Baruch College, Jamie Phillips at Clarion University of Pennsylvania, Aleksandar Pjevalica at the University of Texas at El Paso, Philip Robbins at the University of Missouri, Nathan Rockwood at Virginia Tech, Dave Schmidtz at the University of Arizona, David Shoemaker at Tulane University, David Sobel at Syracuse University, Daniel Star at Boston University, Stephen Sullivan at Edinboro University, Timothy A. Torgerson at the University of Wisconsin-Superior, Mark van Roojen at the University of Nebraska, Lincoln, Paul Wagner at the University of Houston Clear Lake, Brian Wagoner at Davis and Elkins College, Kit Wellman at Washington University in St. Louis, John Weyls at the University of Akron, Jason Zinser at the University of Florida, and Christopher Zurn at the University of Kentucky. I am very grateful for their assistance. Finally, the work for previous editions' ancillary materials were undertaken by my stellar research assistants Justin Horn, Ben Schwan, and Emma Prendergast. The ancillary materials for this edition were done by Stephanie Hoffmann and Lukas Myers. I am very grateful for their dedicated efforts in making these first-rate resources.

R.S.L.
Madison, Wisconsin

A NOTE ON THE COMPANION VOLUME

This collection can be used as a self-standing introduction to ethics. It includes readings from each of the major divisions within moral philosophy. Together with the General Introduction, an Introduction to each reading, study questions, and all of the supplementary materials available at the book's website, I hope that readers are able to get a very good feel for just how interesting moral philosophy can be.

This collection is designed to serve as a natural partner to *Fundamentals of Ethics* (Oxford University Press), an introduction to moral philosophy that I have written. *Fundamentals* is a textbook, though I hope that it is a bit more lively than such a label implies. Both books offer coverage of the good life, the nature of duty and virtue, and the status of morality. The book you have in your hands also offers extensive coverage of many practical ethical problems, such as abortion, gun control, famine relief, etc. My hope, of course, is that the two books work neatly in tandem. The theories and positions I present and analyze in *Fundamentals* are here represented by some of their finest defenders. For those who are content to get the view directly from the source, this book should do. But if you would like a moral theory or an ethical position placed in a broader context, its main lines of argument laid out clearly and then critically assessed, then a dip into the companion volume might not be a bad idea.

I am very interested in hearing from readers who are willing to offer me their feedback, both positive and negative. Perhaps you have found some pieces dull or uninspired, or some that were especially exciting and challenging. For teachers who are familiar with this terrain, perhaps you've been disappointed at seeing a beloved piece gone missing, or would like to pass along the success of a given selection in sparking conversation. The easiest way to reach me is by email: *RussShaferlandau@gmail.com*. I'd be very pleased to receive your thoughts on how this book might be improved.

R. S. L.

The Ethical Life

INTRODUCTION

M oral philosophy, or ethics—I use the terms interchangeably—is, in its widest application, the study of what we should aspire to in our lives, and of how we should live.

There is no agreed-upon definition of morality, or even of philosophy. We can offer vague (very vague) platitudes, on the order of: philosophy is the love of wisdom; morality is the code that we should live by. It isn't clear to me that we can do *much* better than that. More instructive, I think, is to describe the specific fields within ethics. Through an understanding of these areas, we can better appreciate what moral philosophy is all about.

Nowadays, it is standard to distinguish four different areas of moral philosophy. And (surprise!) the four parts of this book correspond to each of these areas.

The first is known as *value theory*. This is the part of ethics that tries to determine what is valuable in and of itself, what a good life consists in. Is happiness, for instance, the ultimate good? Our first author, the Englishman John Stuart Mill, certainly think so. But others are skeptical. These include the late Harvard philosopher Robert Nozick. Perhaps what is most important is simply that we get what we want out of life—no matter what we want? That's what Chris Heathwood argues, in an article that he has written especially for this book. Yet others (represented here by Brad Hooker and Susan Wolf) reject this idea, and offer a variety of things (self-determination, moral virtue, happiness, loving relationships, etc.) that are said to be good in their own right.

In Part II we turn to that area of moral philosophy known as *normative ethics*. This large branch of philosophy is devoted to identifying the supreme principle(s) of right action. Many philosophers have sought just a single, fundamental principle that will unify the entire field, that will explain, for instance, why keeping your word, telling the truth, and helping the poor, are each morally right.

There are many important contenders that seek to fill this role. Consider, for instance, the Divine Command Theory, which tells us that acts are right just because God commands them. The first extended discussion of this view appears in Plato's dialogue *Euthyphro*, a large portion of which is presented here. Socrates, Plato's teacher and mouthpiece in this work, doesn't look too kindly on this view. Though Socrates assumes that there are many gods rather than one, and focuses on what makes actions pious rather than right, the central philosophical concerns about the Divine Command Theory that worry philosophers today are just the ones that Socrates advanced 2,400 years ago.

If God is not the ultimate source of morality, what is? Many have looked to nature—and human nature, in particular—to answer this question. *Natural law theory* takes this idea most seriously, and in one form or another (there are many varieties), it tries to show that moral action is a matter of acting in a way that respects our nature. Thomas Aquinas is the greatest of the natural lawyers; a small selection from his magnum opus, *Summa Theologica*, is reprinted here.

We next turn to *utilitarianism* (presented here by its most elegant defender, John Stuart Mill), which instructs us always to produce the greatest happiness for the greatest number. Utilitarianism focuses on an action's results—did it yield the greatest happiness of all available actions?—to determine its morality. The German philosopher Immanuel Kant, by contrast, tells us that results are morally irrelevant. Acts are right, he says, just because we can use their guiding principles consistently, without involving ourselves in contradiction. This isn't an easy thought to understand, but the basic idea is pretty simple. The essence of morality, Kant thinks, is fairness and justice. Immorality is a matter of making an exception of yourself, of living by rules that, in some sense, cannot possibly serve as the basis of everyone's actions.

Kant's view shares some features with another important normative ethic, the *social contract theory*. Though this theory was briefly discussed as far back as the ancient Greeks, it was not fully developed until well into the sixteenth century. It was brilliantly set forth in the work of

Thomas Hobbes, whose book *Leviathan* is excerpted here. The social contract theory tells us that morality is essentially a cooperative enterprise, and that the moral rules are those that self-interested people would obey on the condition that all others do so as well. Both Kantianism and the social contract theory take the natural ethical question—What if everyone did that?—quite seriously, and both use an answer to this question as a foundation of their normative ethical theory.

One thing that each of the theories canvassed so far has in common is that it tries to identify just a single, supreme moral rule that serves as the ultimate basis of all of our moral duties. But what if there is no such thing? British philosopher W. D. Ross took this question very seriously, and argued against the existence of any such moral rule in developing his ethic of *prima facie duties*. Prima facie duties are those that can be outweighed by competing duties. If Ross is right, *every* general duty is like this. We have a standing duty to keep our word, to do justice, to prevent harm, etc. But sometimes these duties conflict with one another. When they do, only one can be our "all-things-considered" duty, the thing we really must do on that particular occasion. The problem, though, is that there is no fixed ranking of the moral principles, and so it can be very difficult to know what to do when they conflict. Sometimes it is more important to prevent harm than to keep our word, but sometimes the reverse is true. The same is true of all conflicts of duty. While Ross thinks that we can know each prima facie moral duty just through careful reflection, things get much more complicated when it comes to knowing what our final, all-things-considered duty is in specific situations.

Aristotle is next. By many accounts, he is the greatest philosopher who ever lived. He developed the first elaborate version of *virtue ethics*, the view that places the virtues at center stage in ethical inquiry. Virtue theorists reject the idea of a single formula that can provide ethical advice for every occasion. They instead tell us to look to virtuous role models and imagine what they would do if they were in our shoes. It is tempting to begin ethical thinking by selecting a standard (such as the utilitarian standard), and saying that a virtue is a steady commitment that tends to produce right action, as measured by that standard. Virtue ethicists turn this on its head, and argue that we can understand the nature of right action only by first understanding the virtues.

Some of the most exciting recent work in normative ethics has been done by those who consider morality from the perspective of *feminist ethics*. This is best understood as an approach to ethics, rather than as a single view that is a direct competitor with the normative ethical theories we have briefly looked at thus far. In her selection here, philosopher Hilde Lindemann sketches the distinctive features of a feminist outlook on morality. These include an emphasis on taking the experience of women seriously when developing one's ethical ideas and ideals, and eliminating the many ways in which sexist assumptions creep into traditional philosophizing. Lindemann offers a variety of examples and interesting points as a way of introducing us to the large family of feminist approaches to ethics.

We have thus far canvassed those areas of ethics that deal with the good and the right, value theory, and normative ethics. But there is another part of ethics that takes a step back from these debates, and asks, more generally, about the *status* of moral views in both areas. Philosophers call this branch of moral theory *metaethics*, and it is the focus of Part III.

Metaethics studies such questions as these: Is morality just a convenient fiction? If not, can moral standards be true? Suppose they are: Does their truth depend on personal opinion, social consensus, God's commands, or something else? If there are genuine moral truths, how can we know them? And do they have any authority over us—is it always rational to be moral, or is it sometimes reasonable to take the immoral path?

I have divided the authors in this section into two camps—those who are skeptical of objective morality, and those who defend it. As I understand it, morality is objective just in case there are some moral standards that apply to us regardless of what any human being believes.

Opponents of moral objectivity get the first hearing. The Scottish Enlightenment thinker David Hume starts us off. His criticisms of reason's place in ethics have been extremely influential across the past two and a half centuries, and rightly so. Most of today's important critiques of moral objectivity have their ancestors in one or more of the arguments that Hume provided. Hume thought that if moral claims were objectively true, then we should be able to discover our moral duty just by thinking hard about it. But Hume argues that no amount of careful reasoning could do that. And therefore morality cannot be objective.

Hume did not seek to undermine ethics, but rather to offer a diagnosis of its true nature. J. L. Mackie seeks to go further, and to show that there are no moral truths. He argues that all of our moral thinking is based on an error. Mackie believes that moral thought starts from the view that morality is objective. He offers some important arguments to try to show that it isn't. He sees morality as a product of human insecurity and imagination, with no real authority over us. If we all do assume that morality is objective, and if Mackie is right about its being (at best) a useful fiction, then morality really is bankrupt.

Another form of doubt about moral objectivity is given by *cultural relativism*—the view, roughly, that morality is like the law in being a product of human endorsement, legitimately differing from culture to culture, with no objective moral standards to use as a measure for the legitimacy of any given cultural code. This new piece, like the two that follow, was written especially for this book. After helpfully distinguishing two forms of cultural relativism, and identifying some of the reasons that many find it attractive, Jeske proceeds to argue that it's not all it's cracked up to be. Specifically, it provides a poor basis for supporting tolerance, and fails to make good sense of how and why members of different cultures disagree with one another about moral matters.

We then move from a critique of relativism to a positive case on behalf of ethical objectivism. David Enoch argues that almost all of us, whether we realize it or not, are committed to some form of objectivity about morality. He devises a number of tests to help us see the extent of this commitment. That we are committed to morality's objectivity does not prove that our commitments are correct. But we should assume that they are until such time as we have excellent reason to reject them. Enoch considers a number of arguments designed to show that morality is not in fact objective, and then offers his reasons for rejecting those critiques.

The section on metaethics concludes with a selection by Sarah McGrath, who neither criticizes nor defends the objectivity of morality, but rather takes us on a fascinating exploration of various issues connected with the possibility of moral knowledge. Many of us think that it's obvious that we have some such knowledge—for instance, that slavery and genocide are immoral, or that kindness and compassion are morally good. But how, if at all, can we gain such knowledge? And how might we respond to some powerful skeptical arguments that threaten the possibility of our ever knowing right from wrong? Read McGrath's piece for a nuanced and engaging look at these issues.

No philosopher sees his field in just the same way that others do. My take on what really matters in ethics is bound to be personal and, to some degree, not shared by my fellow practitioners. Still, I have aimed in this volume to respect standard divisions within this large field, and have tried to balance selections from classic works with some relatively unfamiliar material that strikes me as important and provocative.

Whether beginners or old pros, each of us improves our moral thinking by being exposed to a variety of viewpoints on the deep questions that interest us. The ideal philosophical introduction, therefore, would present at least the main competitors within the various subfields that make up ethics, thereby giving newcomers a taste of the different perspectives that have shaped debates within this rich area of philosophy. I hope that I have managed some success on this front, but in at least one case, it would have been clearly impossible to achieve this within a reasonable amount of space.

I am thinking here of the last and largest section of the book, Part IV, the one devoted to a variety of *moral problems*. There are far too many interesting moral conundrums to fit them all into a collection of this size. I hope that the topics on offer are compelling, but I recognize that many exciting subjects and insightful articles have been left behind. Short of greatly increasing the size of this collection, I see no way to avoid this, and must hope that the thirty-one offerings available here are of sufficient interest and importance to do what they are meant to do—inspire you to grapple with their puzzles, thought experiments, and arguments, and to appreciate a bit of the complexity of the moral issues that take center stage in this part of the book. What you have in this section (and all the others) is just a small sampling of possible positions and supporting arguments. The readings throughout this book are designed to whet your appetite, not to sate it.

There is no theoretical unity to this half of the volume. The authors here represent a variety of different theoretical approaches, and some, as you will see, do not argue directly from any normative theory at all.

This might be surprising, because a time-honored picture of how to argue about moral problems is to claim that you must first identify the correct normative theory, take note of the relevant nonmoral facts, and presto!—out comes your moral verdict. This way of arguing actually happens less often than you may think, which is why the more common term for this sort of moral philosophy—"applied ethics"—is a bit misleading. That label implies that all practical moral problems can all be solved in a top-down way, by first selecting the proper normative ethic, and then just "applying" it—as if that were a straightforward matter of cranking out its implications.

One reason that philosophers don't always proceed this way is because there is still huge disagreement about which normative ethic is the correct one. And so any philosopher who restricted her arguments to applying a single normative theory would be losing a good deal of her audience—specifically, the large segment of it that disagreed with her normative ethic. As a result, most philosophers who grapple with real-life moral problems begin not with the grand normative theories but rather with more concrete principles (keep your word, don't violate patient confidentiality, avoid imposing unnecessary pain, etc.) or examples that we are already expected to accept. Armed with these, the author then tries to show that a commitment to them implies some specific view about the problem at hand.

The topics covered in this last section are of the first importance: poverty and hunger, euthanasia, immigration, animal rights, environmental ethics, abortion, the death penalty, gun control, the legacy of racism, drugs, genetic engineering, and sexual morality. Are there other topics that deserve a place at the table? Absolutely. But these strike me as being worthy of our attention, and the pieces I have selected all present interesting sets of arguments that deserve careful scrutiny. Some of these pieces do represent pretty direct applications of the normative theories discussed in the second part of this book. In these cases, you can use the arguments contained here as a way of testing those normative theories. In other cases, as I mentioned above, the arguments will be theoretically more free-standing. In any event, I hope that there will be plenty to inspire your interest, curiosity, and, occasionally, your outrage. I have found that each of these reactions can be an excellent catalyst to serious philosophical thinking.

PART I

The Good Life

1

Hedonism

John Stuart Mill

John Stuart Mill (1806–1873) was one of the great hedonistic thinkers. In this excerpt from his long pamphlet *Utilitarianism* (1863), Mill
defends his complex version of hedonism. Sensitive to criticisms that it
counsels us to pursue a life of brutish pleasure, Mill distinguishes
between "higher and lower pleasures" and claims, famously, that it is
"better to be Socrates dissatisfied, than a fool satisfied." He also offers
here his much-discussed "proof" of hedonism, by drawing a parallel
between the evidence we have for something's being visible (that all of
us see it) and something's being desirable (that all of us desire it). He
also argues for the claim that we do and can desire nothing but pleasure,
and uses this conjecture as a way of defending the view that pleasure is
the only thing that is always worth pursuing for its own sake.

The creed which accepts, as the foundation of morals, Utility, or the
Greatest-happiness Principle, holds that actions are right in proportion as they tend to promote happiness, wrong as they tend to
produce the reverse of happiness. By happiness is intended pleasure and
the absence of pain; by unhappiness, pain and the privation of pleasure. To
give a clear view of the moral standard set up by the theory, much more
requires to be said; in particular, what things it includes in the ideas of pain
and pleasure, and to what extent this is left an open question. But these
supplementary explanations do not affect the theory of life on which this

theory of morality is grounded,—namely, that pleasure, and freedom from pain, are the only things desirable as ends; and that all desirable things (which are as numerous in the utilitarian as in any other scheme) are desirable either for the pleasure inherent in themselves, or as means to the promotion of pleasure and the prevention of pain.

Now, such a theory of life excites in many minds, and among them in some of the most estimable in feeling and purpose, inveterate dislike. To suppose that life has (as they express it) no higher end than pleasure,—no better and nobler object of desire and pursuit,—they designate as utterly mean and groveling; as a doctrine worthy only of swine, to whom the followers of Epicurus were, at a very early period, contemptuously likened: and modern holders of the doctrine are occasionally made the subject of equally polite comparisons by its German, French, and English assailants.

When thus attacked, the Epicureans have always answered, that it is not they, but their accusers, who represent human nature in a degrading light, since the accusation supposes human beings to be capable of no pleasures except those of which swine are capable. If this supposition were true, the charge could not be gainsaid, but would then be no longer an imputation; for, if the sources of pleasure were precisely the same to human beings and to swine, the rule of life which is good enough for the one would be good enough for the other. The comparison of the Epicurean life to that of beasts is felt as degrading, precisely because a beast's pleasures do not satisfy a human being's conceptions of happiness. Human beings have faculties more elevated than the animal appetites; and, when once made conscious of them, do not regard any thing as happiness which does not include their gratification. I do not, indeed, consider the Epicureans to have been by any means faultless in drawing out their scheme of consequences from the utilitarian principle. To do this in any sufficient manner, many Stoic as well as Christian elements require to be included. But there is no known Epicurean theory of life which does not assign to the pleasures of the intellect, of the feeling and imagination, and of the moral sentiments, a much higher value as pleasures than to those of mere sensation. It must be admitted, however, that utilitarian writers in general have placed the superiority of mental over bodily pleasures chiefly in the greater permanency, safety, uncostliness, &c., of the former,—that is, in their circumstantial advantages rather than in their intrinsic nature. And, on all these points, utilitarians have fully proved their case; but they might have taken the other, and, as it may be called, higher ground, with entire consistency. It is quite compatible with the principle of utility to recognize the fact, that some kinds of pleasure are more desirable and more valuable than others. It would be absurd, that while, in estimating all other things, quality is considered as well as quantity, the estimation of pleasures should be supposed to depend on quantity alone.

If I am asked what I mean by difference of quality in pleasures, or what makes one pleasure more valuable than another, merely as a pleasure, except its being greater in amount, there is but one possible answer. Of two pleasures, if there be one to which all or almost all who have experience of both give a decided preference, irrespective of any feeling of moral obligation to prefer it, that is the more desirable pleasure. If one of the two is, by those who are competently acquainted with both, placed so far above the other that they prefer it, even though knowing it to be attended with a greater amount of discontent, and would not resign it for any quantity of the other pleasure which their nature is capable of, we are justified in ascribing to the preferred enjoyment a superiority in quality, so far outweighing quantity, as to render it, in comparison, of small account.

Now, it is an unquestionable fact, that those who are equally acquainted with and equally capable of appreciating and enjoying both do give a most marked preference to the manner of existence which employs their higher faculties. Few human creatures would consent to be changed into any of the lower animals, for a promise of the fullest allowance of a beast's pleasures: no intelligent human being would consent to be a fool, no instructed person would be an ignoramus, no person of feeling and conscience would be selfish and base, even though they should be persuaded that the fool, the dunce, or the rascal is better satisfied with his lot than they are with theirs. They would not resign what they possess more than he for the most complete satisfaction of all the desires which they have in common with him. If they ever fancy they would, it is only in cases of unhappiness so extreme, that, to escape from it, they would exchange their lot for almost any other, however undesirable in their own eyes. A being of higher faculties requires more to make him happy, is capable probably of more acute suffering, and certainly accessible to it at more points, than one of an inferior type; but, in spite of these liabilities, he can never really wish to sink into what he feels to be a lower grade of existence. We may give what explanation we please of this unwillingness; we may attribute it to pride, a name which is given indiscriminately to some of the most and to some of the least estimable feelings of which mankind are capable; we may refer it to the love of liberty and personal independence,—an appeal to which was with the Stoics one of the most effective means for the inculcation of it;

to the love of power, or to the love of excitement, both of which do really enter into and contribute to it: but its most appropriate appellation is a sense of dignity, which all human beings possess in one form or other, and in some, though by no means in exact, proportion to their higher faculties, and which is so essential a part of the happiness of those in whom it is strong, that nothing which conflicts with it could be, otherwise than momentarily, an object of desire to them. Whoever supposes that this preference takes place at a sacrifice of happiness; that the superior being, in any thing like equal circumstances, is not happier than the inferior— confounds the two very different ideas of happiness and content. It is indisputable, that the being whose capacities of enjoyment are low has the greatest chance of having them fully satisfied; and a highly endowed being will always feel that any happiness which he can look for, as the world is constituted, is imperfect. But he can learn to bear its imperfections, if they are at all bearable; and they will not make him envy the being who is indeed unconscious of the imperfections, but only because he feels not at all the good which those imperfections qualify. It is better to be a human being dissatisfied, than a pig satisfied; better to be Socrates dissatisfied, than a fool satisfied. And if the fool or the pig are of a different opinion, it is because they only know their own side of the question. The other party to the comparison knows both sides.

It may be objected, that many who are capable of the higher pleasures, occasionally, under the influence of temptation, postpone them to the lower. But this is quite compatible with a full appreciation of the intrinsic superiority of the higher. Men often, from infirmity of character, make their election for the nearer good, though they know it to be the less valuable, and this no less when the choice is between two bodily pleasures than when it is between bodily and mental. They pursue sensual indulgences to the injury of health, though perfectly aware that health is the greater good. It may be further objected, that many who begin with youthful enthusiasm for everything noble, as they advance in years sink into indolence and selfishness. But I do not believe that those who undergo this very common change voluntarily choose the lower description of pleasures in preference to the higher. I believe, that, before they devote themselves exclusively to the one, they have already become incapable of the other. Capacity for the nobler feelings is in most natures a very tender plant, easily killed, not only by hostile influences, but by mere want of sustenance; and, in the majority of young persons, it speedily dies away if the occupations to which their position in life has devoted them, and the society into which it has thrown them, are not favorable to keeping that higher capacity in exercise. Men lose their high aspirations as they lose their intellectual tastes, because they have not time or opportunity for indulging them; and they addict themselves to inferior pleasures, not because they deliberately prefer them, but because they are either the only ones to which they have access, or the only ones which they are any longer capable of enjoying. It may be questioned whether any one, who has remained equally susceptible to both classes of pleasures, ever knowingly and calmly preferred the lower; though many in all ages have broken down in an ineffectual attempt to combine both.

From this verdict of the only competent judges, I apprehend there can be no appeal. On a question, which is the best worth having of two pleasures, or which of two modes of existence is the most grateful to the feelings, apart from its moral attributes and from its consequences, the judgment of those who are qualified by knowledge of both, or, if they differ, that of the majority among them, must be admitted as final. And there needs be the less hesitation to accept this judgment respecting the quality of pleasures, since there is no other tribunal to be referred to even on the question of quantity. What means are there of determining which is the acutest of two pains, or the intensest of two pleasurable sensations, except the general suffrage of those who are familiar with both? Neither pains nor pleasures are homogeneous, and pain is always heterogeneous with pleasure. What is there to decide whether a particular pleasure is worth purchasing at the cost of particular pain, except the feelings and judgment of the experienced? When, therefore, those feelings and judgment declare the pleasures derived from the higher faculties to be preferable in kind, apart from the question of intensity, to those of which the animal nature, disjoined from the higher faculties, is susceptible, they are entitled on this subject to the same regard. . . .

It has already been remarked, that questions of ultimate ends do not admit of proof, in the ordinary acceptation of the term. To be incapable of proof by reasoning is common to all first principles; to the first premises of our knowledge, as well as to those of our conduct. But the former, being matters of fact, may be the subject of a direct appeal to the faculties which judge of fact—namely, our senses, and our internal consciousness. Can an appeal be made to the same faculties on questions of practical ends? Or by what other faculty is cognisance taken of them?

Questions about ends are, in other words, questions of what things are desirable. The utilitarian doctrine is, that happiness is desirable, and the only thing desirable, as an end; all other things being only desirable as means to that end. What ought to be required of this doctrine—what conditions is it requisite that the doctrine should fulfil—to make good its claim to be believed?

The only proof capable of being given that an object is visible, is that people actually see it. The only proof that a sound is audible, is that people hear it: and so of the other sources of our experience. In like manner, I apprehend, the sole evidence it is possible to produce that anything is desirable, is that people do actually desire it. If the end which the utilitarian doctrine proposes to itself were not, in theory and in practice, acknowledged to be an end, nothing could ever convince any person that it was so. No reason can be given why the general happiness is desirable, except that each person, so far as he believes it to be attainable, desires his own happiness. This, however, being a fact, we have not only all the proof which the case admits of, but all which it is possible to require, that happiness is a good: that each person's happiness is a good to that person, and the general happiness, therefore, a good to the aggregate of all persons. Happiness has made out its title as one of the ends of conduct, and consequently one of the criteria of morality. But it has not, by this alone, proved itself to be the sole criterion. To do that, it would seem, by the same rule, necessary to show, not only that people desire happiness, but that they never desire anything else. Now it is palpable that they do desire things which, in common language, are decidedly distinguished from happiness. They desire, for example, virtue, and the absence of vice, no less really than pleasure and the absence of pain. The desire of virtue is not as universal, but it is as authentic a fact, as the desire of happiness. And hence the opponents of the utilitarian standard deem that they have a right to infer that there are other ends of human action besides happiness, and that happiness is not the standard of approbation and disapprobation.

But does the utilitarian doctrine deny that people desire virtue, or maintain that virtue is not a thing to be desired? The very reverse. It maintains not only that virtue is to be desired, but that it is to be desired disinterestedly, for itself. Whatever may be the opinion of utilitarian moralists as to the original conditions by which virtue is made virtue; however they may believe (as they do) that actions and dispositions are only virtuous because they promote another end than virtue; yet this being granted, and it having been decided, from considerations of this description, what is virtuous, they not only place virtue at the very head of the things which are good as means to the ultimate end, but they also recognise as a psychological fact the possibility of its being, to the individual, a good in itself, without looking to any end beyond it; and hold, that the mind is not in a right state, not in a state conformable to Utility, not in the state most conducive to the general happiness, unless it does love virtue in this manner—as a thing desirable in itself, even although, in the individual instance, it should not produce those other desirable consequences which it tends to produce, and on account of which it is held to be virtue. This opinion is not, in the smallest degree, a departure from the Happiness principle. The ingredients of happiness are very various, and each of them is desirable in itself, and not merely when considered as swelling an aggregate. The principle of utility does not mean that any given pleasure, as music, for instance, or any given exemption from pain, as for example health, is to be looked upon as means to a collective something termed happiness, and to be desired on that account. They are desired and desirable in and for themselves; besides being means, they are a part of the end. Virtue, according to the utilitarian doctrine, is not naturally and originally part of the end, but it is capable of becoming so; and in those who love it disinterestedly it has become so, and is desired and cherished, not as a means to happiness, but as a part of their happiness.

To illustrate this farther, we may remember that virtue is not the only thing, originally a means, and which if it were not a means to anything else, would be and remain indifferent, but which by association with what it is a means to, comes to be desired for itself, and that too with the utmost intensity. What, for example, shall we say of the love of money? There is nothing originally more desirable about money than about any heap of glittering pebbles. Its worth is solely that of the things which it will buy; the desires for other things than itself, which it is a means of gratifying. Yet the love of money is not only one of the strongest moving forces of human life, but money is, in many cases, desired in and for itself; the desire to possess it is often stronger than the desire to use it, and goes on increasing when all the desires which point to ends beyond it, to be compassed by it, are falling off. It may, then, be said truly, that money is desired not for the sake of an end, but as part of the end. From being a means to happiness, it has come to be itself a principal ingredient of the individual's conception of happiness. The same may be said of the majority of the great objects of human life—power, for example, or fame; except that to each of these there is a certain amount of immediate pleasure annexed, which has at least the semblance of being naturally inherent in them; a thing which cannot be said of money. Still, however, the strongest natural attraction, both of power and of fame, is the immense aid they give to the attainment of our other wishes; and it is the strong association thus generated between them and all our objects of desire, which gives to the direct desire of them the intensity it often assumes, so as in some characters to surpass in strength all other desires. In these cases the means have become a part of the end, and a more important part of it than any of the things which they are means to. What was once desired as an instrument for the attainment of happiness, has come to be desired for its own sake. In being desired for its own sake it is, however, desired as part of happiness. The person is made, or thinks he would be made, happy by its mere possession; and is made unhappy by failure to obtain it. The desire of it is not a different thing from the desire of happiness, any more than the love of music, or the desire of health. They are included in happiness. They are some of the elements of which the desire of happiness is made up. Happiness is not an abstract idea, but a concrete whole; and these are some of its parts. And the utilitarian standard sanctions and approves their being so. Life would be a poor thing, very ill provided with sources of happiness, if there were not this provision of nature, by which things originally indifferent, but conducive to, or otherwise associated with, the satisfaction of our primitive desires, become in themselves sources of pleasure more valuable than the primitive pleasures, both in permanency, in the space of human existence that they are capable of covering, and even in intensity.

Virtue, according to the utilitarian conception, is a good of this description. There was no original desire of it, or motive to it, save its conduciveness to pleasure, and especially to protection from pain. But through the association thus formed, it may be felt a good in itself, and desired as such with as great intensity as any other good; and with this difference between it and the love of money, of power, or of fame, that all of these may, and often do, render the individual noxious to the other members of the society to which he belongs, whereas there is nothing which makes him so much a blessing to them as the cultivation of the disinterested love of virtue. And consequently, the utilitarian standard, while it tolerates and approves those other acquired desires, up to the point beyond which they would be more injurious to the general happiness than promotive of it, enjoins and requires the cultivation of the love of virtue up to the greatest strength possible, as being above all things important to the general happiness.

It results from the preceding considerations, that there is in reality nothing desired except happiness. Whatever is desired otherwise than as a means to some end beyond itself, and ultimately to happiness, is desired as itself a part of happiness, and is not desired for itself until it has become so. Those who desire virtue for its own sake, desire it either because the consciousness of it is a pleasure, or because the consciousness of being without it is a pain, or for both reasons united; as in truth the pleasure and pain seldom exist separately, but almost always together, the same person feeling pleasure in the degree of virtue attained, and pain in not having attained more. If one of these gave him no pleasure, and the other no pain, he would not love or desire virtue, or would desire it only for the other benefits which it might produce to himself or to persons whom he cared for. We have now, then, an answer to the question, of what sort of proof the principle of utility is susceptible. If the opinion which I have now stated is psychologically true—if human nature is so constituted as to desire nothing which is not either a part of happiness or a means of happiness, we can have no other proof, and we require no other, that these are the only things desirable. If so, happiness is the sole end of human action, and the promotion of it the test by which to judge of all human conduct; from whence it necessarily follows that it must be the criterion of morality, since a part is included in the whole. . . .

John Stuart Mill: Hedonism

1. Mill claims that "Pleasure, and freedom from pain, are the only things desirable as ends." Are there any examples that can challenge this claim?
2. What does Mill propose as a standard to determine which kinds of pleasure are more valuable than others? Is this a plausible standard?
3. Mill states that it is "Better to be Socrates dissatisfied, than a fool satisfied." What reasons does he give for thinking this?
4. In order to show that an object is visible, it is enough to show that people actually see it. Mill claims, similarly, "The sole evidence it is possible to produce that anything is desirable, is that people do actually desire it." Are visibility and desirability similar in this way?
5. Mill claims that "Each person's happiness is a good to that person." He then concludes from this that "the general happiness" is therefore "a good to the aggregate of all persons." Is this a good argument?

6. According to Mill, "The ingredients of happiness are very various, and each of them is desirable in itself." Does this contradict his earlier claim, given in question 1?

7. At the beginning of this selection, Mill says that pleasure and the absence of pain are the only things desirable as ends. Toward the end he claims that "Happiness is the sole end of human action." Are happiness and pleasure the same thing?

2

The Experience Machine

Robert Nozick

In this brief selection from his book *Anarchy, State, and Utopia* (1974), the late Harvard philosopher Robert Nozick (1938–2002) invites us to contemplate a life in which we are placed within a very sophisticated machine that is capable of simulating whatever experiences we find most valuable. Such a life, Nozick argues, cannot be the best life for us, because it fails to make contact with reality. This is meant to show that the good life is not entirely a function of the quality of our inner experiences. Since hedonism measures our well-being in precisely this way, hedonism, says Nozick, must be mistaken.

... Suppose there were an experience machine that would give you any experience you desired. Superduper neuropsychologists could stimulate your brain so that you would think and feel you were writing a great novel, or making a friend, or reading an interesting book. All the time you would be floating in a tank, with electrodes attached to your brain. Should you plug into this machine for life, preprogramming your life's experiences? If you are worried about missing out on desirable experiences, we can suppose that business enterprises have researched thoroughly the lives of many others. You can pick and choose from their large library or smorgasbord of such experiences, selecting your life's experiences for, say, the next two years. After two years have passed, you will have ten minutes or ten hours out of the tank, to select the experiences of your *next* two years. Of course, while in the tank you won't know that you're there; you'll think it's all actually happening. Others can also plug in to have the experiences they want, so there's no need to stay unplugged to serve them. (Ignore problems such as who will service the machines if everybody plugs in.) Would you plug in? *What else can matter to us, other than how our lives feel from the inside?* Nor should you refrain because of the few moments of distress between the moment you've decided and the moment you're plugged. What's a few moments of distress compared to a lifetime of bliss (if that's what you choose), and why feel any distress at all if your decision is the best one?

What does matter to us in addition to our experiences? First, we want to do certain things, and not just have the experience of doing them. In the case of certain experiences, it is only because first we want to do the actions that we want the experiences of doing them or thinking we've done them. (But *why* do we want to do the activities rather than merely to experience them?) A second reason for not plugging in is that we want to be a certain way, to be a certain sort of person. Someone floating in a tank is an indeterminate blob. There is no answer to the question of what a person is like who has long been in the tank. Is he courageous, kind, intelligent, witty, loving? It's not merely that it's difficult to tell; there's no way he is. Plugging into the machine is a kind of suicide. It will seem to some, trapped by a picture, that nothing about what we are like can matter except as it gets reflected in our experiences. But should it be surprising that what we are is important to us? Why should we be concerned only with how our time is filled, but not with what we are?

Thirdly, plugging into an experience machine limits us to a man-made reality, to a world no deeper or more important than that which people can construct. There is no *actual* contact with any deeper reality, though the experience of it can be simulated. Many persons desire to leave themselves open to such contact and to a plumbing of deeper significance.[1] This clarifies

---

1. Traditional religious views differ on the point of contact with a transcendent reality. Some say that contact yields eternal bliss or Nirvana, but they have not distinguished this sufficiently from merely a very long run on the experience machine. Others think it is intrinsically desirable to do the will of a higher being which created us all, though presumably no one would think this if we discovered we had been created as an object of amusement by some superpowerful child from another galaxy or dimension. Still others imagine an eventual merging with a higher reality, leaving unclear its desirability, or where that merging leaves us.

the intensity of the conflict over psychoactive drugs, which some view as mere local experience machines, and others view as avenues to a deeper reality; what some view as equivalent to surrender to the experience machine, others view as following one of the reasons *not* to surrender!

We learn that something matters to us in addition to experience by imagining an experience machine and then realizing that we would not use it. We can continue to imagine a sequence of machines each designed to fill lacks suggested for the earlier machines. For example, since the experience machine doesn't meet our desire to *be* a certain way, imagine a transformation machine which transforms us into whatever sort of person we'd like to be (compatible with our staying us). Surely one would not use the transformation machine to become as one would wish, and thereupon plug into the experience machine![2] So something matters in addition to one's experiences *and* what one is like. Nor is the reason merely that one's experiences are unconnected with what one is like. For the experience machine might be limited to provide only experiences possible to the sort of person plugged in. Is it that we want to make a difference in the world? Consider then the result machine, which produces in the world any result you would produce and injects your vector input into any joint activity. We shall not pursue here the fascinating details of these or other machines. What is most disturbing about them is their living of our lives for us. Is it misguided to search for *particular* additional functions beyond the competence of machines to do for us? Perhaps what we desire is to live (an active verb) ourselves, in contact with reality. (And this, machines cannot do *for* us.) Without elaborating on the implications of this, which I believe connect surprisingly with issues about free will and causal accounts of knowledge, we need merely note the intricacy of the question of what matters *for people* other than their experiences. Until one finds a satisfactory answer, and determines that this answer does not also apply to animals, one cannot reasonably claim that only the felt experiences of animals limit what we may do to them.

---

2. Some wouldn't use the transformation machine at all; it seems like cheating. But the one-time use of the transformation machine would not remove all challenges; there would still be obstacles for the new us to overcome, a new plateau from which to strive even higher. And is this plateau any the less earned or deserved than that provided by genetic endowment and early childhood environment? But if the transformation machine could be used indefinitely often, so that we could accomplish anything by pushing a button to transform ourselves into someone who could do it easily, there would remain no limits we need to strain against or try to transcend. Would there be anything left to do? Do some theological views place God outside of time because an omniscient omnipotent being couldn't fill up his days?

Robert Nozick: The Experience Machine

1. Nozick suggests that most people would choose not to plug in to an "experience machine" if given the opportunity. Would you plug in? Why or why not?

2. Hedonists such as Epicurus and Mill claim that pleasure is the only thing worth pursuing for its own sake. If some people would choose not to plug in to the experience machine, does this show that hedonism is false?

3. One reason Nozick gives for not getting into the experience machine is that "We want to do certain things, and not just have the experience of doing them." Do some activities have value independent of the experiences they produce? If so, what is an example of such an activity?

4. Nozick claims that "Plugging into the machine is a kind of suicide." What does he mean by this? Do you think he is right?

3

Faring Well and Getting What You Want

Chris Heathwood

Chris Heathwood opens his contribution with a very helpful discussion that distinguishes a number of different concerns we may have when talking about the good life. When we speak of a good life, we may be referring to what it is that makes for a *morally* good life. Or we may be asking about how a person can manifest various nonmoral excellences, such as being a great athlete or musician. In asking about the good life, we might also be wondering about life's meaning, and how we can live a meaningful life (if we can). While these are all interesting topics for reflection, Heathwood focuses elsewhere: he wants to know what it is that, in and of itself, makes our lives go better. What, in other words, is intrinsically good for us?

Objectivists answer this question by presenting a list of things whose possession, all by themselves, is supposed to make us better off. Familiar candidates include pleasure, friendship, knowledge, freedom, and virtue. The idea is that no matter our attitude toward such things, our lives go better to the extent that we have more of these items on the list.

Heathwood rejects all objective views about what is intrinsically good for us. He endorses *subjectivism about welfare*: the view "that something we get in life benefits us when and only when we have an interest in it, or want it, or have some other positive attitude towards it (or it causes us to get something else that we have, or will have, a positive attitude towards)." Heathwood asks us to imagine a scenario in which, for any supposedly objective good, a person feels no attraction to it at all. If a person doesn't like, care about, or want (say) freedom, then how could freedom, in itself, improve her lot in life? If Heathwood is right, the answer is: it can't.

....

The Question of Welfare

One of the greatest and oldest questions we can ask ourselves is, What is the good life? What is the best kind of life for a person to live? What are the things in a life that make it worth choosing over other possible lives one could lead? It's hard to imagine a more important question. However, I want to focus on what I take to be a narrower question, namely, What things in life are ultimately to our *benefit*? Or to put it a few other ways, What things make us *better off*?, What makes a life a good life *for us*?, What is it to *fare well*? Taking our cue from this last expression, let's call this *the question of welfare*. In what follows, I'm going to offer my answer to the question of welfare. But first, let's clarify the question further.

I think that the question of welfare is a narrower question than the question of the good life because there are things that make a life a better kind of life to live without necessarily being of any benefit to the person living it. That it would be beneficial to you is one reason for you to choose a life, but not the only reason. Another reason is that the life would be beneficial to others, or, more generally, would exhibit *moral virtue*. Although it is often in a person's self-interest to do the right thing, sometimes doing good is of no benefit to the do-gooder. Imagine a bystander who saves a child in a flash flood, but loses her life in the process. This praiseworthy deed was of great benefit to the child, but, sadly, not to the hero who did it.

Another way a life can be good without being good for the person living it is by manifesting *excellence*. People manifest excellence when they excel at certain worthwhile activities, such as playing the cello, proving interesting mathematical theorems, or mastering Szechuan cooking. As with moral virtue, a life that manifests excellence seems to be in that way better, but an activity's being excellent isn't the same thing as its benefitting the person doing it. Someone might have an amazing talent for basketball, but find the sport boring and repetitive, and claim to "get nothing out of it."

This is likely a case in which manifesting excellence in a certain aspect of life would be of no benefit to the person.

A third value that we should distinguish from welfare is *meaning*. When I ask what things are of ultimate benefit or harm to us, I don't intend to be asking about the meaning of life. Whatever having a meaningful life consists in, I take it that it can vary independently from how well off one is.

There is another important clarification of the question of welfare. If someone asks what things improve the quality of a person's life, he is likely to have in mind the question of what things *tend to cause* a person's life to be improved. He might be wondering, for example, whether all the new technology in our lives really makes us better off; or he might be wondering whether he would have been better off now had he gone to graduate school years ago. These causal questions, while immensely important, are not our question. Our question is rather the question of what things make us better off *in themselves*, independent of any other changes that these things might cause in our lives. In terms philosophers use, we are asking what things are *intrinsically good* for us rather than what things are merely *instrumentally good* for us (i.e., good for us because of what they lead to). The question of intrinsic value has a kind of priority over the question of instrumental value, in that any answer to the question of instrumental value will presuppose, if only implicitly, an answer to the question about intrinsic value.

Preliminary Steps in Answering the Question of Welfare

Now that we have a clearer understanding of the question of welfare, how do we go about answering it? One natural way to begin is to devise a list of things whose presence in our lives seems intuitively to make our lives better. In developing such a list, we should keep in mind the distinction just introduced between intrinsic and instrumental value. Since the question of welfare is the question of intrinsic welfare value, we want to include on the list intuitive *intrinsic* goods only. Consider an example: while medicine can certainly make our lives better, there is no plausibility to the claim that possessing or taking medicine is good *in itself* for us. If medicine benefits us, this is due to the effects that it has on our health. We can also ask, in turn, whether being healthy is an intrinsic or merely an instrumental good. My own view is that bodily health, like medicine, is of merely instrumental value; we'll get to that view shortly.

So what might such a list include? Here are some natural candidates: happiness, knowledge, love, freedom, friendship, the appreciation of beauty, creative activity, being respected. Why think that the presence of such things in themselves makes our lives better? One reason is that these are things that we tend to want or value in our lives, and, moreover, to want or value *for their own sakes*—not merely for their effects. Next, note that such desires *seem reasonable*. These aren't crazy things to want in your life; it makes sense to want them. If it does, what explains this? The view that these things are intrinsically good for us would explain it.

Subjective vs. Objective Theories of Welfare

But now I want to ask a question, consideration of which, I believe, pulls us in the opposite direction—that is, away from the view that all of the items above are intrinsically good for us. It's true that many of us, much of the time, want the above things in our lives, and that we are glad to have them when we get them. But do we want them because it is good to have them, or is it good to have them because we want them? To put the question slightly differently, Do the items on our list above make our lives better only because they are things that we want and are glad to have in our lives, or do these things make our lives better even if we have no interest in them? This question—one of the deepest and most central questions in the philosophy of welfare—is the question of whether welfare is objective or subjective.

Subjectivists hold that something we get in life benefits us when and only when we have an interest in it, or want it, or have some other positive attitude towards it (or it causes us to get something else that we have, or will have, a positive attitude towards). *Objectivists* about welfare deny this, and maintain that at least some of the intrinsically beneficial things in our lives are good for us even if we don't want them, don't like them, don't care about them, and even if they fail to get us anything else that we want or care about. They are good for us "whether we like it or not."

The debate over whether welfare is objective or subjective should not be confused with the debate over whether *morality* is objective or subjective. In my view, morality is pretty clearly objective. It is wrong to light a cat on fire for one's amusement. And the fact that this is wrong does not—as subjectivists about morality would have it—depend upon my or anyone else's negative attitudes towards this kind of act. It's not wrong to light cats on fire because we disapprove of this; rather, we disapprove of it because it's wrong. I feel pretty confident about that. Much less obvious is the notion that a person can be *benefitted*, can have her own interests advanced, when she gets things that she herself in no way wants, things that leave her cold. Indeed, it seems to me that this cannot happen. It seems to me to be a truth about welfare that if something is truly a benefit to someone, it must be something she wants, likes, or cares about, or something that helps her get something she wants, likes, or cares about.

If I am right that this is a truth about welfare, I think that it is probably a foundational truth. That means that there are no deeper truths about welfare from which we can derive it, and hence argue for it. But there are still considerations that can help us to see it. Concrete examples can help do this. Consider the following case:

> Charlie wants to improve his quality of life. He has heard that it is philosophers who claim to be experts on this topic, so he looks through some philosophy journals at his library. He finds an article claiming to have discovered the correct account of welfare. It is an objective theory that includes the items on our list above. The paper is in a pretty good journal, so Charlie decides to go about trying to increase his share of some of the items on the list. For example, to increase his freedom, he moves to a state with higher speed limits. Charlie is careful to make sure that the move won't have any detrimental side effects—that it won't cause him to fail to get less of any of the other goods on the list.
>
> After succeeding in increasing his freedom, Charlie finds that he doesn't care about it, that he is completely indifferent to it. Although he is free to drive faster, he never does (he never wants to). Nor does the freedom to drive faster get him anything else that he is interested in. Charlie considers whether he is any better off as a result of the increase in his freedom. He concludes that he is no better off.

Do you agree with Charlie's own assessment of his situation? I do. I feel confident that Charlie is right that his gains in freedom turned out to be of no benefit to him. Note that the objective theory in question implies otherwise. For according to that theory, *freedom itself*—not freedom that you happen to want, but freedom itself—makes your life better. Since (i) this objective theory implies that Charlie's life is going better as a result of this increase in freedom, but (ii) in fact Charlie's life is not going any better as a result of this increase in freedom, the theory must be mistaken.

Importantly, the point here generalizes. For any of the alleged goods on the list, so long as it is an objective putative good—i.e., a putative good that bears no necessary connection to any positive attitudes on the part of the person for whom it is supposed to be good—we could construct a case similar in all relevant respects to Charlie's case. This would be a case in which someone gets the supposed good, but is in no way glad to have it, and is in no way glad to have anything else that it gets her. I believe that we would again feel confident that this person receives no benefit. And the reason we can always construct such a case, I submit, is the idea mentioned earlier: that if something is truly a benefit to someone, it must be something she wants, likes, or cares about, or something that helps her get such a thing. This is why I'm inclined to believe that whereas objectivism is the correct view of morality, subjectivism is the correct view of welfare.

If there are such good reasons to be a subjectivist, why would anyone reject the view? One of the main reasons that some are driven to reject subjectivism about welfare is that, intuitively, it's possible for a person to want, like, or care about getting *the wrong things*. Some pursuits, for example, strike us as pointless or meaningless. What if someone wants never to step on a crack when he walks on the sidewalk? Would his life really be going better for him each time he satisfies this desire?

But the objection may be most forceful when it appeals to pursuits that are positively bad. Consider, to take a real life example, the serial rapist and murderer Ted Bundy. What Bundy wanted most in his life was to inflict pain on innocent strangers, to wield power over them, and to watch them beg, suffer, and die at his own hand. For quite a number of years, Bundy got just what he wanted. According to subjectivism, when it comes to welfare, anything you take an interest in is as good as any other; that is, it doesn't matter what you want, so long as you get it, and so long as your getting it doesn't conflict with your getting other things that you want. Thus, assuming that Bundy wasn't plagued with guilt or regret during his reign of terror, and that he avoided other unwanted side-effects of his lifestyle, subjectivists must say that Bundy benefitted greatly in doing what he did, that he was quite well off, at least before he got caught. Objectivists, by contrast, have the resources to condemn Bundy's behavior, not just morally, but from the point of view of his own self-interest. They can say that Bundy would himself have been better off if he had had, and had achieved, more admirable goals.

Thus we need to ask ourselves a question. Consider the years before Bundy was caught, the years in which he lived just the sort of life he most wanted to live. Were these years good years for Bundy? Did he live a life that was in his interest to live? Was he just as well off as he would have been during these years had he had morally acceptable interests, and successfully pursued those? Note that our question is not, Did Bundy's lifestyle *make him happy*? Objectivists can agree that it did. Our question is not, Did Bundy *get just what he wanted*? Objectivists agree that he did. Nor should we be distracted by the fact that Bundy's lifestyle led to his eventual ruin. Subjectivists agree that his choices harmed him later on, after he got caught. (Bundy was eventually executed for his crimes.) Rather, our question is, Were the years before he got caught good years for Bundy?

I agree that Bundy was a monster. I condemn what he did in the strongest terms. But it strikes me as a false hope to think that Bundy could not have benefitted from doing what he did. Thus, I "bite the bullet" and maintain that Bundy in fact was quite well off before he got caught. To be honest, I don't even think of this as biting a bullet. It strikes me as the genuinely correct verdict. Remember that all we are saying is that Bundy benefitted, for a time, from his lifestyle. We are not saying that his lifestyle was morally acceptable or that it was worth emulating. Indeed, the claim that Bundy *benefitted* from his monstrous lifestyle helps explain something. It helps explain why we find the whole situation so sickening: here is this monster, doing the most unspeakable things, and all the while living large because of it.

The Desire Theory of Welfare

Subjectivists maintain that being well off has to do with the attitudes we have towards what we get in life rather than the nature of the things themselves. Being benefitted is a matter of having a positive attitude towards things, whatever these things are. Subjectivists often hold that *desire* or *wanting* is the special positive attitude here. Desire may even be an element in all positive attitudes, attitudes such as liking, preferring, caring about something, or having something as a goal.

According to the desire theory of welfare, human welfare consists in the satisfaction of desire. Whenever what a person wants to be the case is in fact the case, this constitutes a benefit for the person. Whenever a person's desires are frustrated, this constitutes a basic harm. The theory recognizes no other fundamental sources of benefit and harm. Many other kinds of event—making money, becoming sick, gaining freedom, appreciating beauty—can cause our lives to go better or worse, but only by being things that we want or don't want, or by causing us to get, or fail to get, other things that we want or don't want. *How* good or bad a desire satisfaction or frustration is for its subject, according to the theory, is a function of the strength of the desire; the more deeply we want something to be the case, the better it is for us if it is the case, and the worse it is if it's not. How well things go for us overall in life is determined by the extent to which we get what we want throughout our lives, both on a day-to-day basis and with respect to larger life goals.

We can distinguish two different things we might mean by the term "want." One sense of the term is merely behavioral. If we voluntarily do something, it follows, on the behavioral sense of the term, that it is some-thing we wanted to do. According to a second sense of the term, we count as wanting something only if we are genuinely attracted to it, only if it gen-uinely appeals to us. Sometimes a person voluntarily does something that holds no appeal for him. On the behavioral sense of the term, it follows that he wanted to do it. But this kind of desire satisfaction does not seem to be of any benefit to the person faced with doing the unappealing thing. Thus I believe that the best version of the desire theory of welfare is one that understands "desire" or "want"—I use these terms interchangeably—in the "genuine attraction" sense mentioned above. Only when we get, or get to do, those things that we are genuinely attracted to or that genuinely appeal to us—the things we "really want"—are we made better off.

What about Pleasure and Happiness?

One of the simplest and oldest theories of human welfare is hedonism, the view that pleasure is the only thing that is intrinsically good for us. Almost everyone accepts that pleasure is an intrinsic welfare good. Hedonism is controversial mainly because it claims that there are no other such goods. How does the desire satisfaction theory of welfare accommodate the value of pleasure?

Whether it can make such an accommodation, and whether it should, depends upon what pleasure is. On one view of the nature of pleasure, pleasure is an indefinable feeling or sensation, in the same general category as the indefinable sensations of seeing red, of the taste of chocolate, or of nausea. If this is what pleasure is, I don't think that pleasure is good in itself for anyone. For imagine a creature who is completely indifferent to this feeling, or even finds it unbearable. It is not plausible to suggest that such a creature would be having a good experience—an experience that is good for it, and makes its life better—when it experiences this indifferent, or even reviled, sensation. Rather, if this view of the nature of pleasure is right, then pleasure's value depends entirely on the creature's wanting it, liking it, or taking an interest in it. It would be just like the taste of chocolate, which (ignoring side effects) is good for a creature to taste when, but only when, the creature wants to be tasting it.

On a competing account of the nature of pleasure, pleasure is a positive attitude, an attitude that one can take up towards things like the chocolate taste one is currently experiencing, the music one is hearing, or the fact that one has gotten a raise. The attitude of being pleased that something is the case is certainly a good state to be in, but it is one that, in my view, ultimately involves desire. Taking pleasure in a chocolate taste sensation just is to be wanting to be experiencing it as you are experiencing it. To be pleased that you have gotten a raise is to want the raise while seeing that you have gotten it. Thus, if pleasure turns out to be a kind of state that is indeed intrinsically valuable, it is a kind of state whose value the desire theory of welfare can recognize, and even explain.

The desire theory can also accommodate the irresistible idea that it's good to be happy. Consider being happy that one has gotten a raise, or that the sun is shining, or that one is living in Barcelona. These are good states to be in. But, just as above, I believe that they are states that essentially involve desire. They involve, respectively, the desire for a raise, the desire that the sun be shining, and the desire to be living in Barcelona. If one gets a raise, and is happy about this, one will necessarily be receiving a desire satisfaction. In this way the value of happiness can be accommodated by the desire theory of welfare.

Refining the Desire Theory

Sometimes our desires are based on ignorance or confused thinking. When they are, it can seem doubtful that satisfying them benefits us. Thus we have a potential problem for the desire theory of welfare, and probably for any subjective theory. To take a simple example, suppose that I have a strong craving for cherry pie, not knowing that I have recently developed a serious allergy to cherries. If I satisfy my desire, I'll need a shot of adrenaline to avoid suffocating to death. Still, in my ignorant state, cherry pie is what I want most. The desire theory of welfare seems to imply, absurdly, that it is most in my interest to have cherry pie.

For this reason, many subjectivists revise the theory so that what determines our welfare is not our actual desires but our *idealized* desires. These are the desires we would have if we knew all the facts, were vividly appreciating them, and were thinking rationally. If I knew, and vividly appreciated, what eating cherry pie would do to me, I would prefer not to have it; the informed desire theory thus does not imply that it would be most in my interest to satisfy my desire for cherry pie.

Subjectivists who are troubled by the problems caused by pointless or immoral desires may hope that the move to idealized desires will help here as well. Perhaps if Ted Bundy had appreciated the effects that his actions would have on his victims, and had been thinking rationally about it, he would not have desired to do the horrible things he did. Perhaps he would have instead wanted the things on the objectivist's list. This is a nice thought, but for it to be true, it would have to be that no one who was fully informed, vividly appreciating the facts, and thinking clearly could have pointless or immoral desires. But surely it's just wishful thinking to believe that.

In any case, the move to ideal desires faces a problem: it begins to abandon the core idea of subjectivism. That idea is simple: what is good for you must be connected to what *you yourself* want, like, or care about—not what someone else wants for you, even if that someone else is an improved version of yourself. If you had full knowledge and appreciation of all of what was possible for you, perhaps you would prefer caviar and experimental music. As it happens, you prefer peanuts and baseball. Surely you benefit when you receive the things you actually want (peanuts and baseball) rather than the things (caviar and experimental music) that you merely would want if you were fully informed and rational. For this reason, I believe that we should regard our actual desires as the ones whose satisfaction directly benefits us.

Fortunately, the problem that motivated the move to idealization—the problem to do with desires based on ignorance—can be solved within the original theory, the theory that appeals to one's actual desires. Recall the case of the allergenic cherry pie. The actual desire theory can say that it is in fact not in my interest to eat the pie. The theory does imply that I'll receive *some* benefit from doing so, but that is plausible—I crave the pie, after all, and I will be very glad to be eating it. But the theory doesn't imply that I'll receive a *net* benefit. For I also have strong desires not to be sent to an emergency room and not to be suffocating. Eating the pie will frustrate these very strong desires. The theory thus delivers the desired result: that overall I'm better off not eating the cherry pie. The move to idealization, which violates the spirit of subjectivism, is not necessary in the first place.

Other objections pose more serious problems for the desire theory and may require that we refine it. Here is one such objection. Suppose that my uncle must go into exile, and I know that I will never see him again. Whenever I think of him, I think of him fondly, hoping very much that he is happy and healthy. As a matter of fact, though I couldn't know this, my uncle *is* happy and healthy. According to the desire theory of welfare, a person benefits whenever a desire of his is satisfied. For a desire to be satisfied, all that is required is that the desired event actually occur; the person need not know this and need derive no satisfaction from it for it to be true that his desire was satisfied. The desire theory thus implies that I am made better off when my uncle achieves happiness and health.

Many (though not all) desire theorists regard this as an unacceptably counterintuitive implication of the theory. They think that I have not been benefitted in the example. I agree, though there is little agreement on how best to handle such a case. One popular solution is to revise the theory so that it counts only desires that are *about one's own life*. My uncle's being happy and healthy is an event in his life, not mine, and thus when it occurs, this revised theory denies that I am benefitted even though I wanted the event to occur. But I believe this restriction excludes too much; it excludes, for example, the desires of fans for their team to win. In my view, the lesson of the exiled uncle is rather that in order to be benefitted, we must *be aware* that the desired event has occurred, or is occurring.

This raises all sorts of issues that we cannot explore here. But I hope I have made a decent case for the ideas that subjectivism is the better approach to welfare, that the desire theory is the way for the subjectivist to go, that the desire theory should appeal to desires in the "genuine attraction" sense of the term, and that your actual rather than ideal desires are plausibly regarded as what determines how well you fare in life.

Chris Heathwood: Faring Well and Getting What You Want

1. Heathwood claims that the meaningfulness of a life can vary independently from how well off the person living it is. To see whether you agree, try to describe an example of (a) a life that you think is meaningful that is not beneficial to the person living it, and (b) a life that is beneficial to the person living it without being a meaningful life.

2. Suppose someone claims that being healthy is intrinsically good for us. Can you think of a way to test whether this is true? Here is one idea:

describe a pair of cases that are exactly alike except that in one of the cases, the person involved has greater health than in the other case. It's crucial that there be no other differences between the cases. What do you think this tells us about the intrinsic value of being healthy?

3. Do you agree that Charlie's gains in freedom turned out to be of no benefit to him? If they are of no benefit to him, is that enough to show that objectivism about well-being is mistaken? If not, what more is required?

4. What is an ideal desire as opposed to an actual desire? Which kind of desire does Heathwood think is connected to welfare? Why does he think this?

5. Do you believe that Heathwood benefits when, unbeknownst to him, his exiled uncle achieves happiness and health? Why or why not?

6. According to one version of the desire theory of welfare, a person is benefited just when a desire that is about her own life is satisfied. Is this theory plausible? Explain.

7. Heathwood thinks that our life is a good life for us to the extent that we get what we want, so long as we are aware of it, and so long as this is a want in the "genuine attraction" sense of "want." Are there any cases in which your life goes better for you even though no such want is satisfied? Are there any cases in which such wants are satisfied, but one fails to be benefited as a result?

4

The Elements of Well-Being

Brad Hooker

··

After a brief discussion of the merits of hedonism and the "desire-fulfilment" theory of well-being, Brad Hooker investigates what he takes to be the most plausible version of an objective list view. Such a view endorses the idea that there are several elements of well-being that are non-instrumentally valuable. In other words, these elements make a direct contribution to a person's well-being, regardless of what other improvements in a life they happen to cause.

There are two central questions we must ask of any objective list view. Perhaps obviously, the first is this: What *are* the elements of well-being? The second asks how to justify the elements of the list: What arguments can be given for thinking that some things really are elements of well-being while other, perhaps popular, candidates for such elements are best left off the list?

Hooker answers the first question by citing pleasure, friendship, significant achievement, important knowledge, and autonomy. Each of these is a *distinct* good—the value of friendship, for instance, cannot be reduced to the amount of pleasure it causes. And each of these is an *objective* good—each one is good for a person even if he or she fails to affirm its value. On this view, a misanthrope who despises friendship, or a lazy person who denies the value of significant achievement, is making a mistake.

Journal of Practical Ethics, Vol. 3, June 2015, pp. 15–35.

Hooker answers the second question by arguing for a kind of controlled experiment to determine whether something qualifies as an element of well-being. He asks us to imagine two situations that are identical in every respect but one—namely, that there is more of the candidate element. So, for instance, imagine yourself just as you are now. And then imagine things exactly the same, except for one change: you are enjoying more pleasure than you were in the first scenario. If you are no better off in the second case, then pleasure is *not* an element of well-being. But Hooker, like most people, thinks that you are better off in the second case than the first. And he thinks that the best explanation of this improvement is that pleasure is an element of well-being.

Interestingly, when Hooker applies this test to living a moral life, he argues that it fails to qualify as the sort of thing that directly makes your life go better. Of course being morally virtuous makes your life *morally* better. And living a moral life often brings with it other valuable things—it is often a path to firmer friendships and significant achievement, for instance. But in two situations where everything is the same except for the fact that in one you are morally admirable and in the other you are not, Hooker argues that you are no better off in the second case than in the first.

....

Clarifications

Like most philosophers, I will take the term 'well-being' to be synonymous with 'welfare,' 'personal good,' and 'individual utility.' Contributions to well-being I refer to as benefits or gains. Subtractions from well-being I refer to as harms, losses, or costs. The elements of well-being are whatever constitutes benefits, that is, contributions to well-being.

Absolutely essential is the distinction between non-instrumental value, which is sometimes called final value, and instrumental value. Examples of things with merely instrumental value are money, medicine, and sleep. This paper focuses on non-instrumental value. When I refer to contributions to well-being, I mean *non-instrumental* contributions, that is, things that are good for us in their own right as opposed to good only because they are means to other things. The main focus of the paper is on the question of what constitutes non-instrumental contributions to a person's well-being. Definitely, all of the values I will be discussing do have instrumental value. But I will be focusing on these values not for their instrumental benefits but as putative elements of well-being.

Hedonism

Hedonism is the theory that well-being consists in pleasures minus pains. Pleasures are experiences found attractive solely because of their experiential quality, rather than for other reasons. Pains are experiences found aversive solely because of their experiential quality, rather than for other reasons.

The focus on experiential quality brings out a defining feature of pleasures and pains, namely that they are *introspectively discernible* (which is not to say that they are *actually* discerned). Imagine someone who fails in the central project of her life but never finds out about this failure. An example might be the amateur sleuth who spent the last five years of her life trying to discover how and why the child Madeleine McCann disappeared. The sleuth died thinking that she had made the crucial discovery that solved the case. But in fact her 'discovery' turned out to be quite mistaken. Because she didn't find out that she failed, her pleasures were what they would have been had her project instead been a success. Hedonists hold that the failure of a life project does not, in itself, reduce the person's welfare. Hedonists think that a person's welfare is determined solely by how this person's life feels from the inside. How her life feels from the inside may depend in part on whether she *believes* her desires have been fulfilled. How her life feels from the inside does not necessarily depend on whether her desires *really* have been fulfilled.

I have contended that introspective discernibility is essential to pleasure and that success in one's projects is not. This is true whether the project is relatively discrete, such as finding out how and why a small child suddenly disappeared, or much more complex and general, such as the goals of having lots of good friends and of being knowledgeable about science, history, and metaphysics and of creating things of enduring value. Consider someone who believes that he has enough good friends and that he is knowledgeable about science, history, and metaphysics and that he has created things of enduring value. This person is likely to feel some satisfaction with his life.

Perhaps this sort of satisfaction is the most important kind of pleasure. Nevertheless, getting this kind of pleasure is possible even if one is deluded about whether one's desires for good friends, for knowledge of science, history, and metaphysics, and for creative success have actually been fulfilled. Feeling satisfied with one's life is compatible with delusion about pretty much everything except whether one feels satisfied with one's life.

Desire-Fulfilment

Another main view of welfare holds that a person's well-being is constituted by the fulfilment of his or her desires, whether or not the person knows the desires have been fulfilled. This view is often called the desire-fulfilment (or preference-satisfaction) theory of well-being.

The main argument in favour of the desire-fulfilment theory over hedonism is that many people's self-interested concern extends beyond their own pleasures and pains, enjoyments and frustrations. For example, many people have stronger self-interested concern for knowing the truth (especially about whether their other desires are fulfilled) than for blissful ignorance.

The main argument against the desire-fulfilment theory is that some desires are so wacky that their fulfilment would not itself constitute a benefit for the people who have them (even if whatever associated pleasure these people derived from believing their desires were fulfilled *would* constitute a benefit for them). Imagine someone who wants a saucer of mud, or to count all the blades of grass in the lawns along a street, or to turn on as many radios as possible (Anscombe, 1958, p. 70; Rawls, 1971, p. 432; Quinn 1993, p. 236). Suppose this person wants these things *for their own sakes*, i.e., non-instrumentally. Fulfilment of such desires in itself would not be of any benefit to this person, we intuitively think.

Objective List Theory

A third theory of welfare agrees with hedonism that pleasure constitutes a benefit. Where this third theory departs from hedonism is over the question of whether there is only one element of well-being or more than one. The third theory claims that other things can also constitute benefits—for example, knowledge of important matters, friendship, significant achievement, and autonomy. Derek Parfit (1984, pp. 493–502) dubbed this theory the 'objective list theory,' but often the name is shortened to the 'list theory.' According to this objective list theory, a life contains more welfare to the extent that it contains pleasure, knowledge of important matters, friendship, significant achievement, and autonomy. A life full of pleasure and fulfilment of desires for things other than the goods just listed could still be of low quality precisely because it lacked the goods just listed.

What makes one achievement more significant than another? Thomas Hurka (1993, chs. 8–10; 2011, ch. 5) argues persuasively that extended and difficult achievements are more significant than narrow and easy ones. Admittedly, a narrower and less difficult achievement might benefit you more than one that is more extended and difficult, because the narrower one brings you greater pleasure or because it helps develop your friendships or because you learn more from it. In other words, when instrumental as well as intrinsic value is considered, a narrower and less difficult achievement can be on balance more beneficial to you than a wider and more difficult achievement. But when we ignore the instrumental benefits of different achievements, we should conclude that extended and difficult achievements are more significant than narrow and easy ones.

We might likewise follow Hurka (1993, chs. 8–10; 2011, ch. 4) in holding that extended and explanatory knowledge is better than narrow and shallow knowledge. For example, knowledge of the basic truths of physics or biology or metaphysics is more important than knowledge of the batting averages achieved by the middle-ranking players on a particular team in a particular month thirty-three years ago. But knowledge about yourself or things closely connected to you can sometimes constitute a larger benefit to you than would more general knowledge about things with no special connection to you. Knowing important facts about yourself—having self-knowledge—is a more important element of your well-being than knowing general truths about physics or biology or metaphysics or other people. For example, knowing your own failings is more important than knowing other people's failings. On the other hand, knowing that something is true not only of you but also of everyone else would constitute a larger benefit than knowing merely the truth about yourself.

Even more contestable than which kind of achievement or knowledge is most valuable as an element of well-being is the question of exactly what comprises autonomy. Does autonomy consist merely in having one's actions be guided by desires that one desires to have? Or does autonomy consist in having one's decisions be guided by one's own value judgements? Or does autonomy require that one's value judgements be themselves autonomously produced? Or does autonomy require that one's value judgements be at least minimally sensible?

These questions are fascinating but, alas, too difficult to address here. Hence, I must simply assume an answer. This is that someone's life contains autonomy to the extent to which she has a variety of important options to choose among, her choices reflect her value judgements, and her value judgements are at least minimally reflective (i.e., she has at least once considered them rather than merely always accepted them without consideration). If Jack severely constricted Jill's set of important options, or if he controlled her choices by controlling her value judgements, she would lack autonomy. The same would be true if a brain injury or mental illness controlled her value judgements or prevented her from being able to assess them.

Now, how can we ascertain whether any given putative good is an item on the objective list? We must run the following kind of thought experiment. We imagine two possible lives for someone that are as much alike as possible except that one of these lives contains more of some candidate good than the other. We then think about whether the life containing more of the candidate good would be more beneficial to the person living it than the other life. If the correct answer is no, then definitely the candidate good in question is not an element of well- being. On the other hand, if the correct answer is instead that the life with more of the candidate good is more beneficial, then we inquire what is the right explanation of this life's being more beneficial. One possible explanation is that the candidate good in question really is an element of well-being.

Pleasure

Here is an illustrative example. We imagine two possible lives for someone that are as much alike as possible except that one of these lives contains a larger amount of innocent pleasure than the other. We are trying to hold everything equal as much as possible with the single variable being the amount of innocent pleasure in the two possible lives. We then think about whether the life containing the larger amount of innocent pleasure would be more beneficial to the person living it than would be the as similar as possible life with a smaller amount of innocent pleasure. If the correct answer is that the life containing the larger amount of innocent pleasure would *not* be more beneficial to the person living it than would be the as similar as possible life with a smaller amount of innocent pleasure, then innocent pleasure is not an element of well-being. On the other hand, if the correct answer is that the life with a larger amount of innocent pleasure *is* more beneficial, then we need to inquire what is the right explanation of this life's being more beneficial. The explanation that suggests itself is that innocent pleasure is indeed an element of well-being.

For that possible explanation to be correct, rival possible explanations must be mistaken. Perhaps the leading rival possible explanation is that, although by hypothesis the two lives being compared are as much alike as possible with the exception that one includes a larger amount of innocent pleasure than the other, the fact that one of these possible lives contains a larger amount of innocent pleasure brings with it differences in the levels of *other* goods and these differences are what account for the superiority of one possible life to the other. In short, although our thought experiment was supposed to isolate one variable, the rival possible explanation claims that other variables are not only ineliminable but also pivotal.

Here is an example of such a rival explanation. This explanation begins with the proposal that the life with the larger amount of innocent pleasure must also have contained a larger amount of significant achievement or friendship or important knowledge or autonomy, as sources of the extra innocent pleasure. This rival explanation then adds that what makes the life with the larger amount of innocent pleasure more beneficial to the person who lives it than the life with a smaller amount of innocent pleasure is not the extra innocent pleasure but instead the larger amount of significant achievement or friendship or important knowledge or autonomy.

This rival explanation starts from a false supposition—namely, that the life with the larger amount of innocent pleasure *must* also have contained a larger amount of significant achievement or friendship or important knowledge or autonomy, as sources of the extra innocent pleasure. This supposition is false because the extra pleasure might have come from insignificant achievement or unimportant knowledge or false beliefs or the satisfaction of physiological urges. The source of innocent pleasure can be trivial or misconceived or merely physiological. There is no necessity that the source of innocent pleasure is itself something valuable, much less an element of well-being.

We can conclude, then, that innocent pleasure is definitely an element of well-being. This is the best explanation of why a life containing a larger amount of innocent pleasure would be more beneficial to the person living it than another possible life as much as possible like the first one except that this life contains a smaller amount of innocent pleasure.

I am aware that, to many people, the thesis that innocent pleasure is an element of well-being seems completely obvious. However, there are some people who do not find innocent pleasure obviously valuable. My argument above is aimed at these people. Later in this essay, there is an argument aimed at people who think innocent pleasure is valuable only if obtained in the course of a worthwhile activity.

Significant Achievement

The structure of the argument above can be applied to other candidate elements of well-being. Let us apply it to significant achievement. We imagine two possible lives for someone that are as much alike as possible except that one of these lives contains a larger amount of significant achievement than the other. We are trying to hold everything equal as much as possible with the single variable being the amount of significant achievement in the two possible lives. We then think about whether the life containing the larger amount of significant achievement would be more beneficial to the person living it than the life that contains a smaller amount of significant achievement but is otherwise as similar as possible. If the correct answer is no, then significant achievement is not an element of well-being. However, the correct answer seems to me to be that the life with a larger amount of significant achievement is more beneficial to the person who leads that life than the life that contains a smaller amount of significant achievement but is otherwise as similar as possible.

Now, what is the best explanation of this life's being more beneficial? One possible explanation is that significant achievement is indeed an element of well-being. The rival possible explanation starts from the supposition that the life with the larger amount of significant achievement must also have contained a larger amount of innocent pleasure or friendship or important knowledge or autonomy. From this supposition, the rival explanation infers that what makes the life with the larger amount of significant achievement more beneficial to the person who lives it is not the extra significant achievement but instead the larger amount of pleasure or friendship or important knowledge or autonomy.

Lives containing a larger amount of significant achievements often do also have more pleasure, friendship, important knowledge, or autonomy in them than they would have had if they had contained a smaller amount of significant achievement. But this certainly is not always true. Sometimes people sacrifice pleasure, friendship, and important knowledge for the sake of pursuing significant achievement. Indeed, obsession about a goal can be instrumental to achieving it but at the same time in conflict with obtaining pleasure, alienating to friends and potential friends, and a blinder to information not relevant to the goal. For such reasons, there is no necessity that a larger amount of significant achievement correlates perfectly with a larger amount of pleasure, friendship, or important knowledge. This is especially obvious in cases where the person who made a significant achievement never found out about it, and thus could not have gained lots of pleasure from knowing about the achievement.

So what is the correct explanation of the fact that the life containing the larger amount of significant achievement would be more beneficial to the person living it than the life that is as similar as possible except that it contains a smaller amount of significant achievement? The correct explanation cannot be that the life with the larger amount of significant achievement *must* also have contained a larger amount of innocent pleasure or friendship or important knowledge or autonomy. The correct explanation is instead that significant achievement is an element of well-being.

Important Knowledge

The same kind of argument can be run for concluding that important knowledge is an element of well-being. Imagine that two lives are as much alike as possible except that one of those lives has important knowledge and the other life does not or one life contains a considerably larger amount of important knowledge than the other. The life containing no or a considerably smaller amount of important knowledge is worse for the agent than a life as much as possible like that one except that it contains at least some or a considerably larger amount of important knowledge.

Again, we have to ask, what is the best explanation of the greater benefit in the life with a larger amount of important knowledge? One possible explanation is that important knowledge is indeed an element of well-being. The rival possible explanation starts from the supposition that the life with the larger amount of important knowledge must also have contained a larger amount of innocent pleasure or more friendship or a larger amount of significant achievement or greater autonomy. From this supposition, the rival explanation infers that what makes the life with the larger amount of important knowledge more beneficial to the person who lives it is not the extra important knowledge but instead the greater pleasure or friendship or significant achievement or autonomy.

We should not accept the supposition that the life with the larger amount of important knowledge must also have contained a larger amount of innocent pleasure or friendship or significant achievement or autonomy. Sometimes important knowledge reduces rather than increases innocent pleasure. Sometimes important knowledge harms friendships. Sometimes important knowledge is not a significant achievement because it was not something that was pursued and thus not an achievement at all. Hence the life with the larger amount of important knowledge *might not* also contain greater innocent pleasure or friendship or significant achievement or autonomy.

Thus, the best explanation of the fact that a life containing no or a considerably smaller amount of important knowledge is worse for the agent than a life as much as possible like that one except that it contains a larger amount of important knowledge *cannot* be that the life with the larger amount of important knowledge must also contain greater innocent pleasure or friendship or significant achievement or autonomy. The best explanation must instead be that important knowledge is an element of well-being.

Autonomy

Concerning autonomy, we can try an argument with the same structure as the arguments above. We imagine two possible lives for someone as similar as possible except that one contains more autonomy and the other less. Then we ask which of these two possible lives is more beneficial to the person who lives it. The autonomous life seems better. Since we have imagined that the two lives are as equal as possible in terms of the other elements of well-being, we minimize the extent to which the superiority of the more autonomous life can be explained by the instrumental value of autonomy.

Again, we face the objection that there are multiple, though correlative, variables here. The objection is that, if one possible life contains greater autonomy than another possible life that is otherwise as similar as possible, the possible life with greater autonomy in it *must* also contain greater pleasure or knowledge or friendship or achievement than the other life. From this supposition, the objection infers that the greater pleasure or knowledge or friendship or achievement, and not the greater autonomy, is what makes this life better.

However, it just is not true that if one possible life contains greater autonomy than another life that is otherwise as similar as possible, then the possible life with greater autonomy in it must also contain greater pleasure or knowledge or friendship or achievement. Greater autonomy might lead to some successes but also, of course, to some failures—some missed opportunities for pleasure, some lack of knowledge, some ruined friendships, and some unsuccessful projects. So, on balance, greater autonomy might not lead to greater pleasure or knowledge or friendship or achievement. So there is nothing to prevent our imagining two possible lives that are equal in terms of pleasure, friendship, achievement, and knowledge and yet one of these lives contains more autonomy than the other.

We thus ask which of these two possible lives is more beneficial to the person who lives it. The more autonomous life seems better. Since we have imagined that the two lives are as equal as possible in terms of the other elements of well-being, the best explanation of the superiority of the more autonomous life in this comparison is that autonomy is an element of well-being.

Appreciating Beauty

Experiencing something as beautiful can definitely be instrumental to other benefits. Most obviously, experiencing something as beautiful can produce pleasure, even ecstasy. Experiencing something as beautiful can also lead to other goods, such as love and knowledge. But is experiencing something as beautiful a non-instrumental good such that a life containing such appreciation must be pro tanto better than a life without?

Well, are judgements of beauty like judgements of taste, i.e., merely subjective? Whether a food is delicious or not is merely subjective. For example, if you judge pears to be delicious and I do not, neither of us need be mistaken. If beauty is like deliciousness, then while you can be correct about whether you find something's aesthetic qualities attractive, you cannot be correct about whether these qualities *really* are attractive or about whether they ought to attract. If beauty is like deliciousness, then what would make a possible life in which you find more beauty better for you than a possible life in which you find less beauty would be the additional pleasure or friendship that the extra beauty would bring you. If beauty is like deliciousness, then appreciating beauty is not itself an element of well-being.

If beauty is not like deliciousness but is instead an objective value, then you can be correct not merely about whether certain qualities attract you and others but also about whether certain qualities *really* are attractive or about whether they *ought* to attract. In that case, you can have knowledge of aesthetic properties. If this is correct, perhaps we should classify appreciation of beauty as a kind of important knowledge. If appreciation of beauty is a kind of important knowledge, then we have grounds for holding that appreciation of beauty is an element of well-being—under the heading of important knowledge.

Living a Morally Good Life

Let us now turn to the question of whether living a morally good life is an element of well-being. Even if it is not, living a morally good life is of course *morally* good. And living a morally good life might be what there is strongest reason to do even where living a morally good life involves self-sacrifice. We can be interested in the question of whether living a morally good life is an element of well-being even if we are committed to sacrificing our own good either for the sake of benefiting others or because moral restrictions get in the way of doing what is most beneficial to oneself.

Living a morally good life is rewarding in terms of the other elements of well-being. Living a morally good life definitely constitutes a significant achievement. And living a morally good life can bring pleasure and ferment friendship. And knowing what morality requires is important knowledge. But is living a morally good life in itself—not under the heading of achievement, or as an instrument to pleasure or friendship, or in its connection with knowledge—an element of well-being?

This is not a question to which the answer seems to me directly apparent. The best I can do is approach the question indirectly, via what I call the sympathy test.

Suppose we ask ourselves whether we are inclined to feel sympathy for someone whose life lacks a particular property. Sympathy is a judgement-sensitive attitude. Our having sympathy for someone whose life lacks a particular property makes sense only if we judge that a life's lacking that property makes the life less beneficial to the person whose life it is than would be a life as similar as possible except that it has this property. So if we *do* feel sympathy for someone whose life lacks the property, this attitude makes sense only if deep down we think that a life's having that property *is* an element of well-being. And if we do *not* feel sympathy for someone whose life lacks the property, one possible explanation is that deep down we think that a life's having that property is not an element of well-being.

We do feel sympathy for people whose lives lack pleasure, friendships, autonomy, significant achievement, or important knowledge without some sort of compensation in terms of a greater amount of one or more of these other goods. In contrast, we do not feel sympathy for people who fail to live morally good lives. One possible explanation of the absence of sympathy is that deep down we really do not believe that living a morally good life is an element of well-being.

Is the sympathy test a good one? If we do have sympathy for someone, we can legitimately make inferences about our beliefs. To be more specific, if we do feel sympathy for someone whose life lacks a particular property, then we must think that a life's lacking this property makes the life less beneficial to the person whose life it is than would be a life as similar as possible except that it has this property. The limitation of the sympathy test appears in cases where we do not feel sympathy for someone whose life lacks a particular property. Yes, one possible explanation for our lack of sympathy is that we really think that a life's having that property is not an element of well-being. However, another possible explanation is that something else prevents us from feeling sympathy. For example, we might think that the person under consideration deserves a life with lower well-being.

We might initially suspect that feeling sympathy for someone is difficult to combine with the condemnation and blame and indignation that we feel towards those we believe have failed to lead morally good lives. Moral blame is regularly accompanied by a kind of hostility, which can get in the way of sympathy.

And yet, blaming someone does not necessarily get in the way of feeling sympathy for that person. Sometimes we have to blame someone about whom we care very strongly. When we blame someone about whom we care very strongly, the blame *can* be accompanied by sympathy. For example, we might blame ourselves for something but at the same time feel sorry for the harm we have caused to ourselves.

So far in this argument I have assumed that we do not feel sympathy for people who fail to live morally good lives. I have cast suspicion on the attempt to explain this lack of sympathy as an effect of blame for those who fail to live morally good lives. Blame for people who fail to live morally good lives does not always prevent sympathy for them. So I *tentatively* surmise that the best explanation of our lack of sympathy for people who fail to lead morally good lives is that we do not really think that living such a life is a distinct element of well-being. (This conclusion should be tempered by the recognition that living a morally good life can be instrumentally beneficial to the person who lives it and can constitute a significant achievement.)

For Well-Being, Friendship Is More Than a Kind of Achievement

Earlier, I argued that friendship should be listed as a distinct element of well-being. I have just now appealed to the sympathy test to argue that we do not really believe that living a morally good life is a distinct element of well-being, though living a morally good life is a kind of significant achievement, which is an element of well-being. With that conclusion in mind, someone might appeal to the fact that forming and sustaining friendships is also an important kind of achievement, albeit one less multidimensional than living a morally good life.

I do not see how it could plausibly be denied that forming and sustaining friendships is also an important kind of achievement. Here is an example. Imagine someone named Frieda who has found the good in a friend named Markus and forgiven him and sustained her interest in him for decades. This really is an impressive achievement on her part, given how conflicted and moody and self-deluded and intermittently self-destructive Markus is. (In contrast, that he has continued to love her is no achievement on his part, given how breathtakingly easy she is to admire and appreciate.)

Now consider the following argument:

> *Premise 1: Forming and sustaining friendships is like living a morally good life in being an important kind of achievement.*
>
> *Premise 2: Living a moral life is not a distinct element of well-being.*
>
> *Premise 3: If forming and sustaining friendships is like living a morally good life in being an important kind of achievement, and if living a morally good life is not a distinct element of well-being, then forming and sustaining friendships is not a distinct element of well-being.*
>
> *Conclusion: Forming and sustaining friendships is not a distinct element of well-being.*

Since this argument's conclusion does follow from the premises, we should assess the premises. Premise 1 is clearly true. Premise 2 is the conclusion we reached via application of the sympathy test, and so let us accept this premise. Premise 3 presumes that different things that are alike in one relevant respect are also alike in other relevant respects. We should not accept this premise, since different things are sometimes not alike in more than one relevant respect. Rejecting premise 3, we must reject the above argument as unsound.

To show that an argument is unsound is not to show that its conclusion is false. In the case of the above argument, however, I think there is an argument showing that its conclusion is false. In other words, this is an argument to show that forming and sustaining friendships is in fact a distinct element of well-being.

This argument begins with the premise that there is diminishing marginal benefit in each element of well-being (this argument was inspired by Hurka, 1993, pp. 84–96; 2011, pp. 166–74). For example, a life with no achievement but a lot of pleasure would benefit a great deal from gaining a significant achievement. Let us dub this achievement A of size S. Compare a very different life, one with lots of achievement already. This second life would not benefit as much from gaining the same achievement A of the same size S. In other words, the two lives we are comparing each gain an achievement A of size S; but, in the life where this is the *only* significant achievement, achievement A of size S constitutes a large benefit, and, in the life where there were already lots of other achievements, achievement A of size S constitutes a smaller benefit.

The diminishing marginal benefit to a life of its containing more instances of a kind of value of which it already contains a lot is relevant for the following reason. Imagine a life that already contained a lot of achievement but as yet no friendship. Suppose now this life gains one friendship. If friendship were not a distinct element of well-being but instead merely a subcategory of achievement, then a life that already contained a lot of achievement but as yet no friendship would *not benefit much* from the addition of one friendship. However, a life that already had a lot of achievement but as yet no friendship would *benefit hugely* from the addition of one friendship. So friendship is not merely a subcategory of achievement but instead is a distinct element of well-being.

References

Anscombe, E. 1958. *Intention*, Oxford, Blackwell Publishers.

Hurka, T. 1993. *Perfectionism*, Oxford, Clarendon Press.

_____ 2011. *The Best Things in Life*, Oxford, Oxford University Press.

Parfit, D. 1984. *Reasons and Persons*, Oxford, Clarendon Press.

Quinn, W. 1993. *Morality and Action*, Cambridge, Cambridge University Press.

Rawls, J. 1971. *A Theory of Justice*, *Cambridge*, MA, Harvard University Press.

Brad Hooker: The Elements of Well-Being

1. What is the difference between instrumental and non-instrumental value?
2. Hooker thinks that we can assess the non-instrumental value of something by comparing two situations. Describe his method and apply it to a candidate element of well-being that he does not consider. How does the method fare?
3. What is Hooker's "sympathy test"? Is it a plausible test for whether something qualifies as an element of well-being?
4. Some people deny that autonomy is an element of well-being—they think autonomy is valuable only when it leads to something else that is good. Hooker disagrees. On what ground do you (or don't you) find his argument compelling?
5. Many people think that moral virtue is an element of well-being. Present and assess Hooker's argument against this view.

5

Happiness and Meaning: Two Aspects of the Good Life

Susan Wolf

....

In this wide-ranging essay, Susan Wolf argues that an essential element of a life that is good for the person living it is that her life be *meaningful*. As Wolf defines it, a meaningful life is one where "subjective attraction meets objective attractiveness"—in other words, it is a life lived by someone who derives fulfilment from engagement in objectively worthwhile activities. For Wolf, both elements here are essential to meaningfulness. One can have a great deal of pleasure in one's life without its being meaningful, since those pleasures may be taken in worthless activities. Alternatively, one can be engaged in truly valuable activities but derive no pleasure thereby. In such a case, one's life is meaningless as well.

Wolf does not deny the hedonist's claim that pleasure is an element of well-being. But given the importance she places on living a meaningful life, Wolf does deny that pleasure is the *only* such element. Wolf also takes issue with preference-satisfaction theorists, who claim that something contributes to your well-being when, and only when, it fulfils one of your desires or preferences. It is possible, she thinks, for people to prefer only worthless activities to worthwhile ones. Even if they then get everything they want, their lives will be meaningless, since they are not engaged with things of genuine value.

Social Policy and Philosophy (1997), pp. 207–225 abridged, with notes edited and renumbered.

Once we appreciate the essential role that living a meaningful life plays in well-being, we encounter some difficult questions: How should the balance between happiness and meaningfulness be struck when having to choose between the two? How can we measure (if we can) degrees of meaningfulness in a life? How meaningful must a life be in order for it to qualify as a good one? Wolf concludes her essay by considering such questions and arguing, among other things, that the very notion of self-interest diminishes in importance once we recognize the distinction between happiness and meaning in a life.

....

The topic of self-interest raises large and intractable philosophical questions—most obviously, the question "In what does self-interest consist?" The concept, as opposed to the content of self-interest, however, seems clear enough. Self-interest is interest in one's own good. To act self-interestedly is to act on the motive of advancing one's own good. Whether what one does actually is in one's self-interest depends on whether it actually does advance, or at least, minimize the decline of, one's own good. Though it may be difficult to tell whether a person is motivated by self-interest in a particular instance, and difficult also to determine whether a given act or decision really is in one's self-interest, the meaning of the claims in question seems unproblematic.

My main concern in this essay is to make a point about the content of self-interest. Specifically I shall put forward the view that meaningfulness, in a sense I shall elaborate, is an important element of a good life. It follows, then, that it is part of an enlightened self-interest that one wants to secure meaning in one's life, or, at any rate, to allow and promote meaningful activity within it. Accepting this substantial conception of self-interest, however, carries with it a curious consequence: the concept of self-interest which formerly seemed so clear begins to grow fuzzy. Fortunately, it comes to seem less important as well.

I. Theories of Self-Interest

In *Reasons and Persons*,[1] Derek Parfit distinguishes three sorts of theories about self-interest—hedonistic theories, preference theories, and what he

---

1. Derek Parfit, *Reasons and Persons* (Oxford: Oxford University Press, 1984).

calls "objective-list theories." *Hedonistic theories* hold that one's good is a matter of the felt quality of one's experiences. The most popular theory of self-interest, which identifies self-interest with happiness, and happiness with pleasure and the absence of pain, is a prime example of a hedonistic theory. Noting that some people do not care that much about their own happiness, however—and, importantly, that they do not even regard their own happiness as the exclusive element of their own good—has led some to propose a *preference theory* of self-interest, which would identify a person's good with what the person most wants for herself. Thus, for example, if a person cares more about being famous, even posthumously famous, than about being happy, then a preference theory would accord fame a proportionate weight in the identification of her self-interest. If a person cares more about knowing the truth than about believing what it is pleasant or comfortable to believe, then it is in her self-interest to have the truth, unpleasant as it may be.

A person's preferences regarding herself, however, may be self-destructive or otherwise bizarre, and it may be that some things (including pleasure) are good for a person whether the person prefers them or not. It is not absurd to think that being deceived is bad for a person (and thus that not being deceived is good for a person) whether or not the person in question consciously values this state. Friendship and love may also seem to be things whose goodness explains, rather than results from, people's preferences for them. The plausibility of these last thoughts explains the appeal of *objective-list theories*, according to which a person's good includes at least some elements that are independent of or prior to her preferences and to their effect on the felt quality of her experience. On this view, there are some items, ideally specifiable on an "objective list," whose relevance to a fully successful life are not conditional on the subject's choice.

The view that I shall be advancing, that meaningfulness is an ingredient of the good life, commits one to a version of this last kind of theory, for my claim is that meaningfulness is a nonderivative aspect of a good life—its goodness does not result from its making us happy or its satisfying the preferences of the person whose life it is. Thus, it follows that any theory that takes self-interest to be a wholly subjective matter, either in a sense that identifies self-interest with the subjective quality of a person's experiences or in a sense that allows the standards of self-interest to be set by a person's subjective preferences, must be inadequate. At the same time, it would be a mistake to think that the objective good of a meaningful life is one that is wholly independent of the subject's experience or preferences, as if it could be good for a person to live a meaningful life whether or not it makes her happy or satisfies her preferences. Indeed, as we will see, the very idea that activities can make a life meaningful without the subject's endorsement is a dubious one.

II. Meaning in Life

What is a meaningful life? Spelling it out will constitute the bulk of my essay, for my hope is that once the idea is spelled out, it will be readily agreed that it is an element of a fully successful life.

A meaningful life is, first of all, one that has within it the basis for an affirmative answer to the needs or longings that are characteristically described as needs for meaning. I have in mind, for example, the sort of questions people ask on their deathbeds, or simply in contemplation of their eventual deaths, about whether their lives have been (or are) worth living, whether they have had any point, and the sort of questions one asks when considering suicide and wondering whether one has any reason to go on. These questions are familiar from Russian novels and existentialist philosophy, if not from personal experience. Though they arise most poignantly in times of crisis and intense emotion, they also have their place in moments of calm reflection, when considering important life choices. Moreover, paradigms of what are taken to be meaningful and meaningless lives in our culture are readily available. Lives of great moral or intellectual accomplishment—Gandhi, Mother Teresa, Albert Einstein—come to mind as unquestionably meaningful lives (if any are); lives of waste and isolation—Thoreau's "lives of quiet desperation," typically anonymous to the rest of us, and the mythical figure of Sisyphus—represent meaninglessness.

To what general characteristics of meaningfulness do these images lead us and how do they provide an answer to the longings mentioned above? Roughly, I would say that meaningful lives are lives of active engagement in projects of worth. Of course, a good deal needs to be said in elaboration of this statement. Let me begin by discussing the two key phrases, "active engagement" and "projects of worth."

A person is actively engaged by something if she is gripped, excited, involved by it. Most obviously, we are actively engaged by the things and people about which and whom we are passionate. Opposites of active engagement are boredom and alienation. To be actively engaged in something is not always pleasant in the ordinary sense of the word. Activities in which people are actively engaged frequently involve stress, danger, exertion, or sorrow (consider, for example: writing a book, climbing a mountain, training for a marathon, caring for an ailing friend). However, there is something good about the feeling of engagement: one feels (typically without thinking about it) especially alive.

That a meaningful life must involve "projects of worth" will, I expect, be more controversial, for the phrase hints of a commitment to some sort of objective value. This is not accidental, for I believe that the idea of meaningfulness, and the concern that our lives possess it, are conceptually linked to such a commitment. Indeed, it is this linkage that I want to defend, for I have neither a philosophical theory of what objective value is nor a substantive theory about what has this sort of value. What is clear to me is that there can be no sense to the idea of meaningfulness without a distinction between more and less worthwhile ways to spend one's time, where the test of worth is at least partly independent of a subject's ungrounded preferences or enjoyment.

Consider first the longings or concerns about meaning that people have, their wondering whether their lives are meaningful, their vows to add more meaning to their lives. The sense of these concerns and resolves cannot fully be captured by an account in which what one does with one's life doesn't matter, as long as one enjoys or prefers it. Sometimes people have concerns about meaning despite their knowledge that their lives to date have been satisfying. Indeed, their enjoyment and "active engagement" with activities and values they now see as shallow seems only to heighten the sense of meaninglessness that comes to afflict them. Their sense that their lives so far have been meaningless cannot be a sense that their activities have not been chosen or fun. When they look for sources of meaning or ways to add meaning to their lives, they are searching for projects whose justifications lie elsewhere.

Second, we need an explanation for why certain sorts of activities and involvements come to mind as contributors to meaningfulness while others seem intuitively inappropriate. Think about what gives meaning to your own life and the lives of your friends and acquaintances. Among the things that tend to come up on such lists, I have already mentioned moral and intellectual accomplishments and the ongoing activities that lead to them. Relationships with friends and relatives are perhaps even more important for most of us. Aesthetic enterprises (both creative and appreciative), the cultivation of personal virtues, and religious practices frequently loom large. By contrast, it would be odd, if not bizarre, to think of crossword puzzles, sitcoms, or the kind of computer games to which I am fighting off addiction as providing meaning in our lives, though there is no question that they afford a sort of satisfaction and that they are the objects of choice. Some things, such as chocolate and aerobics class, I choose even at considerable cost to myself (it is irrelevant that these particular choices may be related), so I must find them worthwhile in a sense. But they are not the sorts of things that make life worth living.

"Active engagement in projects of worth," I suggest, answers to the needs an account of meaningfulness in life must meet. If a person is or has been thus actively engaged, then she does have an answer to the question of whether her life is or has been worthwhile, whether it has or has had a point. When someone looks for ways to add meaning to her life, she is looking (though perhaps not under this description) for worthwhile projects about which she can get enthused. The account also explains why some activities and projects but not others come to mind as contributors to meaning in life. Some projects, or at any rate, particular acts, are worthwhile but too boring or mechanical to be sources of meaning. People do not get meaning from recycling or from writing checks to Oxfam and the ACLU. Other acts and activities, though highly pleasurable and deeply involving, like riding a roller coaster or meeting a movie star, do not seem to have the right kind of value to contribute to meaning.

Bernard Williams once distinguished categorical desires from the rest. Categorical desires give us reasons for living—they are not premised on the assumption that we will live. The sorts of things that give meaning to life tend to be objects of categorical desire. We desire them, at least so I would suggest, because we think them worthwhile. They are not worthwhile simply because we desire them or simply because they make our lives more pleasant.

Roughly, then, according to my proposal, a meaningful life must satisfy two criteria, suitably linked. First, there must be active engagement, and second, it must be engagement in (or with) projects of worth. A life is meaningless if it lacks active engagement with anything. A person who is bored or alienated from most of what she spends her life doing is one whose life can be said to lack meaning. Note that she may in fact be performing functions of worth. A housewife and mother, a doctor, or a bus-driver may be competently doing a socially valuable job, but because she is not engaged by her work (or, as we are assuming, by anything else in her life), she has no categorical desires that give her a reason to live. At the same time, someone who is actively engaged may also live a meaningless life, if the objects of her involvement are utterly worthless. It is difficult to come up with examples of such lives that will be uncontroversial without being bizarre. But both bizarre and controversial examples have their place. In the bizarre category, we might consider pathological cases: someone whose sole passion in life is collecting rubber bands, or memorizing the dictionary, or making handwritten copies of *War and Peace*. Controversial cases will include the corporate lawyer who sacrifices her private life and health for success along the professional ladder, the devotee of a religious cult, or—an example offered by Wiggins[2]—the pig farmer who buys more land to grow more corn to feed more pigs to buy more land to grow more corn to feed more pigs.

We may summarize my proposal in terms of a slogan: "Meaning arises when subjective attraction meets objective attractiveness." The idea is that in a world in which some things are more worthwhile than others, meaning arises when a subject discovers or develops an affinity for one or typically several of the more worthwhile things and has and makes use of the opportunity to engage with it or them in a positive way.

An advantage of the slogan is that it avoids the somewhat misleading reference to "projects." That term is less than ideal in its suggestion of well-defined and goal-oriented tasks. To be sure, many projects do add meaning to life—mastering a field of study, building a house, turning a swamp into a garden, curing cancer—but much of what gives meaning to life consists in ongoing relationships and involvements—with friends, family, the scientific community, with church or ballet or chess. These ongoing strands of life give rise to and are partly constituted by projects—you plan a surprise party for your spouse, coach a little league team, review an article for a journal—but the meaning comes less from the individuated projects than from the larger involvements of which they are parts. The slogan, moreover, is intentionally vague, for if pretheoretical judgments about meaning even approximate the truth, then not only the objects of worth but also the sorts of interaction with them that are capable of contributing to meaning are immensely variable. One can get meaning from creating, promoting, protecting (worthwhile) things, from helping people one loves and people in need, from achieving levels of skill and excellence, from overcoming obstacles, from gaining understanding, and even from just communing with or actively appreciating what is there to be appreciated.

---

2. See David Wiggins, "Truth, Invention, and the Meaning of Life," *Proceedings of the British Academy*, vol. 62 (1976), p. 342.

It is part of our job, if not our natural bent, as philosophers to be skeptical—about the correctness of these pretheoretical judgments, about our ability reliably to distinguish meaningful from meaningless activities, and about the very coherence of the distinction. About the first two worries I am not very concerned. Assuming that the distinctions are coherent and that some activities are more worthwhile than others, our culture-bound, contemporary judgments of which activities are worthwhile are bound to be partly erroneous. History is full of unappreciated geniuses, of artists, inventors, explorers whose activities at their time were scorned, as it is full of models of behavior and accomplishment that later seem to have been overrated. Though we may improve our judgments, both particular and general, by an open-minded, concentrated, and communal effort to examine and articulate the basis for them (a project that strikes me as both worthwhile and intrinsically interesting), the hope or expectation that such scrutiny will yield a reliable method for generally distinguishing worthwhile from worthless activities seems overly optimistic. Why do we respect people who devote themselves to chess more than those who become champions at pinball? Why do we admire basketball stars more than jump-rope champions? What is more worthwhile about writing a book on the philosophy of language than writing one on Nicole Brown Simpson's sex life? It is useful to ask and to answer such questions, so far as we can, both to widen and correct our horizons and to increase our understanding. But our inability to give complete and adequate answers, or to be confident in the details of our assessments, need not be a serious problem. The point of recognizing the distinction, after all, is not to give rankings of meaningful lives. There is no need, in general, to pass judgment on individuals or even on activities in which people want to engage. The point is rather at a more general level to understand the ingredients of our own and others' good, and to get a better idea of the sorts of considerations that provide reasons for living our lives one way rather than another.

The point, which I am in the midst of developing, is that meaningfulness is a nonderivative part of an individual's good, and that meaningfulness consists in active engagement in projects or activities of worth. Though it seems to me that the point and most of its usefulness can stand despite acknowledged difficulties with identifying precisely which projects or activities these are, it would be utterly destroyed if it turned out that there were no such things as projects or activities of worth at all—if it turned out, in other words, as Bentham thought, that pushpin were as good as poetry, not because of some heretofore undiscovered excellences in the game of pushpin, but because the very idea of distinctions in worth is bankrupt or incoherent. If there are no projects of worth (in contrast to other projects), then there are no such things as what I have in mind by more and less meaningful lives, and so it cannot be a part of one's good to live a more meaningful rather than a less meaningful life. If the idea of a worthwhile project is just a fraud or a hoax, then my account of self-interest is undone by it.

Since I have no *theory* of worth by which to prove the coherence of the concept or refute all skeptical challenges, I can only acknowledge the vulnerability of my account of self-interest in this regard. That we do, most of us, believe that some activities and projects are more worthwhile than others, that we regard certain activities as wastes of time (or near wastes of time) and others as inherently valuable, seems undeniable. These beliefs lie behind dispositions to feel proud or disgusted with ourselves for time spent well or badly, and they account for at least some of our efforts to steer our children and our friends toward some activities and away from others. When I try to take up a point of view that denies the distinction between worthwhile and worthless activity, I cannot find it convincing. Still, it is an article of faith that these untheoretical judgments, or some core of them, are philosophically defensible. It is on the assumption that they are defensible that my views about meaningfulness and self-interest are built.

III. Two Challenges

My proposal so far has been that meaningfulness in life arises from engagement in worthwhile activity. I have argued for the plausibility of this account on the grounds that it fits well both with the needs that are typically referred to as needs for meaning and with the concrete judgments of meaningful and meaningless activity that are most commonly made. Before proceeding with an examination of the relation between meaning and self-interest, two challenges to this account of meaning should be answered.

The first objects that, contrary to my claims, my account of meaning fails to meet the requirements I have set up for it. It fails, more particularly, to answer to the needs of at least one type of longing for meaning that members of our species tend to have. Traditional worries about the meaning of life, often set off by reflections on our own mortality and on the indifference of the cosmos in which we occupy so tiny a place, are rarely appeased by the reflection that one can actively engage in projects of worth. At least, they are not appeased by reflection on the availability of the kind of projects I have been talking about, like taking up the cello, writing a novel, volunteering at a child's day-care center or a nursing home. Tolstoy, the publicly acclaimed author of some of the greatest works of literature ever written, the father and spouse of what he described (perhaps inaccurately) as a loving and successful family, could have had no doubt that, relatively speaking, his life was spent in projects as worthwhile as any. Yet he was plagued by the thought that it was all for naught.[3] Nothing he did seemed to save his life from meaninglessness.

Among those who think that meaning in life, or the lack of it, is primarily concerned with facts about the human condition, some disagree not with my general account of meaning but with, if you will, its application. Their position, in other words, shares my view that meaning comes from engagement in projects of worth, but assigns certain facts about the human condition a crucial role in settling whether there are any such projects. If God does not exist, they think, then nothing is any more worthwhile than anything else. Within this group, some believe that God is the only possible standard for judgments of nonsubjective value. If God does not exist, they think, then neither does moral or aesthetic value or any other sort of value that could distinguish some projects as better than others. Others believe that though there may be a difference between great literature and junk, and between virtue and vice, there is no point in bothering about which you occupy yourself with. Nothing lasts forever; the human race will be destroyed; the earth will crash into the sun. Only God, and the promise of an eternal life either for ourselves or for the universe in which our accomplishments have a place, can give a point to our living lives one way rather than another. Only God can make meaningful life so much as a possibility.

My own view about this position is that it expresses an irrational obsession with permanence; but it is enough for the purposes of this essay to note that it does not really challenge the account of meaning I have offered. I have already acknowledged that the usefulness of my account rests on the assumption that the distinction between worthwhile and worthless projects is defensible, and on the assumption that at least a core of our beliefs about what is worthwhile and what is worthless is roughly

---

3. See Leo Tolstoy, "My Confession," in E. D. Klemke, ed., *The Meaning of Life* (New York: Oxford University Press, 1981).

correct. Those who think that God is a necessary grounding for these assumptions and who believe in Him may still find my account of meaning acceptable. Those who think that God is a necessary grounding that unfortunately does not exist will reject my substantive claims about meaning for reasons we have already admitted.

The second challenge to my account of meaningfulness is more directly relevant to the issue of the nature of self-interest. It consists of an alternative subjective account of meaning. According to this position, meaning is not a matter of one's projects in life being worthwhile from some objective point of view. Rather, a person's life is meaningful, one might say, if it is meaningful *to her*, and it is meaningful to her if she thinks or feels it is.

The suggestion that something is meaningful to someone as long as she thinks it is can be of no help to us in developing an account of meaningfulness, for we cannot understand what it would be for someone to think her life meaningful until we have an account of what meaningfulness is. The view I want to discuss, however, is, strictly speaking, more concerned with a feeling or, better, a sense or qualitative character that some of our experiences have. We may use the term "fulfillment" to refer to it. It is pleasant to be or to feel fulfilled or to find an activity or a relationship fulfilling, but it is a pleasure of a specific sort, one that seems closely associated with the thought that our lives or certain activities within them are meaningful. Recognizing this, it may be suggested, gives us all the basis we need for an account of meaning that meets my requirements. We may understand people's longing for meaning as a longing for this particular feeling, a longing which other sorts of pleasure cannot satisfy. We can also explain why some activities characteristically answer the call of meaning better than others. Some yield the feeling of fulfillment while others do not. Chocolate is filling but not fulfilling; it gives pleasure but not of this particular kind. When a person steps back, wondering whether her life has had meaning, or searching for a way to give it more meaning, she may simply be surveying her life for its quotient of fulfillment or looking for ways to increase it.

The very close ties between meaningfulness and fulfillment on which this account of meaning relies are important for understanding both the concept of meaning and its value. That meaningful activity or a meaningful life is at least partly fulfilling is, as this account suggests, a conceptual truth. To *identify* meaningfulness with fulfillment, however, neglects aspects of our use of the terms, and aspects of the experiences that are described by them, that my more objective account of meaningfulness better accommodates.

For one thing, fulfillment is not a brute feeling but one with some cognitive content or concomitant. That certain activities tend to be fulfilling and others not seems connected to features of the relevant activities that make this fact intelligible. There is a fittingness between certain kinds of activities and the potential for fulfillment. When a relationship or a job is fulfilling, there is something about it that makes it so. One feels appreciated or loved, or has the sense of doing good, or finds the challenge of the work rewarding. It is not just that the activities in question meet our expectations, though that is a part of it. Some things are fine but not fulfilling—my relationship with my hairdresser, for example, or my weekly trips to the supermarket.

These considerations suggest that we find things fulfilling only if we can think about them in a certain way. It is difficult precisely to identify a single belief that is always associated with the experience of fulfillment. Still, I propose that there is some association between finding an activity fulfilling and believing, or at least dimly, inarticulately perceiving, there to be something independently worthwhile or good about it.

If we accept the idea that the feeling of fulfillment is necessarily connected with beliefs about its objects—if we accept that an activity or relationship can be fulfilling only if one believes it to be somehow independently good—then we can distinguish two hypotheses about the relationship between meaning and fulfillment. Does meaning come from the experience of fulfillment, no matter what its cause, or is a meaningful life one in which a subject is fulfilled by activities suitable to the experience? The subjective account opts for the former; but the latter seems to square better with our ordinary use of the concept.

We can construct a test case by considering someone whose judgment of an aspect of her life has changed. A woman previously blissfully in love discovers that the man she loved has been using her. She had found the relationship fulfilling before she learned of his deceits. She would have said, had you asked her earlier, that the relationship contributed to the meaningfulness of her life. What would she say now, however, and what should we say about her? No one can take away the feelings of fulfillment she experienced during the period she was deceived; but it seems unlikely that she would say, after the fact, that the relationship truly had given meaning to her life. Indeed, part of what makes this sort of event so sad is that, in addition to the pain that is caused when the deception is discovered, it undermines the value of all the pleasure that came before.

[Consider] cases of addicts or inductees of religious cults whose feelings of contentment are caused, but not justified, by the things that bring them about. Though we should be cautious about passing judgment on the activities that others take to be worthwhile, this is no reason to rule out the possibility that people are sometimes mistaken, that their finding something fulfilling can be wrongly induced, either through the establishment of false factual beliefs (such as belief in a loved one's fidelity or in the divine status of a charismatic leader) or by drugs or electrodes. If, moreover, they are led by such mind-altering means to spend their lives occupied by some equivalent of stone-rolling—watching endless reruns of *Leave It to Beaver* or counting and recounting the number of tiles on the bathroom floor— then it seems to me most in line with ordinary language to describe them as leading meaningless lives, however fulfilled they may feel themselves to be. If, further, such people wake up or snap out of it—if they come to occupy a point of view that devalues their former lives—then their later descriptions would not, I think, grant meaning to the things in which they had found contentment before.

IV. Meaningfulness and Self-Interest

So far I have been occupied with spelling out a conception of what meaningfulness in life is. My point in doing so, in the present context, is to bring it to bear on the idea of self-interest. Meaningfulness seems to me an important ingredient of a good life, and one that is too often either neglected or distorted by contemporary accounts of individual well-being.

Most people—at least most people within a certain group, bounded perhaps by class or education as well as by culture and history—behave in ways that suggest that they are looking for worthwhile things to do with their lives. They actively seek projects or, more typically, happily seize upon activities, from among those to which they are attracted, that they believe to be worthwhile. Explicit thoughts about worth and meaning often occur in connection with major life decisions, in addition to those moments of crisis to which I referred before. Some people decide to have children because they think it will give meaning to their lives. Others decide not to have children because they fear that the attendant responsibilities will deprive them of the time and resources and peace of mind that they need for other things in which they do find meaning. Deliberations about whether to pursue a particular career, or any career, may similarly involve concerns about whether the job is worthwhile, or whether it would demand time and energy that would distract one from what is worthwhile. Even many who do not talk explicitly in terms of meaning or worth make choices that are best explained by reference to them. In other words, our behavior, including some of our speech, seems to reveal a preference for a meaningful life.

We are, however, more apt to explain our choices in terms of fulfillment than meaning. A man opts for the more challenging of two possible careers, even at the cost of stress and insecurity. A woman chooses to work for less pay at a job she believes is morally valuable. People arrange their lives so as to give a few hours a week to Meals on Wheels, or to practicing piano, or to keeping up with their book group, even though it means going with a little less sleep, less flexibility, less straightforward fun. Why? Because, they will say, they find these things fulfilling. They choose to live this way because they regard it as, in some sense, best for them.

Since a meaningful life is necessarily at least partly fulfilling, and since fulfillment is a major component of happiness, a very important reason for taking meaningfulness to be in our interest is that it brings fulfillment with it. It would be misleading, however, to draw from this the conclusion that meaningfulness is an instrumental good for us. To think of meaning as good because it is a means to an independent good of fulfillment would be a mistake.

It is doubtful that fulfillment is an independent good, although feeling fulfilled is pleasant and feeling unfulfilled unpleasant. If fulfillment were an independent good, it would follow that the feeling of fulfillment would be desirable no matter what its cause. It would have to be better to be Sisyphus happy (or, more precisely, Sisyphus fulfilled) than Sisyphus unhappy (unfulfilled), even if this required that Sisyphus was perpetually stoned out of his normal mind. Opinion, however, divides on this matter. Many value fulfillment only on the condition that it be based on appropriate thoughts or perceptions. Moreover, even among those who believe that feeling fulfilled is unconditionally better than the alternative, many would still prefer that these feelings were suitably caused. Better to be Sisyphus happy than Sisyphus unhappy, they may say, but better still not to be Sisyphus at all.

A proponent of a purely hedonistic theory of self-interest may point out that reports of such intuitions prove nothing. People's thinking that justified or appropriate fulfillment is better than unjustified inappropriate fulfillment doesn't make it so. To those who have these intuitions, however, the burden of proof seems to lie with the hedonist. Unless one is committed to a purely hedonistic account of value ahead of time, there seems no reason to doubt that what is principally desirable is getting fulfillment from genuinely fulfilling activities, from activities, that is, whose accompanying feeling of fulfillment comes from the correct perception of their value. There seems no reason to doubt, in other words, that what is principally desirable is living a meaningful life and not living a life that seems or feels meaningful. Insofar as we prefer a truly meaningful life to one that merely seems or feels meaningful, a purely hedonistic theory of self-interest will not account for it.

A preference theory of self-interest, however, would not have to account for it—preference theorists simply accept our preferences and go on to compute our self-interest from there. This suggests an alternative account of the relation between meaning and self-interest. According to preference theories, meaning is important to our well-being if and only if meaning matters to us. Since many of us do want to live meaningful lives—since we think it is better for us if we do—preference theorists will agree that it is in our interest that our lives are meaningful. From their point of view, there is no need to make any more objective claims than that.

From a practical perspective, it matters little whether we accept this theory or a more objective one, particularly if you think, as I do, that the preference for a meaningful life is widespread and deep. If it is accepted as a fact of human nature (even a statistical fact, and even of a culturally created human nature) that people just do care about meaning in their lives, then this gives us reason enough to shape our lives in ways that will encourage not just fulfillment but meaningfulness, and it gives us reason enough to shape our social and political institutions in ways that will increase the opportunities for everyone to live not just happily and comfortably but meaningfully as well.

A preference theory does not, however, seem accurately to reflect the status a meaningful life has for most of us. Most of us, it seems, do not regard our preference for a meaningful life as an ungrounded preference we just happen to have. If we did think so, then we would judge it a matter of indifference whether anyone else had or lacked this preference, and indeed, we would have no reason to want to keep this preference ourselves if we were convinced that we would be better off without it. For most people, however, at least so it seems to me, having a meaningful life is a value and not just a preference. We do not just want our lives to be meaningful, we think it good that we want it. Indeed, our interest and concern for meaning is sometimes mentioned as a mark of our humanity, as an aspect of what raises us above brutes. We think that we would be diminished as a species if we lost the aspiration, or the interest, in living meaningful lives and not just happy ones. Individuals who lack the desire that their lives be meaningful we regard with regret or even pity.

Again it may be noted that our believing something is no proof of its being true, and again I must acknowledge that I have no proof of the value or objective desirability of meaningfulness. At the same time, the claim that a meaningful life is preferable (and not just brutely preferred) to a meaningless one may seem so nearly self-evident as to require no proof. Once one is willing to apply the terms of meaningfulness and meaning-lessness at all, it may seem unstable to believe that a life that lacks meaning is no worse than one that possesses it. Even if we can logically distinguish the position that some lives are more meaningful than others from the position which adds that (some) meaningfulness is a good, this latter position seems more natural than one which denies it. Though we may be unable to argue for caring about meaning in a way that would convince someone who doesn't care to begin with, the concern or the desire for meaningful activity is, for those who have it, more rationally coherent with other values and dispositions than its absence would be.

In response to the question "Why care about living a meaningful life rather than a meaningless one?" the answer that I believe best expresses reflective common sense will begin with the connection between meaning and happiness: Nine times out of ten, perhaps ninety-nine times out of a hundred, a meaningful life will be happier than a meaningless one. The feelings of fulfillment one gets from interacting positively and support-ively with things or creatures (or "realms") whose love seems deserved are wonderful feelings, worth more, on qualitative grounds alone, than many other sorts of pleasure, and worth the cost of putting up with considerable quantities of pain. Moreover, the awareness, even dim and inarticulate, of a lack of anything that can constitute a source of pride or a source of con-nection to anything valuable outside of oneself can be awful, making one irritable, restless, and contemptuous of oneself.

Except in an academic philosophical context such as this, it is perhaps unnatural to press further. If we do press further, however, it seems to me that the strength and character of these feelings of pleasure and pain are not best explained as mere quirks of our natural or culturally conditioned psyches. Rather, that we feel so good or so bad in accordance with our sense of connection to value outside ourselves seems to me best explained in terms of an underlying belief that a life is better when it possesses such connections. What precisely is better about it is difficult to say. But perhaps it has to do with our place in the universe: since we are, each of us, occu-pants in a world full of value independent of our individual selves, living in such a way as to connect positively and supportively with some nonsubjective value harmonizes better with our objective situation than would a life whose chief occupations can be only subjectively defended.

V. The Deconstruction of Self-Interest

I have in this essay been concerned to defend, or rather to elaborate, what I take to be a deeply and widely held view about individual human good, namely, that a fully successful life is, among other things, a meaningful one. Further, I have urged that this claim is distorted if it is understood as an element of either a hedonistic or a preference theory of self-interest. Properly understood, it requires a rejection of both of these sorts of theories.

As a substantive claim, I do not expect that the point that a good life must be meaningful will be surprising. We are not used to thinking very explicitly or very analytically about it, however; and in popular unreflective consciousness, a substantive interest in a meaningful life often sits side by side with assumptions that are incompatible with it. How often have you heard someone say, "What's the point of doing something if it isn't fun, or if you don't enjoy it?" I hear this sentiment expressed quite frequently, despite living on the East Coast. To be fair, such expressions tend to be limited to contexts of self-interest. They are not intended as rejections of the rational authority of moral or legal obligation. Moreover, there is often a point behind such remarks that I would strongly endorse. Against a kind of workaholism and related neurotic obsessions with some forms of success and achievement, it can be useful to step back and reflect in the way these remarks would invoke. Still, the suggestion that there can be no point to things if they are neither duties nor fun is, strictly speaking, both false and dangerous.

Much of what we do would be inexplicable, or at least indefensible, if its justification depended either on its being a duty or, even in the long run, on its maximally contributing to our net fun. Relationships with friends and family, nonobligatory aspects of professional roles, and long-term commitments to artistic, scholarly, or athletic endeavors typically lead us to devote time and energy to things that are difficult and unpleasant, and to forgo opportunities for relaxation and enjoyment. It is arguable that many of these choices advance our happiness (in the broadest sense, our fun) in the long run, but such arguments are at best uncertain, and the thought that they are necessary for the defense of these choices puts a regrettable kind of pressure on the commitments that give rise to them. There is, however, a point—even a self-interested point—to doing things that fall outside the categories both of duty and of fun. One can find a reason, or at least a justifying explanation, for doing something in the fact that the act or activity in question contributes to the meaningfulness of one's life.

Once we have ceased to identify self-interest with happiness, however, other assumptions are also undermined. The concept of self-interest becomes more difficult to work with. Specifically, a conception of self-interest that recognizes the importance of meaning to a good life admits of much greater indeterminacy than the more traditional conceptions. This is partly a function of indeterminacy within the category of meaningfulness itself. Though meaningfulness is not an all-or-nothing concept—some lives are more meaningful than others, a person's life may not have *enough* meaning in it to be satisfactory—there is no well-formed system for making comparative judgments. The meaningfulness of a life may vary depending on how much of it is spent in meaningful activity, on how worthwhile the activities in question are, or on how fully engaged (or attracted) the individual is. In many instances, however, it seems absurd to think there is a correct comparison to be made. Is the life of a great but lonely philosopher more or less meaningful than that of a beloved housekeeper? There seems to be no reason to assume that there is a fact of the matter about this. Moreover, from a self-interested point of view, it is unclear whether, beyond a certain point, it matters whether one's life is more meaningful. A meaningful life is better than a meaningless one, but once it is meaningful enough, there may be no self-interested reason to want, as it were, to squeeze more meaning into it. Finally, the mix between meaning and felt happiness may have no determinate ideal. A person often has to choose between taking a path that would strengthen or expand a part of his or her life that contributes to its meaningfulness (going to graduate school, adopting a child, getting politically involved) and taking an easier or more pleasant road. Once one has accepted a conception of self-interest that recognizes meaningfulness as an independent aspect of one's personal good, one may have to admit that in such cases there may be no answer to the question of what is most in one's self-interest.

Susan Wolf: Happiness and Meaning: Two Aspects of the Good Life

1. How does Wolf define a meaningful life? Do you agree with her definition?
2. The mythical Sisyphus was condemned by the gods to roll a huge boulder up a hill, watch it inevitably fall to the bottom, and then repeat his

efforts—forever. Imagine that this is just the life that Sisyphus prefers for himself and that he is happy with his fate. Why does Wolf think that such a life would nevertheless be meaningless? Do you agree?

3. Wolf identifies both happiness and meaning as elements in a good life. Do you think that there are any others? If so, state and argue for them.

4. Wolf concedes that if nothing were objectively valuable, then her theory would imply that our lives are meaningless. Are you persuaded by her claims and examples to share her view that there are indeed objectively worthwhile activities? Why or why not?

5. Suppose that nothing is objectively valuable and that our lives are therefore (according to Wolf) meaningless. Imagine, though, that we found much of what we did fulfilling and were engaged in our activities in a way that led to a sense of personal satisfaction. How bad for us would it be to lack meaning in our lives?

PART II

Normative Ethics

Theories of Right Conduct

6

Euthyphro

Plato

In an early section (omitted here) of this dialogue about the nature of piety, Socrates bumps into Euthyphro in front of the law courts of Athens. Socrates is on trial for his life; Euthyphro is there to prosecute a murderer. It turns out that Euthyphro is prosecuting his own father, an act that would shock ancient Greek audiences as much as it would shock us in our own time. When Socrates asks him why he would do such a thing, Euthyphro replies that he is privy to many secrets of the gods, and that piety demands that he seek his father's conviction.

Our excerpt picks up at this point. Socrates immediately begs Euthyphro to reveal the essence of piety, its true nature, so that Socrates and others may live more pious lives. Euthyphro first provides some examples of pious actions, but this is not what Socrates is after. He wants to know what is common to all instances of piety. Euthyphro then says that piety is what the gods love.

Socrates then asks what has since come to be known as the Euthyphro Question: Are acts pious because the gods love them, or do the gods love actions because they are pious? We can modify the question a bit to get the following puzzle: Is an action morally right because God commands it, or does God command an action because it is right?

From *Five Dialogues*, 2nd ed., trans. G. M. A. Grube, rev. by John Cooper (Indianapolis: Hackett Publishers, 2002), pp. 7–14.

Many who think that religion is essential to morality endorse the first option—God's commands are what make actions right, so that if God does not exist, or does not issue commands, then nothing is morally right. Plato's arguments are designed to cast doubt on this view.

....

Socrates: . . . So tell me now, by Zeus, what you just now maintained you clearly knew: what kind of thing do you say that godliness and ungodliness are, both as regards murder and other things; or is the pious not the same and alike in every action, and the impious the opposite of all that is pious and like itself, and everything that is to be impious presents us with one form or appearance insofar as it is impious?

Euthyphro: Most certainly, Socrates.

Socrates: Tell me then, what is the pious, and what the impious, do you say?

Euthyphro: I say that the pious is to do what I am doing now, to prosecute the wrongdoer, be it about murder or temple robbery or anything else, whether the wrongdoer is your father or your mother or anyone else; not to prosecute is impious. And observe, Socrates, that I can cite powerful evidence that the law is so. I have already said to others that such actions are right, not to favor the ungodly, whoever they are. These people themselves believe that Zeus is the best and most just of the gods, yet they agree that he bound his father because he unjustly swallowed his sons, and that he in turn castrated his father for similar reasons. But they are angry with me because I am prosecuting my father for his wrongdoing. They contradict themselves in what they say about the gods and about me. . . .

Socrates: And do you believe that there really is war among the gods, and terrible enmities and battles, and other such things as are told by the poets, and other sacred stories such as are embroidered by good writers and by representations of which the robe of the goddess is adorned when it is carried up to the Acropolis? Are we to say these things are true, Euthyphro?

Euthyphro: Not only these, Socrates, but, as I was saying just now, I will, if you wish, relate many other things about the gods which I know will amaze you.

Socrates: I should not be surprised, but you will tell me these at leisure some other time. For now, try to tell me more clearly what I was asking just now, for, my friend, you did not teach me adequately when I asked you what the pious was, but you told me that what you are doing now, in prosecuting your father for murder, is pious.

EUTHYPHRO: And I told the truth, Socrates.

SOCRATES: Perhaps. You agree, however, that there are many other pious actions.

EUTHYPHRO: There are.

SOCRATES: Bear in mind then that I did not bid you tell me one or two of the many pious actions but that form itself that makes all pious actions pious, for you agreed that all impious actions are impious and all pious actions pious through one form, or don't you remember?

EUTHYPHRO: I do.

SOCRATES: Tell me then what this form itself is, so that I may look upon it and, using it as a model, say that any action of yours or another's that is of that kind is pious, and if it is not that it is not.

EUTHYPHRO: If that is how you want it, Socrates, that is how I will tell you.

SOCRATES: That is what I want.

EUTHYPHRO: Well then, what is dear to the gods is pious, what is not is impious.

SOCRATES: Splendid, Euthyphro! You have now answered in the way I wanted. Whether your answer is true I do not know yet, but you will obviously show me that what you say is true.

EUTHYPHRO: Certainly.

SOCRATES: Come then, let us examine what we mean. An action or a man dear to the gods is pious, but an action or a man hated by the gods is impious. They are not the same, but quite opposite, the pious and the impious. Is that not so?

EUTHYPHRO: It is indeed.

SOCRATES: And that seems to be a good statement?

EUTHYPHRO: I think so, Socrates.

SOCRATES: We have also stated that the gods are in a state of discord, that they are at odds with each other, Euthyphro, and that they are at enmity with each other. Has that, too, been said?

EUTHYPHRO: It has.

SOCRATES: What are the subjects of difference that cause hatred and anger? Let us look at it this way. If you and I were to differ about numbers as to which is the greater, would this difference make us enemies and angry with each other, or would we proceed to count and soon resolve our difference about this?

EUTHYPHRO: We would certainly do so.

SOCRATES: Again, if we differed about the larger and the smaller, we would turn to measurement and soon cease to differ.

EUTHYPHRO: That is so.

SOCRATES: And about the heavier and the lighter, we would resort to weighing and be reconciled.

EUTHYPHRO: Of course.

SOCRATES: What subject of difference would make us angry and hostile to each other if we were unable to come to a decision? Perhaps you do not have an answer ready, but examine as I tell you whether these subjects are the just and the unjust, the beautiful and the ugly, the good and the bad. Are these not the subjects of difference about which, when we are unable to come to a satisfactory decision, you and I and other men become hostile to each other whenever we do?

EUTHYPHRO: That is the difference, Socrates, about those subjects.

SOCRATES: What about the gods, Euthyphro? If indeed they have differences, will it not be about these same subjects?

EUTHYPHRO: It certainly must be so.

SOCRATES: Then according to your argument, my good Euthyphro, different gods consider different things to be just, beautiful, ugly, good, and bad, for they would not be at odds with one another unless they differed about these subjects, would they?

EUTHYPHRO: You are right.

SOCRATES: And they like what each of them considers beautiful, good, and just, and hate the opposites of these?

EUTHYPHRO: Certainly.

SOCRATES: But you say that the same things are considered just by some gods and unjust by others, and as they dispute about these things they are at odds and at war with each other. Is that not so?

EUTHYPHRO: It is.

SOCRATES: The same things then are loved by the gods and hated by the gods, and would be both god-loved and god-hated.

EUTHYPHRO: It seems likely.

SOCRATES: And the same things would be both pious and impious, according to this argument?

EUTHYPHRO: I'm afraid so.

SOCRATES: So you did not answer my question, you surprising man. I did not ask you what same thing is both pious and impious, and it appears that what is loved by the gods is also hated by them. So it is in no way surprising if your present action, namely punishing your father, may be pleasing to Zeus but displeasing to Cronus and Uranus, pleasing to Hephaestus but displeasing to Hera, and so with any other gods who differ from each other on this subject.

EUTHYPHRO: I think, Socrates, that on this subject no gods would differ from one another, that whoever has killed anyone unjustly should pay the penalty.

SOCRATES: Well now, Euthyphro, have you ever heard any man maintaining that one who has killed or done anything else unjustly should not pay the penalty?

EUTHYPHRO: They never cease to dispute on this subject, both elsewhere and in the courts, for when they have committed many wrongs they do and say anything to avoid the penalty.

SOCRATES: Do they agree they have done wrong, Euthyphro, and in spite of so agreeing do they nevertheless say they should not be punished?

EUTHYPHRO: No, they do not agree on that point.

SOCRATES: So they do not say or do just anything. For they do not venture to say this, or dispute that they must not pay the penalty if they have done wrong, but I think they deny doing wrong. Is that not so?

EUTHYPHRO: That is true.

SOCRATES: Then they do not dispute that the wrongdoer must be punished, but they may disagree as to who the wrongdoer is, what he did, and when.

EUTHYPHRO: You are right.

SOCRATES: Do not the gods have the same experience, if indeed they are at odds with each other about the just and the unjust, as your argument maintains? Some assert that they wrong one another, while others deny it, but no one among gods or men ventures to say that the wrongdoer must not be punished.

EUTHYPHRO: Yes, that is true, Socrates, as to the main point.

SOCRATES: And those who disagree, whether men or gods, dispute about each action, if indeed the gods disagree. Some say it is done justly, others unjustly. Is that not so?

EUTHYPHRO: Yes, indeed.

SOCRATES: Come now, my dear Euthyphro, tell me, too, that I may become wiser, what proof you have that all the gods consider that man to have been killed unjustly who became a murderer while in your service, was bound by the master of his victim, and died in his bonds before the one who bound him found out from the seers what was to be done with him, and that it is right for a son to denounce and to prosecute his father on behalf of such a man. Come, try to show me a clear sign that all the gods definitely believe this action to be right. If you can give me adequate proof of this, I shall never cease to extol your wisdom.

Euthyphro: This is perhaps no light task, Socrates, though I could show you very clearly.

Socrates: I understand that you think me more dull-witted than the jury, as you will obviously show them that these actions were unjust and that all the gods hate such actions.

Euthyphro: I will show it to them clearly, Socrates, if only they will listen to me.

Socrates: They will listen if they think you show them well. But this thought came to me as you were speaking, and I am examining it, saying to myself: "If Euthyphro shows me conclusively that all the gods consider such a death unjust, to what greater extent have I learned from him the nature of piety and impiety? This action would then, it seems, be hated by the gods, but the pious and the impious were not thereby now defined, for what is hated by the gods has also been shown to be loved by them." So I will not insist on this point; let us assume, if you wish, that all the gods consider this unjust and that they all hate it. However, is this the correction we are making in our discussion, that what all the gods hate is impious, and what they all love is pious, and that what some gods love and others hate is neither or both? Is that how you now wish us to define piety and impiety?

Euthyphro: What prevents us from doing so, Socrates?

Socrates: For my part nothing, Euthyphro, but you look whether on your part this proposal will enable you to teach me most easily what you promised.

Euthyphro: I would certainly say that the pious is what all the gods love, and the opposite, what all the gods hate, is the impious.

Socrates: Then let us again examine whether that is a sound statement, or do we let it pass, and if one of us, or someone else, merely says that something is so, do we accept that it is so? Or should we examine what the speaker means?

Euthyphro: We must examine it, but I certainly think that this is now a fine statement.

Socrates: We shall soon know better whether it is. Consider this: Is the pious being loved by the gods because it is pious, or is it pious because it is being loved by the gods?

EUTHYPHRO: I don't know what you mean, Socrates.

SOCRATES: I shall try to explain more clearly: we speak of something carried and something carrying, of something led and something leading, of something seen and something seeing, and you understand that these things are all different from one another and how they differ?

EUTHYPHRO: I think I do.

SOCRATES: So there is also something loved and—a different thing—something loving.

EUTHYPHRO: Of course.

SOCRATES: Tell me then whether the thing carried is a carried thing because it is being carried, or for some other reason?

EUTHYPHRO: No, that is the reason.

SOCRATES: And the thing led is so because it is being led, and the thing seen because it is being seen?

EUTHYPHRO: Certainly.

SOCRATES: It is not being seen because it is a thing seen but on the contrary it is a thing seen because it is being seen; nor is it because it is something led that it is being led but because it is being led that it is something led; nor is something being carried because it is something carried, but it is something carried because it is being carried. Is what I want to say clear, Euthyphro? I want to say this, namely, that if anything is being changed or is being affected in any way, it is not being changed because it is something changed, but rather it is something changed because it is being changed; nor is it being affected because it is something affected, but it is something affected because it is being affected. Or do you not agree?

EUTHYPHRO: I do.

SOCRATES: Is something loved either something changed or something affected by something?

EUTHYPHRO: Certainly.

SOCRATES: So it is in the same case as the things just mentioned; it is not being loved by those who love it because it is something loved, but it is something loved because it is being loved by them?

EUTHYPHRO: Necessarily.

SOCRATES: What then do we say about the pious, Euthyphro? Surely that it is being loved by all the gods, according to what you say?

EUTHYPHRO: Yes.

SOCRATES: Is it being loved because it is pious, or for some other reason?

EUTHYPHRO: For no other reason.

Socrates: It is being loved then because it is pious, but it is not pious because it is being loved?

Euthyphro: Apparently.

Socrates: And yet it is something loved and god-loved because it is being loved by the gods?

Euthyphro: Of course.

Socrates: Then the god-loved is not the same as the pious, Euthyphro, nor the pious the same as the god-loved, as you say it is, but one differs from the other.

Euthyphro: How so, Socrates?

Socrates: Because we agree that the pious is being loved for this reason, that it is pious, but it is not pious because it is being loved. Is that not so?

Euthyphro: Yes.

Socrates: And that the god-loved, on the other hand, is so because it is being loved by the gods, by the very fact of being loved, but it is not being loved because it is god-loved.

Euthyphro: True.

Socrates: But if the god-loved and the pious were the same, my dear Euthyphro, then if the pious was being loved because it was pious, the god-loved would also be being loved because it was god-loved; and if the god-loved was god-loved because it was being loved by the gods, then the pious would also be pious because it was being loved by the gods. But now you see that they are in opposite cases as being altogether different from each other: the one is such as to be loved because it is being loved, the other is being loved because it is such as to be loved. I'm afraid, Euthyphro, that when you were asked what piety is, you did not wish to make its nature clear to me, but you told me an affect or a quality of it, that the pious has the quality of being loved by all the gods, but you have not yet told me what the pious is.

Plato: Euthyphro

1. What is Euthyphro's first answer to Socrates's question about the nature of piety? Why does Socrates find this answer to be inadequate?

2. In his second attempt to answer Socrates's question, Euthyphro suggests that "what is dear to the gods is pious, what is not is impious." Socrates points out that the gods sometimes disagree (according to the traditional religious views of ancient Greece). Why does this raise a problem

for the view in question? Is there any analogous problem for the monotheistic theory that what God commands is morally right?

3. The most famous question of the dialogue comes when Socrates asks: "Is the pious being loved by the gods because it is pious, or is it pious because it is being loved by the gods?" How does Socrates attempt to explain this question when Euthyphro does not understand? What exactly does the question mean?

4. When Euthyphro suggests that the gods love the pious because it is pious, Socrates responds with the complaint, "you have not yet told me what the pious is." Why does Socrates say this? Is he correct?

5. Suppose Euthyphro were to claim that the pious is pious because it is loved by the gods. What objections might Socrates raise to this proposal?

7

Natural Law

Thomas Aquinas

· ·

This is a short excerpt from St. Thomas Aquinas's magnum opus, *Summa Theologica*, which has served as a central basis of Roman Catholic theology since Aquinas wrote it over seven hundred years ago. Here Aquinas offers some of the essentials of his understanding of natural law. The text is difficult for contemporary readers but repays careful study. In it, Aquinas develops his conception of natural law by considering a series of objections to various aspects of it, then offering three sorts of reply: first, one that cites a biblical text in support of his position; second, a general reply that sets the objection in context; and third, a specific reply to each of the objections he considers.

In this selection Aquinas develops his views on natural law by first asking (and answering) the question of whether there is an unchanging, eternal law. He answers affirmatively, arguing that God (whose existence is presupposed throughout this selection) is himself unchanging and eternal, and that since God governs the entire universe by means of various principles (he calls these "dictates of practical reason"), these laws themselves are eternal and unchanging. The natural law is a subset of the eternal laws and is therefore itself eternal and in some respects unchanging. Aquinas divides the natural law into first principles—the fundamental ones that are taken as self-evident axioms

From *Summa Theologica*, First Part of the Second Part, Question 91, Articles 1 and 2; Question 94, Articles 2–6. Benziger Brothers edition, 1947. Translated by Fathers of the English Dominican Province.

and are entirely unchanging—and secondary ones, which might sometimes be difficult to discern and in rare cases admit of change.

Aquinas argues that everyone has God-given, innate knowledge of the basic principles of natural law, though our understanding may be clouded by various things. He then argues that virtuous acts are those prescribed by the natural law. He claims that we are naturally inclined to act in accordance with reason; acting in accordance with reason is always virtuous; and so acting naturally is always virtuous. And acting unnaturally—as, he claims, people do when having intercourse with others of the same sex—is invariably immoral. Aquinas then considers whether natural law might be different for those in different societies or for those of different temperaments. He argues that its general principles are universally binding on all human beings at all times, but allows that certain secondary principles might subtly differ depending on circumstances.

....

Whether There Is an Eternal Law?

Objection 1: It would seem that there is no eternal law. Because every law is imposed on someone. But there was not someone from eternity on whom a law could be imposed: since God alone was from eternity. Therefore no law is eternal.

Objection 2: Further, promulgation is essential to law. But promulgation could not be from eternity: because there was no one to whom it could be promulgated from eternity. Therefore no law can be eternal.

On the contrary, Augustine says (De Lib. Arb. i, 6): "That Law which is the Supreme Reason cannot be understood to be otherwise than unchangeable and eternal."

I answer that a law is nothing else but a dictate of practical reason emanating from the ruler who governs a perfect community. Now it is evident, granted that the world is ruled by Divine Providence . . . that the whole community of the universe is governed by Divine Reason. Wherefore the very Idea of the government of things in God the Ruler of the universe, has the nature of a law. And since the Divine Reason's conception of things is not subject to time but is eternal, according to Prov. 8:23, therefore it is that this kind of law must be called eternal.

Reply to Objection 1: Those things that are not in themselves, exist with God, inasmuch as they are foreknown and preordained by Him, according to Rm. 4:17: "Who calls those things that are not, as those that are." Accordingly the eternal concept of the Divine law bears the character of an eternal law, in so far as it is ordained by God to the government of things foreknown by Him.

Reply to Objection 2: Promulgation is made by word of mouth or in writing; and in both ways the eternal law is promulgated: because both the Divine Word and the writing of the Book of Life are eternal. But the promulgation cannot be from eternity on the part of the creature that hears or reads.

Whether There Is in Us a Natural Law?

Objection 1: It would seem that there is no natural law in us. Because man is governed sufficiently by the eternal law: for Augustine says (De Lib. Arb. i) that "the eternal law is that by which it is right that all things should be most orderly." But nature does not abound in superfluities as neither does she fail in necessaries. Therefore no law is natural to man.

Objection 2: Further, by the law man is directed, in his acts, to the end. But the directing of human acts to their end is not a function of nature, as is the case in irrational creatures, which act for an end solely by their natural appetite; whereas man acts for an end by his reason and will. Therefore no law is natural to man.

Objection 3: Further, the more a man is free, the less is he under the law. But man is freer than all the animals, on account of his free-will, with which he is endowed above all other animals. Since therefore other animals are not subject to a natural law, neither is man subject to a natural law.

On the contrary, a gloss on Rm. 2:14: "When the Gentiles, who have not the law, do by nature those things that are of the law," comments as follows: "Although they have no written law, yet they have the natural law, whereby each one knows, and is conscious of, what is good and what is evil."

I answer that law, being a rule and measure, can be in a person in two ways: in one way, as in him that rules and measures; in another way, as in that which is ruled and measured, since a thing is ruled and measured, in so far as it partakes of the rule or measure. Wherefore, since all things subject to Divine providence are ruled and measured by the eternal law; it is evident that all things partake somewhat of the eternal law, in so far as, namely, from its being imprinted on them, they derive their respective inclinations to their proper acts and ends. Now among all others, the rational creature is subject to Divine providence in the most excellent way, in so far as it partakes of a share of providence, by being provident both for itself and for others. Wherefore it has a share of the Eternal Reason, whereby it has a natural inclination to its proper act and end: and this participation of the eternal law in the rational creature is called the natural law. Hence the Psalmist: "The light of Thy countenance, O Lord, is signed upon us": thus implying that the light of natural reason, whereby we discern what is good and what is evil, which is the function of the natural law, is nothing else than an imprint on us of the Divine light. It is therefore evident that the natural law is nothing else than the rational creature's participation of the eternal law.

Reply to Objection 1: This argument would hold, if the natural law were something different from the eternal law: whereas it is nothing but a participation thereof.

Reply to Objection 2: Every act of reason and will in us is based on that which is according to nature: for every act of reasoning is based on principles that are known naturally, and every act of appetite in respect of the means is derived from the natural appetite in respect of the last end. Accordingly the first direction of our acts to their end must be in virtue of the natural law.

Reply to Objection 3: Even irrational animals partake in their own way of the Eternal Reason, just as the rational creature does. But because the rational creature partakes thereof in an intellectual and rational manner, therefore the participation of the eternal law in the rational creature is properly called a law, since a law is something pertaining to reason. Irrational creatures, however, do not partake thereof in a rational manner, wherefore there is no participation of the eternal law in them, except by way of similitude.

Whether the Natural Law Contains Several Precepts, or Only One?

Objection 1: It would seem that the natural law contains, not several precepts, but one only. For law is a kind of precept. If therefore there were many precepts of the natural law, it would follow that there are also many natural laws.

Objection 2: Further, the natural law is consequent to human nature. But human nature, as a whole, is one; though, as to its parts, it is manifold.

Therefore, either there is but one precept of the law of nature, on account of the unity of nature as a whole; or there are many, by reason of the number of parts of human nature. The result would be that even things relating to the inclination of the concupiscible faculty belong to the natural law.

Objection 3: Further, law is something pertaining to reason. Now reason is but one in man. Therefore there is only one precept of the natural law.

On the contrary, the precepts of the natural law in man stand in relation to practical matters, as the first principles to matters of demonstration. But there are several first indemonstrable principles. Therefore there are also several precepts of the natural law.

I answer that the precepts of the natural law are to the practical reason, what the first principles of demonstrations are to the speculative reason; because both are self-evident principles. Now a thing is said to be self-evident in two ways: first, in itself; secondly, in relation to us. Any proposition is said to be self-evident in itself, if its predicate is contained in the notion of the subject: although, to one who knows not the definition of the subject, it happens that such a proposition is not self-evident. For instance, this proposition, "Man is a rational being," is, in its very nature, self-evident, since who says "man," says "a rational being": and yet to one who knows not what a man is, this proposition is not self-evident. Hence it is that, as Boethius says (De Hebdom.), certain axioms or propositions are universally self-evident to all; and such are those propositions whose terms are known to all, as, "Every whole is greater than its part," and, "Things equal to one and the same are equal to one another." But some propositions are self-evident only to the wise, who understand the meaning of the terms of such propositions: thus to one who understands that an angel is not a body, it is self-evident that an angel is not circumscriptively in a place: but this is not evident to the unlearned, for they cannot grasp it.

Now a certain order is to be found in those things that are apprehended universally. For that which, before aught else, falls under apprehension, is "being," the notion of which is included in all things whatsoever a man apprehends. Wherefore the first indemonstrable principle is that "the same thing cannot be affirmed and denied at the same time," which is based on the notion of "being" and "not-being": and on this principle all others are based. Now as "being" is the first thing that falls under the apprehension simply, so "good" is the first thing that falls under the apprehension of the practical reason, which is directed to action: since every agent acts for an end under the aspect of good. Consequently the first principle of practical reason is one founded on the notion of good, viz. that "good is that which all things seek after." Hence this is the first precept of law, that "good is to be done and pursued, and evil is to be avoided." All other precepts of the natural law are based upon this: so that whatever the practical reason naturally apprehends as man's good (or evil) belongs to the precepts of the natural law as something to be done or avoided.

Since, however, good has the nature of an end, and evil, the nature of a contrary, hence it is that all those things to which man has a natural inclination, are naturally apprehended by reason as being good, and consequently as objects of pursuit, and their contraries as evil, and objects of avoidance. Wherefore according to the order of natural inclinations, is the order of the precepts of the natural law. Because in man there is first of all an inclination to good in accordance with the nature which he has in common with all substances: inasmuch as every substance seeks the preservation of its own being, according to its nature: and by reason of this inclination, whatever is a means of preserving human life, and of warding off its obstacles, belongs to the natural law. Secondly, there is in man an inclination to things that pertain to him more specially, according to that nature which he has in common with other animals: and in virtue of this inclination, those things are said to belong to the natural law, "which nature has taught to all animals" [Pandect. Just. I, tit. i], such as sexual intercourse, education of offspring and so forth. Thirdly, there is in man an inclination to good, according to the nature of his reason, which nature is proper to him: thus man has a natural inclination to know the truth about God, and to live in society: and in this respect, whatever pertains to this inclination belongs to the natural law; for instance, to shun ignorance, to avoid offending those among whom one has to live, and other such things regarding the above inclination.

Reply to Objection 1: All these precepts of the law of nature have the character of one natural law, inasmuch as they flow from one first precept.

Reply to Objection 2: All the inclinations of any parts whatsoever of human nature, e.g. of the concupiscible and irascible parts, in so far as they are ruled by reason, belong to the natural law, and are reduced to one first precept, as stated above: so that the precepts of the natural law are many in themselves, but are based on one common foundation.

Reply to Objection 3: Although reason is one in itself, yet it directs all things regarding man; so that whatever can be ruled by reason, is contained under the law of reason.

Whether All Acts of Virtue Are Prescribed by the Natural Law?

Objection 1: It would seem that not all acts of virtue are prescribed by the natural law. Because it is essential to a law that it be ordained to the common good. But some acts of virtue are ordained to the private good of the individual, as is evident especially in regards to acts of temperance. Therefore not all acts of virtue are the subject of natural law.

Objection 2: Further, every sin is opposed to some virtuous act. If therefore all acts of virtue are prescribed by the natural law, it seems to follow that all sins are against nature: whereas this applies [only] to certain special sins.

Objection 3: Further, those things which are according to nature are common to all. But acts of virtue are not common to all, since a thing is virtuous in one, and vicious in another. Therefore not all acts of virtue are prescribed by the natural law.

On the contrary, Damascene says (De Fide Orth. iii, 4) that "virtues are natural." Therefore virtuous acts also are a subject of the natural law.

I answer that, We may speak of virtuous acts in two ways: first, under the aspect of virtuous; secondly, as such and such acts considered in their proper species. If then we speak of acts of virtue, considered as virtuous, thus all virtuous acts belong to the natural law. For to the natural law belongs everything to which a man is inclined according to his nature. Now each thing is inclined naturally to an operation that is suitable to it according to its form: thus fire is inclined to give heat. Wherefore, since the rational soul is the proper form of man, there is in every man a natural inclination to act according to reason: and this is to act according to virtue. Consequently, considered thus, all acts of virtue are prescribed by the natural law: since each one's reason naturally dictates to him to act virtuously. But if we speak of virtuous acts, considered in themselves, i.e. in their proper species, then not all virtuous acts are prescribed by the natural law: for many things are done virtuously, to which nature does not incline at first; but which, through the inquiry of reason, have been found by men to be conducive to well-living.

Reply to Objection 1: Temperance is about the natural concupiscences of food, drink and sexual matters, which are indeed ordained to the natural common good, just as other matters of law are ordained to the moral common good.

Reply to Objection 2: By human nature we may mean either that which is proper to man—and in this sense all sins, as being against reason, are also against nature: or we may mean that nature which is common to man and other animals; and in this sense, certain special sins are said to be against nature; thus contrary to sexual intercourse, which is natural to all animals, is unisexual lust, which has received the special name of the unnatural crime.

Reply to Objection 3: This argument considers acts in themselves. For it is owing to the various conditions of men, that certain acts are virtuous for some, as being proportionate and becoming to them, while they are vicious for others, as being out of proportion to them.

Whether the Natural Law Is the Same in All Men?

Objection 1: It would seem that the natural law is not the same in all. For it is stated in the Decretals (Dist. i) that "the natural law is that which is contained in the Law and the Gospel." But this is not common to all men; because, as it is written (Rm. 10:16), "not all obey the gospel." Therefore the natural law is not the same in all men.

Objection 2: Further, "Things which are according to the law are said to be just," as stated in [Aristotle's] Ethic. v. But it is stated in the same book that nothing is so universally just as not to be subject to change in regard to some men. Therefore even the natural law is not the same in all men.

Objection 3: Further, to the natural law belongs everything to which a man is inclined according to his nature. Now different men are naturally inclined to different things; some to the desire of pleasures, others to the desire of honors, and other men to other things. Therefore there is not one natural law for all.

On the contrary, Isidore says (Etym. v, 4): "The natural law is common to all nations."

I answer that, to the natural law belongs those things to which a man is inclined naturally: and among these it is proper to man to be inclined to act according to reason. Now the process of reason is from the common to the proper, as stated in [Aristotle's] Phys. i. The speculative reason, however, is differently situated in this matter, from the practical reason. For, since the speculative reason is busied chiefly with the necessary things, which cannot be otherwise than they are, its proper conclusions, like the universal principles, contain the truth without fail. The practical reason, on the other hand, is busied with contingent matters, about which human actions are concerned: and consequently, although there is necessity in the general principles, the more we descend to matters of detail, the more frequently we encounter defects. Accordingly then in speculative matters truth is the same in all men, both as to principles and as to conclusions: although the truth is not known to all as regards the conclusions, but only as regards the principles which are called common notions. But in matters of action, truth or practical rectitude is not the same for all, as to matters of detail, but only as to the general principles: and where there is the same rectitude in matters of detail, it is not equally known to all.

It is therefore evident that, as regards the general principles whether of speculative or of practical reason, truth or rectitude is the same for all, and is equally known by all. As to the proper conclusions of the speculative reason, the truth is the same for all, but is not equally known to all: thus it is true for all that the three angles of a triangle are together equal to two right angles, although it is not known to all. But as to the proper conclusions of the practical reason, neither is the truth or rectitude the same for all, nor, where it is the same, is it equally known by all. Thus it is right and true for all to act according to reason: and from this principle it follows as a proper conclusion, that goods entrusted to another should be restored to their owner. Now this is true for the majority of cases: but it may happen in a particular case that it would be injurious, and therefore unreasonable, to restore goods held in trust; for instance, if they are claimed for the purpose of fighting against one's country. And this principle will be found to fail the more, according as we descend further into detail, e.g. if one were to say that goods held in trust should be restored with such and such a guarantee, or in such and such a way; because the greater the number of conditions added, the greater the number of ways in which the principle may fail, so that it be not right to restore or not to restore.

Consequently we must say that the natural law, as to general principles, is the same for all, both as to rectitude and as to knowledge. But as to certain matters of detail, which are conclusions, as it were, of those general principles, it is the same for all in the majority of cases, both as to rectitude and as to knowledge; and yet in some few cases it may fail, both as to rectitude, by reason of certain obstacles (just as natures subject to generation and corruption fail in some few cases on account of some obstacle), and as to knowledge, since in some the reason is perverted by passion, or evil habit, or an evil disposition of nature; thus formerly, theft, although it is expressly contrary to the natural law, was not considered wrong among the Germans, as Julius Caesar relates (De Bello Gall. vi).

Reply to Objection 1: The meaning of the sentence quoted is not that whatever is contained in the Law and the Gospel belongs to the natural law, since they contain many things that are above nature; but that whatever belongs to the natural law is fully contained in them. Wherefore Gratian, after saying that "the natural law is what is contained in the Law and the Gospel," adds at once, by way of example, "by which everyone is commanded to do to others as he would be done by."

Reply to Objection 2: The saying of the Philosopher [Aristotle] is to be understood of things that are naturally just, not as general principles, but as conclusions drawn from them, having rectitude in the majority of cases, but failing in a few.

Reply to Objection 3: As, in man, reason rules and commands the other powers, so all the natural inclinations belonging to the other powers must needs be directed according to reason. Wherefore it is universally right for all men, that all their inclinations should be directed according to reason.

Whether the Natural Law Can Be Changed?

Objection 1: It would seem that the natural law can be changed. Because on Ecclus. 17:9, "He gave them instructions, and the law of life," the gloss says: "He wished the law of the letter to be written, in order to correct the law of nature." But that which is corrected is changed. Therefore the natural law can be changed.

Objection 2: Further, the slaying of the innocent, adultery, and theft are against the natural law. But we find these things changed by God: as when God commanded Abraham to slay his innocent son (Gen. 22:2); and when he ordered the Jews to borrow and purloin the vessels of the Egyptians (Ex. 12:35); and when He commanded Osee to take to himself "a wife of fornications" (Osee 1:2). Therefore the natural law can be changed.

Objection 3: Further, Isidore says (Etym. 5:4) that "the possession of all things in common, and universal freedom, are matters of natural law." But these things are seen to be changed by human laws. Therefore it seems that the natural law is subject to change.

On the contrary, It is said in the Decretals (Dist. v): "The natural law dates from the creation of the rational creature. It does not vary according to time, but remains unchangeable."

I answer that, A change in the natural law may be understood in two ways. First, by way of addition. In this sense nothing hinders the natural law from being changed: since many things for the benefit of human life have been added over and above the natural law, both by the Divine law and by human laws.

Secondly, a change in the natural law may be understood by way of subtraction, so that what previously was according to the natural law, ceases to be so. In this sense, the natural law is altogether unchangeable in its first principles: but in its secondary principles, which are certain detailed proximate conclusions drawn from the first principles, the natural law is not changed so that what it prescribes be not right in most cases. But it may be changed in some particular cases of rare occurrence, through some special causes hindering the observance of such precepts.

Reply to Objection 1: The written law is said to be given for the correction of the natural law, either because it supplies what was wanting to the natural law; or because the natural law was perverted in the hearts of some men, as to certain matters, so that they esteemed those things good which are naturally evil; which perversion stood in need of correction.

Reply to Objection 2: All men alike, both guilty and innocent, die the death of nature: which death of nature is inflicted by the power of God on account of original sin, according to 1 Kgs. 2:6: "The Lord killeth and maketh alive." Consequently, by the command of God, death can be inflicted on any man, guilty or innocent, without any injustice whatever. In like manner adultery is intercourse with another's wife; who is allotted to him by the law emanating from God. Consequently intercourse with any woman, by the command of God, is neither adultery nor fornication. The same applies to theft, which is the taking of another's property. For whatever is taken by the command of God, to Whom all things belong, is not taken against the will of its owner, whereas it is in this that theft consists. Nor is it only in human things, that whatever is commanded by God is right; but also in natural things, whatever is done by God, is, in some way, natural.

Reply to Objection 3: A thing is said to belong to the natural law in two ways. First, because nature inclines thereto: e.g. that one should not do harm to another. Secondly, because nature did not bring in the contrary: thus we might say that for man to be naked is of the natural law, because nature did not give him clothes, but art invented them. In this sense, "the possession of all things in common and universal freedom" are said to be of the natural law, because, to wit, the distinction of possessions and slavery were not brought in by nature, but devised by human reason for the benefit of human life. Accordingly the law of nature was not changed in this respect, except by addition.

Whether the Law of Nature Can Be Abolished from the Heart of Man?

Objection 1: It would seem that the natural law can be abolished from the heart of man. Because on Rm. 2:14, "When the Gentiles who have not the law," etc. a gloss says that "the law of righteousness, which sin had blotted out, is graven on the heart of man when he is restored by grace." But the law of righteousness is the law of nature. Therefore the law of nature can be blotted out.

Objection 2: Further, the law of grace is more efficacious than the law of nature. But the law of grace is blotted out by sin. Much more therefore can the law of nature be blotted out.

Objection 3: Further, that which is established by law is made just. But many things are enacted by men, which are contrary to the law of nature. Therefore the law of nature can be abolished from the heart of man.

On the contrary, Augustine says (Confessions ii): "Thy law is written in the hearts of men, which iniquity itself effaces not." But the law which is written in men's hearts is the natural law. Therefore the natural law cannot be blotted out.

I answer that there belong to the natural law, first, certain most general precepts, that are known to all; and secondly, certain secondary and more detailed precepts, which are, as it were, conclusions following closely from first principles. As to those general principles, the natural law, in the abstract, can nowise be blotted out from men's hearts. But it is blotted out in the case of a particular action, in so far as reason is hindered from applying the general principle to a particular point of practice, on account of concupiscence or some other passion. But as to the other, i.e. the secondary precepts, the natural law can be blotted out from the human heart, either by evil persuasions, just as in speculative matters errors occur in respect of necessary conclusions; or by vicious customs and corrupt habits, as among some men, theft, and even unnatural vices, as the Apostle states (Rm. i), were not esteemed sinful.

Reply to Objection 1: Sin blots out the law of nature in particular cases, not universally, except perchance in regard to the secondary precepts of the natural law, in the way stated above.

Reply to Objection 2: Although grace is more efficacious than nature, yet nature is more essential to man, and therefore more enduring.

Reply to Objection 3: This argument is true of the secondary precepts of the natural law, against which some legislators have framed certain enactments which are unjust.

Thomas Aquinas: Natural Law

1. Aquinas believes that acting in accordance with one's natural inclinations is virtuous and that acting contrary to those inclinations is vicious (i.e., exemplifies a vice). What sense of "natural" is required in order to make these claims as plausible as they can be?
2. Aquinas says that the natural law is a "dictate of practical reason." What do you think he means by this?
3. Aquinas's version of natural law clearly depends on its having been authored by God. Can you think of a way to defend a version of natural law theory that does not depend on divine authorship?
4. Aquinas believes that the general principles of the natural law apply to all human beings at all times. Do you find this view of the fundamental moral principles appealing? Why or why not?
5. What can be said on behalf of Aquinas's claim that the first principles of morality are known by everyone?

======= 🔖 =======

8

Utilitarianism

John Stuart Mill

....

Though written over a hundred and fifty years ago in the form of a long pamphlet, Mill's *Utilitarianism* is the most influential presentation of the doctrine yet to appear. In this excerpt from its second chapter, Mill identifies the essential core of the moral theory, namely, its Greatest Happiness Principle: "actions are right in proportion as they tend to promote happiness, wrong as they tend to produce the reverse of happiness." Mill is keen to say that one's own happiness is no more important than another's—the utilitarian creed insists that a virtuous person will be concerned with the general happiness and align her own interests with those of the larger population to the extent possible.

The discussion here takes the form of replies to a series of objections; along the way, Mill takes the opportunity to identify positive attractions of the view. One objection is that utilitarianism demands too much of us by requiring that we always be motivated to promote the greater good. Mill replies by denying this and distinguishing between the standard of right action—the Greatest Happiness Principle—and the standard by which we assess people's motives and character. An act that yields only avoidable harm is wrong, even though the person who did it tried hard to do good. In such a case we need not blame the person, even though he acted immorally. Mill claims that only a small handful of people are in a position to do good on a large scale; as a result, most of us would do best not to ordinarily have the Greatest Happiness Principle as our primary motivation.

Mill, *Utilitarianism* (1861), ch. 2.

Indeed, rather than always ask ourselves which of our options will produce the greatest happiness, Mill thinks that we should rely on a battery of familiar moral rules to guide our actions and in most cases don't even need to reflect much in order to know which of our actions is the right one. We will do more good by relying on these familiar rules (e.g., don't lie, don't kill others, keep your promises) than on frequent, direct calculations of utility. But these rules are themselves justified because following them usually leads to increases in happiness or decreases in unhappiness. Further, these rules will sometimes conflict; when they do, Mill touts as a significant advantage of utilitarianism that its Greatest Happiness Principle provides a principled basis for determining how to resolve such conflicts.

....

The creed which accepts as the foundation of morals, Utility, or the Greatest Happiness Principle, holds that actions are right in proportion as they tend to promote happiness, wrong as they tend to produce the reverse of happiness. By happiness is intended pleasure, and the absence of pain; by unhappiness, pain, and the privation of pleasure. To give a clear view of the moral standard set up by the theory, much more requires to be said; in particular, what things it includes in the ideas of pain and pleasure; and to what extent this is left an open question. But these supplementary explanations do not affect the theory of life on which this theory of morality is grounded—namely, that pleasure, and freedom from pain, are the only things desirable as ends; and that all desirable things (which are as numerous in the utilitarian as in any other scheme) are desirable either for the pleasure inherent in themselves, or as means to the promotion of pleasure and the prevention of pain. . . .

[T]he happiness which forms the utilitarian standard of what is right in conduct, is not the agent's own happiness, but that of all concerned. As between his own happiness and that of others, utilitarianism requires him to be as strictly impartial as a disinterested and benevolent spectator. In the golden rule of Jesus of Nazareth, we read the complete spirit of the ethics of utility. To do as you would be done by, and to love your neighbour as yourself, constitute the ideal perfection of utilitarian morality. As the means of making the nearest approach to this ideal, utility would enjoin, first, that laws and social arrangements should place the happiness, or (as speaking practically it may be called) the interest, of every individual, as nearly as possible in harmony with the interest of the whole; and secondly, that education and opinion, which have so vast a power over human character, should so use that power as to establish in the mind of every individual an indissoluble association between his own happiness and the good of the whole; especially between his own happiness and the practice of such modes of conduct, negative and positive, as regard for the universal happiness prescribes; so that not only may he be unable to conceive the possibility of happiness to himself, consistently with conduct opposed to the general good, but also that a direct impulse to promote the general good may be in every individual one of the habitual motives of action, and the sentiments connected therewith may fill a large and prominent place in every human being's sentient existence. If the impugners of the utilitarian morality represented it to their own minds in this, its true character, I know not what recommendation possessed by any other morality they could possibly affirm to be wanting to it; what more beautiful or more exalted developments of human nature any other ethical system can be supposed to foster, or what springs of action, not accessible to the utilitarian, such systems rely on for giving effect to their mandates.

The objectors to utilitarianism cannot always be charged with representing it in a discreditable light. On the contrary, those among them who entertain anything like a just idea of its disinterested character, sometimes find fault with its standard as being too high for humanity. They say it is exacting too much to require that people shall always act from the inducement of promoting the general interests of society. But this is to mistake the very meaning of a standard of morals, and confound the rule of action with the motive of it. It is the business of ethics to tell us what are our duties, or by what test we may know them; but no system of ethics requires that the sole motive of all we do shall be a feeling of duty; on the contrary, ninety-nine hundredths of all our actions are done from other motives, and rightly so done, if the rule of duty does not condemn them. It is the more unjust to utilitarianism that this particular misapprehension should be made a ground of objection to it, inasmuch as utilitarian moralists have gone beyond almost all others in affirming that the motive has nothing to do with the morality of the action, though much with the worth of the agent. He who saves a fellow creature from drowning does what is morally right, whether his motive be duty, or the hope of being paid for his trouble; he who betrays the friend that trusts him, is guilty of a crime, even if his object be to serve another friend to whom he is under greater obligations.

But to speak only of actions done from the motive of duty, and in direct obedience to principle: it is a misapprehension of the utilitarian mode of thought, to conceive it as implying that people should fix their minds upon so wide a generality as the world, or society at large. The great majority of good actions are intended not for the benefit of the world, but for that of individuals, of which the good of the world is made up; and the thoughts of the most virtuous man need not on these occasions travel beyond the particular persons concerned, except so far as is necessary to assure himself that in benefiting them he is not violating the rights, that is, the legitimate and authorised expectations, of any one else. The multiplication of happiness is, according to the utilitarian ethics, the object of virtue: the occasions on which any person (except one in a thousand) has it in his power to do this on an extended scale, in other words to be a public benefactor, are but exceptional; and on these occasions alone is he called on to consider public utility; in every other case, private utility, the interest or happiness of some few persons, is all he has to attend to. Those alone the influence of whose actions extends to society in general, need concern themselves habitually about so large an object. In the case of abstinences indeed—of things which people forbear to do from moral considerations, though the consequences in the particular case might be beneficial—it would be unworthy of an intelligent agent not to be consciously aware that the action is of a class which, if practised generally, would be generally injurious, and that this is the ground of the obligation to abstain from it. The amount of regard for the public interest implied in this recognition is no greater than is demanded by every system of morals, for they all enjoin to abstain from whatever is manifestly pernicious to society.

The same considerations dispose of another reproach against the doctrine of utility, founded on a still grosser misconception of the purpose of a standard of morality, and of the very meaning of the words right and wrong. It is often affirmed that utilitarianism renders men cold and unsympathising; that it chills their moral feelings towards individuals; that it makes them regard only the dry and hard consideration of the consequences of actions, not taking into their moral estimate the qualities from which those actions emanate. If the assertion means that they do not allow their judgment respecting the rightness or wrongness of an action to be influenced by their opinion of the qualities of the person who does it, this is a complaint not against utilitarianism, but against having any standard of morality at all; for certainly no known ethical standard decides an action to be good or bad because it is done by a good or a bad man, still less because done by an amiable, a brave, or a benevolent man, or the contrary. These considerations are relevant, not to the estimation of actions, but of persons; and there is nothing in the utilitarian theory inconsistent with the fact that there are other things which interest us in persons besides the rightness and wrongness of their actions. The Stoics, indeed, with the paradoxical misuse of language which was part of their system, and by which they strove to raise themselves above all concern about anything but virtue, were fond of saying that he who has that has everything; that he, and only he, is rich, is beautiful, is a king. But no claim of this description is made for the virtuous man by the utilitarian doctrine. Utilitarians are quite aware that there are other desirable possessions and qualities besides virtue, and are perfectly willing to allow to all of them their full worth. They are also aware that a right action does not necessarily indicate a virtuous character, and that actions which are blamable, often proceed from qualities entitled to praise. When this is apparent in any particular case, it modifies their estimation, not certainly of the act, but of the agent. I grant that they are, notwithstanding, of opinion, that in the long run the best proof of a good character is good actions; and resolutely refuse to consider any mental disposition as good, of which the predominant tendency is to produce bad conduct. This makes them unpopular with many people; but it is an unpopularity which they must share with every one who regards the distinction between right and wrong in a serious light; and the reproach is not one which a conscientious utilitarian need be anxious to repel.

If no more be meant by the objection than that many utilitarians look on the morality of actions, as measured by the utilitarian standard, with too exclusive a regard, and do not lay sufficient stress upon the other beauties of character which go towards making a human being lovable or admirable, this may be admitted. Utilitarians who have cultivated their moral feelings, but not their sympathies nor their artistic perceptions, do fall into this mistake; and so do all other moralists under the same conditions. What can be said in excuse for other moralists is equally available for them, namely, that, if there is to be any error, it is better that it should be on that side. As a matter of fact, we may affirm that among utilitarians as among adherents of other systems, there is every imaginable degree of rigidity and of laxity in the application of their standard: some are even puritanically rigorous, while others are as indulgent as can possibly be desired by sinner or by sentimentalist. But on the whole, a doctrine which brings prominently forward the interest that mankind have in the repression and prevention of conduct which violates the moral law, is likely to be inferior to no other in turning the sanctions of opinion against such violations. It is true, the question, What does violate the moral law? is one on which those who recognise different standards of morality are likely now and then to differ. But difference of opinion on moral questions was not first introduced into the world by utilitarianism, while that doctrine does supply, if not always an easy, at all events a tangible and intelligible mode of deciding such differences.

It may not be superfluous to notice a few more of the common misapprehensions of utilitarian ethics. We not uncommonly hear the doctrine of utility inveighed against as a godless doctrine. If it be necessary to say anything at all against so mere an assumption, we may say that the question depends upon what idea we have formed of the moral character of the Deity. If it be a true belief that God desires, above all things, the happiness of his creatures, and that this was his purpose in their creation, utility is not only not a godless doctrine, but more profoundly religious than any other. If it be meant that utilitarianism does not recognise the revealed will of God as the supreme law of morals, I answer, that a utilitarian who believes in the perfect goodness and wisdom of God, necessarily believes that whatever God has thought fit to reveal on the subject of morals, must fulfil the requirements of utility in a supreme degree. But others besides utilitarians have been of opinion that the Christian revelation was intended, and is fitted, to inform the hearts and minds of mankind with a spirit which should enable them to find for themselves what is right, and incline them to do it when found, rather than to tell them, except in a very general way, what it is; and that we need a doctrine of ethics, carefully followed out, to interpret to us the will of God. Whether this opinion is correct or not, it is superfluous here to discuss; since whatever aid religion, either natural or revealed, can afford to ethical investigation, is as open to the utilitarian moralist as to any other. He can use it as the testimony of God to the usefulness or hurtfulness of any given course of action, by as good a right as others can use it for the indication of a transcendental law, having no connection with usefulness or with happiness.

Again, Utility is often summarily stigmatised as an immoral doctrine by giving it the name of Expediency, and taking advantage of the popular use of that term to contrast it with Principle. But the Expedient, in the sense in which it is opposed to the Right, generally means that which is expedient for the particular interest of the agent himself; as when a minister sacrifices the interests of his country to keep himself in place. When it means anything better than this, it means that which is expedient for some immediate object, some temporary purpose, but which violates a rule whose observance is expedient in a much higher degree. The Expedient, in this sense, instead of being the same thing with the useful, is a branch of the hurtful. Thus, it would often be expedient, for the purpose of getting over some momentary embarrassment, or attaining some object immediately useful to ourselves or others, to tell a lie. But inasmuch as the cultivation in ourselves of a sensitive feeling on the subject of veracity, is one of the most useful, and the enfeeblement of that feeling one of the most hurtful, things to which our conduct can be instrumental; and inasmuch as any, even unintentional, deviation from truth, does that much towards weakening the trustworthiness of human assertion, which is not only the principal support of all present social well-being, but the insufficiency of which does more than any one thing that can be named to keep back civilisation, virtue, everything on which human happiness on the largest scale depends; we feel that the violation, for a present advantage, of a rule of such transcendant expediency, is not expedient, and that he who, for the sake of a convenience to himself or to some other individual, does what depends on him to deprive mankind of the good, and inflict upon them the evil, involved in the greater or less reliance which they can place in each other's word, acts the part of one of their worst enemies. Yet that even this rule, sacred as it is, admits of possible exceptions, is acknowledged by all moralists; the chief of which is when the withholding of some fact (as of information from a malefactor, or of bad news from a person dangerously ill) would save an individual (especially an individual other than oneself) from great and unmerited evil, and when the withholding can only be effected by denial. But in order that the exception may not extend itself beyond the need, and may have the least possible effect in weakening reliance on veracity, it ought to be recognised, and, if possible, its limits defined; and if the principle of utility is good for anything, it must be good for weighing these conflicting utilities against one another, and marking out the region within which one or the other preponderates.

Again, defenders of utility often find themselves called upon to reply to such objections as this—that there is not time, previous to action, for calculating and weighing the effects of any line of conduct on the general happiness. This is exactly as if any one were to say that it is impossible to guide our conduct by Christianity, because there is not time, on every occasion on which anything has to be done, to read through the Old and New Testaments. The answer to the objection is, that there has been ample time, namely, the whole past duration of the human species. During all that time, mankind have been learning by experience the tendencies of actions; on which experience all the prudence, as well as all the morality of life, are dependent. People talk as if the commencement of this course of experience had hitherto been put off, and as if, at the moment when some man feels tempted to meddle with the property or life of another, he had to begin considering for the first time whether murder and theft are injurious to human happiness. Even then I do not think that he would find the question very puzzling; but, at all events, the matter is now done to his hand.

It is truly a whimsical supposition that, if mankind were agreed in considering utility to be the test of morality, they would remain without any agreement as to what is useful, and would take no measures for having their notions on the subject taught to the young, and enforced by law and opinion. There is no difficulty in proving any ethical standard whatever to work ill, if we suppose universal idiocy to be conjoined with it; but on any hypothesis short of that, mankind must by this time have acquired positive beliefs as to the effects of some actions on their happiness; and the beliefs which have thus come down are the rules of morality for the multitude, and for the philosopher until he has succeeded in finding better. That philosophers might easily do this, even now, on many subjects; that the received code of ethics is by no means of divine right; and that mankind have still much to learn as to the effects of actions on the general happiness, I admit, or rather, earnestly maintain. The corollaries from the principle of utility, like the precepts of every practical art, admit of indefinite improvement, and, in a progressive state of the human mind, their improvement is perpetually going on.

But to consider the rules of morality as improvable, is one thing; to pass over the intermediate generalisations entirely, and endeavour to test each individual action directly by the first principle, is another. It is a strange notion that the acknowledgment of a first principle is inconsistent with the admission of secondary ones. To inform a traveller respecting the place of his ultimate destination, is not to forbid the use of landmarks and direction-posts on the way. The proposition that happiness is the end and aim of morality, does not mean that no road ought to be laid down to that goal, or that persons going thither should not be advised to take one direction rather than another. Men really ought to leave off talking a kind of nonsense on this subject, which they would neither talk nor listen to on other matters of practical concernment. Nobody argues that the art of navigation is not founded on astronomy, because sailors cannot wait to calculate the Nautical Almanack. Being rational creatures, they go to sea with it ready calculated; and all rational creatures go out upon the sea of life with their minds made up on the common questions of right and wrong, as well as on many of the far more difficult questions of wise and foolish. And this, as long as foresight is a human quality, it is to be presumed they will continue to do. Whatever we adopt as the fundamental principle of morality, we require subordinate principles to apply it by; the impossibility of doing without them, being common to all systems, can afford no argument against any one in particular; but gravely to argue as if no such secondary principles could be had, and as if mankind had remained till now, and always must remain, without drawing any general conclusions from the experience of human life, is as high a pitch, I think, as absurdity has ever reached in philosophical controversy.

The remainder of the stock arguments against utilitarianism mostly consist in laying to its charge the common infirmities of human nature, and the general difficulties which embarrass conscientious persons in shaping their course through life. We are told that a utilitarian will be apt to make his own particular case an exception to moral rules, and, when under temptation, will see a utility in the breach of a rule, greater than he will see in its observance. But is utility the only creed which is able to furnish us with excuses for evil doing, and means of cheating our own conscience? They are afforded in abundance by all doctrines which recognise as a fact in morals the existence of conflicting considerations; which all doctrines do, that have been believed by sane persons. It is not the fault of any creed, but of the complicated nature of human affairs, that rules of conduct cannot be so framed as to require no exceptions, and that hardly any kind of action can safely be laid down as either always obligatory or always condemnable. There is no ethical creed which does not temper the rigidity of its laws, by giving a certain latitude, under the moral responsibility of the agent, for accommodation to peculiarities of circumstances; and under every creed, at the opening thus made, self-deception and dishonest casuistry get in. There exists no moral system under which there do not arise unequivocal cases of conflicting obligation. These are the real difficulties, the knotty points both in the theory of ethics, and in the conscientious guidance of personal conduct. They are overcome practically, with greater or with less success, according to the intellect and virtue of the individual; but it can hardly be pretended that any one will be the less qualified for dealing with them, from possessing an ultimate standard to which conflicting rights and duties can be referred. If utility is the ultimate source of moral obligations, utility may be invoked to decide between them when their demands are incompatible. Though the application of the standard may be difficult, it is better than none at all: while in other systems, the moral laws all claiming independent authority, there is no common umpire entitled to interfere between them; their claims to precedence one over another rest on little better than sophistry, and unless determined, as they generally are, by the unacknowledged influence of considerations of utility, afford a free scope for the action of personal desires and partialities. We must remember that only in these cases of conflict between secondary principles is it requisite that first principles should be appealed to. There is no case of moral obligation in which some secondary principle is not involved; and if only one, there can seldom be any real doubt which one it is, in the mind of any person by whom the principle itself is recognised.

John Stuart Mill: Utilitarianism

1. Utilitarianism claims that my happiness is no more important than yours. This kind of impartiality seems highly appealing. But this also appears to prohibit us from giving ourselves or our family priority over the interests of others. Is this appearance correct? Can utilitarianism allow for partiality to oneself or one's family?
2. Mill claims that virtuous people will rarely have the Greatest Happiness Principle in mind when acting. Why does he say this? Is his claim plausible? And is it what a utilitarian really should say?
3. Mill believes that the motives that prompt an action are irrelevant to that action's morality. Is this claim plausible? Why or why not?
4. Many critics of utilitarianism claim that the theory requires that we sacrifice too much for others. Mill counters by saying that only a very few people are in a position to do much good for many others; as a result, most of us are not required to focus our efforts in ways that require significant self-sacrifice. Is Mill's view too rosy, especially now that we are so easily able to learn of how unfortunate others are and are easily able to give to charities that can help improve the lives of those who are less well off than we are?
5. Some have argued that utilitarianism is a godless doctrine. What is Mill's reply to this? Do you find it plausible?

9

The Good Will and the Categorical Imperative

Immanuel Kant

Immanuel Kant (1724–1804) was the greatest German philosopher who ever lived. In this excerpt from his *Groundwork of the Metaphysics of Morals*, Kant introduces two key elements of his moral philosophy. According to Kant, the first of these, the good will, is the only thing possessed of unconditional value: it is valuable in its own right, in every possible circumstance. The good will is the steady commitment to do our duty for its own sake. Our actions possess moral worth if, but only if, they are prompted by the good will.

The second important element is the *categorical imperative*, Kant's term for a requirement of reason that applies to us regardless of what we care about. Moral requirements are categorical imperatives—we must, for instance, sometimes give help to others in need, even if we don't want to, and even if such help gets us nothing that we care about. Kant believed that moral action is rational action. Each of us has a compelling reason to obey morality, even when doing so only frustrates our deepest desires.

Kant here sets out two tests for morally acceptable action. The first says that actions are morally acceptable only when the principles that inspire them can be acted on by everyone consistently. The second requires us to treat humanity always as an end in itself, and never as

From *Groundwork of the Metaphysics of Morals*, trans. Mary Gregor (1998). Reprinted with the permission of Cambridge University Press.

a mere means. Kant realizes that such formulations are somewhat abstract, and so here offers us a number of illustrations that are meant to help us understand and apply them.

....

The Good Will

It is impossible to think of anything at all in the world, or indeed even beyond it, that could be considered good without limitation except a **good will**. Understanding, wit, judgment and the like, whatever such *talents* of mind may be called, or courage, resolution, and perseverance in one's plans, as qualities of *temperament*, are undoubtedly good and desirable for many purposes, but they can also be extremely evil and harmful if the will which is to make use of these gifts of nature, and whose distinctive constitution is therefore called *character*, is not good. It is the same with *gifts of fortune*. Power, riches, honor, even health and that complete well-being and satisfaction with one's condition called *happiness*, produce boldness and thereby often arrogance as well unless a good will is present which corrects the influence of these on the mind and, in so doing, also corrects the whole principle of action and brings it into conformity with universal ends—not to mention that an impartial rational spectator can take no delight in seeing the uninterrupted prosperity of a being graced with no feature of a pure and good will, so that a good will seems to constitute the indispensable condition even of worthiness to be happy.

Some qualities are even conducive to this good will itself and can make its work much easier; despite this, however, they have no inner unconditional worth but always presuppose a good will, which limits the esteem one otherwise rightly has for them and does not permit their being taken as absolutely good. Moderation in affects and passions, self-control, and calm reflection are not only good for all sorts of purposes but even seem to constitute a part of the *inner* worth of a person; but they lack much that would be required to declare them good without limitation (however unconditionally they were praised by the ancients); for, without the basic principles of a good will they can become extremely evil, and the coolness of a scoundrel makes him not only far more dangerous but also immediately more abominable in our eyes than we would have taken him to be without it.

A good will is not good because of what it effects or accomplishes, because of its fitness to attain some proposed end, but only because of its volition, that is, it is good in itself and, regarded for itself, is to be valued incomparably higher than all that could merely be brought about by it in favor of some inclination and indeed, if you will, of the sum of all inclinations. Even if, by a special disfavor of fortune or by the niggardly provision of a stepmotherly nature, this will should wholly lack the capacity to carry out its purpose—if with its greatest efforts it should yet achieve nothing and only the good will were left (not, of course, as a mere wish but as the summoning of all means insofar as they are in our control)—then, like a jewel, it would still shine by itself, as something that has its full worth in itself. Usefulness or fruitlessness can neither add anything to this worth nor take anything away from it. Its usefulness would be, as it were, only the setting to enable us to handle it more conveniently in ordinary commerce or to attract to it the attention of those who are not yet expert enough, but not to recommend it to experts or to determine its worth. . . .

We have, then, to explicate the concept of a will that is to be esteemed in itself and that is good apart from any further purpose, as it already dwells in natural sound understanding and needs not so much to be taught as only to be clarified—this concept that always takes first place in estimating the total worth of our actions and constitutes the condition of all the rest. In order to do so, we shall set before ourselves the concept of **duty**, which contains that of a good will though under certain subjective limitations and hindrances, which, however, far from concealing it and making it unrecognizable, rather bring it out by contrast and make it shine forth all the more brightly.

I here pass over all actions that are already recognized as contrary to duty, even though they may be useful for this or that purpose; for in their case the question whether they might have been done *from duty* never arises, since they even conflict with it. I also set aside actions that are really in conformity with duty but to which human beings have *no inclination* immediately and which they still perform because they are impelled to do so through another inclination. For in this case it is easy to distinguish whether an action in conformity with duty is done *from duty* or from a self-seeking purpose. It is much more difficult to note this distinction when an action conforms with duty and the subject has, besides, an *immediate* inclination to it. For example, it certainly conforms with duty that a shopkeeper not overcharge an inexperienced customer, and where there is a good deal of trade a prudent merchant does not overcharge but keeps a fixed general price for everyone, so that a child can buy from him as well as everyone else. People are thus served *honestly*; but this is not nearly enough for us to believe that the merchant acted in this way from duty and basic principles of honesty; his advantage required it; it cannot be assumed here that he had, besides, an immediate inclination toward his customers, so as from love, as it were, to give no one preference over another in the matter of price. Thus the action was done neither from duty nor from immediate inclination but merely for purposes of self-interest.

On the other hand, to preserve one's life is a duty, and besides everyone has an immediate inclination to do so. But on this account the often anxious care that most people take of it still has no inner worth and their maxim has no moral content. They look after their lives *in conformity with duty* but not *from duty*. On the other hand, if adversity and hopeless grief have quite taken away the taste for life; if an unfortunate man, strong of soul and more indignant about his fate than despondent or dejected, wishes for death and yet preserves his life without loving it, not from inclination or fear but from duty, then his maxim has moral content.

To be beneficent where one can is a duty, and besides there are many souls so sympathetically attuned that, without any other motive of vanity or self-interest they find an inner satisfaction in spreading joy around them and can take delight in the satisfaction of others so far as it is their own work. But I assert that in such a case an action of this kind, however it may conform with duty and however amiable it may be, has nevertheless no true moral worth but is on the same footing with other inclinations, for example, the inclination to honor, which, if it fortunately lights upon what is in fact in the common interest and in conformity with duty and hence honorable, deserves praise and encouragement but not esteem; for the maxim lacks moral content, namely that of doing such actions not from inclination but *from duty*. Suppose, then, that the mind of this philanthropist were overclouded by his own grief, which extinguished all sympathy with the fate of others, and that while he still had the means to benefit others in distress their troubles did not move him because he had enough to do with his own; and suppose that now, when no longer incited to it by any inclination, he nevertheless tears himself out of this deadly insensibility and does the action without any inclination, simply from duty; then the action first has its genuine moral worth. Still further: if nature had put little sympathy in the heart of this or that man; if (in other respects an honest man) he is by temperament cold and indifferent to the sufferings of others, perhaps because he himself is provided with the special gift of patience and endurance toward his own sufferings and presupposes the same in every other or even requires it; if nature had not properly fashioned such a man (who would in truth not be its worst product) for a philanthropist, would he not still find within himself a source from which to give himself a far higher worth than what a mere good-natured temperament might have? By all means! It is just then that the worth of character comes out, which is moral and incomparably the highest, namely that he is beneficent not from inclination but from duty. . . .

Thus the moral worth of an action does not lie in the effect expected from it and so too does not lie in any principle of action that needs to borrow its motive from this expected effect. For, all these effects (agreeableness of one's condition, indeed even promotion of others' happiness) could have been also brought about by other causes, so that there would have been no need, for this, of the will of a rational being, in which, however, the highest and unconditional good alone can be found. Hence nothing other than the *representation of the law* in itself, *which can of course occur only in a rational being,* insofar as it and not the hoped-for effect is the determining ground of the will, can constitute the preeminent good we call moral, which is already present in the person himself who acts in accordance with this representation and need not wait upon the effect of his action.

But what kind of law can that be, the representation of which must determine the will, even without regard for the effect expected from it, in order for the will to be called good absolutely and without limitation? Since I have deprived the will of every impulse that could arise for it from obeying some law, nothing is left but the conformity of actions as such with universal law, which alone is to serve the will as its principle, that is, *I ought never to act except in such a way that I could also will that my maxim should become a universal law.* Here mere conformity to law as such, without having as its basis some law determined for certain actions, is what serves the will as its principle, and must so serve it, if duty is not to be everywhere an empty delusion and a chimerical concept. Common human reason also agrees completely with this in its practical appraisals and always has this principle before its eyes. Let the question be, for example: may I, when hard pressed, make a promise with the intention not to keep it? Here I easily distinguish two significations the question can have: whether it is prudent or whether it is in conformity with duty to make a false promise. The first can undoubtedly often be the case. I see very well that it is not enough to get out of a present difficulty by means of this subterfuge but that I must reflect carefully whether this lie may later give rise to much greater inconvenience for me than that from which I now extricate myself; and since, with all my supposed *cunning*, the results cannot be so easily foreseen but that once confidence in me is lost this could be far more prejudicial to me than all the troubles I now think to avoid, I must reflect whether the matter might be handled *more prudently* by proceeding on a general maxim and making it a habit to promise nothing except with the intention of keeping it. But it is soon clear to me that such a maxim will still be based only on results feared. To be truthful from duty, however, is something entirely different from being truthful from anxiety about detrimental results, since in the first case the concept of the action in itself already contains a law for me while in the second I must first look about elsewhere to see what effects on me might be combined with it. For, if I deviate from the principle of duty this is quite certainly evil; but if I am unfaithful to my maxim of prudence this can sometimes be very advantageous to me, although it is certainly safer to abide by it. However, to inform myself in the shortest and yet infallible way about the answer to this problem, whether a lying promise is in conformity with duty, I ask myself: would I indeed be content that my maxim (to get myself out of difficulties by a false promise) should hold as a universal law (for myself as well as for others)? and could I indeed say to myself that every one may make a false promise when he finds himself in a difficulty he can get out of in no other way? Then I soon become aware that I could indeed will the lie, but by no means a universal law to lie; for in accordance with such a law there would properly be no promises at all, since it would be futile to avow my will with regard to my future actions to others who would not believe this avowal or, if they rashly did so, would pay me back in like coin; and thus my maxim, as soon as it were made a universal law, would have to destroy itself.

I do not, therefore, need any penetrating acuteness to see what I have to do in order that my volition be morally good. Inexperienced in the course of the world, incapable of being prepared for whatever might come to pass in it, I ask myself only: can you also will that your maxim become a universal law? If not, then it is to be repudiated, and that not because of a disadvantage to you or even to others forthcoming from it but because it cannot fit as a principle into a possible giving of universal law, for which lawgiving reason, however, forces from me immediate respect. Although I do not yet *see* what this respect is based upon (this the philosopher may investigate), I at least understand this much: that it is an estimation of a worth that far outweighs any worth of what is recommended by inclination, and that the necessity of my action from *pure* respect for the practical law is what constitutes duty, to which every other motive must give way because it is the condition of a will good in itself, the worth of which surpasses all else. . . .

The Categorical Imperative

Now, all imperatives command either *hypothetically* or *categorically*. The former represent the practical necessity of a possible action as a means to achieving something else that one wills (or that it is at least possible for one to will). The categorical imperative would be that which represented an action as objectively necessary of itself, without reference to another end.

Since every practical law represents a possible action as good and thus as necessary for a subject practically determinable by reason, all imperatives are formulae for the determination of action that is necessary in accordance with the principle of a will which is good in some way. Now, if the action would be good merely as a means *to something else* the imperative is *hypothetical*; if the action is represented as in itself good, hence as necessary in a will in itself conforming to reason, as its principle, *then it is categorical*. . . .

There is one imperative that, without being based upon and having as its condition any other purpose to be attained by certain conduct, commands this conduct immediately. This imperative is **categorical**. It has to do not with the matter of the action and what is to result from it, but with the form and the principle from which the action itself follows; and the essential good in the action consists in the disposition, let the result be what it may. This imperative may be called the imperative of **morality**. . . .

When I think of a *hypothetical* imperative in general I do not know beforehand what it will contain; I do not know this until I am given the condition. But when I think of a *categorical* imperative I know at once what it contains. For, since the imperative contains, beyond the law, only the necessity that the maxim[1] be in conformity with this law, while the law contains no condition to which it would be limited, nothing is left with which the maxim of action is to conform but the universality of a law as such; and this conformity alone is what the imperative properly represents as necessary.

---

1. A maxim is the subjective principle of acting, and must be distinguished from the objective principle, namely the practical law. The former contains the practical rule determined by reason conformably with the conditions of the subject (often his ignorance or also his inclinations), and is therefore the principle in accordance with which the subject acts; but the law is the objective principle valid for every rational being, and the principle in accordance with which he ought to act, i.e., an imperative.

There is, therefore, only a single categorical imperative and it is this: *act only in accordance with that maxim through which you can at the same time will that it become a universal law.*

Now, if all imperatives of duty can be derived from this single imperative as from their principle, then, even though we leave it undecided whether what is called duty is not as such an empty concept, we shall at least be able to show what we think by it and what the concept wants to say.

Since the universality of law in accordance with which effects take place constitutes what is properly called *nature* in the most general sense (as regards its form)—that is, the existence of things insofar as it is determined in accordance with universal laws—the universal imperative of duty can also go as follows: *act as if the maxim of your action were to become by your will a* **universal law of nature.**

We shall now enumerate a few duties in accordance with the usual division of them into duties to ourselves and to other human beings and into perfect and imperfect duties.[2]

(1) Someone feels sick of life because of a series of troubles that has grown to the point of despair, but is still so far in possession of his reason that he can ask himself whether it would not be contrary to his duty to himself to take his own life. Now he inquires whether the maxim of his action could indeed become a universal law of nature. His maxim, however, is: from self-love I make it my principle to shorten my life when its longer duration threatens more troubles than it promises agreeableness. The only further question is whether this principle of self-love could become a universal law of nature. It is then seen at once that a nature whose law it would be to destroy life itself by means of the same feeling whose destination is to impel toward the furtherance of life would contradict itself and would therefore not subsist as nature; thus that maxim could not possibly be a law of nature and, accordingly, altogether opposes the supreme principle of all duty.

(2) Another finds himself urged by need to borrow money. He well knows that he will not be able to repay it but sees also that nothing will be lent him unless he promises firmly to repay it within a determinate time. He would like to make such a promise, but he still has enough conscience to ask himself: is it not forbidden and contrary to duty to help oneself out of need in such a way? Supposing that he still decided to do so, his maxim of action would go as follows: when I believe myself to be in need of money

---

2. I understand here by a perfect duty one that admits no exception in favor of inclination.

I shall borrow money and promise to repay it, even though I know that this will never happen. Now this principle of self-love or personal advantage is perhaps quite consistent with my whole future welfare, but the question now is whether it is right. I therefore turn the demand of self-love into a universal law and put the question as follows: how would it be if my maxim became a universal law? I then see at once that it could never hold as a universal law of nature and be consistent with itself, but must necessarily contradict itself. For, the universality of a law that everyone, when he believes himself to be in need, could promise whatever he pleases with the intention of not keeping it would make the promise and the end one might have in it itself impossible, since no one would believe what was promised him but would laugh at all such expressions as vain pretenses.

(3) A third finds in himself a talent that by means of some cultivation could make him a human being useful for all sorts of purposes. However, he finds himself in comfortable circumstances and prefers to give himself up to pleasure than to trouble himself with enlarging and improving his fortunate natural predispositions. But he still asks himself whether his maxim of neglecting his natural gifts, besides being consistent with his propensity to amusement, is also consistent with what one calls duty. He now sees that a nature could indeed always subsist with such a universal law, although (as with the South Sea Islanders) the human being should let his talents rust and be concerned with devoting his life merely to idleness, amusement, procreation—in a word, to enjoyment; only he cannot possibly will that this become a universal law or be put in us as such by means of natural instinct. For, as a rational being he necessarily wills that all the capacities in him be developed, since they serve him and are given to him for all sorts of possible purposes.

(4) Yet a *fourth*, for whom things are going well while he sees that others (whom he could very well help) have to contend with great hardships, thinks: what is it to me? let each be as happy as heaven wills or as he can make himself; I shall take nothing from him nor even envy him; only I do not care to contribute anything to his welfare or to his assistance in need! Now, if such a way of thinking were to become a universal law the human race could admittedly very well subsist, no doubt even better than when everyone prates about sympathy and benevolence and even exerts himself to practice them occasionally, but on the other hand also cheats where he can, sells the right of human beings or otherwise infringes upon it. But although it is possible that a universal law of nature could very well subsist in accordance with such a maxim, it is still impossible to will that such a

principle hold everywhere as a law of nature. For, a will that decided this would conflict with itself, since many cases could occur in which one would need the love and sympathy of others and in which, by such a law of nature arisen from his own will, he would rob himself of all hope of the assistance he wishes for himself. . . .

If we now attend to ourselves in any transgression of a duty, we find that we do not really will that our maxim should become a universal law, since that is impossible for us, but that the opposite of our maxim should instead remain a universal law, only we take the liberty of making an *exception* to it for ourselves (or just for this once) to the advantage of our inclination. Consequently, if we weighed all cases from one and the same point of view, namely that of reason, we would find a contradiction in our own will, namely that a certain principle be objectively necessary as a universal law and yet subjectively not hold universally but allow exceptions. . . .

Suppose there were something the *existence of which in itself* has an absolute worth, something which as *an end in itself* could be a ground of determinate laws; then in it, and in it alone, would lie the ground of a possible categorical imperative, that is, of a practical law.

Now I say that the human being and in general every rational being exists as an end in itself, *not merely as a means* to be used by this or that will at its discretion; instead he must in all his actions, whether directed to himself or also to other rational beings, always be regarded *at the same time as an end*. All objects of the inclinations have only a conditional worth; for, if there were not inclinations and the needs based on them, their object would be without worth. But the inclinations themselves, as sources of needs, are so far from having an absolute worth, so as to make one wish to have them, that it must instead be the universal wish of every rational being to be altogether free from them. Thus the worth of any object *to be acquired* by our action is always conditional. Beings the existence of which rests not on our will but on nature, if they are beings without reason, still have only a relative worth, as means, and are therefore called *things*, whereas rational beings are called *persons* because their nature already marks them out as an end in itself, that is, as something that may not be used merely as a means, and hence so far limits all choice (and is an object of respect). These, therefore, are not merely subjective ends, the existence of which as an effect of our action has a worth *for us*, but rather *objective ends*, that is, beings the existence of which is in itself an end, and indeed one such that no other end, to which they would serve *merely* as means, can be put in its place, since without it nothing of *absolute worth* would be found anywhere; but if all worth were conditional and therefore contingent, then no supreme practical principle for reason could be found anywhere.

If, then, there is to be a supreme practical principle and, with respect to the human will, a categorical imperative, it must be one such that, from the representation of what is necessarily an end for everyone because it is an *end in itself*, it constitutes an *objective* principle of the will and thus can serve as a universal practical law. The ground of this principle is: *rational nature exists as an end in itself.* The human being necessarily represents his own existence in this way; so far it is thus a *subjective* principle of human actions. But every other rational being also represents his existence in this way consequent on just the same rational ground that also holds for me; thus it is at the same time an *objective* principle from which, as a supreme practical ground, it must be possible to derive all laws of the will. The practical imperative will therefore be the following: *So act that you use humanity, whether in your own person or in the person of any other, always at the same time as an end, never merely as a means.* We shall see whether this can be carried out.

To keep to the preceding examples:

First, as regards the concept of necessary duty to oneself, someone who has suicide in mind will ask himself whether his action can be consistent with the idea of humanity *as an end in itself.* If he destroys himself in order to escape from a trying condition he makes use of a person *merely as a means* to maintain a tolerable condition up to the end of life. A human being, however, is not a thing and hence not something that can be used *merely* as a means, but must in all his actions always be regarded as an end in itself. I cannot, therefore, dispose of a human being in my own person by maiming, damaging or killing him. (I must here pass over a closer determination of this principle that would prevent any misinterpretation, e.g., as to having limbs amputated in order to preserve myself, or putting my life in danger in order to preserve my life, and so forth; that belongs to morals proper.)

Second, as regards necessary duty to others or duty owed them, he who has it in mind to make a false promise to others sees at once that he wants to make use of another human being *merely as a means,* without the other at the same time containing in himself the end. For, he whom I want to use for my purposes by such a promise cannot possibly agree to my way of behaving toward him, and so himself contain the end of this action. This conflict with the principle of other human beings is seen more distinctly if examples of assaults on the freedom and property of others are brought forward. For then it is obvious that he who transgresses the rights of human beings intends to make use of the person of others merely as means, without taking into consideration that, as rational beings, they are always to be valued at the same time as ends, that is, only as beings who must also be able to contain in themselves the end of the very same action.

Third, with respect to contingent (meritorious) duty to oneself, it is not enough that the action does not conflict with humanity in our person as an end in itself; it must also *harmonize with it.* Now there are in humanity predispositions to greater perfection, which belong to the end of nature with respect to humanity in our subject; to neglect these might admittedly be consistent with the *preservation* of humanity as an end in itself but not with the *furtherance* of this end.

Fourth, concerning meritorious duty to others, the natural end that all human beings have is their own happiness. Now, humanity might indeed subsist if no one contributed to the happiness of others but yet did not intentionally withdraw anything from it; but there is still only a negative and not a positive agreement with *humanity as an end in itself* unless everyone also tries, as far as he can, to further the ends of others. For, the ends of a subject who is an end in itself must as far as possible be also *my* ends, if that representation is to have its *full* effect in me. . . .

Immanuel Kant: The Good Will and the Categorical Imperative

1. Kant claims that a good will is the only thing that can be considered "good without limitation." What does he mean by this? Do you find this claim plausible?

2. Unlike hedonists, Kant believes that happiness is not always good. What reasons does he give for thinking this? Do you agree with him?

3. What is the difference between doing something "in conformity with duty" and doing something "from duty"? Is Kant correct in saying that only actions done from duty have moral worth?

4. Kant claims to have discovered a categorical imperative, a moral requirement that we have reason to follow regardless of what we happen to desire. Can people have reasons for action that are completely independent of their desires?

5. According to Kant, it is morally permissible to act on a particular principle (or "maxim") only if "you can at the same time will that it become a universal law." Do you think this is a good test of whether an action is morally permissible? Can you think of any immoral actions that would pass this test, or any morally permissible actions that would fail it?

6. Kant later gives another formulation of the categorical imperative: "So act that you use humanity, whether in your own person or in the person of any other, always at the same time as an end, never merely as a means." What does it mean to treat someone as an end? Are we always morally required to treat humans in this way?

10

Leviathan

Thomas Hobbes

Thomas Hobbes (1588–1679) was the most brilliant of the modern social contract theorists. His theory, important in both ethics and political philosophy, views the basic moral rules of society as ones that rational people would adopt in order to protect their own interests. Without obedience to such rules, the situation deteriorates into a "war of all against all, in which the life of man is solitary, poor, nasty, brutish and short."

Hobbes was an ethical egoist—someone who thinks that our fundamental duty is to look after our own interests—as well as a social contract theorist. Many commentators have found a tension in this combination. See for yourself whether Hobbes succeeded in justifying the basic moral rules by reference to self-interest.

Among the many interesting features in this excerpt from Hobbes's classic *Leviathan* is his discussion of the fool. The fool is someone who allows that breaking one's promises is unjust, but who thinks that it may sometimes be rational to do so anyway. Hobbes resists this idea. He wants to show that it is always rational to do one's duty—to live by the laws of cooperation that would be accepted by free and rational people. His overall view is motivated by the thought that moral duties must provide each of us with excellent reasons to obey them, and that these reasons must ultimately stem from self-interest. As a result, Hobbes's discussion casts fascinating light on the perennial question of why we should be moral.

Of the Natural Condition of Mankind as Concerning Their Felicity and Misery

Nature hath made men so equal in the faculties of body and mind as that, though there be found one man sometimes manifestly stronger in body or of quicker mind than another, yet when all is reckoned together the difference between man and man is not so considerable as that one man can thereupon claim to himself any benefit to which another may not pretend as well as he. For as to the strength of body, the weakest has strength enough to kill the strongest, either by secret machination or by confederacy with others that are in the same danger with himself.

And as to the faculties of the mind, setting aside the arts grounded upon words, and especially that skill of proceeding upon general and infallible rules, called science, which very few have and but in few things, as being not a native faculty born with us, nor attained, as prudence, while we look after somewhat else, I find yet a greater equality amongst men than that of strength. For prudence is but experience, which equal time equally bestows on all men in those things they equally apply themselves unto. That which may perhaps make such equality incredible is but a vain conceit of one's own wisdom, which almost all men think they have in a greater degree than the vulgar; that is, than all men but themselves, and a few others, whom by fame, or for concurring with themselves, they approve. For such is the nature of men that howsoever they may acknowledge many others to be more witty, or more eloquent or more learned, yet they will hardly believe there be many so wise as themselves; for they see their own wit at hand, and other men's at a distance. But this proveth rather that men are in that point equal, than unequal. For there is not ordinarily a greater sign of the equal distribution of anything than that every man is contented with his share.

From this equality of ability ariseth equality of hope in the attaining of our ends. And therefore if any two men desire the same thing, which nevertheless they cannot both enjoy, they become enemies; and in the way to their end (which is principally their own conservation, and sometimes their delectation only) endeavour to destroy or subdue one another. And from hence it comes to pass that where an invader hath no more to fear than another man's single power, if one plant, sow, build, or possess a convenient seat, others may probably be expected to come prepared with forces united to dispossess and deprive him, not only of the fruit of his labour, but also of his life or liberty. And the invader again is in the like danger of another.

And from this diffidence of one another, there is no way for any man to secure himself so reasonable as anticipation; that is, by force, or wiles, to master the persons of all men he can so long till he see no other power great enough to endanger him: and this is no more than his own conservation requireth, and is generally allowed. Also, because there be some that, taking pleasure in contemplating their own power in the acts of conquest, which they pursue farther than their security requires, if others, that otherwise would be glad to be at ease within modest bounds, should not by invasion increase their power, they would not be able, long time, by standing only on their defence, to subsist. And by consequence, such augmentation of dominion over men being necessary to a man's conservation, it ought to be allowed him.

Again, men have no pleasure (but on the contrary a great deal of grief) in keeping company where there is no power able to overawe them all. For every man looketh that his companion should value him at the same rate he sets upon himself, and upon all signs of contempt or undervaluing naturally endeavours, as far as he dares (which amongst them that have no common power to keep them in quiet is far enough to make them destroy each other), to extort a greater value from his contemners, by damage; and from others, by the example.

So that in the nature of man, we find three principal causes of quarrel. First, competition; secondly, diffidence; thirdly, glory.

The first maketh men invade for gain; the second, for safety; and the third, for reputation. The first use violence, to make themselves masters of other men's persons, wives, children, and cattle; the second, to defend them; the third, for trifles, as a word, a smile, a different opinion, and any other sign of undervalue, either direct in their persons or by reflection in their kindred, their friends, their nation, their profession, or their name.

Hereby it is manifest that during the time men live without a common power to keep them all in awe, they are in that condition which is called war; and such a war as is of every man against every man. For war consisteth not in battle only, or the act of fighting, but in a tract of time, wherein the will to contend by battle is sufficiently known: and therefore the notion of time is to be considered in the nature of war, as it is in the nature of weather. For as the nature of foul weather lieth not in a shower or two of rain, but in an inclination thereto of many days together: so the nature of war consisteth not in actual fighting, but in the known disposition thereto during all the time there is no assurance to the contrary. All other time is peace.

Whatsoever therefore is consequent to a time of war, where every man is enemy to every man, the same consequent to the time wherein men live without other security than what their own strength and their own invention shall furnish them withal. In such condition there is no place for industry, because the fruit thereof is uncertain: and consequently no culture of the earth; no navigation, nor use of the commodities that may be imported by sea; no commodious building; no instruments of moving and removing such things as require much force; no knowledge of the face of the earth; no account of time; no arts; no letters; no society; and which is worst of all, continual fear, and danger of violent death; and the life of man, solitary, poor, nasty, brutish, and short.

It may seem strange to some man that has not well weighed these things that Nature should thus dissociate and render men apt to invade and destroy one another: and he may therefore, not trusting to this inference, made from the passions, desire perhaps to have the same confirmed by experience. Let him therefore consider with himself: when taking a journey, he arms himself and seeks to go well accompanied; when going to sleep, he locks his doors; when even in his house he locks his chests; and this when he knows there be laws and public officers, armed, to revenge all injuries shall be done him; what opinion he has of his fellow subjects, when he rides armed; of his fellow citizens, when he locks his doors; and of his children, and servants, when he locks his chests. Does he not there as much accuse mankind by his actions as I do by my words? But neither of us accuse man's nature in it. The desires, and other passions of man, are in themselves no sin. No more are the actions that proceed from those passions till they know a law that forbids them; which till laws be made they cannot know, nor can any law be made till they have agreed upon the person that shall make it.

It may peradventure be thought there was never such a time nor condition of war as this; and I believe it was never generally so, over all the world: but there are many places where they live so now. For the savage people in many places of America, except the government of small families, the concord whereof dependeth on natural lust, have no government at all, and live at this day in that brutish manner, as I said before. Howsoever, it may be perceived what manner of life there would be, where there were no common power to fear, by the manner of life which men that have formerly lived under a peaceful government use to degenerate into a civil war.

But though there had never been any time wherein particular men were in a condition of war one against another, yet in all times kings and persons of sovereign authority, because of their independency, are in continual jealousies, and in the state and posture of gladiators, having their weapons pointing, and their eyes fixed on one another; that is, their forts, garrisons, and guns upon the frontiers of their kingdoms, and continual spies upon their neighbours, which is a posture of war. But because they uphold thereby the industry of their subjects, there does not follow from it that misery which accompanies the liberty of particular men.

To this war of every man against every man, this also is consequent; that nothing can be unjust. The notions of right and wrong, justice and injustice, have there no place. Where there is no common power, there is no law; where no law, no injustice. Force and fraud are in war the two cardinal virtues. Justice and injustice are none of the faculties neither of the body nor mind. If they were, they might be in a man that were alone in the world, as well as his senses and passions. They are qualities that relate to men in society, not in solitude. It is consequent also to the same condition that there be no propriety, no dominion, no mine and thine distinct; but only that to be every man's that he can get, and for so long as he can keep it. And thus much for the ill condition which man by mere nature is actually placed in; though with a possibility to come out of it, consisting partly in the passions, partly in his reason.

The passions that incline men to peace are: fear of death; desire of such things as are necessary to commodious living; and a hope by their industry to obtain them. And reason suggesteth convenient articles of peace upon which men may be drawn to agreement. These articles are they which otherwise are called the laws of nature, whereof I shall speak more particularly in the two following chapters.

Of the First and Second Natural Laws, and of Contracts

The right of nature, which writers commonly call *jus naturale*, is the liberty each man hath to use his own power as he will himself for the preservation of his own nature; that is to say, of his own life; and consequently, of doing anything which, in his own judgement and reason, he shall conceive to be the aptest means thereunto.

By liberty is understood, according to the proper signification of the word, the absence of external impediments; which impediments may oft take away part of a man's power to do what he would, but cannot hinder him from using the power left him according as his judgement and reason shall dictate to him.

A law of nature, *lex naturalis*, is a precept, or general rule, found out by reason, by which a man is forbidden to do that which is destructive of his life, or taketh away the means of preserving the same, and to omit that by which he thinketh it may be best preserved.

And because the condition of man ... is a condition of war of every one against every one, in which case every one is governed by his own reason, and there is nothing he can make use of that may not be a help unto him in preserving his life against his enemies; it followeth that in such a condition every man has a right to every thing, even to one another's body. And therefore, as long as this natural right of every man to every thing endureth, there can be no security to any man, how strong or wise soever he be, of living out the time which nature ordinarily alloweth men to live. And consequently it is a precept, or general rule of reason: that every man ought to endeavour peace, as far as he has hope of obtaining it; and when he cannot obtain it, that he may seek and use all helps and advantages of war. The first branch of which rule containeth the first and fundamental law of nature, which is: to seek peace and follow it. The second, the sum of the right of nature, which is: by all means we can to defend ourselves.

From this fundamental law of nature, by which men are commanded to endeavour peace, is derived this second law: that a man be willing, when others are so too, as far forth as for peace and defence of himself he shall think it necessary, to lay down this right to all things; and be contented with so much liberty against other men as he would allow other men against himself. For as long as every man holdeth this right, of doing anything he liketh; so long are all men in the condition of war. But if other men will not lay down their right, as well as he, then there is no reason for anyone to divest himself of his: for that were to expose himself to prey, which no man is bound to, rather than to dispose himself to peace. This is that law of the gospel: Whatsoever you require that others should do to you, that do ye to them.

Whensoever a man transferreth his right, or renounceth it, it is either in consideration of some right reciprocally transferred to himself, or for some other good he hopeth for thereby. For it is a voluntary act: and of the voluntary acts of every man, the object is some good to himself. And therefore there be some rights which no man can be understood by any words, or other signs, to have abandoned or transferred. As first a man cannot lay down the right of resisting them that assault him by force to take away his life, because he cannot be understood to aim thereby at any good to himself. The same may be said of wounds, and chains, and imprisonment, both because there is no benefit consequent to such patience, as there is to the patience of suffering another to be wounded or imprisoned, as also because a man cannot tell when he seeth men proceed against him by violence whether they intend his death or not. And lastly the motive and end for which this renouncing and transferring of right is introduced is nothing else but the security of a man's person, in his life, and in the means of so preserving life as not to be weary of it. And therefore if a man by words, or other signs, seem to despoil himself of the end for which those signs were intended, he is not to be understood as if he meant it, or that it was his will, but that he was ignorant of how such words and actions were to be interpreted.

The mutual transferring of right is that which men call contract. . . .

Signs of contract are either express or by inference. Express are words spoken with understanding of what they signify: and such words are either of the time present or past; as, I give, I grant, I have given, I have granted, I will that this be yours: or of the future; as, I will give, I will grant, which words of the future are called promise.

Signs by inference are sometimes the consequence of words; sometimes the consequence of silence; sometimes the consequence of actions; sometimes the consequence of forbearing an action: and generally a sign by inference, of any contract, is whatsoever sufficiently argues the will of the contractor.

Words alone, if they be of the time to come, and contain a bare promise, are an insufficient sign of a free gift and therefore not obligatory. For if they be of the time to come, as, tomorrow I will give, they are a sign I have not given yet, and consequently that my right is not transferred, but remaineth till I transfer it by some other act. . . .

If a covenant be made wherein neither of the parties perform presently, but trust one another, in the condition of mere nature (which is a condition of war of every man against every man) upon any reasonable suspicion, it is void: but if there be a common power set over them both, with right and force sufficient to compel performance, it is not void. For he that performeth first has no assurance the other will perform after, because the bonds of words are too weak to bridle men's ambition, avarice, anger, and other passions, without the fear of some coercive power; which in the condition of mere nature, where all men are equal, and judges of the justness of their own fears, cannot possibly be supposed. And therefore he which performeth first does but betray himself to his enemy, contrary to the right he can never abandon of defending his life and means of living.

But in a civil estate, where there is a power set up to constrain those that would otherwise violate their faith, that fear is no more reasonable; and for that cause, he which by the covenant is to perform first is obliged so to do.

Of Other Laws of Nature

From that law of nature by which we are obliged to transfer to another such rights as, being retained, hinder the peace of mankind, there followeth a third; which is this: that men perform their covenants made; without which covenants are in vain, and but empty words; and the right of all men to all things remaining, we are still in the condition of war.

And in this law of nature consisteth the fountain and original of justice. For where no covenant hath preceded, there hath no right been transferred, and every man has right to everything and consequently, no action can be unjust. But when a covenant is made, then to break it is unjust and the definition of injustice is no other than the not performance of covenant. And whatsoever is not unjust is just.

But because covenants of mutual trust, where there is a fear of not performance on either part (as hath been said in the former chapter), are invalid, though the original of justice be the making of covenants, yet injustice actually there can be none till the cause of such fear be taken away; which, while men are in the natural condition of war, cannot be done. Therefore before the names of just and unjust can have place, there must be some coercive power to compel men equally to the performance of their covenants, by the terror of some punishment greater than the benefit they expect by the breach of their covenant, and to make good that propriety which by mutual contract men acquire in recompense of the universal right they abandon: and such power there is none before the erection of a Commonwealth. And this is also to be gathered out of the ordinary definition of justice in the Schools, for they say that justice is the constant will of giving to every man his own. And therefore where there is no own, that is, no propriety, there is no injustice; and where there is no coercive power erected, that is, where there is no Commonwealth, there is no propriety, all men having right to all things: therefore where there is no Commonwealth, there nothing is unjust. So that the nature of justice consisteth in keeping of valid covenants, but the validity of covenants begins not but with the constitution of a civil power sufficient to compel men to keep them: and then it is also that propriety begins.

The fool hath said in his heart, there is no such thing as justice, and sometimes also with his tongue, seriously alleging that every man's conservation and contentment being committed to his own care, there could be no reason why every man might not do what he thought conduced thereunto: and therefore also to make, or not make; keep, or not keep, covenants was not against reason when it conduced to one's benefit. He does not therein deny that there be covenants; and that they are sometimes broken, sometimes kept; and that such breach of them may be called injustice, and the observance of them justice: but he questioneth whether injustice, taking away the fear of God (for the same fool hath said in his heart there is no God), may not sometimes stand with that reason which dictateth to every man his own good; and particularly then, when it conduceth to such a benefit as shall put a man in a condition to neglect not only the dispraise and revilings, but also the power of other men. The kingdom of God is gotten by violence: but what if it could be gotten by unjust violence? Were it against reason so to get it, when it is impossible to receive hurt by it? And if it be not against reason, it is not against justice: or else justice is not to be approved for good. From such reasoning as this, successful wickedness hath obtained the name of virtue: and some that in all other things have disallowed the violation of faith, yet have allowed it when it is for the getting of a kingdom. And the heathen that believed that Saturn was deposed by his son Jupiter believed nevertheless the same Jupiter to be the avenger of injustice, somewhat like to a piece of law in Coke's Commentaries on Littleton; where he says if the right heir of the crown be attainted of treason, yet the crown shall descend to him, and eo instante the attainder be void: from which instances a man will be very prone to infer that when the heir apparent of a kingdom shall kill him that is in possession, though his father, you may call it injustice, or by what other name you will; yet it can never be against reason, seeing all the voluntary actions of men tend to the benefit of themselves; and those actions are most reasonable that conduce most to their ends. This specious reasoning is nevertheless false.

For the question is not of promises mutual, where there is no security of performance on either side, as when there is no civil power erected over the parties promising; for such promises are no covenants: but either where one of the parties has performed already, or where there is a power to make him perform, there is the question whether it be against reason; that is, against the benefit of the other to perform, or not. And I say it is not against reason. For the manifestation whereof we are to consider; first, that when a man doth a thing, which notwithstanding anything can be foreseen and reckoned on tendeth to his own destruction, howsoever some accident, which he could not expect, arriving may turn it to his benefit; yet such events do not make it reasonably or wisely done. Secondly, that in a condition of war, wherein every man to every man, for want of a common power to keep them all in awe, is an enemy, there is no man can hope by his own strength, or wit, to defend himself from destruction without the help of confederates; where every one expects the same defence by the confederation that any one else does: and therefore he which declares he thinks it reason to deceive those that help him can in reason expect no other means of safety than what can be had from his own single power. He, therefore, that breaketh his covenant, and consequently declareth that he thinks he may with reason do so, cannot be received into any society that unite themselves for peace and defence but by the error of them that receive him; nor when he is received be retained in it without seeing the danger of their error; which errors a man cannot reasonably reckon upon as the means of his security: and therefore if he be left, or cast out of society, he perisheth; and if he live in society, it is by the errors of other men, which he could not foresee nor reckon upon, and consequently against the reason of his preservation; and so, as all men that contribute not to his destruction forbear him only out of ignorance of what is good for themselves.

As for the instance of gaining the secure and perpetual felicity of heaven by any way, it is frivolous; there being but one way imaginable, and that is not breaking, but keeping of covenant.

And for the other instance of attaining sovereignty by rebellion; it is manifest that, though the event follow, yet because it cannot reasonably be expected, but rather the contrary, and because by gaining it so, others are taught to gain the same in like manner, the attempt thereof is against reason. Justice therefore, that is to say, keeping of covenant, is a rule of reason by which we are forbidden to do anything destructive to our life, and consequently a law of nature.

Thomas Hobbes: Leviathan

1. At the beginning of the selection, Hobbes argues that all humans are fundamentally equal. In what ways does Hobbes claim that we are equal? Do you agree with him?
2. Hobbes claims that without a government to enforce law and order, we would find ourselves in a "war . . . of every man against every man." What reasons does he give for believing this? Do you think he is right?

3. According to Hobbes, if there were no governments to establish laws, nothing would be just or unjust. Does this seem plausible? Would some actions be unjust even if there were no authority around to punish those who committed them?

4. Hobbes says, "Of the voluntary acts of every man, the object is some good to himself." Is Hobbes correct in thinking that self-interest is what motivates every voluntary action?

5. Hobbes claims that it is always unjust to violate our covenants (or contracts), provided that there is a government with the power to enforce them. He also claims that any action that does not violate a covenant is just. Can you think of any counterexamples to either of these claims?

6. The "fool" claims that it is rational to unjustly break one's covenants in cases where doing so promotes one's self-interest. How does Hobbes respond to this claim? Do you find Hobbes's replies convincing?

===== ❧ =====

11

What Makes Right Acts Right?

W. D. Ross

....

W. D. Ross (1877–1971) developed a truly novel moral theory in his book *The Right and the Good* (1930), from which this selection is taken. He found something attractive about both utilitarianism and Kantianism, the major theoretical competitors of his day, but found that each had a major flaw. Ross applauded utilitarianism's emphasis on benevolence, but rejected its idea that maximizing goodness is our sole moral duty. Kantianism, on the other hand, preserved the attractive idea that justice is independently important, but erred in claiming that the moral rules that specify such duties are absolute (never to be broken).

Ross created a kind of compromise theory, in which he identified a number of distinct grounds for moral duty (benevolence, fidelity to promises, truth-telling, avoiding harm, gratitude, justice, reparation). Each of these is a basis for a *prima facie duty*—an always-important reason that generates an "all-things-considered" duty, provided that no other reason or set of reasons is weightier in the situation. In other words, it is sometimes acceptable to violate a prima facie duty.

But when? We cannot offer a permanent ranking of these prima facie duties. Sometimes, for instance, it is right to promote the general happiness even if we have to commit an injustice to do so. But at other times, the balance should be struck in the opposite way.

W. D. Ross, "What Makes Right Acts Right?" from *The Right and the Good* (1930), pp. 16–32. By permission of Oxford University Press, Inc.

Ross insisted that these prima facie duties are self-evident. Here he offers some very influential (and controversial) remarks on how we can gain moral knowledge, both of the moral principles themselves and of the correct verdicts to reach in particular cases.

....

The point at issue is that to which we now pass, viz. whether there is any general character which makes right acts right, and if so, what it is. Among the main historical attempts to state a single characteristic of all right actions which is the foundation of their rightness are those made by egoism and utilitarianism. But I do not propose to discuss these, not because the subject is unimportant, but because it has been dealt with so often and so well already, and because there has come to be so much agreement among moral philosophers that neither of these theories is satisfactory. A much more attractive theory has been put forward by Professor Moore: that what makes actions right is that they are productive of more *good* than could have been produced by any other action open to the agent.

This theory is in fact the culmination of all the attempts to base rightness on productivity of some sort of result. The first form this attempt takes is the attempt to base rightness on conduciveness to the advantage or pleasure of the agent. This theory comes to grief over the fact, which stares us in the face, that a great part of duty consists in an observance of the rights and a furtherance of the interests of others, whatever the cost to ourselves may be. Plato and others may be right in holding that a regard for the rights of others never in the long run involves a loss of happiness for the agent, that 'the just life profits a man.' But this, even if true, is irrelevant to the rightness of the act. As soon as a man does an action *because* he thinks he will promote his own interests thereby, he is acting not from a sense of its rightness but from self-interest.

To the egoistic theory hedonistic utilitarianism supplies a much-needed amendment. It points out correctly that the fact that a certain pleasure will be enjoyed by the agent is no reason why he ought to bring it into being rather than an equal or greater pleasure to be enjoyed by another, though, human nature being what it is, it makes it not unlikely that he will try to bring it into being. But hedonistic utilitarianism in its turn needs a correction. On reflection it seems clear that pleasure is not the only thing in life that we think good in itself, that for instance we think the possession of a good character, or an intelligent understanding of the world, as good or better. A great advance is made by the substitution of 'productive of the greatest good' for 'productive of the greatest pleasure.'

Not only is this theory more attractive than hedonistic utilitarianism, but its logical relation to that theory is such that the latter could not be true unless it were true, while it might be true though hedonistic utilitarianism were not. It is in fact one of the logical bases of hedonistic utilitarianism. For the view that what produces the maximum pleasure is right has for its bases the views (1) that what produces the maximum good is right, and (2) that pleasure is the only thing good in itself. If, therefore, it can be shown that productivity of the maximum good is not what makes all right actions right, we shall *a fortiori* have refuted hedonistic utilitarianism.

When a plain man fulfils a promise because he thinks he ought to do so, it seems clear that he does so with no thought of its total consequences, still less with any opinion that these are likely to be the best possible. He thinks in fact much more of the past than of the future. What makes him think it right to act in a certain way is the fact that he has promised to do so—that and, usually, nothing more. That his act will produce the best possible consequences is not his reason for calling it right. What lends colour to the theory we are examining, then, is not the actions (which form probably a great majority of our actions) in which some such reflection as 'I have promised' is the only reason we give ourselves for thinking a certain action right, but the exceptional cases in which the consequences of fulfilling a promise (for instance) would be so disastrous to others that we judge it right not to do so. It must of course be admitted that such cases exist. If I have promised to meet a friend at a particular time for some trivial purpose, I should certainly think myself justified in breaking my engagement if by doing so I could prevent a serious accident or bring relief to the victims of one. And the supporters of the view we are examining hold that my thinking so is due to my thinking that I shall bring more good into existence by the one action than by the other. A different account may, however, be given of the matter, an account which will, I believe, show itself to be the true one. It may be said that besides the duty of fulfilling promises I have and recognize a duty of relieving distress, and that when I think it right to do the latter at the cost of not doing the former, it is not because I think I shall produce more good thereby but because I think it the duty which is in the circumstances more of a duty. This account surely corresponds much more closely with what we really think in such a situation.

If, so far as I can see, I could bring equal amounts of good into being by fulfilling my promise and by helping some one to whom I had made no promise, I should not hesitate to regard the former as my duty. Yet on the view that what is right is right because it is productive of the most good I should not so regard it.

There are two theories, each in its way simple, that offer a solution of such cases of conscience. One is the view of Kant, that there are certain duties of perfect obligation, such as those of fulfilling promises, of paying debts, of telling the truth, which admit of no exception whatever in favour of duties of imperfect obligation, such as that of relieving distress. The other is the view of, for instance, Professor Moore and Dr. Rashdall, that there is only the duty of producing good, and that all 'conflicts of duties' should be resolved by asking 'by which action will most good be produced?' But it is more important that our theory fit the facts than that it be simple, and the account we have given above corresponds (it seems to me) better than either of the simpler theories with what we really think, viz. that normally promise-keeping, for example, should come before benevolence, but that when and only when the good to be produced by the benevolent act is very great and the promise comparatively trivial, the act of benevolence becomes our duty.

In fact the theory of 'ideal utilitarianism,' if I may for brevity refer so to the theory of Professor Moore, seems to simplify unduly our relations to our fellows. It says, in effect, that the only morally significant relation in which my neighbours stand to me is that of being possible beneficiaries by my action. They do stand in this relation to me, and this relation is morally significant. But they may also stand to me in the relation of promisee to promiser, of creditor to debtor, of wife to husband, of child to parent, of friend to friend, of fellow countryman to fellow countryman, and the like; and each of these relations is the foundation of a *prima facie* duty, which is more or less incumbent on me according to the circumstances of the case. When I am in a situation, as perhaps I always am, in which more than one of these *prima facie* duties is incumbent on me, what I have to do is to study the situation as fully as I can until I form the considered opinion (it is never more) that in the circumstances one of them is more incumbent than any other; then I am bound to think that to do this *prima facie* duty is my duty *sans phrase* in the situation.

I suggest '*prima facie* duty' or 'conditional duty' as a brief way of referring to the characteristic (quite distinct from that of being a duty proper) which an act has, in virtue of being of a certain kind (e.g. the keeping of a promise), of being an act which would be a duty proper if it were not at the same time of another kind which is morally significant. Whether an act is a duty proper or actual duty depends on *all* the morally significant kinds it is an instance of.

The phrase '*prima facie* duty' must be apologized for, since (1) it suggests that what we are speaking of is a certain kind of duty, whereas it is in fact not a duty, but something related in a special way to duty. Strictly speaking, we want not a phrase in which duty is qualified by an adjective, but a separate noun. (2) '*Prima' facie* suggests that one is speaking only of an appearance which a moral situation presents at first sight, and which may turn out to be illusory; whereas what I am speaking of is an objective fact involved in the nature of the situation, or more strictly in an element of its nature, though not, as duty proper does, arising from its whole nature.

There is nothing arbitrary about these *prima facie* duties. Each rests on a definite circumstance which cannot seriously be held to be without moral significance. Of prima facie duties I suggest, without claiming completeness or finality for it, the following division.

1. Some duties rest on previous acts of my own. These duties seem to include two kinds.
   A. Those resting on a promise or what may fairly be called an implicit promise, such as the implicit undertaking not to tell lies which seems to be implied in the act of entering into conversation (at any rate by civilized men), or of writing books that purport to be history and not fiction. These may be called the duties of fidelity.
   B. Those resting on a previous wrongful act. These may be called the duties of reparation.
2. Some rest on previous acts of other men, i.e. services done by them to me. These may be loosely described as the duties of gratitude.
3. Some rest on the fact or possibility of a distribution of pleasure or happiness (or of the means thereto) which is not in accordance with the merit of the persons concerned; in such cases there arises a duty to upset or prevent such a distribution. These are the duties of justice.
4. Some rest on the mere fact that there are beings in the world whose condition we can make better in respect of virtue, or of intelligence, or of pleasure. These are the duties of beneficence.

5. Some rest on the fact that we can improve our own condition in respect of virtue or of intelligence. These are the duties of self-improvement.

6. I think that we should distinguish from (4) the duties that may be summed up under the title of 'not injuring others.' No doubt to injure others is incidentally to fail to do them good; but it seems to me clear that non-maleficence is apprehended as a duty distinct from that of beneficence, and as a duty of a more stringent character.

The essential defect of the 'ideal utilitarian' theory is that it ignores, or at least does not do full justice to, the highly personal character of duty. If the only duty is to produce the maximum of good, the question who is to have the good—whether it is myself, or my benefactor, or a person to whom I have made a promise to confer that good on him, or a mere fellow man to whom I stand in no such special relation—should make no difference to my having a duty to produce that good. But we are all in fact sure that it makes a vast difference.

If the objection be made, that this catalogue of the main types of duty is an unsystematic one resting on no logical principle, it may be replied, first, that it makes no claim to being ultimate. It is a *prima facie* classification of the duties which reflection on our moral convictions seems actually to reveal. And if these convictions are, as I would claim that they are, of the nature of knowledge, and if I have not misstated them, the list will be a list of authentic conditional duties, correct as far as it goes though not necessarily complete. The list of *goods* put forward by the rival theory is reached by exactly the same method—the only sound one in the circumstances—viz. that of direct reflection on what we really think. Loyalty to the facts is worth more than a symmetrical architectonic or a hastily reached simplicity. If further reflection discovers a perfect logical basis for this or for a better classification, so much the better.

It may, again, be objected that our theory that there are these various and often conflicting types of *prima facie* duty leaves us with no principle upon which to discern what is our actual duty in particular circumstances. But this objection is not one which the rival theory is in a position to bring forward. For when we have to choose between the production of two heterogeneous goods, say knowledge and pleasure, the 'ideal utilitarian' theory can only fall back on an opinion, for which no logical basis can be offered, that one of the goods is the greater; and this is no better than a similar opinion that one of two duties is the more urgent. And again, when we consider the infinite variety of the effects of our actions in the way of pleasure, it must surely be admitted that the claim which *hedonism* sometimes makes, that it offers a readily applicable criterion of right conduct, is quite illusory.

I am unwilling, however, to content myself with *an argumentum ad hominem*, and I would contend that in principle there is no reason to anticipate that every act that is our duty is so for one and the same reason. Why should two sets of circumstances, or one set of circumstances, not possess different characteristics, any one of which makes a certain act our *prima facie* duty? When I ask what it is that makes me in certain cases sure that I have a *prima facie* duty to do so and so, I find that it lies in the fact that I have made a promise; when I ask the same question in another case, I find the answer lies in the fact that I have done a wrong. And if on reflection I find (as I think I do) that neither of these reasons is reducible to the other, I must not on *any a priori* ground assume that such a reduction is possible.

It is necessary to say something by way of clearing up the relation between *prima facie* duties and the actual or absolute duty to do one particular act in particular circumstances. If, as almost all moralists except Kant are agreed, and as most plain men think, it is sometimes right to tell a lie or to break a promise, it must be maintained that there is a difference between *prima facie* duty and actual or absolute duty. When we think ourselves justified in breaking, and indeed morally obliged to break, a promise in order to relieve someone's distress, we do not for a moment cease to recognize a *prima facie* duty to keep our promise, and this leads us to feel, not indeed shame or repentance, but certainly compunction, for behaving as we do; we recognize, further, that it is our duty to make up somehow to the promisee for the breaking of the promise. We have to distinguish from the characteristic of being our duty that of tending to be our duty. Any act that we do contains various elements in virtue of which it falls under various categories. In virtue of being the breaking of a promise, for instance, it tends to be wrong; in virtue of being an instance of relieving distress it tends to be right.

Something should be said of the relation between our apprehension of the *prima facie* rightness of certain types of act and our mental attitude towards particular acts. It is proper to use the word 'apprehension' in the former case and not in the latter. That an act, *qua* fulfilling a promise, or *qua* effecting a just distribution of good, or *qua* returning services rendered, or *qua* promoting the good of others, or *qua* promoting the virtue or insight of the agent, is *prima facie* right, is self-evident; not in the sense that it is evident from the beginning of our lives, or as soon as we attend to the proposition for the first time, but in the sense that when we have reached sufficient mental maturity and have given sufficient attention to the proposition it is evident without any need of proof, or of evidence beyond itself. It is self-evident just as a mathematical axiom, or the validity of a form of inference, is evident. The moral order expressed in these propositions is just as much part of the fundamental nature of the universe (and, we may add, of any possible universe in which there were moral agents at all) as is the spatial or numerical structure expressed in the axioms of geometry or arithmetic. In our confidence that these propositions are true there is involved the same trust in our reason that is involved in our confidence in mathematics; and we should have no justification for trusting it in the latter sphere and distrusting it in the former. In both cases we are dealing with propositions that cannot be proved, but that just as certainly need no proof.

Our judgements about our actual duty in concrete situations have none of the certainty that attaches to our recognition of the general principles of duty. A statement is certain, i.e. is an expression of knowledge, only in one or other of two cases: when it is either self-evident, or a valid conclusion from self-evident premisses. And our judgements about our particular duties have neither of these characters. (1) They are not self-evident. Where a possible act is seen to have two characteristics, in virtue of one of which it is *prima facie* right, and in virtue of the other *prima facie* wrong, we are (I think) well aware that we are not certain whether we ought or ought not to do it; that whether we do it or not, we are taking a moral risk. We come in the long run, after consideration, to think one duty more pressing than the other, but we do not feel certain that it is so. And though we do not always recognize that a possible act has two such characteristics, and though there may be cases in which it has not, we are never certain that any particular possible act has not, and therefore never certain that it is right, nor certain that it is wrong. For, to go no further in the analysis, it is enough to point out that any particular act will in all probability in the course of time contribute to the bringing about of good or of evil for many human beings, and thus have a *prima facie* rightness or wrongness of which we know nothing. (2) Again, our judgements about our particular duties are not logical conclusions from self-evident premisses. The only possible premisses would be the general principles stating their *prima facie* rightness or wrongness *qua* having the different characteristics they do have; and even if we could (as we cannot) apprehend the extent to which an act will tend on the one hand, for example, to bring about advantages for our benefactors, and on the other hand to bring about disadvantages for fellow men who are not our benefactors, there is no principle by which we can draw the conclusion that it is on the whole right or on the whole wrong. In this respect the judgement as to the rightness of a particular act is just like the judgement as to the beauty of a particular natural object or work of art. A poem is, for instance, in respect of certain qualities beautiful and in respect of certain others not beautiful; and our judgement as to the degree of beauty it possesses on the whole is never reached by logical reasoning from the apprehension of its particular beauties or particular defects. Both in this and in the moral case we have more or less probable opinions which are not logically justified conclusions from the general principles that are recognized as self-evident.

There is therefore much truth in the description of the right act as a fortunate act. If we cannot be certain that it is right, it is our good fortune if the act we do is the right act. This consideration does not, however, make the doing of our duty a mere matter of chance. There is a parallel here between the doing of duty and the doing of what will be to our personal advantage. We never *know* what act will in the long run be to our advantage. Yet it is certain that we are more likely in general to secure our advantage if we estimate to the best of our ability the probable tendencies of our actions in this respect, than if we act on caprice. And similarly we are more likely to do our duty if we reflect to the best of our ability on the *prima facie* rightness or wrongness of various possible acts in virtue of the characteristics we perceive them to have, than if we act without reflection. With this greater likelihood we must be content.

The general principles of duty are obviously not self-evident from the beginning of our lives. How do they come to be so? The answer is, that they come to be self-evident to us just as mathematical axioms do. We find by experience that this couple of matches and that couple make four matches, that this couple of balls on a wire and that couple make four balls: and by reflection on these and similar discoveries we come to see that it is of the nature of two and two to make four. In a precisely similar way, we see the *prima facie* rightness of an act which would be the fulfilment of a particular promise, and of another which would be the fulfilment of another promise, and when we have reached sufficient maturity to think in general terms, we apprehend *prima facie* rightness to belong to the nature of any fulfilment of promise. What comes first in time is the apprehension of the self-evident *prima facie* rightness of an individual act of a particular type. From this we come by reflection to apprehend the self-evident general principle of *prima facie* duty. From this, too, perhaps along with the apprehension of the self-evident *prima facie* rightness of the same act in virtue of its having another characteristic as well, and perhaps in spite of the apprehension of its *prima facie* wrongness in virtue of its having some third characteristic, we come to believe something not self-evident at all, but an object of probable opinion, viz. that this particular act is (not *prima facie* but) actually right.

In what has preceded, a good deal of use has been made of 'what we really think' about moral questions; a certain theory has been rejected because it does not agree with what we really think. It might be said that this is in principle wrong; that we should not be content to expound what our present moral consciousness tells us but should aim at a criticism of our existing moral consciousness in the light of theory. Now I do not doubt that the moral consciousness of men has in detail undergone a good deal of modification as regards the things we think right, at the hands of moral theory. But if we are told, for instance, that we should give up our view that there is a special obligatoriness attaching to the keeping of promises because it is self-evident that the only duty is to produce as much good as possible, we have to ask ourselves whether we really, when we reflect, are convinced that this is self-evident, and whether we really can get rid of our view that promise-keeping has a bindingness independent of productiveness of maximum good. In my own experience I find that I cannot, in spite of a very genuine attempt to do so; and I venture to think that most people will find the same.

I would maintain, in fact, that what we are apt to describe as 'what we think' about moral questions contains a considerable amount that we do not think but know, and that this forms the standard by reference to which the truth of any moral theory has to be tested, instead of having itself to be tested by reference to any theory. I hope that I have in what precedes indicated what in my view these elements of knowledge are that are involved in our ordinary moral consciousness.

It would be a mistake to found a natural science on 'what we really think,' i.e. on what reasonably thoughtful and well-educated people think about the subjects of the science before they have studied them scientifically. For such opinions are interpretations, and often misinterpretations, of sense-experience; and the man of science must appeal from these to sense-experience itself, which furnishes his real data. In ethics no such appeal is possible. We have no more direct way of access to the facts about rightness and goodness and about what things are right or good, than by thinking about them; the moral convictions of thoughtful and well-educated people are the data of ethics just as sense-perceptions are the data of a natural science. Just as some of the latter have to be rejected as illusory, so have some of the former; but as the latter are rejected only when they are in conflict with other more accurate sense-perceptions, the former are rejected only when they are in conflict with other convictions which stand better the test of reflection. The existing body of moral convictions of the best people is the cumulative product of the moral reflection of many generations, which has developed an extremely delicate power of appreciation of moral distinctions; and this the theorist cannot afford to treat with anything other than the greatest respect. The verdicts of the moral consciousness of the best people are the foundation on which he must build; though he must first compare them with one another and eliminate any contradictions they may contain.

W. D. Ross: What Makes Right Acts Right?

1. Ross begins by considering the view that the right action is the one that is "productive of more *good* than could have been produced by any other action open to the agent." What objections does he offer to this view? Do you think they are good ones?

2. Ross also considers Kant's view, according to which there are certain moral rules that must be followed without exception. What does Ross think is wrong with this theory? Do you agree with his criticism?

3. What does Ross mean by "*prima facie* duties," and how do these differ from "duty proper"? How does he think we should use our knowledge of *prima facie* duties to determine what our duty is in a particular situation?

4. How does Ross think we come to know *prima facie* duties? Do you find his view plausible?

5. What reasons does Ross give for his claim that we can never be certain about what the right thing to do is in a particular situation? Do you agree with him about this?

6. Ross claims that "the moral convictions of thoughtful and well-educated people are the data of ethics just as sense-perceptions are the data of a natural science." Is beginning with our own moral convictions the best way of doing ethics, or do you think there is a better way?

12

Nicomachean Ethics

Aristotle

....

Aristotle (384–322 bce) was perhaps the greatest philosopher who ever lived. He worked in a variety of philosophical areas (logic, metaphysics, philosophy of mind, epistemology, ethics, rhetoric), and in each field produced work that exerted an influence across many centuries.

His seminal work in moral philosophy is *Nicomachean Ethics*, believed to be a set of carefully recorded lecture notes taken down by Aristotle's students. In this excerpt, from book 2 of the *Nicomachean Ethics*, Aristotle discusses the nature of virtue, its role in a good human life, and its relation to happiness and to "the golden mean." Aristotle's thoughts on the virtues have served as the basis of almost every version of virtue ethics developed in Western philosophy over the past two millennia.

....

Aristotle, from *Nicomachean Ethics* (1998), trans. W. D. Ross, pp. 28–47. By permission of Oxford University Press.

Moral Virtue

Moral Virtue, How Produced, in What Medium and in What Manner Exhibited

Moral virtue, like the arts, is acquired by repetition of the corresponding acts

Virtue, . . . being of two kinds, intellectual and moral, intellectual virtue in the main owes both its birth and its growth to teaching (for which reason it requires experience and time), while moral virtue comes about as a result of habit, whence also its name (ἠθική) is one that is formed by a slight variation from the word ἔθος (habit). From this it is also plain that none of the moral virtues arises in us by nature; for nothing that exists by nature can form a habit contrary to its nature. For instance the stone which by nature moves downwards cannot be habituated to move upwards, not even if one tries to train it by throwing it up ten thousand times; nor can fire be habituated to move downwards, nor can anything else that by nature behaves in one way be trained to behave in another. Neither by nature, then, nor contrary to nature do the virtues arise in us; rather we are adapted by nature to receive them, and are made perfect by habit.

Again, of all the things that come to us by nature we first acquire the potentiality and later exhibit the activity (this is plain in the case of the senses; for it was not by often seeing or often hearing that we got these senses, but on the contrary we had them before we used them, and did not come to have them by using them); but the virtues we get by first exercising them, as also happens in the case of the arts as well. For the things we have to learn before we can do them, we learn by doing them, e.g. men become builders by building and lyre-players by playing the lyre; so too we become just by doing just acts, temperate by doing temperate acts, brave by doing brave acts.

These acts cannot be prescribed exactly, but must avoid excess and defect

Since, then, the present inquiry does not aim at theoretical knowledge like the others (for we are inquiring not in order to know what virtue is, but in order to become good, since otherwise our inquiry would have been of no use), we must examine the nature of actions, namely how we ought to do them; for these determine also the nature of the states of character that are produced, as we have said. Now, that we must act according to the right rule is a common principle and must be assumed—it will be discussed later, i.e. both what the right rule is, and how it is related to the other virtues. But this must be agreed upon beforehand, that the whole account of matters of conduct must be given in outline and not precisely, . . . that the accounts we demand must be in accordance with the subject-matter; matters concerned with conduct and questions of what is good for us have no fixity, any more than matters of health. The general account being of this nature, the account of particular cases is yet more lacking in exactness; for they do not fall under any art or precept, but the agents themselves must in each case consider what is appropriate to the occasion, as happens also in the art of medicine or of navigation.

But though our present account is of this nature we must give what help we can. First, then, let us consider this, that it is the nature of such things to be destroyed by defect and excess, as we see in the case of strength and of health (for to gain light on things imperceptible we must use the evidence of sensible things); exercise either excessive or defective destroys the strength, and similarly drink or food which is above or below a certain amount destroys the health, while that which is proportionate both produces and increases and preserves it. So too is it, then, in the case of temperance and courage and the other virtues. For the man who flies from and fears everything and does not stand his ground against anything becomes a coward, and the man who fears nothing at all but goes to meet every danger becomes rash; and similarly the man who indulges in every pleasure and abstains from none becomes self-indulgent, while the man who shuns every pleasure, as boors do, becomes in a way insensible; temperance and courage, then, are destroyed by excess and defect, and preserved by the mean.

But not only are the sources and causes of their origination and growth the same as those of their destruction, but also the sphere of their actualization will be the same; for this is also true of the things which are more evident to sense, e.g. of strength; it is produced by taking much food and undergoing much exertion, and it is the strong man that will be most able to do these things. So too is it with the virtues; by abstaining from pleasures we become temperate, and it is when we have become so that we are most able to abstain from them; and similarly too in the case of courage; for by being habituated to despise things that are fearful and to stand our ground against them we become brave, and it is when we have become so that we shall be most able to stand our ground against them.

Pleasure in doing virtuous acts is a sign that the virtuous disposition has been acquired: a variety of considerations show the essential connexion of moral virtue with pleasure and pain

We must take as a sign of states of character the pleasure or pain that supervenes upon acts; for the man who abstains from bodily pleasures and delights in this very fact is temperate, while the man who is annoyed at it is self-indulgent, and he who stands his ground against things that are terrible and delights in this or at least is not pained is brave, while the man who is pained is a coward. For moral excellence is concerned with pleasures and pains; it is on account of the pleasure that we do bad things, and on account of the pain that we abstain from noble ones. Hence we ought to have been brought up in a particular way from our very youth, as Plato says, so as both to delight in and to be pained by the things that we ought; this is the right education.

We assume, then, that this kind of excellence tends to do what is best with regard to pleasures and pains, and vice does the contrary.

That virtue, then, is concerned with pleasures and pains, and that by the acts from which it arises it is both increased and, if they are done differently, destroyed, and that the acts from which it arose are those in which it actualizes itself—let this be taken as said.

The actions that produce moral virtue are not good in the same sense as those that flow from it: the latter must fulfil certain conditions not necessary in the case of the arts

The question might be asked, what we mean by saying that we must become just by doing just acts, and temperate by doing temperate acts; for if men do just and temperate acts, they are already just and temperate, exactly as, if they do what is in accordance with the laws of grammar and of music, they are grammarians and musicians.

Or is this not true even of the arts? It is possible to do something that is in accordance with the laws of grammar, either by chance or under the guidance of another. A man will be a grammarian, then, only when he has both said something grammatical and said it grammatically; and this means doing it in accordance with the grammatical knowledge in himself.

Again, the case of the arts and that of the virtues are not similar; for the products of the arts have their goodness in themselves, so that it is enough that they should have a certain character, but if the acts that are in accordance with the virtues have themselves a certain character it does not follow that they are done justly or temperately. The agent also must be in a certain condition when he does them; in the first place he must have knowledge, secondly he must choose the acts, and choose them for their own sakes, and thirdly his action must proceed from a firm and unchangeable character. These are not reckoned in as conditions of the possession of the arts except the bare knowledge; but as a condition of the possession of the virtues knowledge has little or no weight, while the other conditions count not for a little but for everything, i.e. the very conditions which result from often doing just and temperate acts.

Actions, then, are called just and temperate when they are such as the just or the temperate man would do; but it is not the man who does these that is just and temperate, but the man who also does them as just and temperate men do them. It is well said, then, that it is by doing just acts that the just man is produced, and by doing temperate acts the temperate man; without doing these no one would have even a prospect of becoming good.

Definition of Moral Virtue

The genus of moral virtue: it is a state of character,
not a passion, nor a faculty

Next we must consider what virtue is. Since things that are found in the soul are of three kinds—passions, faculties, states of character—virtue must be one of these. By passions I mean appetite, anger, fear, confidence, envy, joy, friendly feeling, hatred, longing, emulation, pity, and in general the feelings that are accompanied by pleasure or pain; by faculties the things in virtue of which we are said to be capable of feeling these, e.g. of becoming angry or being pained or feeling pity; by states of character the things in virtue of which we stand well or badly with reference to the passions, e.g. with reference to anger we stand badly if we feel it violently or too weakly, and well if we feel it moderately; and similarly with reference to the other passions.

Now neither the virtues nor the vices are *passions*, because we are not called good or bad on the ground of our passions, but are so called on the ground of our virtues and our vices, and because we are neither praised nor blamed for our passions (for the man who feels fear or anger is not praised, nor is the man who simply feels anger blamed, but the man who feels it in a certain way), but for our virtues and our vices we *are* praised or blamed.

Again, we feel anger and fear without choice, but the virtues are modes of choice or involve choice. Further, in respect of the passions we are said to be moved, but in respect of the virtues and the vices we are said not to be moved but to be disposed in a particular way.

For these reasons also they are not *faculties*; for we are neither called good or bad, nor praised or blamed, for the simple capacity of feeling the passions; again, we have the faculties by nature, but we are not made good or bad by nature; we have spoken of this before.

If, then, the virtues are neither passions nor faculties, all that remains is that they should be *states of character*.

Thus we have stated what virtue is in respect of its genus.

The differentia of moral virtue: it is a disposition to choose the mean

We must, however, not only describe virtue as a state of character, but also say what sort of state it is. We may remark, then, that every virtue or excellence both brings into good condition the thing of which it is the excellence and makes the work of that thing be done well; e.g. the excellence of the eye makes both the eye and its work good; for it is by the excellence of the eye that we see well. Similarly the excellence of the horse makes a horse both good in itself and good at running and at carrying its rider and at awaiting the attack of the enemy. Therefore, if this is true in every case, the virtue of man also will be the state of character which makes a man good and which makes him do his own work well.

How this is to happen we have stated already, but it will be made plain also by the following consideration of the specific nature of virtue. In everything that is continuous and divisible it is possible to take more, less, or an equal amount, and that either in terms of the thing itself or relatively to us; and the equal is an intermediate between excess and defect. By the intermediate in the object I mean that which is equidistant from each of the extremes, which is one and the same for all men; by the intermediate relatively to us that which is neither too much nor too little—and this is not one, nor the same for all. For instance, if ten is many and two is few, six is the intermediate, taken in terms of the object; for it exceeds and is exceeded by an equal amount; this is intermediate according to arithmetical proportion. But the intermediate relatively to us is not to be taken so; if ten pounds are too much for a particular person to eat and two too little, it does not follow that the trainer will order six pounds; for this also is perhaps too much for the person who is to take it, or too little—too little for Milo, too much for the beginner in athletic exercises. The same is true of running and wrestling. Thus a master of any art avoids excess and defect, but seeks the intermediate and chooses this—the intermediate not in the object but relatively to us.

If it is thus, then, that every art does its work well—by looking to the intermediate and judging its works by this standard (so that we often say of good works of art that it is not possible either to take away or to add anything, implying that excess and defect destroy the goodness of works of art, while the mean preserves it; and good artists, as we say, look to this in their work), and if, further, virtue is more exact and better than any art, as nature also is, then virtue must have the quality of aiming at the intermediate. I mean moral virtue; for it is this that is concerned with passions and actions, and in these there is excess, defect, and the intermediate. For instance, both fear and confidence and appetite and anger and pity and in general pleasure and pain may be felt both too much and too little, and in both cases not well; but to feel them at the right times, with reference to the right objects, towards the right people, with the right motive, and in the right way, is what is both intermediate and best, and this is characteristic of virtue. Similarly with regard to actions also there is excess, defect, and the intermediate. Now virtue is concerned with passions and actions, in which excess is a form of failure, and so is defect, while the intermediate is praised and is a form of success; and being praised and being successful are both characteristics of virtue. Therefore virtue is a kind of mean, since, as we have seen, it aims at what is intermediate.

Again, it is possible to fail in many ways (for evil belongs to the class of the unlimited, as the Pythagoreans conjectured, and good to that of the limited), while to succeed is possible only in one way (for which reason also one is easy and the other difficult—to miss the mark easy, to hit it difficult); for these reasons also, then, excess and defect are characteristic of vice, and the mean of virtue;

For men are good in but one way, but bad in many.

Virtue, then, is a state of character concerned with choice, lying in a mean, i.e. the mean relative to us, this being determined by a rational principle, and by that principle by which the man of practical wisdom would determine it. Now it is a mean between two vices, that which depends on excess and that which depends on defect; and again it is a mean because the vices respectively fall short of or exceed what is right in both passions and actions, while virtue both finds and chooses that which is intermediate. Hence in respect of what it is, i.e. the definition which states its essence, virtue is a mean, with regard to what is best and right an extreme.

But not every action nor every passion admits of a mean; for some have names that already imply badness, e.g. spite, shamelessness, envy, and in the case of actions adultery, theft, murder; for all of these and suchlike things imply by their names that they are themselves bad, and not the excesses or deficiencies of them. It is not possible, then, ever to be right with regard to them; one must always be wrong. Nor does goodness or badness with regard to such things depend on committing adultery with the right woman, at the right time, and in the right way, but simply to do any of them is to go wrong. It would be equally absurd, then, to expect that in unjust, cowardly, and voluptuous action there should be a mean, an excess, and a deficiency; for at that rate there would be a mean of excess and of deficiency, an excess of excess, and a deficiency of deficiency. But as there is no excess and deficiency of temperance and courage because what is intermediate is in a sense an extreme, so too of the actions we have mentioned there is no mean nor any excess and deficiency, but however they are done they are wrong; for in general there is neither a mean of excess and deficiency, nor excess and deficiency of a mean.

The above proposition illustrated by reference to particular virtues

We must, however, not only make this general statement, but also apply it to the individual facts. For among statements about conduct those which are general apply more widely, but those which are particular are more true, since conduct has to do with individual cases, and our statements must harmonize with the facts in these cases. We may take these cases from our table. With regard to feelings of fear and confidence courage is the mean; of the people who exceed, he who exceeds in fearlessness has no name (many of the states have no name), while the man who exceeds in confidence is rash, and he who exceeds in fear and falls short in confidence is a coward. With regard to pleasures and pains—not all of them, and not so much with regard to the pains—the mean is temperance, the excess self-indulgence. Persons deficient with regard to the pleasures are not often found; hence such persons also have received no name. But let us call them 'insensible.'

With regard to giving and taking of money the mean is liberality, the excess and the defect prodigality and meanness. In these actions people exceed and fall short in contrary ways; the prodigal exceeds in spending and falls short in taking, while the mean man exceeds in taking and falls short in spending. (At present we are giving a mere outline or summary, and are satisfied with this; later these states will be more exactly determined.) With regard to money there are also other dispositions—a mean, magnificence (for the magnificent man differs from the liberal man; the former deals with large sums, the latter with small ones), an excess, tastelessness and vulgarity, and a deficiency, niggardliness; these differ from the states opposed to liberality, and the mode of their difference will be stated later.

With regard to honour and dishonour the mean is proper pride, the excess is known as a sort of 'empty vanity', and the deficiency is undue humility; and as we said liberality was related to magnificence, differing from it by dealing with small sums, so there is a state similarly related to proper pride, being concerned with small honours while that is concerned with great. For it is possible to desire honour as one ought, and more than one ought, and less, and the man who exceeds in his desires is called ambitious, the man who falls short unambitious, while the intermediate person has no name. The dispositions also are nameless, except that that of the ambitious man is called ambition. Hence the people who are at the extremes lay claim to the middle place; and we ourselves sometimes call the intermediate person ambitious and sometimes unambitious, and sometimes praise the ambitious man and sometimes the unambitious. The reason of our doing this will be stated in what follows; but now let us speak of the remaining states according to the method which has been indicated.

With regard to anger also there is an excess, a deficiency, and a mean. Although they can scarcely be said to have names, yet since we call the intermediate person good-tempered let us call the mean good temper; of the persons at the extremes let the one who exceeds be called irascible, and his vice irascibility, and the man who falls short an unirascible sort of person, and the deficiency unirascibility.

Characteristics of the Extreme and Mean States: Practical Corollaries

The extremes are opposed to each other and to the mean
There are three kinds of disposition, then, two of them vices, involving excess and deficiency respectively, and one a virtue, viz. the mean, and all are in a sense opposed to all; for the extreme states are contrary both

to the intermediate state and to each other, and the intermediate to the extremes; as the equal is greater relatively to the less, less relatively to the greater, so the middle states are excessive relatively to the deficiencies, deficient relatively to the excesses, both in passions and in actions. For the brave man appears rash relatively to the coward, and cowardly relatively to the rash man; and similarly the temperate man appears self-indulgent relatively to the insensible man, insensible relatively to the self-indulgent, and the liberal man prodigal relatively to the mean man, mean relatively to the prodigal. Hence also the people at the extremes push the intermediate man each over to the other, and the brave man is called rash by the coward, cowardly by the rash man, and correspondingly in the other cases.

These states being thus opposed to one another, the greatest contrariety is that of the extremes to each other, rather than to the intermediate; for these are further from each other than from the intermediate, as the great is further from the small and the small from the great than both are from the equal. Again, to the intermediate some extremes show a certain likeness, as that of rashness to courage and that of prodigality to liberality; but the extremes show the greatest unlikeness to each other; now contraries are defined as the things that are furthest from each other, so that things that are further apart are more contrary.

To the mean in some cases the deficiency, in some the excess, is more opposed; e.g. it is not rashness, which is an excess, but cowardice, which is a deficiency, that is more opposed to courage, and not insensibility, which is a deficiency, but self-indulgence, which is an excess, that is more opposed to temperance. This happens from two reasons, one being drawn from the thing itself; for because one extreme is nearer and liker to the intermediate, we oppose not this but rather its contrary to the intermediate. E.g., since rashness is thought liker and nearer to courage, and cowardice more unlike, we oppose rather the latter to courage; for things that are further from the intermediate are thought more contrary to it. This, then, is one cause, drawn from the thing itself; another is drawn from ourselves; for the things to which we ourselves more naturally tend seem more contrary to the intermediate. For instance, we ourselves tend more naturally to pleasures, and hence are more easily carried away towards self-indulgence than towards propriety. We describe as contrary to the mean, then, rather the directions in which we more often go to great lengths; and therefore self-indulgence, which is an excess, is the more contrary to temperance.

The mean is hard to attain, and is grasped by perception, not by reasoning

That moral virtue is a mean, then, and in what sense it is so, and that it is a mean between two vices, the one involving excess, the other deficiency, and that it is such because its character is to aim at what is intermediate in passions and in actions, has been sufficiently stated. Hence also it is no easy task to be good. For in everything it is no easy task to find the middle, e.g. to find the middle of a circle is not for everyone but for him who knows; so, too, anyone can get angry—that is easy—or give or spend money; but to do this to the right person, to the right extent, at the right time, with the right motive, and in the right way, *that* is not for everyone, nor is it easy; wherefore goodness is both rare and laudable and noble.

Hence he who aims at the intermediate must first depart from what is the more contrary to it, as Calypso advises—

Hold the ship out beyond that surf and spray.

For of the extremes one is more erroneous, one less so; therefore, since to hit the mean is hard in the extreme, we must as a second best, as people say, take the least of the evils; and this will be done best in the way we describe.

But we must consider the things towards which we ourselves also are easily carried away; for some of us tend to one thing, some to another; and this will be recognizable from the pleasure and the pain we feel. We must drag ourselves away to the contrary extreme; for we shall get into the intermediate state by drawing well away from error, as people do in straightening sticks that are bent.

Now in everything the pleasant or pleasure is most to be guarded against; for we do not judge it impartially. We ought, then, to feel towards pleasure as the elders of the people felt towards Helen, and in all circumstances repeat their saying; for if we dismiss pleasure thus we are less likely to go astray. It is by doing this, then, (to sum the matter up) that we shall best be able to hit the mean.

But this is no doubt difficult, and especially in individual cases; for it is not easy to determine both how and with whom and on what provocation and how long one should be angry; for we too sometimes praise those who fall short and call them good-tempered, but sometimes we praise those who get angry and call them manly. The man, however, who deviates little from goodness is not blamed, whether he do so in the direction of the more or of the less, but only the man who deviates more widely; for *he* does not fail to be noticed. But up to what point and to what extent a man must deviate before he becomes blameworthy it is not easy to determine by reasoning, any more than anything else that is perceived by the senses; such things depend on particular facts, and the decision rests with perception. So much, then, is plain, that the intermediate state is in all things to be praised, but that we must incline sometimes towards the excess, sometimes towards the deficiency; for so shall we most easily hit the mean and what is right.

Aristotle: Nicomachean Ethics

1. Some philosophers have maintained that people are naturally morally good, while others have held that people are naturally wicked. Aristotle takes a middle ground, saying, "Neither by nature, then, nor contrary to nature do the virtues arise in us." Which view do you think is correct, and why?
2. What do you think Aristotle means when he says that "matters concerned with conduct and questions of what is good for us have no fixity"? Do you agree with this statement?
3. What is the difference, according to Aristotle, between performing virtuous actions and being a virtuous person? Do you agree with him that the latter is more valuable?
4. Aristotle says that virtue is a "mean" between extremes. For instance, the virtue of courage consists of the disposition to feel neither too much nor too little fear, but rather some appropriate amount in between. Is this consistent with his claim that some actions (such as stealing or adultery) are always wrong in all circumstances?
5. What advice does Aristotle give regarding how we should go about seeking the mean between extremes? Do you think this is good advice?

13

What Is Feminist Ethics?

Hilde Lindemann

....

Hilde Lindemann offers us a brief overview of feminist ethics in this selection. She first discusses the nature of feminism and identifies some of the various ways that people have defined it. Lindemann argues against thinking of feminism as focused primarily on equality, women, or the differences between the sexes. She instead invites us to think of feminism as based on considerations of gender—specifically, considerations to do with the lesser degree of power that women have, largely the world over, as compared with men.

Lindemann proceeds to discuss the sex/gender distinction and to identify the central tasks of feminist ethics: to understand, criticize, and correct the inaccurate gender assumptions that underlie our moral thinking and behavior. An important approach of most feminists is a kind of skepticism about the ability to distinguish political commitments from intellectual ones. Lindemann concludes by discussing this skepticism and its implications for feminist thought.

....

A few years ago, a dentist in Ohio was convicted of having sex with his female patients while they were under anesthesia. I haven't been able to discover whether he had to pay a fine or do jail time,

Hilde Lindemann, "What Is Feminist Ethics?" from *An Invitation to Feminist Ethics* (2004), pp. 2–3, 6–16. Reproduced with the permission of The McGraw-Hill Companies.

but I do remember that the judge ordered him to take a course in ethics. And I recall thinking how odd that order was. Let's suppose, as the judge apparently did, that the dentist really and truly didn't know it was wrong to have sex with anesthetized patients (this will tax your imagination, but try to suppose it anyway). Can we expect—again, as the judge apparently did—that on completing the ethics course, the dentist would be a better, finer man?

Hardly. If studying ethics could make you good, then the people who have advanced academic degrees in the subject would be paragons of moral uprightness. I can't speak for all of them, of course, but though the ones I know are nice enough, they're no more moral than anyone else. Ethics doesn't improve your character. Its *subject* is morality, but its relationship to morality is that of a scholarly study to the thing being studied. In that respect, the relationship is a little like the relationship between grammar and language.

Let's explore that analogy. People who speak fluent English don't have to stop and think about the correctness of the sentence "He gave it to *her.*" But here's a harder one. Should you say, "He gave it to *her* who must be obeyed?" or "He gave it to *she* who must be obeyed?" To sort this out, it helps to know a little grammar—the systematic, scholarly description of the structure of the language and the rules for speaking and writing in it. According to those rules, the object of the preposition "to" is the entire clause that comes after it, and the subject of that clause is "she." So, even though it sounds peculiar, the correct answer is "He gave it to she who must be obeyed."

In a roughly similar vein, morally competent adults don't have to stop and think about whether it's wrong to have sex with one's anesthetized patients. But if you want to understand whether it's wrong to have large signs in bars telling pregnant women not to drink, or to sort out the conditions under which it's all right to tell a lie, it helps to know a little ethics. The analogy between grammar and ethics isn't exact, of course. For one thing, there's considerably more agreement about what language is than about what morality is. For another, grammarians are concerned only with the structure of language, not with the meaning or usage of particular words. In both cases, however, the same point can be made: You already have to know quite a lot about how to behave—linguistically or morally—before there's much point in studying either grammar or ethics. . . .

What Is Feminism?

What, then, is feminism? As a social and political movement with a long, intermittent history, feminism has repeatedly come into public awareness, generated change, and then disappeared again. As an eclectic body of theory, feminism entered colleges and universities in the early 1970s as a part of the women's studies movement, contributing to scholarship in every academic discipline, though probably most heavily in the arts, social sciences, literature, and the humanities in general. Feminist ethics is a part of the body of theory that is being developed primarily in colleges and universities.

Many people in the United States think of feminism as a movement that aims to make women the social equals of men, and this impression has been reinforced by references to feminism and feminists in the newspapers, on television, and in the movies. But bell hooks has pointed out in *Feminist Theory from Margin to Center* (1984, 18–19) that this way of defining feminism raises some serious problems. Which men do women want to be equal to? Women who are socially well off wouldn't get much advantage from being the equals of the men who are poor and lower class, particularly if they aren't white. hooks's point is that there are no women and men in the abstract. They are poor, black, young, Latino/a, old, gay, able-bodied, upper class, down on their luck, Native American, straight, and all the rest of it. When a woman doesn't think about this, it's probably because she doesn't have to. And that's usually a sign that her own social position is privileged. In fact, privilege often means that there's something uncomfortable going on that others have to pay attention to but you don't. So, when hooks asks which men women want to be equal to, she's reminding us that there's an unconscious presumption of privilege built right in to this sort of demand for equality.

There's a second problem with the equality definition. Even if we could figure out which men are the ones to whom women should be equal, that way of putting it suggests that the point of feminism is somehow to get women to measure up to what (at least some) men already are. Men remain the point of reference; theirs are the lives that women would naturally want. If the first problem with the equality definition is "Equal to *which* men?" the second problem could be put as "Why equal to *any* men?" Reforming a system in which men are the point of reference by allowing women to perform as their equals "forces women to focus on men and address men's conceptions of women rather than creating and developing women's values about themselves," as Sarah Lucia Hoagland puts it in *Lesbian Ethics* (1988, 57). For that reason, Hoagland and some other feminists believe that feminism is first and foremost about women.

But characterizing feminism as about women has its problems too. What, after all, is a woman? In her 1949 book, *The Second Sex*, the French feminist philosopher Simone de Beauvoir famously observed, "One is not born, but becomes a woman. No biological, psychological, or economic fate determines the figure that the human female presents in society: it is civilization as a whole that produces this creature, intermediate between male and eunuch, which is described as feminine" (301). Her point is that while plenty of human beings are born female, 'woman' is not a natural fact about them—it's a social invention. According to that invention, which is widespread in "civilization as a whole," man represents the positive, typical human being, while woman represents only the negative, the not-man. She is the Other against whom man defines himself—he is all the things that she is not. And she exists only in relation to him. In a later essay called "One Is Not Born a Woman," the lesbian author and theorist Monique Wittig (1981, 49) adds that because women belong to men sexually as well as in every other way, women are necessarily heterosexual. For that reason, she argued, lesbians aren't women.

But, you are probably thinking, everybody knows what a woman is, and lesbians certainly *are* women. And you're right. These French feminists aren't denying that there's a perfectly ordinary use of the word *woman* by which it means exactly what you think it means. But they're explaining what this comes down to, if you look at it from a particular point of view. Their answer to the question "What is a woman?" is that women are different from men. But they don't mean this as a trite observation. They're saying that 'woman' refers to *nothing but* difference from men, so that apart from men, women aren't anything. 'Man' is the positive term, 'woman' is the negative one, just like 'light' is the positive term and 'dark' is nothing but the absence of light.

A later generation of feminists have agreed with Beauvoir and Wittig that women are different from men, but rather than seeing that difference as simply negative, they put it in positive terms, affirming feminine qualities as a source of personal strength and pride. For example, the philosopher Virginia Held thinks that women's moral experience as mothers, attentively nurturing their children, may serve as a better model for social relations than the contract model that the free market provides. The poet Adrienne Rich celebrated women's passionate nature (as opposed, in stereotype, to the rational nature of men), regarding the emotions as morally valuable rather than as signs of weakness.

But defining feminism as about the positive differences between men and women creates yet another set of problems. In her 1987 *Feminism Unmodified*, the feminist legal theorist Catharine A. MacKinnon points out that this kind of difference, as such, is a symmetrical relationship: If I am different from you, then you are different from me in exactly the same respects and to exactly the same degree. "Men's differences from women are equal to women's differences from men," she writes. "There is an *equality* there. Yet the sexes are not socially equal" (MacKinnon 1987, 37). No amount of attention to the differences between men and women explains why men, as a group, are more socially powerful, valued, advantaged, or free than women. For that, you have to see differences as counting in certain ways, and certain differences being created precisely because they give men *power* over women.

Although feminists disagree about this, my own view is that feminism isn't—at least not directly—about equality, and it isn't about women, and it isn't about difference. It's about power. Specifically, it's about the social pattern, widespread across cultures and history, that distributes power asymmetrically to favor men over women. This asymmetry has been given many names, including the subjugation of women, sexism, male dominance, patriarchy, systemic misogyny, phallocracy, and the oppression of women. A number of feminist theorists simply call it gender, and throughout this book, I will too.

What Is Gender?

Most people think their gender is a natural fact about them, like their hair and eye color: "Jones is 5 foot 8, has red hair, and is a man." But gender is a *norm*, not a fact. It's a prescription for how people are supposed to act; what they must or must not wear; how they're supposed to sit, walk, or stand; what kind of person they're supposed to marry; what sorts of things they're supposed to be interested in or good at; and what they're entitled to. And because it's an *effective* norm, it creates the differences between men and women in these areas.

Gender doesn't just tell women to behave one way and men another, though. It's a *power* relation, so it tells men that they're entitled to things that women aren't supposed to have, and it tells women that they are supposed to defer to men and serve them. It says, for example, that men are supposed to occupy positions of religious authority and women are supposed to run the church suppers. It says that mothers are supposed to take care of their children but fathers have more important things to do. And it says that the things associated with femininity are supposed to take a back seat to the things that are coded masculine. Think of the many tax dollars allocated to the military as compared with the few tax dollars allocated to the arts. Think about how kindergarten teachers are paid as compared to how stockbrokers are paid. And think about how many presidents of the United States have been women. Gender operates through social institutions (like marriage and the law) and practices (like education and medicine) by disproportionately conferring entitlements and the control of resources on men, while disproportionately assigning women to subordinate positions in the service of men's interests.

To make this power relation seem perfectly natural—like the fact that plants grow up instead of down, or that human beings grow old and die—gender constructs its norms for behavior around what is supposed to be the natural biological distinction between the sexes. According to this distinction, people who have penises and testicles, XY chromosomes, and beards as adults belong to the male sex, while people who have clitorises and ovaries, XX chromosomes, and breasts as adults belong to the female sex, and those are the only sexes there are. Gender, then, is the complicated set of cultural meanings that are constructed around the two sexes. Your sex is either male or female, and your gender—either masculine, or feminine—corresponds socially to your sex.

As a matter of fact, though, sex isn't quite so simple. Some people with XY chromosomes don't have penises and never develop beards, because they don't have the receptors that allow them to make use of the male hormones that their testicles produce. Are they male or female? Other people have ambiguous genitals or internal reproductive structures that don't correspond in the usual manner to their external genitalia. How should we classify them? People with Turner's syndrome have XO chromosomes instead of XX. People with Klinefelter's syndrome have three sex chromosomes: XXY. Nature is a good bit looser in its categories than the simple male/female distinction acknowledges. Most human beings can certainly be classified as one sex or the other, but a considerable number of them fall somewhere in between.

The powerful norm of gender doesn't acknowledge the existence of the in-betweens, though. When, for example, have you ever filled out an application for a job or a driver's license or a passport that gave you a choice other than M or F? Instead, by basing its distinction between masculine and feminine on the existence of two and only two sexes, gender makes the inequality of power between men and women appear natural and therefore legitimate.

Gender, then, is about power. But it's not about the power of just one group over another. Gender always interacts with other social markers—such as race, class, level of education, sexual orientation, age, religion, physical and mental health, and ethnicity—to distribute power unevenly among women positioned differently in the various social orders, and it does the same to men. A man's social status, for example, can have a great deal to do with the extent to which he's even perceived as a man. There's a wonderful passage in the English travel writer Frances Trollope's *Domestic Manners of the Americans* (1831), in which she describes the exaggerated delicacy of middle-class young ladies she met in Kentucky and Ohio. They wouldn't dream of sitting in a chair that was still warm from contact with a gentleman's bottom, but thought nothing of getting laced into their corsets in front of a male house slave. The slave, it's clear, didn't count as a man—not in the relevant sense, anyway. Gender is the force that makes it matter whether you are male or female, but it always works hand in glove with all the other things about you that matter at the same time. It's one power relation intertwined with others in a complex social system that distinguishes your betters from your inferiors in all kinds of ways and for all kinds of purposes.

Power and Morality

If feminism is about gender, and gender is the name for a social system that distributes power unequally between men and women, then you'd expect feminist ethicists to try to *understand, criticize,* and *correct* how gender operates within our moral beliefs and practices. And they do just that. In the first place, they challenge, on moral grounds, the powers men have over women, and they claim for women, again on moral grounds, the powers that gender denies them. As the moral reasons for opposing gender are similar to the moral reasons for opposing power systems based on social markers other than gender, feminist ethicists also offer moral arguments against systems based on class, race, physical or mental ability, sexuality, and age. And because all these systems, including gender, are powerful enough to *conceal* many of the forces that keep them in place, it's often necessary to make the forces visible by explicitly identifying—and condemning—the various ugly ways they allow some people to treat others. This is a central task for feminist ethics.

Feminist ethicists also produce theory about the moral meaning of various kinds of *legitimate* relations of unequal power, including relationships of dependency and vulnerability, relationships of trust, and relationships based on something other than choice. Parent–child relationships, for example, are necessarily unequal and for the most part unchosen. Parents can't help having power over their children, and while they may have chosen to have children, most don't choose to have the particular children they do, nor do children choose their parents. This raises questions about the responsible use of parental power and the nature of involuntary obligations, and these are topics for feminist ethics. Similarly, when you trust someone, that person has power over you. Whom should you trust, for what purposes, and when is trust not warranted? What's involved in being trustworthy, and what must be done to repair breaches of trust? These too are questions for feminist ethics.

Third, feminist ethicists look at the various forms of power that are required for morality to operate properly at all. How do we learn right from wrong in the first place? We usually learn it from our parents, whose power to permit and forbid, praise and punish, is essential to our moral training. For whom or what are we ethically responsible? Often this depends on the kind of power we have over the person or thing in question. If, for instance, someone is particularly vulnerable to harm because of something I've done, I might well have special duties toward that person. Powerful social institutions—medicine, religion, government, and the market, to take just a few examples—typically dictate what is morally required of us and to whom we are morally answerable. Relations of power set the terms for who must answer to whom, who has authority over whom, and who gets excused from certain kinds of accountability to whom. But because so many of these power relations are illegitimate, in that they're instances of gender, racism, or other kinds of bigotry, figuring out which ones are morally justified is a task for feminist ethics.

Description and Prescription

So far it sounds as if feminist ethics devotes considerable attention to *description*—as if feminist ethicists were like poets or painters who want to show you something about reality that you might otherwise have missed. And indeed, many feminist ethicists emphasize the importance of understanding how social power actually works, rather than concentrating solely on how it ought to work. But why, you might ask, should ethicists worry about how power operates within societies? Isn't it up to sociologists and political scientists to describe how things *are*, while ethicists concentrate on how things *ought* to be?

As the philosopher Margaret Urban Walker has pointed out in *Moral Contexts*, there is a tradition in Western philosophy, going all the way back to Plato, to the effect that morality is something ideal and that ethics, being the study of morality, properly examines only that ideal. According to this tradition, notions of right and wrong as they are found in the world are unreliable and shadowy manifestations of something lying outside of human experience—something to which we ought to aspire but can't hope to reach. Plato's Idea of the Good, in fact, is precisely not of this earth, and only the gods could truly know it. Christian ethics incorporates Platonism into its insistence that earthly existence is fraught with sin and error and that heaven is our real home. Kant too insists that moral judgments transcend the histories and circumstances of people's actual lives, and most moral philosophers of the twentieth century have likewise shown little interest in how people really live and what it's like for them to live that way. "They think," remarks Walker (2001), "that there is little to be learned from what is about what ought to be" (3).

In Chapter Four [omitted here—ed.] we'll take a closer look at what goes wrong when ethics is done that way, but let me just point out here that if you don't know how things are, your prescriptions for how things ought to be won't have much practical effect. Imagine trying to sail a ship without knowing anything about the tides or where the hidden rocks and shoals lie. You might have a very fine idea of where you are trying to go, but if you don't know the waters, at best you are likely to go off course, and at worst you'll end up going down with all your shipmates. If, as many feminists have noted, a crucial fact about human selves is that they are always embedded in a vast web of relationships, then the forces at play within those relationships must be understood. It's knowing how people are situated with respect to these forces, what they are going through as they are subjected to them, and what life is like in the face of them, that lets us decide which of the forces are morally justified. Careful description of how things are is a crucial part of feminist methodology, because the power that puts certain groups of people at risk of physical harm, denies them full access to the good things their society has to offer, or treats them as if they were useful only for other people's purposes is often hidden and hard to see. If this power isn't seen, it's likely to remain in place, doing untold amounts of damage to great numbers of people.

All the same, feminist ethics is *normative* as well as descriptive. It's fundamentally about how things ought to be, while description plays the crucial but secondary role of helping us to figure that out. Normative language is the language of "ought" instead of "is," the language of "worth" and "value," "right" and "wrong," "good" and "bad." Feminist ethicists differ on a number of normative issues, but as the philosopher Alison Jaggar (1991) has famously put it, they all share two moral commitments: "that the subordination of women is morally wrong and that the moral experience of women is worthy of respect" (95). The first commitment—that women's interests ought not systematically to be set in the service of men's—can be understood as a moral challenge to power under the guise of gender. The second commitment—that women's experience must be taken seriously—can be understood as a call to acknowledge how that power operates. These twin commitments are the two normative legs on which any feminist ethics stands. . . .

Morality and Politics

If the idealization of morality goes back over two thousand years in Western thought, a newer tradition, only a couple of centuries old, has split off morality from politics. According to this tradition, which can be traced to Kant and some other Enlightenment philosophers, morality concerns the relations between persons, whereas politics concerns the relations among nation-states, or between a state and its citizens. So, as Iris Marion Young (1990) puts it, ethicists have tended to focus on intentional actions by individual persons, conceiving of moral life as "conscious, deliberate, a rational weighing of alternatives," whereas political philosophers have focused on impersonal governmental systems, studying "laws, policies, the large-scale distribution of social goods, countable quantities like votes and taxes" (149).

For feminists, though, the line between ethics and political theory isn't quite so bright as this tradition makes out. It's not always easy to tell where feminist ethics leaves off and feminist political theory begins. There are two reasons for this. In the first place, while ethics certainly concerns personal behavior, there is a long-standing insistence on the part of feminists that the personal *is* political. In a 1970 essay called "The Personal Is Political," the political activist Carol Hanisch observed that "personal problems are political problems. There are no personal solutions at this time" (204–205). What Hanisch meant is that even the most private areas of everyday life, including such intensely personal areas as sex, can function to maintain abusive power systems like gender. If a heterosexual woman believes, for example, that contraception is primarily her responsibility because she'll have to take care of the baby if she gets pregnant, she is propping up a system that lets men evade responsibility not only for pregnancy, but for their own offspring as well. Conversely, while unjust social arrangements such as gender and race invade every aspect of people's personal lives, "there are no personal solutions," either when Hanisch wrote those words or now, because to shift dominant understandings of how certain groups may be treated, and what other groups are entitled to expect of them, requires concerted political action, not just personal good intentions.

The second reason why it's hard to separate feminist ethics from feminist politics is that feminists typically subject the ethical theory they produce to critical political scrutiny, not only to keep untoward political biases out, but also to make sure that the work accurately reflects their feminist politics. Many nonfeminist ethicists, on the other hand, don't acknowledge that their work reflects their politics, because they don't think it should. Their aim, by and large, has been to develop ideal moral theory that applies to all people, regardless of their social position or experience of life, and to do that objectively, without favoritism, requires them to leave their own personal politics behind. The trouble, though, is that they aren't really leaving their own personal politics behind. They're merely refusing to notice that their politics is inevitably built right in to their theories. (This is an instance of Lindemann's ad hoc rule Number 22: Just because you think you are doing something doesn't mean you're actually doing it.) Feminists, by contrast, are generally skeptical of the idealism nonfeminists favor, and they're equally doubtful that objectivity can be achieved by stripping away what's distinctive about people's experiences or commitments. Believing that it's no wiser to shed one's political allegiances in the service of ethics than it would be to shed one's moral allegiances, feminists prefer to be transparent about their politics as a way of keeping their ethics intellectually honest. . . .

Hilde Lindemann: What Is Feminist Ethics?

1. Near the beginning of her piece, Lindemann claims that studying ethics "doesn't improve your character." Do you think she is right about this? If so, what is the point of studying ethics?

2. What problems does Lindemann raise for the view that feminism is fundamentally about equality between men and women? Can these problems be overcome, or must we admit that feminism is concerned with equality?
3. What is the difference between sex and gender? Why does Lindemann think that gender is essentially about power? Do you think she is right about this?
4. Lindemann claims that feminist ethics is "*normative* as well as descriptive." What does she mean by this? In what ways is feminist ethics more descriptive than other approaches to ethics? Do you see this as a strength or a weakness?
5. What is meant by the slogan "The personal is political"? Do you agree with the slogan?
6. Lindemann claims that one should not set aside one's political views when thinking about ethical issues. What reasons does she give for thinking this? Do you agree with her?

For Further Reading

Baier, Annette. 1994. *Moral Prejudices: Essays on Ethics.* Cambridge, MA: Harvard University Press.

Beauvoir, Simone de. 1949 [1974]. *The Second Sex.* Trans. and ed. H. M. Parshley. New York: Modern Library.

Hanisch, Carol. 1970. "The Personal Is Political." In *Notes from the Second Year.* New York: Radical Feminism.

Hoagland, Sarah Lucia. 1988. *Lesbian Ethics: Toward New Value.* Palo Alto, CA: Institute of Lesbian Studies.

hooks, bell. 1984. *Feminist Theory from Margin to Center.* Boston: South End Press.

Jaggar, Alison. 1991. "Feminist Ethics: Projects, Problems, Prospects." In *Feminist Ethics*, ed. Claudia Card. Lawrence: University Press of Kansas.

MacKinnon, Catharine A. 1987. *Feminism Unmodified.* Cambridge, MA: Harvard University Press.

Plumwood, Val. 2002. *Environmental Culture: The Ecological Crisis of Reason.* London: Routledge.

Walker, Margaret Urban. 2001. "Seeing Power in Morality: A Proposal for Feminist Naturalism in Ethics." In *Feminists Doing Ethics*, ed. Peggy DesAutels and Joanne Waugh. Lanham, MD: Rowman & Littlefield. 2003.

Walker, Margaret Urban. 2003. *Moral Contexts.* Lanham, MD: Rowman & Littlefield.

Wittig, Monique. 1981. "One Is Not Born a Woman." *Feminist Issues* 1, no. 2.

Young, Iris Marion. 1990. *Justice and the Politics of Difference.* Princeton, NJ: Princeton University Press.

PART III

Metaethics

The Status of Morality

14

Moral Distinctions Not Derived from Reason

David Hume

David Hume (1711–1776) sought to offer a wholly naturalistic account of the nature and origins of morality. He rejected the idea of eternal moral truths, graspable by reason alone. He thought that morality is essentially a way of organizing our emotional responses to a value-free world. In this excerpt from his first masterpiece, *A Treatise of Human Nature* (1737), Hume offers several influential arguments against moral rationalism— the idea that reason is the basis of morality, our primary means of gaining moral knowledge, and the source of moral motivation. Also included here is perhaps his most famous claim about morality, namely, that one cannot derive an *ought* from an *is*. According to Hume, it is impossible to substantiate a claim about what ought to be done, or ought to be the case, solely from claims about how the world actually is. Since reason is confined to telling us what is the case, it cannot, by itself, supply us with advice about our duty, or about which ideals we should aspire to.

. . . It has been observed, that nothing is ever present to the mind but its perceptions; and that all the actions of seeing, hearing, judging, loving, hating, and thinking, fall under this denomination. The mind can never exert itself in any action which we may not comprehend under the term of *perception*; and consequently that term is no less applicable to those judgments by which we distinguish moral good and evil, than to every other operation of the mind. To approve of one character, to condemn another, are only so many different perceptions.

Now, as perceptions resolve themselves into two kinds, viz. *impressions* and *ideas*, this distinction gives rise to a question, with which we shall open up our present inquiry concerning morals, *whether it is by means of our ideas or impressions we distinguish betwixt vice and virtue, and pronounce an action blamable or praise-worthy?* This will immediately cut off all loose discourses and declamations, and reduce us to something precise and exact on the present subject.

Those who affirm that virtue is nothing but a conformity to reason; that there are eternal fitnesses and unfitnesses of things, which are the same to every rational being that considers them; that the immutable measure of right and wrong impose an obligation, not only on human creatures, but also on the Deity himself: all these systems concur in the opinion, that morality, like truth, is discerned merely by ideas, and by their juxtaposition and comparison. In order, therefore, to judge of these systems, we need only consider whether it be possible from reason alone, to distinguish betwixt moral good and evil, or whether there must concur some other principles to enable us to make that distinction.

If morality had naturally no influence on human passions and actions, it were in vain to take such pains to inculcate it; and nothing would be more fruitless than that multitude of rules and precepts with which all moralists abound. Philosophy is commonly divided into *speculative* and *practical*; and as morality is always comprehended under the latter division, it is supposed to influence our passions and actions, and to go beyond the calm and indolent judgments of the understanding. And this is confirmed by common experience, which informs us that men are often governed by their duties, and are deterred from some actions by the opinion of injustice, and impelled to others by that of obligation.

Since morals, therefore, have an influence on the actions and affections, it follows that they cannot be derived from reason; and that because reason alone, as we have already proved, can never have any such influence. Morals excite passions, and produce or prevent actions. Reason of itself is utterly impotent in this particular. The rules of morality, therefore, are not conclusions of our reason.

No one, I believe, will deny the justness of this inference; nor is there any other means of evading it, than by denying that principle on which it is founded. As long as it is allowed, that reason has no influence on our passions and actions, it is in vain to pretend that morality is discovered only by a deduction of reason. An active principle can never be founded on an inactive; and if reason be inactive in itself, it must remain so in all its shapes and appearances, whether it exerts itself in natural or moral subjects, whether it considers the powers of external bodies, or the actions of rational beings.

It would be tedious to repeat all the arguments by which I have proved that reason is perfectly inert, and can never either prevent or produce any action or affection. It will be easy to recollect what has been said upon that subject. I shall only recall on this occasion one of these arguments, which I shall endeavour to render still more conclusive, and more applicable to the present subject.

Reason is the discovery of truth or falsehood. Truth or falsehood consists in an agreement or disagreement either to the *real* relations of ideas, or to *real* existence and matter of fact. Whatever therefore is not susceptible of this agreement or disagreement, is incapable of being true or false, and can never be an object of our reason. Now, it is evident our passions, volitions, and actions, are not susceptible of any such agreement or disagreement; being original facts and realities, complete in themselves, and implying no reference to other passions, volitions, and actions. It is impossible, therefore, they can be pronounced either true or false, and be either contrary or conformable to reason.

This argument is of double advantage to our present purpose. For it proves *directly*, that actions do not derive their merit from a conformity to reason, nor their blame from a contrariety to it; and it proves the same truth more *indirectly*, by showing us, that as reason can never immediately prevent or produce any action by contradicting or approving of it, it cannot be the source of moral good and evil, which are found to have that influence. Actions may be laudable or blamable; but they cannot be reasonable or unreasonable: laudable or blamable, therefore, are not the same with reasonable or unreasonable. The merit and demerit of actions frequently contradict, and sometimes control our natural propensities. But reason has no such influence. Moral distinctions, therefore, are not the offspring of reason. Reason is wholly inactive, and can never be the source of so active a principle as conscience, or a sense of morals.

But perhaps it may be said, that though no will or action can be immediately contradictory to reason, yet we may find such a contradiction in some of the attendants of the actions, that is, in its causes or effects. The action may cause a judgment, or may be *obliquely* caused by one, when the judgment concurs with a passion; and by an abusive way of speaking, which philosophy will scarce allow of, the same contrariety may, upon that account, be ascribed to the action. How far this truth or falsehood may be the source of morals, it will now be proper to consider.

It has been observed that reason, in a strict and philosophical sense, can have an influence on our conduct only after two ways: either when it excites a passion, by informing us of the existence of something which is a proper object of it; or when it discovers the connection of causes and effects, so as to afford us means of exerting any passion. These are the only kinds of judgment which can accompany our actions, or can be said to produce them in any manner; and it must be allowed, that these judgments may often be false and erroneous. A person may be affected with passion, by supposing a pain or pleasure to lie in an object which has no tendency to produce either of these sensations, or which produces the contrary to what is imagined. A person may also take false measures for the attaining of his end, and may retard, by his foolish conduct, instead of forwarding the execution of any object. These false judgments may be thought to affect the passions and actions, which are connected with them, and may be said to render them unreasonable, in a figurative and improper way of speaking. But though this be acknowledged, it is easy to observe, that these errors are so far from being the source of all immorality, that they are commonly very innocent, and draw no manner of guilt upon the person who is so unfortunate as to fall into them. They extend not beyond a mistake of *fact*, which moralists have not generally supposed criminal, as being perfectly involuntary. I am more to be lamented than blamed, if I am mistaken with regard to the influence of objects in producing pain or pleasure, or if I know not the proper means of satisfying my desires. No one can ever regard such errors as a defect in my moral character. A fruit, for instance, that is really disagreeable, appears to me at a distance, and, through mistake, I fancy it to be pleasant and delicious. Here is one error. I choose certain means of reaching this fruit, which are not proper for my end. Here is a second error; nor is there any third one, which can ever possibly enter into our reasonings concerning actions. I ask, therefore, if a man in this situation, and guilty of these two errors, is to be regarded as vicious and criminal, however unavoidable they might have been? Or if it be possible to imagine that such errors are the sources of all immorality?

And here it may be proper to observe, that if moral distinctions be derived from the truth or falsehood of those judgments, they must take place wherever we form the judgments; nor will there be any difference, whether the question be concerning an apple or a kingdom, or whether the error be avoidable or unavoidable.

For as the very essence of morality is supposed to consist in an agreement or disagreement to reason, the other circumstances are entirely arbitrary, and can never either bestow on any action the character of virtuous or vicious, or deprive it of that character. To which we may add, that this agreement or disagreement, not admitting of degrees, all virtues and vices would of course be equal.

Should it be pretended, that though a mistake of *fact* be not criminal, yet a mistake of right often is; and that this may be the source of immorality: I would answer, that it is impossible such a mistake can ever be the original source of immorality, since it supposes a real right and wrong; that is, a real distinction in morals, independent of these judgments. A mistake, therefore, of right, may become a species of immorality; but it is only a secondary one, and is founded on some other antecedent to it.

As to those judgments which are the *effects* of our actions, and which, when false, give occasion to pronounce the actions contrary to truth and reason; we may observe, that our actions never cause any judgment, either true or false, in ourselves, and that it is only on others they have such an influence. It is certain that an action, on many occasions, may give rise to false conclusions in others; and that a person, who, through a window, sees any lewd behaviour of mine with my neighbour's wife, may be so simple as to imagine she is certainly my own. In this respect my action resembles somewhat a lie or falsehood; only with this difference, which is material, that I perform not the action with any intention of giving rise to a false judgment in another, but merely to satisfy my lust and passion. It causes, however, a mistake and false judgment by accident; and the falsehood of its effects may be ascribed, by some odd figurative way of speaking, to the action itself. But still I can see no pretext of reason for asserting, that the tendency to cause such an error is the first spring or original source of all immorality.

Thus, upon the whole, it is impossible that the distinction betwixt moral good and evil can be made by reason; since that distinction has an influence upon our actions, of which reason alone is incapable. Reason and judgment may, indeed, be the mediate cause of an action, by prompting or by directing a passion; but it is not pretended that a judgment of this kind, either in its truth or falsehood, is attended with virtue or vice. And as to the judgments, which are caused by our judgments, they can still less bestow those moral qualities on the actions which are their causes.

But, to be more particular, and to show that those eternal immutable fitnesses and unfitnesses of things cannot be defended by sound philosophy, we may weigh the following considerations.

If the thought and understanding were alone capable of fixing the boundaries of right and wrong, the character of virtuous and vicious either must lie in some relations of objects, or must be a matter of fact which is discovered by our reasoning. This consequence is evident. As the operations of human understanding divide themselves into two kinds, the comparing of ideas, and the inferring of matter of fact, were virtue discovered by the understanding, it must be an object of one of these operations; nor is there any third operation of the understanding which can discover it. There has been an opinion very industriously propagated by certain philosophers, that morality is susceptible of demonstration; and though no one has ever been able to advance a single step in those demonstrations, yet it is taken for granted that this science may be brought to an equal certainty with geometry or algebra. Upon this supposition, vice and virtue must consist in some relations; since it is allowed on all hands, that no matter of fact is capable of being demonstrated. Let us therefore begin with examining this hypothesis, and endeavour, if possible, to fix those moral qualities which have been so long the objects of our fruitless researches; point out distinctly the relations which constitute morality or obligation, that we may know wherein they consist, and after what manner we must judge of them.

If you assert that vice and virtue consist in relations susceptible of certainty and demonstration, you must confine yourself to those *four* relations which alone admit of that degree of evidence; and in that case you run into absurdities from which you will never be able to extricate yourself. For as you make the very essence of morality to lie in the relations, and as there is no one of these relations but what is applicable, not only to an irrational but also to an inanimate object, it follows that even such objects must be susceptible of merit or demerit. *Resemblance, contrariety, degrees in quality*, and *proportions in quantity and number*; all these relations belong as properly to matter as to our actions, passions, and volitions. It is unquestionable, therefore, that morality lies not in any of these relations, nor the sense of it in their discovery.

Should it be asserted, that the sense of morality consists in the discovery of some relation distinct from these, and that our enumeration was not complete when we comprehended all demonstrable relations under four general heads; to this I know not what to reply, till some one be so good as to point out to me this new relation. It is impossible to refute a system which has never yet been explained. In such a manner of fighting in the dark, a man loses his blows in the air, and often places them where the enemy is not present.

I must therefore, on this occasion, rest contented with requiring the two following conditions of any one that would undertake to clear up this system. *First*, as moral good and evil belong only to the actions of the mind, and are derived from our situation with regard to external objects, the relations from which these moral distinctions arise must lie only betwixt internal actions and external objects, and must not be applicable either to internal actions, compared among themselves, or to external objects, when placed in opposition to other external objects. For as morality is supposed to attend certain relations, if these relations could belong to internal actions considered singly, it would follow, that we might be guilty of crimes in ourselves, and independent of our situation with respect to the universe; and in like manner, if these moral relations could be applied to external objects, it would follow that even inanimate beings would be susceptible of moral beauty and deformity. Now, it seems difficult to imagine that any relation can be discovered betwixt our passions, volitions, and actions, compared to external objects, which relation might not belong either to these passions and volitions, or to these external objects, compared among *themselves*.

But it will be still more difficult to fulfil the *second* condition, requisite to justify this system. According to the principles of those who maintain an abstract rational difference betwixt moral good and evil, and a natural fitness and unfitness of things, it is not only supposed, that these relations, being eternal and immutable, are the same, when considered by every rational creature, but their *effects* are also supposed to be necessarily the same; and it is concluded they have no less, or rather a greater, influence in directing the will of the Deity, than in governing the rational and virtuous of our own species. These two particulars are evidently distinct. It is one thing to know virtue, and another to conform the will to it. In order, therefore, to prove that the measures of right and wrong are eternal laws, *obligatory* on every rational mind, it is not sufficient to show the relations upon which they are founded: we must also point out the connection betwixt the relation and the will; and must prove that this connection is so necessary, that in every well-disposed mind, it must take place and have its influence; though the difference betwixt these minds be in other respects immense and infinite. Now, besides what I have already proved, that even in human nature no relation can ever alone produce any action; besides this, I say, it has been shown, in treating of the understanding, that there is no connection of cause and effect, such as this is supposed to be, which is discoverable otherwise than by experience, and of which we can pretend to have any security by the simple consideration of the objects. All beings in the universe, considered in themselves, appear entirely loose and independent of each other. It is only by experience we learn their influence and connection; and this influence we ought never to extend beyond experience.

Thus it will be impossible to fulfil the *first* condition required to the system of eternal rational measures of right and wrong; because it is impossible to show those relations, upon which such a distinction may be founded: and it is as impossible to fulfil the *second* condition: because we cannot prove *a priori*, that these relations, if they really existed and were perceived, would be universally forcible and obligatory. . . .

Nor does this reasoning only prove, that morality consists not in any relations that are the objects of science; but if examined, will prove with equal certainty, that it consists not in any *matter of fact*, which can be discovered by the understanding. This is the *second* part of our argument; and if it can be made evident, we may conclude that morality is not an object of reason. But can there be any difficulty in proving that vice and virtue are not matters of fact, whose existence we can infer by reason? Take any action allowed to be vicious; wilful murder, for instance. Examine it in all lights, and see if you can find that matter of fact, or real existence, which you call *vice*. In whichever way you take it, you find only certain passions, motives, volitions, and thoughts. There is no other matter of fact in the case. The vice entirely escapes you, as long as you consider the object. You never can find it, till you turn your reflection into your own breast, and find a sentiment of disapprobation, which arises in you, towards this action. Here is a matter of fact; but it is the object of feeling, not of reason. It lies in yourself, not in the object. So that when you pronounce any action or character to be vicious, you mean nothing, but that from the constitution of your nature you have a feeling or sentiment of blame from the contemplation of it. Vice and virtue, therefore, may be compared to sounds, colours, heat, and cold, which, according to modern philosophy, are not qualities in objects, but perceptions in the mind: and this discovery in morals, like that other in physics, is to be regarded as a considerable advancement of the speculative sciences; though, like that too, it has little or no influence on practice. Nothing can be more real, or concern us more, than our own sentiments of pleasure and uneasiness; and if these be favourable to virtue, and unfavourable to vice, no more can be requisite to the regulation of our conduct and behaviour.

I cannot forbear adding to these reasonings an observation, which may, perhaps, be found of some importance. In every system of morality which I have hitherto met with, I have always remarked, that the author proceeds for some time in the ordinary way of reasoning, and establishes the being of a God, or makes observations concerning human affairs; when of a sudden I am surprised to find, that instead of the usual copulations of propositions, *is*, and *is not*, I meet with no proposition that is not connected with an *ought*, or an *ought not*. This change is imperceptible; but is, however, of the last consequence. For as this ought, or ought not, expresses some new relation or affirmation, it is necessary that it should be observed and explained; and at the same time that a reason should be given, for what seems altogether inconceivable, how this new relation can be a deduction from others, which are entirely different from it. But as authors do not commonly use this precaution, I shall presume to recommend it to the readers; and am persuaded, that this small attention would subvert all the vulgar systems of morality, and let us see that the distinction of vice and virtue is not founded merely on the relations of objects, nor is perceived by reason.

David Hume: Moral Distinctions Not Derived from Reason

1. According to Hume, "reason has no influence on our passions and actions." What does Hume mean by this? Do you think he is right?
2. Hume claims that the rules of morality "are not conclusions of our reason." How does he argue for this? Do you find his argument convincing?
3. Hume admits that "false judgments" may influence our behavior, but argues that the truth of our judgments does not determine whether actions are morally right or wrong. What is his argument for thinking this?
4. According to Hume, to say that an action is wrong is equivalent to saying that "from the constitution of your nature you have a feeling or sentiment of blame from the contemplation of it." Is this a plausible account of what we mean when we say that an action is wrong? Does this imply that different actions are wrong for different people, depending on how they feel?
5. Hume claims it is "inconceivable" that we can deduce claims about what *ought* to be the case from claims about what is the case. What exactly does he mean by this? Do you think there are any counterexamples to this claim?

═══ ❧ ═══

15

The Subjectivity of Values

J. L. Mackie

....

J. L. Mackie (1917–1981), who taught for many years at Oxford University, regarded all ethical views as bankrupt. In this excerpt from his book *Ethics: Inventing Right and Wrong* (1977), Mackie outlines the basic ideas and the central motivating arguments for his *error theory*— the view that all positive moral claims are mistaken. All moral talk, as Mackie sees it, is based on a false assumption: that there are objective moral values. This fundamental error infects the entire system of morality. The foundations are corrupt, and so the entire moral edifice must come tumbling down.

Mackie offers a number of important arguments to substantiate his critique of morality. The argument from relativity claims that the extent of moral disagreement is best explained by the claim that there are no objective values. The argument from queerness contends that objective moral values would be objectionably different from any other kind of thing in the universe, possessed of strange powers that are best rejected. Mackie concludes with his account of why so many people, for so long, have fallen into error by succumbing to the temptation to think of morality as objective.

....

Moral Scepticism

There are no objective values. This is a bald statement of the thesis of this chapter, but before arguing for it I shall try to clarify and restrict it in ways that may meet some objections and prevent some misunderstanding. . . .

The claim that values are not objective, are not part of the fabric of the world, is meant to include not only moral goodness, which might be most naturally equated with moral value, but also other things that could be more loosely called moral values or disvalues—rightness and wrongness, duty, obligation, an action's being rotten and contemptible, and so on. It also includes non-moral values, notably aesthetic ones, beauty and various kinds of artistic merit. I shall not discuss these explicitly, but clearly much the same considerations apply to aesthetic and to moral values, and there would be at least some initial implausibility in a view that gave the one a different status from the other. . . .

The claim to objectivity, however ingrained in our language and thought, is not self-validating. It can and should be questioned. But the denial of objective values will have to be put forward not as the result of an analytic approach, but as an 'error theory,' a theory that although most people in making moral judgements implicitly claim, among other things, to be pointing to something objectively prescriptive, these claims are all false. It is this that makes the name 'moral scepticism' appropriate.

But since this is an error theory, since it goes against assumptions ingrained in our thought and built into some of the ways in which language is used, since it conflicts with what is sometimes called common sense, it needs very solid support. It is not something we can accept lightly or casually and then quietly pass on. If we are to adopt this view, we must argue explicitly for it. Traditionally it has been supported by arguments of two main kinds, which I shall call the argument from relativity and the argument from queerness. . . .

The Argument from Relativity

The argument from relativity has as its premiss the well-known variation in moral codes from one society to another and from one period to another, and also the differences in moral beliefs between different groups and classes within a complex community. Such variation is in itself merely a truth of descriptive morality, a fact of anthropology which entails neither first order nor second order ethical views. Yet it may indirectly support second order subjectivism: radical differences between first order moral judgements make it difficult to treat those judgements as apprehensions of objective truths. But it is not the mere occurrence of disagreements that tells against the objectivity of values. Disagreement on questions in history or biology or cosmology does not show that there are no objective issues in these fields for investigators to disagree about. But such scientific disagreement results from speculative inferences or explanatory hypotheses based on inadequate evidence, and it is hardly plausible to interpret moral disagreement in the same way. Disagreement about moral codes seems to reflect people's adherence to and participation in different ways of life. The causal connection seems to be mainly that way round: it is that people approve of monogamy because they participate in a monogamous way of life rather than that they participate in a monogamous way of life because they approve of monogamy. Of course, the standards may be an idealization of the way of life from which they arise: the monogamy in which people participate may be less complete, less rigid, than that of which it leads them to approve. This is not to say that moral judgements are purely conventional. Of course there have been and are moral heretics and moral reformers, people who have turned against the established rules and practices of their own communities for moral reasons, and often for moral reasons that we would endorse. But this can usually be understood as the extension, in ways which, though new and unconventional, seemed to them to be required for consistency, of rules to which they already adhered as arising out of an existing way of life. In short, the argument from relativity has some force simply because the actual variations in the moral codes are more readily explained by the hypothesis that they reflect ways of life than by the hypothesis that they express perceptions, most of them seriously inadequate and badly distorted, of objective values.

But there is a well-known counter to this argument from relativity, namely to say that the items for which objective validity is in the first place to be claimed are not specific moral rules or codes but very general basic principles which are recognized at least implicitly to some extent in all society—such principles as provide the foundations of what Sidgwick has called different methods of ethics: the principle of universalizability, perhaps, or the rule that one ought to conform to the specific rules of any way of life in which one takes part, from which one profits, and on which one relies, or some utilitarian principle of doing what tends, or seems likely, to promote the general happiness. It is easy to show that such general principles, married with differing concrete circumstances, different existing social patterns or different preferences, will beget different specific moral rules; and there is some plausibility in the claim that the specific rules thus generated will vary from community to community or from group to group in close agreement with the actual variations in accepted codes.

The argument from relativity can be only partly countered in this way. To take this line the moral objectivist has to say that it is only in these principles that the objective moral character attaches immediately to its descriptively specified ground or subject: other moral judgements are objectively valid or true, but only derivatively and contingently—if things had been otherwise, quite different sorts of actions would have been right. And despite the prominence in recent philosophical ethics of universalization, utilitarian principles, and the like, these are very far from constituting the whole of what is actually affirmed as basic in ordinary moral thought. Much of this is concerned rather with what Hare calls 'ideals' or, less kindly, 'fanaticism.' That is, people judge that some things are good or right, and others are bad or wrong, not because—or at any rate not only because—they exemplify some general principle for which widespread implicit acceptance could be claimed, but because something about those things arouses certain responses immediately in them, though they would arouse radically and irresolvably different responses in others. 'Moral sense' or 'intuition' is an initially more plausible description of what supplies many of our basic moral judgements than 'reason.' With regard to all these starting points of moral thinking the argument from relativity remains in full force.

The Argument from Queerness

Even more important, however, and certainly more generally applicable, is the argument from queerness. This has two parts, one metaphysical, the other epistemological. If there were objective values, then they would be entities or qualities or relations of a very strange sort, utterly different from anything else in the universe. Correspondingly, if we were aware of them, it would have to be by some special faculty of moral perception or intuition, utterly different from our ordinary ways of knowing everything else. These points were recognized by Moore when he spoke of non-natural qualities, and by the intuitionists in their talk about a 'faculty of moral intuition.' Intuitionism has long been out of favour, and it is indeed easy to point out its implausibilities. What is not so often stressed, but is more important, is that the central thesis of intuitionism is one to which any objectivist view of values is in the end committed: intuitionism merely makes unpalatably plain what other forms of objectivism wrap up. Of course the suggestion that moral judgements are made or moral problems solved by just sitting down and having an ethical intuition is a travesty of actual moral thinking. But, however complex the real process, it will require (if it is to yield authoritatively prescriptive conclusions) some input of this distinctive sort, either premises or forms of argument or both. When we ask the awkward question, how we can be aware of this authoritative prescriptivity, of the truth of these distinctively ethical premises or of the cogency of this distinctively ethical pattern of reasoning, none of our ordinary accounts of sensory perception or introspection or the framing and confirming of explanatory hypotheses or inference or logical construction or conceptual analysis, or any combination of these, will provide a satisfactory answer; 'a special sort of intuition' is a lame answer, but it is the one to which the clear-headed objectivist is compelled to resort.

Indeed, the best move for the moral objectivist is not to evade this issue, but to look for companions in guilt. For example, Richard Price argues that it is not moral knowledge alone that such an empiricism as those of Locke and Hume is unable to account for, but also our knowledge and even our ideas of essence, number, identity, diversity, solidity, inertia, substance, the necessary existence and infinite extension of time and space, necessity and possibility in general, power, and causation. If the understanding, which Price defines as the faculty within us that discerns truth, is also a source of new simple ideas of so many other sorts, may it not also be a power of immediately perceiving right and wrong, which yet are real characters of actions?

This is an important counter to the argument from queerness. The only adequate reply to it would be to show how, on empiricist foundations, we can construct an account of the ideas and beliefs and knowledge that we have of all these matters. I cannot even begin to do that here, though I have undertaken some parts of the task elsewhere. I can only state my belief that satisfactory accounts of most of these can be given in empirical terms. If some supposed metaphysical necessities or essences resist such treatment, then they too should be included, along with objective values, among the targets of the argument from queerness.

This queerness does not consist simply in the fact that ethical statements are 'unverifiable.' Although logical positivism with its verifiability theory of descriptive meaning gave an impetus to non-cognitive accounts of ethics, it is not only logical positivists but also empiricists of a much more liberal sort who should find objective values hard to accommodate. Indeed, I would not only reject the verifiability principle but also deny the conclusion commonly drawn from it, that moral judgements lack descriptive meaning. The assertion that there are objective values or intrinsically prescriptive entities or features of some kind, which ordinary moral judgements presuppose, is, I hold, not meaningless but false.

Plato's Forms give a dramatic picture of what objective values would have to be. The Form of the Good is such that knowledge of it provides the knower with both a direction and an overriding motive; something's being good both tells the person who knows this to pursue it and makes him pursue it. An objective good would be sought by anyone who was acquainted with it, not because of any contingent fact that this person, or every person, is so constituted that he desires this end, but just because the end has to-be-pursuedness somehow built into it. Similarly, if there were objective principles of right and wrong, any wrong (possible) course of action would have not-to-be-doneness somehow built into it. Or we should have something like Clarke's necessary relations of fitness between situations and actions, so that a situation would have a demand for such-and-such an action somehow built into it.

The need for an argument of this sort can be brought out by reflection on Hume's argument that 'reason'—in which at this stage he includes all sorts of knowing as well as reasoning—can never be an 'influencing motive of the will.' Someone might object that Hume has argued unfairly from the lack of influencing power (not contingent upon desires) in ordinary objects of knowledge and ordinary reasoning, and might maintain that values differ from natural objects precisely in their power, when known, automatically to influence the will. To this Hume could, and would need to, reply that this objection involves the postulating of value-entities or value-features of quite a different order from anything else with which we are acquainted, and of a corresponding faculty with which to detect them. That is, he would have to supplement his explicit argument with what I have called the argument from queerness.

Another way of bringing out this queerness is to ask, about anything that is supposed to have some objective moral quality, how this is linked with its natural features. What is the connection between the natural fact that an action is a piece of deliberate cruelty—say, causing pain just for fun—and the moral fact that it is wrong? It cannot be an entailment, a logical or semantic necessity. Yet it is not merely that the two features occur together. The wrongness must somehow be 'consequential' or 'supervenient'; it is wrong because it is a piece of deliberate cruelty. But just what *in the world* is signified by this 'because'? And how do we know the relation that it signifies, if this is something more than such actions being socially condemned, and condemned by us too, perhaps through our having absorbed attitudes from our social environment? It is not even sufficient to postulate a faculty which 'sees' the wrongness: something must be postulated which can see at once the natural features that constitute the cruelty, and the wrongness, and the mysterious consequential link between the two. Alternatively, the intuition required might be the perception that wrongness is a higher order property belonging to certain natural properties; but what is this belonging of properties to other properties, and how can we discern it? How much simpler and more comprehensible the situation would be if we could replace the moral quality with some sort of subjective response which could be causally related to the detection of the natural features on which the supposed quality is said to be consequential.

It may be thought that the argument from queerness is given an unfair start if we thus relate it to what are admittedly among the wilder products of philosophical fancy—Platonic Forms, non-natural qualities, self-evident relations of fitness, faculties of intuition, and the like. Is it equally forceful if applied to the terms in which everyday moral judgements are more likely to be expressed—though still, as has been argued in the original work, with a claim to objectivity—'you must do this,' 'you can't do that,' 'obligation,' 'unjust,' 'rotten,' 'disgraceful,' 'mean,' or talk about good reasons for or against possible actions? Admittedly not; but that is because the objective prescriptivity, the element a claim for whose authoritativeness is embedded in ordinary moral thought and language, is not yet isolated in these forms of speech, but is presented along with relations to desires and feelings, reasoning about the means to desired ends, interpersonal demands, the injustice which consists in the violation of what are in the context the accepted standards of merit, the psychological constituents of meanness, and so on. There is nothing queer about any of these, and under cover of them the claim for moral authority may pass unnoticed. But if I am right in arguing that it is ordinarily there, and is therefore very likely to be incorporated almost automatically in philosophical accounts of ethics which systematize our ordinary thought even in such apparently innocent terms as these, it needs to be examined, and for this purpose it needs to be isolated and exposed as it is by the less cautious philosophical reconstructions.

Patterns of Objectification

Considerations of these kinds suggest that it is in the end less paradoxical to reject than to retain the common-sense belief in the objectivity of moral values, provided that we can explain how this belief, if it is false, has become established and is so resistant to criticisms. This proviso is not difficult to satisfy.

On a subjectivist view, the supposedly objective values will be based in fact upon attitudes which the person has who takes himself to be recognizing and responding to those values. If we admit what Hume calls the mind's 'propensity to spread itself on external objects,' we can understand the supposed objectivity of moral qualities as arising from what we can call the projection or objectification of moral attitudes. This would be analogous to what is called the 'pathetic fallacy,' the tendency to read our feelings into their objects. If a fungus, say, fills us with disgust, we may be inclined to ascribe to the fungus itself a non-natural quality of foulness. But in moral contexts there is more than this propensity at work. Moral attitudes themselves are at least partly social in origin: socially established— and socially necessary—patterns of behaviour put pressure on individuals, and each individual tends to internalize these pressures and to join in requiring these patterns of behaviour of himself and of others. The attitudes that are objectified into moral values have indeed an external source, though not the one assigned to them by the belief in their absolute authority. Moreover, there are motives that would support objectification. We need morality to regulate interpersonal relations, to control some of the ways in which people behave towards one another, often in opposition to contrary inclinations. We therefore want our moral judgements to be authoritative for other agents as well as for ourselves: objective validity would give them the authority required. Aesthetic values are logically in the same position as moral ones; much the same metaphysical and epistemological considerations apply to them. But aesthetic values are less strongly objectified than moral ones; their subjective status, and an 'error theory' with regard to such claims to objectivity as are incorporated in aesthetic judgements, will be more readily accepted, just because the motives for their objectification are less compelling.

But it would be misleading to think of the objectification of moral values as primarily the projection of feelings, as in the pathetic fallacy. More important are wants and demands. As Hobbes says, 'whatsoever is the object of any man's Appetite or Desire, that is it, which he for his part calleth *Good* '; and certainly both the adjective 'good' and the noun 'goods' are used in non-moral contexts of things because they are such as to satisfy desires. We get the notion of something's being objectively good, or having intrinsic value, by reversing the direction of dependence here, by making the desire depend upon the goodness, instead of the goodness on the desire. And this is aided by the fact that the desired thing will indeed have features that make it desired, that enable it to arouse a desire or that make it such as to satisfy some desire that is already there. It is fairly easy to confuse the way in which a thing's desirability is indeed objective with its having in our sense objective value. The fact that the word 'good' serves as one of our main moral terms is a trace of this pattern of objectification. . . .

J. L. Mackie: The Subjectivity of Values

1. Why does Mackie refer to his view as an "error theory"? What is the "error" that Mackie takes himself to be pointing out?

2. Mackie cites widespread disagreement about morality as evidence for his view that there are no objective moral values. Yet he admits that the existence of scientific disagreement does not suggest that there are no objective scientific truths. Why does Mackie think that ethics is different from science in this regard? Do you think he is right about this?

3. One might object to Mackie's argument from disagreement by noting that some moral prohibitions (against killing innocent people, against adultery, etc.) are widely shared across cultures. Does this show that there is something wrong with the argument from disagreement? How do you think Mackie would respond to such an objection?

4. Mackie claims that objective values, if they existed, would be entities "of a very strange sort, utterly different from anything else in the universe." What feature of moral values would make them so strange? Do you agree with Mackie that the "queerness" of moral properties is a good reason to deny their existence?

5. Mackie suggests that his view is "simpler and more comprehensible" than accepting objective values. In what ways is his view simpler? Is this a good reason to reject the existence of objective values?

6. Mackie thinks that for his error theory to succeed, he must explain how people come to think that there are objective moral values in the first place. How does he attempt to do so? Do you think he is successful?

16

Cultural Relativism

Diane Jeske

We often hesitate before judging members of another culture whose moral views seem to differ greatly from our own. This hesitation has been supported by at least two forms of cultural relativism. The first assesses others by reference to the standards of a speaker's own culture. When you say, for instance, that female circumcision is wrong, your judgment is correct just in case members of your own culture disapprove of that practice. The second sort of relativism—the one that author Diane Jeske focuses on—makes the morality of actions depend on the standards of the culture that the action is performed in. In that case, your judgment that this practice is wrong would be true if you were judging a person who performed that action in the U.S., but false if your judgment focused on the actions of those in various parts of Africa.

Cultural relativism implies that no action has a moral nature in itself. Moral standards, like those of the law or etiquette, may legitimately differ from culture to culture. The idea that actions are properly judged only relative to the local standards where they are performed has seemed to make good sense of how people can disagree about the morality of actions. It has also seemed to support a policy of tolerance and open-mindedness about cultural practices that differ from our own. But as Jeske argues, careful examination shows both of these claims to be problematic.

This essay was commissioned for the sixth edition of *The Ethical Life*.

Jeske has us imagine Thomas Jefferson claiming that slavery is morally okay, while we deny that. It seems that we have a disagreement here. But we don't, if cultural relativism is true. If we're focused on whether slavery in eighteenth-century America is acceptable, then if cultural relativism is true, we'd have to agree with Jefferson. If we're instead focused on whether slavery is acceptable in contemporary America, Jefferson would have to agree with us. There would be no basis for disagreement once we saw what the local standards really said about slavery.

When it comes to tolerance, cultural relativism tells us that the standards of the culture in which an act is performed are the ones that determine the action's morality. As we know, however, many cultures deeply endorse discrimination that targets members of various groups. If cultural relativism is true, then such discrimination is morally acceptable—in fact, opposing such discrimination would be immoral, since attempts to create greater equality would violate the existing standards of that culture. Cultural relativism endorses intolerance in cultures that stand behind discrimination and oppression, and endorses tolerance only in cultures that celebrate it. Jeske claims that cultural relativism therefore fails to offer a solid basis for supporting tolerance.

....

In the southern United States prior to the Civil War, the law considered many people of African descent to be property. A large majority of white people, rich and poor, in those southern states regarded the practice of African slavery as morally justified, and any form of abolitionist activity as morally wrong. Many of the revered figures of the early Republic, including Madison, Washington, and Jefferson, were slave-holders. The reverence of these figures continues in our contemporary world, a world that strongly condemns racism of any form. Many people will morally judge a person in 2020 who makes a racist joke more harshly than they will morally condemn Jefferson for having been a slave-holder.

Female circumcision is still widely practiced in parts of Africa, the Middle East, and Asia, with more than 200 million women alive today in 30 countries having been circumcised. Most forms of female circumcision have serious and irrevocable impacts on the physical, particularly reproductive, health and psychological and sexual well-being of the women who undergo the operation, which is usually carried out, without anesthesia, on girls under the age of sixteen. While people in the communities that circumcise their daughters morally condemn a failure to do so, those who live in countries such as the U.S., the U.K., and Canada, judge the practice to be morally wrong. However, many people in these latter countries will hesitate to morally judge those in, say, remote villages of Africa, who have their daughters circumcised.

These cases provide examples of the ways in which cultural practices have varied across cultures. They also illustrate the ways in which people in different cultures disagree in the moral judgments they make of such practices. With respect to non-moral matters (e.g., whether there is life on other planets, or whether the diversity of species is a result of evolution), when two people disagree, we simply assume that either one or both of them is wrong about the matter at hand. But many people are uncomfortable with such an approach to moral disagreement, and that discomfort in many cases results from the fact that moral disagreement is seen as a function of the persons at issue being from different cultures. Hence, we are reluctant to judge those in other cultures according to the same moral standards we use to judge members of our own culture.

After all, we are encouraged to celebrate diversity and tolerance. In particular, we are encouraged to celebrate diversity in and toleration of cultural practices that differ from our own. But practices such as female circumcision and slavery have a long history in and are regarded as having an important function in the cultures in which they are or have been found. Given our commitment to diversity and tolerance, then, we find ourselves hesitating in making moral judgments in such cases. Ought we to judge people in other cultures according to the same standards we use with respect to those in our own culture, or ought we to judge them according to different criteria?

One natural approach to these questions is to regard moral judgment as nothing more than a matter of how people feel about various practices. Around here, now, we reject and disapprove of both female circumcision and slavery, and so we say of those practices that they are morally wrong. But in other times or places, people have accepted and approved of female circumcision or slavery, and so they say of those practices that they are morally right. This is the approach taken by those who support the theory known as *cultural relativism*.

In this chapter we consider how best to understand cultural relativism so as to accommodate the way in which many people are tempted to talk about moral disagreement across cultures (section I). We will then consider whether acceptance of cultural relativism is the only or best way to handle our hesitancy in judging members of other cultures in the same way in which we judge members of our own culture and whether it provides the best explanation of moral disagreement across cultures (section II). We will also evaluate whether our commitment to diversity and tolerance is best served by or even compatible with a commitment to cultural relativism (section III). Finally, we will see that matters about culture and disagreement are perhaps not as straightforward as they initially seem (section IV).

I. Relativity and Moral Judgment

A familiar response to members of other cultures engaging in practices of which we disapprove is to say "that is the right thing *for them* to do even if it is not the right thing *for us* to do." It is certainly wrong *for me* to hold slaves, but, it might be said, that does not imply that it was wrong *for Thomas Jefferson* to hold slaves. Claims of this form suggest the view that moral judgment is in some way relative to an individual's cultural placement: it would be wrong *of me* to have my daughter circumcised, but it is not wrong *for women in certain African communities* to have their daughters circumcised.

Relativity in judgment is a phenomenon with which we are familiar outside of the domain of morality. Consider the following exchange between me and my brother: Me: "White chocolate is delicious." My brother: "White chocolate is not delicious. It is disgusting!" At first, it looks like my brother is contradicting me, and that he and I are engaged in a disagreement about the nature of white chocolate. But it takes very little reflection to see that that is not the case. Almost nobody thinks that there is some property, "being delicious," that white chocolate either has or doesn't have, and that one of us has made a mistake as to whether white chocolate has that property. Rather, my saying "White chocolate is delicious" is another way for me to say something like "I really enjoy the taste of white chocolate." My brother, then, is saying that he does not enjoy the taste of white chocolate. After we have restated our claims, we can see that not only are we not disagreeing with one another, we are not even really talking about the same thing: I am talking about what I like, while my brother is talking about what he likes.

When I declared that white chocolate is delicious, my brother might have responded, "Well, maybe *for you* it's delicious, but it certainly isn't *for me*," just as someone might say of the woman in the remote African village who has her daughter circumcised, "Well, it was the right thing *for her* to do." So some philosophers and non-philosophers have proposed that judgments about an action's being right or wrong are like judgments that some food is delicious: just as "being delicious" is not a property of any food considered in itself, so "being right/wrong" is not a property of any action considered in itself.

There are two importantly different versions of cultural relativism. One renders the truth or falsity (what philosophers call the truth value) of a moral judgment relative to the *speaker's* culture. The other version relativizes the truth values of moral judgments to the culture of the person whose action is being morally assessed. Let's begin with a more formal statement of the first form of the view:

> **Cultural Relativism with Speaker-Relativity**: For person S to judge that person T's action is right (wrong) is for S to judge that *members of S's culture* approve (disapprove) of T's action.

When a friend and I are talking about forcing women to wear head coverings in public, we will say to each other, "That is wrong!" and take ourselves to have made a true claim. But if we were to note that members of Hasidic Jewish communities claim that it is not wrong to force women to wear head coverings in public, we might at least hesitate to judge that person to have said something false. Cultural relativism with speaker-relativity can make sense of this: the claim is true when made by me or my friend (twenty-first-century secular American academics), but false when made by a Hasidic Jew, because the truth value of a moral judgment is relative to the attitudes of the members of the speaker's culture.

So, according to the version of cultural relativism that makes the truth value of moral judgments relative to the attitudes of the speaker's culture, the standard by which any person is to judge the actions of anyone else are the standards of the person making the judgment. But that does not allow us to say of people in other cultures, "that's right *for them* even though it's not right *for us*." According to cultural relativism with speaker-relativity, when *I* make moral judgments, what is right for the members of my culture is right for everyone, and what is wrong for the members of my culture is wrong for everyone. In order to avoid this result, we can adopt:

> **Cultural Relativism with Agent-Relativity**: For person S to judge that person T's action is right (wrong) is for S to judge that *members of T's culture* approve (disapprove) of T's action.

Consider the case of Thomas Jefferson's being a slave-holder. When I judge that Thomas Jefferson's having been a slave-holder is wrong, according to cultural relativism with speaker-relativity, what I have said is true, because people in my culture disapprove of slave-holding. However, according to cultural relativism with agent-relativity, that judgment is false, because Thomas Jefferson's culture (white Americans in the southern states in the 1700s and 1800s) did not disapprove of slavery. So cultural relativism with agent-relativity allows us to make sense of saying, of slave-holding and Thomas Jefferson, "it was not wrong *for him*." What we are saying, according to this version of cultural relativism, is that people in Jefferson's culture did not disapprove of slave-holding.

Cultural relativism with agent-relativity accommodates and explains both of the features of moral judgment that we discussed in the introduction. First, if we accept cultural relativism with agent-relativity, we can see why we ought to be hesitant about making negative moral judgments about people in other cultures for engaging in practices that we, here and now, reject: to engage in moral judgment about a person's action is to assess whether her performing such an action is approved or disapproved of by members of *her* culture. According to this view, while it is certainly wrong *for me* to have *my daughter* circumcised, it is not wrong *for members of various African societies* to have *their daughters* circumcised. What is wrong for us here and now is not necessarily wrong for other people in other times or places.

Second, cultural relativism with agent-relativity makes sense of moral disagreement without forcing us to say that someone must be wrong when such disagreement occurs. Moral disagreement, like disagreement about whether white chocolate is delicious, is only apparent disagreement. When I say that it is wrong to hold slaves, while Thomas Jefferson (at least in the latter years of his life) said that it is not wrong to hold slaves, it looks as if we are disagreeing with one another, that the truth of my claim implies the falsity of his (and vice versa). But that appearance is misleading, according to cultural relativism with agent-relativity. For on that view, a claim such as "it is wrong to hold slaves" is importantly incomplete: in order to assign a truth value to the judgment, we have to know when and where the slave-holding is taking place. If I clarify by saying that I mean slavery is wrong for people in my culture, then my judgment is true. But if I am saying that slavery is wrong for members of Jefferson's culture, then my judgment is false. Once we understand that in making moral judgments we are really just talking about how an agent's culture regards her actions, we can recognize that what looks like disagreement across cultures is really just a matter of people in different cultures having different attitudes to various practices.

So cultural relativism (from here on, whenever I refer to cultural relativism I will be talking about the version with agent-relativity) seems to capture some aspects of our moral thought and discourse. But does it do so in the most plausible way? Do we need to relativize moral judgment to cultures in order to do so?

II. Knowledge and the Relativity of Judgment

Cultural relativists defend their view by appealing to the ways in which they handle two aspects of our moral thought and discourse: (i) the fact that we tend to judge people in other cultures differently from how we judge members of our own culture, and (ii) the fact that moral disagreement is common across cultures. But there are other ways of accounting for these two features of our moral practice that do not require us to assume the truth of cultural relativism.

II.i Making Moral Judgments Relative to Culture

Consider the following case: Alfred is a physician in the eighteenth century, when it was widely believed that blood-letting was the medically appropriate treatment for an array of illnesses. Physicians would open a vein and allow a significant amount of blood to drain from a patient's body. We now know that blood-letting will not only not cure disease but that it will make the patient weaker and less well-equipped to fight her illness. If a physician today tried to utilize blood-letting to treat a serious illness such as cancer, we would judge him as acting immorally and would hold him responsible for any harm caused to his patient. However, we would not judge Alfred in the same way. In fact, we might say of Alfred's opening his patient's vein, "it was the right thing *for him* to do."

Why do we judge that what was right for Alfred to do in this case is different from what it is right for a contemporary physician, Abigail, to do? The obvious answer is that Alfred is working in a context in which it is reasonable for him to believe that blood-letting will aid his patient: it is the accepted go-to treatment, and all of the respected experts and textbooks endorse that treatment. Abigail, however, knows, or at least ought to know, that blood-letting will have adverse effects on her patient, because the practice is rejected by all of the relevant experts and textbooks. So our differing judgments of Alfred and of Abigail are the result of our differing judgments about what beliefs it is reasonable for each to have and to act on.

Now let us reconsider our case of a community in which girls are circumcised. One reason for finding cultural relativism plausible is that it allows us to say that what is right for parents in this community is different from what is right for parents in our communities as a result of differing cultural attitudes toward the practice of female circumcision. But our case of Alfred and Abigail offers us another possibility as to why we might judge that what is right for an agent is relative to her cultural placement. That possibility involves an appeal to differences in background, non-moral knowledge. Our own moral rejection of the practice of female circumcision is to a large extent a result of a recognition of the ways in which the practice harms women. But in many of the communities in which the practice is approved, people have false views about the effects of circumcising girls and young women: some believe that circumcision makes child birth easier, and some believe that the clitoris, which is usually removed as a part of the circumcision operation, poses serious and potentially lethal dangers to the men who have intercourse with uncircumcised women, and to the infants they give birth to. If these false beliefs were true, then we would probably have quite different moral views about female circumcision, given that our views about the potential harms and benefits to the people involved underlie our moral views about the rightness or wrongness of circumcision. So we might think that if members of communities that practice circumcision believe it to be beneficial to all involved, then we should not view them as acting wrongly, just as we do not judge Alfred to have acted wrongly, given his belief that he is doing what is best for his patients.

We can notice, however, that an agent's beliefs, no matter how sincerely held, are not always enough to cause us to judge her actions to be right. For example, many people still hold racist beliefs; very likely, some of those people sincerely believe that members of certain other races are emotionally or intellectually stunted or exceptionally dangerous. Now, if there were some race such that members of that race were, in the vast majority of cases, dangerous, then we would be justified in treating members of that race as a threat. Nonetheless, we do not say of contemporary racists that their racist actions are right. That's because we do not think that contemporary racists are justified in viewing members of other races in this way: racist thinking has been debunked quite decisively. Further, it seems that those who still have racist beliefs ought to know that their beliefs are false: they have access to all of the same data as the rest of us here and now, and have, in most cases, sufficient education to evaluate that data rationally. In most cases, such people are guided by illicit motives, such as a need to feel superior, and this leads them to deceive themselves into holding racist beliefs. Such people choose not to examine evidence that could undermine the beliefs that support their self-image, and they are culpable for making such a choice.

Consider again the case of Thomas Jefferson, slave-holder. Some people are inclined to say that it was right for him to hold slaves, but not all are willing to do so. After all, there were plenty of abolitionists whom Jefferson knew personally, and his younger self had advocated on behalf of the slaves and denounced the institution of slavery. In his later years, his views shifted, and they shifted, it seemed, the more financially dependent upon slavery Jefferson became. As we learn these facts about Jefferson, our willingness to say that it was right for him to hold slaves at least starts to waver, if not to disappear entirely. He starts to look less like Alfred and more like the contemporary racists who have self-interested reasons that motivate them to accept racist ideology.

Our moral beliefs are often a function of our non-moral beliefs. For example, our beliefs about how doctors ought to respond to their patients are a function of our beliefs about what sorts of treatments will best promote the patient's physical well-being. Our beliefs about the wrongness of African slavery are, at least in part, a function of our belief that slave-owners had mistaken non-moral views about the emotional and intellectual capacities of the people they enslaved. We morally reject female circumcision because we reject the beliefs about the harms it prevents that its practitioners use to justify it. But we also recognize that what a person is justified in believing is to a large extent a function of her time and culture. Thus, moral judgment ought to be sensitive to the culture of the agent being evaluated, because that culture is relevant to what it is rational for that agent to believe. But the case of Thomas Jefferson shows that we need to be sensitive to the *particular* facts about the *particular* person we are evaluating. After all, there is a sense in which Jefferson and a poor, uneducated white Southerner belonged to the same culture, but it is quite clear that what it was rational for Jefferson to believe was, in many cases, quite different from what it was rational for the poor, uneducated person to believe. So particularities of background knowledge may do a better job of accommodating some of our judgments about agents in other times or places than does an appeal to mere cultural placement.

II.ii Explaining Moral Disagreement

In the previous subsection, we saw that our tendency to relativize our moral judgments to an agent's culture can be explained by an appeal to cultural differences with respect to background, non-moral beliefs. This disagreement with respect to non-moral beliefs can, of course, also explain cultural divergence with respect to moral judgment. If our moral beliefs are often a function of our non-moral beliefs, then divergence with respect to the latter will cause divergence with respect to the former. For example, in the nineteenth-century court case *Bradwell v. Illinois*, it was held that it was legitimate to prevent women from practicing law. One of several reasons given was that every defendant deserved a good defense, and women, given their inferior intellectual capabilities and emotional instability, would not provide such a defense. We now believe that women are just as capable as men of being effective lawyers; if we did not, we would also be more likely to sympathize with barring women from the legal profession.

In fact, this explanation of moral disagreement might seem preferable to the way in which cultural relativism handles disagreement. As we saw in section I, the cultural relativist thinks that it will often turn out that there actually isn't any disagreement. When I claim that slavery is wrong, we need to specify where and when the slave-holding takes place. It is true that slavery is wrong for me, but it is false that slavery is wrong for Jefferson. So when Jefferson says that slavery is not wrong, if he is talking about his holding of slaves, then he is not, contrary to appearances, disagreeing with me. So if we think that there is genuine disagreement between me and Jefferson, then we would need to reject cultural relativism.

Let us now consider how cultural relativism handles diversity and toleration.

III. Multiculturalism and Ethical Theory

We live in a world where we are encouraged to be tolerant of and to attempt to preserve cultural diversity. We condemn those in previous times who invaded other lands and tried to force indigenous persons to conform to the conquerors' own ways of life. Of course, much of this drive to colonize resulted from greed and a desire to dominate, but there were also those who sincerely believed that the indigenous persons lived in morally disreputable ways and needed to be brought to the moral light that the colonizers believed that they possessed. As a result, many ways of life were destroyed and entire peoples deprived of their cultural traditions—and, sometimes, of their very existence. Our response now is to view the colonizers as smug, arrogant people driven by a belief that there was only one correct way to live—their own.

Rejection of this sort of arrogance has motivated many of those who accept cultural relativism. If cultural relativism is true, then the conquerors are simply wrong to claim that there is one true moral code that transcends cultures—morality, according to the cultural relativist, is nothing over and above the attitudes of people in the agent's culture. So, when Westerners encountered other peoples who had different sorts of (for example) modes of dress or marital and family arrangements, their negative moral judgments of such people were just false: they were failing to judge those cultural practices relative to the attitudes of the people in those cultures. While it would be wrong for a British missionary woman in the 1800s to wander around in public in nothing more than a skirt made of animal skin or grasses, it was not wrong for women in certain African or Pacific Islander cultures to do so. Thus, it seems that cultural relativism discourages the sort of judgmental arrogance that has so often led (and continues to lead) to intolerance.

Before we embrace cultural relativism, however, there are a few questions that we need to address: (1) Do we believe that toleration ought to extend to all cultural practices? (2) Does denial of cultural relativism encourage the sort of smug arrogance that cultural relativists denounce? (3) Does cultural relativism actually support tolerance of diversity?

Let's begin with (1): Do we believe that toleration ought to extend to all cultural practices? The obvious answer is that of course we do not. African slavery in the American South was a deeply entrenched feature of the life of white culture in the southern states, as was the white supremacist worldview that undergirded it. After the American Civil War, the lynching of Black people (mainly men) became a cultural ritual in which entire communities participated: this ritual reinforced the culture of white supremacy in southern states. But slavery and lynching and other institutions supporting white supremacy caused, and continue to cause, immense amounts of harm to Black Americans. Today we are struggling with the aftermaths of slavery and lynching, and we firmly believe that such practices ought to be condemned in the harshest terms.

We can notice that there is a vast difference between cultural practices such as slavery and those concerning how one dresses. Slavery was a practice that caused great harm to a vast number of people. Whether a woman is expected to bare or not to bare her breasts in public is quite different. Whereas the latter really does seem to be nothing more than a matter of cultural expectation and history, the former does not. Often, those who went to other lands and criticized and attempted to change aspects of the cultures that they encountered failed to give adequate consideration to the needs and conditions of people in those cultures. For example, what is regarded as appropriate dress is often a function of climate and of available materials. Marital and child-care arrangements are sometimes a function of the size of a community and the need to reproduce and to care for children in ways compatible with meeting the community's goal of survival. But slavery such as it was practiced in the American South was simply a way for a class of people (white land-owners) to benefit from the labor of others (people of African descent) in the most profitable manner possible. Understanding the motivations for cultural practices can reveal a great difference between those such as slavery and those such as smoking peyote: it is the difference between the motivation of benefitting oneself at the expense of others and merely creating rituals that bind a group together or benefit the group as a whole, given existing conditions.

It is not always a straightforward matter to figure out which category a given cultural practice falls into. For many cultures that practice female circumcision, it is viewed as a rite of passage that helps to integrate girls into the community. But it is also an undeniable fact that the practice serves the function of denigrating the sexual autonomy and well-being of women in order to protect male control over lineage and other forms of property. In this respect, then, female circumcision is like slavery in being a practice that benefits one class of society at the cost of great harm to another. Toleration of such a practice would seem to be a form of complicity with exploitation and pain. Thus, such toleration does not seem at all admirable.

Let's move on to (2): Does denial of cultural relativism encourage the sort of smug arrogance that cultural relativists denounce? It might seem that if we commit ourselves to a moral code that transcends cultural attitudes and that can be used as a basis of criticism of existing moral codes, then we will proceed to criticize any cultural practice that does not meet our own standards, and will then regard ourselves as justified in using coercive force to change the ways of life of other peoples. Adherence to a culture-independent moral code, then, seems to encourage colonialism, violence, and other forms of intolerance that demean and harm those who are different from us.

However, these sorts of responses to other cultures are not the result of acceptance of a culture-independent moral code on its own. They are the result of acceptance of such a code coupled with either of the following assumptions: (i) that one's code is entirely and obviously correct, or (ii) that a judgment that a person or persons is acting wrongly justifies coercive interference.

But both assumptions are unjustified. First, one can accept that there is a culture-independent moral code without assuming that one's own culture's way of life completely accords with that moral code. There were, for example, white Southerners even in Jefferson's day who regarded slavery as highly immoral and who worked to abolish it. To be a good person, one needs to approach conventional practices, in one's own culture as well as in other cultures, with an open mind and a critical eye. Cultural practices are often a result of class interests and self-deception, and are often sustained through propaganda motivated by greed and other vices. Every person, in every culture, needs to recognize that they can learn from the different ways in which other cultures live and that their own cultural practices ought not to be accepted uncritically.

We also need to remind ourselves of the fact, discussed in the previous section, that moral truth is dependent on non-moral truth in important ways. So when we see people in other cultures doing things in ways that seem wrong to us, we need to stop and ask whether, in fact, those ways might actually be appropriate responses to the different circumstances in which those people find themselves. In past ages Inuit peoples in Greenland would sometimes kill infants whose fathers died. This seems morally horrific to us, until we remember that Greenlanders used to live always on the brink of starvation and that their survival depended upon successful hunting by male members of the group. If an infant had no father to hunt for it, then it would have to be fed by the efforts of other men who had their own families to sustain. The Greenlanders had to sacrifice someone given their circumstances, and so they chose to sacrifice those who presented a burden without being able to simultaneously contribute to the group's survival. Whether or not we agree with the choices they made, we can certainly see how complicated and heart-breaking their situation was, and how we ourselves, in their circumstances, might make the very same choice.

Finally, the second assumption above is just false. Even if we decide that a practice like female circumcision is wrong, regardless of the circumstances of the communities in which it is practiced, it does not follow that it is right for us to intervene, and it certainly does not follow that we are justified in intervening in a violent manner. If female circumcision is wrong, it is wrong because it causes so much harm to so many women and girls. So our response ought to involve trying to figure out how to end that harm. What sort of intervention would be best in the long run? Harsh criticism, for example, sometimes only produces a defensive reaction, and violence often just causes yet more suffering. Sometimes, unfortunately, our best response is no response. The wrongness of others' actions is never sufficient, in itself, to render our intervention right.

So denial of cultural relativism does not necessarily generate smug arrogance. Further, acceptance of it may well be compatible with smug arrogance and intolerance. Consider (3): Does cultural relativism actually support tolerance of diversity? Recall our British missionaries encountering cultures in which women appeared in public with bare breasts. The missionaries responded with deep disapproval, which reflected the dominant attitude in their own culture. In trying to change the ways in which the indigenous women dressed, the missionaries were acting in ways approved of by their own culture, and so (according to cultural relativism) were acting morally. If we accept cultural relativism, the following two claims are entirely compatible with one another: (i) S, in baring her breasts, is doing what it is right for her to do, and (ii) It is right for T to attempt to prevent S from baring her breasts. S's culture may approve of her appearing in public with bare breasts, and T's culture may approve of her trying to prevent S from appearing in public with bare breasts.

According to the cultural relativist, what is right for me to do is determined by the attitudes of my culture. So if my culture approves of conquering by violence and then colonizing other cultures, then it is right for me to be a violent, colonizing conqueror. If my culture disapproves of tolerance of diversity, then it is wrong of me to be tolerant and accepting. White Southerners disapproved of abolitionist activity, so if I were a white woman in 1830s Alabama, it would be wrong for me to work to end slavery. If Black Lives Matter activists are correct in saying that our culture is one of white supremacy, then it is wrong for us who are members of this culture to strive for racial equality. One cannot have a culture-independent commitment to tolerance and equality if one is a cultural relativist, because cultural relativists reject any culture-independent moral truths. Two conclusions follow directly. First, rejection of cultural relativism does not entail intolerance. Second, acceptance of cultural relativism is, under certain circumstances, incompatible with tolerance.

IV. How Much Moral Disagreement Is There?

Suppose that we were in discussion with an American slave-holder from 1850s South Carolina who claims that African slavery is morally justified. How would he attempt to defend his view? He would claim that Black persons are not capable of caring for themselves, that slavery really does benefit his slaves, that emancipating Black people would result in a serious danger to society, etc. Of course, we would respond that he is just wrong: Black people are as capable as white people, slavery is no benefit to the enslaved, and that emancipation would bring about no serious dangers (except for those caused by disgruntled ex-slave-holders).

What is significant is that, if the slave-holder were to genuinely attempt to defend his moral position, he would not claim that harm to the slaves is just irrelevant, or that greed on the part of white slave-holders is a perfectly acceptable justification for the institution of slavery. He would recognize, just as we do, that moral justification ultimately requires showing how human well-being is promoted by a given action or practice. He would also recognize that moral justification cannot involve a mere appeal to how much money slavery will bring him. Similarly, in defending female circumcision, a member of a culture that approves of it would try to show how it promotes goods such as family stability and how it actually is better for the health of all involved. The point is that even in what appear to be extreme disagreements, there is usually some common ground, some agreement about the nature of moral justification and about what sorts of considerations are morally relevant. If we are open-minded and willing to listen to each other, we can hope to find that common ground and to see what exactly it is we are disagreeing about. That does not mean that we will always be able to resolve that disagreement, but it offers us a place to begin.

Diane Jeske: Cultural Relativism

1. Imagine what appears to be a moral disagreement between a slave-holder and an abolitionist. How does cultural relativism with speaker relativity analyze this exchange? Does relativism with agent relativity do any better?

2. Cultural relativism implies that the correct moral standards are those endorsed by collectives of actual people, with their various intellectual and emotional limitations. Is this a limitation or an attraction of relativism? State the reasons behind your reply.

3. If cultural relativism is true, then we know whether a given action is right or wrong so long as we are familiar with the standards of the society in which it is performed. Is this a plausible view of how to gain moral knowledge? Why or why not?
4. Jeske argues that Thomas Jefferson can be rightly criticized for holding slaves, even though most members of his culture endorsed slavery. What is her basis for thinking this? Is her position plausible?
5. Many people endorse cultural relativism because they believe that it is needed to support the value of tolerance. Jeske gives some reasons to doubt this rationale. Do you think that her critique is plausible? Why or why not?

17

Why I Am an Objectivist about Ethics (And Why You Are, Too)

David Enoch

David Enoch claims that almost all of us are committed to the objectivity of ethics. When we reflect on our attitudes toward ethical claims and ethical practices, it is clear that we are assuming that there are correct answers to moral questions, and correct standards of moral evaluation, whose truth and authority do not depend on our beliefs or attitudes about them. In the first half of his paper, Enoch presents three tests that attempt to reveal our commitment to moral objectivity. Even if these tests succeed in their aim—and Enoch thinks that they clearly do—he realizes that this is not enough to prove that morality is objective. For, as he says, religious commitments also aspire to objectivity. And yet this does not show that any religious claim is objectively true (or true at all).

Still, the compelling appearance of objectivity in morality gives us good reason to think that morality is indeed objective—unless, of course, there are even stronger arguments that undermine this appearance. Enoch devotes the second half of his paper to considering a few of the most important of these arguments. Some critics argue that the extent of moral disagreement undermines moral objectivity. Critics also argue that those who defend the existence of objective truths need to provide a way of coming to know them, but that there is no plausible way to gain moral knowledge, if morality is indeed objective. Critics also worry that ethical objectivity supports intolerance and dogmatism. Enoch carefully presents each criticism and then offers sharp replies to the objections.

You may think that you're a moral relativist or subjectivist—many people today seem to. But I don't think you are. In fact, when we start doing metaethics—when we start, that is, thinking philosophically about our moral discourse and practice—thoughts about morality's objectivity become almost irresistible. Now, as is always the case in philosophy, that some thoughts seem irresistible is only the starting point for the discussion, and under argumentative pressure we may need to revise our relevant beliefs. Still, it's important to get the starting points right. So it's important to understand the deep ways in which rejecting morality's objectivity is unappealing. What I want to do, then, is to highlight the ways in which accepting morality's objectivity is appealing, and to briefly address some common worries about it, worries that may lead some to reject—or to think they reject—such objectivity. In the final section, I comment on the (not obvious) relation between the underlying concerns about morality's objectivity and the directions in which current discussion in metaethics are developing. As it will emerge, things are not (even) as simple as the discussion below seems to suggest. This is just one reason why metaethics is so worth doing.

Why Objectivity? Three (Related) Reasons

In the next section we're going to have to say a little more about what objectivity is. But sometimes it's helpful to start by engaging the underlying concerns, and return to more abstract, perhaps conceptual, issues later on.

The Spinach Test

Consider the following joke (which I borrow from Christine Korsgaard): A child hates spinach. He then reports that he's glad he hates spinach. To the question "Why?" he responds: "Because if I liked it, I would have eaten it, and it's yucky!"

In a minute we're going to have to annoyingly ask why the joke is funny. For now, though, I want to highlight the fact that similar jokes are not always similarly funny. Consider, for instance, someone who grew up in the twentieth-century West and who believes that the earth revolves around the sun. Also, she reports to be happy she wasn't born in the Middle Ages, "because had I grown up in the Middle Ages, I would have believed that the earth is in the center of the universe, and that belief is false!"

To my ears, the joke doesn't work in this latter version (try it on your friends!). The response in the earth-revolves-around-the-sun case sounds perfectly sensible, precisely in a way in which the analogous response does not sound sensible in the spinach case.

We need one last case. Suppose someone grew up in the United States in the late twentieth century and rejects any manifestation of racism as morally wrong. He then reports that he's happy that that's when and where he grew up, "because had I grown up in the eighteenth century, I would have accepted slavery and racism. And these things are wrong!" How funny is this third, last version of the joke? To my ears, it's about as (un) funny as the second one, and nowhere nearly as amusing as the first. The response to the question in this last case (why he is happy that he grew up in the twentieth century) seems to me to make perfect sense, and I suspect it makes sense to you too. And this is why there's nothing funny about it.

OK, then, why is the spinach version funny and the others are not? Usually, our attitude towards our own likings and dislikings (when it comes to food, for instance) is that it's all about us. If you don't like spinach, the reason you shouldn't have it is precisely that you don't like it. So if we're imagining a hypothetical scenario in which you do like it, then you no longer have any reason not to eat it. This is what the child in the first example gets wrong: he's holding fixed his dislike for spinach, even in thinking about the hypothetical case in which he likes spinach. But because these issues are all about him and what he likes and dislikes, this makes no sense.

But physics is different: What we want, believe or do—none of this affects the earth's orbit. The fact that the earth revolves around the sun is just not about us at all. So it makes sense to hold this truth fixed even when thinking about hypothetical cases in which you don't believe it. And so it makes sense to be happy that you aren't in the Middle Ages, since you'd then be in a situation in which your beliefs about the earth's orbit would be false (even if you couldn't know that they were). And because this makes sense, the joke isn't funny.

And so we have the spinach test: About any relevant subject matter, formulate an analogue of the spinach joke. If the joke works, this seems to indicate that the subject matter is all about us and our responses, our likings and dislikings, our preferences, and so on. If the joke doesn't work, the subject matter is much more objective than that, as in the astronomy case. And when we apply the spinach test to a moral issue (like the moral status of racism), it seems to fall squarely on the objective side.

(Exercise: Think about your taste in music, and formulate the spinach test for it. Is the joke funny?)

Disagreement and Deliberation

We sometimes engage in all sorts of disagreements. Sometimes, for instance, we may engage in a disagreement about even such silly things as whether bitter chocolate is better than milk chocolate. Sometimes we disagree about such things as whether human actions influence global warming. But these two kinds of disagreement are very different. One way of seeing this is thinking about what it feels like from the inside to engage in such disagreements. In the chocolate case, it feels like stating one's own preference, and perhaps trying to influence the listener into getting his own preferences in line. In the global warming case, though, it feels like trying to get at an objective truth, one that is there anyway, independently of our beliefs and preferences. (Either human actions contribute to global warming, or they don't, right?)

And so another test suggests itself, a test having to do with what it *feels like* to engage in disagreement (or, as we sometimes say, with the *phenomenology* of disagreement).

But now think of some serious moral disagreement—about the moral status of abortion, say. Suppose, then, that you are engaged in such disagreement. (It's important to imagine this from the inside, as it were. Don't imagine looking from the outside at two people arguing over abortion; think what it's like to be engaged in such argument yourself—if not about abortion, then about some other issue you care deeply about.) Perhaps you think that there is nothing wrong with abortion, and you're arguing with someone who thinks that abortion is morally wrong. What does such disagreement feel like? In particular, does it feel more like disagreeing over which chocolate is better, or like disagreeing over factual matters (such as whether human actions contribute to global warming)?

Because this question is a phenomenological one (that is, it's about what something feels like from the inside), I can't answer this question for you. You have to think about what it feels like for you when you are engaged in moral disagreement. But I can say that in my case such moral disagreement feels exactly like the one about global warming—it's about an objective matter of fact, that exists independently of us and our disagreement. It is in no way like disagreeing over the merits of different kinds of chocolate. And I think I can rather safely predict that this is how it feels for you too.

So on the phenomenology-of-disagreement test as well, morality seems to fall on the objective side.

In fact, we may be able to take disagreement out of the picture entirely. Suppose there is no disagreement—perhaps because you're all by yourself trying to make up your mind about what to do next. In one case, you're thinking about what kind of chocolate to get. In another, you're choosing between buying a standard car and a somewhat more expensive hybrid car (whose effect on global warming, if human actions contribute to global warming, is less destructive). Here, too, there's a difference. In the first case, you seem to be asking questions about yourself and what you like more (in general, or right now). In the second case, you need to make up your mind about your own action, of course, but you're asking yourself questions about objective matters of fact that do not depend on you at all—in particular, about whether human actions affect global warming.

Now consider a third case, in which you're trying to make up your mind about having an abortion, or advising a friend who is considering an abortion. So you're wondering whether abortion is wrong. Does it feel like asking about your own preferences or like an objective matter of fact? Is it more like the chocolate case or like the hybrid car case? If, like me, you answer that it's much more like the hybrid car case, then you think, like me, that the phenomenology of deliberation too indicates that morality is objective.

(Exercise: think about your taste in music again. In terms of the phenomenology of disagreement and deliberation, is it on the objective side?)

Would It Still Have Been Wrong If . . .?

Top hats are out of fashion. This may be an interesting, perhaps even practically relevant, fact—it may, for instance, give you reason to wear a top hat (if you want to be special) or not to (if not). But think about the following question: Had our fashion practices been very different—had we all worn top hats, thought they were cool, and so on—would it still have been true that top hats are out of fashion? The answer, it seems safe to assume, is "no."

Smoking causes cancer. This is an interesting, practically relevant fact—it most certainly gives you a reason not to smoke, or perhaps to stop smoking. Now, had our relevant practices and beliefs regarding smoking been different—had we been OK with it, had we not banned it, had we thought smoking was actually quite harmless—would it still have been true that smoking causes cancer? I take it to be uncontroversial that the answer is "yes." The effects of smoking on our health do not depend on our beliefs and practices in anything like the way in which the fashionability of top hats does. Rather, it is an objective matter of fact.

And so we have a third objectivity test, one in terms of the relevant "what if" sentences (or *counterfactuals*, as they are often called), such as

"Had our beliefs and practices been very different, would it still have been true that so-and-so?" Let's apply this test to morality.

Gender-based discrimination is wrong. I hope you agree with me on this (if you don't, replace this with a moral judgment you're rather confident in). Would it still have been wrong had our relevant practices and beliefs been different? Had we been all for gender-based discrimination, would that have made gender-based discrimination morally acceptable? Of course, in such a case we would have *believed* that there's nothing wrong with gender-based discrimination. But would it *be* wrong? To me it seems very clear that the answer is "Yes!" Gender-based discrimination is just as wrong in a society where everyone believes it's morally permissible. (This, after all, is why we would want such a society to change, and why, if we are members, we would fight for reform.) The problem in such a society is precisely that its members miss something so important—namely, the wrongness of gender-based discrimination. Had we thought gender-based discrimination was okay, we would have been mistaken. The morality of such discrimination does not depend on our opinion of it. The people in that hypothetical society may accept gender-based discrimination, but that doesn't make such discrimination acceptable.

In this respect too, then, morality falls on the objective side. When it comes to the counterfactual test, moral truths behave more like objective, actual truths (like whether smoking causes cancer) than like purely subjective, perhaps conventional claims (say, that top hats are unfashionable).

(Exercises: Can you see how the counterfactual test relates to the spinach test? And think about your favorite music, the kind of music that you don't just like, but that you think is *good*. Had you not liked it, would it still have been good?)

What's At Issue?

We have, then, three tests for objectivity—the spinach test, the phenomenology-of-disagreement-and-deliberation test, and the counterfactual test. And though we haven't yet said much about what objectivity comes to, these tests test for something that is recognizably in the vicinity of what we're after with our term "objectivity."

Objectivity, like many interesting philosophical terms, can be understood in more than one way. As a result, when philosophers affirm or deny the objectivity of some subject matter, it's not to be taken for granted that they're asserting or denying the same thing. But we don't have to go through a long list of what may be meant by morality's objectivity. It will be more productive, I think, to go about things in a different way. We can start by asking, why does it matter whether morality is objective? If we have a good enough feel for the answer to this question, we can then use it to find the sense of objectivity that we care about.

I suggest that we care about the objectivity of morality for roughly the reasons specified in the previous section. We want morality's objectivity to support our responses in those cases. We want morality's objectivity to vindicate the phenomenology of deliberation and disagreement, and our relevant counterfactual judgments. We want morality's objectivity to explain why the moral analogue of the spinach test isn't funny.

Very well, then, in what sense must morality be objective in order for the phenomenology of disagreement and deliberation and our counterfactual judgments to be justified? The answer, it seems to me, is that a subject matter is objective if the truths or facts in it exist independently of what we think or feel about them.

This notion of objectivity nicely supports the counterfactual test. If a certain truth (say, that smoking causes cancer) doesn't depend on our views about it, then it would have been true even had we not believed it. Not so for truths that do depend on our beliefs, practices, or emotions (such as the truth that top hats are unfashionable). And if moral truths are similarly independent of our beliefs, desires, preferences, emotions, points of view, and so on—if, as is sometimes said, moral truths are *response-independent*—then it's clear why gender-based discrimination would have been wrong even had we approved of it.

Similarly, if it's our responses that make moral claims true, then in a case of disagreement, it seems natural to suppose that both sides may be right. Perhaps, in other words, your responses make it the case that abortion is morally permissible ("for you," in some sense of this very weird phrase?), and your friend's responses make it the case that abortion is morally wrong ("for her"?). But if the moral status of abortion is response-*independent*, we understand why moral disagreement feels like factual disagreement—only one of you is right, and it's important to find out who. And of course, the whole point of the spinach test was to distinguish between caring about things just because we care about them (such as not eating spinach, if you find it yucky) and caring about things that seem to us important independently of us caring about them (such as the wrongness of racism).

Another way of making the same point is as follows: Objective facts are those we seek to discover, not those we make true. And in this respect too, when it comes to moral truths, we are in a position more like that of the scientist who tries to discover the laws of nature (which exist independently of her investigations) than that of the legislator (who creates laws).

Now, in insisting that morality is objective in this sense—for instance, by relying on the reasons given in the previous section—it's important to see what has and what has not been established. In order to see this, it may help to draw an analogy with religious discourse. So think of your deeply held religious beliefs, if you have any. (If, like me, you do not, try to think what it's like to be deeply committed to a religious belief, or perhaps think of your commitment to atheism.) And try to run our tests—does it make sense to be happy that you were brought up under the religion in which you deeply believe, even assuming that with a different education you would have believed another religion, or no religion at all? What do you think of the phenomenology of religious deliberation and disagreement? And had you stopped believing, would the doctrines of your faith still have been true?

Now, perhaps things are not obvious here, but it seems to me that for many religious people, religious discourse passes all these objectivity tests. But from this it does not follow that atheism is false, much less that a specific religion is true. When they are applied to some specific religious discourse, the objectivity tests show that such discourse *aspires* to objectivity. In other words, the tests show what the world must be like for the commitments of the discourse to be vindicated: if (say) a Catholic's religious beliefs are to be true, what must be the case is that the doctrines of the Catholic Church hold objectively, that is, response-independently. This leaves entirely open the question whether these doctrines do in fact hold.

Back to morality, then. Here too, what the discussion of objectivity (tentatively) establishes is just something about the *aspirations* of moral discourse: namely, that it aspires to objectivity. If our moral judgments are to be true, it must be the case that things have value, that people have rights and duties, that there are better and worse ways to live our lives— and all of this must hold objectively, that is, response-independently. But establishing that moral discourse *aspires* to objectivity is one thing. Whether *there actually are* objective moral truths is quite another.

And now you may be worried. Why does it matter, you may wonder, what morality's aspirations are, if (for all I've said so far) they may not be met? I want to offer two replies here. First, precisely in order to check whether morality's aspirations are in fact fulfilled, we should understand them better. If you are trying to decide, for instance, whether the commitments of Catholicism are true, you had better understand them first. Second, and more importantly, one of the things we are trying to do here is to gain a better understanding of what we are already committed to. You may recall that I started with the hypothesis that you may think you're a relativist or a subjectivist. But if the discussion so far gets things right (if, that is, morality aspires to this kind of objectivity), and if you have any moral beliefs at all (don't you think that some things are wrong? do we really need to give gruesome examples?), then it follows that you yourself are already committed to morality's objectivity. And this is already an interesting result, at least for you.

That morality aspires in this way to objectivity also has the implication that any full metaethical theory—any theory, that is, that offers a full description and explanation of moral discourse and practice—has to take this aspiration into account. Most likely, it has to accommodate it. Less likely, but still possibly, such a theory may tell us that this aspiration is futile, explaining why even though morality is not objective, we tend to think that it is, why it manifests the marks of objectivity that the tests above catch on, and so on. What no metaethical theory can do, however, is ignore the very strong appearance that morality is objective. I get back to this in the final section, below.

Why Not?

As I already mentioned, we cannot rule out the possibility that under argumentative pressure we're going to have to revise even some of our most deeply held beliefs. Philosophy, in other words, is hard. And as you can imagine, claims about morality's objectivity have not escaped criticism. Indeed, perhaps some such objections have already occurred to you. In this section, I quickly mention some of them, and hint at the ways in which I think they can be coped with. But let me note how incomplete the discussion here is. There are, of course, other objections, objections that I don't discuss here. More importantly, there are many more things to say—on both sides—regarding the objections that I do discuss. The discussion here is meant as an introduction to these further discussions, no more than that. (Have I mentioned that philosophy is hard?)

Disagreement

I have been emphasizing ways in which moral disagreement may motivate the thought that morality is objective. But it's very common to think that something about moral disagreement actually goes the other way. For if there are perfectly objective moral truths, why is there so much disagreement about them? Wouldn't we expect, if there are such objective truths, to see everyone converging on them? Perhaps such convergence cannot be expected to be perfect and quick, but still—why is there so much persistent, apparently irreconcilable disagreement in morality, but not in subject matters whose objectivity is less controversial? If there is no answer to this question, doesn't this count heavily against morality's objectivity?

It is not easy to see exactly what this objection comes to. (Exercise: Can you try and formulate a precise argument here?) It may be necessary to distinguish between several possible arguments. Naturally, different ways of understanding the objection will call for different responses. But there are some things that can be said in general here. First, the objection seems to underrate the extent of disagreement in subject matters whose objectivity is pretty much uncontroversial (think of the causes and effects of global warming again). It may also overrate the extent of disagreement in morality. Still, the requirement to explain the scope and nature of moral disagreements seems legitimate. But objectivity-friendly explanations seem possible.

Perhaps, for instance, moral disagreement is sometimes best explained by noting that people tend to accept the moral judgments that it's in their interest to accept, or that tend to show their lives and practices in good light. Perhaps this is why the poor tend to believe in the welfare state, and the rich tend to believe in property rights.

Perhaps the most important general lesson here is that not all disagreements count against the objectivity of the relevant discourse. So what we need is a criterion to distinguish between objectivity-undermining and non-objectivity-undermining disagreements. And then we need an argument showing that moral disagreement is of the former kind. I don't know of a fully successful way of filling in these details here.

Notice, by the way, that such attempts are going to have to overcome a natural worry about *self-defeat*. Some theories defeat themselves, that is, roughly, fail even by their own lights. Consider, for instance, the theory "All theories are false," or the belief "No belief is justified." (Exercise: Can you think of other self-defeating theories?) Now, disagreement in philosophy has many of the features that moral disagreement seems to have. In particular, so does metaethical disagreement. Even more in particular, so does disagreement about *whether disagreement undermines objectivity*. If moral disagreement undermines the objectivity of moral conclusions, metaethical disagreement seems to undermine the objectivity of meta-ethical conclusions, including the conclusion that disagreement of this kind undermines objectivity. And this starts to look like self-defeat. So if some disagreement-objection to the objectivity of morality is going to succeed, it must show how moral disagreement undermines the objectivity of morality, but metaethical disagreement does *not* undermine the objectivity of metaethical claims. Perhaps it's possible to do so. But it's not going to be easy.

But How Do We Know?

Even if there are these objective moral truths—for instance, the kind of objective moral truth that both sides to a moral disagreement typically lay a claim to—how can we ever come to know them? In the astronomical case of disagreement about the relative position and motion of the earth and the sun, there are things we can say in response to a similar question—we can talk about perception, and scientific methodology, and progress. Similarly in other subject matters where we are very confident that objective truths await our discovery. Can anything at all be said in the moral case? We do not, after all, seem to possess something worth calling moral perception, a direct perception of the moral status of things. And in the moral case it's hard to argue that we have an established, much less uncontroversial, methodology either. (Whether there is moral progress is, I'm sure you've already realized, highly controversial.)

In other words, what we need is a moral epistemology, an account of how moral knowledge is possible, of how moral beliefs can be more or less justified, and the like. And I do not want to belittle the need for a moral epistemology, in particular an epistemology that fits well with an objectivist understanding of moral judgments. But the objectivist is not without resources here. After all, morality is not the only subject matter where perception and empirical methodology do not seem to be relevant. Think, for instance, of mathematics, and indeed of philosophy. But we do not often doubt the reality of mathematical knowledge. (Philosophical knowledge is a harder case, perhaps. Exercise: Can you see how claiming that we do not have philosophical knowledge may again give rise to a worry about self-defeat?)

Perhaps, then, what is really needed is a general epistemology of the a priori—of those areas, roughly, where the empirical method seems out of place. And perhaps it's not overly optimistic to think that any plausible epistemology of the a priori will vindicate moral knowledge as well.

Also, to say that there is no methodology of doing ethics is at the very least an exaggeration. Typically, when facing a moral question, we do not just stare at it helplessly. Perhaps we're not always very good at morality. But this doesn't mean that we never are. And perhaps at our best, when we employ our best ways of moral reasoning, we manage to attain moral knowledge.

(Exercise: There is no *uncontroversial* method of doing ethics. What, if anything, follows from this?)

Who Decides?

Still, even if moral knowledge is not especially problematic, even if moral disagreement can be explained in objectivity-friendly ways, and even if there are perfectly objective moral truths, what should we do in cases of disagreement and conflict? Who gets to decide what the right way of pro-ceeding is? Especially in the case of intercultural disagreement and con-flict, isn't saying something like "We're right and you're wrong about what is objectively morally required" objectionably dogmatic, intolerant, per-haps an invitation to fanaticism?

Well, in a sense, no one decides. In another sense, everyone does. The situation here is precisely as it is everywhere else: no one gets to decide whether smoking causes cancer, whether human actions contribute to global warming, whether the earth revolves around the sun. Our decisions do not make these claims true or false. But everyone gets (roughly speak-ing) to decide what they are going to believe about these matters. And this is so for moral claims as well.

How about intolerance and fanaticism? If the worry is that people are likely to become dangerously intolerant if they believe in objective moral-ity, then first, such a prediction would have to be established. After all, many social reformers (think, for instance, of Martin Luther King, Jr.) who fought *against* intolerance and bigotry seem to have been inspired by the thought that their vision of equality and justice was objectively correct. Further, even if it's very dangerous for people to believe in the objectivity of their moral convictions, this doesn't mean that morality isn't objective. Such danger would give us reasons not to let people know about morality's objectivity. It would not give us a reason to believe that morality is not objective. (Compare: even if it were the case that things would go rapidly downhill if atheism were widely believed, this wouldn't prove that atheism is false.)

More importantly, though, it's one thing to believe in the objectivity of morality, it's quite another to decide what to do about it. And it's quite possible that the right thing to do, given morality's objectivity, is hardly ever to respond with "I am simply right and you are simply wrong!" or to be intolerant. In fact, if you think that it's wrong to be intolerant, aren't you committed to the objectivity of this very claim? (Want to run the three tests again?) So it seems as if the only way of accommodating the importance of toleration is actually to *accept* morality's objectivity, not to *reject* it.

Conclusion

As already noted, much more can be said—about what objectivity is, about the reasons to think that morality is objective, and about these (and many other) objections to morality's objectivity. Much more work remains to be done.

And one of the ways in which current literature addresses some of these issues may sound surprising, for a major part of the debate *assumes* something like morality's aspiration to objectivity in the sense above, but refuses to infer from such observations quick conclusions about the nature of moral truths and facts. In other words, many metaethicists today deny the most straightforward objectivist view of morality, according to which moral facts are a part of response-independent reality, much like mathematical and physical facts. But they do not deny morality's objectivity—they care, for instance, about passing the three tests above. And so they attempt to show how even on other metaethical views, morality's objectivity can be accommodated. As you can imagine, philosophers disagree about the success (actual and potential) of such accommodation projects.

Naturally, such controversies also lead to attempts to better understand what the objectivity at stake exactly is, and why it matters (if it matters) whether morality is objective. As is often the case, attempts to evaluate answers to a question make us better understand—or wonder about—the question itself.

Nothing here, then, is simple. But I hope that you now see how you are probably a moral objectivist, at least in your intuitive starting point. Perhaps further philosophical reflection will require that you abandon this starting point. But this will be an *abandoning*, and a very strong reason is needed to justify it. Until we get such a conclusive argument against moral objectivity, then, objectivism should be the view to beat.

David Enoch: Why I Am an Objectivist about Ethics (And Why You Are, Too)

1. In what ways does our attitude to morality seem to be different from our attitude to matters of taste?
2. In what ways does our attitude to morality seem to be different from our attitude to matters of convention, like fashion?
3. How can the phenomenon of moral disagreement count against the objectivity of morality?
4. Can the dangerousness of belief in moral objectivity give us reason to believe that morality is not after all objective? If so, how? If not, why not?
5. In what ways do we treat our aesthetic commitments and our moral ones on a par? In what ways do they seem to differ?

18

Moral Knowledge
Sarah McGrath

···

Sarah McGrath opens her article with a series of questions that you may have asked yourself at some point: do we have any moral knowledge? If so, how much? Where does it come from? How can we get it? She proceeds to address these questions by first considering what the source of moral knowledge might be. Many have thought that such knowledge must originate in evidence from the senses, since (according to these philosophers) all knowledge stems from this source. Critics of this empiricist view have frequently insisted that moral knowledge comes, instead, from our intuitions about what is right and wrong. Some critics of both views have argued that these are the only two options for explaining where moral knowledge comes from, that both options are deeply implausible, and that therefore no one has any moral knowledge at all!

McGrath next considers the method of reflective equilibrium, which tells us that moral knowledge is acquired by balancing our considered judgments—those formed in good conditions—to yield a coherent body of moral and nonmoral beliefs. This is by far the most widely endorsed view among philosophers. But while it has many virtues, it also has two serious drawbacks—it can ratify some moral beliefs that are clearly false, while also excluding some moral views that are clearly true.

The last section of McGrath's article is devoted to discussing three prominent skeptical challenges. The first focuses on cases of deference,

---

This essay was commissioned for the fifth edition of *The Ethical Life*.

where a person forms her beliefs solely on the basis of someone else's say-so. This seems perfectly fine when it comes to nonmoral matters. By contrast, it seems problematic to form your *moral* beliefs just by taking over those of someone else. The second challenge stems from the fact of widespread moral disagreement: in the face of such disagreement, should we give up the moral beliefs we currently hold? The third challenge comes from evolutionary considerations: if the explanation for why we hold our moral beliefs is that it was beneficial to our ancestors' survival, should that make us worry about whether those beliefs are actually true? McGrath does not seek to provide definitive answers to these skeptical challenges, but rather clearly explains them and invites our further reflection on their merits.

....

I. Introduction

Imagine that you have accidentally discovered that your roommate's new best friend says terrible things about her behind her back. If you tell her, there will be drama. She will be very upset, and she might even end up getting mad at *you.* If you don't tell her, then maybe she will never find out. Maybe if she never finds out, this "wrinkle" in the new friendship will work itself out, and the friendship will be long-lasting and wonderful. Maybe it is none of your business! You really care about your roommate, and you really want to do the right thing. But what *is* the right thing? What should you do?

When you are wondering what to do in this kind of situation, it seems as though there is something that you *don't know* that you *want* to know and are *trying to figure out.* Sometimes when we try to figure out what to do we are trying to figure out what would be most expedient—most effective in achieving our personal goals. But other times, we are trying to figure out what is *morally* right—what we *morally* ought to do. And that might be what is happening in the roommate example: you might be asking a moral question, and seeking what philosophers would call "moral knowledge."

On the one hand, it seems that ordinary people have a lot of moral knowledge—we know it is wrong to give cigarettes to kids, we know we should return lost wallets when we find them, etc. On the other hand, it seems that there are a lot of hard questions. In addition to the daily-life quandaries like the one I described above, there are controversial moral issues such as: could it ever be morally permissible to torture a suspected terrorist in order to get information? Is it wrong to use factory farmed animals for food? Under what circumstances (if any) is it permissible to abort a fetus? What do we owe to future generations, or to distant strangers in need?

Moral philosophy concerns questions about how we may treat others—about what particular kinds of action are permissible, forbidden or required. *Epistemology* is the branch of philosophy that concerns whether and how we know the various kinds of things that we take ourselves to know. *Moral epistemology* lies at the intersection of these two branches of philosophy. Some of the questions within the field of moral epistemology include: assuming that you have moral knowledge, where does it come from? And to the extent that there are difficult questions, about which you are uncertain, how can you get answers? Presumably, when it comes to many of your deeply held moral convictions, there are smart people who would disagree with you. In the face of this, does it make sense for you to stick to your guns, or should you reduce your confidence?

Another question within moral epistemology is: how much moral knowledge do we actually have? Perhaps it is obvious that what a philosopher says about the *sources* of moral knowledge will have an impact on what she says about its *extent*. If moral knowledge is a matter of common sense, then presumably most people have a lot of it. The Scottish philosopher Thomas Reid thought:

> There are some intricate cases in morals which admit of disputation; but these seldom occur in practice; and when they do, the learned disputant has no great advantage. In order to know what is right and what is wrong in human conduct, we need only listen to the dictates of our conscience, when the mind is calm and unruffled, or attend to the judgment we form of others in like circumstances. (1788/2003, 645)

But, on the other hand, if getting in touch with moral reality would require a kind of sixth-sense that we do not in fact have, then perhaps we have no moral knowledge at all. The Australian philosopher J. L. Mackie thought that moral knowledge required "some special faculty of moral perception or intuition, utterly different from our ordinary ways of knowing everything else."[1] Since Mackie thought that we clearly don't have any such faculty, he concluded that we do not have any moral knowledge at all.

---

1. See Mackie, "The Subjectivity of Values" (this volume).

Offhand, you might think neither of these positions is correct. The existence of seemingly irresolvable moral controversies with sincere and intelligent people on both sides makes it hard to believe that the answers to moral questions are easily available to all of us. That said, the claim that we have no moral knowledge at all is hard to believe in the face of the fact that many people seem to know at least the basics (e.g., that slavery is wrong).

II. Traditional Epistemological Worries about the Source of Moral Knowledge

Let's start by thinking about some cases of *non*-moral knowledge. Imagine that you are uncertain about whether it is going to rain today, and also, where you left your umbrella. You might: look outside at the sky, check the forecast, poke around in the closet, and text your friend whose house you were at last night. When you want to know answers to ordinary factual questions like these, you investigate by seeking relevant evidence in the world around us.

And in some ways, these ordinary cases are similar to cases of scientific investigation. A physicist wants to know whether there is a proton in the cloud chamber. She looks to see whether she can observe a vapor trail; if yes, then she takes this as evidence for the claim that there is a proton.[2]

But now suppose that we are uncertain about whether a *moral* claim is true. For example, suppose we are uncertain whether:

(1) It would be wrong to torture a suspected terrorist in order to get information.

If we want to figure out whether *that's* true, how might we proceed? What kind of test could we do? What kind of evidence would we be looking for?

A striking thing about moral uncertainty is that, at least in many cases, our problem is not that we are missing some piece of *empirical information*. Even if we knew exactly what torture would do to the suspected terrorist, and what kind of outcome we would prevent by getting him to talk, still, we might not know whether torture is ever morally okay. It does not seem that we can discover the answers to moral questions in the same way that we can discover the answers to straightforward factual or scientific questions.

---

2. The example is from Harman, "Ethics and Observation" (*The Ethical Life*, Fifth Edition. Oxford University Press, 2020).

Now, we should be careful not to overstate the point: there is a way in which our knowledge of many moral claims *does* depend on our knowledge of empirical claims. For example, the truth of

(2) It is wrong to encourage children to smoke.

depends on the effects of smoking on health; clearly, *smoking is detrimental to health* is an empirical claim. But in this case, while our knowledge that (2) is true does depend in part on non-moral, empirical knowledge, it also depends on some prior piece of *moral* knowledge that is not itself empirical. (In this case: "it is wrong to encourage children to do things that would be detrimental to their health.")

According to the formidable *empiricist* tradition, experience plays a primary or even an exclusive role in accounting for all the knowledge that we possess. And while empiricism has enjoyed great popularity in the Western philosophical tradition, empiricism about moral knowledge has been strikingly *un*popular. John Stuart Mill stands out as a notable exception.[3] Mill thought that claims about moral rightness actually are empirically testable, because he thought they can be translated into empirical claims about *which actions would produce the most happiness for the greatest number of individuals*. According to Mill's analysis, facts about what is right just *are* facts about what would maximize happiness for the greatest number of people.

Notice how much easier it is to explain where moral knowledge comes from if moral facts are facts about which actions would make the most people the happiest. For then it seems that moral investigation, far from being methodologically obscure, simply becomes a part of psychology or sociology. If moral properties just are "natural" properties—the kinds of properties that can be investigated by the social sciences—then the vexing difficulties about moral knowledge go away.

But here is an important objection to Mill's theory. Suppose that we knew for sure that performing some action would be conducive to the general happiness. So for example, suppose we knew for sure that torturing the suspected terrorist would make the most people happiest. Even if we knew that, we could still *wonder* whether doing it would be right. But if "right" just means "conducive to the general happiness," our wondering makes no sense: the question should seem "closed" to us. (Compare the question: "Yes, I *know* he is a bachelor, but is he unmarried???") In 1903, G.E. Moore used this argument to convince nearly everyone that Mill's

---

3. See Mill, "Utilitarianism" (this volume).

theory was wrong. But he believed his argument showed more than that: he thought it showed that *no* version of "ethical naturalism"—the view that moral properties can be defined in terms of natural properties—could possibly be right. Moore thought that for *any* natural property, you could know that something has that property, and still wonder whether the thing was morally good.[4] And for the next fifty-odd years, most philosophers agreed: they thought Moore's argument could refute *any* theory that says moral terms can be translated into natural ones.

Though Moore's "Open Question Argument" was strikingly influential, his views about how we *do* gain moral knowledge did not win many fans. If we asked Moore, "Okay, so where *does* moral knowledge come from?" Moore would say something like this: some moral truths are "self-evident"—we know them just by having intuitions about them, which happens when they strike us forcefully after we consider them.[5] But many of Moore's contemporaries found this story, which gives central place to self-evidence and intuition, about as *un*convincing as the open question argument was convincing. An obvious question they had is: what if my intuitions differ from yours? How do we know who is right? About this problem, A. J. Ayer complained:

> [I]t is notorious that what seems intuitively certain to one person may seem doubtful, or even false, to another.... Some moralists claim to settle the matter by saying that they "know" that their own moral judgements are correct. But such an assertion is of purely psychological interest, and has not the slightest tendency to prove the validity of any moral judgement. For dissenting moralists may equally well "know" that their ethical views are correct. And as far as subjective certainty goes, there will be nothing to choose between them. When such differences of opinion arise in connexion with an ordinary empirical proposition, one may attempt to resolve them by referring to, or actually carrying out, some relevant empirical test. But with regard to ethical statements, there is, on the.... "intuitionist" theory, no relevant empirical test. (1936/1954, 106)

Ayer agrees with Moore that moral claims are not empirical claims, to be tested, "out in the world." But since he finds it equally clear that they can't be "tested," unscientifically, *inside our heads* (i.e., by intuition), he concludes: *we have no moral knowledge at all!*

---

4. Moore argued against attempts to define "good" in natural terms, but analogous versions of the argument can be run against other moral properties, like "right" and "wrong."

5. *Principia Ethica* Chapter VI; sections 112 and 113.

Perhaps this sort of pessimism about the prospects for moral knowledge is ultimately correct. But a notable feature of the philosophical landscape today is that a lot of contemporary philosophers are doing ethics: they are weighing in on actual moral issues, such as the permissibility of abortion, torture, and the death penalty. It seems that a basic presupposition of this activity is that moral knowledge can be gained or extended by reasoning and argument. Within moral epistemology, the prominence of ethical theorizing has prompted renewed interest in our questions: where could moral knowledge come from, and how could we extend it?

III. The Method of Reflective Equilibrium

Let us take stock. On the one hand, moral knowledge does not appear to be empirical knowledge; on the other, Moore's intuitionism seems unsatisfying, especially in the face of disagreement. But Moore's intuitionism is not the only alternative to empiricism about morality.

Looking to the actual practice of philosophers working in applied ethics, many moral philosophers have come to believe that *the method of reflective equilibrium* is the correct account of how moral inquiry should ideally be conducted. The term "reflective equilibrium" is due to John Rawls, who gave the method its canonical articulation in his seminal book *A Theory of Justice* (1971). While there are significant differences in how the method is understood by its proponents, there are common themes and commitments. One is that when we engage in moral inquiry, we are never "starting from scratch." Instead, we begin the process of moral theorizing by bringing to the table moral beliefs that we already have. The first step in applying the method is to sift through these beliefs for those that count as "considered judgments"—those that seem clearly true when you carefully reflect upon them under conditions that are conducive to judging well. These conditions are specified differently by different theorists, but they typically include: being calm rather than upset, being able to concentrate, not having a personal interest in how the issue is settled, and focusing on judgments that are stable rather than fleeting.

The considered judgments that a person starts with will be at different "levels of generality": some will be about particular cases (e.g., "I should tell my roommate what was said behind her back"); some will concern more general claims (e.g., "it is wrong to encourage children to smoke"); some may be at a higher level of generality still ("when faced with a choice, always do the thing that will minimize loss of life").

The next step is to try to come up with general principles that could account for or systematize these considered judgments. Applying the method of reflective equilibrium involves working back and forth between principles and judgments at different levels of generality, resolving the conflicts that come up along the way. The goal is to get yourself into what Rawls calls a "state of reflective equilibrium," in which the principles that you hold and the judgments that you make fit together, and the more general principles help to explain the more particular judgments.[6] Your beliefs will count as being *reasonable, justified*, or even *things that you know*, to the extent that they have survived this process.

This story may feel familiar: it might sound not only like a description of what professional ethicists do, but also like a description of what *you* do when you sit down to figure out what to think about some moral question or problem. And while it is in many ways accessible, it doesn't make moral justification *too* easy to come by: being justified in holding a moral opinion requires more than just having an intuition.

So the method of reflective equilibrium has a lot going for it, but it also faces serious objections.[7] Some critics worry that the method is *too liberal*: that a person could apply the method perfectly, but still end up with beliefs that are *un*reasonable or *un*justified. To see this, notice that there is nothing in the description of the method that rules out that someone's *considered judgments* could include:

(3) One is morally required to occasionally kill randomly.

And there is nothing that rules out that (3) could *survive* this person's flawless application of the method. She might believe (3) in a state of Reflective Equilibrium. But we might think: that is not enough to make (3) reasonable to believe! That someone can make (3) fit in with everything *else* she believes just means she holds many more unreasonable beliefs as well!

Normally, when proponents of the method explain it, they use examples of considered judgments that look very reasonable—the kinds of judgments that ordinary people will share. But since the method is supposed to be a method for *achieving* reasonableness or justification, it seems important to consider examples that do not look obviously reasonable or

---

6. For an example of what this kind of reasoning might look like, see the opening paragraphs of Harman's "Ethics and Observation" (*The Ethical Life*, Fifth Edition. Oxford University Press, 2020).

7. The objections discussed here are drawn from Kelly and McGrath (2010).

justified at the outset. And once we do that, the worry is that the theory needs tighter restrictions on the starting points (i.e., considered judgments). For it is always possible that someone will make terrible judgments even though she is in conditions suitable for making great judgments (she is calm, she is not emotional, etc.), just as it is always possible that someone could play a terrible soccer game in the best of possible conditions.

A natural solution to this problem is to modify the criteria for considered judgments, so that to count as "considered," a judgment must *be a reasonable thing to believe*. But this cannot work. For it gets things backwards: we are supposed to be using the method of reflective equilibrium as the way to figure out whether judgments get to count as reasonable in the first place.

There is also an objection from the opposite direction: the method may be *too strict*. In other words, it may exclude beliefs that are already reasonable or justified. Suppose that a person of color believes

(4) A person of color should not be disadvantaged on the basis of her skin color.

It seems that the method instructs her to bracket this belief when engaging in moral reasoning, since she is personally invested in whether it is true. But surely, (4) is something she shouldn't set aside! Another example: suppose you are walking through a crowded mall and you see a crying toddler who is obviously lost. You know *immediately* that you should help; you don't need reflective equilibrium reasoning to figure it out.

The problem here seems to be that the method over-intellectualizes knowledge of basic, obvious moral truths: ordinary people who have never used the method nevertheless might know with a high degree of certainty that, say, slavery is wrong. But if ordinary people *already* know that, then "reflective equilibrium" cannot, at any rate, be the whole story about where moral knowledge comes from. Perhaps the method is most plausible as a story about how we might extend our moral knowledge, or deepen our moral understanding.

IV. Further Puzzles and Challenges: Deference, Disagreement, and Debunking

Deference

We ended the last section by noting that the method of reflective equilibrium may over-intellectualize moral knowledge. Reflection on the question of how we know basic moral truths like "slavery is wrong" might point our attention to some obvious facts: each of us is born into a social world in which others follow moral norms and hold moral views; parents teach that certain practices (e.g., sharing) are right and others (e.g., hitting) are wrong; children also observe that certain kinds of behavior are punished or met with disapproval, and others rewarded. Maybe we uncritically *inherit* a great deal of our moral knowledge from our social environment.

Granted, this couldn't be the whole story! The obvious question arises: supposing that you inherited moral knowledge from your parents, how did *they* acquire it? If they inherited it from *their* parents, this just pushes the relevant question back.

But we can still ask: could absorbing the moral views of others nevertheless be an important way of acquiring moral knowledge? Is it plausible that, starting as young children, we begin to acquire full-fledged moral knowledge by simply adopting beliefs that are presupposed by the thoughts and practices of those around us?

Certainly, a great deal of our knowledge about *other* subject matters comes to us from testimony. Take, for example, geography. It seems safe to assume that children acquire most of their geographical beliefs from testimony. And it is natural to say that the relevant beliefs amount to knowledge, provided that what the kids believe about geography is true, and that the adults who are teaching them are reliable sources. Children who learn in this way do not have to subject their geographical beliefs to any kind of scrutiny to count as knowing.

Returning now to the case of morality: when it comes to the moral beliefs that a child acquires or absorbs from her parents and her social environment, are the standards for knowing different?

On the one hand, it seems as though the answer to this question should be "no." It certainly seems as though children pick up a lot of moral information from their social environments, starting at a very early age. And, as a more general theoretical matter, it seems that we should not expect standards for moral knowledge to differ from standards for knowledge in other domains, like geography.

But on the other hand, it does seem as though there is an interesting asymmetry in our attitudes toward moral versus other kinds of deference. Consider the following case:

> **Ally and Brad**. At lunch, Brad notices that Ally has ordered the vegetarian sandwich. They start to talk about vegetarianism. Ally explains that she is a vegetarian because she thinks eating meat is wrong.

"Why?" Brad asks. Ally explains that she learned this from her Intro to Ethics professor. "What reasons did the professor give?" Brad asks. Ally says, "I'm not sure! I was doing my physics problem set during the lecture, but I am sure he said it was wrong. I wrote it down."

There is something very odd about this kind of case. Whereas many people do in fact pick up their geographic beliefs by deferring to others, there seems to be something strange about Ally's simply absorbing the belief that eating meat is wrong from her Ethics professor, without being able to say anything about the reasons why.

What could explain our sense that there is something odd about this? Are moral beliefs special, in that they are beliefs that we must arrive at *autonomously*—on our own? In fact, there is a venerable philosophical tradition of thinking so. R.M. Hare once claimed that one of the things that distinguishes "any serious moral problem" from a purely factual question is that:

> . . . a man who is faced with such a problem knows that it is his own problem, and that nobody can answer it for him. He may, it is true, ask the advice of other people; and he may also ascertain more facts about the circumstances and consequences of a proposed action, and other facts of this sort. But there will come a time when he does not hope to find anything else of relevance by factual inquiry, and when he knows that, whatever others may say about the answer to this problem, *he* has to answer it. (1962, 1)

Of course, there is some sense in which a person must ultimately make up her own mind about *any* question that she considers. But Hare explicitly says that this sense is stronger for moral convictions (1962, 2).

So here are some questions: First, is it true that one must in some sense arrive at one's moral convictions for oneself? If it is true, then what is it about the nature of morality, and our relationship to it, that explains this? Notice that if Ayer were right that moral judgments express feelings rather than facts, then we might have an easy explanation: deference only makes sense when there actually are some facts to defer about! Another possibility is that Ally's deferring to her professor looks strange because the question of whether eating animals is wrong is highly *controversial*: wouldn't it be equally odd to defer to your physics professor about the mechanism of high-Tc superconductivity, if you knew that this was an issue the physicists themselves disagreed about?

Disagreement

This raises the question: how does the possibility of your having moral knowledge interact with the fact that many people would disagree with your moral convictions?

Most of us have deeply held moral convictions which are highly controversial. We have strong views about abortion rights, animal rights, the death penalty, our obligations to future generations and to distant strangers in need. With respect to these issues, opinion is substantially divided: there are sincere and intelligent people who have thought a great deal about the questions but disagree with one another.

Henry Sidgwick, in *The Methods of Ethics*, makes the following provocative claim about disagreement:

> If I find any of my judgments, intuitive or inferential, in direct conflict with a judgment of some other mind, there must be error somewhere: and if I have no more reason to suspect error in the other mind than in my own, reflective comparison between the two judgments necessarily reduces me temporarily to a state of neutrality. (1907/1981, 342)

Sidgwick goes on to say that "the absence of such disagreement must remain an indispensable negative condition on the certainty of our knowledge" (1907/1981, 342).

Sidgwick is talking about *certainty*, but a parallel claim about knowledge also seems plausible. Call someone who meets the condition that "you have no more reason to suspect error [in her] mind than in your own" your "epistemic peer." When you find out that your epistemic peer about moral questions disagrees with you about one of your deeply held moral convictions, is that consistent with your knowing you are right? Is it reasonable for you to stick to your guns, or should you be reduced to a "state of neutrality," as Sidgwick suggests?

Let's first consider a non-moral example. Suppose you are working on a problem set with a friend whom you take to be your epistemic peer when it comes to math. When you compare answers to problem three, you discover that you disagree. If you have no special reason to think that it is your peer who has made a mistake—she is not distracted, or otherwise impaired—it seems like you should become less confident in your answer. The thought here is that even if she made the mistake, *you* still do not *know*, because the fact that your peer disagrees with you in these circumstances should make you suspend judgment.

Generally speaking, when you find yourself in a situation like this one, you will often become less confident in what you originally believed. The discovery that opinion about some matter of fact is divided among sensible smart people who have studied the matter long and hard might make you suspend judgment. But, returning now to the moral case: we already know that many of our moral beliefs are hugely controversial! We know that very smart people disagree with us about abortion rights, animal rights, the death penalty, our obligations to future generations, and to distant strangers in need. So here are some questions we might ask: Are any of those people our epistemic peers? And if so, should this have the kind of neutralizing effect that Sidgwick describes? Or is there some reason to think that the moral domain is special—that in the face of moral disagreement, we are justified in standing by our deeply held convictions, irrespective of the distribution of the opinions of others?

Debunking

Our final challenge begins with the fact that there are many moral beliefs that do not seem to be controversial: parents ought to care for their children; we should try to help those who have helped us; we should punish cheaters and thieves. These seem like familiar, relatively *un*controversial, basic moral beliefs. But a striking feature of these beliefs is this: they look very much like what we *would* have believed if we had simply let evolution pick our moral beliefs for us. If our beliefs had been shaped by the facts about what would be conducive to the survival and propagation of our species, wouldn't we feel very strongly that we should care for our young? It seems quite plausible that, had our ancestors not been the kind of creatures who were moved by the needs of their children, we wouldn't be around to think about it!

So it is plausible that evolutionary forces played a strong role in shaping our moral beliefs. But if the explanation for why we hold our moral beliefs is that it was beneficial to our ancestors' survival, should that make us worry about whether those beliefs are actually true? Could this explanation of why we hold the moral beliefs that we do actually undermine them?[8]

There are many circumstances in which learning about why you hold a belief you hold can undermine it, returning you to a "state of neutrality" in Sidgwick's sense. Imagine, for example, that toward the end of the

---

8. This kind of challenge has been pressed most influentially by Street (2006) and Joyce (2006).

summer you receive an email stating that roommate assignments for the Fall have been made, and your roommate will be Robert A. Zimmerman from Minnesota. On the basis of this email, you believe that your new roommate will be a person named Robert (or possibly "Bob") from Minnesota. But fifteen minutes later, you receive an email from the University's Information Technology desk apologizing for any inconvenience caused by the fake emails about roommate assignments sent out as a prank. When you find out that the first email was a prank, you no longer have any reason for believing that your roommate will be a guy named Robert from Minnesota. You return to a state of neutrality with respect to the question of who your roommate will be.

Our question is: does the evolutionary explanation of our moral beliefs undermine or "debunk" those beliefs, in the same way that learning that the email was a prank debunks your belief about who your roommate will be? If our moral values are basically just the values that it would be beneficial for creatures like us to have, does that mean that we are hopelessly in the dark about which moral values are actually *true*?

There are many possible responses to this evolutionary challenge. One response is to reject the assumption that if there is a moral truth, that truth must exist independently of what we value. If moral truth is not independent of human psychology, but is rather a function of it, then it may seem as though this skeptical challenge cannot get going in the first place. But one might worry: if we go this route, does morality lose the kind of objectivity and authority that we might have taken it to have?

V. Conclusion

By way of conclusion, let's try to connect our theme of empiricism to the issues that we have discussed in sections III and IV.

Notice that reflective equilibrium appears on the scene as a method for moral inquiry, not as a method for *scientific* inquiry. It might be instructive to step back and ask: How does the method of reflective equilibrium differ from the scientific method? A natural thought is that while scientists surely do seek to make their theories cohere with their considered judgments, this is not the whole story: any description of the scientific method that neglects to mention the role of *observation* would be radically incomplete.

Perhaps the source of the "too liberal" and "too strict" problems for Reflective Equilibrium are the same: nothing in the method plays the tethering role of observation. Nothing rules *out* wildly unreasonable starting points, and nothing rules *in* the things we know prior to engaging in any reasoning at all. Similarly, it seems that it would at least *help* with the unsettling problem of moral disagreement if there were some independent way to confirm which one of us is getting things right. Presumably, disagreeing scientists have something that helps, namely, observation, which can (presumably) "push-back" against conflicting theories and nudge them toward consensus. If we could know which of the opinionated Ethics professors to trust by waiting to see who turns out to be right, in the same way that we can pick our weather forecasters or sports odds-makers based on the accuracy of their predictions, then perhaps moral deference wouldn't seem odd. And if there was a way of confirming that in spite of our evolutionary history, our moral beliefs are still spot-on, rather than off-base, we would have a satisfactory reply to the evolutionary debunker.

This essay has focused on some of the pervasive worries about the sources of moral knowledge. One very general strategy for responding to these worries is what Mackie calls "companions in guilt." If what makes moral knowledge suspect is its shaky connection to experience, then it isn't just moral knowledge we should worry about; the lines of attack that we have discussed may imply skepticism about the possibility of kinds of knowledge as well. For example, when you figure out the answers to a math problem set, you do it by thinking hard and applying the concepts you learned in class. You do not do experiments in a math lab. If the fact that you can learn math this way doesn't make mathematical knowledge shaky, why should the standards for moral knowledge be any different? Another general strategy is to resist the assumption that nothing stands to morality as observation stands to science. Many contemporary moral epistemologists favor intuitionist views that are descendants of Moore's intuitionism; perhaps moral intuitions or "moral appearances" can be the "data" to which moral theories must answer. More radically, one might deny that moral beliefs are entirely cut off from empirical observation, and look for compelling examples to the contrary.[9]

---

9. One such example might be this: over the course of the last decade a large number of Americans have changed their minds about the morality of same-sex relationships (http://www.gallup.com/poll/1651/gay-lesbian-rights.aspx). The main reason that people give for changing their minds was finding out that someone they knew personally or professionally participated in same-sex relationships (2013 Pew Research Center Report, "Growing Support for Gay Marriage: Changed Minds and Changing Demographics"). Could this be a case in which empirical evidence ("My good friend Bob is in a same-sex relationship") could provide disconfirming evidence for a moral claim ("Same-sex relationships are morally wrong")?

Sarah McGrath: Moral Knowledge

1. How plausible do you find the empiricist claim that all moral knowledge has its source in the evidence of our senses?
2. Can our moral intuitions provide a good basis for forming our moral beliefs? Why or why not?
3. Do you think that we have any moral knowledge? If so, give some examples, and explain how you have acquired that knowledge. If not, explain why you and others fail to know (for instance) that genocide is immoral or that kindness is good.
4. Construct an argument that starts from the fact of widespread moral disagreement and concludes that we have no moral knowledge. Is such an argument sound? Why or why not?
5. Construct an argument that starts from the assumption that our moral beliefs are largely influenced by past evolutionary considerations, and concludes with the claim that we have no moral knowledge. Is such an argument sound? Why or why not?

References

Ayer, A. J. 1936. *Language, Truth, and Logic*. New York: Dover.

Hare, R. M. 1962. *Freedom and Reason*. Oxford: Oxford University Press.

Harman, G. 1977. *The Nature of Morality: An Introduction to Ethics*. Oxford: Oxford University Press.

Joyce, R. 2006. *The Evolution of Morality*. Cambridge: MIT Press.

Kelly, T. and S. McGrath. 2010. "Is Reflective Equilibrium Enough?" *Philosophical Perspectives* 24: 325–59.

Mackie, J. L. 1977. *Ethics: Inventing Right and Wrong*. New York: Penguin.

Mill, J. S. 1861/1979. *Utilitarianism*. Indianapolis: Hackett.

Moore, G. E. 1903/2004. *Principia Ethica*. Mineola, NY: Dover.

Rawls, J. 1971. *A Theory of Justice*. Cambridge, MA: Harvard University Press.

Reid, T. 1788/2003. *Essays on the Active Powers of the Human Mind*. Excerpt reprinted in *Moral Philosophy from Montaigne to Kant*, ed. J. Schneewind. New York: Cambridge University Press.

Sidgwick, H. 1907/1981. *The Methods of Ethics*. Indianapolis: Hackett.

Street, S. 2006. "A Darwinian Dilemma for Realist Theories of Value." *Philosophical Studies* 127.1: 109–66.

PART IV

Moral Problems

19

What Will Future Generations Condemn Us For?

Kwame Anthony Appiah

In this provocative short piece, the distinguished philosopher Kwame Anthony Appiah invites us to reflect on the morality of our current practices by asking what future generations would think of them. He notes that we are puzzled at how our ancestors allowed and even positively supported such practices as slavery, the exclusion of women from the voting rolls, and racist lynchings—practices that nowadays strike us as abhorrent.

The underlying idea behind Appiah's thought experiment is that we may be able to uncover our moral blind spots by reflecting on how future generations will regard us. He identifies three signs that a contemporary practice may draw the condemnation of future generations. First, there are already contemporary arguments leveled against the practice, even if those arguments are currently doing little to sway broad public opinion. Second, defenders of these practices tend not to offer arguments but rather appeals to tradition, necessity, or human nature. Third, supporters of these questionable practices tend to engage in what Appiah calls "strategic ignorance," turning their attention away from the unsavory aspects of the practices that they enjoy or otherwise take for granted.

Appiah identifies four contemporary practices that he thinks exemplify all three of these features and are likely to be the target of future moral condemnation: our prison system, industrial meat production, the institutionalization of the elderly, and our treatment of the environment.

....

Once, pretty much everywhere, beating your wife and children was regarded as a father's duty, homosexuality was a hanging offense, and waterboarding was approved—in fact, invented—by the Catholic Church. Through the middle of the 19th century, the United States and other nations in the Americas condoned plantation slavery. Many of our grandparents were born in states where women were forbidden to vote. And well into the 20th century, lynch mobs in this country stripped, tortured, hanged and burned human beings at picnics.

Looking back at such horrors, it is easy to ask: What were people thinking?

Yet, the chances are that our own descendants will ask the same question, with the same incomprehension, about some of our practices today.

Is there a way to guess which ones? After all, not every disputed institution or practice is destined to be discredited. And it can be hard to distinguish in real time between movements, such as abolition, that will come to represent moral common sense and those, such as prohibition, that will come to seem quaint or misguided. Recall the book-burners of Boston's old Watch and Ward Society or the organizations for the suppression of vice, with their crusades against claret, contraceptives and sexually candid novels.

Still, a look at the past suggests three signs that a particular practice is destined for future condemnation.

First, people have already heard the arguments against the practice. The case against slavery didn't emerge in a blinding moment of moral clarity, for instance; it had been around for centuries.

Second, defenders of the custom tend not to offer moral counterarguments but instead invoke tradition, human nature or necessity. (As in, "We've always had slaves, and how could we grow cotton without them?")

And third, supporters engage in what one might call strategic ignorance, avoiding truths that might force them to face the evils in which they're complicit. Those who ate the sugar or wore the cotton that the slaves grew simply didn't think about what made those goods possible.

That's why abolitionists sought to direct attention toward the conditions of the Middle Passage, through detailed illustrations of slave ships and horrifying stories of the suffering below decks.

With these signs in mind, here are four contenders for future moral condemnation.

Our Prison System

We already know that the massive waste of life in our prisons is morally troubling; those who defend the conditions of incarceration usually do so in non-moral terms (citing costs or the administrative difficulty of reforms); and we're inclined to avert our eyes from the details. Check, check and check.

Roughly 1 percent of adults in this country are incarcerated. We have 4 percent of the world's population but 25 percent of its prisoners. No other nation has as large a proportion of its population in prison; even China's rate is less than half of ours. What's more, the majority of our prisoners are non-violent offenders, many of them detained on drug charges. (Whether a country that was truly free would criminalize recreational drug use is a related question worth pondering.)

And the full extent of the punishment prisoners face isn't detailed in any judge's sentence. More than 100,000 inmates suffer sexual abuse, including rape, each year; some contract HIV as a result. Our country holds at least 25,000 prisoners in isolation in so-called supermax facilities, under conditions that many psychologists say amount to torture.

Industrial Meat Production

The arguments against the cruelty of factory farming have certainly been around a long time; it was Jeremy Bentham, in the 18th century, who observed that, when it comes to the treatment of animals, the key question is not whether animals can reason but whether they can suffer. People who eat factory-farmed bacon or chicken rarely offer a moral justification for what they're doing. Instead, they try not to think about it too much, shying away from stomach-turning stories about what goes on in our industrial abattoirs.

Of the more than 90 million cattle in our country, at least 10 million at any time are packed into feedlots, saved from the inevitable diseases of overcrowding only by regular doses of antibiotics, surrounded by piles of their own feces, their nostrils filled with the smell of their own urine. Picture it—and then imagine your grandchildren seeing that picture. In the European Union, many of the most inhumane conditions we allow are already illegal or—like the sow stalls into which pregnant pigs are often crammed in the United States—will be illegal soon.

The Institutionalized and Isolated Elderly

Nearly 2 million of America's elderly are warehoused in nursing homes, out of sight and, to some extent, out of mind. Some 10,000 for-profit facilities have arisen across the country in recent decades to hold them. Other elderly Americans may live independently, but often they are isolated and cut off from their families. (The United States is not alone among advanced democracies in this. Consider the heat wave that hit France in 2003: While many families were enjoying their summer vacations, some 14,000 elderly parents and grandparents were left to perish in the stifling temperatures.) Is this what Western modernity amounts to—societies that feel no filial obligations to their inconvenient elders?

Sometimes we can learn from societies much poorer than ours. My English mother spent the last 50 years of her life in Ghana, where I grew up. In her final years, it was her good fortune not only to have the resources to stay at home, but also to live in a country where doing so was customary. She had family next door who visited her every day, and she was cared for by doctors and nurses who were willing to come to her when she was too ill to come to them. In short, she had the advantages of a society in which older people are treated with respect and concern.

Keeping aging parents and their children closer is a challenge, particularly in a society where almost everybody has a job outside the home (if not across the country). Yet the three signs apply here as well: When we see old people who, despite many living relatives, suffer growing isolation, we know something is wrong. We scarcely try to defend the situation; when we can, we put it out of our minds. Self-interest, if nothing else, should make us hope that our descendants will have worked out a better way.

The Environment

Of course, most transgenerational obligations run the other way—from parents to children—and of these the most obvious candidate for opprobrium is our wasteful attitude toward the planet's natural resources and ecology. Look at a satellite picture of Russia, and you'll see a vast expanse of parched wasteland where decades earlier was a lush and verdant landscape. That's the Republic of Kalmykia, home to what was recognized in the 1990s as Europe's first man-made desert. Desertification, which is primarily the result of destructive land-management practices, threatens a third of the Earth's surface; tens of thousands of Chinese villages have been overrun by sand drifts in the past few decades.

It's not as though we're unaware of what we're doing to the planet: We know the harm done by deforestation, wetland destruction, pollution, overfishing, greenhouse gas emissions—the whole litany. Our descendants, who will inherit this devastated Earth, are unlikely to have the luxury of such recklessness. Chances are, they won't be able to avert their eyes, even if they want to.

Let's not stop there, though. We will all have our own suspicions about which practices will someday prompt people to ask, in dismay: What were they thinking?

Even when we don't have a good answer, we'll be better off for anticipating the question.

Kwame Anthony Appiah: What Will Future Generations Condemn Us For?

1. Appiah identifies three signs that a practice will be targeted for condemnation by future generations. Do you agree that these are good indicators that something is morally suspect?
2. Can you think of other such signs?
3. Which contemporary practices, other than the four that Appiah mentions, do you think will be the target of future moral criticism?
4. Can you think of good signs that a contemporary practice will earn the *respect* of future generations? If so, what are these signs?
5. Which current practices possess these features and so, to your mind, are likely to earn the respect of future generations?

20

The Singer Solution to World Poverty

Peter Singer

....

Peter Singer argues that our ordinary patterns of spending money on ourselves are immoral. Such spending involves the purchase of many things that are not essential to preserving our lives or health. The money we spend on fancy dinners, new clothes, or vacations could instead be sent to relief agencies that save people's lives. We don't know our potential beneficiaries, but that is morally irrelevant. Our decision not to spend money to save their lives is morally inexcusable.

Singer offers us a series of fascinating examples in which people have the opportunity to prevent an innocent person's death but fail to do so. We regard the person in each example as having done something extremely immoral. Singer argues that we who spend money on inessential personal pleasures are no better.

But what if most of the people we know are also failing to give anything to famine relief or aid agencies? That doesn't let us off the hook—it just means that they are also behaving in a deeply immoral way.

Perhaps the money sent overseas will not do as much good as advertised? Singer mentions some very reliable aid agencies (and provides contact information) that will not squander your money. For a couple hundred dollars, you can save a child's life, or purchase a few

Reprinted by permission of the author. © Peter Singer, 1999. This article first appeared under the title "The Singer Solution to World Poverty," *New York Times Magazine* (Sept 5, 1999), pp. 60–63.

new additions to your wardrobe. If Singer is right, then choosing to spend that money on yourself means knowingly allowing an innocent person to die. Given the relatively small sacrifice you would be making if you sent that money overseas, and given the great benefit you would be providing if you did, morality gives you no choice. World poverty could largely be solved if we in the wealthier nations did our moral duty and gave much more than we currently do to those in greatest need.

....

In the Brazilian film *Central Station*, Dora is a retired schoolteacher who makes ends meet by sitting at the station writing letters for illiterate people. Suddenly she has an opportunity to pocket $1,000. All she has to do is persuade a homeless 9-year-old boy to follow her to an address she has been given. (She is told he will be adopted by wealthy foreigners.) She delivers the boy, gets the money, spends some of it on a television set, and settles down to enjoy her new acquisition. Her neighbor spoils the fun, however, by telling her that the boy was too old to be adopted—he will be killed and his organs sold for transplantation. Perhaps Dora knew this all along, but after her neighbor's plain speaking, she spends a troubled night. In the morning Dora resolves to take the boy back.

Suppose Dora had told her neighbor that it is a tough world, other people have nice new TVs too, and if selling the kid is the only way she can get one, well, he was only a street kid. She would then have become, in the eyes of the audience, a monster. She redeems herself only by being prepared to bear considerable risks to save the boy.

At the end of the movie, in cinemas in the affluent nations of the world, people who would have been quick to condemn Dora if she had not rescued the boy go home to places far more comfortable than her apartment. In fact, the average family in the United States spends almost one-third of its income on things that are no more necessary to them than Dora's new TV was to her. Going out to nice restaurants, buying new clothes because the old ones are no longer stylish, vacationing at beach resorts—so much of our income is spent on things not essential to the preservation of our lives and health. Donated to one of a number of charitable agencies, that money could mean the difference between life and death for children in need.

All of which raises a question: In the end, what is the ethical distinction between a Brazilian who sells a homeless child to organ peddlers and an American who already has a TV and upgrades to a better one—knowing that the money could be donated to an organization that would use it to save the lives of kids in need?

Of course, there are several differences between the two situations that could support different moral judgments about them. For one thing, to be able to consign a child to death when he is standing right in front of you takes a chilling kind of heartlessness; it is much easier to ignore an appeal for money to help children you will never meet. Yet for a utilitarian philosopher like myself—that is, one who judges whether acts are right or wrong by their consequences—if the upshot of the American's failure to donate the money is that one more kid dies on the streets of a Brazilian city, then it is, in some sense, just as bad as selling the kid to the organ peddlers. But one doesn't need to embrace my utilitarian ethic to see that, at the very least, there is a troubling incongruity in being so quick to condemn Dora for taking the child to the organ peddlers while, at the same time, not regarding the American consumer's behavior as raising a serious moral issue.

In his 1996 book, *Living High and Letting Die*, the New York University philosopher Peter Unger presented an ingenious series of imaginary examples designed to probe our intuitions about whether it is wrong to live well without giving substantial amounts of money to help people who are hungry, malnourished or dying from easily treatable illnesses like diarrhea. Here's my paraphrase of one of these examples:

Bob is close to retirement. He has invested most of his savings in a very rare and valuable old car, a Bugatti, which he has not been able to insure. The Bugatti is his pride and joy. In addition to the pleasure he gets from driving and caring for his car, Bob knows that its rising market value means that he will always be able to sell it and live comfortably after retirement. One day when Bob is out for a drive, he parks the Bugatti near the end of a railway siding and goes for a walk up the track. As he does so, he sees that a runaway train, with no one aboard, is running down the railway track. Looking farther down the track, he sees the small figure of a child very likely to be killed by the runaway train. He can't stop the train and the child is too far away to warn of the danger, but he can throw a switch that will divert the train down the siding where his Bugatti is parked. Then nobody will be killed—but the train will destroy his Bugatti. Thinking of his joy in owning the car and the financial security it represents, Bob decides not to throw the switch. The child is killed. For many years to come, Bob enjoys owning his Bugatti and the financial security it represents.

Bob's conduct, most of us will immediately respond, was gravely wrong. Unger agrees. But then he reminds us that we, too, have opportunities to save the lives of children. We can give to organizations like UNICEF or Oxfam America. How much would we have to give one of these organizations to have a high probability of saving the life of a child threatened by easily preventable diseases? (I do not believe that children are more worth saving than adults, but since no one can argue that children have brought their poverty on themselves, focusing on them simplifies the issues.) Unger called up some experts and used the information they provided to offer some plausible estimates that include the cost of raising money, administrative expenses and the cost of delivering aid where it is most needed. By his calculation, $200 in donations would help a sickly 2-year-old transform into a healthy 6-year-old—offering safe passage through childhood's most dangerous years. To show how practical philosophical argument can be, Unger even tells his readers that they can easily donate funds by using their credit card and calling one of these toll-free numbers: (800) 367-5437 for Unicef; (800) 693-2687 for Oxfam America. [http://supportunicef.org/forms/whichcountry2.html for Unicef and https://give.oxfamamerica.org/page/46459/donate/1 for Oxfam—PS.]

Now you, too, have the information you need to save a child's life. How should you judge yourself if you don't do it? Think again about Bob and his Bugatti. Unlike Dora, Bob did not have to look into the eyes of the child he was sacrificing for his own material comfort. The child was a complete stranger to him and too far away to relate to in an intimate, personal way. Unlike Dora, too, he did not mislead the child or initiate the chain of events imperiling him. In all these respects, Bob's situation resembles that of people able but unwilling to donate to overseas aid and differs from Dora's situation.

If you still think that it was very wrong of Bob not to throw the switch that would have diverted the train and saved the child's life, then it is hard to see how you could deny that it is also very wrong not to send money to one of the organizations listed above. Unless, that is, there is some morally important difference between the two situations that I have overlooked.

Is it the practical uncertainties about whether aid will really reach the people who need it? Nobody who knows the world of overseas aid can doubt that such uncertainties exist. But Unger's figure of $200 to save a child's life was reached after he had made conservative assumptions about the proportion of the money donated that will actually reach its target.

One genuine difference between Bob and those who can afford to donate to overseas aid organizations but don't is that only Bob can save the child on the tracks, whereas there are hundreds of millions of people who can give $200 to overseas aid organizations. The problem is that most of them aren't doing it. Does this mean that it is all right for you not to do it?

Suppose that there were more owners of priceless vintage cars—Carol, Dave, Emma, Fred, and so on, down to Ziggy—all in exactly the same situation as Bob, with their own siding and their own switch, all sacrificing the child in order to preserve their own cherished car. Would that make it all right for Bob to do the same? To answer this question affirmatively is to endorse follow-the-crowd ethics—the kind of ethics that led many Germans to look away when the Nazi atrocities were being committed. We do not excuse them because others were behaving no better.

We seem to lack a sound basis for drawing a clear moral line between Bob's situation and that of any reader of this article with $200 to spare who does not donate it to an overseas aid agency. These readers seem to be acting at least as badly as Bob was acting when he chose to let the runaway train hurtle toward the unsuspecting child. In the light of this conclusion, I trust that many readers will reach for the phone and donate that $200. Perhaps you should do it before reading further.

Now that you have distinguished yourself morally from people who put their vintage cars ahead of a child's life, how about treating yourself and your partner to dinner at your favorite restaurant? But wait. The money you will spend at the restaurant could also help save the lives of children overseas! True, you weren't planning to blow $200 tonight, but if you were to give up dining out just for one month, you would easily save that amount. And what is one month's dining out, compared to a child's life? There's the rub. Since there are a lot of desperately needy children in the world, there will always be another child whose life you could save for another $200. Are you therefore obliged to keep giving until you have nothing left? At what point can you stop?

Hypothetical examples can easily become farcical. Consider Bob. How far past losing the Bugatti should he go? Imagine that Bob had got his foot stuck in the track of the siding, and if he diverted the train, then before it rammed the car it would also amputate his big toe. Should he still throw the switch? What if it would amputate his foot? His entire leg?

As absurd as the Bugatti scenario gets when pushed to extremes, the point it raises is a serious one: only when the sacrifices become very significant indeed would most people be prepared to say that Bob does nothing wrong when he decides not to throw the switch. Of course, most people could be wrong; we can't decide moral issues by taking opinion polls. But consider for yourself the level of sacrifice that you would demand of Bob, and then think about how much money you would have to give away in order to make a sacrifice that is roughly equal to that. It's almost certainly much, much more than $200. For most middle-class Americans, it could easily be more like $200,000.

Isn't it counterproductive to ask people to do so much? Don't we run the risk that many will shrug their shoulders and say that morality, so conceived, is fine for saints but not for them? I accept that we are unlikely to see, in the near or even medium-term future, a world in which it is normal for wealthy Americans to give the bulk of their wealth to strangers. When it comes to praising or blaming people for what they do, we tend to use a standard that is relative to some conception of normal behavior. Comfortably off Americans who give, say, 10 percent of their income to overseas aid organizations are so far ahead of most of their equally comfortable fellow citizens that I wouldn't go out of my way to chastise them for not doing more. Nevertheless, they should be doing much more, and they are in no position to criticize Bob for failing to make the much greater sacrifice of his Bugatti.

At this point various objections may crop up. Someone may say: "If every citizen living in the affluent nations contributed his or her share I wouldn't have to make such a drastic sacrifice, because long before such levels were reached, the resources would have been there to save the lives of all those children dying from lack of food or medical care. So why should I give more than my fair share?" Another, related, objection is that the Government ought to increase its overseas aid allocations, since that would spread the burden more equitably across all taxpayers.

Yet the question of how much we ought to give is a matter to be decided in the real world—and that, sadly, is a world in which we know that most people do not, and in the immediate future will not, give substantial amounts to overseas aid agencies. We know, too, that at least in the next year, the United States Government is not going to meet even the very modest United Nations-recommended target of 0.7 percent of gross national product; at the moment it lags far below that, at 0.09 percent, not even half of Japan's 0.22 percent or a tenth of Denmark's 0.97 percent.

Thus, we know that the money we can give beyond that theoretical "fair share" is still going to save lives that would otherwise be lost. While the idea that no one need do more than his or her fair share is a powerful one, should it prevail if we know that others are not doing their fair share and that children will die preventable deaths unless we do more than our fair share? That would be taking fairness too far.

Thus, this ground for limiting how much we ought to give also fails. In the world as it is now, I can see no escape from the conclusion that each one of us with wealth surplus to his or her essential needs should be giving most of it to help people suffering from poverty so dire as to be life-threatening. That's right: I'm saying that you shouldn't buy that new car, take that cruise, redecorate the house or get that pricey new suit. After all, a $1,000 suit could save five children's lives.

So how does my philosophy break down in dollars and cents? An American household with an income of $50,000 spends around $30,000 annually on necessities, according to the Conference Board, a nonprofit economic research organization. Therefore, for a household bringing in $50,000 a year, donations to help the world's poor should be as close as possible to $20,000. The $30,000 required for necessities holds for higher incomes as well. So a household making $100,000 could cut a yearly check for $70,000. Again, the formula is simple: whatever money you're spending on luxuries, not necessities, should be given away.

Now, evolutionary psychologists tell us that human nature just isn't sufficiently altruistic to make it plausible that many people will sacrifice so much for strangers. On the facts of human nature, they might be right, but they would be wrong to draw a moral conclusion from those facts. If it is the case that we ought to do things that, predictably, most of us won't do, then let's face that fact head-on. Then, if we value the life of a child more than going to fancy restaurants, the next time we dine out we will know that we could have done something better with our money. If that makes living a morally decent life extremely arduous, well, then that is the way things are. If we don't do it, then we should at least know that we are failing to live a morally decent life—not because it is good to wallow in guilt but because knowing where we should be going is the first step toward heading in that direction.

When Bob first grasped the dilemma that faced him as he stood by that railway switch, he must have thought how extraordinarily unlucky he was to be placed in a situation in which he must choose between the life of an innocent child and the sacrifice of most of his savings. But he was not unlucky at all. We are all in that situation.

Peter Singer: The Singer Solution to World Poverty

1. Was it morally wrong of Bob to refrain from throwing the switch, thus allowing the child to die? Is there any moral difference between Bob's decision and the decision of well-off people to spend money on luxuries rather than the alleviation of poverty?

2. One difference between the case of Bob and the case of someone not giving to charity is that Bob is the only person in a position to prevent the child's death, while many people are in a position to give to charity. Why doesn't Singer think that this is a morally relevant difference? Do you agree with him?

3. How much of our income does Singer think we are morally required to give away? Do you find his standard reasonable?

4. How does Singer respond to the objection that his theory is too demanding, and that people will never make the sacrifices he suggests? Do you find his response convincing?

5. One might respond to Singer's proposals by claiming that instead of individuals contributing money to alleviate world poverty, governments should be responsible for handling such efforts. Why doesn't Singer think that this undermines his view that middle-class people should give large percentages of their income to charity?

========= ❧ =========

21

A Kantian Approach
to Famine Relief

Onora O'Neill

....

Onora O'Neill opens this selection by providing a very helpful summary of the central ideas of Kant's principle of humanity, which calls on us to treat human beings as ends, and never as mere means. These dual notions require interpretation, as O'Neill (one of the preeminent scholars of Kantian ethics in the last several decades) well recognizes. To treat someone as a means is innocent enough—it is simply to rely on her to help you to achieve one of your goals. But to treat someone as a mere means is to treat her in a way that she cannot in principle consent to. Treating someone as an end is to show her the respect that she is due, owing to her rationality and autonomy. This amounts to treating her in ways that she *can* consent to.

The question here is whether, in spending money on our own pleasures rather than on giving to aid agencies that will save the lives of famine victims, we are thereby violating our moral obligations. O'Neill applies the rudiments of the Kantian ethic to provide an answer. Our moral obligations to aid others are discretionary—we must do some good, but we are allowed to choose the times and the ways in which we offer such help. Of course, we must treat no such victims as mere means—we must not coerce or deceive them, for instance. But how much (if anything) must we do for them?

From Onora O'Neill, "A Kantian Approach to Famine Relief," in Tom Regan, ed., *Matters of Life and Death*, second edition (New York: Random House, 1986), pp. 322–329.

In addressing this question, O'Neill contrasts the Kantian view with a utilitarian one, which requires that we give such aid until the point at which, were we to give any more, we would become as badly off as our intended beneficiaries. The Kantian view is less demanding. As O'Neill indicates, the Kantian can offer no precise formula for specifying the amount and kind of aid that one must give to victims of famine relief. Still, because of its emphasis on the importance of developing one's capacities for autonomous choice, and because of the severe ways in which famine threatens those capacities, Kantian ethics places a high priority on providing such aid.

The Formula of the End in Itself

Kant states the Formula of the End in Itself as follows:

> Act in such a way that you always treat humanity, whether in your own person or in the person of any other, never simply as a means but always at the same time as an end.

To understand this we need to know what it is to treat a person as a means or as an end. According to Kant, each of our acts reflects one or more *maxims*. The maxim of the act is the principle on which one sees oneself as acting. A maxim expresses a person's policy, or if he or she has no settled policy, the principle underlying the particular intention or decision on which he or she acts. Thus, a person who decides "This year I'll give 10 percent of my income to famine relief " has as a maxim the principle of tithing his or her income for famine relief.

Whenever we act intentionally, we have at least one maxim and can, if we reflect, state what it is. When we want to work out whether an act we propose to do is right or wrong, according to Kant, we should look at our maxims. We just have to check that the act we have in mind will not use anyone as a mere means, and, if possible, that it will treat other persons as ends in themselves.

Using Persons as Mere Means

To use someone as a *mere means* is to involve them in a scheme of action *to which they could not in principle consent*. Kant does not say that there is anything wrong about using someone as a means. Evidently we have to do so in any cooperative scheme of action. If I cash a check I use the teller as a means, without whom I could not lay my hands on the cash; the teller in turn uses me as a means to earn his or her living. But in this case, each party consents to her or his part in the transaction. Kant would say that though they use one another as means, they do not use one another as *mere* means. Each person assumes that the other has maxims of his or her own and is not just a thing or a prop to be manipulated.

But there are other situations where one person uses another in a way to which the other could not in principle consent. For example, one person may make a promise to another with every intention of breaking it. If the promise is accepted, then the person to whom it was given must be ignorant of what the promisor's intention (maxim) really is. Successful false promising depends on deceiving the person to whom the promise is made about what one's real maxim is. And since the person who is deceived doesn't know that real maxim, he or she can't in principle consent to his or her part in the proposed scheme of action. The person who is deceived is, as it were, a prop or a tool—a mere means—in the false promisor's scheme. In Kant's view, it is this that makes false promising wrong.

In Kant's view, acts that are done on maxims that require deception or coercion of others, and so cannot have the consent of those others, are wrong. When we act on such maxims, we treat others as mere means, as things rather than as ends in themselves. If we act on such maxims, our acts are not only wrong but unjust: such acts wrong the particular others who are deceived or coerced.

Treating Persons as Ends in Themselves

To treat someone as an end in him- or herself requires in the first place that one not use him or her as mere means, that one respect each as a rational person with his or her own maxims. But beyond that, one may also seek to foster others' plans and maxims by sharing some of their ends. To act beneficently is to seek others' happiness, therefore to intend to achieve some of the things that those others aim at with their maxims. Beneficent acts try to achieve what others want. However, we cannot seek everything that others want; their wants are too numerous and diverse, and, of course, sometimes incompatible. It follows that beneficence has to be selective.

There is a sharp distinction between the requirements of justice and of beneficence in Kantian ethics. Justice requires that we act on *no* maxims that use others as mere means. Beneficence requires that we act on *some* maxims that foster others' ends, though it is a matter for judgment and discretion which of their ends we foster. Kantians will claim that they have done nothing wrong if none of their acts is unjust, and that their duty is complete if in addition their life plans have been reasonably beneficent.

Kantian Deliberations on Famine Problems

The theory I have just sketched may seem to have little to say about famine problems. For it is a theory that forbids us to use others as mere means but does not require us to direct our benevolence first to those who suffer most. A conscientious Kantian, it seems, has only to avoid being unjust to those who suffer famine and can then be beneficent to those nearer home. He or she would not be obliged to help the starving, even if no others were equally distressed.

Kant's moral theory does make less massive demands on moral agents than utilitarian moral theory. On the other hand, it is somewhat clearer just what the more stringent demands are, and they are not negligible. We have here a contrast between a theory that makes massive but often indeterminate demands and a theory that makes fewer but less unambiguous demands and leaves other questions, in particular the allocation of beneficence, unresolved.

Kantian Duties of Justice in Times of Famine

In famine situations, Kantian moral theory requires unambiguously that we do no injustice. We should not act on any maxim that uses another as mere means, so we should neither deceive nor coerce others. Such a requirement can become quite exacting when the means of life are scarce, when persons can more easily be coerced, and when the advantage of gaining more than what is justly due to one is great.

First, where there is a rationing scheme, one ought not to cheat and seek to get more than one's share—any scheme of cheating will use someone as mere means. Nor may one take advantage of others' desperation to profiteer or divert goods onto the black market or to accumulate a fortune out of others' misfortunes. Transactions that are outwardly sales and purchases can be coercive when one party is desperate. All the forms of corruption that deceive or put pressure on others are also wrong: hoarding unallocated food, diverting relief supplies for private use, corruptly using one's influence to others' disadvantage. Such requirements are far from trivial and frequently violated in hard times. In severe famines, refraining from coercing and deceiving may risk one's own life and require the greatest courage.

Second, justice requires that in famine situations one still try to fulfill one's duties to particular others. For example, even in times of famine, a person has duties to try to provide for dependents. These duties may, tragically, be unfulfillable. If they are, Kantian ethical theory would not judge wrong the acts of a person who had done her or his best. A conscientious attempt to meet the particular obligations one has undertaken may also require of one many further maxims of self-restraint and of endeavor—for example, it may require a conscientious attempt to avoid having (further) children; it may require contributing one's time and effort to programs of economic development. Where there is no other means to fulfill particular obligations, Kantian principles may require a generation of sacrifice.

The obligations of those who live with or near famine are undoubtedly stringent and exacting; for those who live further off it is harder to see what a Kantian moral theory demands. Might it not, for example, be permissible to do nothing at all about those suffering famine? Might one not ensure that one does nothing unjust to the victims of famine by adopting no maxims whatsoever that mention them? To do so would, at the least, require one to refrain from certain deceptive and coercive practices frequently employed during the European exploration and economic penetration of the now underdeveloped world and still not unknown. For example, it would be unjust to "purchase" valuable lands and resources from persons who don't understand commercial transactions or exclusive property rights or mineral rights, and so do not understand that their acceptance of trinkets destroys their traditional economic pattern and way of life. The old adage "trade follows the flag" reminds us to how great an extent the economic penetration of the less-developed countries involved elements of coercion and deception, so was on Kantian principles unjust (regardless of whether or not the net effect has benefited the citizens of those countries).

Few persons in the developed world today find themselves faced with the possibility of adopting on a grand scale maxims of deceiving or coercing persons living in poverty. But at least some people find that their jobs require them to make decisions about investment and aid policies that enormously affect the lives of those nearest to famine. What does a commitment to Kantian moral theory demand of such persons?

It has become common in writings in ethics and social policy to distinguish between one's *personal responsibilities* and one's *role responsibilities*. So a person may say, "As an individual I sympathize, but in my official capacity I can do nothing"; or we may excuse persons' acts of coercion because they are acting in some particular capacity—e.g., as a soldier or a jailer. On the other hand, this distinction isn't made or accepted by everyone. At the Nuremberg trials of war criminals, the defense "I was only doing my job" was disallowed, at least for those whose command position meant that they had some discretion in what they did. Kantians generally would play down any distinction between a person's own responsibilities and his or her role responsibilities. They would not deny that in any capacity one is accountable for certain things for which as a private person one is not accountable. For example, the treasurer of an organization is accountable to the board and has to present periodic reports and to keep specified records. But if she fails to do one of these things for which she is held accountable she will be held responsible for that failure—it will be imputable to her as an individual. When we take on positions, we *add* to our responsibilities those that the job requires; but we do not lose those that are already required of us. Our social role or job gives us, on Kant's view, no license to use others as mere means.

If persons are responsible for all their acts, it follows that it would be unjust for aid officials to coerce persons into accepting sterilization, wrong for them to use coercive power to achieve political advantages (such as military bases) or commercial advantages (such as trade agreements that will harm the other country). Where a less-developed country is pushed to exempt a multinational corporation from tax laws, or to construct out of its meager tax revenues the infrastructure of roads, harbors, or airports (not to mention executive mansions) that the corporation—but perhaps not the country—needs, then one suspects that some coercion has been involved.

The problem with such judgments—and it is an immense problem—is that it is hard to identify coercion and deception in complicated institutional settings. It is not hard to understand what is coercive about one person threatening another with serious injury if he won't comply with the first person's suggestion. But it is not at all easy to tell where the outward forms of political and commercial negotiation—which often involve an element of threat—have become coercive.

Kantian Duties of Beneficence in Times of Famine

The grounds of duties of beneficence are that such acts develop or promote others' ends and, in particular, foster others' capacities to pursue ends, to be autonomous beings.

Clearly there are many opportunities for beneficence. But one area in which the *primary* task of developing others' capacity to pursue their own ends is particularly needed is in the parts of the world where extreme poverty and hunger leave people unable to pursue any of their other ends. Beneficence directed at putting people in a position to pursue whatever ends they may have has, for Kant, a stronger claim on us than beneficence directed at sharing ends with those who are already in a position to pursue varieties of ends. It would be nice if I bought a tennis racquet to play with my friend who is tennis mad and never has enough partners; but it is more important to make people able to plan their own lives to a minimal extent. It is nice to walk a second mile with someone who requests one's company; better to share a cloak with someone who may otherwise be too cold to make any journey. Though these suggestions are not a detailed set of instructions for the allocation of beneficence by Kantians, they show that relief of famine must stand very high among duties of beneficence.

The Limits of Kantian Ethics: Intentions and Results

Kantian ethics differs from utilitarian ethics both in its scope and in the precision with which it guides action. Every action, whether of a person or of an agency, can be assessed by utilitarian methods, provided only that information is available about all the consequences of the act. The theory has unlimited scope, but, owing to lack of data, often lacks precision. Kantian ethics has a more restricted scope. Since it assesses actions by looking at the maxims of agents, it can only assess intentional acts. This means that it is most at home in assessing individuals' acts; but it can be extended to assess acts of agencies that (like corporations and governments and student unions) have decision-making procedures.

It may seem a great limitation of Kantian ethics that it concentrates on intentions to the neglect of results. It might seem that all conscientious Kantians have to do is to make sure that they never intend to use others as mere means, and that they sometimes intend to foster others' ends. And, as we all know, good intentions sometimes lead to bad results, and correspondingly, bad intentions sometimes do no harm, or even produce good.

If Hardin is right, the good intentions of those who feed the starving lead to dreadful results in the long run. If some traditional arguments in favor of capitalism are right, the greed and selfishness of the profit motive have produced unparalleled prosperity for many.

But such discrepancies between intentions and results are the exception and not the rule. For we cannot just *claim* that our intentions are good and do what we will. Our intentions reflect what we expect the immediate results of our action to be. Nobody credits the "intentions" of a couple who practice neither celibacy nor contraception but still insist "we never meant to have (more) children." Conception is likely (and known to be likely) in such cases. Where people's expressed intentions ignore the normal and predictable results of what they do, we infer that (if they are not amazingly ignorant) their words do not express their true intentions. The Formula of the End in Itself applies to the intentions on which one acts—not to some prettified version that one may avow. Provided this intention—the agent's real intention—uses no other as mere means, he or she does nothing unjust. If some of his or her intentions foster others' ends, then he or she is sometimes beneficent. It is therefore possible for people to test their proposals by Kantian arguments even when they lack the comprehensive causal knowledge that utilitarianism requires. Conscientious Kantians can work out whether they will be doing wrong by some act even though they know that their foresight is limited and that they may cause some harm or fail to cause some benefit.

Utilitarianism and Respect for Life

Utilitarians value happiness and the absence or reduction of misery. As a utilitarian one ought (if conscientious) to devote one's life to achieving the best possible balance of happiness over misery. If one's life plan remains in doubt, this will be because the means to this end are often unclear. But whenever the causal tendency of acts is clear, utilitarians will be able to discern the acts they should successively do in order to improve the world's balance of happiness over unhappiness.

This task is not one for the faint-hearted. First, it is dauntingly long, indeed interminable. Second, it may at times require the sacrifice of happiness, and even of lives, for the sake of a greater happiness. As our control over the means of ending and preserving human life has increased, analogous dilemmas have arisen in many areas for utilitarians. Should life be preserved at the cost of pain when modern medicine makes this possible?

Should life be preserved without hope of consciousness? Should triage policies, because they may maximize the number of survivors, be used to determine who should be left to starve? All these questions can be fitted into utilitarian frameworks and answered *if* we have the relevant information. And sometimes the answer will be that human happiness demands the sacrifice of unwilling lives. Further, for most utilitarians, it makes no difference if the unwilling sacrifices involve acts of injustice to those whose lives are to be lost. Utilitarians do not deny these possibilities, though the imprecision of our knowledge of consequences often blurs the implications of the theory. If we peer through the blur, we see that the utilitarian view is that lives may indeed be sacrificed for the sake of a greater good even when the persons are not willing. There is nothing wrong with using another as a mere means provided that the end for which the person is so used is a happier result than could have been achieved any other way, taking into account the misery the means have caused. In utilitarian thought, persons are not ends in themselves. Their special moral status derives from their being means to the production of happiness. Human life has therefore a high though derivative value, and one life may be taken for the sake of greater happiness in other lives, or for ending misery in that life. Nor is there any deep difference between ending a life for the sake of others' happiness by not helping (e.g., by triaging) and doing so by harming.

Utilitarian moral theory has then a rather paradoxical view of the value of human life. Living, conscious humans are (along with other sentient beings) necessary for the existence of everything utilitarians value. But it is not their being alive but the state of their consciousness that is of value. Hence, the best results may require certain lives to be lost—by whatever means—for the sake of the total happiness and absence of misery that can be produced.

Kant and Respect for Persons

Kantians reach different conclusions about human life. Human life is valuable because humans (and conceivably other beings, e.g., angels or apes) are the bearers of rational life. Humans are able to choose and to plan. This capacity and its exercise are of such value that they ought not to be sacrificed, for anything of lesser value. Therefore, no one rational or autonomous creature should be treated as mere means for the enjoyment or even the happiness of another. We may in Kant's view justifiably—even nobly— risk or sacrifice our lives for others. For in doing so we follow our own maxim and nobody uses us as mere means. But no others may use either our lives or our bodies for a scheme that they have either coerced or deceived us into joining. For in doing so they would fail to treat us as rational beings; they would use us as mere means and not as ends in ourselves.

Onora O'Neill: A Kantian Approach to Famine Relief

1. O'Neill contrasts the Kantian and utilitarian views about the nature and extent of our moral obligations to famine victims. Which elements of these views do you find especially attractive or objectionable?
2. The Kantian offers people a lot of discretion about how to fulfill their general obligation to benefiting others. How appealing do you find such discretion?
3. Contrast the Kantian and utilitarian views about respect for life. Which do you find more attractive and why?
4. O'Neill does not discuss the Kantian principle of universalizability (see Chapter 9). What are the implications of this principle for our duties to give to famine relief?
5. How does the importance of autonomy and rationality figure into the Kantian picture of our obligations to famine victims?

======= ❧ =======

22

International Aid: Not the Cure You're Hoping For

Jason Brennan

....

Jason Brennan focuses on two questions in this piece. First: Why are some countries rich and others poor? Second: Does international aid actually succeed in lifting people out of poverty? The answers he offers may be surprising.

Brennan thinks that many people, and most philosophers, mistake their way when thinking about these questions because they fail to appreciate the relevant economic facts about how nations become wealthy and about how ineffective international aid really is. In this selection he emphasizes the importance of relying on claims that have achieved consensus among economists.

Many people think that some countries are rich, and others poor, either because rich countries have much greater natural resources than poor ones, or have gained their riches by exploiting poor countries. Brennan claims instead that wealthy countries got that way, and stay that way (when they do), because they have excellent institutions. A poor country can transform its wealth if it reorganizes itself to reduce corruption, increase the freedoms of its citizens, and free its markets of needless government control.

In answer to the second question, Brennan claims that international aid does very little good. It can, he concedes, save some lives in

---

Jason Brennan, "International Aid: Not the Cure You Were Hoping For," in Robert Fischer, ed., *Ethics, Left and Right: The Moral Issues that Divide Us.* Oxford University Press 2019, pp. 160-168.

emergency situations. But the chance that it leads to long-term benefits for poor populations is slim to none. It's a common assumption, but mistaken nonetheless, that we can easily end world poverty if rich countries simply gave some portion of their wealth to the poor. The problem with this thinking, according to Brennan, is that it fails to appreciate how crucial good institutions are to sustaining the health and well-being of a nation's population. Giving money or food aid directly to impoverished countries rarely improves their institutions, and so does little, in the end, to improve the lives of the needy.

....

Many people are too poor to meet their basic needs. The good news is that extreme poverty (defined as living on less than $1.90 per capita per day) is disappearing before our eyes. In 1820, about 95% of people lived in extreme poverty. By 1960, that had only dropped to about 66%. Now, less than 10% of the world lives in extreme poverty. Perhaps most remarkably, these numbers are proportions. There are many more people around, and they're living better than ever before.[1] This is a miracle, but hardly anyone notices it.

Nevertheless, many remain mired in poverty. Surely, most of us think, something must be done. Immediately, a facile solution comes to mind: Some countries—Germany or the United States—have more than enough. (Even a person at the "poverty line" in the US is, despite the high cost of US living, among the top 14% of income earners worldwide.) So, it seems, curing world poverty is easy: The rich countries could just donate a bunch of money to the poor countries. Voila!

I wish it were that simple. This is a topic where normative reasoning and moral philosophy, in isolation, tend to lead us astray. If we genuinely care about solving world poverty, we need the tools of economics to help us answer two questions:

Why are some countries rich and others poor?

Does international aid, whether through private charities, government-to-government aid, or government-to-charity aid, actually succeed in lifting people out of poverty?

---

1. Max Roser and Esteban Ortiz-Ospina, "Global Extreme Poverty," in *Our World in Data*, accessed Feb. 2, 2018, https://ourworldindata.org/extreme-poverty/.

Philosophy might uncover what our obligations are in light of the facts, but it does not help us discover what the facts are. Unfortunately, philosophers of global justice are uninterested in or even hostile to learning the facts. Philosophers tend to advocate the policies economists know don't work, and tend to reject the institutions economists know work.

The overwhelming consensus in economics is that rich countries are rich because they have good institutions, while poor countries are poor because they have bad institutions. Further, the consensus is that aid generally doesn't work. Under special conditions, certain targeted forms of aid can prevent death during an immediate crisis, but that's about it. I'll explain both of these points below.

False Starts

Many people believe that global justice requires wealth redistribution from rich to poor countries. Most who find redistributive views appealing do so because they also hold mistaken beliefs about empirical matters. They usually accept one or more the following claims:

1. The reason some countries are rich and others are poor is that natural resources are unevenly distributed around the globe. The rich are rich because they have or had access to more or better resources than the poor countries did.
2. The reason some countries are rich and others are poor is that the rich countries (through conquest, colonialism, and empire) *extracted* resources from the poor countries.
3. We can easily end world poverty if rich countries simply gave some portion of their wealth to the poor.

These are *economic* claims. But they play an important role in many people's normative reasoning. People who accept these claims regard world poverty as a simple problem of misallocation: too much here, too little there. The obvious next step is to argue for redistribution in order to fix the misallocation. But the problem here is that each of these three claims is *false*.

The first two claims hold that differences in wealth result from a zero-sum process. I'll take a closer look below. But here, let's pause to note that wealth has been made, not simply moved around. We've seen an explosion of wealth and income over the past two hundred years. In 1990 US dollars, GDP/capita in 1 AD was about $457, rising to $712 by 1820. But look what's happened since:

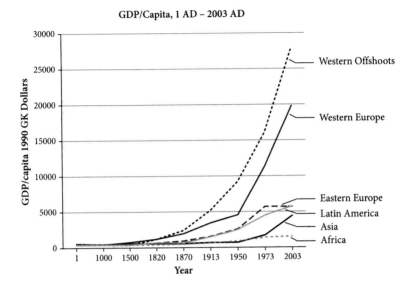

FIGURE 1[2]

When the history of economic growth is drawn on a chart, as in Fig. 1, it looks like a hockey stick. In the past 200 years, *real* (that is, inflation and cost-of-living adjusted) per capita world product has increased by a factor of at least 30. The United States' economy this year will produce *more*, in real terms, than the entire world did in 1950.

When the Great Enrichment began, Western Europe and the Western European offshoots grew faster than the rest of the world. As a result, the gap between Europe's standard of living and the rest of the world also grew. But even the poorest regions enjoyed *some* growth. It's not that Western Europe and the European offshoots grew rich while the other countries became even poorer. It's not as though Western Europe grew rich at the rate others grew poor, which would suggest a zero-sum reallocation of a fixed stock of wealth. Rather, all countries started off as poor; some got *slightly* richer over time, while the European countries and their offshoots got *much* richer over time.

Why?

---

2. Chart made using data from Angus Maddison, *Contours of the World Economy, 1–2030 AD: Essays in Macro-Economic History* (New York: Oxford University Press 2007), 70.

Wrong Answer One: Natural Resources

Philosopher Thomas Pogge claims the world's rich have excluded the poor from their fair share of the world's natural resources. Pogge thinks this unjust. He claims people worldwide have a right to "a proportional resource share."[3]

Philosophers often assume differential natural resources explain why some countries are rich and others poor. But, as economist David Weil summarizes the empirical literature in his widely used textbook *Economic Growth*, "the effect of natural resources on income is weak at best."[4] For instance, China after the 1950s was and remains poorer (in per capita income and other standard measures) than Singapore or Hong Kong, though the latter have almost *no* natural resources to speak of. The USSR was much poorer than the USA, though the USSR had far better natural resources. In Adam Smith's time, the Netherlands and England were richer than France, though France had far better natural resources. And so on.

Indeed, while natural resources can sometimes spur growth, they more frequently *inhibit* growth. Economists refer to this problem as the "resource curse": countries with a high concentration of easily extractable natural resources frequently suffer from economic stagnation.

Just why this is so is debated. One explanation may be that countries with abundant natural resources "do not develop the cultural attributes necessary for economic success," in part because necessity is the mother of invention.[5] Another theory is that countries that enjoy resource booms tend to consume the sudden influx income in an unsustainable way. They don't develop capital, but eat away the extra income until it's gone. (See, e.g., Venezuela.) Perhaps the most popular theory (or, more precisely, the theory thought to identify the most significant set of causes) is that when a country enjoys abundant resources, this encourages governments to act in destructive ways. Regardless, the idea that resources explain wealth is widely accepted by laypeople, but widely rejected by economists.

---

3. Thomas Pogge, "Eradicating Systemic Poverty: Brief for a Global Resources Dividend," *Journal of Human Development* 2(2001): 59–77, p. 65.
4. David Weil, *Economic Growth*, 3rd Edition (New York: Pearson, 2013), 453.
5. Weil, *Economic Growth*, 450.

Wrong Answer Two: Imperialism

A second popular view holds that that rich countries are rich because they (or their predecessors), through policies of colonialism, imperialism, and resource extraction, stole from the so-called third world. ... As Pogge says,

> [E]xisting radical inequality is deeply tainted by how it accumulated through one historical process that was deeply pervaded by enslavement, colonialism, even genocide. The rich are quick to point out that they cannot inherit their ancestor's sins. Indeed. But how can they then be entitled to the fruits of these sins: to their huge inherited advantage in power and wealth over the rest of the world?[6]

On this view, imperialist extraction explains (or helps to explain) why developed countries became wealthy and why undeveloped countries are poor. Our wealth is inherited stolen wealth.

European countries indeed conquered Africans, Asians, and Native Americans, murdered and enslaved them, and stole their resources for use back home. Does such theft explain why European countries and some of their offshoots are rich? If you've never taken an economics class, you'll probably presume, as Pogge does, that the answer is yes.

But economists think the answer is no. Indeed, Adam Smith's 1776 *Wealth of Nations*—the book that founded modern economics—is fundamentally an economic critique of imperialism. Smith carefully surveyed the economic value of the goods Britain and other countries had extracted from the Americas and elsewhere, and then compared that to the costs these countries incurred to create and maintain those empires. Smith concluded:

> The rulers of Great Britain have, for more than a century past, amused the people with the imagination that they possessed a great empire on the west side of the Atlantic. This empire, however, [is] ... not a gold mine, but the project of a gold mine; a project which has cost, which continues to cost, and which, if pursued in the same way as it has been hitherto, is likely to cost, immense expense, without being likely to bring any profit; for the effects of the monopoly of the colony trade, it has been shown, are, to the great body of the people, mere loss instead of profit.[7]

---

6. Thomas Pogge, "Poverty and Human Rights," accessed Feb. 2, 2018, http://www2.ohchr.org/english/issues/poverty/expert/docs/Thomas_Pogge_Summary.pdf
7. Adam Smith, *The Wealth of Nations*, V.3.92.

Smith found that a minority of politically well-connected people benefitted from the empire, but the majority of British subjects *lost* money. The losers lost more than the winners won. The costs of creating and maintaining the empire greatly *exceeded* the value of the raw materials obtained. (To illustrate: Imagine you paid $50K to buy a gun to rob people, but you only got $25K in earnings from all your muggings. You thereby *lost* money on your robberies.) Further, Smith showed, imperialism distorted the economy (by encouraging inefficient production methods) and so further hurt Britain and other imperial powers. Britain was getting richer despite its empire, not because of it.

The thrust of Smith's views is widely accepted. The general view among economists—who have better data today than Smith did back then—is that empires do not pay for themselves, even if we focus narrowly on the economic interests of imperial powers and ignore the harm they did to those they conquered.

However, while imperialism does not explain why some countries are rich, it may partly explain why some now remain poor. When imperialist powers established colonies, they replaced existing institutions with new institutions. As economists Daron Acemoglu, Simon Johnson, and James Robinson show, the kinds of institutions imperial powers set up depended on whether Europeans could settle in the colonies. In places such as North America, where European settlers faced low mortality rates (because there were low risks of disease), imperial powers exported well-functioning, growth-creating institutions.[8] In places such as the Congo, where Europeans faced high mortality rates (because of disease), imperial powers established growth-inhibiting extractive institutions. When the European powers abandoned or lost their colonies, these bad institutions remained behind, and generally morphed into the dysfunctional institutions those countries have today.

You might think this concession justifies redistribution: "Aha! Belgium should redistribute some of its wealth to the Congo. After all, even if the Belgians lost money in their rape, murder, and robbery of the Congo, it's still their fault that the Congo is doing badly today." In the same way, this argument goes, suppose I spent $500 to buy a gun, and then rob you,

---

8. Or better, ended up being forced to set up inclusive institutions. See Daron Acemoglu, Simon Johnson, and James Robinson, "The Colonial Origins of Comparative Development: An Empirical Investigation," *American Economic Review* 91 (2001): 1369–1401; Daron Acemoglu and James Robinson, *Why Nations Fail* (New York: Crown Business, 2013).

but only get $250 from doing so. Even though I lost money when I robbed you, I still owe you compensation.

But this argument treats countries as if they were people, and it obscures morally important facts. It's not that the Belgian or British people chose, as a group, to steal from Africans or Native Americans. Rather, what really happened was that, years ago, in what were non-democratic countries, the kings and queens, plus some political insiders, taxed the Belgian and British subjects to buy guns, soldiers, and warships, and then used those to steal from the Africans and Native Americans. The Belgian and British subjects were *also* victims of imperialism—their leaders exploited them (through taxes and conscription) to then exploit others (through conquest and theft). So, demanding the Belgians pay restitution to the Congo is demanding the descendants of some victims pay restitution to the descendants of other victims. Imagine Queen Isabella robs my grandpa to buy a gun, which she then uses to kill your grandpa. It's bizarre to hold that this would require me to compensate you.

Institutions Are the Answer, Unfortunately

The dominant view in mainstream development economics is that sustained economic growth results mainly from having good economic and political institutions. Institutions "are the rules of the game in a society or, more formally, are the humanly devised constraints that shape human interaction."[9] As economist Dani Rodrik summarizes, when it comes to explaining economic growth and why some countries are rich and others poor, "the quality of institutions trumps everything else."[10]

Which institutions produce growth? Countries with A) robust systems of private property and B) open markets, C) protected by the rule of law enforced by D) stable and inclusive governments, offer much better prospects for significant and sustained development than those that lack such institutions. The countries with institutions A–D, such as Switzerland, Canada, Singapore, or Hong Kong, are nearly always rich; the countries that lack A–D are nearly always poor. The reasons why are well understood, though I can only summarize them here.

---

9. Douglas North, *Institutions, Institutional Change, and Economic Performance* (Cambridge: Cambridge University Press, 1990), 3.

10. Dani Rodrik, Arvind Subramanian, and Francisco Trebbi, "Institutions Rule: The Primacy of Institutions over Geography and Integration in Economic Development," *Journal of Economic Growth* 9 (2004): 131–165.

As Acemoglu and Robinson argue in *Why Nations Fail*, the main difference between good and bad institutions concerns the degree to which they foster extractive activity or instead encourage cooperation and productivity. The main difference concerns whom the institutions empower, and thus whom the institutions benefit. What they call *inclusive* institutions, such as open markets and strong protections for private property, empower people across society, and thus tend to benefit all. They give people a stake in and ability to invest long term and engage in mutually beneficial capital accumulation. By contrast, *extractive* institutions—such as dictatorships where the government owns the natural resources, or overly regulated economies where rent seekers rig the rules—empower only some, and thus tend to benefit only small groups of people at others' expense.

It's "unfortunate" that the institutional theory of wealth is correct. The reason it's unfortunate is that while we know which institutions create growth and which impede it, we don't know how to induce social change. We don't know how to get countries with bad institutions to switch to good institutions. Part of the reason institutional change is so difficult is that the leaders of countries with bad institutions nearly always have a stake in those bad institutions—they make their living by exploiting their subjects or selling favors.

The Aid Illusion

Though developed countries didn't get rich at the expense of poor countries, you might still hope we could solve world poverty by giving away money. It's a simple idea. We're rich. They're poor. We give them some cash. They stop being poor.

As Nobel Laureate economist Angus Deaton (himself an aid skeptic) notes, if that argument were sound, then curing world poverty would require barely anything from us:

> One of the stunning facts about global poverty is how little it would take to fix it, at least if we could magically transfer money into the bank accounts of the world's poor. In 2008, there were about 800 million people in the world living on less than $1.00 a day. On average, each of these people is "short" about $0.28 a day. ... We could make up that shortfall with less than a quarter billion dollars a day ... Taking ... into account [differences in purchasing power in poor countries], ... world poverty could be eliminated if every American adult donated $0.30 a day; or, if we could build a coalition of the willing from all the adults of

Britain, France, Germany, and Japan, each would need to give only $0.15 a day.[11]

People may be selfish, but surely no one would balk at 15 cents a day to end extreme world poverty. It seems so easy!

But it's not easy, as Deaton then explains. In the past 50 years, hundreds of billions of dollars have been spent on government-to-government and other forms of international aid. Just between 2000 and 2010, governments provided $128 billion in foreign aid.[12] Has it done any good?

Looking at Africa over the past 50 years, Deaton finds an inverse relationship between growth and aid. He summarizes the empirics:

> Growth *decreased* steadily while aid *increased* steadily. When aid fell off, after the end of the Cold War, growth picked up; the end of the Cold War took away one of the main rationales for aid to Africa, and African growth rebounded. ... [A] more accurate punchline would be "the Cold War is over, and Africa won," because the West reduced aid.[13]

Economists Left and Right generally agree. (Philosophers of global justice generally ignore such economics, or cherry pick the minority dissenting studies.) In a comprehensive review of the existing empirical literature, Hristos Doucouliagos and Martin Paldam conclude that, overall, "after 40 years of years of development aid, the evidence indicates that aid has not been effective."[14] Overall, the research generally finds that aid is more likely to hurt than help. In general, economists find that aid helps a bit in countries that have pretty good institutions, but tends to hurt in countries with bad institutions.[15]

Why would it *hurt*? Acemoglu and Robinson write,

> The idea that rich Western countries should provide large amounts of "development aid" in order to solve the problem of [world] poverty ... is based on an incorrect understanding of what causes poverty. Countries such as Afghanistan are poor because of their extractive institutions—which result in a lack of property rights, law and order, or well-functioning legal systems and the stifling domination of national

11. Angus Deaton, *The Great Escape* (Princeton: Princeton University Press, 2013), 268–269.

12. Christopher Coyne, *Doing Bad by Doing Good: Why Humanitarian Aid Fails* (Stanford: Stanford University Press, 2013), 47.

13. Deaton, *Great Escape*, 285.

14. Hristos Doucouliagos and Martin Paldam, "Aid Effectiveness on Accumulation: A Meta Study," *Kyklos* 59 (2006): 227–254.

15. Here, I draw from Coyne, *Doing Bad by Doing Good*, 51.

and, more often, local elites over political and economic life. The same institutional problems mean that foreign aid will be ineffective, as it will be plundered and is unlikely to be delivered where it is supposed to go. In the worst-case scenario, it will prop up the regimes that are the very root of the problems of those societies.[16]

The problem is that poor countries suffer negative feedback loops. They are governed by abusive elites, people who make a living (and stay in power) by extracting resources from their countries and people. In such conditions, to pour more money into a country usually means lining the pockets of the abusers, not feeding the hungry.

When rulers make a living by extracting resources from their societies, sending more money means increasing the rewards of being in power. Foreign aid tends to make bad governments thrive without the support of their citizens, encourage factions within those countries (different agencies, bureaucracies, strongmen) to compete for power in order to gain control of the incoming aid, and tends to subsidize corruption. It escalates conflicts, civil wars, and human rights violations. Rather than inducing development and growth, aid often prolongs and worsens the conditions that produce poverty and need in the first place.

No one denies that aid *can* do good sometimes. Christopher Coyne, himself another major critic of foreign aid, finds that aid seems to be most effective in increasing pre-determined outputs in response to clear-cut crises. If there's a sudden famine, buying and distributing food stops starvation. (Though, as Coyne documents, it can also fail at that, and sometimes even makes things worse.[17])

But there is distinction between *aid* and *development*. Development happens when a society begins to grow economically, and the conditions that cause people's poverty start to disappear. There is simply no track record of aid helping to spur economic development. The reasons why are clear: To get rich, countries need good institutions, but you can't export good institutions the way you can send a sack of rice.

An Obligation to Help Is an Obligation to Help

Philosophers of global justice spend their time debating which normative principles would ground duties of international aid. To induce their

16. Acemoglu and Robinson, *Why Nations Fail*, 452–453.
17. Coyne, *Doing Bad by Doing Good*.

readers to have moral intuitions which favor redistribution, they often rely on thought experiments like these:

1. If grandma gave 20 of her grandchildren 80% of the pie, and the other 166 grandkids only 20%, should the rich 20 give the poor 166 more pie?
2. Suppose my grandpa stole your grandpa's watch, which I then inherit. Should I give it "back" to you?
3. If I see a kid drowning in a puddle, shouldn't I save him, even if saving him ruins my expensive shoes?

Philosophers think the actual world is analogous to thought experiments like these. This makes foreign aid seem morally mandatory.

But economics, surprisingly, tells us that philosophers are bad at philosophy. The problem is that these three thought experiments, and all the variations on them, are *irrelevant*. The gap between rich and poor did not result from an unfair initial distribution of resources or from theft. And saving the world's poor from poverty looks almost nothing like pulling a drowning kid from a pond.

In 1799, US President George Washington got a bad sore throat. His family called in doctors, who then killed him. Yes, killed him. His doctors (the best available in his day) subscribed to false and counterproductive beliefs about medicine. They bled him multiple times, extracting at least forty-eight ounces of blood. They also blistered his skin, induced vomiting, and administered an enema. The dehydrated president then died. When Martha Washington sent for the doctors, despite her best intentions, she was ordering a death sentence.

An obligation to help the poor is an obligation to actually help them. Good intentions don't matter. Too often, developed countries play the part of Washington's doctors, killing instead of helping, administering a medicine worse than the disease. Philosophers of global justice today play the role of Martha Washington. They mean well, but they're calling in the bad doctors.

I'm not saying we should do nothing. I'm instead claiming we should do what works. "We" (the people in the developed world) helped Taiwan, Hong Kong, South Korea, and Japan—countries that were poor in the 1950s but are rich today—become rich not by giving them aid, but by buying their products as they liberalized their economies. If we want to help, we will open borders to immigrants and we'll increase international trade. We'll confine foreign aid to its rightful place and stop pretending it's the solution.

Jason Brennan: International Aid: Not the Cure You Were Hoping For

1. If Brennan is right, the solution to world poverty requires massive change to the institutions of poorer countries. Assuming that is correct, what, if anything, are the obligations of richer countries to help with such institutional change?

2. Brennan allows that many rich nations have a history of exploiting ones that are now poor, but denies that this generates any duty of compensation or reparation. Do you agree with his reasoning? Why or why not?

3. Does the dire need of others ever, by itself, impose a moral duty to assist them? If not, why not? If so, does this justify some duty to provide aid to distant strangers?

4. Would it be morally acceptable for wealthier countries to provide aid to poorer ones, but only on the condition that the poorer nations improved their institutions?

5. Brennan says that, when it comes to foreign aid, "good intentions don't matter"—results do. If an aid program fails to help the needy, then it is unjustified, no matter how well-meaning the donors. Do you agree? Why or why not?

23

═══ ❧ ═══

The Morality of Euthanasia

James Rachels

....

James Rachels (1941–2003) argues that active euthanasia is sometimes morally permissible. Active euthanasia occurs when someone (typically a medical professional) takes action to deliberately end a patient's life, at the patient's request, for the patient's own good. Rachels argues that considerations of mercy play a vital role in justifying active euthanasia in many cases.

He first considers a utilitarian argument on behalf of active euthanasia, but finds problems with utilitarianism that are weighty enough to undermine this argument. However, Rachels believes that a different version can succeed. In this one, Rachels claims that any action that promotes the best interests of all concerned, and that violates no rights, is morally acceptable. Since, he claims, active euthanasia sometimes satisfies this description, it is sometimes morally acceptable.

....

The single most powerful argument in support of euthanasia is the argument from mercy. It is also an exceptionally simple argument, at least in its main idea, which makes one uncomplicated point. Terminally ill patients sometimes suffer pain so horrible that it is beyond the comprehension of those who have not actually experienced it. Their

---

From "Euthanasia," in Tom Beauchamp, ed., *Matters of Life and Death*, 2nd ed. (McGraw-Hill, 1986), pp. 49–52.

suffering can be so terrible that we do not like even to read about it or think about it; we recoil even from the descriptions of such agony. The argument from mercy says euthanasia is justified because it provides an end to *that*.

The great Irish satirist Jonathan Swift took eight years to die, while, in the words of Joseph Fletcher, "His mind crumbled to pieces." At times the pain in his blinded eyes was so intense he had to be restrained from tearing them out with his own hands. Knives and other potential instruments of suicide had to be kept from him. For the last three years of his life, he could do nothing but sit and drool: and when he finally died it was only after convulsions that lasted thirty-six hours.

Swift died in 1745. Since then, doctors have learned how to eliminate much of the pain that accompanies terminal illness, but the victory has been far from complete. So, here is a more modern example.

Stewart Alsop was a respected journalist who died in 1975 of a rare form of cancer. Before he died, he wrote movingly of his experiences as a terminal patient. Although he had not thought much about euthanasia before, he came to approve of it after rooming briefly with someone he called Jack:

> The third night that I roomed with Jack in our tiny double room in the solid-tumor ward of the cancer clinic of the National Institutes of Health in Bethesda, Md., a terrible thought occurred to me.
>
> Jack had a melanoma in his belly, a malignant solid tumor that the doctors guessed was about the size of a softball. The cancer had started a few months before with a small tumor in his left shoulder, and there had been several operations since. The doctors planned to remove the softball-sized tumor, but they knew Jack would soon die. The cancer had metastasized—it had spread beyond control.
>
> Jack was good-looking, about 28, and brave. He was in constant pain, and his doctor had prescribed an intravenous shot of a synthetic opiate—a pain-killer, or analgesic—every four hours. His wife spent many of the daylight hours with him, and she would sit or lie on his bed and pat him all over, as one pats a child, only more methodically, and this seemed to help control the pain. But at night, when his pretty wife had left (wives cannot stay overnight at the NIH clinic) and darkness fell, the pain would attack without pity.
>
> At the prescribed hour, a nurse would give Jack a shot of the synthetic analgesic, and this would control the pain for perhaps two hours or a bit more. Then he would begin to moan, or whimper, very low, as though he didn't want to wake me. Then he would begin to howl, like a dog.

When this happened, either he or I would ring for a nurse, and ask for a pain-killer. She would give him some codeine or the like by mouth, but it never did any real good—it affected him no more than half an aspirin might affect a man who had just broken his arm. Always the nurse would explain as encouragingly as she could that there was not long to go before the next intravenous shot—"Only about 50 minutes now." And always poor Jack's whimpers and howls would become more loud and frequent until at last the blessed relief came.

The third night of this routine the terrible thought occurred to me. "If Jack were a dog," I thought, "what would be done with him?" The answer was obvious: the pound, and chloroform. No human being with a spark of pity could let a living thing suffer so, to no good end.

The NIH clinic is, of course, one of the most modern and best-equipped hospitals we have. Jack's suffering was not the result of poor treatment in some backward rural facility; it was the inevitable product of his disease, which medical science was powerless to prevent.

I have quoted Alsop at length not for the sake of indulging in gory details but to give a clear idea of the kind of suffering we are talking about. We should not gloss over these facts with euphemistic language or squeamishly avert our eyes from them. For only by keeping them firmly and vividly in mind can we appreciate the full force of the argument from mercy: If a person prefers—and even begs for—death as the only alternative to lingering on *in this kind of torment*, only to die anyway after a while, then surely it is not immoral to help this person die sooner. As Alsop put it, "No human being with a spark of pity could let a living thing suffer so, to no good end."

The Utilitarian Version of the Argument

In connection with this argument, the utilitarians deserve special mention. They argued that actions and social policies should be judged right or wrong *exclusively* according to whether they cause happiness or misery; and they argued that when judged by this standard, euthanasia turns out to be morally acceptable. The utilitarian argument may be elaborated as follows:

(1) Any action or social policy is morally right if it serves to increase the amount of happiness in the world or to decrease the amount of misery. Conversely, an action or social policy is morally wrong if it serves to decrease happiness or to increase misery.

(2) The policy of killing, at their own request, hopelessly ill patients who are suffering great pain would decrease the amount of misery in the world. (An example could be Alsop's friend Jack.)

(3) Therefore, such a policy would be morally right.

The first premise of this argument, (1), states the Principle of Utility, which is the basic utilitarian assumption. Today most philosophers think that this principle is wrong, because they think that the promotion of happiness and the avoidance of misery are not the *only* morally important things. Happiness, they say, is only one among many values that should be promoted: freedom, justice, and a respect for people's rights are also important. To take one example: people *might* be happier if there were no freedom of religion, for if everyone adhered to the same religious beliefs, there would be greater harmony among people. There would be no unhappiness caused within families by Jewish girls marrying Catholic boys, and so forth. Moreover, if people were brainwashed well enough, no one would mind not having freedom of choice. Thus happiness would be increased. But, the argument continues, even if happiness *could* be increased this way, it would not be right to deny people freedom of religion, because people have a right to make their own choices. Therefore, the first premise of the utilitarian argument is unacceptable.

There is a related difficulty for utilitarianism, which connects more directly with the topic of euthanasia. Suppose a person is leading a miserable life—full of more unhappiness than happiness—but does *not* want to die. This person thinks that a miserable life is better than none at all. Now I assume that we would all agree that the person should not be killed; that would be plain, unjustifiable murder. Yet it *would* decrease the amount of misery in the world if we killed this person—it would lead to an increase in the balance of happiness over unhappiness—and so it is hard to see how, on strictly utilitarian grounds, it could be wrong. Again, the Principle of Utility seems to be an inadequate guide for determining right and wrong. So we are on shaky ground if we rely on *this* version of the argument from mercy for a defense of euthanasia.

Doing What Is in Everyone's Best Interests

Although the foregoing utilitarian argument is faulty, it is nevertheless based on a sound idea. For even if the promotion of happiness and avoidance of misery are not the *only* morally important things, they are still very important. So, when an action or a social policy would decrease misery, that is *a* very strong reason in its favor. In the cases of voluntary euthanasia we are now considering, great suffering is eliminated, and since the patient requests it, there is no question of violating individual rights. That is why, regardless of the difficulties of the Principle of Utility, the utilitarian version of the argument still retains considerable force.

I want now to present a somewhat different version of the argument from mercy, which is inspired by utilitarianism but which avoids the difficulties of the foregoing version by not making the Principle of Utility a premise of the argument. I believe that the following argument is sound and proves that active euthanasia *can* be justified:

1. If an action promotes the best interests of everyone concerned and violates *no one's* rights, then that action is morally acceptable.
2. In at least some cases, active euthanasia promotes the best interests of everyone concerned and violates no one's rights.
3. Therefore, in at least some cases, active euthanasia is morally acceptable.

It would have been in everyone's best interests if active euthanasia had been employed in the case of Stewart Alsop's friend Jack. First, and most important, it would have been in Jack's own interests, since it would have provided him with an easier, better death, without pain. (Who among us would choose Jack's death, if we had a choice, rather than a quick painless death?) Second, it would have been in the best interests of Jack's wife. Her misery, helplessly watching him suffer, must have been almost unbearable. Third, the hospital staff's best interests would have been served, since if Jack's dying had not been prolonged, they could have turned their attention to other patients whom they could have helped. Fourth, other patients would have benefited, since medical resources would no longer have been used in the sad, pointless maintenance of Jack's physical existence. Finally, if Jack himself requested to be killed, the act would not have violated his rights. Considering all this, how can active euthanasia in this case be wrong? How can it be wrong to do an action that is merciful, that benefits everyone concerned, and that violates no one's rights?

James Rachels: The Morality of Euthanasia

1. Would someone in circumstances like Jack's be better off dead? That is, would dying quickly and painlessly be in his best interest?

2. What are Rachels's objections to the principle of utility? Do you find them convincing?
3. How does Rachels's second argument differ from the utilitarian argument? Do you agree with Rachels that it is a stronger argument?
4. Rachels claims that euthanasia cannot be said to violate anyone's rights, given that the patient requests it. Do you find this claim plausible? Is it possible to do something that violates someone's rights even if he or she consents to it?
5. Rachels claims that (in some cases) active euthanasia promotes the interests of everyone concerned. If our society were to allow active euthanasia, would this be harmful to anyone's interests? Why or why not?

24

The Survival Lottery

John Harris

In this paper, John Harris invites us to consider the merits of a special sort of organ transplant scheme, which he calls the survival lottery. Each year, many thousands of people die because of organ failure and the lack of a suitable donor organ. Harris proposes that we remedy this situation by instituting a lottery among (almost) all citizens. Whenever two or more people are in need of a vital organ, we pick a citizen at random to be vivisected (dissected while alive—though presumably under anesthesia!), so that his or her organs can be distributed to those who need them to survive.

We don't do this with any sort of punitive intent, but rather in order to minimize the number of people who die, through no fault of their own, because of organ failure. True, the organ donor being killed is wholly innocent. But then so are those who are dying for lack of a donor organ.

Harris is well aware that the lottery sounds like outright murder, and he devotes the bulk of the article to presenting, and then countering, a great many objections to it. He acknowledges that there may be problems with making such a system feasible in practice. If these problems could be ironed out, however, Harris thinks that rational and morally enlightened people would endorse this proposal for their own society.

John Harris, "The Survival Lottery" from *Philosophy* 50 (1975), pp. 81–87. Reprinted with the permission of Cambridge University Press.

Let us suppose that organ transplant procedures have been perfected; in such circumstances if two dying patients could be saved by organ transplants then, if surgeons have the requisite organs in stock and no other needy patients, but nevertheless allow their patients to die, we would be inclined to say, and be justified in saying, that the patients died because the doctors refused to save them. But if there are no spare organs in stock and none otherwise available, the doctors have no choice, they cannot save their patients and so must let them die. In this case we would be disinclined to say that the doctors are in any sense the cause of their patients' deaths. But let us further suppose that the two dying patients, Y and Z, are not happy about being left to die. They might argue that it is not strictly true that there are no organs which could be used to save them. Y needs a new heart and Z new lungs. They point out that if just one healthy person were to be killed his organs could be removed and both of them be saved. We and the doctors would probably be alike in thinking that such a step, while technically possible, would be out of the question. We would not say that the doctors were killing their patients if they refused to prey upon the healthy to save the sick. And because this sort of surgical Robin Hoodery is out of the question we can tell Y and Z that they cannot be saved, and that when they die they will have died of natural causes and not of the neglect of their doctors. Y and Z do not however agree, they insist that if the doctors fail to kill a healthy man and use his organs to save them, then the doctors will be responsible for their deaths.

Many philosophers have for various reasons believed that we must not kill even if by doing so we could save life. They believe that there is a moral difference between killing and letting die. On this view, to kill A so that Y and Z might live is ruled out because we have a strict obligation not to kill but a duty of some lesser kind to save life. A. H. Clough's dictum "Thou shalt not kill but need'st not strive officiously to keep alive" expresses bluntly this point of view. The dying Y and Z may be excused for not being much impressed by Clough's dictum. They agree that it is wrong to kill the innocent and are prepared to agree to an absolute prohibition against so doing. They do not agree, however, that A is more innocent than they are. Y and Z might go on to point out that the currently acknowledged right of the innocent not to be killed, even where their deaths might give life to others, is just a decision to prefer the lives of the fortunate to those of the unfortunate. A is innocent in the sense that he has done nothing to deserve death, but Y and Z are also innocent in this sense. Why should they be the ones to die simply because they are so unlucky as to have diseased organs?

Why, they might argue, should their living or dying be left to chance when in so many other areas of human life we believe that we have an obligation to ensure the survival of the maximum number of lives possible?

Y and Z argue that if a doctor refuses to treat a patient, with the result that the patient dies, he has killed that patient as sure as shooting, and that, in exactly the same way, if the doctors refuse Y and Z the transplants that they need, then their refusal will kill Y and Z, again as sure as shooting. The doctors, and indeed the society which supports their inaction, cannot defend themselves by arguing that they are neither expected, nor required by law or convention, to kill so that lives may be saved (indeed, quite the reverse) since this is just an appeal to custom or authority. A man who does his own moral thinking must decide whether, in these circumstances, he ought to save two lives at the cost of one, or one life at the cost of two. The fact that so called "third parties" have never before been brought into such calculations, have never before been thought of as being involved, is not an argument against their now becoming so. There are of course, good arguments against allowing doctors simply to haul passers-by off the streets whenever they have a couple of patients in need of new organs. And the harmful side-effects of such a practice in terms of terror and distress to the victims, the witnesses and society generally, would give us further reasons for dismissing the idea. Y and Z realize this and have a proposal, which they will shortly produce, which would largely meet objections to placing such power in the hands of doctors and eliminate at least some of the harmful side-effects.

In the unlikely event of their feeling obliged to reply to the reproaches of Y and Z, the doctors might offer the following argument: they might maintain that a man is only responsible for the death of someone whose life he might have saved, if, in all the circumstances of the case, he ought to have saved the man by the means available. This is why a doctor might be a murderer if he simply refused or neglected to treat a patient who would die without treatment, but not if he could only save the patient by doing something he ought in no circumstances to do—kill the innocent. Y and Z readily agree that a man ought not to do what he ought not to do, but they point out that if the doctors, and for that matter society at large, ought on balance to kill one man if two can thereby be saved, then failure to do so will involve responsibility for the consequent deaths. The fact that Y's and Z's proposal involves killing the innocent cannot be a reason for refusing to consider their proposal, for this would just be a refusal to face the question at issue and so avoid having to make a decision as to what ought to be done in circumstances like these. It is Y's and Z's claim that failure to adopt their plan will also involve killing the innocent, rather more of the innocent than the proposed alternative.

To back up this last point, to remove the arbitrariness of permitting doctors to select their donors from among the chance passers-by outside hospitals, and the tremendous power this would place in doctors' hands, to mitigate worries about side-effects and lastly to appease those who wonder why poor old A should be singled out for sacrifice, Y and Z put forward the following scheme: they propose that everyone be given a sort of lottery number. Whenever doctors have two or more dying patients who could be saved by transplants, and no suitable organs have come to hand through "natural" deaths, they can ask a central computer to supply a suitable donor. The computer will then pick the number of a suitable donor at random and he will be killed so that the lives of two or more others may be saved. No doubt if the scheme were ever to be implemented a suitable euphemism for "killed" would be employed. Perhaps we would begin to talk about citizens being called upon to "give life" to others. With the refinement of transplant procedures such a scheme could offer the chance of saving large numbers of lives that are now lost. Indeed, even taking into account the loss of the lives of donors, the numbers of untimely deaths each year might be dramatically reduced, so much so that everyone's chance of living to a ripe old age might be increased. If this were to be the consequence of the adoption of such a scheme, and it might well be, it could not be dismissed lightly. It might of course be objected that it is likely that more old people will need transplants to prolong their lives than will the young, and so the scheme would inevitably lead to a society dominated by the old. But if such a society is thought objectionable, there is no reason to suppose that a program could not be designed for the computer that would ensure the maintenance of whatever is considered to be an optimum age distribution throughout the population.

Suppose that inter-planetary travel revealed a world of people like ourselves, but who organized their society according to this scheme. No one was considered to have an absolute right to life or freedom from interference, but everything was always done to ensure that as many people as possible would enjoy long and happy lives. In such a world a man who attempted to escape when his number was up or who resisted on the grounds that no one had a right to take his life, might well be regarded as a murderer. We might or might not prefer to live in such a world, but the morality of its inhabitants would surely be one that we could respect. It would not be obviously more barbaric or cruel or immoral than our own.

Y and Z are willing to concede one exception to the universal application of their scheme. They realize that it would be unfair to allow people who have brought their misfortune on themselves to benefit from the lottery. There would clearly be something unjust about killing the abstemious B so that W (whose heavy smoking has given him lung cancer) and X (whose drinking has destroyed his liver) should be preserved to overindulge again.

What objections could be made to the lottery scheme? A first straw to clutch at would be the desire for security. Under such a scheme we would never know when we would hear *them* knocking at the door. Every post might bring a sentence of death, every sound in the night might be the sound of boots on the stairs. But, as we have seen, the chances of actually being called upon to make the ultimate sacrifice might be slimmer than is the present risk of being killed on the roads, and most of us do not lie trembling a-bed, appalled at the prospect of being dispatched on the morrow. The truth is that lives might well be more secure under such a scheme.

If we respect individuality and see every human being as unique in his own way, we might want to reject a society in which it appeared that individuals were seen merely as interchangeable units in a structure, the value of which lies in its having as many healthy units as possible. But of course Y and Z would want to know why A's individuality was more worthy of respect than theirs.

Another plausible objection is the natural reluctance to play God with men's lives, the feeling that it is wrong to make any attempt to re-allot the life opportunities that fate has determined, that the deaths of Y and Z would be "natural," whereas the death of anyone killed to save them would have been perpetrated by men. But if we are able to change things, then to elect not to do so is also to determine what will happen in the world.

Neither does the alleged moral differences between killing and letting die afford a respectable way of rejecting the claims of Y and Z. For if we really want to counter proponents of the lottery, if we really want to answer Y and Z and not just put them off, we cannot do so by saying that the lottery involves killing and object to it for that reason, because to do so would, as we have seen, just beg the question as to whether the failure to save as many people as possible might not also amount to killing.

To opt for the society which Y and Z propose would be then to adopt a society in which saintliness would be mandatory. Each of us would have to recognize a binding obligation to give up his own life for others when called upon to do so. In such a society anyone who reneged upon this duty would be a murderer. The most promising objection to such a society, and indeed to any principle which required us to kill A in order to save Y and Z, is, I suspect, that we are committed to the right of self-defence. If I can kill A to save Y and Z then he can kill me to save P and Q, and it is only if I am prepared to agree to this that I will opt for the lottery or be prepared to agree to a man's being killed if doing so would save the lives of more than one other man. Of course there is something paradoxical about basing objections to the lottery scheme on the right of self-defence since, *ex hypothesi*, each person would have a better chance of living to a ripe old age if the lottery scheme were to be implemented. None the less, the feeling that no man should be required to lay down his life for others makes many people shy away from such a scheme, even though it might be rational to accept it on prudential grounds, and perhaps even mandatory on utilitarian grounds. Again, Y and Z would reply that the right of self-defence must extend to them as much as to anyone else; and while it is true that they can only live if another man is killed, they would claim that it is also true that if they are left to die, then someone who lives on does so over their dead bodies.

It might be argued that the institution of the survival lottery has not gone far to mitigate the harmful side-effects in terms of terror and distress to victims, witnesses and society generally, that would be occasioned by doctors simply snatching passers-by off the streets and disorganizing them for the benefit of the unfortunate. Donors would after all still have to be procured, and this process, however it was carried out, would still be likely to prove distressing to all concerned. The lottery scheme would eliminate the arbitrariness of leaving the life and death decisions to the doctors, and remove the possibility of such terrible power falling into the hands of any individuals, but the terror and distress would remain. The effect of having to apprehend presumably unwilling victims would give us pause. Perhaps only a long period of education or propaganda could remove our abhorrence. What this abhorrence reveals about the rights and wrongs of the situation is however more difficult to assess. We might be inclined to say that only monsters could ignore the promptings of conscience so far as to operate the lottery scheme. But the promptings of conscience are not necessarily the most reliable guide. In the present case Y and Z would argue that such promptings are mere squeamishness, an over-nice self-indulgence that costs lives. Death, Y and Z would remind us, is a distressing experience whenever and to whomever it occurs, so the less it occurs the better. Fewer victims and witnesses will be distressed as part of the side-effects of the lottery scheme than would suffer as part of the side-effects of not instituting it.

Lastly, a more limited objection might be made, not to the idea of killing to save lives, but to the involvement of "third parties." Why, so the objection goes, should we not give X's heart to Y or Y's lungs to X, the same number of lives being thereby preserved and no one else's life set at risk? Y's and Z's reply to this objection differs from their previous line of argument. To amend their plan so that the involvement of so called "third parties" is ruled out would, Y and Z claim, violate their right to equal concern and respect with the rest of society. They argue that such a proposal would amount to treating the unfortunate who need new organs as a class within society whose lives are considered to be of less value than those of its more fortunate members. What possible justification could there be for singling out one group of people whom we would be justified in using as donors but not another? The idea in the mind of those who would propose such a step must be something like the following: since Y and Z cannot survive, since they are going to die in any event, there is no harm in putting their names into the lottery, for the chances of their dying cannot thereby be increased and will in fact almost certainly be reduced. But this is just to ignore everything that Y and Z have been saying. For if their lottery scheme is adopted they are not going to die anyway—their chances of dying are no greater and no less than those of any other participant in the lottery whose number may come up. This ground for confining selection of donors to the unfortunate therefore disappears. Any other ground must discriminate against Y and Z as members of a class whose lives are less worthy of respect than those of the rest of society.

It might more plausibly be argued that the dying who cannot themselves be saved by transplants, or by any other means at all, should be the priority selection group for the computer programme. But how far off must death be for a man to be classified as "dying"? Those so classified might argue that their last few days or weeks of life are as valuable to them (if not more valuable) than the possibly longer span remaining to others. The problem of narrowing down the class of possible donors without discriminating unfairly against some sub-class of society is, I suspect, insoluble.

Such is the case for the survival lottery. Utilitarians ought to be in favour of it, and absolutists cannot object to it on the ground that it involves killing the innocent, for it is Y's and Z's case that any alternative must also involve killing the innocent. If the absolutist wishes to maintain his objection he must point to some morally relevant difference between positive and negative killing. This challenge opens the door to a large topic with a whole library of literature, but Y and Z are dying and do not have time to explore it exhaustively. In their own case the most likely candidate for some feature which might make this moral difference is the malevolent intent of Y and Z themselves. An absolutist might well argue that while no one intends the deaths of Y and Z, no one necessarily wishes them dead, or aims at their demise for any reason, they do mean to kill A (or have him killed). But Y and Z can reply that the death of A is no part of their plan, they merely wish to use a couple of his organs, and if he cannot live without them . . . tant pis! None would be more delighted than Y and Z if artificial organs would do as well, and so render the lottery scheme otiose.

One form of absolutist argument perhaps remains. This involves taking an Orwellian stand on some principle of common decency. The argument would then be that even to enter into the sort of "macabre" calculations that Y and Z propose displays a blunted sensibility, a corrupted and vitiated mind. Forms of this argument have recently been advanced by Noam Chomsky (*American Power and the New Mandarins*) and Stuart Hampshire (*Morality and Pessimism*). The indefatigable Y and Z would of course deny that their calculations are in any sense "macabre," and would present them as the most humane course available in the circumstances. Moreover they would claim that the Orwellian stand on decency is the product of a closed mind, and not susceptible to rational argument. Any reasoned defence of such a principle must appeal to notions like respect for human life, as Hampshire's argument in fact does, and these Y and Z could make conformable to their own position.

Can Y and Z be answered? Perhaps only by relying on moral intuition, on the insistence that we do feel there is something wrong with the survival lottery and our confidence that this feeling is prompted by some morally relevant difference between our bringing about the death of A and our bringing about the deaths of Y and Z. Whether we could retain this confidence in our intuitions if we were to be confronted by a society in which the survival lottery operated, was accepted by all, and was seen to save many lives that would otherwise have been lost, it would be interesting to know.

There would of course be great practical difficulties in the way of implementing the lottery. In so many cases it would be agonizingly difficult to decide whether or not a person had brought his misfortune on himself. There are numerous ways in which a person may contribute to his predicament, and the task of deciding how far, or how decisively, a person is himself responsible for his fate would be formidable. And in those cases where we can be confident that a person is innocent of responsibility for his predicament, can we acquire this confidence in time to save him? The lottery scheme would be a powerful weapon in the hands of someone willing and able to misuse it. Could we ever feel certain the lottery was safe from unscrupulous computer programmers? Perhaps we should be thankful that such practical difficulties make the survival lottery an unlikely consequence of the perfection of transplants. Or perhaps we should be appalled.

It may be that we would want to tell Y and Z that the difficulties and dangers of their scheme would be too great a price to pay for its benefits. It is as well to be clear, however, that there is also a high, perhaps an even higher, price to be paid for the rejection of the scheme. That price is the lives of Y and Z and many like them, and we delude ourselves if we suppose that the reason why we reject their plan is that we accept the sixth commandment.

John Harris: The Survival Lottery

1. What exactly is a survival lottery, and how would it work? Do you think it would be morally permissible to institute one?
2. Some people might object to Harris's proposal by claiming that it is never morally permissible to kill innocent people. Why doesn't Harris think this is a good objection? Do you find his criticisms of this objection convincing?
3. Another objection to the survival lottery claims that any such policy would cause widespread terror, since anyone could be selected to have his or her organs harvested. Is this a good objection? How does Harris respond?
4. Harris allows one exception to the universal application of the survival lottery. What is the exception? Do you agree that these individuals should be excluded from the lottery?
5. Some might think that instituting a survival lottery amounts to "playing God." What does it mean to "play God"? Is it always wrong to do so?
6. What "practical difficulties" does Harris think we would face if we tried to institute a survival lottery? Could these difficulties be overcome?

25

Refugees and the Right to Control Immigration
Christopher Heath Wellman

....

Christopher Heath Wellman's article is an extended defense of the moral rights of legitimate states to exclude outsiders, including those who hope to immigrate to such states. The right to exclude is not, he thinks, absolute. But while there may be some exceptions, the right is more robust and extensive than many assume. It is so strong that legitimate states typically have a moral right to exclude even refugees from their borders, should they choose to do so.

Wellman's core argument is built upon three assumptions. First, legitimate states are morally entitled to self-determination. Second, freedom of association is a very important element of self-determination. And, third, freedom of association entitles one to refuse to associate with others. Together, these support the view that legitimate states are morally entitled to refuse to "associate" with non-citizens, which means, in practical terms, that such states may deny outsiders entry to the state's territory or an offer of citizenship.

Wellman uses an argument from analogy to support his views. A person has a right to self-determination, which entitles her to freedom of association, which gives her a right to refuse to associate with others at her discretion. This right explains why it would be wrong to force a person to get married against her will, or to take someone into her

---

This essay was commissioned for the fifth edition of *The Ethical Life*.

home when she wants to bar the door against him. Legitimate states possess these rights as well, and they entitle such states to refuse, at their discretion, to extend citizenship or residence to outsiders.

Wellman realizes that many wealthier countries have a history of exploiting the countries whose citizens are seeking to emigrate. But he believes that there are usually ways, other than by allowing immigration, by which those wealthier states can fulfill their duties of justice to those they have wronged.

....

I believe that legitimate states have a right to political self-determination which entitles them to design and enforce their own immigration policies.[1] This right is admittedly not absolute, but I do not think it is outweighed as easily or as often as most presume. To support these claims, I shall defend a legitimate state's right to exclude outsiders and then argue that this right is typically not outweighed by the competing claims of refugees.

The Right to Exclude

My argument for a legitimate state's right to exclude outsiders is built on three foundational premises: (1) legitimate states are entitled to self-determination, (2) freedom of association is an integral component of self-determination, and (3) freedom of association entitles one to refuse to associate with others as one sees fit. Based on this reasoning, I conclude that, just as an individual's right to self-determination explains why she may choose whether or not to marry any given suitor, the citizens of a legitimate state are free collectively to offer or refuse membership in their political community to any given prospective immigrant.

It is not difficult to establish the truth of the second and third premises. To see that freedom of association is integral to self-determination and that enjoying freedom of association requires that one be free to refuse to associate with others, we need only imagine a setting in which one's

---

1. This paper utilizes excerpts from my book (co-authored with Phillip Cole), *Debating the Ethics of Immigration: Is There a Right to Exclude?* (New York: Oxford University Press, 2011), in which these ideas and arguments are developed and defended at greater length.

father, say, has sole discretion to choose who his children will marry. Whatever one might think of this type of arrangement, it clearly does not respect rights to self-determination. Freedom of association involves more than merely the right to get married, it includes the right to reject any and all suitors one prefers not to marry. And this explains why those of us who value individual autonomy take such offense at the thought of institutions which bestow upon parents the authority to force spouses on their children.

But while few deny that individuals have a right to freedom of association in the marital realm, some may question whether corporate political entities are the types of things that could have such a right. To see that states are entitled to an analogous sphere of political self-determination, think of a country like Norway and its relations with Sweden and the European Union. Norway is currently an associate member of the EU, and it enjoys close relations with Sweden, the country from which it seceded in 1905. But now imagine that Sweden (inspired, perhaps by the reunification of Germany) wanted to reunite with Norway or that the EU wanted Norway to become a full member. Would Sweden or the EU have the right to unilaterally annex Norway, or would it be impermissible for them to do so without Norway's consent? It seems clear that neither Sweden nor the EU is morally entitled to forcibly annex Norway. If either wants to merge with Norway, it may invite Norway to join forces, but Norway is free to either accept or decline such an invitation. Indeed, even if it is clear to all that the Norwegians would be better off after the merger, it remains Norway's decision to make, and no other country or international organization may permissibly force itself onto Norway without its consent.

And notice that one cannot insist upon Norway's right to remain independent of Sweden without implicitly affirming its right to self-determination, because the best explanation for the impermissibility of Sweden's unilateral annexation of Norway is that it violates Norway's sovereign right to independence. But if Norway's right to self-determination entitles it to refuse to associate with other corporate political entities like Sweden or the EU, then why is it not similarly within its rights to refuse to associate with any given Swedish or European citizen? It seems to me, then, that just as an individual has a right to determine whom (if anyone) he or she would like to marry, a group of fellow-citizens has a right to determine whom (if anyone) it would like to invite into its political community. And just as an individual's freedom of association entitles one to remain single, a legitimate state's freedom of association entitles it to exclude all foreigners from its political community.

Here two potential objections present themselves. First, it may strike some as misleading to compare having discretion over one's partner in marriage to the selection of potential immigrants, because having control over one's associates is plainly paramount in marital relations but seems of little consequence within the relatively impersonal context of political life. Second, even if we concede that a legitimate state's right to freedom of association applies in its relations to other countries or international institutions, this seems quite different from alleging that large political regimes enjoy freedom of association with respect to individual foreigners.

In response to the first worry, I admit that freedom of association is considerably more important in intimate relations. Acknowledging this is unproblematic, however, since it amounts to conceding only that rights to freedom of association are more valuable in intimate contexts, not that they do not exist elsewhere. At most, then, this objection merely highlights that it may require more to defeat the presumptive right in intimate contexts. Notice, however, that there are many non-intimate associations where we rightly value freedom of association very highly. Religious associations in which people attend to matters of conscience and political groups through which members express themselves can often be large and impersonal, and yet we are extremely reluctant to restrict their associative rights.

Despite the admitted lack of intimacy, freedom of association is also clearly important for political states. To appreciate this, notice that even members of relatively insignificant associations like golf clubs are often (understandably) concerned about their control over potential members. These members typically care about their club's membership rules for at least two sets of reasons. First and most obviously, the size of the club affects one's experience as a member. In the case of a private golf club, for instance, some may want to expand membership, so that each individual will be required to pay less in dues, while others might well be against adding new members for fear that the increased number of golfers will result in limited access to, and more wear and tear on, the golf course. In short, whereas some might be motivated to cut costs, others will be happy to pay higher fees for a more exclusive golfing experience. Second and perhaps less obviously, members will care about the rules of membership because all new members will subsequently have a say in how the club is organized. In other words, caring about one's experience as a club member gives one reason to care about the rules for admitting new members, because, once admitted, new members will typically have a say in determining the future course of the club.

And if the reasons to concern oneself with the membership rules of one's golf club are straightforward, there is nothing curious about people caring so much about the rules governing who may enter their political communities, even though a citizen will typically never meet, let alone have anything approaching intimate relations with, the vast majority of her compatriots. Indeed, there are a number of obvious reasons why citizens would care deeply about how many and which type of immigrants can enter their country. Even if we put to one side all concerns about the state's culture, economy, and political functioning, for instance, people's lives are obviously affected by substantial changes in population density, so it seems only natural that citizens who like higher population density would welcome huge numbers of immigrants, while those with contrary tastes would prefer a more exclusive policy. And in the real world, of course, a substantial influx of foreigners will also almost invariably affect the host state's cultural make-up, the way its economy functions, and/or how its political system operates. And let me be clear: I am not assuming that all of these changes will necessarily be for the worse. More modestly, I am emphasizing only that citizens will often care deeply about their country's culture, economy and political arrangements, and thus, depending upon their particular preferences, may well seek more or fewer immigrants, or perhaps more or fewer immigrants of a given linguistic, cultural, economic and/or political profile.

In the case of Mexican immigrants into the United States, for instance, it is not the least bit surprising that some favor a more open policy, while others lobby for the government to heighten its efforts to stem what they regard as a "flood" of unwelcome newcomers. Without taking a stand on this particular controversy, here I wish to stress only the obvious point that, even with large anonymous groups like contemporary bureaucratic states, the number and types of constituents have an obvious and direct effect upon what it is like to be a member of these groups. Thus, unless one questions why anyone would care about their experience as citizens, there is no reason to doubt that we should be so concerned about our country's immigration policy. What is more, as in the case of golf clubs, the crucial point is that—whether one interacts personally with them or not—one's fellow citizens play roles in charting the course that one's country takes. And since a country's immigration policy determines who has the opportunity to join the current citizens in shaping the country's future, this policy will matter enormously to any citizen who cares what course her political community will take.

This connection between a group's membership and its future direction underscores why freedom of association is such an integral component of self-determination. No collective can be fully self-determining without enjoying freedom of association because, when the members of a group can change, an essential part of group self-determination is exercising control over what the "self" is. To appreciate this point, consider again the controversy over Mexican immigration into the United States. It is not merely that large numbers of these immigrants would almost certainly change the culture of those areas where they tend to relocate *en masse*; it is also that (if legally admitted and given the standard voting rights of citizenship) these new members will help determine future laws in the United States, including its immigration policy toward other potential immigrants from Mexico (and elsewhere). Thus, if I am right that legitimate political states are entitled to political self-determination, there appears to be every reason to conclude that this privileged position of sovereignty includes a weighty presumptive right to freedom of association, a right which entitles these states to include or exclude foreigners as they see fit.

Consider now the worry that, while legitimate states are indeed entitled to freedom of association, this right applies only against other corporate entities, such as foreign countries or international institutions; it does not hold against individual persons who would like to enter a given political community. An objector of this stripe shies away from a blanket denial of political freedom of association in recognition of the unpalatable implications such a position would allow. Think again of contemporary Norway, for instance. If one denied Norway's right to freedom of association, then there seems to be no principled way to explain why Sweden or the European Union would act impermissibly if either were to forcibly annex it. Presumably neither Sweden nor the EU may unilaterally merge with Norway; rather, Norway has the right to either accept or refuse these unions. But affirming Norway's right to reject these mergers is just to say that Norway enjoys a right to freedom of association which holds against foreign countries like Sweden and international organizations like the EU. It does not necessarily follow, this objection continues, that Norway therefore has the right to deny admittance to any given Swede or citizen of an EU country who would like to enter Norway. Indeed, in terms of self-determination, the contrast between merging with Sweden and admitting an individual Swede is striking, in that only the former would appear to seriously impact Norway's control over its internal affairs. Thus, insofar as freedom of association is defended as an important component of self-determination, perhaps sovereign states enjoy freedom of association only with respect to macro institutions and not in their micro dealings with individual persons.

An individual immigrant would admittedly not have anything like the impact on Norway's political self-determination that a forced merger with Sweden or the EU would. Nonetheless, I am unmoved by this objection for at least two basic reasons. First, we routinely (and rightly, I think) ascribe rights of freedom of association against individuals to large, non-political institutions. Second, political states would lose a crucial portion of their self-determination if they were unable to refuse to associate with individuals. Consider these points in turn.

Let us begin by considering two garden-variety large institutions like Microsoft Corporation and Harvard University. Presumably each of these institutions enjoys freedom of association, and thus Microsoft could choose to either accept or reject an offer to merge with Cisco Systems and Harvard would have the discretion as to whether or not to accept an offer to form a cooperative alliance with, say, Stanford University. But notice that we do not restrict their freedom of association exclusively to their dealings with other corporate entitles; Microsoft's and Harvard's rights to self-determination also give them discretion over their relations with individuals. No matter how qualified I may be, I may not simply assign myself a paying job at Microsoft, for instance, nor may I unilaterally decide to enroll in Harvard as a student or assume a position on their faculty. And if large bureaucratic organizations like Microsoft and Harvard are perfectly within their rights to refuse to associate with various individuals, why should we think that freedom of association would operate any differently for political states? At the very least, it seems as though anyone who wanted to press this second objection would owe us an explanation as to why the logic of freedom of association does not apply to political states as it plainly does in other contexts.

The best way to make this case would presumably be to point out that, because political states are so enormous, an individual's immigration will have no discernible impact upon any given country's capacity for self-determination. I acknowledge that one person's immigration is typically insignificant, but this fact strikes me as insufficient to vindicate the objection. Notice, for instance, that one unilaterally appointed student at

Harvard or a single employee at Microsoft would not make much of a difference at either institution, but we would never conclude from this that Harvard and Microsoft lack discretion over their respective admissions and hiring processes. What is more, as the example of Mexican immigrants into the U.S. illustrates, even if a solitary immigrant would be unlikely to have much of an impact on any given state, a sufficient number of immigrants certainly could make an enormous difference. And unless a state is able to exercise authority over the individuals who might immigrate, it is in no position to control its future self-determination. Thus, the very same principle of political self-determination which entitles Norway to either join or reject an association with other countries like those in the EU also entitles Norway to set its own immigration policy for potential individual immigrants.

To summarize our discussion of these two potential objections: Even though (1) the association among compatriots may be far less important than the intimate relations among family members, and (2) a single immigrant is likely to have no discernible influence upon a political community's capacity to be self-determining, legitimate political states have weighty presumptive rights to freedom of association which entitle them to either accept or reject individual applicants for immigration as they see fit. In short, the principle of political self-determination explains why countries have a right to design and enforce their own immigration policies. Whether any given (legitimate) state wants to have entirely open borders, exclude all outsiders, or enact some intermediate policy, it has a presumptive right to do so.

As mentioned earlier, though, this right is merely presumptive and thus remains liable to being overridden in any given set of circumstances. Below I will consider whether this presumptive right is necessarily outweighed by the competing claims of refugees. First, though, I want to emphasize that I am arguing on behalf of a *deontological* right to limit immigration rather than a *consequential* recommendation as to how any given state should act.

There is a big difference between defending an agent's right to X and recommending that this agent actually do X. One can defend Norway's right to remain independent of Sweden or the EU, for instance, without taking a stand on the separate question of whether Norway would be wise to join. This combination of positions may at first seem contradictory, but it is not. What Norway ought to do and who is entitled to decide what Norway does are two separate issues. Thus, it is important to bear in mind that, in defending a legitimate state's right to exclude potential immigrants, I am offering no opinion on the separate question as to how countries might best exercise this right.

There are several reasons I am not comfortable making any recommendations as to how jealously states should guard their borders. First and most obviously, determining what immigration policy would be best for a country's citizens and/or humanity as a whole requires knowledge of a great deal of detailed empirical information that I simply lack. Just as importantly, though, it seems to me that there is unlikely to be any "one size fits all" prescription which would be appropriate for every country in the world. On the contrary, there is no reason why a certain number and type of immigrants could not be beneficial in one country and yet quite harmful in another; it all depends on the particular social, cultural, economic and political circumstances of the host country. Consider, for instance, the economic impact of immigration. While some writers warn that opening a country's markets to outsiders will have potentially disastrous effects, others counter that the impact of open borders will (in the long run, at least) invariably be beneficial, since removing any artificial boundary will allow the market to operate more efficiently. I would guess, however, that the truth lies somewhere between these two polar positions. Even if we restrict our focus exclusively to the economic impact upon those who were initially in the host state (as these debates often implicitly presume we should), how helpful any given influx of newcomers would be seems to me to depend upon a number of factors, such as this country's antecedent level of unemployment and the types of skills and work ethic these immigrants have. In addition to determining what the overall effect of the immigrants would be, it is important to consider how the various costs and benefits are distributed. In many cases the influx of relatively unskilled workers may disproportionately help relatively wealthy business owners (who benefit from the increased supply of labor) and hurt working-class people (who now face greater competition for jobs whose wages have been decreased). Thus, if one believes that we should be especially concerned about our worst-off compatriots, then this might provide a reason of justice to limit immigration even in circumstances in which the overall net economic impact of more porous borders would be positive.

In light of these observations, I am reluctant to recommend a specific immigration policy as the ideal solution for any given (let alone every) state to follow. If forced to show my hand, however, I must confess that I would generally favor more open borders than the status quo. I appreciate that countries have a variety of good reasons to refrain from completely opening their borders, but I suspect that many of the world's current policies are more the result of unprincipled politicians' exploiting the xenophobia of their constituents for short-term political gain than of well-reasoned assessments of what will be to the long-term advantage. In saying this, however, I am in no way retreating from my contention that legitimate regimes may set their own immigration policy. In my view, there are deontological reasons to respect a legitimate state's rights of political self-determination, and so those countries which qualify have a deontologically based moral right to freedom of association. Thus, whether they exercise this right rationally or not, it is their call to make. Just as my friends and family may not forcibly interfere with my imprudent decisions to get married or divorced, for instance, external parties must respect a legitimate state's dominion over its borders, even if the resulting policy seems plainly irrational.

To recapitulate the highlights of what has been a relatively long discussion: One cannot adequately capture why it is in principle wrong for an external body such as Sweden or the EU to forcibly annex a country like Norway without invoking a state's right to political self-determination. But if legitimate political regimes enjoy a sphere of self-determination which allows them to refuse relations with foreign countries and international organizations, it seems only natural to conclude that they are similarly entitled to reject associating with individual foreigners. Thus, any regime which satisfactorily protects and respects human rights is entitled to unilaterally design and enforce its own immigration policy. In sum, just as an individual has the right to determine whom (if anyone) she would like to marry, a group of fellow-citizens has a right to determine whom (if anyone) it would like to invite into its political community. And just as an individual's freedom of association entitles her to remain single, a corporate political entity's freedom of association entitles it to exclude all foreigners.

As striking as this conclusion may sound, it is not ultimately all that controversial once one recalls that the right in question is not absolute, but merely presumptive. Many who insist that morality requires (more) open borders might happily concede all of the conclusions for which I have argued to this point, for instance, because they are confident that whatever presumptive rights legitimate states have to exclude foreigners are often (if not always) overridden by more weighty moral concerns. Space limitations do not allow me to attend to the many powerful arguments that have been offered in defense of open borders, but I will argue below that even refugees do not necessarily have as strong of a claim to immigrate as one might initially suspect. This will not establish that legitimate states may exclude all prospective immigrants, of course, but hopefully it will lend credence to my claim that a state's presumptive right to exclude outsiders holds up quite well against the competing claims of outsiders.

Refugees

Following the 1951 Convention Relating to the Status of Refugees, international law defines a refugee as someone who "owing to a well-founded fear of being persecuted for reasons of race, religion, nationality, membership of a particular social group, or political opinion, is outside the country of his nationality, and is unable to or, owing to such fear, is unwilling to avail himself of the protection of that country."[2] Critics have protested that this definition is too narrow in at least three important ways.[3] First, why focus exclusively on victims of group-based persecution? And even if we do think in terms of groups, why restrict ourselves to these particular groups? What if someone is persecuted *qua* woman or *qua* homosexual, for instance? Second, given the variety of threats to living a minimally decent human life, why insist that only those vulnerable to persecution can qualify as refugees? What about so-called economic refugees or those who are fleeing a civil war, for instance? Third, why think that someone must already be "outside the country of his nationality" in order to qualify? What if an individual is being detained at the border or is too frail or impoverished to migrate without assistance, for example?

I share these worries about this restricted definition of refugees. If human rights are best understood as the protections humans need against the standard threats to living a minimally decent life, then it strikes me that anyone whose human rights are in jeopardy should qualify as a refugee. Defined thusly, a refugee would be anyone who has a particularly urgent claim to help because her current state is either unable or unwilling to protect her human rights. I will not press this issue here, however, because our interest in refugees is as a potential exception to my claim that legitimate states have the right to exclude outsiders. Retaining the

---

2. Convention, art. 1A(2).
3. For an excellent discussion of these matters, see Andrew E. Shacknove, "Who Is a Refugee?" *Ethics* 95 (January 1985): 274–284.

traditional, narrow definition seems appropriate, then, since this provides the toughest challenge to my account.

It is not difficult to see why refugees are thought to be an especially compelling counterexample to anyone who seeks to defend a state's discretion over immigration. First, unlike someone who merely wants to migrate to improve an already good life (such as an artist who wants to live in New York, for example), the refugee is unable to live a minimally decent human life in her home country. More importantly, insofar as this person specifically needs protection from her state, she cannot be helped from abroad. Unlike a poor Chadian to whom Norwegians might ship resources, for instance, an Iraqi Kurd persecuted by Saddam Hussein's Baathist regime apparently could not be helped in any other way than by being given refuge in a foreign country. Finally, given that the refugee has fled her home country and is requesting asylum from the new state, the latter is now involved in the situation. As regrettable as it might be for Norway to refuse to send funds to starving Chadians, for instance, Norway is not thought to be implicated in their starvation in the same way it would be if it forcibly returned a Kurdish asylum seeker to Iraq, where she was subsequently tortured. Combining these points, a refugee's plight appears morally tantamount to that of a baby who has been left on one's doorstep in the dead of winter. Only a moral monster would deny the duty to bring this infant into her home, and no theorist who endorses human rights could deny that states must admit refugees.

I agree that the citizens of wealthy states are obligated to help refugees, but I am not convinced that this assistance must come in the form of more open admissions. Just as we might send food and other resources to the world's poor, we can try to help persecuted foreigners in their home state. Imagine that Iraqi Kurds request asylum in Norway, for instance. Assuming that these Kurds are in fact being persecuted, it is natural to conclude that Norway has no choice but to allow them to immigrate. But this conclusion is too hasty. While there would presumably be nothing wrong with welcoming these Iraqis into the Norwegian political community, there are other options if the Norwegians would prefer not to expand their citizenship. If Norway were able to protect these Kurds in their homeland, creating a safe haven with a no-fly zone in Northern Iraq, for instance, then there would be nothing wrong with Norway's assisting them in this fashion. (Indeed, in many ways, helping in this manner seems preferable.) The core point, of course, is that if these persecuted Kurds have a right against Norwegians, it is a general right to protection from their persecutors, not the more specific right to refuge *in Norway*. If Norway provides these Kurds refuge in Iraq, then the Kurds cease to qualify as refugees and thus no longer have any special claim to migrate to Norway.

Some will resist my proposal on the grounds that Norway should not meddle in Iraq's domestic affairs, but this objection wrongly presumes an orientation in which every *de facto* state occupies a privileged position of moral dominion over all matters on its territory. On my view, only *legitimate* states are entitled to political self-determination, where legitimacy is understood in terms of satisfactorily protecting the rights of one's constituents and respecting the rights of all others. And any state that persecutes its own citizens (as the Baathist regime did when it targeted Kurds) clearly does not adequately secure the human rights of its citizens and thus is manifestly not entitled to the normal sovereign rights which typically make humanitarian intervention in principle wrong. And note: I am not saying that it will always be easy or advisable to intervene and fix a refugee's problem at its source. (On the contrary, I would think that countries would more often prefer to admit refugees than to forcibly intervene on their behalf.) I allege only there is nothing in principle which necessarily prohibits foreign states like Norway from providing refuge to persecuted groups like Iraqi Kurds in their native countries.

At this point, one might protest that Norway must admit these Kurdish refugees at least until it has adequately secured a safe haven in Northern Iraq. This may be right: No matter how jealously the Norwegians might guard their political membership, the Kurds must not be returned until their protection against persecution can be guaranteed. It is important to notice, however, that Norwegians need not extend the benefits of political membership to these temporary visitors any more than it must give citizenship to other guests, like tourists, who are in the country for only a short time. What is more, if I am right that there is nothing wrong with Norway's intervening in Iraq once the Kurdish refugees have already arrived on Norway's doorstep, then presumably it would equally be permissible for Norway to intervene preemptively, so as to avert the mass migration. After all, Norway's intervention is justified by the initial acts of Iraqi persecution, not by the subsequent migration of masses of refugees.

Before closing, I would like to return to the analogy of the baby on the doorstep, not to insist that it is inapt, but because I think reflecting upon this domestic case actually confirms my analysis of refugees. Suppose, then, that I open my front door in the dead of winter and find a newborn baby wrapped in blankets. Clearly, I must bring the infant in from the cold, but it does not follow that I must then adopt the child and raise her as my own. Perhaps it would be permissible to do so, but it seems clear that I would not be required to incorporate this child into my family if I would prefer not to. This child has a right to a decent future, and its arrival on my doorstep may well obligate me to attend to her needs until I can find her a satisfactory home, but the infant's valid claim not to be left out in the cold does not entail the entirely distinct right to permanent inclusion in my family. I thus conclude that the analogy between a refugee and a baby left on one's doorstep is both apt and instructive. In both cases, one can non-voluntarily incur a stringent duty to help the imperiled individual. But just as one can satisfactorily discharge one's duty to the vulnerable child without permanently adopting it, a state can entirely fulfill its responsibility to persecuted refugees without allowing them to immigrate into its political community.

In the end, then, I respond to the challenge posed by the plight of refugees by conceding a stringent duty to help but insisting that this obligation is disjunctive. Just as wealthy states may permissibly respond to global poverty either by opening their borders or by helping to eliminate this poverty at its source, countries that receive refugees on their political doorstep are well within their rights either to invite these refugees into their political communities or to intervene in the refugees' home state to ensure that they are effectively protected from persecution there. I thus conclude that, as tragic as the cases of many refugees no doubt are, they do not necessarily constitute an exception to my thesis that legitimate states are entitled to exclude all outsiders, even those who desperately seek to gain admission.

Christopher Heath Wellman: Refugees and the Right to Control Immigration

1. Reconstruct Wellman's central argument for allowing legitimate states to refuse entry or citizenship to outsiders. Which premise do you think most vulnerable, and why?
2. How plausible is Wellman's analogy between, on the one hand, an individual's right to refuse to marry a suitor or refuse to let someone into her home, and, on the other, a state's right to refuse entry or citizenship to outsiders?
3. Here is another analogy: you are lost in the woods, starving, and see a cabin. It's locked, but through a window you see that there is food inside.

You can either remain outside and die of exposure or starvation, or break into the cabin and save yourself. Many would say that you are morally permitted to save yourself, and—here's the analogy—refugees are in exactly the same position with regard to wealthy countries. What are the implications of Wellman's view for this case? Do you find those implications plausible or implausible?

4. Many states have become wealthy through a long history of exploiting other countries, some of whose citizens are now seeking to emigrate. Does this history impose any duties on wealthy states to open their borders? Why or why not?

5. Some argue that an open borders policy is morally problematic because it creates "brain drain"—a situation in which a significant proportion of the most educated and talented within a struggling nation decide to emigrate, leaving the struggling country in even worse shape. Does this constitute a good reason for restricting immigration?

26

Open Borders
Javier Hidalgo

Imagine that you wake up one morning and see a wall of barbed wire surrounding your neighborhood. When you try to cross, in order to look for work, go to church, or visit a relative, a guard forbids you from doing so. In anything but a very unusual, emergency situation, enforcing this barrier violates your freedom of movement and your freedom of association. And that, in turn, threatens your freedom to seek an occupation, practice your religion, and sustain family relations.

Javier Hidalgo introduces this thought experiment to draw a clear parallel with immigration policies that place barriers against migrant entry. He allows that there may be exceptional cases where, all things considered, it is justified to block a migrant from entering a country, but those special cases aside, every country (including our own) should have open borders. Failing to do so, he argues, violates rights to freedom of movement, association, occupational choice, and religious freedom.

Hidalgo then confronts various criticisms of an open borders policy. Some claim that while it would be generous to open borders to non-citizens, we have no moral duty to do so. Hidalgo replies that we owe everyone, citizen and non-citizen alike, a wide variety of duties that require us not to interfere with their rights (including the right to

This essay was commissioned for the sixth edition of *The Ethical Life* and draws heavily on my past work, particularly: Javier Hidalgo, "The Libertarian Case for Open Borders," in *The Routledge Handbook of Libertarianism*, ed. Jason Brennan, Bas Van der Vossen, and David Schmidtz (New York, NY: Routledge, 2017), 377–389; Javier Hidalgo, *Unjust Borders: Individuals and the Ethics of Immigration* (New York, NY: Routledge, 2018), chapter 1.

move about freely). Others argue that immigration ends up costing citizens more, in order to pay for various social benefits of the new entrants. But Hidalgo points to data that indicates that more immigration tends to make societies wealthier and better off. Some claim that crime rates rise with immigration; Hidalgo denies that this is so. He then argues that closing borders would be immoral even if immigration had unavoidably negative overall social costs for existing citizens, as there are strict limits on what governments may do to help their citizens. Hidalgo once more argues by analogy: "If it's wrong for me to coerce and assault strangers in order to benefit my children, then it is hard to see why it would be fine for the government to coerce and assault foreigners for the benefit of citizens. But that's just what immigration restrictions do." Another argument is that the preservation of culture allows us to close our borders if we choose. Hidalgo replies that many immigrants assimilate to the prevailing culture, that many countries, such as the U.S., are already highly multicultural, and that we are not allowed to preserve a culture if doing so requires denying the important rights of others. Finally, he considers the objection that countries are like private clubs, and are therefore allowed to forbid others from becoming members. Hidalgo argues that this analogy is flawed; while private clubs may restrict what people wear, what they say, and the religion they practice, governments are forbidden from doing these things. This shows, says Hidalgo, that the analogy between governments and private associations is misleading.

....

1. Introduction

Gabriel Hernández Cortez is a Mexican citizen from Guanajuato in central Mexico. In Guanajuato, Gabriel worked in construction and earned a few dollars daily. Gabriel's son, Carlos, became ill and was hospitalized. The cost of Carlos's medical care was ruinous for his family's finances. His wife and two children had to move in with her parents. Meanwhile, Gabriel set out for the United States to earn more money. Gabriel says: "I prefer to stay home. But the only way to make it is to come north. . . . I just want a very tiny slice of pie. I just want to work for a little bit of money."

But Gabriel couldn't reach the United States. Gabriel tried crossing the border four times. Each time, American immigrant agents caught him and turned him back. In one case, border agents caught Gabriel as he was climbing a barbed-wire fence. An agent grabbed Gabriel by his hair and the barbed wire cut his leg. He says, "I don't blame *la migra*. They're just doing their jobs, enforcing the laws that come down from above." Gabriel remained in Naco, Sonora, and slept out in a central plaza in the city, pondering how to cross the border. I don't know what happened to him.[1]

Here's another case. Gloria lived in Phoenix with her four children where she worked as a housekeeper. She was a single mom and she was also undocumented. One day she was arrested. Her employer had been operating drop houses where unauthorized migrants would stay after crossing the border. Gloria says that she had nothing to do with it, but she was charged as an accomplice. After serving time in prison, she was deported to Mexico and lost custody of her children. The children were separated and put into foster care. Gloria now lives in Nogales, Mexico. She works in a factory for $15 per day and lives in a plywood shed. Gloria rarely sees her children. Gloria says, "When I was young and my kids were little, I thought that I could never live without them. I never thought that one day they'd grow up and I'd be far away from them. But you have to learn how to live like this." Her children visit her at the border where they can talk through a mesh fence, but these visits are infrequent. Gloria's son says, "I just sometimes feel like I'm a stranger to her. And sometimes she's a stranger to me."[2]

The laws and policies that forbid migrants like Gabriel from crossing borders and that deport migrants like Gloria are immigration restrictions. Immigration restrictions stop foreigners from crossing borders and permanently residing in another state's territory. There's nothing special about the United States, of course. Every state enforces immigration restrictions.

Are immigration restrictions justified? My answer: generally speaking, no. My overall argument goes like this. Immigration restrictions interfere with valuable freedoms, such as freedom of association and occupational choice. So, there's a presumption against immigration restrictions. Other moral considerations can in principle defeat this presumption. But they usually don't. We thus have reason to conclude that actual immigration restrictions are unjust.

---

1. This story is reported in: Margaret Regan, *The Death of Josseline: Immigration Stories from the Arizona Borderlands* (Boston, Mass.: Beacon Press, 2010), pp. 16–20.
2. This story is from: "The Walls," *This American Life*, March 16, 2018, accessed June 1, 2018, https://www.thisamericanlife.org/641/the-walls.

2. Freedom of Movement Is Valuable

Let's start with the claim that immigration restrictions interfere with valuable freedoms. To motivate this claim, let's consider a thought experiment.

Imagine that tomorrow you wake up in the morning and you start getting ready for work, just like every other day. As you're pulling out of your driveway, you notice something strange. You see walls topped with barbed wire encircling your neighborhood. You also notice police officers patrolling the area around the walls, and pulling down people who try to scale them.

You angrily ask the police officers why they're doing this. They respond: "The local government has determined that the members of your community are taking jobs from other citizens and using too many welfare benefits. Besides, your community is culturally distinct from the broader community and we can't have your community changing our culture in bad ways. Finally, doesn't the rest of the community have a right to self-determination? We can decide who we want to associate with and we've decided that we don't want to associate with you!"

Needless to say, you don't accept these arguments and you're eager to escape your neighborhood. You need to get to work, for one thing. But you also want to visit friends and family members in other parts of the city, attend concerts and classes, eventually move to a new apartment across the city, and so on. But state officials stop you from leaving. You might be injured if you evade these officials and scale the walls. Maybe you'll cut yourself on barbed wire. If you are undeterred and try to leave anyway, these officers will overpower and imprison you. Moreover, state officials will probably track you down and return you to your neighborhood even if you do manage to escape. Finally, let's suppose that public officials make it illegal for people outside of your neighborhood to interact with you by employing or sheltering you. Let's call this case *Neighborhood*.

At first glance, the actions of state officials in Neighborhood seem seriously wrong. Why's that? Well, we have strong moral reasons to refrain from coercing and harming other people. Almost everyone thinks that assault and violent threats are usually wrong. The reasons against coercion and violence speak against the actions of the state employees. After all, state officials threaten you with physical force in Neighborhood and deploy this force against you if you disobey their commands.

The deeper story is that state employees infringe on valuable liberties when they prohibit you from leaving your neighborhood. If you're unable to leave your neighborhood, you can't search for work, you can't associate with your friends and family, you can't attend your church, and you can't explore cultural opportunities outside of your neighborhood. So, state employees seem to violate your rights to freedom of association, occupational choice, religious freedom, and so on. Your personal liberties in Neighborhood are curtailed by restrictions on freedom of movement.

Reflection on Neighborhood suggests that freedom of movement is intimately connected with core freedoms. To exercise occupational freedom or religious liberty, we must have the freedom to move around. Your religious freedom is impaired if the state forbids you from traveling to the church of your choice. You lack occupational freedom if other people stop you from searching for a job or traveling to employers who are willing to hire you. The state should respect basic liberal freedoms like freedom of conscience, freedom of association, freedom of speech, and occupational freedom. And, if the state should respect these basic liberties and freedom of movement is necessary for people to exercise their basic liberties, then the state should allow freedom of movement. So, we can conclude that the state should allow freedom of movement.

You might concede that it's wrong for state officials to restrict your freedom of movement in Neighborhood. But you might argue that this is an extreme case. Sure, it's wrong for governments to put you in prison without justification. It hardly follows from this that states are obligated to respect your freedom of movement in general. Instead, maybe states are only obligated to ensure that you have an adequate range of options. The government avoids violating your rights if it restricts your freedom of movement *and* you already have an adequate range of options to live a decent life. So, this objection says that it's wrong to restrict your freedom of movement if you lack enough options to live a decent life. Otherwise, though, it can be permissible to restrict your freedom of movement.

The problem with this line of argument is that we have strong reasons to avoid restricting freedom of movement even when people already have adequate or decent options. Let's consider a new variation on Neighborhood. Imagine that you live in a major city—say, Los Angeles. You have plenty of good options in this city. You can access a range of jobs, associate with a wide variety of people, and access many different cultural opportunities. After all, there are more people in Los Angeles county than there are in many countries, such as Denmark or New Zealand. So, you can have a decent life if you stay in Los Angeles. But imagine that state officials decide to stop you from leaving the city or that all other towns and cities in the United States deny you admission. If you try to get to San Francisco, the police will track you down and force you to come back to Los Angeles. Let's call this case *City*.

It's less bad for officials to stop you from leaving Los Angeles than it is for someone to prevent you from leaving your neighborhood. It's still wrong, though. This indicates that, even if you have decent options where you live, states should still respect your freedom to move. To drive this point home, let's compare freedom of movement to other freedoms, such as freedom of occupational choice. Suppose that you already have a good job and you can easily satisfy your basic needs. You are a tenured college professor, say. But you want to pursue a new career in a different industry because you are bored with your work and you want a career that you'll find more meaningful. Let's imagine that the government forbids you from changing jobs. Government officials explain, "You already have a job, plenty of decent options, and you already have enough options to live a good life. So, it's permissible for us to prohibit you from quitting your tenured professorship."

This is a bad argument. It's wrong to stop you from exercising your occupational freedom even if you can already satisfy your basic needs or have decent options. The same point again applies to other valuable liberties. Take freedom of religion. It's unjust for the government to forbid me from practicing the Jedi religion, despite the fact that I have plenty of other religious options. We can apply this point to freedom of movement too. States should still respect your freedom of movement regardless of whether you are already well off or not.

With these clarifications on the table, let's now turn to immigration restrictions.

3. Against Immigration Restrictions

Immigration restrictions infringe on freedom of movement. Immigration restrictions coercively stop many millions of people from moving to other countries, and they in effect forbid citizens of states that restrict immigration from associating with foreigners.

Let's return to the case that I discussed in the beginning of this chapter: the case of Gabriel Hernández Cortez. To recap: Gabriel is a Mexican citizen who lives in poverty and who wants to immigrate to the United States. He tried to cross the border, but border agents used physical force to stop him, imprison him, and deport him back to Mexico. Most people would judge that the conduct of state officials in Neighborhood and City is wrong. But many people also endorse immigration restrictions that prevent people like Gabriel from crossing borders.

Why, though? If it's wrong to restrict your freedom of movement in Neighborhood and City, then why is it permissible for American officials to prevent people like Gabriel from immigrating to the United States? Here's my view: the same reasons bear on each of these cases. Public officials have strong moral reasons to refrain from restricting your freedom of movement in Neighborhood and City and, if public officials have these reasons, then the United States government has strong moral reasons to refrain from restricting Gabriel's freedom of movement, too.

Let's consider some different ways of blocking this conclusion. An objector might argue that governments lack obligations to maximize the freedoms of foreigners. This critic might reason as follows: "It would be *nice* if the United States allowed Gabriel to immigrate. But the United States only has obligations to expand and protect the freedom of Americans, not the freedoms of foreigners. So, it's permissible for the United States to refuse to allow Gabriel to immigrate. In contrast, state officials have duties to respect the liberties of their citizens. These duties explain why it's wrong for state employees to forbid you from leaving your neighborhood or city."

It's false, though, that governments only have obligations to respect the freedom of their own citizens. They are obligated to respect the liberty of foreigners too. This is so because we have "negative" duties to other people. Negative duties are duties to refrain from harming or coercing people. Negative duties are universal. They apply to all other people simply in virtue of their humanity. The reason I ought to refrain from beating other people up is simply that they're people, rather than because they're my compatriots.

Here are some other examples to illustrate the point that our reasons to avoid coercing and harming people don't depend on whether they're foreigners or not:

(A) A Mexican police officer, Fernando, decides to assault and imprison an American tourist, Tracy, while she is visiting Mexico.

(B) An American public official, Roy, goes on a vacation to Mexico and he assaults Mexican citizens without provocation.

(C) American public officials decide to forcibly round up foreign tourists in the United States and place them in a prison camp.

(D) The president of the United States orders a military strike on a Mexican city, killing hundreds of non-combatants. This strike is unprovoked.

The actions A–D seem wrong. But why? The answer again is that we have negative duties to refrain from interfering with other people, even if they're foreigners. We might say that the negative duty to refrain from harmful interference is a "general" duty, a duty that we *prima facie* owe to all other people. So, we can't coerce, assault, or imprison foreigners without a good justification.

What about Gabriel's case, though? It looks like state officials in this example are violating negative duties here, too—in particular, their negative duties to refrain from coercing Gabriel. Maybe this duty is overridden by other considerations. But at first glance officials do have these duties. After all, if the people in A–D have duties to respect the rights and liberties of foreigners, then it stands to reason that immigration agents have these duties, too. The point generalizes. The United States government has obligations to respect the freedom of Gabriel and others who want to immigrate. These obligations are moral reasons to oppose immigration restrictions.

You might object to my argument by pointing out that rights to immigrate involve more than just the permission to enter a territory. When someone immigrates, they also become entitled to public services, such as police protection and access to the courts, and eventually other resources, like welfare benefits. These benefits can be costly. Citizens might need to foot the bill for public benefits in the form, say, of higher taxes. So, the decision about whether to admit Gabriel into the United States is not just about the decision to refrain from forcibly stopping him from immigrating. It's also about whether citizens are obligated to bear the costs of allowing Gabriel to immigrate. For this reason, you might reasonably doubt whether we can ground the right to immigrate solely in the negative duty to refrain from coercing foreigners.

Maybe allowing Gabriel to immigrate would impose costs on citizens. Yet this fails to break the analogy between immigration and Neighborhood and City. If the police allow you to leave your neighborhood or city, then your movement might impose costs on other people. Suppose that, if the government lets you leave your neighborhood or city, then you will move to a nearby city. And, once you live in this town, you'll become entitled to public services there. You will be entitled to police protection, access to the courts, and so on. This may impose costs on the other residents of the town where you now live. Yet the actions of state officials in Neighborhood are unjust nevertheless. Gabriel's immigration seems no different. It looks like it's wrong to deny a person freedom of movement just because this person *might* impose costs on others.

Suppose that you agree with me that it seems unjust for the United States to exclude people like Gabriel. But you could deny that this judgment generalizes to immigration restrictions more broadly. You could argue that it's wrong to exclude Gabriel, because Gabriel is unable to satisfy his basic needs or the basic needs of his child where he is currently situated. Maybe Gabriel lacks adequate options to live a decent life. He's unable to find a decent job and source of income. However, you might claim that it's permissible to restrict the immigration of someone who is already well off. Thus, Gabriel's case fails to ground a *general* objection to immigration restrictions. So, on this line of argument, it's wrong to deny admission to foreigners if this imperils their ability to satisfy their basic needs, but it may be permissible to restrict their entry otherwise.

Yet it seems wrong to restrict the immigration even of people who are already well off. Let's return to my thought experiment City. To recap, you live in Los Angeles, you are already well off, and you have plenty of options for living a decent life. Nonetheless, it seems unjust for government officials to trap you in Los Angeles. Thus, despite the fact that you have decent options where you live, the government should still respect your freedom to move. The same goes for foreigners. Even if Gabriel were well off, there would still be strong reasons to allow him to immigrate to the United States. Like other liberties such as occupational freedom, states have good reasons to respect your freedom of movement regardless of whether you already have plenty of options.

That said, it *is* morally worse for the United States to stop Gabriel from immigrating than it is for United States to prevent the immigration of someone who is already well off. Everything else being equal, it's worse to coercively stop a person from moving from one place to another if this person's interest in doing so is stronger. Gabriel has a strong interest in moving to the United States. If Gabriel had the chance to immigrate to the United States, this would make him much better off. Thus, the United States has an especially strong reason to admit him. And it turns out the same point applies for millions and millions of foreigners. Migrants like Gabriel are desperate and destitute. These cases are not exceptional. States prohibit many destitute and desperate foreigners from immigrating. So, actual immigration restrictions set back the urgent interests of many people.

To get a sense of how harmful immigration restrictions are, let's consider how much people would benefit from immigrating. The economist Branko Milanovic finds that location of birth is the biggest predictor of a person's lifetime income.[3] Your prospects in life are probably determined less by your class or sex than by the place where you were born. If location determines your prospects in life, then this suggests that moving your location could improve your prospects. And this is what economists find. Estimates indicate that low-skilled immigrants from Mexico raise their wages by over 400 percent after they migrate to the United States. Unskilled Salvadorians increase their annual incomes from about $1,200 to $18,000 by moving to the United States.[4] In general, low-skilled workers in poor countries can more than triple their real earnings by moving to the United States or a similar country.

Why do migrants benefit from immigrating? Here're a few reasons. Richer states tend to have better institutions. They do a *relatively* good job of protecting property rights, implementing the rule of law, and avoiding inefficient regulations. Rich states also tend to have more human capital, better technology, and superior infrastructure. These attributes help people to become more productive when they move to rich countries. Productivity is the main determinant of income. So, we should expect that moving people from a poor to a rich country would significantly increase their incomes. In fact, migration from, say, Nigeria or Chad to an affluent country massively boosts people's standard of living. To take another example, computer programmers earn dramatically more in the United States than they do in India, even though they're performing similar tasks.[5] Thus, to the extent that immigration restrictions prevent these people from moving, these restrictions deny foreigners large benefits.

There is more to life than money, of course. People want to immigrate for non-economic reasons, too. People move in order to escape authoritarian governments, political instability, and violence. Authoritarian regimes rule a large fraction of the human race. The residents of these countries often want to immigrate to states that protect civil and political liberties. Many people also live in societies with high rates of violence. For example, many Latin American countries experience high rates of drug-related

---

3. Branko Milanovic, "Global Inequality of Opportunity: How Much of Our Income Is Determined by Where We Live?" *Review of Economics and Statistics*, 97, no. 2 (2015): 452–460.

4. Lant Pritchett, *Let Their People Come: Breaking the Gridlock on Global Labor Mobility* (Washington, D.C.: Center for Global Development, 2006), p. 22.

5. Michael A. Clemens, "Why Do Programmers Earn More in Houston than Hyderabad? Evidence from Randomized Processing of US Visas," *American Economic Review* 103, no. 3 (2013): 198–202.

violence. This violence has caused hundreds of thousands of people to immigrate to other countries, such as the United States. Civil wars in the Middle East have recently generated millions of refugees who desperately want to find safety abroad.

So, it appears that a large number of people would benefit a great deal if they could immigrate, but they cannot do so. But you may still harbor doubts that borders should be left relatively open even if immigration is such a good deal for the global poor. One common concern is that, if states allowed more immigration, then skilled workers from poor countries would immigrate. If skilled workers left, this would deprive poor countries of human capital. The most talented entrepreneurs and the most educated citizens would seek their fortunes in rich countries. Poor countries would thus lose their most skilled citizens. Wouldn't this make the global poor worse off?

Economists actually disagree about the effects of skilled migration. While some economists think that the emigration of skilled workers has negative effects on poor countries, others believe that this emigration has neutral or even positive impacts.[6] Skilled workers may benefit the compatriots that they leave behind by forming technological and trade networks between their new and old countries. They also spread valuable ideas and send home remittances. Also, migration is often circular. Skilled people might work in, say, Britain for a few years and return home with more education and skills. Anyway, the current order makes it much easier for skilled workers to immigrate to rich countries. Rich countries are eager to recruit doctors and computer programmers from poor countries while they shun construction workers and taxi drivers. Even if skilled migration creates more overall harm than benefit for the global poor, people in poor countries would benefit if more *unskilled* workers had the legal opportunity to immigrate to rich countries.

To sum up, immigration has large benefits for migrants and immigration restrictions deny these benefits to many millions of people. This information is relevant because it tells us something about the magnitude of the harms that immigration restrictions inflict. Immigration restrictions

---

6. For contrasting perspectives on skilled immigration, see: Devesh Kapur and John McHale, *Give Us Your Best and Brightest: The Global Hunt for Talent and Its Impact on the Developing World* (Baltimore, MD: Brookings Institution Press, 2005); Michael Clemens, "Losing Our Minds? New Research Directions on Skilled Emigration and Development," *International Journal of Manpower* 37, no. 7 (2016): 1227–1248.

curtail valuable freedoms and this fact grounds a powerful objection to these restrictions. I think that immigration restrictions are unjust even if they avoid trapping people in poverty or oppression. But it's morally worse to coercively stop people from immigrating if their interest in doing so is stronger. People have weighty interests in substantially improving their standard of living, escaping authoritarian governments, and living in conditions free from violence. Actual immigration restrictions trample on these interests.

4. Objections and Responses

Commentators in public debate often defend immigration restrictions by pointing out that immigration can harm our fellow citizens. Immigrants compete with citizens for jobs and this competition drives down wages, which creates more poverty. Immigrants end up using welfare and other public benefits and this strains government budgets. And maybe immigrants cause other problems too, such as crime and terrorism. Many people say that governments should restrict immigration to prevent these bad things from happening. Let's call this *the bad consequences objection* to open borders.

The bad consequences objection says that immigrants harm the societies that admit them. Yet people frequently exaggerate the costs of immigration. Consider the effects of immigration on wages. Most economists who study the labor market effects of immigration conclude that immigration has small effects on the wages of citizens.[7] Foreigners often don't compete with citizens for jobs. Instead, foreigners have different skills and attributes than many citizens and this leads them to complement the labor of citizens. Consequently, immigration can actually raise the wages of citizens. Or take the fiscal effects of immigration. Many people worry that immigrants will end up using a lot of public services and welfare benefits, thereby imposing costs on the rest of us. But, in reality, researchers find that the effects of immigration on public finances are small and hard to detect.[8] Most immigrants find work and pay taxes; immigrants usually pay their own way.

---

7. Giovanni Peri, "Do Immigrant Workers Depress the Wages of Native Workers?" *IZA World of Labor* 42 (2014): 1–10.

8. The National Academy of Sciences, ed., *The Economic and Fiscal Consequences of Immigration* (National Academies Press, 2017).

Think about it this way. Imagine that half of the population of the country where you lived disappeared right now. Would you be better off economically? Probably not. That's because all those other people add something to the economy. They buy stuff, which creates demand for your labor. And their talents and knowledge on the whole make your country more productive, which increases your wages in the long-run, too. Immigrants are people, too. It stands to reason that they also add something to a society's prosperity. And this is what economists find. More immigration tends to make societies wealthier and better-off.[9]

What about the threat that immigration poses to our physical security? Popular opinion is also wrong about the relationship between immigration and crime. Most studies on the relationship between immigration and crime conclude that immigration does not increase crime and may in fact reduce it.[10] Or consider terrorism. The number of immigrants who are terrorists is infinitesimal. The United States admitted 3.25 million refugees over the past four decades and only twenty of them have been convicted of attempting or committing terrorism on U.S. territory. The chance of an American being killed by a foreign terrorist is about 1 in 3,600,000.[11] Falling furniture is much more likely to kill you than an immigrant terrorist, to say nothing of car accidents, ordinary homicides, or heart disease. The lesson is that, when you review the evidence and compare this evidence to popular perceptions about immigration, you'll find that people tend to overestimate the costs of immigration and underestimate its benefits.

Let's suppose though that immigration does have serious costs for citizens. We still need to ask ourselves: is it necessary to restrict immigration in order to prevent bad outcomes or is there another alternative? For example, let's assume that immigrants end up consuming a lot of welfare benefits and straining the government's budget. It doesn't follow that we should restrict immigration. Here's another option: states can deny immigrants access to public services and welfare benefits. You might object, "That's unfair!" But surely it's better than excluding immigrants outright.

---

9. Amandine Aubry, Michał Burzyński, and Frédéric Docquier, "The Welfare Impact of Global Migration in OECD Countries," *Journal of International Economics* 101 (July 2016): 1–21.

10. Graham C. Ousey and Charis E. Kubrin, "Immigration and Crime: Assessing a Contentious Issue," *Annual Review of Criminology* 1, no. 1 (2018): 63–84.

11. Alex Nowrasteh, "Terrorism and Immigration: A Risk Analysis" (Washington, D.C.: CATO Institute, 2016), https://www.cato.org/publications/policy-analysis/terrorism-immigration-risk-analysis.

If so, we can address the problem without restricting immigration. And the same goes for most other potential costs of immigration.

Let's assume, though, that immigration does harm some citizens and that we can't find a feasible way to avoid these costs. Even then, immigration restrictions would be unjustified. Notice that the bad consequences objection assumes that, if immigration imposes costs on citizens, then that's a good reason to restrict immigration. Yet there's a problem with this assumption: it ignores immigrants. The rights and interests of immigrants matter, too. As I argued earlier, we have obligations to refrain from harming and coercing other people, including foreigners. And these obligations can trump our obligations to our fellow citizens.

Here's an analogy. I think that I owe more to my children than I owe to random strangers. I should show more concern for my children than I should show for other people's children. Nonetheless, it would be wrong for me to coerce, kidnap, or assault strangers in order to benefit my children. Suppose that, if I mugged strangers on the street, I could afford to buy my children presents that they really wanted. Obviously though, that wouldn't be okay. The economist Bryan Caplan observes that "almost everyone knows that 'it would help my son' is not a good reason for even petty offenses—like judging a Tae Kwon Do tournament unfairly because your son's a contestant."[12]

The same point applies to governments. Many of us think that governments owe more to their citizens than they owe to foreigners. Governments have stronger obligations to benefit their own citizens. But there are strict limits on what governments can do to help their citizens. If it's wrong for me to coerce and assault strangers in order to benefit my children, then it is hard to see why it would be fine for the government to coerce and assault foreigners for the benefit of citizens. But that's just what immigration restrictions do: immigration restrictions involve coercion and violence. So, even if immigration restrictions are necessary to benefit citizens, we should still doubt whether it's morally okay to enforce them.

Here's another common objection to open borders: some people argue that states should restrict immigration in order to preserve a society's national culture. Foreigners have different values and cultural practices. If they immigrate, then this will change a society's culture and identity. But

---

12. Bryan Caplan, "Patria, Parenti, Amici," *Econlog* (blog), December 25, 2011, http://econlog.econlib.org/archives/2011/12/patria_parenti.html.

we have good reasons to preserve our culture. So, we should restrict immigration. Let's call this: *the cultural objection* to open borders.

One response to the cultural objection is to point out that most immigrants assimilate and adopt the cultural practices of recipient societies.[13] Another response to the cultural objection is to ask, "So what if immigration causes cultural change?" The exercise of many individual rights can change a society's culture and identity. Consider rights to free speech. Free speech can change a society's culture by encouraging people to adopt new values and practices. Suppose that Mormons are successful at persuading many Americans to convert. This could change a society's culture—let's assume that Mormons have somewhat different values and practices than the dominant culture. But it would clearly be wrong to forbid Mormons from proselytizing.

Or consider rights to reproductive freedom. Imagine that Muslims are a minority in a society, but Muslims have more children than the rest of the population and most of these children adopt the practices and values of their parents. As a result, Muslims' exercise of reproductive freedom generates cultural change. We should clearly condemn any restrictions on Muslim's reproductive freedom that aim to stop this change. Individual rights trump the goal of cultural preservation. Foreigners' rights to immigrate should override this goal as well. Thus, the cultural objection to open borders is unsound.

Let's consider one final objection to open borders. Some people think of states like private clubs or property. We can rightfully exclude people from our private associations and property. Suppose that you and your friends form a chess club. It seems okay for you to refuse to allow strangers to join your club. Or assume that you own your house. You are within your rights to prevent homeless people from sleeping in your home. Maybe we can defend immigration restrictions on similar grounds. States might be analogous to private clubs or perhaps states have property rights in their national territories. If that's true, then we can exclude immigrants just as we can exclude people from our clubs and houses. Let's call this the *rights-based objection* to open borders.

But here's the problem with the rights-based objection. If states have rights to freedom of association or property rights over their territories, then states can permissibly do more than just restrict immigration.

---

13. Jack Citrin et al., "Testing Huntington: Is Hispanic Immigration a Threat to American Identity?" *Perspectives on Politics* 5, no. 1 (2007): 31–48.

They can restrict all individual rights. To illustrate, consider that private associations, such as clubs, churches, or businesses, can permissibly exclude non-members. For example, the Catholic Church can permissibly refuse to baptize Satanists. In this sense, the Catholic Church has the right to exclude people. But private associations can also regulate the behavior of their members in illiberal ways. This is why the Catholic Church can forbid its members from using birth control, having sex out of wedlock, worshipping Satan, and so on.

Now, suppose you think that states are like private associations in that both can permissibly exclude non-members. Well, if states really are like private associations, then states should also be able to regulate the behavior of their members in the same way that private associations do. States should also have the right to forbid citizens from using birth control, having sex out of wedlock, or worshipping Satan. Thus, the same logic that justifies immigration restrictions also implies that states can restrict any liberty, such as freedom of speech or sexual freedom. If states are like clubs, they might exercise their rights by excluding outsiders. Or states may exercise their rights to freedom of association by curtailing the individual liberties of their members.

Suppose, alternatively, you think that citizens collectively own their territories or institutions and that these property rights permit the exclusion of outsiders. On this view, countries are like big private estates. And aren't private estates well within their rights to exclude trespassers? The problem is, once again, that this justifies too much. Consider a private establishment, like a restaurant. A restaurant may have a dress code that forbids customers from taking off their shirt, wearing clothes with profanity on them, or wearing baggy pants, and that requires workers to wear a uniform. They can also forbid people from such activities as staging a political protest in their restaurant. Why is it permissible for a restaurant to do this? Ownership rights. Private property rights give people the right to control what happens on their property, within some limits. If countries are essentially private property, then they should be able to forbid residents from wearing baggy pants, uttering profanity, holding political protests, and so on.

I submit that these are not policies that we should accept. It would be unjust for states to behave in these ways. But, to reject the implications that countries can act in illiberal ways, we must also reject the view that countries are analogous to private property or private clubs. And, if countries are not like private property or clubs, then we can't appeal to these analogies to justify immigration restrictions. For this reason, the rights-based objection to open borders fails.

5. Conclusion

Advocates of open borders aren't crazy. They acknowledge that immigration can cause problems and that, in rare cases, there are good arguments for immigration restrictions. If allowing immigration would cause disaster, then that's a solid reason for restricting it. But open borders advocates just happen to believe that a careful evaluation of the evidence reveals that immigration has far fewer downsides and many more upsides than most people think. Once you work through the evidence, you find that most people's fears about immigration are exaggerated or even baseless.

So, what would a world with open borders look like? You're already familiar with it. You know how you can just move around your country freely? Tomorrow you can wake up and decide to move to another city or town. I live in Richmond, Virginia. If I wanted to, I could get up right now, buy a plane ticket to Alaska, and move there. Advocates of open borders say that the whole world should be like that.

Sometimes when I lecture about immigration, I show the audience pictures of what open and closed borders look like. Photo 1 is a picture of an

PHOTO 1

PHOTO 2

open border.[14] This is the border between Germany and Switzerland. Germany is on the left side of the street and Switzerland is on the right side.

Photo 2 is the border between Spain and Portugal.[15] Spain and Portugal are members of the European Union, which has open borders between member states. What do we observe in these two pictures? Not much. Just countryside and open roads. It's peaceful. No walls, guns, or border guards.

Now, contrast these pictures with Photo 3.[16] This is the border between Hungary and Serbia, which is not an open border. Notice the high fences topped with razor wires and the police officer ready to stop migrants from crossing.

---

14. Hansueli Krapf, "Canton of Schaffhausen, Swiss/German Border in Dörflingen," *Wikipedia Commons*, April 22, 2012, https://commons.wikimedia.org/wiki/File:2012-04-22_19-33-46_Switzerland_Kanton_Schaffhausen_D%C3%B6rflingen,_Hinterdorf.JPG (accessed July 3, 2020).

15. M.Peinado, "España-Portugal," *Wikipedia Commons*, May 3, 2013, https://commons.wikimedia.org/wiki/File:007422_-_Espa%C3%B1a-Portugal_(8735025539).jpg (accessed July 3, 2020).

16. Bőr Benedek, "Police Car Near Hungary-Serbia Border Barrier," *Wikipedia Commons*, September 14, 2015, https://commons.wikimedia.org/wiki/File:Police_car_at_Hungary-Serbia_border_barrier.jpg (accessed July 3, 2020).

PHOTO 3

PHOTO 4

Or consider Photo 4.[17] This is the border between Texas and the Mexican state of Chihuahua. Also not an open border.

Think about what kind of world you want to live in. Do we want to live in a world where borders look like the first two pictures? Or do want to live in a world where borders look like the third and fourth pictures? I hope to have given you some reason to prefer the first two.

---

17. Dicklyon, "Border Wall between Sunland Park, New Mexico, United States, and Anapra, Chihuaha, Mexico" *Wikipedia Commons*, January 26, 2019, https://commons.wikimedia.org/wiki/File:Border_wall_at_Anapra.jpg (accessed July 3, 2020).

Javier Hidalgo: Open Borders

1. Hidalgo presents the thought experiment he calls Neighborhood. Do you think that Neighborhood is a good analogy for closed borders? Can we justifiably draw lessons for immigration policy from this thought experiment? Why or why not?

2. Hidalgo argues that freedom of association supports open borders. Others have argued that freedom of association supports immigration limits. Their thinking goes like this: Freedom of association protects your right to refuse marriage or friendship with a suitor, so it likewise protects a country's right to decline to be associated with migrants who seek entry. Do you find this analogy plausible? Does freedom of association better support open borders or immigration restrictions (or neither)?

3. Many fear that open borders will result in the destruction of a nation's culture. How important is it to protect such culture? What, if any, are the permissible limits a nation can take in order to preserve its culture? Do immigration limits fall within those limits?

4. Hidalgo writes that "if it's wrong for me to coerce and assault strangers in order to benefit my children, then it is hard to see why it would be fine for the government to coerce and assault foreigners for the benefit of citizens. But that's just what immigration restrictions do." What do you think of this claim? If you agree with this claim, offer your reasons in support of it; if you disagree, offer the reasons that lead you to reject it.

5. There's an old saying: a picture's worth a thousand words. Consider the photos at the end of Hidalgo's article. Are these legitimate philosophical devices for trying to persuade readers? Why or why not?

27

Our Moral Duty to Eat Meat
Nick Zangwill

Here is Nick Zangwill, succinctly stating his article's central line of reasoning: "[G]iven the world as it is, the only way for animals to benefit in large numbers is to kill and eat them. Therefore, we should kill and eat them." It might seem paradoxical to justify a duty to kill animals on the basis of seeking to benefit them, but that is Zangwill's ambition. He doesn't argue that killing the animals actually benefits them. Nor is he concerned to justify killing animals that experience only a very low quality of life. If animals raised on factory farms meet that description, then his argument doesn't apply to them. But for all animals that enjoy at least a decent quality of life, Zangwill believes that we have a moral duty to eventually kill and eat them.

Why is that? Because doing so is required in order to sustain a practice that benefits animals. We have a moral duty to support practices that confer great benefits on others, humans and animals alike. Many farming practices do this; therefore, we have a moral duty to support those practices. Crucially, though, those practices require that animals be killed and sold at market. Farmers cannot simply grow and grow their flocks without limit. The economic viability of such farming depends on the animals being killed and sold at the end of the process. If farmers weren't able to earn their keep, then they wouldn't create the conditions that allow farm animals to be born and thrive. For instance, if it weren't in the interests of New Zealand shepherds to raise their

Nick Zangwill, "Our Moral Duty to Eat Meat," from *Journal of the American Philosophical Association* (2021), pp. 1-17.

millions of sheep, then those sheep, which for the most part live decent lives, wouldn't exist, and so wouldn't be around to enjoy the benefits of their lives. The flourishing of these sheep, which is a good thing and which we have a moral duty to support, depends on a practice that requires eventually killing them and selling their meat.

After making some important clarifications and responding to objections, Zangwill argues that even ethical vegetarians and vegans have a moral duty to eat meat, and are acting immorally if they maintain their refusal to do so.

E ating nonhuman animal meat is not merely permissible but also good. It is what we ought to do, and it is our moral duty. So I argue. I shall not distinguish the claim that eating meat is good from the claim that we ought to eat meat. The claim that it is our *duty* is a stronger claim. The claim that it is good and the claim that it is what we ought to do are closely related to the claim that it is our duty: if something is our duty, then it is good to do it, and we ought to do it. Furthermore, I take the goods, oughts, and duties here to be moral ones. Note also that by the word 'animals' in what follows, I mean nonhuman animals, and by 'meat' I mean nonhuman animal meat.

1. The Benefit to Animals of Eating Meat

Why is eating meat good? That is, what makes it good? The basic claim, to put it crudely at first, is that eating meat is morally good primarily because it benefits animals. Of course, the practice does not benefit a particular animal that we eat at the time that we eat it. Nevertheless, the existence of that animal and animals of that kind depends on human beings eating animals of its kind and, hence, that meat-eating practice benefits them. Domesticated animals exist in the numbers that they do only if there is a practice of eating them. For example, the many millions of sheep in New Zealand would not begin to survive in the wild. They exist only because we have a practice of eating them. The meat-eating practice benefits them greatly. Therefore, we should eat them.

The argument, to be more precise, is that we should eat meat where meat-eating is part of a past and ongoing practice that benefits animals. The animals we eat should have good lives, and their pleasures and happiness are part of that. It is an empirical question how much of actual current meat-eating fits this description. It may be that only animals reared in decent ways have good lives, and that so-called factory-farmed animals have little or no quality of life, or that their pain outweighs their pleasure. If so, the argument from benefit to animals does not apply to factory-farmed animals. Perhaps we should not eat factory-farmed animals. Nevertheless, very many animals we eat do not live dismal lives, and the argument clearly applies to them. For example, the millions of sheep in New Zealand that graze outdoors overall have good lives. Therefore, we should eat them. A great deal of meat is not factory farmed, and is, as it were, fair game. The argument does not justify participating in practices where there is no quality in animals' lives. However, it is not seriously questionable that much meat-eating of the more 'free-range' kind of animals does enable a significant quality of life for the animals in question. It is hard to get reliable and impartial information about how much of each kind there is, but it seems that at least around 5 percent of actual meat production is of the more benign sort. That justifies an awful lot of meat-eating. When I speak of eating meat being justified in what follows, I shall mean only meat from animals that overall have a good life. A minority of meat produced in the world today involves such happy animals. But it is a significant minority, one that justifies much eating of those animals.

It is a relatively uncontroversial empirical premise that if the market for meat dried up, farmers would stop caring for animals and breeding them (Scruton 2000). Of course, if human beings were radically different—perhaps if they were immaterial or immortal or could draw nutrition from the air—then our obligations to animals would be different. But so what? We are dealing with our world or a world like our world. Of course, there are various barely possible utopian visions or fantasies in which large numbers of animals somehow get cared for without being killed and eaten. However, given the world as it is, the only way for animals to benefit in large numbers is to kill and eat them. Therefore, we should kill and eat them.

2. Consciousness, Happiness, Suffering, and Death

It seems to be obvious and intuitive that benefitting animals is good. But what if the question is asked: why, exactly, is it good to benefit animals? What is the ground of the obligation to benefit animals, whether individual animals or animals of a kind? We can also benefit bacteria. But we do not think that this something we should do. Why not?

On *this* point, I agree with those, such as Peter Singer (Singer 1975), who think that what is important is animal consciousness. They think that animal consciousness means we ought not to eat animals, whereas I think the very opposite. Nevertheless, we can agree that the ground of our obligations concerning animals is consciousness—there is something it is like to be many animals—which is why those animals have interests that matter morally: the quality of their consciousness can be better or worse. By contrast, bacteria have interests; they can be benefitted or harmed, and they can flourish or not. However, there is nothing it is like to be bacteria; they are not conscious. It is also unlikely that there is something it is like to be an earthworm. Therefore, we do not have obligations to bacteria and earthworms, or at least not this kind of obligation. Because some animals are conscious, they have interests and can flourish in a way that matters morally. But for many kinds of animals (cows, sheep, chickens), in order to exist and flourish in that way there must be a practice of eating them. Therefore, we should eat them.

I do not deny that animal pain and suffering matter. However, we should insist, and strongly so, that animal pleasure and happiness also matter—something almost entirely overlooked by huge numbers of those who write with apparent concern for animals. The emphasis among the defenders of so-called animal liberation or animal rights on animal pain and suffering rather than on animal pleasure and happiness is bizarre and disturbing (for example, Singer 1975; Regan 1983). The only explanation I can think of is that this emphasis is a form of what is called speciesism: animal pleasure and happiness are discounted just because they are not of our species. There is an impressive inconsistency in this because those who present themselves as having great concern for animals somehow omit to factor in the benefit to animals of pleasure and happiness. This looks like speciesism because they think human pleasure and happiness matters, and yet, while they do think the same of animal pleasure and happiness, they care only about animal pain and suffering.

It is imperative that moral issues about suffering and death are separated. There are moral issues about the suffering and happiness of animals, and there are moral issues about whether we can or should kill animals. These issues are clearly separate in principle. Killing could ideally be completely painless and free of suffering. Of course, the fact that animals feel pain and pleasure is relevant to how we should care for them and nurture their interests during their lives, and it is also relevant to *how* we should kill them. But that fact is not in itself relevant to *whether* we may kill animals for food if their death is painless. These two issues are often confused. In fact, killing animals and eating them is not merely compatible with kindness and benefit to animals but is required if we are to be kind to animals and to benefit them. Otherwise there would be no such animals to be kind to or to benefit. The goal of kindness to animals dictates that we should kill and eat them.

The ideal of painless death may not be achieved in many cases. The animals we eat may incur *some* pain or suffering at the end of their lives, which is regrettable. Nevertheless, it is vastly less than the overall good in their lives. Therefore, even if they feel pain or suffering at the end, it is not remotely plausible that pain and suffering at the end of their lives somehow negates all the good in their lives that they had before that. That would be a strange fetishization of their last few moments. It is also true that many human beings have miserable painful deaths, but that hardly means that their lives before that were not worth living. Nevertheless, we should certainly strive to minimize animals' pain and suffering in the process of killing them.

Some people think that how life ends matters for human beings in a way that it does not matter for animals. If this is true, it is presumably due to our cognitive sophistication, which allows us to conceive of our life as having something like a narrative structure. But without that cognitive sophistication, the end of life cannot carry the special weight it does for many people who argue that we should not eat animals. Because animals lack the cognitive sophistication of human beings, no special weight can attach to their last moments when considered in the light of their lives as a totality.

Like human beings, animals have pains and miseries, but like human beings, a great many of the animals we eat also have considerably more pleasure and happiness in their lives than pain and misery. Therefore, we should eat them.

3. Two Comments

(A) A complication is that different animals have different degrees of consciousness. Different animals also have different kinds of consciousness. Consciousness varies in vividness, fine-grainedness, and so on. It is plausible that we have greater obligations to advance the interests of animals further up the hierarchy of consciousness. This means that we should concentrate our efforts on breeding, killing, and eating animals with higher levels of consciousness if those lives are good overall. Suppose there were evidence that an animal, such as a sheep, feels more pleasure and distress than does a chicken. Then we would have greater duties to sheep than to chickens. And if so, other things being equal, given a choice between lamb and chicken, we should eat lamb and not chicken.

(B) What about the argument that calves and their mothers incur psychological suffering when they are separated in the process of meat production? I already conceded that there is suffering in the lives and deaths of domesticated animals, but I downplayed its importance in the overall balance of things. The worry is that we cannot do this so easily with the more sophisticated emotional suffering of animals like cows, where significant attachments develop. Nevertheless, the important question remains: is the cow's life as a whole good? There is no reason to believe that the sophisticated trauma of separation in the life of a cow makes a cow's whole life not worth living, any more than the many traumas in the lives of human beings make their lives not worth living. Indeed, quite the opposite: human grief is proof that human life is worth living, despite the trauma of loss. Grief is an eloquent testament to the value of life. The same goes for the cow's separation trauma. The argument runs exactly the other way from the way it is assumed to run. If cows can grieve or suffer separation trauma, that is proof of the sophistication and high quality of the cow's mental life, which provides all the more reason to eat cows as part of a practice whereby they benefit. Of course, the grief of animals matters, and it should be factored into our assessment of the value of their lives; the fact that they feel grief makes a difference to our behavior with respect to animals via the practices that sustain or have sustained the quality of life for those animals. However, animal grief speaks *in favor* of eating animals, not against it.

4. Beneficial Historical Practices: Wild and Domesticated Animals

The above is half of the positive argument: the appeal to the benefit to animals and the appeal to consciousness. What needs to be added is the fact that our *relationship* with domesticated animals, by contrast with wild animals, makes a significant moral difference.

We are in ongoing symbiotic relationships with many types of animals (such as cows, sheep, and chickens), and there are long-standing practices whereby we benefit them and they benefit us. It is as if we were in a relationship of friendship with them—and that is why we should eat them! We have *duties* to benefit our friends in virtue of our special relationship with them; benefitting them is not merely virtuous or praiseworthy. Likewise, in virtue of the ongoing mutual dependency of animals on us and of us on them, it is our duty to eat them, and this is not something merely virtuous or praiseworthy. If there turn out to be creatures on Mars that would be benefitted by our eating them, then it would be virtuous or praiseworthy to eat them, not our duty. We actually stand in an ongoing relationship of mutual dependence with many earthly species, and thus eating them is not merely virtuous or praiseworthy—we have a duty to eat them, just as we have special duties to our friends. It is true that it is not usual to eat our friends, and so, in this respect, the two situations are indeed different. I concede that. But the situations are similar in that duties arise in the context of a relationship of mutual dependence.

This marks a significant difference between domesticated and wild animals. Consider the billions of nondomesticated animals in the wild who kill and eat each other. These animals have pleasures and pains; does that mean that we also have obligations to them? Should we intervene to prevent the lion from eating the gazelle? But this aspect of these animals' lives is an unalterable part of nature ('Nature red in tooth and claw'). This is not true of domesticated animals that are mostly spared the fear of predators, thanks to human beings.

The fate of wild animals is not entirely disconnected from us. The actions of human beings affect them. That is not the issue here—the issue is the lack of a mutually beneficial symbiotic relationship with them. Because of that, we are not obligated to interfere with the endless cycle of life and death in the wild. Indeed, we should probably not interfere unless it is to undo previous wrongful intervention. By contrast, it is our duty to eat the animals we have domesticated because we are in an ongoing relationship of mutual dependence with those domesticated animals. Furthermore, it is a relationship that benefits the domesticated animals. In virtue of their ongoing consciousness and its quality, the lives of many domesticated animals are good. But that good depends on our eating them. This is not true of the conscious lives of wild animals. Therefore, we have a duty to eat domesticated farm animals but not wild animals.

Suppose that due to some disease the animals we have cared for and caused to exist would have no descendants. For example, there would be no more sheep in the future. Then we may still eat the last generation of sheep in virtue of their participation in a practice that has benefitted those sheep and many of their forbears. *Must* we eat them? Perhaps not in that situation although we *may* do so.

Carnivorism has been immensely beneficial to its practitioners, both human beings and the animals they eat. If there are present duties to continue the practice, the practice must have been beneficial: Chinese foot-binding was a long-standing cultural practice but not a beneficial one; thus, that history confers no present duty to persist. But carnivorism is and has been highly beneficial to both the eater and the eaten. Therefore, that practice generates duties.

There is a question about the identity conditions of carnivorous practices. The animals we eat should be of the same kind as the animals that were benefitted by that practice in the past: a practice that benefits chickens cannot justify us in eating ducks. If a carnivorous practice benefits chickens but not ducks, then that practice generates duties to eat chickens and not ducks. It would be unfair to chickens to eat ducks instead of chickens.

Do we have a duty to breed huge numbers of animals to feel pleasure and happiness? No, the argument is not a consequentialist one. We have a duty to be the gentle custodians of happy animals that we eat because of our ongoing beneficial relationship of mutual dependence. Perhaps larger herds or flocks of domesticated animals are better than smaller ones. But there is no requirement to maximize. The best way to do our duty, given what the world is like, is probably to continue a tradition of breeding, tending, and eating animals that have lives that are good overall. New Zealand famously has ten sheep for every person. Right now, the people of New Zealand are pursuing a morally righteous policy, which must be almost optimal given the limits imposed by facts about human beings, society, and economics. New Zealand farmers may or may not be motivated by the cause of animal welfare. Irrespective of their motivations, they have contributed and are contributing very substantially to the cause of animal welfare, which is what matters. New Zealand sheep farming is a noble practice, and New Zealand sheep farmers are heroic benefactors of animal kind.

The ongoing history of mutual benefit is the ground of the present moral duty of human beings to eat animals. If the practice were beneficial only to one of the two parties, that would perhaps not justify persisting in it. But both parties benefit—and animals benefit a lot more than human beings. For human beings could survive as vegetarians or vegans, but domesticated animals could not survive human beings being vegetarians or vegans. Indeed, if most human beings became vegetarians or vegans, it would be the greatest disaster ever for animal kind since an asteroid strike precipitated an ice age that wiped out the dinosaurs and many other species.

5. Killing and Eating Enslaved Human Beings?

There is one counterargument that has not been addressed thus far, which is likely to have occurred to the reader. This is the argument that if the argument from historic benefit to animals were good, it would have the consequence that we should at least sometimes kill and eat enslaved human beings if doing so were part of a practice that has benefitted them. This counter-argument needs to be neutralized; otherwise it will fester unhealthily in the background and be a distraction from the main thrust of the argument for eating meat.

My view is that there are special considerations, arising from human rationality, that block the extension of the argument: human beings, including many severely mentally disabled human beings, have distinctive rights that animals lack, and this means that we cannot kill and eat enslaved human beings, not even for their own good. The rational activity that is in play is not merely a high state of consciousness but a self-reflective activity in which a creature reflectively assesses its own mental life, which it changes in accordance with that self-assessment. Rational activity is different in kind from consciousness.

I shall not and need not argue for a rationality view here and spell out the specific way that a rationality view invokes rational activity and delivers rights, or consider its scope of application (for example, encompassing severely mentally disabled human beings). There are two points that can be made. First, even if an argument of the sort pursued here were to yield an obligation to kill and eat enslaved human beings, it would only be what philosophers call a *pro tanto* obligation, and such an obligation might or might not be outweighed by the special rights of human beings. Second, a crucial empirical premise of the argument advanced here for killing and eating animals is that these kinds of animals would not exist were it not for the practice of killing and eating them. The parallel premise is not at all plausible for human beings. Even if, counterfactually, groups of human beings were enslaved and eaten, it would remain true that they *could* survive and flourish outside that practice. There are, of course, science-fiction scenarios (such as H. G. Wells's *Time Machine*) where such a practice is imagined as a norm, with different empirical premises. But that is fiction, and it is hard to know the rights and wrongs where we depart so much from actuality. At any rate, because of the empirical fact that no group of human beings actually depends for its existence on a meat-eating practice in which human beings are killed and eaten, it is very unlikely that there is even a *pro tanto* obligation to kill and eat enslaved human beings that needs to be outweighed. No group of human beings actually owes its existence to cannibalistic meat-eating practices in the way that billions of animals do owe their lives to carnivorous meat-eating practices. Therefore, we do not need to worry about the mere possibility too much, especially because it is also plausible that there are distinctive human rights in play that would protect human beings in that merely possible situation.

6. Which Animals?

One familiar objection to appealing to animal benefit is that it means that we have duties at a time to creatures who do not yet exist at that time, which would be odd. But this is not something that the historical benefit view is committed to, and such an objection would misunderstand the view presented here as a consequentialist one. We have duties to present existing animals, to eat them, in virtue of a past and present mutually beneficial relationship between human beings and animals of that kind, where animals 'of that kind' means animals that are the descendants of animals that have actually benefitted from the practice. (We would owe nothing to animals of the same species that have been causally isolated for a long time from those that have benefitted, but this is an unlikely scenario.) The present fact that these animals have a certain history is what imposes the obligation. True, many future animals that do not yet exist will benefit by our eating presently existing animals. But our duties are to present and actual animals, to eat them, not to future or merely possible animals that will benefit. The view is not a consequentialist one because the grounds of duties look backward to the past, not forward to the future. Our duties are to presently existing animals because the existing practice has benefitted animals in the past and continues to benefit them in the present, and that is why we should now eat the animals produced by the beneficial practice.

The duty to eat animals is like the duty to care for one's parents in their old age. The history of benefit matters. What our parents did for us in the past is a ground of our later duty to them. But direct consequentialism allows that it might be fine to bump off our parents regardless of what they have done for us. Moreover, the rationale for respecting our parents is not an indirect consequentialist one: what matters are not the future benefits of a general practice of caring for parents, but the actual history of a particular parent and child pair. In a similar way, farmers should kill and eat or allow others to kill and eat the animals they have cared for because of what the past and ongoing present practice has done for animals and also human beings. That history dictates a bond of loyalty between human beings and the animals they care for, a bond much like that between parents and children. Of course, it is not usual to eat our own parents, and in this respect I concede that the two cases are different. However, they are similar in that systematic historical benefit generates a bond of loyalty and duties of care. It is just that in the case of animals, caring entails killing, unlike in the case of one's parents.

7. Who Is Obligated?

On whom, exactly, does the duty to eat meat fall? I have said that it is *our* duty, where this means human beings whose forebears participated in the carnivorous practice. It is our collective duty. In principle, that means that if enough people eat enough meat to sustain the beneficial practice, then particular people's obligations might lapse or be weakened, just as a person's duty to help a stranger in trouble lapses or weakens if there are already enough other people helping the stranger. However, while it is good to help sustain a beneficial practice, that is not the main reason for eating meat; rather, the main reason is the historical one that the practice has been beneficial to participants. We eat the animals that have benefitted out of respect for the past—a matter of honor, if you like. This duty binds all of us although perhaps we need not eat much meat if others are bearing more of the weight of the duty. It is like carrying a coffin: one does it out of respect for the past, but if there are enough pallbearers, one need not volunteer.

At the time of death, the benefit that a particular sheep has reaped is in the past. Now is the time for this sheep to pay. But why does a particular person have a duty to exact that payment from this sheep? Consider the following analogy. Suppose someone commits a crime and therefore should be punished. Unless people have a special role in the law, perhaps as prison warders, they have no special duty to administer punishment. However, sometimes there is no such division of labor. There might be a shared responsibility for enforcement in some jurisdictions. Consider jurisdictions in which there is a 'duty of rescue' law. Suppose that someone is drowning or suffering a crime. Then a person nearby who is aware of the situation, a bystander, is under an obligation to the person drowning or suffering a crime. Eating meat is, in this respect, like the duty of rescue law: a person is duty-bound to the particular sheep being eaten.

Killing and eating animals seem to differ in this respect. The slaughtering of animals is done by specialists, and the reason for this is that they are probably more skilled in doing this so as to minimize suffering. Therefore, it is permissible to delegate this duty to them. There is no such reason for the duty to eat meat, which falls on all of us. But even in the case of slaughtering, we all have a duty to delegate the duty.

What if some people claim to be altogether exempt from the burden imposed by the carnivorous practice because they are vegans and do not participate in the practice? Perhaps their parents were vegans too. Nevertheless, every vegan has ancestors who were carnivores; indeed, their ancestors were in a meat-eating relationship with animals for thousands of years. A modern vegan is the beneficiary and inheritor of this ancient tradition, and is therefore duty-bound to it and to continue to nurture the animals that depend on that practice. If vegans do not continue the practice, they are selfish free riders, depending for their existence on their ancestors who ate meat. Almost all modern vegans would not exist if their ancestors had not eaten meat. Vegans depend for their existence on their forebears who virtuously benefitted animals and who reaped benefits themselves from the carnivorous practice. Therefore, vegans are individually bound by the same collective duty to eat meat as the rest of us.

8. All Things Considered

My argument has been that the historic and continuing benefit to animals of the practice of eating meat creates a duty to eat animals. Even so, this is not the only duty in the world. Of course. The duty is a *pro tanto* duty. It may be outweighed by other duties and obligations. But if it were not outweighed, it would amount to an all-things-considered or overall duty to eat animals.

What about the rights and wrongs of eating vegetables? Like nonconscious bacteria and earthworms, vegetables are in a different moral category from conscious animals. There is nothing it is like to be a carrot. For this reason, we are not under an obligation to participate in a practice that has promoted and continues to promote the flourishing of carrots by eating them as we are under an obligation to participate in a practice that has promoted and continues to promote the flourishing of conscious animals. Nevertheless, eating vegetables is not morally neutral because it bears on the fulfillment of our other obligations, such as our obligation to eat animals. One argument would be that since eating vegetables distracts us from our obligation to eat animals, in that respect eating vegetables is morally wrong. We should not blithely pass over the opportunity to participate in a practice that has benefitted conscious animals by eating them. If so, we should ideally have a diet entirely of meat, with no vegetables at all! However, there are reputed to be health benefits for human beings from eating vegetables. If so, then eating vegetables helps us fulfill our obligations, such as our obligations to eat animals. That would give us derivative moral obligations to eat vegetables.

In considering the overall moral status of meat eating, we should factor in a variety of other things, such as the positive and negative consequences of meat-eating practices. Perhaps there are harms to the environment caused by farting and burping cows and sheep. This might justify us in eating sheep instead of cows if sheep fart or burp less, or relevantly differently, from cows. However, even if New Zealand sheep farming does cause pollution, these effects should be balanced against the interests of sheep, and, of course, we should try to mitigate that damage while retaining the sheep rearing.

We should not dwell only on additional negative effects. There are other positive aspects to the practice of eating meat that reinforce the argument from the benefit to animals from the carnivorous practice. Many other kinds of considerations also favor eating meat. One is the gustatory pleasure of human beings when they eat meat. We should not ignore human pleasures in eating meat. These provide reasons that should be counted. However, those pleasures do not have much weight compared with the duty arising from historic and present benefit to animals. The human pleasure in eating meat is a welcome part of a good practice.

Other kinds of considerations are aesthetic ones. There is the beauty of meat itself, celebrated in the erotic novel *Le Boucher* by Alina Reyes. There is also the beauty of the countryside where animals live—the beauty of the grassy fenced hills, punctuated by grazing animals, should not be discounted. This beauty depends on our eating meat. Of course, aesthetic considerations sometimes conflict with moral considerations, and then we have a dilemma. Fortunately, in the case of animals, beauty and goodness go hand in hand: aesthetic and moral considerations point in the same direction. Aesthetic considerations provide additional justification for eating meat although, as with human gustatory pleasure, aesthetic considerations do not have much weight when compared with our duty to participate in a beneficial meat-eating practice.

Effects on human welfare and rights need to be weighed carefully. The employment that the meat-eating practice provides for millions of human beings needs to be considered. There are also other additional effects, for example, on other animals—wild animals for example. The calculation will be complex, and it might turn up some surprising results. Nevertheless, considered in itself, the meat-eating practice is clearly good, very good. Thus, it generates a very strong *pro tanto* reason for human beings to participate in it. Many factors need to be considered in arriving at an all-things-considered judgment of the value of participating in the practice of eating meat. However, we should not assume that these extraneous weighable factors are systematically negative. In many discussions, authors do not merely accentuate the negative, but they eliminate the positive. This bias has all the hallmarks of conspiracy-theory reasoning. No one has ever made a convincing case that the overall effects of the meat industry or at least of the nicer (non-factory) parts of it, are negative. The overall assessment would have to be holistic, and it would have to be complex, with numerous interacting factors. We have no reason to believe that the world would be better off if human beings did not eat meat. Those who think they know this are deceiving themselves.

There might be other good consequences of eating meat that we have not considered here. There might also be other positive or negative moral considerations that are not a matter of benefits or harms. However, as far as the practice of eating meat itself is concerned, it is clear that it is good to eat meat, we ought to eat meat, and eating meat is our duty.

9. Coda

Some people do not eat meat. It could be that they put their own self-interest before morality. Perhaps they do not like the taste, for example, or have some irrational taboo against it, just as irrational racial prejudice leads some people not to care about certain kinds of people or to harm them. Or it could be that they do not care about the welfare of conscious animals because speciesism leads them not to value a tradition that benefits those animals, in particular, speciesism causes them to ignore animals' pleasures and happiness. Whatever the psychological explanation, their practice is immoral. Eating meat is good, it is what we ought to do and our duty, and not to do so is bad and wrong. Where duty is in tension with self-interest, we should strive to put self-interest to one side and do our duty. Those happiness-deniers and life-deniers who have speciesist prejudices that prevent them from eating meat should strive to rid themselves of prejudice and do the right thing and eat meat.

Eating meat is creating life. It brings into existence beings with valuable states of consciousness. Or at least eating meat is an essential part of a practice whereby valuable conscious lives have been and are being created. (Recall that the argument is restricted to animals that have good lives overall, rather than including miserable factory-farmed animals.) This is as great a benefit as one can confer on creatures—so excellent an act is eating animals! Did not our parents give us a great gift, if not the greatest gift—life, existence? In a similar way, New Zealand sheep farmers who raise sheep kindly and kill them, minimizing distress, to make room for new generations of happy sheep are great benefactors of animal kind. They give life and happiness. Those who eat that meat should be proud to be part of such an excellent beneficial practice. Eating meat is an act of kindness. Eating meat is primarily about life, not death, and it should be celebrated as such.

References

Regan, Tom. (1983) *The Case for Animal Rights*. Lost Angeles: University of California Press.

Scruton, Roger. (2000) *Animal Right and Wrongs*. 3d ed. London: Continuum.

Singer, Peter. (1975) *Animal Liberation*. New York: Harper Collins.

Nick Zangwill: Our Moral Duty to Eat Meat

1. Are there beneficial actions that we have no moral duty to perform? If so, what distinguishes those beneficial actions that are morally required from those that aren't? Does meat eating fall into the first or second category? Why?

2. Zangwill denies that his argument imposes a moral duty to kill and eat so-called "marginal" human beings. Do you find his reasoning here persuasive? Why or why not?

3. Zangwill allows that the moral duty to eat meat is only *pro tanto* (i.e., able to be outweighed by more pressing duties). What are the competing

moral duties that might oppose eating meat? Do you think these competing duties are weightier than the one to eat meat? Why?

4. Early on in his article Zangwill clarifies that his argument is not intended to apply to those farm animals living miserable lives. The upshot is that his argument does not assign a moral duty to kill such animals, but does impose a moral duty to kill animals that are flourishing. Is this paradoxical? Why or why not?

5. Zangwill argues that those who oppose eating meat on ethical grounds are mistaken, and are morally required to become omnivores. Do you agree with his assessment? Why or why not?

28

~

Puppies, Pigs and People: Eating Meat and Marginal Cases

Alastair Norcross

....

Alastair Norcross opens his provocative piece with a fictional scenario that is both outrageous and meant to make a very serious philosophical point. As he sees it, current practices of factory farming are deeply immoral. One might think that meat-eaters are exempt from blame, though, since for the most part they are not the ones who are actually perpetrating the harms to animals on the factory farms that process the great majority of animal products. Norcross rejects this thought. As he sees it, meat-eaters—at least those who know of the cruelty of the treatment of factory-farmed animals—are fully blameworthy for their indulgence. The good they get from eating meat—primarily the gustatory pleasure they get from eating meat—is far outweighed by the awful suffering of the animals when confined and killed on factory farms.

Norcross considers a wide variety of replies to his charge. These include the claim that individual meat-eaters are off the moral hook because their purchases are so insignificant that they cannot affect the practices on factory farms. Another reply is that meat-eaters do not intend to harm animals, but only foresee animal harm as a result of contemporary farming practices. Norcross extensively criticizes both replies.

Alastair Norcross, "Puppies, Pigs and People: Eating Meat and Marginal Cases," from *Philosophical Perspectives* 18 (2004), pp. 229–234, 239–244.

He then introduces a very popular argument in the literature on animal welfare: the argument from marginal cases. This argument says that we must treat animals and so-called "marginal" human beings as equals, since such humans have mental lives that are no more developed than those of the animals that are killed and eaten for food. He considers several replies to this argument, and finds fault with each of them. If we are unwilling to cruelly confine, prematurely kill, and eat "marginal" human beings, then we should be equally reluctant to do such things to animals.

Norcross concludes with a discussion of the difference between being a moral agent (i.e., someone who can respond to moral reasons and control her behavior by means of such reasons) and a moral patient (i.e., a being to whom we owe duties, even if that being lacks rights or lacks the cognitive powers needed to be a moral agent). Norcross argues that animals qualify as moral patients, even if, because of their diminished or nonexistent rationality, they cannot qualify as moral agents. We therefore owe them duties of respect, which protect them against the current practices involved in factory farming.

1. Fred's Basement

Consider the story of Fred, who receives a visit from the police one day. They have been summoned by Fred's neighbors, who have been disturbed by strange sounds emanating from Fred's basement. When they enter the basement they are confronted by the following scene: Twenty-six small wire cages, each containing a puppy, some whining, some whimpering, some howling. The puppies range in age from newborn to about six months. Many of them show signs of mutilation. Urine and feces cover the bottoms of the cages and the basement floor. Fred explains that he keeps the puppies for twenty-six weeks, and then butchers them while holding them upside-down. During their lives he performs a series of mutilations on them, such as slicing off their noses and their paws with a hot knife, all without any form of anesthesia. Except for the mutilations, the puppies are never allowed out of the cages, which are barely big enough to hold them at twenty-six weeks. The police are horrified, and promptly charge Fred with animal abuse. As details of the case are publicized, the public is outraged. Newspapers are flooded with letters demanding that Fred be severely punished. There are calls for more severe penalties for animal abuse. Fred is denounced as a vile sadist.

Finally, at his trial, Fred explains his behavior, and argues that he is blameless and therefore deserves no punishment. He is, he explains, a great lover of chocolate. A couple of years ago, he was involved in a car accident, which resulted in some head trauma. Upon his release from hospital, having apparently suffered no lasting ill effects, he visited his favorite restaurant and ordered their famous rich dark chocolate mousse. Imagine his dismay when he discovered that his experience of the mousse was a pale shadow of its former self. The mousse tasted bland, slightly pleasant, but with none of the intense chocolaty flavor he remembered so well. The waiter assured him that the recipe was unchanged from the last time he had tasted it, just the day before his accident. In some consternation, Fred rushed out to buy a bar of his favorite Belgian chocolate. Again, he was dismayed to discover that his experience of the chocolate was barely even pleasurable. Extensive investigation revealed that his experience of other foods remained unaffected, but chocolate, in all its forms, now tasted bland and insipid. Desperate for a solution to his problem, Fred visited a renowned gustatory neurologist, Dr. T. Bud. Extensive tests revealed that the accident had irreparably damaged the godiva gland, which secretes cocoamone, the hormone responsible for the experience of chocolate. Fred urgently requested hormone replacement therapy. Dr. Bud informed him that, until recently, there had been no known source of cocoamone, other than the human godiva gland, and that it was impossible to collect cocoamone from one person to be used by another. However, a chance discovery had altered the situation. A forensic veterinary surgeon, performing an autopsy on a severely abused puppy, had discovered high concentrations of cocoamone in the puppy's brain. It turned out that puppies, who don't normally produce cocoamone, could be stimulated to do so by extended periods of severe stress and suffering. The research, which led to this discovery, while gaining tenure for its authors, had not been widely publicized, for fear of antagonizing animal welfare groups. Although this research clearly gave Fred the hope of tasting chocolate again, there were no commercially available sources of puppy-derived cocoamone. Lack of demand, combined with fear of bad publicity, had deterred drug companies from getting into the puppy torturing business. Fred appeals to the court to imagine his anguish, on discovering that a solution to his severe deprivation was possible, but not readily available. But he wasn't inclined to sit around bemoaning his cruel fate. He did what any chocolate lover would do. He read the research, and set up his own cocoamone collection lab in his basement. Six months of intense puppy suffering, followed by a brutal death, produced enough cocoamone to last him a week, hence the twenty-six cages. He isn't a sadist or an animal abuser, he explains. If there were a method of collecting cocoamone without torturing puppies, he would gladly employ it. He derives no pleasure from the suffering of the puppies itself. He sympathizes with those who are horrified by the pain and misery of the animals, but the court must realize that human pleasure is at stake. The puppies, while undeniably cute, are mere animals. He admits that he would be just as healthy without chocolate, if not more so. But this isn't a matter of survival or health. His life would be unacceptably impoverished without the experience of chocolate.

End of story. Clearly, we are horrified by Fred's behavior, and unconvinced by his attempted justification. It is, of course, unfortunate for Fred that he can no longer enjoy the taste of chocolate, but that in no way excuses the imposition of severe suffering on the puppies. I expect near universal agreement with this claim (the exceptions being those who are either inhumanly callous or thinking ahead, and wish to avoid the following conclusion, to which such agreement commits them). No decent person would even contemplate torturing puppies merely to enhance a gustatory experience. However, billions of animals endure intense suffering every year for precisely this end. Most of the chicken, veal, beef, and pork consumed in the US comes from intensive confinement facilities, in which the animals live cramped, stress-filled lives and endure unanaesthetized mutilations. The vast majority of people would suffer no ill health from the elimination of meat from their diets. Quite the reverse. The supposed benefits from this system of factory farming, apart from the profits accruing to agribusiness, are increased levels of gustatory pleasure for those who claim that they couldn't enjoy a meat-free diet as much as their current meat-filled diets. If we are prepared to condemn Fred for torturing puppies merely to enhance his gustatory experiences, shouldn't we similarly condemn the millions who purchase and consume factory-raised meat? Are there any morally significant differences between Fred's behavior and their behavior?

2. Fred's Behavior Compared with Our Behavior

The first difference that might seem to be relevant is that Fred tortures the puppies himself, whereas most Americans consume meat that comes from animals that have been tortured by others. But is this really relevant? What if Fred had been squeamish and had employed someone else to torture the puppies and extract the cocoamone? Would we have thought any better of Fred? Of course not.

Another difference between Fred and many consumers of factory-raised meat is that many, perhaps most, such consumers are unaware of the treatment of the animals, before they appear in neatly wrapped packages on supermarket shelves. Perhaps I should moderate my challenge, then. If we are prepared to condemn Fred for torturing puppies merely to enhance his gustatory experiences, shouldn't we similarly condemn those who purchase and consume factory-raised meat, in full, or even partial, awareness of the suffering endured by the animals? While many consumers are still blissfully ignorant of the appalling treatment meted out to meat, that number is rapidly dwindling, thanks to vigorous publicity campaigns waged by animal welfare groups. Furthermore, any meat-eating readers of this article are now deprived of the excuse of ignorance.

Perhaps a consumer of factory-raised animals could argue as follows: While I agree that Fred's behavior is abominable, mine is crucially different. If Fred did not consume his chocolate, he would not raise and torture puppies (or pay someone else to do so). Therefore Fred could prevent the suffering of the puppies. However, if I did not buy and consume factory-raised meat, no animals would be spared lives of misery. Agribusiness is much too large to respond to the behavior of one consumer. Therefore I cannot prevent the suffering of any animals. I may well regret the suffering inflicted on animals for the sake of human enjoyment. I may even agree that the human enjoyment doesn't justify the suffering. However, since the animals will suffer no matter what I do, I may as well enjoy the taste of their flesh.

There are at least two lines of response to this attempted defense. First, consider an analogous case. You visit a friend in an exotic location, say Alabama. Your friend takes you out to eat at the finest restaurant in Tuscaloosa. For dessert you select the house specialty, "Chocolate Mousse à la Bama," served with a small cup of coffee, which you are instructed to drink before eating the mousse. The mousse is quite simply the most delicious dessert you have ever tasted. Never before has chocolate tasted so rich and satisfying. Tempted to order a second, you ask your friend what makes this mousse so delicious. He informs you that the mousse itself is ordinary, but the coffee contains a concentrated dose of cocoamone, the newly discovered chocolate-enhancing hormone. Researchers at Auburn University have perfected a technique for extracting cocoamone from the brains of freshly slaughtered puppies, who have been subjected to lives of pain and frustration. Each puppy's brain yields four doses, each of which is effective for about fifteen minutes, just long enough to enjoy one serving of mousse. You are, naturally, horrified and disgusted. You will certainly not order another serving, you tell your friend. In fact, you are shocked that your friend, who had always seemed to be a morally decent person, could have both recommended the dessert to you and eaten one himself, in full awareness of the loathsome process necessary for the experience. He agrees that the suffering of the puppies is outrageous, and that the gain in human pleasure in no way justifies the appalling treatment they have to endure. However, neither he nor you can save any puppies by refraining from consuming cocoamone. Cocoamone production is now Alabama's leading industry, so it is much too large to respond to the behavior of one or two consumers. Since the puppies will suffer no matter what either of you does, you may as well enjoy the mousse.

If it is as obvious as it seems that a morally decent person, who is aware of the details of cocoamone production, couldn't order Chocolate Mousse à la Bama, it should be equally obvious that a morally decent person, who is aware of the details of factory farming, can't purchase and consume factory-raised meat. If the attempted excuse of causal impotence is compelling in the latter case, it should be compelling in the former case. But it isn't.

The second response to the claim of causal impotence is to deny it. Consider the case of chickens, the most cruelly treated of all animals raised for human consumption, with the possible exception of veal calves. In 1998, almost 8 billion chickens were slaughtered in the US, almost all of them raised on factory farms. Suppose that there are 250 million chicken eaters in the US, and that each one consumes, on average, 25 chickens per year (this leaves a fair number of chickens slaughtered for nonhuman consumption, or for export). Clearly, if only one of those chicken eaters gave up eating chicken, the industry would not respond. Equally clearly, if they all gave up eating chicken, billions of chickens (approximately 6.25 billion per year) would not be bred, tortured, and killed. But there must also be some number of consumers, far short of 250 million, whose renunciation of chicken would cause the industry to reduce the number of chickens bred in factory farms. The industry may not be able to respond to each individual's behavior, but it must respond to the behavior of fairly large numbers. Suppose that the industry is sensitive to a reduction in demand for chicken equivalent to 10,000 people becoming vegetarians. (This seems like a reasonable guess, but I have no idea what the actual numbers are, nor is it important.) For each group of 10,000 who give up chicken, a quarter of a million fewer chickens are bred per year. It appears, then, that if you give up eating chicken, you have only a one in ten thousand chance of making any difference to the lives of chickens, unless it is certain that fewer than 10,000 people will ever give up eating chicken, in which case you have no chance. Isn't a one in ten thousand chance small enough to render your continued consumption of chicken blameless? Not at all.. . . A one in ten thousand chance of saving 250,000 chickens per year from excruciating lives is morally and mathematically equivalent to the certainty of saving 25 chickens per year. We commonly accept that even small risks of great harms are unacceptable. That is why we disapprove of parents who fail to secure their children in car seats or with seat belts, who leave their small children unattended at home, or who drink or smoke heavily during pregnancy. Or consider commercial aircraft safety measures. The chances that the oxygen masks, the lifejackets, or the emergency exits on any given plane will be called on to save any lives in a given week, are far smaller than one in ten thousand. And yet we would be outraged to discover that an airline had knowingly allowed a plane to fly for a week with non-functioning emergency exits, oxygen masks, and lifejackets. So, even if it is true that your giving up factory-raised chicken has only a tiny chance of preventing suffering, given that the amount of suffering that would be prevented is in inverse proportion to your chance of preventing it, your continued consumption is not thereby excused.

But perhaps it is not even true that your giving up chicken has only a tiny chance of making any difference. Suppose again that the poultry industry only reduces production when a threshold of 10,000 fresh vegetarians is reached. Suppose also, as is almost certainly true, that vegetarianism is growing in popularity in the US (and elsewhere). Then, even if you are not the one, newly converted vegetarian, to reach the next threshold of 10,000, your conversion will reduce the time required before the next threshold is reached. The sooner the threshold is reached, the sooner production, and therefore animal suffering, is reduced. Your behavior, therefore, does make a difference. Furthermore, many people who become vegetarians influence others to become vegetarian, who in turn influence others, and so on. It appears, then, that the claim of causal impotence is mere wishful thinking, on the part of those meat lovers who are morally sensitive enough to realize that human gustatory pleasure does not justify inflicting extreme suffering on animals.

Perhaps there is a further difference between the treatment of Fred's puppies and the treatment of animals on factory farms. The suffering of the puppies is a necessary means to the production of gustatory pleasure, whereas the suffering of animals on factory farms is simply a by-product of the conditions dictated by economic considerations. Therefore, it might be argued, the suffering of the puppies is *intended as a means* to Fred's pleasure, whereas the suffering of factory raised animals is merely *foreseen* as a side-effect of a system that is a means to the gustatory pleasures of millions. The distinction between what is intended, either as a means or as an end in itself, and what is 'merely' foreseen is central to the Doctrine of Double Effect. Supporters of this doctrine claim that it is sometimes permissible to bring about an effect that is merely foreseen, even though the very same effect could not permissibly be brought about if intended. (Other conditions have to be met in order for the Doctrine of Double Effect to judge an action permissible, most notably that there be an outweighing good effect.) Fred acts impermissibly, according to this line of argument, because he intends the suffering of the puppies as a means to his pleasure. Most meat eaters, on the other hand, even if aware of the suffering of the animals, do not intend the suffering.

In response to this line of argument, I could remind the reader that Samuel Johnson said, or should have said, that the Doctrine of Double Effect is the last refuge of a scoundrel. I won't do that, however, since neither the doctrine itself, nor the alleged moral distinction between intending and foreseeing can justify the consumption of factory-raised meat. The Doctrine of Double Effect requires not merely that a bad effect be foreseen and not intended, but also that there be an outweighing good effect. In the case of the suffering of factory-raised animals, whatever good could plausibly be claimed to come out of the system clearly doesn't outweigh the bad. Furthermore, it would be easy to modify the story of Fred to render the puppies' suffering 'merely' foreseen. For example, suppose that the cocoamone is produced by a chemical reaction that can only occur when large quantities of drain-cleaner are forced down the throat of a conscious, unanaesthetized puppy. The consequent appalling suffering, while not itself a means to the production of cocoamone, is nonetheless an unavoidable side-effect of the means. In this variation of the story, Fred's behavior is no less abominable than in the original.

One last difference between the behavior of Fred and the behavior of the consumers of factory-raised meat is worth discussing, if only because it is so frequently cited in response to the arguments of this paper. Fred's behavior is abominable, according to this line of thinking, because it involves the suffering of *puppies*. The behavior of meat-eaters, on the other hand, 'merely' involves the suffering of chickens, pigs, cows, calves, sheep, and the like. Puppies (and probably dogs and cats in general) are morally different from the other animals. Puppies *count* (morally, that is), whereas the other animals don't, or at least not nearly as much.

So, what gives puppies a higher moral status than the animals we eat? Presumably there is some morally relevant property or properties possessed by puppies but not by farm animals. Perhaps puppies have a greater degree of rationality than farm animals, or a more finely developed moral sense, or at least a sense of loyalty and devotion. The problems with this kind of approach are obvious. It's highly unlikely that any property that has even an outside chance of being ethically relevant is both possessed by puppies and not possessed by any farm animals. For example, it's probably true that most puppies have a greater degree of rationality (whatever that means) than most chickens, but the comparison with pigs is far more dubious. Besides, if Fred were to inform the jury that he had taken pains to acquire particularly stupid, morally obtuse, disloyal and undevoted puppies, would they (or we) have declared his behavior to be morally acceptable? Clearly not.

I have been unable to discover any morally relevant differences between the behavior of Fred, the puppy torturer, and the behavior of the millions of people who purchase and consume factory-raised meat, at least those who do so in the knowledge that the animals live lives of suffering and deprivation. If morality demands that we not torture puppies merely to enhance our own eating pleasure, morality also demands that we not support factory farming by purchasing factory-raised meat. . . .

3. Humans' Versus Animals' Ethical Status—The Rationality Gambit

For the purposes of this discussion, to claim that humans have a superior ethical status to animals is to claim that it is morally right to give the interests of humans greater weight than those of animals in deciding how to behave. Such claims will often be couched in terms of rights, such as the rights to life, liberty or respect, but nothing turns on this terminological matter. One may claim that it is generally wrong to kill humans, but not animals, because humans are rational, and animals are not. Or one may claim that the suffering of animals counts less than the suffering of humans (if at all), because humans are rational, and animals are not. . . .

What could ground the claim of superior moral status for humans? Just as the defender of a higher moral status for puppies than for farm animals needs to find some property or properties possessed by puppies but not by farm animals, so the defender of a higher moral status for humans needs to find some property or properties possessed by humans but not by other animals. The traditional view, dating back at least to Aristotle, is that rationality is what separates humans, both morally and metaphysically, from other animals.

One of the most serious challenges to the traditional view involves a consideration of what philosophers refer to as 'marginal cases.' Whatever kind and level of rationality is selected as justifying the attribution of superior moral status to humans will either be lacking in some humans or present in some animals. To take one of the most commonly-suggested features, many humans are incapable of engaging in moral reflection. For some, this incapacity is temporary, as is the case with infants, or the temporarily cognitively disabled. Others who once had the capacity may have permanently lost it, as is the case with the severely senile or the irreversibly comatose. Still others never had and never will have the capacity, as is the case with the severely mentally disabled. If we base our claims for the moral superiority of humans over animals on the attribution of such capacities, won't we have to exclude many humans? Won't we then be forced to the claim that there is at least as much moral reason to use cognitively deficient humans in experiments and for food as to use animals? Perhaps we could exclude the only temporarily disabled, on the grounds of potentiality, though that move has its own problems. Nonetheless, the other two categories would be vulnerable to this objection.

I will consider two lines of response to the argument from marginal cases. The first denies that we have to attribute different moral status to marginal humans, but maintains that we are, nonetheless, justified in attributing different moral status to animals who are just as cognitively sophisticated as marginal humans, if not more so. The second admits that, strictly speaking, marginal humans are morally inferior to other humans, but proceeds to claim pragmatic reasons for treating them, at least usually, as if they had equal status.

As representatives of the first line of defense, I will consider arguments from three philosophers, Carl Cohen, Alan White, and David Schmidtz. First, Cohen:

> [the argument from marginal cases] fails; it mistakenly treats an essential feature of humanity as though it were a screen for sorting humans. The capacity for moral judgment that distinguishes humans from

animals is not a test to be administered to human beings one by one. Persons who are unable, because of some disability, to perform the full moral functions natural to human beings are certainly not for that reason ejected from the moral community. The issue is one of kind. . . . What humans retain when disabled, animals have never had.[1]

Alan White argues that animals don't have rights, on the grounds that they cannot intelligibly be spoken of in the full language of a right. By this he means that they cannot, for example, claim, demand, assert, insist on, secure, waive, or surrender a right. This is what he has to say in response to the argument from marginal cases:

> Nor does this, as some contend, exclude infants, children, the feeble-minded, the comatose, the dead, or generations yet unborn. Any of these may be for various reasons empirically unable to fulfill the full role of right-holder. But . . . they are logically possible subjects of rights to whom the full language of rights can significantly, however falsely, be used. It is a misfortune, not a tautology, that these persons cannot exercise or enjoy, claim, or waive, their rights or do their duty or fulfil their obligations.[2]

David Schmidtz defends the appeal to typical characteristics of species, such as mice, chimpanzees, and humans, in making decisions on the use of different species in experiments. He also considers the argument from marginal cases:

> Of course, some chimpanzees lack the characteristic features in virtue of which chimpanzees command respect as a species, just as some humans lack the characteristic features in virtue of which humans command respect as a species. It is equally obvious that some chimpanzees have cognitive capacities (for example) that are superior to the cognitive capacities of some humans. But whether every human being is superior to every chimpanzee is beside the point. The point is that we can, we do, and we should make decisions on the basis of our recognition that mice, chimpanzees, and humans are relevantly different types. We can have it both ways after all. Or so a speciesist could argue.[3]

---

1. Carl Cohen, "The Case for the Use of Animals in Biomedical Research," *The New England Journal of Medicine*, vol. 315, 1986.
2. Alan White, Rights, (OUP 1984). Reprinted in *Animal Rights and Human Obligations*, 2nd edition, Tom Regan and Peter Singer (eds.) (Prentice Hall, 1989), 120.
3. David Schmidtz, "Are All Species Equal?," *Journal of Applied Philosophy*, Vol. 15, no. 1 (1998), 61, my emphasis.

There is something deeply troublesome about the line of argument that runs through all three of these responses to the argument from marginal cases. A particular feature, or set of features is claimed to have so much moral significance that its presence or lack can make the difference to whether a piece of behavior is morally justified or morally outrageous. But then it is claimed that the presence or lack of the feature in any *particular* case is not important. The relevant question is whether the presence or lack of the feature is *normal*. Such an argument would seem perfectly preposterous in most other cases. Suppose, for example, that ten famous people are on trial in the afterlife for crimes against humanity. On the basis of conclusive evidence, five are found guilty and five are found not guilty. Four of the guilty are sentenced to an eternity of torment, and one is granted an eternity of bliss. Four of the innocent are granted an eternity of bliss, and one is sentenced to an eternity of torment. The one innocent who is sentenced to torment asks why he, and not the fifth guilty person, must go to hell. Saint Peter replies, "Isn't it obvious Mr. Ghandi? You are male. The other four men—Adolph Hitler, Joseph Stalin, George W. Bush, and Richard Nixon—are all guilty. Therefore the normal condition for a male defendant in this trial is guilt. The fact that you happen to be innocent is irrelevant. Likewise, of the five female defendants in this trial, only one was guilty. Therefore the normal condition for female defendants in this trial is innocence. That is why Margaret Thatcher gets to go to heaven instead of you."

As I said, such an argument is preposterous. Is the reply to the argument from marginal cases any better? Perhaps it will be claimed that a biological category such as a species is more 'natural,' whatever that means, than a category like 'all the male (or female) defendants in this trial.' Even setting aside the not inconsiderable worries about the conventionality of biological categories, it is not at all clear why this distinction should be morally relevant. What if it turned out that there were statistically relevant differences in the mental abilities of men and women? Suppose that men were, on average, more skilled at manipulating numbers than women, and that women were, on average, more empathetic than men. Would such differences in what was 'normal' for men and women justify us in preferring an innumerate man to a female math genius for a job as an accountant, or an insensitive woman to an ultra-sympathetic man for a job as a counselor? I take it that the biological distinction between male and female is just as real as that between human and chimpanzee.

A second response to the argument from marginal cases is to concede that cognitively deficient humans really do have an inferior moral status to normal humans. Can we, then, use such humans as we do animals? I know of no-one who takes the further step of advocating the use of marginal humans for food How can we advocate this second response while blocking the further step? Mary Anne Warren suggests that "there are powerful practical and emotional reasons for protecting non-rational human beings, reasons which are absent in the case of most non-human animals."[4] It would clearly outrage common human sensibilities, if we were to raise retarded children for food or medical experiments. Here is Steinbock in a similar vein:

> I doubt that anyone will be able to come up with a concrete and morally relevant difference that would justify, say, using a chimpanzee in an experiment rather than a human being with less capacity for reasoning, moral responsibility, etc. Should we then experiment on the severely retarded? Utilitarian considerations aside, we feel a special obligation to care for the handicapped members of our own species, who cannot survive in this world without such care In addition, when we consider the severely retarded, we think, 'That could be me.' It makes sense to think that one might have been born retarded, but not to think that one might have been born a monkey Here we are getting away from such things as 'morally relevant differences' and are talking about something much more difficult to articulate, namely, the role of feeling and sentiment in moral thinking.[5]

This line of response clearly won't satisfy those who think that marginal humans really do deserve equal moral consideration with other humans. It is also a very shaky basis on which to justify our current practices. What outrages human sensibilities is a very fragile thing. Human history is littered with examples of widespread acceptance of the systematic mistreatment of some groups who didn't generate any sympathetic response from others. That we do feel a kind of sympathy for retarded humans that we don't feel for dogs is, if true, a contingent matter. To see just how shaky a basis this is for protecting retarded humans, imagine that a new kind of

---

4. Mary Anne Warren, "Difficulties with the Strong Animal Rights Position," *Between the Species* 2, no. 4, 1987. Reprinted in *Contemporary Moral Problems*, 5th edition, James E. White (ed.) (Wadsworth, 1997), 482–83.

5. Bonnie Steinbock, "Speciesism and the Idea of Equality," *Philosophy* 53, no. 204 (April 1978), 469–70. Reprinted in *Contemporary Moral Problems*, 5th edition, James E. White (ed.) (Wadsworth, 1997) 467–468.

birth defect (perhaps associated with beef from cows treated with bovine growth hormone) produces severe mental retardation, green skin, and a complete lack of emotional bond between parents and child. Furthermore, suppose that the mental retardation is of the same kind and severity as that caused by other birth defects that don't have the other two effects. It seems likely that denying moral status to such defective humans would not run the same risks of outraging human sensibilities as would the denial of moral status to other, less easily distinguished and more loved defective humans. Would these contingent empirical differences between our reactions to different sources of mental retardation justify us in ascribing different direct moral status to their subjects? The only difference between them is skin color and whether they are loved by others. Any theory that could ascribe moral relevance to differences such as these doesn't deserve to be taken seriously.

Finally, perhaps we could claim that the practice of giving greater weight to the interests of all humans than of animals is justified on evolutionary grounds. Perhaps such differential concern has survival value for the species. Something like this may well be true, but it is hard to see the moral relevance. We can hardly justify the privileging of human interests over animal interests on the grounds that such privileging serves human interests!

6. Agent and Patient—the Speciesist's Central Confusion

Although the argument from marginal cases certainly poses a formidable challenge to any proposed criterion of full moral standing that excludes animals, it doesn't, in my view, constitute the most serious flaw in such attempts to justify the status quo. The proposed criteria are all variations on the Aristotelian criterion of rationality. But what is the moral relevance of rationality? Why should we think that the possession of a certain level or kind of rationality renders the possessor's interests of greater moral significance than those of a merely sentient being? In Bentham's famous words, "The question is not, Can they reason? nor Can they talk? But, Can they suffer?"[6]

What do defenders of the alleged superiority of human interests say in response to Bentham's challenge? Some, such as Carl Cohen, simply reiterate the differences between humans and animals that they claim to carry

---

6. Jeremy Bentham, *Introduction to the Principles of Morals and Legislation*, chapter 17.

moral significance. Animals are not members of moral communities, they don't engage in moral reflection, they can't be moved by moral reasons, *therefore* (?) their interests don't count as much as ours. Others, such as Steinbock and Warren, attempt to go further. Here is Warren on the subject:

> Why is rationality morally relevant? It does not make us "better" than other animals or more "perfect." . . . But it is morally relevant insofar as it provides greater possibilities for cooperation and for the nonviolent resolution of problems.[7]

Warren is certainly correct in claiming that a certain level and kind of rationality is morally relevant. Where she, and others who give similar arguments, go wrong is in specifying what the moral relevance amounts to. If a being is incapable of moral reasoning, at even the most basic level, if it is incapable of being moved by moral reasons, claims, or arguments, then it cannot be a moral agent. It cannot be subject to moral obligations, to moral praise or blame. Punishing a dog for doing something "wrong" is no more than an attempt to alter its future behavior.

All this is well and good, but what is the significance for the question of what weight to give to animal interests? That animals can't be moral agents doesn't seem to be relevant to their status as moral *patients*. Many, perhaps most, humans are both moral agents and patients. Most, perhaps all, animals are only moral patients. Why would the lack of moral agency give them diminished status as moral patients? Full status as a moral patient is not some kind of reward for moral agency. I have heard students complain in this regard that it is *unfair* that humans bear the burdens of moral responsibility, and don't get enhanced consideration of their interests in return. This is a very strange claim. Humans are subject to moral obligations, because they are the kind of creatures who *can* be. What grounds moral agency is simply different from what grounds moral standing as a patient. It is no more unfair that humans and not animals are moral agents, than it is unfair that real animals and not stuffed toys are moral patients.

. . . It seems that any attempt to justify the claim that humans have a higher moral status than other animals by appealing to some version of rationality as the morally relevant difference between humans and animals will fail on at least two counts. It will fail to give an adequate answer to the

---

7. Warren, op. cit. 482.

argument from marginal cases, and, more importantly, it will fail to make the case that such a difference is morally relevant to the status of animals as moral patients as opposed to their status as moral agents.

I conclude that our intuitions that Fred's behavior is morally impermissible are accurate. Furthermore, given that the behavior of those who knowingly support factory farming is morally indistinguishable, it follows that their behavior is also morally impermissible.

Alastair Norcross: Puppies, Pigs and People: Eating Meat and Marginal Cases

1. Do you agree that Fred acts immorally in the case that Norcross describes? If so, what exactly is it about Fred's behavior that is morally objectionable? If not, why not?
2. Some might claim that eating meat from factory farms is relevantly different from Fred's behavior because individual consumers are powerless to change the factory-farming system, whereas Fred is fully in control of the puppies. How does Norcross respond to this claim?
3. Another disanalogy between Fred's behavior and that of most meateaters is that Fred *intends* to make the puppies suffer, while most consumers of meat don't intend to make any animals suffer. Does this disanalogy undermine Norcross's argument? Why or why not?
4. What is the "argument from marginal cases" and what is it supposed to show? What do you think is the strongest objection to the argument?
5. What is the difference between being a moral agent and being a moral patient? Why does Norcross think that nonhuman animals are moral patients? Do you agree with him?

29

The Public and Private Morality of Climate Change

John Broome

....

John Broome begins his essay by introducing two important distinctions. The first is between public morality, which directs government actions, and private morality, which directs those of individuals. The second is between duties of justice, which focus on what we owe to particular people, and duties of goodness, which are duties to make the world better.

Broome argues that when it comes to private morality and what we, as individuals, must do to address climate change, we have only duties of justice. For a variety of reasons, the good we can do to prevent climate change harms is relatively small, and our resources would be better spent in trying to yield greater benefits in non-climate-related areas. Governments, though, *do* have climate-based duties of goodness; given their much greater resources, they can address severe problems, such as medical crises, while also taking steps to reduce damage to the climate.

Both individuals and governments have duties of justice to redress the harms imposed by our emissions. Broome reviews seven different features of the harms that come from our emissions, in support of the claim that such harmful behavior, both on the part of individuals and governments, amounts to an injustice. When it comes to individuals, his verdict is succinct: "Your carbon footprint ought to be zero unless

John Broome, "The Public and Private Morality of Climate Change," from the Tanner Lectures vol. 32, 2013, pp. 5–20.

you make restitution." That said, Broome does not in fact advise individuals to compensate everyone who is harmed by our carbon emissions. That would be too unwieldy. Rather, he proposes that we reduce our emissions where we can, and *offset* the rest. This amounts to taking steps to remove or prevent emissions in proportion to causing them.

Broome then turns his attention to a government's duty of goodness to improve climate conditions. He argues that, as a practical matter, governments can discharge their duties of goodness to future generations without asking current citizens to make any net sacrifice. How is such a thing possible? By reducing greenhouse emissions (a sacrifice), but compensating current citizens by allowing them to use up more non-emissions-generating resources. Future generations would therefore be left with fewer of these other resources, but a cleaner environment.

....

We as individuals are subject to various moral duties. We have a duty to be kind to strangers, to keep our promises, to look after our parents when they are old, and so on. Collective entities, including our governments, are also subject to moral duties, or so I assume. I assume that a government should not imprison innocent people, it should protect refugees, it should support the destitute, and so on, and that these are moral duties.

The moral duties of governments—whatever they are—I call "public morality." They generate derivative moral duties for citizens: we should do what is appropriate to get our government to act rightly, and support it when it does. These duties I call "civic morality." By "private morality," I mean the morality of our private lives; private morality does not include our civic duties.

Climate change creates duties within both public and private morality. I shall describe some of them.

Duties of Justice and Duties of Goodness

Moral duties fall into two broad classes: duties of justice and duties of goodness or beneficence. There may be other sorts of moral duties, too, but I shall be concerned only with these two. I start by making the distinction between them.

The duty of goodness is to make the world better. Some libertarians deny that people as individuals have this duty. I disagree with those libertarians, but I have no need to argue with them here. My conclusions about private morality will not call on this duty of goodness. However, I shall assume that governments have a duty of goodness; I assume they have a duty to make the world better for their own citizens at least. For instance, they should create their country's economic infrastructure and design their banking regulations with that aim in mind.

Improving the world is not our only moral duty. When an action of yours would improve the world, you are not necessarily morally required to do it, and sometimes you are not even morally permitted to do it. A famous example is the case of a surgeon who has five patients, each needing an organ in order to survive: one needs a heart, another a liver, a third a kidney, and so on. Suppose the surgeon kills an innocent visitor to the hospital and distributes her organs to the five patients, thereby saving five lives at the expense of one. That leads to a net benefit; it improves the world. Yet this surgeon's act is not morally permissible.

So there must be some other source of moral duties that can oppose the duty of goodness. There is evidently some sort of a moral duty not to harm people, even for the sake of the greater overall good. . . . The duty not to harm is not unlimited; there are occasions when it is morally permissible to harm someone. For instance, you may do harm in self-defense, and you may harm a person when you are inflicting a deserved punishment on her. I am sorry to say I cannot accurately delineate the boundaries of the duty not to harm, but I hope soon to identify one instance of it convincingly.

I take this duty not to harm to be a duty of justice. Other philosophers may classify it differently, and nothing will turn on the classification. It does have at least one feature that is characteristic of justice. It is a duty *owed* to a particular person, or to particular people. If you breach a duty of justice, you are doing an injustice, and there is always someone to whom you do it. To express this fact, we often say that the person has a *right* to your performing the duty. Rights go along with justice. When you have a duty of justice to do something, someone has a right to your doing it.

By contrast, duties of goodness are not owed to particular people. The difference is nicely illustrated by the views of the eighteenth-century philosopher William Godwin. Godwin thought that the duty to promote good is indeed owed to the people whose good you should promote.[1] He explicitly classified it as a duty of justice. For instance, he thought that if someone else can make better use of your horse than you can, she has a right to it. He thought you do her an injustice if you do not let her have it. Few of us agree with Godwin about that. Most of us think we have a duty to promote goodness, but we think the duty is not owed to particular people, and we therefore do not take it to be a duty of justice.

Justice and Goodness in Public and Private Morality

I am now going to apply this distinction among sorts of duty to the moral duties that arise from climate change. My first point is that the relative importance of justice and goodness differs between private morality and public morality. Justice is relatively more important for private morality, goodness relatively more important for public morality. Indeed, I shall argue that the private morality of climate change is governed entirely by the duty of justice, whereas public morality is also aimed at goodness.

Why do I say this? For two main reasons. The first is known as the "nonidentity problem." It was made prominent by the philosopher Derek Parfit.[2] Remember that a duty of justice is owed to particular people, who have a right to its performance. Take a particular person who is alive 150 years from now—call her "Sarah." Suppose Sarah's life is not very good because we, the current generation, allow climate change to go unchecked. Could she claim we do her an injustice by our profligacy? Could she say she has a right to a better life, which we deny her by emitting so much greenhouse gas? She could not, for a reason I shall now explain.

Suppose we were instead to take the trouble to reduce our emissions. By "we" I am referring to the present generation either in the whole world or within a particular nation. We would live lives of a different sort. The richer among us would travel less by car and plane and buy fewer consumer goods. The poorer would find farming easier and find less need to migrate to the cities; they would also find less need to move to higher ground to escape from the rising sea. There would be many other

---

1. William Godwin, *Enquiry Concerning Political Justice*, 3rd ed. (1798; reprint, Harmondsworth: Penguin Press, 1976).

2. Derek Parfit, *Reasons and Persons* (Oxford: Oxford University Press, 1984), chap. 16.

differences. Indeed, everyone's life would be different. Consequently, many people would have babies with different partners. Even those who would have the same partner as they actually do have would conceive their babies at different times.

The identity of a person depends on the sperm and egg she originates from. No one could have come from a different egg or a different sperm from the one she actually does come from. To put it differently: anyone who originated from a different sperm or a different egg would be a different person. Consequently, even the slightest variation in the timing of conception makes a different person. A slight change in a couple's lives means that they conceive different people. Were we to significantly reduce our emissions of greenhouse gas, it would change the lives of nearly everyone in the world. Within a couple of generations, the entire population of the world would consist of different people. Call this the "nonidentity effect."

Our Sarah would therefore not exist at all, were we to take the trouble to reduce our emissions. If she would not even exist were we to reduce our emissions, she cannot plausibly claim she had a right to a better life, which we violate by not doing so. We could not give Sarah a better life by emitting less gas, so we do not violate a right of hers by emitting profligately. Suppose we did owe a duty to Sarah to reduce emissions. Were we to carry out this duty, there would be no Sarah and therefore no duty. It would be a duty that cannot be satisfied. That makes no sense. We can conclude that our emissions do no injustice to Sarah. The same goes for nearly everyone in her generation.

In a way, the nonidentity effect excuses us as a generation from a charge of injustice toward future generations. Please do not think it excuses us from every moral duty to reduce emissions. Our continued emissions make the lives of future generations much less good than they could be. So they constitute a serious violation of our duty of goodness. This is not in any way a minor violation of morality; making the world less good is a serious moral fault. But it is not a violation of justice.

The nonidentity effect of a generation's or a country's emissions will obviously be much bigger than the nonidentity effect of a single person's emissions. If you reduce your own emissions of greenhouse gas, that will affect the identity of some people in the next few generations, but probably not very many. So the nonidentity effect provides individuals with little excuse against a charge of injustice to future generations. That is the first reason justice is relatively more important for individuals than it is for nations and their governments.

The Harm Done by an Individual

The second reason justice is relatively more important in the private morality of climate change is that the duty of goodness demands very little of an individual. It requires you to reduce your greenhouse gas emissions only insofar as you can do so at a very small cost. Probably it requires you to turn off the light when you leave a room—that sort of thing. The reason is quantitative, and to explain it I need to start by giving you some idea of the quantity of harm a person's emissions do.

I shall use a calculation shown to me by David Frame, now of Victoria University in New Zealand.[3] I must emphasize that Frame means it to be very rough. The figures are intended only to show you the order of magnitude of the harm you do, nothing more. Frame calculates that an average person from a rich country, if she was born in 1950, will emit during the course of her whole life about 800 tonnes of carbon dioxide. This will warm the atmosphere by about half a billionth of a degree. A major part of the harm climate change will do is the killing of people. The World Health Organization has published predictions of the number who will be killed, and on that basis we can estimate that this 800 tonnes will shorten people's lives in total by some months. Each year of a rich person's emissions shortens lives by one or two days. We will not shorten any single person's life that much, but each of us shortens lives in total by that amount.

This is a serious harm. None of us would want to be responsible for shortening people's lives to that extent. This figure shows you, read conversely, how much good you could do by reducing your emissions. Some people despair in the face of climate change. They think the problem is so huge that nothing they can do as individuals will do any good. But they are wrong. By reducing your emissions, you can do significant good through extending people's lives. If you stop your emissions, each year you will extend lives by a day or two.

But the main point I want to make is that the good you can do by reducing your emissions, though significant, is small compared with other opportunities you have. Suppose you reduce your annual emissions to zero in the cheapest possible way (which is by offsetting them, as I shall explain later). It will cost you a few hundred dollars per year. For that you will extend people's lives by one or two days each year. But for a few hundred

---

3. David Frame, "Personal and Intergenerational Carbon Footprints" (forthcoming).

dollars, a charity that treats tuberculosis can cure a person's infection, and thereby extend her life for many years or decades. Of course, reducing emissions will do good in other ways as well as by saving lives, but they are not enough to close this very large gap in benefits. So if you aim to use your resources to improve the world, reducing emissions of greenhouse gas is not the way to do it. To improve the world, you should carry on emitting, and send the money you save by doing so to a tuberculosis charity. This is why I say that the duty of goodness does not require you to reduce your emissions significantly.

Why does the same argument not apply to governments? It's because governments—at least the governments of large countries—control more resources. Like individuals, they have more effective ways of using resources to do good, by treating tuberculosis, controlling malaria and polio, providing clean drinking water around the world, and so on. But even if they were to do all those things, they could *still* improve the world further by using their power to reduce greenhouse gas emissions. A government's duty of goodness requires it to treat tuberculosis, control malaria, provide clean water, and so on, *and* control climate change. That is not so for an individual. If you were to devote all your resources to improving the world, even when they were completely exhausted, the need for tuberculosis treatment would still be more pressing than the need to reduce greenhouse gas emissions.

The Injustice of Emissions

The private morality of climate change therefore does not arise from the duty of goodness. It arises instead from the duty of justice. What justice does the duty of justice require of individuals?

I am concerned with the particular duty of justice not to harm. I have already said that each person's emissions of greenhouse gas do harm. I have even given a rough estimate of the amount of one particular harm they do: the harm of shortening lives. Earlier I pointed out that not all harms are necessarily unjust, but next I shall argue that the harm done by emissions is indeed an injustice. I cannot do this conclusively, because I am not able to identify exactly where the boundary lies between harms that are unjust and those that are not. But I shall mention seven different characteristics of the harm done by our emissions, and by the time I have reached the end of the list, I think it will be clear that this harm lies on the side of injustice. Several points beside the seven are so obvious that I do not include them in the list: the harm caused by emissions is not a merited punishment, it is done without the consent of the person harmed, and so on. Here is the list.

First, the harm done by our emissions is the result of something we *do*. Many of us make a distinction between doing harm and failing to prevent harm. If you fail to donate to a charity that relieves poverty, you fail to prevent the harm of poverty, but many of us do not think this failure is an injustice. Emitting greenhouse gas is different. In living our lives, we *act* in ways that cause greenhouse gases to be emitted. We *cause* carbon dioxide to spew from our chimneys and the exhaust pipes of our cars. These are consequences of things we do, rather than of things we omit to do.

Second, the harm we do by our emissions is serious. It may be permissible to do a trivial amount of harm, but this harm is far from trivial. I have given an idea of its size.

Third, the harm we do is not accidental. Indeed, we do it knowingly, though not deliberately. Few people in the developed world are ignorant of the greenhouse effect. Accidental harms are not an injustice, but emissions are not in that category.

Fourth, we do not compensate the victims of our harm. An injustice can sometimes be canceled by compensation, but our emissions are not canceled in this way.

Fifth, most of us make our emissions for our own benefit. That is not true of all of us. Some people are exceptionally altruistic and act for the sake of others. They may use the money they save by not cutting their emissions to benefit mankind. I am addressing not them, but the less altruistic majority. I said that justice normally prohibits you from harming other people even in order to make the world better. It more strongly prohibits you from harming other people in order to benefit yourself.

Sixth, the harms done by the emissions of the rich are not fully reciprocated. Some environmental harms are reciprocal. Traffic congestion is an example. If you drive to work, the presence of your car on the roads impedes other people on their way to work. They equally impede you. Each of you is significantly harming others by delaying them, but because the harm is reciprocal, we do not think that each of you is doing an injustice to others. Climate change is different. It is mostly a one-way transaction in which the present rich harm the present poor and future generations and are not much harmed in return. When I say that greenhouse gas emissions are an injustice, I am referring to the emissions of the present rich.

A seventh characteristic of greenhouse gas emissions is that we could easily reduce them. I shall soon explain that this is easier than you may think. You might be excused for causing harms that it would be very hard to avoid causing, but emitting greenhouse gas is not in that category.

I conclude from all these considerations that our emissions of greenhouse gas are an injustice.

The Individual Duty Not to Cause Emissions

It follows that each of us is under a duty of justice not to cause the emission of greenhouse gas, at least without compensating the people who are harmed as a result. Your carbon footprint ought to be zero unless you make restitution. This is strong advice, but I find I cannot avoid drawing this conclusion. It puts me in an unusual position for a moral philosopher. Normally, moral philosophers talk in generalities. We avoid preaching to people about particular moral demands. But here I am doing that. Fortunately, you will see in a moment that this duty turns out to be less onerous than it may at first appear.

By what means should you perform this duty of justice? You might try to do it by compensating the people you harm. Doing so would be remarkably cheap. Most of the harm you cause will not happen till far in the future. This means that if you put aside money now to compensate the victims of your harm, you can exploit the power of compound interest before you have to pay it over. William Nordhaus calculates that if you are lucky enough to be able to invest your money at 5.5 percent per year, $7.40 is enough to compensate for the harm done by a tonne of carbon dioxide.[4] Since you emit perhaps twenty or thirty tonnes in a year, a couple of hundred dollars a year will suffice.

However, I do not recommend this means of trying to achieve justice, because it will fail. Remember that duties of justice are owed to particular people. Your emissions of greenhouse gas are an injustice done to a large fraction of the world's population over a long period of time. You will not be able to compensate each of them individually.

You might try to make restitution through a collective international scheme of some sort. That way, you will not compensate all the individuals you harm, but you might manage some sort of surrogate compensation, by compensating large populations rather than individuals. Possibly you

---

4. William Nordhaus, *A Question of Balance* (New Haven, CT: Yale University Press, 2008), 15, 178.

might satisfy justice by other means. But there remains another problem. You do not know how much compensation you actually owe. None of us knows how much harm we cause by our emissions. We may be able to compute how much gas we emit, but the harm that gas does is very uncertain. Predictions of the effects of climate change are recognized to be very uncertain indeed. I have mentioned Nordhaus's figure, but I do not think he would claim it is particularly reliable.

You would do much better not to make the emissions in the first place; no compensation will then be required. This is possible. We all know some steps we might take: do not live wastefully, be frugal with energy in particular, switch off lights, do not waste water, eat less meat, eat local food, and so on. Many of these are steps you can take at little or no cost to yourself, and you should take those ones. However, you could not live in a way that does not cause the emission of any greenhouse gas at all. Virtually anything you buy has been produced using energy from fossil fuels. You can certainly reduce your emissions. But your most effective way of reducing your emissions to zero is to cancel or *offset* the emissions that you will still be causing after you have taken the obvious steps. Offsetting is a good way to fulfill your duty of justice. I shall explain how it works in a moment.

I am not telling you that offsetting is a way to solve the problem of climate change. I have already said that reducing your individual emissions of greenhouse gas—by offsetting or in other ways—is not the most effective way for you to improve the world. Your duty to have a zero carbon footprint does not derive from your duty of goodness. You must do it to avoid committing an injustice to other people—simply that. So far as solving the problem of climate change is concerned, your best route is through political action to induce your government to do what it should.

Offsetting

Offsetting your emissions means ensuring that for every unit of greenhouse gas you cause to be added to the atmosphere, you also cause a unit to be subtracted from it. If you offset, on balance you add nothing. Offsetting does not remove the very molecules that you emit, but the climate does not care which particular molecules are warming it. If you offset all your emissions, you make sure that your presence in the world causes no addition to the greenhouse gas in the atmosphere. You do not contribute to warming the atmosphere, so you do no harm through climate change. It is not that you do harm, which you then compensate for; offsetting is not a sort of compensation. It is a way to avoid harming in the first place.

It will not be easy to calculate the offset you need. You must make sure you offset not just the gas that is directly emitted by your own actions, but also the gas that supplied the energy used in making everything you consume. The average emissions in your own country will not be a good guide, because much of what you consume will have been manufactured abroad. It would be safest to overestimate. But in any case, this calculation is much less pervaded by uncertainty than trying to calculate how much harm your emissions do, with the aim of compensating people for them. This adds to the reasons for preferring offsetting to compensating.

How do you offset in practice? You may be able to subtract gas from the atmosphere yourself. One way of doing so is to grow trees. As they grow, trees remove carbon from the air to build their bodies: they take in carbon dioxide molecules, keep the carbon, and release the oxygen. But you would need to make sure that your trees' carbon is permanently kept out of the air, and that would be hard to achieve. Eventually, your trees will die and decompose, and their carbon will return to the air. Somehow you will have to ensure your forest will be replanted again and again perpetually even after your death. For that reason, effective do-it-yourself offsetting is difficult.

More easily practicable means of offsetting are "preventive," as I call them. Instead of taking carbon dioxide out of the atmosphere, they prevent it from getting into the atmosphere in the first place.

Plenty of commercial organizations offer to prevent carbon emissions on your behalf. You pay them a fee per tonne of offsetting you ask them to do. They use your money to finance projects that diminish emissions somewhere in the world. Most projects create sources of renewable energy. For instance, they build hydroelectric power stations or wind farms. Others promote the efficient use of energy. One installs efficient cooking stoves in people's homes in Africa and Asia. Cooking with firewood is an important cause of carbon emissions, and efficient stoves reduce the quantity that is emitted.

Preventive offsetting is cheap. Responsible companies will offset a tonne of emissions for around ten dollars. This means you can offset all your emissions for a few hundred dollars. That is why I said you can easily avoid harming people through your emissions.

Many environmentalists are strongly opposed to offsetting. Greenpeace is opposed, for example. One of its arguments is: "The truth is, once you've put a tonne of CO2 into the atmosphere, there's nothing off-setting can do to stop it changing our climate."[5] I do not think this is true. If at the same time you put a tonne of carbon dioxide into the atmosphere, you subtract another tonne, your actions together do not change the climate. So, since the climate does not change, the tonne you emit does not change it. Certainly, you do not change the climate, which is what matters.

Still, I recognize there are significant moral and practical problems connected with offsetting. One of them is that it is difficult to be sure that the reduction in emissions you pay for really happens. But I prefer to leave these for our discussion, because I want to get on to public morality.

Governments' Duties of Goodness

Governments, like individuals, bear duties of justice. However, in responding to climate change, they also have duties of goodness. I am going to concentrate on those because I have already talked about justice. I want to survey a different part of the morality of climate change.

When governments try to promote goodness, they must generally do some complex calculations. Their actions, especially over climate change, benefit many people and also impose costs on many people. Different benefits have to be aggregated together somehow, and so do different costs. Then benefits have to be weighed against costs. Cost-benefit analysis of some sort is inevitable. Climate change is a problem on a vast scale, affecting the whole world for centuries, and the quantitative methods of economics are necessary for coping with it.

Cost-benefit analysis also calls for ethical analysis, because the valuing and weighing of benefits and costs raise moral questions of many sorts. How should benefits to the rich be weighed against benefits to the poor? How should we value the loss of a person's life against the mundane good things that life contains? How should we take account of the huge uncertainty that surrounds climate change, including the small chance of total catastrophe? How should we weigh distant future benefits against present costs? How should we take into account the changes in the world's population that climate change will undoubtedly cause, including the small chance that our population will collapse to small numbers or even to extinction?

---

5. Statement by Charlie Kronick of Greenpeace, January 17, 2007.

Efficiency

All of those questions are fertile sources of disagreement and argument. But I have decided to leave them aside and take up one subject that does not involve weighing and aggregating. Instead, it involves what economists call efficiency. Having spent most of this lecture talking about private duties of justice that particularly do not aim to solve the problem of climate change, I am going to spend the rest of it on something that perhaps might solve it. It is a point that I have come to think is extremely important for the practical politics of climate change.

Oddly enough, it is a point of simple economics. When a person engages in some activity that emits greenhouse gas, the gas spreads around the globe and delivers small harms everywhere. These harms are among the costs of what the person does, but the person who causes the gas to be emitted does not bear this cost. It is borne by all people who suffer the harm. In economists' terminology, it is an "external cost" of the activity. Emissions of greenhouse gas constitute an "externality," as economists put it.

Externalities cause *inefficiency*. From the point of view of economics, this is what principally makes climate change a problem. Inefficiency here is what is sometimes called more specifically "Pareto inefficiency." It is defined as a situation in which it would be technically possible to make some people better off without making anyone worse off; a change of this sort is called a "Pareto improvement." Because emissions are an externality, they cause inefficiency in this sense, so a Pareto improvement is possible. I can go further. It would be technically possible to go so far as to remove the externality through a Pareto improvement.

This is a consequence of very elementary economic theory, though I admit I had to be reminded of its implications for climate change by my onetime teacher Duncan Foley.[6] The elementary economics needs to be modified to take account of the nonidentity effect, but it is nevertheless true that no one needs to make any sacrifice to solve the problem caused by the externality of greenhouse gas emissions.

I can describe in broad terms how the externality could be solved without any sacrifices. Although we are bequeathing to our successors a dirty atmosphere, we are doing quite a lot of good things for them in

---

6. See Duncan Foley, "The Economic Fundamentals of Global Warming," in *Twenty-First Century Microeconomics: Responding to the Climate Challenge*, edited by Jonathan M. Harris and Neva R. Goodwin (Cheltenham, UK: Edward Elgar, 2009), 115–126.

other ways. We are leaving them a lot of resources: cities, economic infrastructure, cultivated land, knowledge, and also those natural resources that we do not use up. Suppose we reduce our emissions of greenhouse gas. Other things being equal, that would require a sacrifice on our part. But we could fully compensate ourselves for the sacrifice by consuming more of other resources and leaving less to future generations in other ways. We could compensate ourselves to the extent that we are no worse off on balance. In macroeconomic terms, we could keep our own consumption constant and redirect our investment toward reducing greenhouse gas emissions. Future generations would receive from us fewer resources of other sorts, but they would have a cleaner atmosphere, and they would end up better off on balance.

Here is a slightly more concrete example of how this could be done. We could impose a carbon tax equal to the external damage done by emissions. Then we could compensate each person in some way for the carbon tax she pays. For example, we could reduce her income tax to the extent that she is just as well off as she was before. The carbon tax itself would finance some of the compensation, but it will not be enough to finance full compensation for everybody. The balance could be financed by a loan that will be repaid by future generations.

The externality of climate change could be removed without anyone's making a sacrifice. This raises a puzzle. When delegates come each year to meetings of the United Nations Framework Convention on Climate Change, at Copenhagen or Durban or somewhere else, they take themselves to be negotiating about how to distribute among the nations the burden of reducing climate change. No government will agree to accept a burden—to impose a sacrifice on its people—so the meetings regularly fail to achieve the reductions in emissions that are required. Yet I am saying that eliminating the problem of climate change requires no sacrifices at all. What is going on?

Efficiency Versus Optimization

I am telling the truth. It would indeed be possible in principle to eliminate the externality without any sacrifices. Doing so would be an improvement on the present situation, since some people would be better off and no one would be worse off. But it does not follow that this is the best thing that can be done about climate change. Most of the economists who work on climate change have chosen to look for this best thing, and their thinking has influenced the political process. These economists approach the problem as one of *optimization*. They look for the *best* way of managing our resources: the way that will do the most good. They work out how the international community can best meet its duty of goodness. This involves weighing benefits and costs in the way I have described. It turns out that, if their calculations are correct and founded on correct ethical principles, it would be best if the present generation did make some sacrifices for the future. . . .

Compare these three options:

Business as usual. ("BAU")
Reduce emissions and fully compensate ourselves for doing so, so there is no sacrifice. ("Compensation")
Reduce emissions and do not fully compensate ourselves for doing so, so there is sacrifice. ("Optimum")

. . .

Compensation is unattractive. Not only is it worse than Optimum, but it also incorporates injustice. BAU is an unjust situation: the present rich harm the present poor by our emissions of greenhouse gas, and that is unjust. If we move from there to Compensation, the rich are paid for reducing their emissions by those who suffer from them. This is an improvement for those who suffer, but it nevertheless perpetuates the injustice. If someone unjustly hurts you every day, you may be able to improve your situation by paying her to stop it, but that does not remove the injustice.

So I understand why the political process aims toward Optimum rather than Compensation. But the constant failure of the political process has made me cynical. National leaders will not commit their presently living people—in most cases their electorate—to the sacrifices they must make to achieve Optimum. I no longer think Optimum can be reached through negotiation, and I now favor aiming instead at Compensation. The issue at stake would then be how to distribute the *benefits* of controlling climate change—not the burdens—among the nations. Putting the question in this optimistic form might break the political logjam.

The difference between Compensation and Optimum is a matter of the distribution of resources between people: between the rich and the poor and between present and future generations. This distribution is not primarily determined by climate change, and dealing with climate change need not involve putting it right. If you aim for the very best outcome, you are aiming to correct all the present ills of the world. For example, suppose you think that the correct rate for discounting future commodities is below the interest rate in the market. By implication, you think the market does not pass as many resources to the future as it should; present people are consuming too much and not leaving enough for our successors. If, in dealing with climate change, you choose policies that are optimal according to your lower discount rate, you will find yourself making up for this general failure, as well as for the particular problem of climate change. Now that I have become cynical, I think we should concentrate on solving the particular problem and temporarily leave aside the general one.

Public Morality

Should we understand this as a moral duty of goodness, resting on governments and the international community? It could be argued that promoting efficiency is not even a moral duty at all. It is in everyone's interests. We could think of this task of government as merely one of coordinating people's activities in pursuing their own interests. We might even think a government in this domain acts not as an agent in its own right, but as a mere mechanism through which individual people coordinate their activities by mutual agreement. Many economists claim that ethics has nothing to do with economics, and many of those same economists claim that economics is concerned with efficiency only. I think this idea may be the basis of their thinking.

But governments have too many of the characteristics of agency for this to be plausible. For example, governments clearly have intentions. After two centuries, the Monroe Doctrine still expresses one of the US government's intentions, even though the personnel who constitute the government have changed many times. True, it remains a topic for philosophical research how a collective entity can have intentions, but it is a fact. As agents, governments are potentially bearers of moral duties, and improving the world is one duty they actually bear. Moreover, they cannot be merely a forum where agents coordinate their interests, since many of the relevant interests belong to people who are not yet born. Governments have a moral responsibility toward those people.

If governments cannot achieve the best outcome, Optimum, their duty of goodness requires them at least to aim for Compensation.

This sets a task for the economics profession. The theory tells us that Compensation, where no one makes a sacrifice, is possible. But to make it possible in practice requires some work. We are to reduce our emissions, financing the cost of doing so by loans that will be repaid by future people. But we know well that there is a limit to the amount that governments can borrow, and several governments seem to have already reached their limit. We therefore need new economic institutions that are robust enough to support enough borrowing to achieve Compensation. Economists must design these institutions.

I hope institutions can be created that will make Compensation possible. If so, I hope it will allow progress to be made on climate change. But remember that Compensation is not a good solution. If Compensation can be achieved, Optimum still remains a possibility. Getting from Compensation to Optimum is a matter of the distribution of resources between generations. It could be achieved by canceling the debt that builds up under Compensation. I hope that by making Compensation a real possibility, we might achieve something more like Optimum in the end. In taking the cynical position, I have not abandoned the aim of doing the best.

John Broome: The Public and Private Morality of Climate Change

1. Explain the non-identity effect. Does it have the implications for duties to address climate change that Broome thinks?
2. Broome believes that individuals have no duties of justice to redress climate change harms they cause. Why does he say this? Do you agree with his reasons? Why or why not?
3. What is the difference between efficiency and optimization? Do you agree with the use Broome makes of this distinction?
4. What is offsetting, and is this a plausible way for individuals to fulfill their duties of goodness regarding climate change?
5. Broome emphasizes the possibility of governments addressing their duties of goodness to future generations without asking their citizens to undertake any sacrifices. What are his reasons for this emphasis, and do you find them attractive? Why or why not?

30

Ideals of Human Excellence and Preserving Natural Environments

Thomas Hill, Jr.

....

According to Thomas Hill, Jr., the standard moral theories have difficulty explaining what is wrong with the destruction of the environment. Utilitarianism runs into trouble, because it is possible that overall happiness is maximized when cutting down a virgin forest or bulldozing a field to make way for suburban homes. Kantian and rights-based moral theories have just as much trouble here, because it is very difficult to defend the idea that plants or ecosystems—incapable of reasoning, asserting claims, or even feeling anything—are possessed of rights. Contractarian theories are just as vulnerable on this score. If our basic duties are owed only to our fellow members of the social contract, then plants and ecosystems will again be left out in the cold.

These concerns lead Hill to consider an alternative way of understanding our ethical relations with the environment. Rather than focusing on the question of whether we have any duties directly toward the environment, Hill invites us to consider a virtue ethical approach, which places primary emphasis on the sort of person we should try to become. He argues that those who fail to treat the environment with respect are almost certainly going to be less than fully virtuous. They will fail to be admirable in a number of ways, and will exemplify a variety of vices. In particular, those who are indifferent to the value of

---

Thomas Hill, Jr., "Ideals of Human Excellence and Preserving Natural Environments," from *Environmental Ethics* 5 (1983), pp. 211–224.

nature will almost certainly be ignorant and self-important. They will lack proper humility, and will either fail to have a well-developed sense of beauty, or will be insufficiently grateful for the good things in life. Thus even if we can't defend the claim that nature has rights, or that we owe nature anything, there is still excellent reason to respect and preserve natural environments. For if we don't, we will fall short of plausible ideals of human excellence.

....

I

A wealthy eccentric bought a house in a neighborhood I know. The house was surrounded by a beautiful display of grass, plants, and flowers, and it was shaded by a huge old avocado tree. But the grass required cutting, the flowers needed tending, and the man wanted more sun. So he cut the whole lot down and covered the yard with asphalt. After all it was his property and he was not fond of plants.

It was a small operation, but it reminded me of the strip mining of large sections of the Appalachians. In both cases, of course, there were reasons for the destruction, and property rights could be cited as justification. But I could not help but wonder, "What sort of person would do a thing like that?"

Many Californians had a similar reaction when a recent governor defended the leveling of ancient redwood groves, reportedly saying, "If you have seen one redwood, you have seen them all."

Incidents like these arouse the indignation of ardent environmentalists and leave even apolitical observers with some degree of moral discomfort. The reasons for these reactions are mostly obvious. Uprooting the natural environment robs both present and future generations of much potential use and enjoyment. Animals too depend on the environment; and even if one does not value animals for their own sakes, their potential utility for us is incalculable. Plants are needed, of course, to replenish the atmosphere quite aside from their aesthetic value. These reasons for hesitating to destroy forests and gardens are not only the most obvious ones, but also the most persuasive for practical purposes. But, one wonders, is there nothing more behind our discomfort? Are we concerned solely about the potential use and enjoyment of the forests, etc., for ourselves, later generations, and perhaps animals? Is there not something else which disturbs us when we witness the destruction or even listen to those who would defend it in terms of cost/benefit analysis?

Imagine that in each of our examples those who would destroy the environment argue elaborately that, even considering future generations of human beings and animals, there are benefits in "replacing" the natural environment which outweigh the negative utilities which environmentalists cite. No doubt we could press the argument on the facts, trying to show that the destruction is shortsighted and that its defenders have underestimated its potential harm or ignored some pertinent rights or interests. But is this all we could say? Suppose we grant, for a moment, that the utility of destroying the redwoods, forests, and gardens is equal to their potential for use and enjoyment by nature lovers and animals. Suppose, further, that we even grant that the pertinent human rights and animal rights, if any, are evenly divided for and against destruction. Imagine that we also concede, for argument's sake, that the forests contain no potentially useful endangered species of animals and plants. Must we then conclude that there is no further cause for moral concern? Should we then feel morally indifferent when we see the natural environment uprooted?

II

Suppose we feel that the answer to these questions should be negative. Suppose, in other words, we feel that our moral discomfort when we confront the destroyers of nature is not fully explained by our belief that they have miscalculated the best use of natural resources or violated rights in exploiting them. Suppose, in particular, we sense that part of the problem is that the natural environment is being viewed exclusively as a natural resource. What could be the ground of such a feeling? That is, what is there in our system of normative principles and values that could account for our remaining moral dissatisfaction?

Some may be tempted to seek an explanation by appeal to the interests, or even the rights, of plants. After all, they may argue, we only gradually came to acknowledge the moral importance of all human beings, and it is even more recently that consciences have been aroused to give full weight to the welfare (and rights?) of animals. The next logical step, it may be argued, is to acknowledge a moral requirement to take into account the interests (and rights?) of plants. The problem with the strip miners, redwood cutters, and the like, on this view, is not just that they ignore the welfare and rights of people and animals: they also fail to give due weight to the survival and health of the plants themselves.

The temptation to make such a reply is understandable if one assumes that all moral questions are exclusively concerned with whether *acts* are right or wrong, and that this, in turn, is determined entirely by how the acts impinge on the rights and interests of those directly affected. On this assumption, if there is cause for moral concern, some right or interest has been neglected; and if the rights and interests of human beings and animals have already been taken into account, then there must be some other pertinent interests, for example, those of plants. A little reflection will show that the assumption is mistaken; but, in any case, the conclusion that plants have rights or morally relevant interests is surely untenable. We do speak of what is "good for" plants, and they can "thrive" and also be "killed." But this does not imply that they have "interests" in any morally relevant sense. Some people apparently believe that plants grow better if we talk to them, but the idea that the plants suffer and enjoy, desire and dislike, etc., is clearly outside the range of both common sense and scientific belief. The notion that the forests should be preserved to avoid *hurting* the trees or because they have a *right* to life is not part of a widely shared moral consciousness, and for good reason.

Another way of trying to explain our moral discomfort is to appeal to certain religious beliefs. If one believes that all living things were created by a God who cares for them and entrusted us with the use of plants and animals only for limited purposes, then one has a reason to avoid careless destruction of the forests, etc., quite aside from their future utility. Again, if one believes that a divine force is immanent in all nature, then too one might have reason to care for more than sentient things. But such arguments require strong and controversial premises, and, I suspect, they will always have a restricted audience.

Early in this century, due largely to the influence of G. E. Moore, another point of view developed which some may find promising.[1] Moore introduced, or at least made popular, the idea that certain states of affairs are intrinsically valuable—not just valued, but valuable, and not necessarily because of their effects on sentient beings. The intrinsic goodness of something, he thought, was an objective, nonrelational property of the

---

1. G. E. Moore, *Principia Ethica* (Cambridge: Cambridge University Press, 1903); *Ethics* (London: H. Holt, 1912).

thing, like its texture or color, but not a property perceivable by sense perception or detectable by scientific instruments. In theory at least, a single tree thriving alone in a universe without sentient beings, and even without God, could be intrinsically valuable. . . . The survival of a forest might have worth beyond its worth *to* sentient beings.

Even if we try to . . . think in Moore's terms, it is far from obvious that everyone would agree that the existence of forests, etc., is intrinsically valuable. The test, says Moore, is what we would say when we imagine a universe with just the thing in question, without any effects or accompaniments, and then we ask, "Would its existence be better than its nonexistence?" Be careful. Moore would remind us, not to construe this question as, "Would you *prefer* the existence of that universe to its nonexistence?" The question is, "Would its existence have the objective, nonrelational property, intrinsic goodness?"

Now even among those who have no worries about whether this really makes sense, we might well get a diversity of answers. Those prone to destroy natural environments will doubtless give one answer, and nature lovers will likely give another. When an issue is as controversial as the one at hand, intuition is a poor arbiter.

The problem, then, is this. We want to understand what underlies our moral uneasiness at the destruction of the redwoods, forests, etc., even apart from the loss of these as resources for human beings and animals. But I find no adequate answer by pursuing the questions, "Are rights or interests of plants neglected?" "What is God's will on the matter?" and "What is the intrinsic value of the existence of a tree or forest?" My suggestion, which is in fact the main point of this paper, is that we look at the problem from a different perspective. That is, let us turn for a while from the effort to find reasons why certain *acts* destructive of natural environments are morally wrong to the ancient task of articulating our ideals of human excellence. Rather than argue directly with destroyers of the environment who say, "Show me why what I am doing is *immoral*," I want to ask, "What sort of person would want to do what they propose?" The point is not to skirt the issue with an *ad hominem*, but to raise a different moral question, for even if there is no convincing way to show that the destructive acts are wrong (independently of human and animal use and enjoyment), we may find that the willingness to indulge in them reflects the absence of human traits that we admire and regard as morally important.

This strategy of shifting questions may seem more promising if one reflects on certain analogous situations. Consider, for example, the Nazi who asks, in all seriousness, "Why is it wrong for me to make lampshades out of human skin—provided, of course, I did not myself kill the victims to get the skins?" We would react more with shock and disgust than with indignation, I suspect, because it is even more evident that the question reveals a defect in the questioner than that the proposed act is itself immoral. Sometimes we may not regard an act wrong at all though we see it as reflecting something objectionable about the person who does it. Imagine, for example, one who laughs spontaneously to himself when he reads a newspaper account of a plane crash that kills hundreds. Or, again, consider an obsequious grandson who, having waited for his grandmother's inheritance with mock devotion, then secretly spits on her grave when at last she dies. Spitting on the grave may have no adverse consequences and perhaps it violates no rights. The moral uneasiness which it arouses is explained more by our view of the agent than by any conviction that what he did was immoral. Had he hesitated and asked, "Why shouldn't I spit on her grave?" it seems more fitting to ask him to reflect on the sort of person he is than to try to offer reasons why he should refrain from spitting.

III

What sort of person, then, would cover his garden with asphalt, strip mine a wooded mountain, or level an irreplaceable redwood grove? Two sorts of answers, though initially appealing, must be ruled out. The first is that persons who would destroy the environment in these ways are either shortsighted, underestimating the harm they do, or else are too little concerned for the well-being of other people. Perhaps too they have insufficient regard for animal life. But these considerations have been set aside in order to refine the controversy. Another tempting response might be that we count it a moral virtue, or at least a human ideal, to love nature. Those who value the environment only for its utility must not really love nature and so in this way fall short of an ideal. But such an answer is hardly satisfying in the present context, for what is at issue is why we feel moral discomfort at the activities of those who admittedly value nature only for its utility. That it is ideal to care for nonsentient nature beyond its possible use is really just another way of expressing the general point which is under controversy.

What is needed is some way of showing that this ideal is connected with other virtues, or human excellences, not in question. To do so is difficult and my suggestions, accordingly, will be tentative and subject to qualification. The main idea is that, though indifference to nonsentient nature does not *necessarily* reflect the absence of virtues, it often signals the absence of certain traits which we want to encourage because they are, in most cases, a natural basis for the development of certain virtues. It is often thought, for example, that those who would destroy the natural environment must lack a proper appreciation of their place in the natural order, and so must either be ignorant or have too little humility. Though I would argue that this is not necessarily so, I suggest that, given certain plausible empirical assumptions, their attitude may well be rooted in ignorance, a narrow perspective, inability to see things as important apart from themselves and the limited groups they associate with, or reluctance to accept themselves as natural beings. Overcoming these deficiencies will not guarantee a proper moral humility, but for most of us it is probably an important psychological preliminary. Later I suggest, more briefly, that indifference to nonsentient nature typically reveals absence of either aesthetic sensibility or a disposition to cherish what has enriched one's life and that these, though not themselves moral virtues, are a natural basis for appreciation of the good in others and gratitude.

Consider first the suggestion that destroyers of the environment lack an appreciation of their place in the universe. Their attention, it seems, must be focused on parochial matters, on what is, relatively speaking, close in space and time. They seem not to understand that we are a speck on the cosmic scene, a brief stage in the evolutionary process, only one among millions of species on Earth, and an episode in the course of human history. Of course, they know that there are stars, fossils, insects, and ancient ruins; but do they have any idea of the complexity of the processes that led to the natural world as we find it? Are they aware how much the forces at work within their own bodies are like those which govern all living things and even how much they have in common with inanimate bodies? Admittedly scientific knowledge is limited and no one can master it all; but could one who had a broad and deep understanding of his place in nature really be indifferent to the destruction of the natural environment?

This first suggestion, however, may well provoke a protest from a sophisticated anti-environmentalist. "Perhaps *some* may be indifferent to nature from ignorance," the critic may object, "but I have studied astronomy, geology, biology, and biochemistry, and I still unashamedly regard the nonsentient environment as simply a resource for our use. It should not be wasted, of course, but what should be preserved is decidable by weighing long-term costs and benefits." "Besides," our critic may continue, "as philosophers you should know the old Humean formula, 'You cannot derive an *ought* from an *is*.' All the facts of biology, biochemistry, etc., do not entail that I ought to love nature or want to preserve it. What one understands is one thing; what one values is something else. Just as nature lovers are not necessarily scientists, those indifferent to nature are not necessarily ignorant."

Although the environmentalist may concede the critic's logical point, he may well argue that, as a matter of fact, increased understanding of nature tends to heighten people's concern for its preservation. If so, despite the objection, the suspicion that the destroyers of the environment lack deep understanding of nature is not, in most cases, unwarranted, but the argument need not rest here.

The environmentalist might amplify his original idea as follows: "When I said that the destroyers of nature do not appreciate their place in the universe, I was not speaking of intellectual understanding alone, for, after all, a person can *know* a catalog of facts without ever putting them together and seeing vividly the whole picture which they form. To see oneself as just one part of nature is to look at oneself and the world from a certain perspective which is quite different from being able to recite detailed information from the natural sciences. What the destroyers of nature lack is this perspective, not particular information."

Again our critic may object, though only after making some concessions: "All right," he may say, "*some* who are indifferent to nature may lack the cosmic perspective of which you speak, but again there is no *necessary* connection between this failing, if it is one, and any particular evaluative attitude toward nature. In fact, different people respond quite differently when they move to a wider perspective. When I try to picture myself vividly as a brief, transitory episode in the course of nature, I simply get depressed. Far from inspiring me with a love of nature, the exercise makes me sad and hostile. . . ." In sum, the critic may object, "Even if one should try to see oneself as one small transitory part of nature, doing so does not dictate any particular normative attitude. Some may come to love nature, but others are moved to live for the moment; some sink into sad resignation; others get depressed or angry. So indifference to nature is not necessarily a sign that a person fails to look at himself from the larger perspective."

The environmentalist might respond to this objection in several ways. He might, for example, argue that even though some people who see themselves as part of the natural order remain indifferent to nonsentient nature, this is not a common reaction. Typically, it may be argued, as we become more and more aware that we are parts of the larger whole we come to value the whole independently of its effect on ourselves. Thus, despite the possibilities the critic raises, indifference to nonsentient nature is still in most cases a sign that a person fails to see himself as part of the natural order.

If someone challenges the empirical assumption here, the environmentalist might develop the argument along a quite different line. The initial idea, he may remind us, was that those who would destroy the natural environment fail to *appreciate* their place in the natural order. "Appreciating one's place" is not simply an intellectual appreciation. It is also an attitude, reflecting what one values as well as what one knows. When we say, for example, that both the servile and the arrogant person fail to *appreciate* their place in a society of equals, we do not mean simply that they are ignorant of certain empirical facts, but rather that they have certain objectionable attitudes about their importance relative to other people. Similarly, to fail to appreciate one's place in nature is not merely to lack knowledge or breadth of perspective, but to take a certain attitude about what matters. A person who *understands* his place in nature but still views nonsentient nature merely as a resource takes the attitude that nothing is *important* but human beings and animals. Despite first appearances, he is not so much like the pre-Copernican astronomers who made the intellectual error of treating the Earth as the "center of the universe" when they made their calculations. He is more like the racist who, though well aware of other races, treats all races but his own as insignificant.

So construed, the argument appeals to the common idea that awareness of nature typically has, and should have, a humbling effect. The Alps, a storm at sea, the Grand Canyon, towering redwoods, and "the starry heavens above" move many a person to remark on the comparative insignificance of our daily concerns and even of our species, and this is generally taken to be a quite fitting response. What seems to be missing, then, in those who understand nature but remain unmoved is a proper humility.[2] Absence of proper humility is not the same as selfishness or egoism, for one can be devoted to self-interest while still viewing

---

2. By "proper humility" I mean that sort and degree of humility that is a morally admirable character trait. How precisely to define this is, of course, a controversial matter; but the point for present purposes is just to set aside obsequiousness, false modesty, underestimation of one's abilities, and the like.

one's own pleasures and projects as trivial and unimportant. And one can have an exaggerated view of one's own importance while grandly sacrificing for those one views as inferior. Nor is the lack of humility identical with belief that one has power and influence, for a person can be quite puffed up about himself while believing that the foolish world will never acknowledge him. The humility we miss seems not so much a belief about one's relative effectiveness and recognition as an attitude which measures the importance of things independently of their relation to oneself or to some narrow group with which one identifies. A paradigm of a person who lacks humility is the self-important emperor who grants status to his family because it is *his*, to his subordinates because he appointed them, and to his country because *he* chooses to glorify it. Less extreme but still lacking proper humility is the elitist who counts events significant solely in proportion to how they affect his class. The suspicion about those who would destroy the environment, then, is that what they count important is too narrowly confined insofar as it encompasses only what affects beings who, like us, are capable of feeling.

This idea that proper humility requires recognition of the importance of nonsentient nature is similar to the thought of those who charge meat eaters with "species-ism." In both cases it is felt that people too narrowly confine their concerns to the sorts of beings that are most like them. But, however intuitively appealing, the idea will surely arouse objections from our nonenvironmentalist critic. "Why," he will ask, "do you suppose that the sort of humility I *should* have requires me to acknowledge the importance of nonsentient nature aside from its utility? You cannot, by your own admission, argue that nonsentient nature *is* important, appealing to religious or intuitionist grounds. And simply to assert, without further argument, that an ideal humility requires us to view nonsentient nature as important for its own sake begs the question at issue. If proper humility is acknowledging the relative importance of things as one should, then to show that I must lack this you must first establish that one *should* acknowledge the importance of nonsentient nature."

Though some may wish to accept this challenge, there are other ways to pursue the connection between humility and response to nonsentient nature. For example, suppose we grant that proper humility requires only acknowledging a due status to sentient beings. We must admit, then, that it is logically possible for a person to be properly humble even though he viewed all nonsentient nature simply as a resource. But this logical possibility may be a psychological rarity. It may be that, given the sort of beings we are, we would never learn humility before persons without developing the general capacity to cherish, and regard important, many things for their own sakes. The major obstacle to humility before persons is self-importance, a tendency to measure the significance of everything by its relation to oneself and those with whom one identifies. The processes by which we overcome self-importance are doubtless many and complex, but it seems unlikely that they are exclusively concerned with how we relate to other people and animals. Learning humility requires learning to feel that something matters besides what will affect oneself and one's circle of associates. What leads a child to care about what happens to a lost hamster or a stray dog he will not see again is likely also to generate concern for a lost toy or a favorite tree where he used to live. Learning to value things for their own sake, and to count what affects them important aside from their utility, . . . is necessary to the development of humility and it seems likely to take place in experiences with nonsentient nature as well as with people and animals. If a person views all nonsentient nature merely as a resource, then it seems unlikely that he has developed the capacity needed to over-come self-importance.

IV

This last argument, unfortunately, has its limits. It presupposes an empirical connection between experiencing nature and overcoming self-importance, and this may be challenged. Even if experiencing nature promotes humility before others, there may be other ways people can develop such humility in a world of concrete, glass, and plastic. If not, perhaps all that is needed is limited experience of nature in one's early, developing years; mature adults, having overcome youthful self-importance, may live well enough in artificial surroundings. More importantly, the argument does not fully capture the spirit of the intuition that an ideal person stands humbly before nature. That idea is not simply that experiencing nature tends to foster proper humility before other people; it is, in part, that natural surroundings encourage and are appropriate to an ideal sense of oneself as part of the natural world. Standing alone in the forest, after months in the city, is not merely good as a means of curbing one's arrogance before others; it reinforces and fittingly expresses one's acceptance of oneself as a natural being.

Previously we considered only one aspect of proper humility, namely, a sense of one's relative importance with respect to other human beings. Another aspect, I think, is a kind of *self-acceptance*. This involves acknowledging, in more than a merely intellectual way, that we are the sort of creatures that we are. Whether one is self-accepting is not so much a matter of how one attributes *importance* comparatively to oneself, other people, animals, plants, and other things as it is a matter of understanding, facing squarely, and responding appropriately to who and what one is, e.g., one's powers and limits, one's affinities with other beings and differences from them, one's unalterable nature and one's freedom to change. Self-acceptance is not merely intellectual awareness, for one can be intellectually aware that one is growing old and will eventually die while nevertheless behaving in a thousand foolish ways that reflect a refusal to acknowledge these facts. On the other hand, self-acceptance is not passive resignation, for refusal to pursue what one truly wants within one's limits is a failure to accept the freedom and power one has. Particular behaviors, like dying one's gray hair and dressing like those twenty years younger, do not *necessarily* imply lack of self-acceptance, for there could be reasons for acting in these ways other than the wish to hide from oneself what one really is. One fails to accept oneself when the patterns of behavior and emotion are rooted in a desire to disown and deny features of oneself, to pretend to oneself that they are not there. This is not to say that a self-accepting person makes no value judgments about himself, that he likes all facts about himself, wants equally to develop and display them; he can, and should feel remorse for his past misdeeds and strive to change his current vices. The point is that he does not disown them, pretend that they do not exist or are facts about something other than himself. Such pretense is incompatible with proper humility because it is seeing oneself as better than one is.

Self-acceptance of this sort has long been considered a human excellence, under various names, but what has it to do with preserving nature? There is, I think, the following connection. As human beings we are part of nature, living, growing, declining, and dying by natural laws similar to those governing other living beings; despite our awesomely distinctive human powers, we share many of the needs, limits, and liabilities of animals and plants. These facts are neither good nor bad in themselves, aside from personal preference and varying conventional values. To say this is to utter a truism which few will deny, but to accept these facts, as facts about oneself, is not so easy—or so common. Much of what naturalists deplore about our increasingly artificial world reflects, and encourages, a denial of these facts, an unwillingness to avow them with equanimity. . . .

My suggestion is not merely that experiencing nature causally promotes such self-acceptance, but also that those who fully accept themselves as part of the natural world lack the common drive to disassociate themselves from nature by replacing natural environments with artificial ones. A storm in the wilds helps us to appreciate our animal vulnerability, but, equally important, the reluctance to experience it may *reflect* an unwillingness to accept this aspect of ourselves. The person who is too ready to destroy the ancient redwoods may lack humility, not so much in the sense that he exaggerates his importance relative to others, but rather in the sense that he tries to avoid seeing himself as one among many natural creatures.

V

My suggestion so far has been that, though indifference to nonsentient nature is not itself a moral vice, it is likely to reflect either ignorance, a self-importance, or a lack of self-acceptance which we must overcome to have proper humility. A similar idea might be developed connecting attitudes toward nonsentient nature with other human excellences. For example, one might argue that indifference to nature reveals a lack of either an aesthetic sense or some of the natural roots of gratitude.

When we see a hillside that has been gutted by strip miners or the garden replaced by asphalt, our first reaction is probably, "How ugly!" The scenes assault our aesthetic sensibilities. We suspect that no one with a keen sense of beauty could have left such a sight. Admittedly not everything in nature strikes us as beautiful, or even aesthetically interesting, and sometimes a natural scene is replaced with a more impressive architectural masterpiece. But this is not usually the situation in the problem cases which environmentalists are most concerned about. More often beauty is replaced with ugliness.

At this point our critic may well object that, even if he does lack a sense of beauty, this is no moral vice. His cost/benefit calculations take into account the pleasure others may derive from seeing the forests, etc., and so why should he be faulted?

Some might reply that, despite contrary philosophical traditions, aesthetics and morality are not so distinct as commonly supposed. Appreciation of beauty, they may argue, is a human excellence which morally ideal persons should try to develop. But, setting aside this controversial position, there still may be cause for moral concern about those who have no aesthetic response to nature. Even if aesthetic sensibility is not itself a moral virtue, many of the capacities of mind and heart which it presupposes may be ones which are also needed for an appreciation of other people.

Consider, for example, curiosity, a mind open to novelty, the ability to look at things from unfamiliar perspectives, empathetic imagination, interest in details, variety, and order, and emotional freedom from the immediate and the practical. All these, and more, seem necessary to aesthetic sensibility, but they are also traits which a person needs to be fully sensitive to people of all sorts. The point is not that a moral person must be able to distinguish beautiful from ugly people; the point is rather that unresponsiveness to what is beautiful, awesome, dainty, dumpy, and otherwise aesthetically interesting in nature probably reflects a lack of the openness of mind and spirit necessary to appreciate the best in human beings.

The anti-environmentalist, however, may refuse to accept the charge that he lacks aesthetic sensibility. If he claims to appreciate seventeenth-century miniature portraits, but to abhor natural wildernesses, he will hardly be convincing. Tastes vary, but aesthetic sense is not *that* selective. He may, instead, insist that he *does* appreciate natural beauty. He spends his vacations, let us suppose, hiking in the Sierras, photographing wild-flowers, and so on. He might press his argument as follows: "I enjoy natural beauty as much as anyone, but I fail to see what this has to do with preserving the environment independently of human enjoyment and use. Nonsentient nature is a resource, but one of its best uses is to give us pleasure. I take this into account when I calculate the costs and benefits of preserving a park, planting a garden, and so on. But the problem you raised explicitly set aside the desire to preserve nature as a means to enjoyment. I say, let us enjoy nature fully while we can, but if all sentient beings were to die tomorrow, we might as well blow up all plant life as well. A redwood grove that no one can use or enjoy is utterly worthless."

The attitude expressed here, I suspect, is not a common one, but it represents a philosophical challenge. The beginnings of a reply may be found in the following. When a person takes joy in something, it is a common (and perhaps natural) response to come to cherish it. To cherish something is not simply to be happy with it at the moment, but to care for it for its own sake. This is not to say that one necessarily sees it as having feelings and so wants it to feel good; nor does it imply that one judges the thing to have Moore's intrinsic value. One simply wants the thing to survive and (when appropriate) to thrive, and not simply for its utility. We see this attitude repeatedly regarding mementos. They are not simply valued as a means to remind us of happy occasions; they come to be valued for their own sake. Thus, if someone really took joy in the natural environment, but was prepared to blow it up as soon as sentient life ended, he would lack this common human tendency to cherish what enriches our lives. While this response is not itself a moral virtue, it may be a natural basis of the virtue we call "gratitude." People who have no tendency to cherish things that give them pleasure may be poorly disposed to respond gratefully to persons who are good to them. Again the connection is not one of logical necessity, but it may nevertheless be important. A nonreligious person unable to "thank" anyone for the beauties of nature may nevertheless feel "grateful" in a sense; and I suspect that the person who feels no such "gratitude" toward nature is unlikely to show proper gratitude toward people.

Suppose these conjectures prove to be true. One may wonder what is the point of considering them. Is it to disparage all those who view nature merely as a resource? To do so, it seems, would be unfair, for, even if this attitude typically stems from deficiencies which affect one's attitudes toward sentient beings, there may be exceptions and we have not shown that their view of nonsentient nature is itself blameworthy. But when we set aside questions of blame and inquire what sorts of human traits we want to encourage, our reflections become relevant in a more positive way. The point is not to insinuate that all anti-environmentalists are defective, but to see that those who value such traits as humility, gratitude, and sensitivity to others have reason to promote the love of nature.

Thomas Hill, Jr.: Ideals of Human Excellence and Preserving Natural Environments

1. Why does Hill think it is sometimes difficult to explain what is wrong with destroying the environment in terms of rights and welfare? What alternative framework does he propose for looking at the issue?
2. Hill presents several examples of acts which may not necessarily be immoral, but which would clearly reveal a defect in any person who performed them. Do you find his examples convincing? Is harming the environment relevantly similar to these actions?
3. Hill suggests that many environmentally destructive actions might be performed as a result of ignorance. How does he argue for this claim, and how might an "anti-environmentalist" respond?
4. What exactly is *humility*, and why does Hill claim that those who are unmoved by nature lack it? Do you agree with him?
5. What connection, if any, is there between self-acceptance and preserving nature? Can a person fully accept himself or herself while at the same time destroying natural environments?

31

A Defense of Abortion

Judith Jarvis Thomson

In this article, Judith Thomson does what very few pro-choice advocates have been willing to do—namely, to grant, for the purposes of
argument, that the fetus is as much a moral person as you or I. Still, she
argues, being a person does not, by itself, entitle you to use someone
else's resources, even if those resources are needed in order to preserve
your life. Thus even if we grant that the fetus is a person, that is not
enough to show that the fetus is entitled to the continued use of the
mother's "resources" (her body). A pregnant woman has a right to
bodily autonomy, and that right, in many cases, morally prevails over
any rights possessed by a fetus.

Thomson uses a number of thought experiments to defend this
claim. The most famous of these involves a world-class violinist. Suppose that you wake up one morning and find yourself connected to a
transfusion machine that is providing life support for this musician.
He surely has a right to life. But Thomson says that you would be
within your rights to remove yourself from the apparatus—even
knowing that, by doing this, he will die. The violinist, of course, is
meant to be a stand-in for the fetus. According to Thomson, although
it would be awfully nice of pregnant women to continue carrying their
fetuses to term, they are not usually morally required to do so.

Judith Jarvis Thomson, "A Defense of Abortion," from *Philosophy and Public Affairs* 1 (1971),
pp. 47–66. Copyright © 1971 *Philosophy and Public Affairs*. Reproduced with permission of
Blackwell Publishing Ltd.

Thomson anticipates a variety of objections to this example, and provides further examples to support her view that women usually have a moral right to seek and obtain an abortion.

....

Most opposition to abortion relies on the premise that the fetus is a human being, a person, from the moment of conception. The premise is argued for, but, as I think, not well. Take, for example, the most common argument. We are asked to notice that the development of a human being from conception through birth into childhood is continuous; then it is said that to draw a line, to choose a point in this development and say "before this point the thing is not a person, after this point it is a person" is to make an arbitrary choice, a choice for which in the nature of things no good reason can be given. It is concluded that the fetus is, or anyway that we had better say it is, a person from the moment of conception. But this conclusion does not follow. Similar things might be said about the development of an acorn into an oak tree, and it does not follow that acorns are oak trees, or that we had better say they are. Arguments of this form are sometimes called "slippery slope arguments"—the phrase is perhaps self-explanatory—and it is dismaying that opponents of abortion rely on them so heavily and uncritically.

I am inclined to agree, however, that the prospects for "drawing a line" in the development of the fetus look dim. I am inclined to think also that we shall probably have to agree that the fetus has already become a human person well before birth. Indeed, it comes as a surprise when one first learns how early in its life it begins to acquire human characteristics. By the tenth week, for example, it already has a face, arms and legs, fingers and toes; it has internal organs, and brain activity is detectable. On the other hand, I think that the premise is false, that the fetus is not a person from the moment of conception. A newly fertilized ovum, a newly implanted clump of cells, is no more a person than an acorn is an oak tree. But I shall not discuss any of this. For it seems to me to be of great interest to ask what happens if, for the sake of argument, we allow the premise. How, precisely, are we supposed to get from there to the conclusion that abortion is morally impermissible? Opponents of abortion commonly spend most of their time establishing that the fetus is a person, and hardly any time explaining the step from there to the impermissibility of abortion. Perhaps they think the step too simple and obvious to require much comment. Or perhaps instead they are simply being economical in argument. Many of those who defend abortion rely on the premise that the fetus is not a person, but only a bit of tissue that will become a person at birth; and why pay out more arguments than you have to? Whatever the explanation, I suggest that the step they take is neither easy nor obvious, that it calls for closer examination than it is commonly given, and that when we do give it this closer examination we shall feel inclined to reject it.

I propose, then, that we grant that the fetus is a person from the moment of conception. How does the argument go from here? Something like this, I take it. Every person has a right to life. So the fetus has a right to life. No doubt the mother has a right to decide what shall happen in and to her body; everyone would grant that. But surely a person's right to life is stronger and more stringent than the mother's right to decide what happens in and to her body, and so outweighs it. So the fetus may not be killed; an abortion may not be performed.

It sounds plausible. But now let me ask you to imagine this. You wake up in the morning and find yourself back to back in bed with an unconscious violinist. A famous unconscious violinist. He has been found to have a fatal kidney ailment, and the Society of Music Lovers has canvassed all the available medical records and found that you alone have the right blood type to help. They have therefore kidnapped you, and last night the violinist's circulatory system was plugged into yours, so that your kidneys can be used to extract poisons from his blood as well as your own. The director of the hospital now tells you, "Look, we're sorry the Society of Music Lovers did this to you—we would never have permitted it if we had known. But still, they did it, and the violinist now is plugged into you. To unplug you would be to kill him. But never mind, it's only for nine months. By then he will have recovered from his ailment, and can safely be unplugged from you." Is it morally incumbent on you to accede to this situation? No doubt it would be very nice of you if you did, a great kindness. But do you *have* to accede to it? What if it were not nine months, but nine years? Or longer still? What if the director of the hospital says, "Tough luck, I agree, but you've now got to stay in bed, with the violinist plugged into you, for the rest of your life. Because remember this. All persons have a right to life, and violinists are persons. Granted you have a right to decide what happens in and to your body, but a person's right to life outweighs your right to decide what happens in and to your body. So you cannot ever be unplugged from him." I imagine you would regard this as outrageous, which suggests that something really is wrong with that plausible-sounding argument I mentioned a moment ago.

In this case, of course, you were kidnapped; you didn't volunteer for the operation that plugged the violinist into your kidneys. Can those who oppose abortion on the ground I mentioned make an exception for a pregnancy due to rape? Certainly. They can say that persons have a right to life only if they didn't come into existence because of rape; or they can say that all persons have a right to life, but that some have less of a right to life than others, in particular, that those who came into existence because of rape have less. But these statements have a rather unpleasant sound. Surely the question of whether you have a right to life at all, or how much of it you have, shouldn't turn on the question of whether or not you are the product of a rape. And in fact the people who oppose abortion on the ground I mentioned do not make this distinction, and hence do not make an exception in case of rape.

Nor do they make an exception for a case in which the mother has to spend the nine months of her pregnancy in bed. They would agree that would be a great pity, and hard on the mother; but all the same, all persons have a right to life, the fetus is a person, and so on. I suspect, in fact, that they would not make an exception for a case in which, miraculously enough, the pregnancy went on for nine years, or even the rest of the mother's life.

Some won't even make an exception for a case in which continuation of the pregnancy is likely to shorten the mother's life; they regard abortion as impermissible even to save the mother's life. Such cases are nowadays very rare, and many opponents of abortion do not accept this extreme view. All the same, it is a good place to begin: a number of points of interest come out in respect to it.

1. Let us call the view that abortion is impermissible even to save the mother's life "the extreme view." I want to suggest first that it does not issue from the argument I mentioned earlier without the addition of some fairly powerful premises. Suppose a woman has become pregnant, and now learns that she has a cardiac condition such that she will die if she carries the baby to term. What may be done for her? The fetus, being a person, has a right to life, but as the mother is a person too, so has she a right to life. Presumably they have an equal right to life. How is it supposed to come out that an abortion may not be performed? If mother and child have an equal right to life, shouldn't we perhaps flip a coin? Or should we add to the mother's right to life her right to decide what happens in and to her body,

which everybody seems to be ready to grant—the sum of her rights now outweighing the fetus' right to life?

The most familiar argument here is the following. We are told that performing the abortion would be directly killing[1] the child, whereas doing nothing would not be killing the mother, but only letting her die. Moreover, in killing the child, one would be killing an innocent person, for the child has committed no crime, and is not aiming at his mother's death. And then there are a variety of ways in which this might be continued. (1) But as directly killing an innocent person is always and absolutely impermissible, an abortion may not be performed. Or, (2) as directly killing an innocent person is murder, and murder is always and absolutely impermissible, an abortion may not be performed. Or, (3) as one's duty to refrain from directly killing an innocent person is more stringent than one's duty to keep a person from dying, an abortion may not be performed. Or, (4) if one's only options are directly killing an innocent person or letting a person die, one must prefer letting the person die, and thus an abortion may not be performed.

Some people seem to have thought that these are not further premises which must be added if the conclusion is to be reached, but that they follow from the very fact that an innocent person has a right to life. But this seems to me to be a mistake, and perhaps the simplest way to show this is to bring out that while we must certainly grant that innocent persons have a right to life, the theses in (1) through (4) are all false. Take (2), for example. If directly killing an innocent person is murder, and thus is impermissible, then the mother's directly killing the innocent person inside her is murder, and thus is impermissible. But it cannot seriously be thought to be murder if the mother performs an abortion on herself to save her life. It cannot seriously be said that she *must* refrain, that she *must* sit passively by and wait for her death. Let us look again at the case of you and the violinist. There you are, in bed with the violinist, and the director of the hospital says to you, "It's all most distressing, and I deeply sympathize, but you see this is putting an additional strain on your kidneys, and you'll be dead within the month. But you *have* to stay where you are all the same. Because unplugging you would be directly killing an innocent violinist, and that's murder, and that's impermissible." If anything in the world is true, it is that you do not commit

---

1. The term "direct" in the arguments I refer to is a technical one. Roughly, what is meant by "direct killing" is either killing as an end in itself, or killing as a means to some end, for example, the end of saving someone else's life.

murder, you do not do what is impermissible, if you reach around to your back and unplug yourself from that violinist to save your life.

The main focus of attention in writings on abortion has been on what a third party may or may not do in answer to a request from a woman for an abortion. This is in a way understandable. Things being as they are, there isn't much a woman can safely do to abort herself. So the question asked is what a third party may do, and what the mother may do, if it is mentioned at all, is deduced, almost as an afterthought, from what it is concluded that third parties may do. But it seems to me that to treat the matter in this way is to refuse to grant to the mother that very status of person which is so firmly insisted on for the fetus. For we cannot simply read off what a person may do from what a third party may do. Suppose you find yourself trapped in a tiny house with a growing child. I mean a very tiny house, and a rapidly growing child—you are already up against the wall of the house and in a few minutes you'll be crushed to death. The child on the other hand won't be crushed to death; if nothing is done to stop him from growing he'll be hurt, but in the end he'll simply burst open the house and walk out a free man. Now I could well understand it if a bystander were to say, "There's nothing we can do for you. We cannot choose between your life and his, we cannot be the ones to decide who is to live, we cannot intervene." But it cannot be concluded that you too can do nothing, that you cannot attack it to save your life. However innocent the child may be, you do not have to wait passively while it crushes you to death. Perhaps a pregnant woman is vaguely felt to have the status of house, to which we don't allow the right of self-defense. But if the woman houses the child, it should be remembered that she is a person who houses it.

I should perhaps stop to say explicitly that I am not claiming that people have a right to do anything whatever to save their lives. I think, rather, that there are drastic limits to the right of self-defense. If someone threatens you with death unless you torture someone else to death, I think you have not the right, even to save your life, to do so. But the case under consideration here is very different. In our case there are only two people involved, one whose life is threatened, and one who threatens it. Both are innocent: the one who is threatened is not threatened because of any fault, the one who threatens does not threaten because of any fault. For this reason we may feel that we bystanders cannot intervene. But the person threatened can.

In sum, a woman surely can defend her life against the threat to it posed by the unborn child, even if doing so involves its death. And this shows not merely that the theses in (1) through (4) are false; it shows also that the extreme view of abortion is false, and so we need not canvass any other possible ways of arriving at it from the argument I mentioned at the outset.

2. The extreme view could of course be weakened to say that while abortion is permissible to save the mother's life, it may not be performed by a third party, but only by the mother herself. But this cannot be right either. For what we have to keep in mind is that the mother and the unborn child are not like two tenants in a small house which has, by an unfortunate mistake, been rented to both: the mother *owns* the house. The fact that she does adds to the offensiveness of deducing that the mother can do nothing from the supposition that third parties can do nothing. But it does more than this: it casts a bright light on the supposition that third parties can do nothing. Certainly it lets us see that a third party who says "I cannot choose between you" is fooling himself if he thinks this is impartiality. If Jones has found and fastened on a certain coat, which he needs to keep him from freezing, but which Smith also needs to keep him from freezing, then it is not impartiality that says "I cannot choose between you" when Smith owns the coat. Women have said again and again "This body is *my* body!" and they have reason to feel angry, reason to feel that it has been like shouting into the wind. . . .

3. Where the mother's life is not at stake, the argument I mentioned at the outset seems to have a much stronger pull. "Everyone has a right to life, so the unborn person has a right to life." And isn't the child's right to life weightier than anything other than the mother's own right to life, which she might put forward as ground for an abortion?

This argument treats the right to life as if it were unproblematic. It is not, and this seems to me to be precisely the source of the mistake.

For we should now, at long last, ask what it comes to, to have a right to life. In some views having a right to life includes having a right to be given at least the bare minimum one needs for continued life. But suppose that what in fact *is* the bare minimum a man needs for continued life is something he has no right at all to be given? If I am sick unto death, and the only thing that will save my life is the touch of Henry Fonda's cool hand on my fevered brow, then all the same, I have no right to be given the touch of Henry Fonda's cool hand on my fevered brow. It would be frightfully nice of him to fly in from the West Coast to provide it. It would be less nice, though no doubt well meant, if my friends flew out to the West Coast and carried Henry Fonda back with them. But I have no right at all against anybody that he should do this for me. Or again, to return to the story I told earlier, the fact that for continued life that violinist needs the continued use of your kidneys does not establish that he has a right to be given the continued use of your kidneys. He certainly has no right against you that *you* should give him continued use of your kidneys. For nobody has any right to use your kidneys unless you give him such a right; and nobody has the right against you that you shall give him this right—if you do allow him to go on using your kidneys, this is a kindness on your part, and not something he can claim from you as his due. Nor has he any right against anybody else that *they* should give him continued use of your kidneys. Certainly he had no right against the Society of Music Lovers that they should plug him into you in the first place. And if you now start to unplug yourself, having learned that you will otherwise have to spend nine years in bed with him, there is nobody in the world who must try to prevent you, in order to see to it that he is given something he has a right to be given.

Some people are rather stricter about the right to life. In their view, it does not include the right to be given anything, but amounts to, and only to, the right not to be killed by anybody. But here a related difficulty arises. If everybody is to refrain from killing that violinist, then everybody must refrain from doing a great many different sorts of things. Everybody must refrain from slitting his throat, everybody must refrain from shooting him—and everybody must refrain from unplugging you from him. But does he have a right against everybody that they shall refrain from unplugging you from him? To refrain from doing this is to allow him to continue to use your kidneys. It could be argued that he has a right against us that we should allow him to continue to use your kidneys. That is, while he had no right against us that we should give him the use of your kidneys, it might be argued that he anyway has a right against us that we shall not now intervene and deprive him of the use of your kidneys. I shall come back to third-party interventions later. But certainly the violinist has no right against you that *you* shall allow him to continue to use your kidneys. As I said, if you do allow him to use them, it is a kindness on your part, and not something you owe him.

The difficulty I point to here is not peculiar to the right to life. It reappears in connection with all the other natural rights; and it is something which an adequate account of rights must deal with. For present purposes it is enough just to draw attention to it. But I would stress that I am not arguing that people do not have a right to life—quite to the contrary, it seems to me that the primary control we must place on the acceptability of an account of rights is that it should turn out in that account to be a truth that all persons have a right to life. I am arguing only that having a right to life does not guarantee having either a right to be given the use of or a right to be allowed continued use of another person's body—even if one needs it for life itself. So the right to life will not serve the opponents of abortion in the very simple and clear way in which they seem to have thought it would.

4. There is another way to bring out the difficulty. In the most ordinary sort of case, to deprive someone of what he has a right to is to treat him unjustly. Suppose a boy and his small brother are jointly given a box of chocolates for Christmas. If the older boy takes the box and refuses to give his brother any of the chocolates, he is unjust to him, for the brother has been given a right to half of them. But suppose that, having learned that otherwise it means nine years in bed with that violinist, you unplug yourself from him. You surely are not being unjust to him, for you gave him no right to use your kidneys, and no one else can have given him any such right. But we have to notice that in unplugging yourself, you are killing him; and violinists, like everybody else, have a right to life, and thus in the view we were considering just now, the right not to be killed. So here you do what he supposedly has a right you shall not do, but you do not act unjustly to him in doing it.

The emendation which may be made at this point is this: the right to life consists not in the right not to be killed, but rather in the right not to be killed unjustly. This runs a risk of circularity, but never mind: it would enable us to square the fact that the violinist has a right to life with the fact that you do not act unjustly toward him in unplugging yourself, thereby killing him. For if you do not kill him unjustly, you do not violate his right to life, and so it is no wonder you do him no injustice.

But if this emendation is accepted, the gap in the argument against abortion stares us plainly in the face: it is by no means enough to show that the fetus is a person, and to remind us that all persons have a right to life— we need to be shown also that killing the fetus violates its right to life, i.e., that abortion is unjust killing. And is it?

I suppose we may take it as a datum that in a case of pregnancy due to rape the mother has not given the unborn person a right to the use of her body for food and shelter. Indeed, in what pregnancy could it be supposed that the mother has given the unborn person such a right? It is not as if there were unborn persons drifting about the world, to whom a woman who wants a child says "I invite you in."

But it might be argued that there are other ways one can have acquired a right to the use of another person's body than by having been invited to use it by that person. Suppose a woman voluntarily indulges in intercourse, knowing of the chance it will issue in pregnancy, and then she does become pregnant; is she not in part responsible for the presence, in fact the very existence, of the unborn person inside her? No doubt she did not invite it in. But doesn't her partial responsibility for its being there itself give it a right to the use of her body? If so, then her aborting it would be more like the boy's taking away the chocolates, and less like your unplugging yourself from the violinist—doing so would be depriving it of what it does have a right to, and thus would be doing it an injustice.

And then, too, it might be asked whether or not she can kill it even to save her own life: If she voluntarily called it into existence, how can she now kill it, even in self-defense?

The first thing to be said about this is that it is something new. Opponents of abortion have been so concerned to make out the independence of the fetus, in order to establish that it has a right to life, just as its mother does, that they have tended to overlook the possible support they might gain from making out that the fetus is *dependent* on the mother, in order to establish that she has a special kind of responsibility for it, a responsibility that gives it rights against her which are not possessed by any independent person—such as an ailing violinist who is a stranger to her.

On the other hand, this argument would give the unborn person a right to its mother's body only if her pregnancy resulted from a voluntary act, undertaken in full knowledge of the chance a pregnancy might result from it. It would leave out entirely the unborn person whose existence is due to rape. Pending the availability of some further argument, then, we would be left with the conclusion that unborn persons whose existence is due to rape have no right to the use of their mothers' bodies, and thus that aborting them is not depriving them of anything they have a right to and hence is not unjust killing.

And we should also notice that it is not at all plain that this argument really does go even as far as it purports to. For there are cases and cases, and the details make a difference. If the room is stuffy, and I therefore open a window to air it, and a burglar climbs in, it would be absurd to say, "Ah, now he can stay, she's given him a right to the use of her house—for she is partially responsible for his presence there, having voluntarily done what enabled him to get in, in full knowledge that there are such things as burglars, and that burglars burgle." It would be still more absurd to say this if I had had bars installed outside my windows, precisely to prevent burglars from getting in, and a burglar got in only because of a defect in the bars. It remains equally absurd if we imagine it is not a burglar who climbs in, but an innocent person who blunders or falls in. Again, suppose it were like this: people-seeds drift about in the air like pollen, and if you open your windows, one may drift in and take root in your carpets or upholstery. You don't want children, so you fix up your windows with fine mesh screens, the very best you can buy. As can happen, however, and on very, very rare occasions does happen, one of the screens is defective; and a seed drifts in and takes root. Does the person-plant who now develops have a right to the use of your house? Surely not—despite the fact that you voluntarily opened your windows, you knowingly kept carpets and upholstered furniture, and you knew that screens were sometimes defective. Someone may argue that you are responsible for its rooting, that it does have a right to your house, because after all you *could* have lived out your life with bare floors and furniture, or with sealed windows and doors. But this won't do—for by the same token anyone can avoid a pregnancy due to rape by having a hysterectomy, or anyway by never leaving home without a (reliable!) army.

It seems to me that the argument we are looking at can establish at most that there are *some* cases in which the unborn person has a right to the use of its mother's body, and therefore *some* cases in which abortion is unjust killing. There is room for much discussion and argument as to precisely which, if any. But I think we should sidestep this issue and leave it open, for at any rate the argument certainly does not establish that all abortion is unjust killing.

5. There is room for yet another argument here, however. We surely must all grant that there may be cases in which it would be morally indecent to detach a person from your body at the cost of his life. Suppose you learn that what the violinist needs is not nine years of your life, but only one hour: all you need do to save his life is to spend one hour in that bed with him. Suppose also that letting him use your kidneys for that one hour would not affect your health in the slightest. Admittedly you were kidnapped. Admittedly you did not give anyone permission to plug him into you. Nevertheless it seems to me plain you *ought* to allow him to use your kidneys for that hour—it would be indecent to refuse.

Again, suppose pregnancy lasted only an hour, and constituted no threat to life or health. And suppose that a woman becomes pregnant as a result of rape. Admittedly she did not voluntarily do anything to bring about the existence of a child. Admittedly she did nothing at all which would give the unborn person a right to the use of her body. All the same it might well be said, as in the newly emended violinist story, that she *ought* to allow it to remain for that hour—that it would be indecent in her to refuse. . . .

6. My argument will be found unsatisfactory on two counts by many of those who want to regard abortion as morally permissible. First, while I do argue that abortion is not impermissible, I do not argue that it is always permissible. There may well be cases in which carrying the child to term requires only Minimally Decent Samaritanism[2] of the mother, and this is a standard we must not fall below. I am inclined to think it a merit of my account precisely that it does *not* give a general yes or a general no. It allows for and supports our sense that, for example, a sick and desperately frightened fourteen-year-old schoolgirl, pregnant due to rape, may *of course* choose abortion, and that any law which rules this out is an insane law. And it also allows for and supports our sense that in other cases resort to abortion is even positively indecent. It would be indecent in the woman to request an abortion, and indecent in a doctor to perform it, if she is in her seventh month, and wants the abortion just to avoid the nuisance of postponing a trip abroad. The very fact that the arguments I have been drawing attention to treat all cases of abortion, or even all cases of abortion in which the mother's life is not at stake, as morally on a par ought to have made them suspect at the outset.

Secondly, while I am arguing for the permissibility of abortion in some cases, I am not arguing for the right to secure the death of the unborn child. It is easy to confuse these two things in that up to a certain point in the life of the fetus it is not able to survive outside the mother's body; hence removing it from her body guarantees its death. But they are importantly different. I have argued that you are not morally required to spend nine months in bed, sustaining the life of that violinist; but to say this is by no means to say that if, when you unplug yourself, there is a miracle and he survives, you then have a right to turn round and slit his throat. You may detach yourself even if this costs him his life; you have no right to be guaranteed his death, by some other means, if unplugging yourself does not kill him. There are some people who will feel dissatisfied by this feature of my argument. A woman may be utterly devastated by the thought of a child, a

---

2. Meeting a standard of minimally decent treatment towards those in need.—Ed.

bit of herself, put out for adoption and never seen or heard of again. She may therefore want not merely that the child be detached from her, but more, that it die. Some opponents of abortion are inclined to regard this as beneath contempt—thereby showing insensitivity to what is surely a powerful source of despair. All the same, I agree that the desire for the child's death is not one which anybody may gratify, should it turn out to be possible to detach the child alive.

At this place, however, it should be remembered that we have only been pretending throughout that the fetus is a human being from the moment of conception. A very early abortion is surely not the killing of a person, and so is not dealt with by anything I have said here.

Judith Jarvis Thomson: A Defense of Abortion

1. Thomson's first thought experiment is the case of the violinist. Do you agree that it would be permissible to unplug yourself from the violinist? What conclusions about abortion should we draw from this thought experiment?
2. What is the "extreme view"? What are Thomson's objections to the view? Do you find her objections compelling?
3. Thomson claims that the notion of a "right to life" cannot be interpreted as a right to "the bare minimum one needs for continued life." Why does she claim this? What, according to Thomson, does having a right to life amount to? Do you agree with her about this?
4. Why doesn't Thomson think that abortion always involves unjust killing? What does the justice of abortion depend on, according to Thomson?
5. Under what conditions (if any) do you think a woman grants a fetus the right to use her body?

===== ❧ =====

32

Why Abortion Is Immoral

Don Marquis

....

In this article, Don Marquis argues, from entirely secular premises, to
the conclusion that abortion is, in most circumstances, a form of
murder. He does this by first trying to explain why it is immoral to kill
people like you and me. After canvassing a few popular but mistaken
options, he arrives at his answer. Such killing is immoral because it
deprives us of a future of value.

Human fetuses—most of them, at least—also share this feature.
And therefore it is ordinarily wrong to kill human fetuses. And so
abortion is usually immoral. Marquis considers a variety of objections
to his view, and concludes his article by trying to show how each of
them can be met.

....

The view that abortion is, with rare exceptions, seriously immoral
has received little support in the recent philosophical literature.
No doubt most philosophers affiliated with secular institutions
of higher education believe that the anti-abortion position is either a
symptom of irrational religious dogma or a conclusion generated by
seriously confused philosophical argument. The purpose of this essay is

Don Marquis, "Why Abortion Is Immoral," from *Journal of Philosophy* 86 (1989), pp. 183–202.
Used by permission of Don Marquis and *The Journal of Philosophy*.

to undermine this general belief. This essay sets out an argument that purports to show, as well as any argument in ethics can show, that abortion is, except possibly in rare cases, seriously immoral, that it is in the same moral category as killing an innocent adult human being. . . .

I.

A sketch of standard anti-abortion and pro-choice arguments exhibits how those arguments possess certain symmetries that explain why partisans of those positions are so convinced of the correctness of their own positions, why they are not successful in convincing their opponents, and why, to others, this issue seems to be unresolvable. An analysis of the nature of this standoff suggests a strategy for surmounting it.

Consider the way a typical anti-abortionist argues. She will argue or assert that life is present from the moment of conception or that fetuses look like babies or that fetuses possess a characteristic such as a genetic code that is both necessary and sufficient for being human. Anti-abortionists seem to believe that (1) the truth of all of these claims is quite obvious, and (2) establishing any of these claims is sufficient to show that abortion is morally akin to murder.

A standard pro-choice strategy exhibits similarities. The pro-choicer will argue or assert that fetuses are not persons or that fetuses are not rational agents or that fetuses are not social beings. Pro-choicers seem to believe that (1) the truth of any of these claims is quite obvious, and (2) establishing any of these claims is sufficient to show that an abortion is not a wrongful killing.

In fact, both the pro-choice and the anti-abortion claims do seem to be true, although the "it looks like a baby" claim is more difficult to establish the earlier the pregnancy. We seem to have a standoff. How can it be resolved?

As everyone who has taken a bit of logic knows, if any of these arguments concerning abortion is a good argument, it requires not only some claim characterizing fetuses, but also some general moral principle that ties a characteristic of fetuses to having or not having the right to life or to some other moral characteristic that will generate the obligation or the lack of obligation not to end the life of a fetus. Accordingly, the arguments of the anti-abortionist and the pro-choicer need a bit of filling in to be regarded as adequate.

Note what each partisan will say. The anti-abortionist will claim that her position is supported by such generally accepted moral principles as "It is always prima facie seriously wrong to take a human life" or "It is always prima facie seriously wrong to end the life of a baby." Since these are generally accepted moral principles, her position is certainly not obviously wrong. The pro-choicer will claim that her position is supported by such plausible moral principles as "Being a person is what gives an individual intrinsic moral worth" or "It is only seriously prima facie wrong to take the life of a member of the human community." Since these are generally accepted moral principles, the pro-choice position is certainly not obviously wrong. Unfortunately, we have again arrived at a standoff.

Now, how might one deal with this standoff? The standard approach is to try to show how the moral principles of one's opponent lose their plausibility under analysis. It is easy to see how this is possible. On the one hand, the anti-abortionist will defend a moral principle concerning the wrongness of killing which tends to be broad in scope in order that even fetuses at an early stage of pregnancy will fall under it. The problem with broad principles is that they often embrace too much. In this particular instance, the principle "It is always prima facie wrong to take a human life" seems to entail that it is wrong to end the existence of a living human cancer-cell culture, on the grounds that the culture is both living and human. Therefore, it seems that the anti-abortionist's favored principle is too broad.

On the other hand, the pro-choicer wants to find a moral principle concerning the wrongness of killing which tends to be narrow in scope in order that fetuses will *not* fall under it. The problem with narrow principles is that they often do *not* embrace enough. Hence, the needed principles such as "It is prima facie seriously wrong to kill only persons" or "It is prima facie wrong to kill only rational agents" do not explain why it is wrong to kill infants or young children or the severely retarded or even perhaps the severely mentally ill. Therefore, we seem again to have a stand-off. The anti-abortionist charges, not unreasonably, that pro-choice principles concerning killing are too narrow to be acceptable; the pro-choicer charges, not unreasonably, that anti-abortionist principles concerning killing are too broad to be acceptable. . . .

All this suggests that a necessary condition of resolving the abortion controversy is a more theoretical account of the wrongness of killing. After all, if we merely believe, but do not understand, why killing adult human beings such as ourselves is wrong, how could we conceivably show that abortion is either immoral or permissible?

II.

In order to develop such an account, we can start from the following unproblematic assumption concerning our own case: it is wrong to kill *us*. Why is it wrong? Some answers can be easily eliminated. It might be said that what makes killing us wrong is that a killing brutalizes the one who kills. But the brutalization consists of being inured to the performance of an act that is hideously immoral; hence, the brutalization does not explain the immorality. It might be said that what makes killing us wrong is the great loss others would experience due to our absence. Although such hubris is understandable, such an explanation does not account for the wrongness of killing hermits, or those whose lives are relatively independent and whose friends find it easy to make new friends.

A more obvious answer is better. What primarily makes killing wrong is neither its effect on the murderer nor its effect on the victim's friends and relatives, but its effect on the victim. The loss of one's life is one of the greatest losses one can suffer. The loss of one's life deprives one of all the experiences, activities, projects, and enjoyments that would otherwise have constituted one's future. Therefore, killing someone is wrong, primarily because the killing inflicts (one of) the greatest possible losses on the victim. To describe this as the loss of life can be misleading, however. The change in my biological state does not by itself make killing me wrong. The effect of the loss of my biological life is the loss to me of all those activities, projects, experiences, and enjoyments which would otherwise have constituted my future personal life. These activities, projects, experiences, and enjoyments are either valuable for their own sakes or are means to something else that is valuable for its own sake. Some parts of my future are not valued by me now, but will come to be valued by me as I grow older and as my values and capacities change. When I am killed, I am deprived both of what I now value which would have been part of my future personal life, but also what I would come to value. Therefore, when I die, I am deprived of all of the value of my future. Inflicting this loss on me is ultimately what makes killing me wrong. This being the case, it would seem that what makes killing *any* adult human being prima facie seriously wrong is the loss of his or her future.[1]

How should this rudimentary theory of the wrongness of killing be evaluated? It cannot be faulted for deriving an 'ought' from an 'is,' for it

---

1. I have been most influenced on this matter by Jonathan Glover, *Causing Death and Saving Lives* (New York: Penguin, 1977), ch. 3; and Robert Young, "What Is So Wrong with Killing People?" *Philosophy*, LIV, 210 (1979): 515–528.

does not. The analysis assumes that killing me (or you, reader) is prima facie seriously wrong. The point of the analysis is to establish which natural property ultimately explains the wrongness of the killing, given that it is wrong. A natural property will ultimately explain the wrongness of killing, only if (1) the explanation fits with our intuitions about the matter and (2) there is no other natural property that provides the basis for a better explanation of the wrongness of killing. This analysis rests on the intuition that what makes killing a particular human or animal wrong is what it does to that particular human or animal. What makes killing wrong is some natural effect or other of the killing. Some would deny this. For instance, a divine-command theorist in ethics would deny it. Surely this denial is, however, one of those features of divine-command theory which renders it so implausible.

The claim that what makes killing wrong is the loss of the victim's future is directly supported by two considerations. In the first place, this theory explains why we regard killing as one of the worst of crimes. Killing is especially wrong, because it deprives the victim of more than perhaps any other crime. In the second place, people with AIDS or cancer who know they are dying believe, of course, that dying is a very bad thing for them. They believe that the loss of a future to them that they would otherwise have experienced is what makes their premature death a very bad thing for them. A better theory of the wrongness of killing would require a different natural property associated with killing which better fits with the attitudes of the dying. What could it be?

The view that what makes killing wrong is the loss to the victim of the value of the victim's future gains additional support when some of its implications are examined. In the first place, it is incompatible with the view that it is wrong to kill only beings who are biologically human. It is possible that there exists a different species from another planet whose members have a future like ours. Since having a future like that is what makes killing someone wrong, this theory entails that it would be wrong to kill members of such a species. Hence, this theory is opposed to the claim that only life that is biologically human has great moral worth, a claim which many anti-abortionists have seemed to adopt. This opposition, which this theory has in common with personhood theories, seems to be a merit of the theory.

In the second place, the claim that the loss of one's future is the wrong-making feature of one's being killed entails the possibility that the futures of some actual nonhuman mammals on our own planet are sufficiently like ours that it is seriously wrong to kill them also. Whether some animals do have the same right to life as human beings depends on adding to the account of the wrongness of killing some additional account of just what it is about my future or the futures of other adult human beings which makes it wrong to kill us. No such additional account will be offered in this essay. Undoubtedly, the provision of such an account would be a very difficult matter. Undoubtedly, any such account would be quite controversial. Hence, it surely should not reflect badly on this sketch of an elementary theory of the wrongness of killing that it is indeterminate with respect to some very difficult issues regarding animal rights.

In the third place, the claim that the loss of one's future is the wrong-making feature of one's being killed does not entail, as sanctity of human life theories do, that active euthanasia is wrong. Persons who are severely and incurably ill, who face a future of pain and despair, and who wish to die will not have suffered a loss if they are killed. It is, strictly speaking, the value of a human's future which makes killing wrong in this theory. This being so, killing does not necessarily wrong some persons who are sick and dying. Of course, there may be other reasons for a prohibition of active euthanasia, but that is another matter. Sanctity-of-human-life theories seem to hold that active euthanasia is seriously wrong even in an individual case where there seems to be good reason for it independently of public policy considerations. This consequence is most implausible, and it is a plus for the claim that the loss of a future of value is what makes killing wrong that it does not share this consequence.

In the fourth place, the account of the wrongness of killing defended in this essay does straightforwardly entail that it is prima facie seriously wrong to kill children and infants, for we do presume that they have futures of value. Since we do believe that it is wrong to kill defenseless little babies, it is important that a theory of the wrongness of killing easily account for this. Personhood theories of the wrongness of killing, on the other hand, cannot straightforwardly account for the wrongness of killing infants and young children. Hence, such theories must add special ad hoc accounts of the wrongness of killing the young. The plausibility of such ad hoc theories seems to be a function of how desperately one wants such theories to work. The claim that the primary wrong-making feature of a killing is the loss to the victim of the value of its future accounts for the wrongness of killing young children and infants directly; it makes the wrongness of such acts as obvious as we actually think it is. This is a further merit of this theory. Accordingly, it seems that this value of a future-like-ours theory of the wrongness of killing shares strengths of both sanctity-of-life and person-hood accounts while avoiding weaknesses of both. In addition, it meshes with a central intuition concerning what makes killing wrong.

The claim that the primary wrong-making feature of a killing is the loss to the victim of the value of its future has obvious consequences for the ethics of abortion. The future of a standard fetus includes a set of experiences, projects, activities, and such which are identical with the futures of adult human beings and are identical with the futures of young children. Since the reason that is sufficient to explain why it is wrong to kill human beings after the time of birth is a reason that also applies to fetuses, it follows that abortion is prima facie seriously morally wrong.

This argument does not rely on the invalid inference that, since it is wrong to kill persons, it is wrong to kill potential persons also. The category that is morally central to this analysis is the category of having a valuable future like ours; it is not the category of personhood. The argument to the conclusion that abortion is prima facie seriously morally wrong proceeded independently of the notion of person or potential person or any equivalent. Someone may wish to start with this analysis in terms of the value of a human future, conclude that abortion is, except perhaps in rare circumstances, seriously morally wrong, infer that fetuses have the right to life, and then call fetuses "persons" as a result of their having the right to life. Clearly, in this case, the category of person is being used to state the *conclusion* of the analysis rather than to generate the *argument* of the analysis. . . .

Of course, this value of a future-like-ours argument, if sound, shows only that abortion is prima facie wrong, not that it is wrong in any and all circumstances. Since the loss of the future to a standard fetus, if killed, is, however, at least as great a loss as the loss of the future to a standard adult human being who is killed, abortion, like ordinary killing, could be justified only by the most compelling reasons. The loss of one's life is almost the greatest misfortune that can happen to one. Presumably abortion could be justified in some circumstances, only if the loss consequent on failing to abort would be at least as great. Accordingly, morally permissible abortions will be rare indeed unless, perhaps, they occur so early in pregnancy that a fetus is not yet definitely an individual. Hence, this argument should be taken as showing that abortion is presumptively very seriously wrong, where the presumption is very strong—as strong as the presumption that killing another adult human being is wrong.

III.

How complete an account of the wrongness of killing does the value of a future-like-ours account have to be in order that the wrongness of abortion is a consequence? This account does not have to be an account of the necessary conditions for the wrongness of killing. Some persons in nursing homes may lack valuable human futures, yet it may be wrong to kill them for other reasons. Furthermore, this account does not obviously have to be the sole reason killing is wrong where the victim did have a valuable future. This analysis claims only that, for any killing where the victim did have a valuable future like ours, having that future by itself is sufficient to create the strong presumption that the killing is seriously wrong.

One way to overturn the value of a future-like-ours argument would be to find some account of the wrongness of killing which is at least as intelligible and which has different implications for the ethics of abortion. . . .

One move of this sort is based upon the claim that a necessary condition of one's future being valuable is that one values it. Value implies a valuer. Given this one might argue that, since fetuses cannot value their futures, their futures are not valuable to them. Hence, it does not seriously wrong them deliberately to end their lives.

This move fails, however, because of some ambiguities. Let us assume that something cannot be of value unless it is valued by someone. This does not entail that my life is of no value unless it is valued by me. I may think, in a period of despair, that my future is of no worth whatsoever, but I may be wrong because others rightly see value—even great value—in it. Furthermore, my future can be valuable to me even if I do not value it. This is the case when a young person attempts suicide, but is rescued and goes on to significant human achievements. Such young people's futures are ultimately valuable to them, even though such futures do not seem to be valuable to them at the moment of attempted suicide. A fetus's future can be valuable to it in the same way. Accordingly, this attempt to limit the anti-abortion argument fails.

Another similar attempt to reject the anti-abortion position is based on Tooley's claim that an entity cannot possess the right to life unless it has the capacity to desire its continued existence. It follows that, since fetuses lack the conceptual capacity to desire to continue to live, they lack the right to life. Accordingly, Tooley concludes that abortion cannot be seri- ously prima facie wrong.[2] . . .

One might attempt to defend Tooley's basic claim on the grounds that, because a fetus cannot apprehend continued life as a benefit, its continued life cannot be a benefit or cannot be something it has a right to or cannot be something that is in its interest. This might be defended in terms of the

---

2. Michael Tooley, *Abortion and Infanticide* (New York: Oxford University Press, 1984), pp. 46–47.

general proposition that, if an individual is literally incapable of caring about or taking an interest in some X, then one does not have a right to X or X is not a benefit or X is not something that is in one's interest.

Each member of this family of claims seems to be open to objections. As John C. Stevens[3] has pointed out, one may have a right to be treated with a certain medical procedure (because of a health insurance policy one has purchased), even though one cannot conceive of the nature of the procedure. And, as Tooley himself has pointed out, persons who have been indoctrinated, or drugged, or rendered temporarily unconscious may be literally incapable of caring about or taking an interest in something that is in their interest or is something to which they have a right, or is something that benefits them. Hence, the Tooley claim that would restrict the scope of the value of a future-like-ours argument is undermined by counterexamples. . . .[4]

IV.

In this essay, it has been argued that the correct ethic of the wrongness of killing can be extended to fetal life and used to show that there is a strong presumption that any abortion is morally impermissible. If the ethic of killing adopted here entails, however, that contraception is also seriously immoral, then there would appear to be a difficulty with the analysis of this essay.

But this analysis does not entail that contraception is wrong. Of course, contraception prevents the actualization of a possible future of value. Hence, it follows from the claim that futures of value should be maximized that contraception is prima facie immoral. This obligation to maximize does not exist, however; furthermore, nothing in the ethics of killing in this paper entails that it does. The ethics of killing in this essay would entail that contraception is wrong only if something were denied a human future of value by contraception. Nothing at all is denied such a future by contraception, however.

Candidates for a subject of harm by contraception fall into four categories: (1) some sperm or other, (2) some ovum or other, (3) a sperm and an ovum separately, and (4) a sperm and an ovum together. Assigning the

---

3. "Must the Bearer of a Right Have the Concept of That to Which He Has a Right?" *Ethics*, xcv, 1 (1984): 68–74.
4. See Tooley again in *Abortion and Infanticide*, pp. 47–49.

harm to some sperm is utterly arbitrary, for no reason can be given for making a sperm the subject of harm rather than an ovum. Assigning the harm to some ovum is utterly arbitrary, for no reason can be given for making an ovum the subject of harm rather than a sperm. One might attempt to avoid these problems by insisting that contraception deprives both the sperm and the ovum separately of a valuable future like ours. On this alternative, too many futures are lost. Contraception was supposed to be wrong, because it deprived us of one future of value, not two. One might attempt to avoid this problem by holding that contraception deprives the combination of sperm and ovum of a valuable future like ours. But here the definite article misleads. At the time of contraception, there are hundreds of millions of sperm, one (released) ovum and millions of possible combinations of all of these. There is no actual combination at all. Is the subject of the loss to be a merely possible combination? Which one? This alternative does not yield an actual subject of harm either. Accordingly, the immorality of contraception is not entailed by the loss of a future-like-ours argument simply because there is no nonarbitrarily identifiable subject of the loss in the case of contraception.

Don Marquis: Why Abortion Is Immoral

1. Marquis begins by criticizing some common arguments on both sides of the abortion issue. Do his criticisms succeed in refuting the common arguments? Why or why not?
2. What, according to Marquis, is wrong with killing adult humans? Is his theory the best account of what is wrong with such killing?
3. Marquis claims that abortion is wrong for the same reason that killing adult humans is wrong. Are there any differences between the two that would justify abortion?
4. One might object to Marquis's claim that fetuses have a valuable future by pointing out that fetuses do not have the cognitive capacities to value anything. How does Marquis respond to this objection? Do you find his response convincing?
5. Marquis admits that his theory would be problematic if it led to the view that contraception is seriously morally wrong. How does he argue that his theory does not do this? Do you think he succeeds?

=== ❧ ===

33

The Problem of Abortion and the Doctrine of the Double Effect

Philippa Foot

....

In this article, Philippa Foot (1920–2010) introduces and discusses the merits of the ethical principle known as the doctrine of double effect. The doctrine states that, under certain conditions, it is permitted to cause harm if the harm is merely foreseen, rather than directly intended. Foot offers a variety of fascinating cases to explore the difference between foresight and intention. Many of these cases have become classic examples within moral philosophy, none more so than the Trolley Problem.

The Trolley Problem has generated many variations, but the central case is simple. There is a runaway trolley; you can either allow it to continue on its way, or switch it to a spur. Why would you do either? Well, there are five people on the track ahead, and only one on the spur. All six are innocent. Intuitively, it seems at least permissible, and many think it required, to pull the lever that will send the trolley to the spur. From this example, you might infer that whenever we have to choose between saving a greater and a lesser number of innocent lives, we ought to save the greater number. But, as Foot shows, such a claim is deeply problematic.

Philippa Foot, "The Problem of Abortion and the Doctrine of the Double Effect," from *Oxford Review* 5 (1967), pp. 5–15. Reprinted by permission of the Principal and Fellows of Somerville College Oxford.

In its most general formulation, the challenge is to explain precisely why it is only sometimes, and not always, morally acceptable to minimize harm. The doctrine of double effect has been introduced to do the needed explaining, but Foot finds the doctrine flawed. She concludes with a presentation of her own solution, and an application of it to the issue of abortion.

....

One of the reasons why most of us feel puzzled about the problem of abortion is that we want, and do not want, to allow to the unborn child the rights that belong to adults and children. When we think of a baby about to be born it seems absurd to think that the next few minutes or even hours could make so radical a difference to its status; yet as we go back in the life of the foetus we are more and more reluctant to say that this is a human being and must be treated as such. No doubt this is the deepest source of our dilemma, but it is not the only one. For we are also confused about the general question of what we may and may not do where the interests of human beings conflict. We have strong intuitions about certain cases; saying, for instance, that it is all right to raise the level of education in our country, though statistics allow us to predict that a rise in the suicide rate will follow, while it is not all right to kill the feeble-minded to aid cancer research. It is not easy, however, to see the principles involved, and one way of throwing light on the abortion issue will be by setting up parallels involving adults or children once born. So we will be able to isolate the "equal rights" issue, and should be able to make some advance.

I shall not, of course, discuss all the principles that may be used in deciding what to do where the interests or rights of human beings conflict. What I want to do is to look at one particular theory, known as the "doctrine of the double effect" which is invoked by Catholics in support of their views on abortion but supposed by them to apply elsewhere. As used in the abortion argument this doctrine has often seemed to non-Catholics to be a piece of complete sophistry.... And yet this principle has seemed to some non-Catholics as well as to Catholics to stand as the only defence against decisions on other issues that are quite unacceptable. It will help us in our difficulty about abortion if this conflict can be resolved.

The doctrine of the double effect is based on a distinction between what a man foresees as a result of his voluntary action and what, in the strict sense, he intends. He intends in the strictest sense both those things that he aims at as ends and those that he aims at as means to his ends. The latter may be regretted in themselves but nevertheless desired for the sake of the end, as we may intend to keep dangerous lunatics confined for the sake of our safety. By contrast a man is said not strictly, or directly, to intend the foreseen consequences of his voluntary actions where these are neither the end at which he is aiming nor the means to this end. Whether the word "intention" should be applied in both cases is not of course what matters: Bentham spoke of "oblique intention," contrasting it with the "direct intention" of ends and means, and we may as well follow his terminology. Everyone must recognize that some such distinction can be made, though it may be made in a number of different ways, and it is the distinction that is crucial to the doctrine of the double effect. The words "double effect" refer to the two effects that an action may produce: the one aimed at, and the one foreseen but in no way desired. By "the doctrine of the double effect" I mean the thesis that it is sometimes permissible to bring about by oblique intention what one may not directly intend. Thus the distinction is held to be relevant to moral decision in certain difficult cases. It is said for instance that the operation of hysterectomy involves the death of the foetus as the foreseen but not strictly or directly intended consequence of the surgeon's act, while other operations kill the child and count as the direct intention of taking an innocent life, a distinction that has evoked particularly bitter reactions on the part of non-Catholics. If you are permitted to bring about the death of the child, what does it matter how it is done? The doctrine of the double effect is also used to show why in another case, where a woman in labour will die unless a craniotomy operation is performed, the intervention is not to be condoned. There, it is said, we may not operate, but must let the mother die. We foresee her death but do not directly intend it, whereas to crush the skull of the child would count as direct intention of its death.

This last application of the doctrine has been queried by Professor Hart on the ground that the child's death is not strictly a means to saving the mother's life and should logically be treated as an unwanted but foreseen consequence by those who make use of the distinction between direct and oblique intention. To interpret the doctrine in this way is perfectly reasonable given the language that has been used; it would, however, make nonsense of it from the beginning. A certain event may be desired under one of its descriptions, unwanted under another, but we cannot treat these as two different events, one of which is aimed at and the other not.

And even if it be argued that there are here two different events—the crushing of the child's skull and its death—the two are obviously much too close for an application of the doctrine of the double effect. To see how odd it would be to apply the principle like this we may consider the story, well known to philosophers, of the fat man stuck in the mouth of the cave. A party of potholers have imprudently allowed the fat man to lead them as they make their way out of the cave, and he gets stuck, trapping the others behind him. Obviously the right thing to do is to sit down and wait until the fat man grows thin; but philosophers have arranged that flood waters should be rising within the cave. Luckily (luckily?) the trapped party have with them a stick of dynamite with which they can blast the fat man out of the mouth of the cave. Either they use the dynamite or they drown. In one version the fat man, whose head is *in* the cave, will drown with them; in the other he will be rescued in due course. Problem: may they use the dynamite or not? Later we will find parallels to this example. Here it is introduced for light relief and because it will serve to show how ridiculous one version of the doctrine of the double effect would be. For suppose that the trapped explorers were to argue that the death of the fat man might be taken as a merely foreseen consequence of the act of blowing him up. ("We didn't want to kill him . . . only to blow him into small pieces" or even ". . . only to blast him out of the mouth of the cave.") I believe that those who use the doctrine of the double effect would rightly reject such a suggestion, though they will, of course, have considerable difficulty in explaining where the line is to be drawn. What is to be the criterion of "closeness" if we say that anything very close to what we are literally aiming at counts as if part of our aim?

Let us leave this difficulty aside and return to the arguments for and against the doctrine, supposing it to be formulated in the way considered most effective by its supporters, and ourselves bypassing the trouble by taking what must on any reasonable definition be clear cases of "direct" or "oblique" intention.

The first point that should be made clear, in fairness to the theory, is that no one is suggesting that it does not matter what you bring about as long as you merely foresee and do not strictly intend the evil that follows. We might think, for instance, of the (actual) case of wicked merchants selling, for cooking, oil they knew to be poisonous and thereby killing a number of innocent people, comparing and contrasting it with that of some unemployed gravediggers, desperate for custom, who got hold of this same oil and sold it (or perhaps *they* secretly gave it away) in order to create orders for graves. They strictly (directly) intend the deaths they cause, while the merchants could say that it was not part of their *plan* that anyone should die. In morality, as in law, the merchants, like the gravediggers, would be considered as murderers; nor are the supporters of the doctrine of the double effect bound to say that there is the least difference between them in respect of moral turpitude. What they are committed to is the thesis that *sometimes* it makes a difference to the permissibility of an action involving harm to others that this harm, although foreseen, is not part of the agent's direct intention. An end such as earning one's living is clearly not such as to justify *either* the direct or oblique intention of the death of innocent people, but in certain cases one is justified in bringing about knowingly what one could not directly intend.

It is now time to say why this doctrine should be taken seriously in spite of the fact that it sounds rather odd, that there are difficulties about the distinction on which it depends, and that it seemed to yield one sophistical conclusion when applied to the problem of abortion. The reason for its appeal is that its opponents have often *seemed* to be committed to quite indefensible views. Thus the controversy has raged around examples such as the following. Suppose that a judge or magistrate is faced with rioters demanding that a culprit be found for a certain crime and threatening otherwise to take their own bloody revenge on a particular section of the community. The real culprit being unknown, the judge sees himself as able to prevent the bloodshed only by framing some innocent person and having him executed. Beside this example is placed another in which a pilot whose aeroplane is about to crash is deciding whether to steer from a more to a less inhabited area. To make the parallel as close as possible it may rather be supposed that he is the driver of a runaway tram which he can only steer from one narrow track on to another; five men are working on one track and one man on the other; anyone on the track he enters is bound to be killed. In the case of the riots the mob have five hostages, so that in both the exchange is supposed to be one man's life for the lives of five. The question is why we should say, without hesitation, that the driver should steer for the less occupied track, while most of us would be appalled at the idea that the innocent man could be framed. It may be suggested that the special feature of the latter case is that it involves the corruption of justice, and this is, of course, very important indeed. But if we remove that special feature, supposing that some private individual is to kill an innocent person and pass him off as the criminal, we still find ourselves horrified by the idea. The doctrine of the double effect offers us a way out of the difficulty, insisting that it is one thing to steer towards someone foreseeing that you will kill him and another to aim at his death as part of your plan. Moreover there is one very important element of good in what is here insisted. In real life it would hardly ever be certain that the man on the narrow track would be killed. Perhaps he might find a foothold on the side of the tunnel and cling on as the vehicle hurtled by. The driver of the tram does not then leap off and brain him with a crowbar. The judge, however, needs the death of the innocent man for his (good) purposes. If the victim proves hard to hang he must see to it that he dies another way. To choose to execute him is to choose that this evil *shall come about*, and this must therefore count as a *certainty* in weighing up the good and evil involved. The distinction between direct and oblique intention is crucial here, and is of great importance in an uncertain world. Nevertheless this is no way to defend the doctrine of the double effect. For the question is whether the difference between aiming at something and obliquely intending it is *in itself* relevant to moral decisions; not whether it is important when correlated with a difference of certainty in the balance of good and evil. Moreover we are particularly interested in the application of the doctrine of the double effect to the question of abortion, and no one can deny that in medicine there are sometimes certainties so complete that it would be a mere quibble to speak of the "probable outcome" of this course of action or that. It is not, therefore, with a merely philosophical interest that we should put aside the uncertainty and scrutinize the examples to test the doctrine of the double effect. Why can we not argue from the case of the steering driver to that of the judge?

Another pair of examples poses a similar problem. We are about to give to a patient who needs it to save his life a massive dose of a certain drug in short supply. There arrive, however, five other patients each of whom could be saved by one-fifth of that dose. We say with regret that we cannot spare our whole supply of the drug for a single patient, just as we should say that we could not spare the whole resources of a ward for one dangerously ill individual when ambulances arrive bringing in the victims of a multiple crash. We feel bound to let one man die rather than many if that is our only choice. Why then do we not feel justified in killing people in the interests of cancer research or to obtain, let us say, spare parts for grafting on to those who need them? We can suppose, similarly, that several dangerously ill people can be saved only if we kill a certain individual and make a serum from his dead body. (These examples are not over fanciful considering present controversies about prolonging the life of mortally ill patients whose eyes or kidneys are to be used for others.)

Why cannot we argue from the case of the scarce drug to that of the body needed for medical purposes? Once again the doctrine of the double effect comes up with an explanation. In one kind of case but not the other we aim at the death of the innocent man.

A further argument suggests that if the doctrine of the double effect is rejected this has the consequence of putting us hopelessly in the power of bad men. Suppose for example that some tyrant should threaten to torture five men if we ourselves would not torture one. Would it be our duty to do so, supposing we believed him, because this would be no different from choosing to rescue five men from his torturers rather than one? If so anyone who wants us to do something we think wrong has only to threaten that otherwise he himself will do something we think worse. A mad murderer, known to keep his promises, could thus make it our duty to kill some innocent citizen to prevent him from killing two. From this conclusion we are again rescued by the doctrine of the double effect. If we refuse, we foresee that the greater number will be killed but we do not intend it: it is he who intends (that is strictly or directly intends) the death of innocent persons; we do not.

At one time I thought that these arguments in favour of the doctrine of the double effect were conclusive, but I now believe that the conflict should be solved in another way. The clue that we should follow is that the strength of the doctrine seems to lie in the distinction it makes between what we do (equated with direct intention) and what we allow (thought of as obliquely intended). Indeed it is interesting that the disputants tend to argue about whether we are to be held responsible for what we allow as we are for what we do. Yet it is not obvious that this is what they should be discussing, since the distinction between what one does and what one allows to happen is not the same as that between direct and oblique intention. To see this one has only to consider that it is possible *deliberately* to allow something to happen, aiming at it either for its own sake or as part of one's plan for obtaining something else. So one person might want another person dead, and deliberately allow him to die. And again one may be said to do things that one does not aim at, as the steering driver would kill the man on the track. Moreover there is a large class of things said to be brought about rather than either done or allowed, and either kind of intention is possible. So it is possible to *bring about* a man's death by getting him to go to sea in a leaky boat, and the intention of his death may be either direct or oblique.

Whatever it may, or may not, have to do with the doctrine of the double effect, the idea of *allowing* is worth looking into in this context. I shall leave aside the special case of giving permission, which involves the idea of authority, and consider the two main divisions into which cases of allowing seem to fall. There is firstly the allowing which is forbearing to prevent. For this we need a sequence thought of as somehow already in train, and something that the agent could do to intervene. (The agent must be able to intervene, but does not do so.) So, for instance, he could warn someone, but *allows* him to walk into a trap. He could feed an animal but *allows* it to die for lack of food. He could stop a leaking tap but *allows* the water to go on flowing. This is the case of allowing with which we shall be concerned, but the other should be mentioned. It is the kind of allowing which is roughly equivalent to *enabling*, the root idea being the removal of some obstacle which is, as it were, holding back a train of events. So someone may remove a plug and *allow* water to flow; open a door *and* allow an animal to get out; or give someone money and *allow* him to get back on his feet.

The first kind of allowing requires an omission, but there is no other general correlation between omission and allowing, commission and bringing about or doing. An actor who fails to turn up for a performance will generally spoil it rather than allow it to be spoiled. I mentioned the distinction between omission and commission only to not set it aside.

Thinking of the first kind of allowing (forebearing to prevent), we should ask whether there is any difference, from the moral point of view, between what one does or causes and what one merely allows. It seems clear that on occasions one is just as bad as the other, as is recognized in both morality and law. A man may murder his child or his aged relatives, by allowing them to die of starvation as well as by giving poison; he may also be convicted of murder on either account. In another case we would, however, make a distinction. Most of us allow people to die of starvation in India and Africa, and there is surely something wrong with us that we do; it would be nonsense, however, to pretend that it is only in law that we make a distinction between allowing people in the underdeveloped countries to die of starvation and sending them poisoned food. There is worked into our moral system a distinction between what we owe people in the form of aid and what we owe them in the way of noninterference. Salmond, in his *Jurisprudence*, expressed as follows the distinction between the two.

A positive right corresponds to a positive duty, and is a right that he on whom the duty lies shall do some positive act on behalf of the person entitled. A negative right corresponds to a negative duty, and is a right that the person bound shall refrain from some act which would operate to the prejudice of the person entitled. The former is a right to be positively benefited; the latter is merely a right not to be harmed.[1]

As a general account of rights and duties this is defective, since not all are so closely connected with benefit and harm. Nevertheless for our purposes it will do well. Let us speak of negative duties when thinking of the obligation to refrain from such things as killing or robbing, and of the positive duty, e.g., to look after children or aged parents. It will be useful, however, to extend the notion of positive duty beyond the range of things that are strictly called duties, bringing acts of charity under this heading. These are owed only in a rather loose sense, and some acts of charity could hardly be said to be owed at all, so I am not following ordinary usage at this point.

Let us now see whether the distinction of negative and positive duties explains why we see differently the action of the steering driver and that of the judge, of the doctors who withhold the scarce drug and those who obtain a body for medical purposes, of those who choose to rescue the five men rather than one man from torture and those who are ready to torture the one man themselves in order to save five. In each case we have a conflict of duties, but what kind of duties are they? Are we, in each case, weighing positive duties against positive, negative against negative, or one against the other? Is the duty to refrain from injury, or rather to bring aid?

The steering driver faces a conflict of negative duties, since it is his duty to avoid injuring five men and also his duty to avoid injuring one. In the circumstances he is not able to avoid both, and it seems clear that he should do the least injury he can. The judge, however, is weighing the duty of not inflicting injury against the duty of bringing aid. He wants to rescue the innocent people threatened with death but can do so only by inflicting injury himself. Since one does not *in general* have the same duty to help people as to refrain from injuring them, it is not possible to argue to a conclusion about what he should do from the steering driver case. It is interesting that, even where the strictest duty of positive aid exists, this still does not weigh as if a negative duty were involved. It is not, for instance,

---

permissible to commit a murder to bring one's starving children food. If the choice is between inflicting injury on one or many there seems only one rational course of action; if the choice is between aid to some at the cost of injury to others, and refusing to inflict the injury to bring the aid, the whole matter is open to dispute. So it is not inconsistent of us to think that the driver must steer for the road on which only one man stands while the judge (or his equivalent) may not kill the innocent person in order to stop the riots. Let us now consider the second pair of examples, which concern the scarce drug on the one hand and on the other the body needed to save lives. Once again we find a difference based on the distinction between the duty to avoid injury and the duty to provide aid. Where one man needs a massive dose of the drug and we withhold it from him in order to save five men, we are weighing aid against aid. But if we consider killing a man in order to use his body to save others, we are thinking of doing him injury to bring others aid. In an interesting variant of the model, we may suppose that instead of killing someone we deliberately let him die. (Perhaps he is a beggar to whom we are thinking of giving food, but then we say "No, they need bodies for medical research.") Here it does seem relevant that in allowing him to die we are aiming at his death, but presumably we are inclined to see this as a violation of negative rather than positive duty. If this is right, we see why we are unable in either case to argue to a conclusion from the case of the scarce drug.

In the examples involving the torturing of one man or five men, the principle seems to be the same as for the last pair. If we are bringing aid (rescuing people about to be tortured by the tyrant), we must obviously rescue the larger rather than the smaller group. It does not follow, however, that we would be justified in inflicting the injury, or getting a third person to do so, in order to save the five. We may therefore refuse to be forced into acting by the threats of bad men. To refrain from inflicting injury ourselves is a stricter duty than to prevent other people from inflicting injury, which is not to say that the other is not a very strict duty indeed.

So far the conclusions are the same as those at which we might arrive following the doctrine of the double effect, but in others they will be different, and the advantage seems to be on the side of the alternative. Suppose, for instance, that there are five patients in a hospital whose lives could be saved by the manufacture of a certain gas, but that this inevitably releases lethal fumes into the room of another patient whom for some reason we are unable to move. His death, being of no use to us, is clearly a side effect, and not directly intended. Why then is the case different from that of the scarce drug, if the point about that is that we foresaw but did not strictly intend the death of the single patient? Yet it surely is different. The relatives of the gassed patient would presumably be successful if they sued the hospital and the whole story came out. We may find it particularly revolting that someone should be *used* as in the case where he is killed or allowed to die in the interest of medical research, and the fact of *using* may even determine what we would decide to do in some cases, but the principle seems unimportant compared with our reluctance to bring such injury for the sake of giving aid.

My conclusion is that the distinction between direct and oblique intention plays only a quite subsidiary role in determining what we say in these cases, while the distinction between avoiding injury and bringing aid is very important indeed. I have not, of course, argued that there are no other principles. For instance it clearly makes a difference whether our positive duty is a strict duty or rather an act of charity: feeding our own children or feeding those in far away countries. It may also make a difference whether the person about to suffer is one thought of as uninvolved in the threatened disaster, and whether it is his presence that constitutes the threat to the others. In many cases we find it very hard to know what to say, and I have not been arguing for any general conclusion such as that we may never, whatever the balance of good and evil, bring injury to one for the sake of aid to others, even when this injury amounts to death. I have only tried to show that even if we reject the doctrine of the double effect we are not forced to the conclusion that the size of the evil must always be our guide.

Let us now return to the problem of abortion, carrying out our plan of finding parallels involving adults or children rather than the unborn. We must say something about the different cases in which abortion might be considered on medical grounds.

First of all there is the situation in which nothing that can be done will save the life of child and mother, but where the life of the mother can be saved by killing the child. This is parallel to the case of the fat man in the mouth of the cave who is bound to be drowned with the others if nothing is done. Given the certainty of the outcome, as it was postulated, there is no serious conflict of interests here, since the fat man will perish in either case, and it is reasonable that the action that will save someone should be done. It is a great objection to those who argue that the direct intention of the death of an innocent person is never justifiable that the edict will apply even in this case. The Catholic doctrine on abortion must here conflict with that of most reasonable men. Moreover we would be justified in performing the operation whatever the method used, and it is neither a necessary nor a good justification of the special case of hysterectomy that the child's death is not directly intended, being rather a foreseen consequence of what is done. What difference could it make as to how the death is brought about?

Secondly we have the case in which it is possible to perform an operation which will save the mother and kill the child or kill the mother and save the child. This is parallel to the famous case of the shipwrecked mariners who believed that they must throw someone overboard if their boat was not to founder in a storm, and to the other famous case of the two sailors, Dudley and Stephens, who killed and ate the cabin boy when adrift on the sea without food. Here again there is no conflict of interests so far as the decision to act is concerned; only in deciding whom to save. Once again it would be reasonable to act, though one would respect someone who held back from the appalling action either because he preferred to perish rather than do such a thing or because he held on past the limits of reasonable hope. In real life the certainties postulated by philosophers hardly ever exist, and Dudley and Stephens were rescued not long after their ghastly meal. Nevertheless if the certainty were absolute, as it might be in the abortion case, it would seem better to save one than none. Probably we should decide in favour of the mother when weighing her life against that of the unborn child, but it is interesting that, a few years later, we might easily decide it the other way.

The worst dilemma comes in the third kind of example where to save the mother we must kill the child, say by crushing its skull, while if nothing is done the mother will perish but the child can be safely delivered after her death. Here the doctrine of the double effect has been invoked to show that we may not intervene, since the child's death would be directly intended while the mother's would not. On a strict parallel with cases not involving the unborn we might find the conclusion correct though the reason given was wrong. Suppose, for instance, that in later life the presence of a child was certain to bring death to the mother. We would surely not think ourselves justified in ridding her of it by a process that involved its death. For in general we do not think that we can kill one innocent person to rescue another, quite apart from the special care that we feel is due to children once they have prudently got themselves born. What we would be prepared to do when a great many people were involved is another matter, and this is probably the key to one quite common view of abortion on the part of those who take quite seriously the rights of the unborn child. They probably feel that if *enough* people are involved one must be sacrificed, and they think of the mother's life against the unborn child's life as if it were many against one. But of course many people do not view it like this at all, having no inclination to accord to the foetus or unborn child anything like ordinary human status in the matter of rights. I have not been arguing for or against these points of view but only trying to discern some of the currents that are pulling us back and forth. The levity of the examples is not meant to offend.

Philippa Foot: The Problem of Abortion and the Doctrine of the Double Effect

1. What is the doctrine of double effect? Why does Foot think that the doctrine should be taken seriously?
2. What kinds of cases is the doctrine of double effect supposed to explain? Do you think the doctrine offers the correct moral verdict in these cases?
3. According to Foot, some have suggested that rejecting the doctrine of double effect would have "the consequence of putting us hopelessly in the power of bad men." What reason is there to believe this? Do you find the claim plausible?
4. What alternative to the doctrine of double effect does Foot offer? Does her theory succeed in explaining the cases that the doctrine of double effect was supposed to explain?
5. What advantages does Foot believe her theory has over the doctrine of double effect? Which theory do you think is better?
6. What conclusions does Foot draw about the morality of abortion? What other considerations, besides those Foot discusses, are relevant to the question of when (if ever) abortion is morally permissible?

34

Justifying Legal Punishment

Igor Primoratz

In this excerpt from his book *Justifying Legal Punishment* (1989), Igor Primoratz defends the retributivist idea that a punishment is justified only if it gives a criminal his just deserts. But what do criminals deserve? Primoratz argues for the following principle: criminals deserve to be deprived of the same value that they deprived their victims of. Primoratz regards all human beings as possessed of lives of equal moral worth, and also believes that nothing is as valuable as human life. So murderers deserve to die. Since justice is a matter of giving people what they deserve, it follows that justice demands that murderers be executed.

Primoratz considers the most popular arguments of the opposing camp, and finds problems for each of them. Opponents claim that capital punishment violates a murderer's right to life; that killing murderers is contradictory; that capital punishment is disproportionally harsh; that the innocent are inevitably going to be executed; and that systematic discrimination undermines any chance at moral legitimacy. Primoratz carefully considers each objection and offers his replies. In the end, he thinks that justice requires the death penalty, that justice is the supreme legal virtue, and that none of the objections is strong enough to undermine the case for capital punishment. Therefore the state ought to execute convicted murderers.

... According to the retributive theory, consequences of punishment, however important from the practical point of view, are irrelevant when it comes to its justification; *the* moral consideration is its justice. Punishment is morally justified insofar as it is meted out as retribution for the offense committed. When someone has committed an offense, he deserves to be punished: it is just, and consequently justified, that he be punished. The offense is the sole ground of the state's right and duty to punish. It is also the measure of legitimate punishment: the two ought to be proportionate. So the issue of capital punishment within the retributive approach comes down to the question, Is this punishment ever proportionate retribution for the offense committed, and thus deserved, just, and justified?

The classic representatives of retributivism believed that it was, and that it was the only proportionate and hence appropriate punishment, if the offense was *murder*—that is, criminal homicide perpetrated voluntarily and intentionally or in wanton disregard of human life. In other cases, the demand for proportionality between offense and punishment can be satisfied by fines or prison terms; the crime of murder, however, is an exception in this respect, and calls for the literal interpretation of the *lex talionis*. The uniqueness of this crime has to do with the uniqueness of the value which has been deliberately or recklessly destroyed. We come across this idea as early as the original formulation of the retributive view—the biblical teaching on punishment: "You shall accept no ransom for the life of a murderer who is guilty of death; but he shall be put to death."[1] The rationale of this command—one that clearly distinguishes the biblical conception of the criminal law from contemporaneous criminal law systems in the Middle East—is that man was not only created *by* God, like every other creature, but also, alone among all the creatures, *in the image of God*:

> That man was made in the image of God . . . is expressive of the peculiar and supreme worth of man. Of all creatures, Genesis 1 relates, he alone possesses this attribute, bringing him into closer relation to God than all the rest and conferring upon him the highest value This view of the uniqueness and supremacy of human life places life beyond the reach of other values. The idea that life may be measured in terms of money or other property is excluded. Compensation of any kind is ruled out. The guilt of the murderer is infinite because the murdered life is invaluable; the kinsmen of the slain man are not competent to

---

1. Numbers 35.31 (R.S.V.).

say when he has been paid for. An absolute wrong has been committed, a sin against God which is not subject to human discussion Because human life is invaluable, to take it entails the death penalty.[2]

This view that the value of human life is not commensurable with other values, and that consequently there is only one truly equivalent punishment for murder, namely death, does not necessarily presuppose a theistic outlook. It can be claimed that, simply because we have to be alive if we are to experience and realize any other value at all, there is nothing equivalent to the murderous destruction of a human life except the destruction of the life of the murderer. Any other retribution, no matter how severe, would still be less than what is proportionate, deserved, and just. As long as the murderer is alive, no matter how bad the conditions of his life may be, there are always at least *some* values he can experience and realize. This provides a plausible interpretation of what the classical representatives of retributivism as a philosophical theory of punishment, such as Kant and Hegel, had to say on the subject.[3]

It seems to me that this is essentially correct. With respect to the larger question of the justification of punishment in general, it is the retributive theory that gives the right answer. Accordingly, capital punishment ought to be retained where it obtains, and reintroduced in those jurisdictions that have abolished it, although we have no reason to believe that, as a means of deterrence, it is any better than a very long prison term. It ought to be retained, or reintroduced, for one simple reason: that justice be done in cases of murder, that murderers be punished according to their deserts.

There are a number of arguments that have been advanced against this rationale of capital punishment. . . .

[One] abolitionist argument . . . simply says that capital punishment is illegitimate because it violates the right to life, which is a fundamental,

---

2. M. Greenberg, "Some Postulates of Biblical Criminal Law," in J. Goldin (ed.), *The Jewish Expression* (New York: Bantam, 1970), pp. 25–26. (Post-biblical Jewish law evolved toward the virtual abolition of the death penalty, but that is of no concern here.)

3. "There is no parallel between death and even the most miserable life, so that there is no equality of crime and retribution [in the case of murder] unless the perpetrator is judicially put to death" (I. Kant, "The Metaphysics of Morals," *Kant's Political Writings*, ed. H. Reiss, trans. H. B. Nisbet [Cambridge: Cambridge University Press, 1970], p. 156). "Since life is the full compass of a man's existence, the punishment [for murder] cannot simply consist in a 'value,' for none is great enough, but can consist only in taking away a second life" (G. W. F. Hegel, *Philosophy of Right*, trans. T. M. Knox [Oxford: Oxford University Press, 1965], p. 247).

absolute, sacred right belonging to each and every human being, and therefore ought to be respected even in a murderer.

If any rights are fundamental, the right to life is certainly one of them; but to claim that it is absolute, inviolable under any circumstances and for any reason, is a different matter. If an abolitionist wants to argue his case by asserting an absolute right to life, she will also have to deny moral legitimacy to taking human life in war, revolution, and self-defense. This kind of pacifism is a consistent but farfetched and hence implausible position.

I do not believe that the right to life (nor, for that matter, any other right) is absolute. I have no general theory of rights to fall back upon here; instead, let me pose a question. Would we take seriously the claim to an absolute, sacred, inviolable right to life—coming from the mouth of a *confessed murderer*? I submit that we would not, for the obvious reason that it is being put forward by the person who confessedly denied another human being this very right. But if the murderer cannot plausibly claim such a right for himself, neither can *anyone else* do that in his behalf. This suggests that there is an element of reciprocity in our general rights, such as the right to life or property. I can convincingly claim these rights only so long as I acknowledge and respect the same rights of others. If I violate the rights of others, I thereby lose the same rights. If I am a murderer, I have no *right* to live.

Some opponents of capital punishment claim that a criminal law system which includes this punishment is contradictory, in that it prohibits murder and at the same time provides for its perpetration: "It is one and the same legal regulation which prohibits the individual from murdering, while allowing the state to murder. . . . This is obviously a terrible irony, an abnormal and immoral logic, against which everything in us revolts."[4]

This seems to be one of the more popular arguments against the death penalty, but it is not a good one. If it were valid, it would prove too much. Exactly the same might be claimed of other kinds of punishment: of prison terms, that they are "contradictory" to the legal protection of liberty; of fines, that they are "contradictory" to the legal protection of property. Fortunately enough, it is not valid, for it begs the question at issue. In order to be able to talk of the state as "murdering" the person it executes, and to claim that there is "an abnormal and immoral logic" at work here, which thrives on a "contradiction," one has to use the word "murder" in the very same sense—that is, in the usual sense, which implies the idea of

---

4. S. V. Vulović, *Problem smrtne kazne* (Belgrade: Geca Kon, 1925), pp. 23–24.

the *wrongful* taking the life of another—both when speaking of what the murderer has done to the victim and of what the state is doing to him by way of punishment. But this is precisely the question at issue: whether capital punishment is "murder," whether it is wrongful or morally justified and right.

The next two arguments attack the retributive rationale of capital punishment by questioning the claim that it is only this punishment that satisfies the demand for proportion between offense and punishment in the case of murder. The first points out that any two human lives are different in many important respects, such as age, health, physical and mental capability, so that it does not make much sense to consider them equally valuable. What if the murdered person was very old, practically at the very end of her natural life, while the murderer is young, with most of his life still ahead of him, for instance? Or if the victim was gravely and incurably ill, and thus doomed to live her life in suffering and hopelessness, without being able to experience almost anything that makes a human life worth living, while the murderer is in every respect capable of experiencing and enjoying things life has to offer? Or the other way round? Would not the death penalty in such cases amount either to taking a more valuable life as a punishment for destroying a less valuable one, or *vice versa*? Would it not be either too much, or too little, and in both cases disproportionate, and thus unjust and wrong, from the standpoint of the retributive theory itself?

Any plausibility this argument might appear to have is the result of a conflation of differences between, and value of, human lives. No doubt, any two human lives are *different* in innumerable ways, but this does not entail that they are not *equally valuable*. I have no worked-out general theory of equality to refer to here, but I do not think that one is necessary in order to do away with this argument. The modern humanistic and democratic tradition in ethical, social, and political thought is based on the idea that all human beings are equal. This finds its legal expression in the principle of equality of people under the law. If we are not willing to give up this principle, we have to stick to the assumption that, all differences notwithstanding, any two human lives, *qua* human lives, are equally valuable. If, on the other hand, we allow that, on the basis of such criteria as age, health, or mental or physical ability, it can be claimed that the life of one person is more or less valuable than the life of another, and we admit such claims in the sphere of law, including criminal law, we shall thereby give up the principle of equality of people under the law. In all consistency, we shall not be able to demand that property, physical and personal integrity, and all other rights and interests of individuals be given equal consideration in courts of law either—that is, we shall have to accept systematic discrimination between individuals on the basis of the same criteria across the whole field. I do not think anyone would seriously contemplate an overhaul of the whole legal system along these lines.

The second argument having to do with the issue of proportionality between murder and capital punishment draws our attention to the fact that the law normally provides for a certain period of time to elapse between the passing of a death sentence and its execution. It is a period of several weeks or months; in some cases it extends to years. This period is bound to be one of constant mental anguish for the condemned. And thus, all things considered, what is inflicted on him is disproportionately hard and hence unjust. It would be proportionate and just only in the case of "a criminal who had warned his victim of the date at which he would inflict a horrible death on him and who, from that moment onward, had confined him at his mercy for months."[5]

The first thing to note about this argument is that it does not support a full-fledged abolitionist stand; if it were valid, it would not show that capital punishment is *never* proportionate and just, but only that it is *very rarely* so. Consequently, the conclusion would not be that it ought to be abolished outright, but only that it ought to be restricted to those cases that would satisfy the condition cited above. Such cases do happen, although, to be sure, not very often; the murder of Aldo Moro, for instance, was of this kind. But this is not the main point. The main point is that the argument actually does not hit at capital punishment itself, although it is presented with that aim in view. It hits at something else: a particular way of carrying out this punishment, which is widely adopted in our time. Some hundred years ago and more, in the Wild West, they frequently hanged the man convicted to die almost immediately after pronouncing the sentence. I am not arguing here that we should follow this example today; I mention this piece of historical fact only in order to show that the interval between sentencing someone to death and carrying out the sentence is not a part of capital punishment itself. However unpalatable we might find those Wild West hangings, whatever objections we might want to voice against the speed with which they followed the sentencing, surely

---

5. A. Camus, "Reflections on the Guillotine," *Resistance, Rebellion and Death*, trans. J. O'Brien (London: Hamish Hamilton, 1961), p. 143.

we shall not deny them the *description* of "executions." So the implication of the argument is not that we ought to do away with capital punishment altogether, nor that we ought to restrict it to those cases of murder where the murderer had warned the victim weeks or months in advance of what he was going to do to her, but that we ought to reexamine the procedure of carrying out this kind of punishment. We ought to weigh the reasons for having this interval between the sentencing and executing, against the moral and human significance of the repercussions such an interval inevitably carries with it.

These reasons, in part, have to do with the possibility of miscarriages of justice and the need to rectify them. Thus we come to the argument against capital punishment which, historically, has been the most effective of all: many advances of the abolitionist movement have been connected with discoveries of cases of judicial errors. Judges and jurors are only human, and consequently some of their beliefs and decisions are bound to be mistaken. Some of their mistakes can be corrected upon discovery; but precisely those with most disastrous repercussions—those which result in innocent people being executed—can never be rectified. In all other cases of mistaken sentencing we can revoke the punishment, either completely or in part, or at least extend compensation. In addition, by exonerating the accused we give moral satisfaction. None of this is possible after an innocent person has been executed; capital punishment is essentially different from all other penalties by being completely irrevocable and irreparable. Therefore, it ought to be abolished.

A part of my reply to this argument goes along the same lines as what I had to say on the previous one. It is not so far-reaching as abolitionists assume; for it would be quite implausible, even fanciful, to claim that there have *never* been cases of murder which left no room whatever for reasonable doubt as to the guilt and full responsibility of the accused. Such cases may not be more frequent than those others, but they do happen. Why not retain the death penalty at least for them?

Actually, this argument, just as the preceding one, does not speak out against capital punishment itself, but against the existing procedures for trying capital cases. Miscarriages of justice result in innocent people being sentenced to death and executed, even in the criminal-law systems in which greatest care is taken to ensure that it never comes to that. But this does not stem from the intrinsic nature of the institution of capital punishment; it results from deficiencies, limitations, and imperfections of the criminal law procedures in which this punishment is meted out. Errors of justice do not demonstrate the need to do away with capital punishment; they simply make it incumbent on us to do everything possible to improve even further procedures of meting it out.

To be sure, this conclusion will not find favor with a diehard abolitionist. "I shall ask for the abolition of Capital Punishment until I have the infallibility of human judgement demonstrated to me," that is, as long as there is even the slightest possibility that innocent people may be executed because of judicial errors, Lafayette said in his day.[6] Many an opponent of this kind of punishment will say the same today. The demand to do away with capital punishment altogether, so as to eliminate even the smallest chance of that ever happening—the chance which, admittedly, would remain even after everything humanly possible has been done to perfect the procedure, although then it would be very slight indeed—is actually a demand to give a privileged position to murderers as against all other offenders, big and small. For if we acted on this demand, we would bring about a situation in which proportionate penalties would be meted out for all offenses, *except* for murder. Murderers would not be receiving the only punishment truly proportionate to their crimes, the punishment of death, but some other, lighter, and thus disproportionate penalty. All other offenders would be punished according to their deserts; only murderers would be receiving less than *they* deserve. In all other cases justice would be done in full; only in cases of the gravest of offenses, the crime of murder, justice would not be carried out in full measure. It is a great and tragic miscarriage of justice when an innocent person is mistakenly sentenced to death and executed, but systematically giving murderers advantage over all other offenders would also be a grave injustice. Is the fact that, as long as capital punishment is retained, there is a possibility that over a number of years, or even decades, an injustice of the first kind may be committed, unintentionally and unconsciously, reason enough to abolish it altogether, and thus end up with a system of punishments in which injustices of the second kind are perpetrated daily, consciously, and inevitably?

There is still another abolitionist argument that actually does not hit out against capital punishment itself, but against something else. Figures are sometimes quoted which show that this punishment is much more often meted out to the uneducated and poor than to the educated, rich,

---

6. Quoted in E. R. Calvert, *Capital Punishment in the Twentieth Century* (London: G. P. Putnam's Sons, 1927), p. 132.

and influential people; in the United States, much more often to blacks than to whites. These figures are adduced as a proof of the inherent injustice of this kind of punishment. On account of them, it is claimed that capital punishment is not a way of doing justice by meting out deserved punishment to murderers, but rather a means of social discrimination and perpetuation of social injustice.

I shall not question these findings, which are quite convincing, and anyway, there is no need to do that in order to defend the institution of capital punishment. For there seems to be a certain amount of discrimination and injustice not only in sentencing people to death and executing them, but also in meting out other penalties. The social structure of the death rows in American prisons, for instance, does not seem to be basically different from the general social structure of American penitentiaries. If this argument were valid, it would call not only for abolition of the penalty of death, but for doing away with other penalties as well. But it is not valid; as Burton Leiser has pointed out,

> . . . this is not an argument, either against the death penalty or against any other form of punishment. It is an argument against the unjust and inequitable distribution of penalties. If the trials of wealthy men are less likely to result in convictions than those of poor men, then something must be done to reform the procedure in criminal courts. If those who have money and standing in the community are less likely to be charged with serious offenses than their less affluent fellow citizens, then there should be a major overhaul of the entire system of criminal justice But the maldistribution of penalties is no argument against any particular form of penalty.[7]

Igor Primoratz: Justifying Legal Punishment

1. Retributivists such as Primoratz hold that the punishment of a crime ought to be proportional to the offense. Do you find such a view plausible? Are there any other morally relevant considerations when considering how someone should be punished?
2. Primoratz argues that the only punishment proportional to the offense of murder is the death penalty. What reasons does he give for thinking this? Do you think he is correct?

---

7. B. M. Leiser, *Liberty, Justice and Morals: Contemporary Value Conflicts* (New York: Macmillan, 1973), p. 225.

3. Some argue that capital punishment violates the right to life. Primoratz responds that the right to life is not "absolute." What does he mean by this, and how does he argue for it? Do you agree with him?

4. How does Primoratz respond to the objection that the death penalty is hypocritical because it involves killing people for the offense of killing other people? Do you find his response convincing?

5. Many people object to the death penalty on the grounds that it sometimes results in innocent people being executed, and is often applied in a discriminatory way. Why doesn't Primoratz think these concerns justify abolishing the death penalty? Do you agree?

35

An Eye for an Eye?

Stephen Nathanson

In this excerpt from his book *An Eye for an Eye?* (1987), Stephen Nathanson argues against the classic retributivist principle of punishment: *lex talionis*. This principle tells us to treat criminals just as they treated their victims—an eye for an eye, a tooth for a tooth. Nathanson finds two major problems for *lex talionis*. First, it advises us to commit highly immoral actions—raping a rapist, for instance, or torturing a torturer. Second, it is impossible to apply in many cases of deserved punishment—for instance, the principle offers no advice about what to do with drunk drivers, air polluters, embezzlers, or spies.

Retributivists might replace *lex talionis* with a principle of proportional punishment, according to which increasingly bad crimes must be met with increasingly harsher punishment. This proposal is plausible, says Nathanson, but it offers no justification for the death penalty. All it tells us is that the worst crimes ought to be met with the harshest punishments. But it says nothing about how harsh those punishments should be.

Nathanson concludes by discussing the symbolism of abolishing the death penalty, and claims that we express a respect for each person's inalienable rights by refraining from depriving a murderer of his life.

"An Eye for an Eye?" from *An Eye for an Eye?* by Stephen Nathanson (1987). Reprinted with permission of Rowman & Littlefield.

Suppose we . . . try to determine what people deserve from a strictly moral point of view. How shall we proceed?

The most usual suggestion is that we look at a person's actions because what someone deserves would appear to depend on what he or she does. A person's actions, it seems, provide not only a basis for a moral appraisal of the person but also a guide to how he should be treated. According to the *lex talionis* or principle of "an eye for an eye," we ought to treat people as they have treated others. What people deserve as recipients of rewards or punishments is determined by what they do as agents.

This is a powerful and attractive view, one that appears to be backed not only by moral common sense but also by tradition and philosophical thought. The most famous statement of philosophical support for this view comes from Immanuel Kant, who linked it directly with an argument for the death penalty. Discussing the problem of punishment, Kant writes,

> What kind and what degree of punishment does legal justice adopt as its principle and standard? None other than the principle of equality . . . the principle of not treating one side more favorably than the other. Accordingly, any undeserved evil that you inflict on someone else among the people is one that you do to yourself. If you vilify, you vilify yourself; if you steal from him, you steal from yourself; if you kill him, you kill yourself. Only the law of retribution (*jus talionis*) can determine exactly the kind and degree of punishment.[1]

Kant's view is attractive for a number of reasons. First, it accords with our belief that what a person deserves is related to what he does. Second, it appeals to a moral standard and does not seem to rely on any particular legal or political institutions. Third, it seems to provide a measure of appropriate punishment that can be used as a guide to creating laws and instituting punishments. It tells us that the punishment is to be identical with the crime. Whatever the criminal did to the victim is to be done in turn to the criminal.

In spite of the attractions of Kant's view, it is deeply flawed. When we see why, it will be clear that the whole "eye for an eye" perspective must be rejected.

---

1. Kant, *Metaphysical Elements of Justice*, translated by John Ladd (Indianapolis: Bobbs-Merrill, 1965), p. 101.

Problems with the Equal Punishment Principle

. . . [Kant's view] does not provide an adequate criterion for determining appropriate levels of punishment.

. . . We can see this, first, by noting that for certain crimes, Kant's view recommends punishments that are not morally acceptable. Applied strictly, it would require that we rape rapists, torture torturers, and burn arsonists whose acts have led to deaths. In general, where a particular crime involves barbaric and inhuman treatment, Kant's principle tells us to act barbarically and inhumanly in return. So, in some cases, the principle generates unacceptable answers to the question of what constitutes appropriate punishment.

This is not its only defect. In many other cases, the principle tells us nothing at all about how to punish. While Kant thought it obvious how to apply his principle in the case of murder, his principle cannot serve as a general rule because it does not tell us how to punish many crimes. Using the Kantian version or the more common "eye for an eye" standard, what would we decide to do to embezzlers, spies, drunken drivers, airline hijackers, drug users, prostitutes, air polluters, or persons who practice medicine without a license? If one reflects on this question, it becomes clear that there is simply no answer to it. We could not in fact design a system of punishment simply on the basis of the "eye for an eye" principle.

In order to justify using the "eye for an eye" principle to answer our question about murder and the death penalty, we would first have to show that it worked for a whole range of cases, giving acceptable answers to questions about amounts of punishment. Then, having established it as a satisfactory general principle, we could apply it to the case of murder. It turns out, however, that when we try to apply the principle generally, we find that it either gives wrong answers or no answers at all. Indeed, I suspect that the principle of "an eye for an eye" is no longer even a principle. Instead, it is simply a metaphorical disguise for expressing belief in the death penalty. People who cite it do not take it seriously. They do not believe in a kidnapping for a kidnapping, a theft for a theft, and so on. Perhaps "an eye for an eye" once was a genuine principle, but now it is merely a slogan. Therefore, it gives us no guidance in deciding whether murderers deserve to die.

In reply to these objections, one might defend the principle by saying that it does not require that punishments be strictly identical with crimes. Rather, it requires only that a punishment produce an amount of suffering in the criminal which is equal to the amount suffered by the victim. Thus, we don't have to hijack airplanes belonging to airline hijackers, spy on spies, etc. We simply have to reproduce in them the harm done to others.

Unfortunately, this reply really does not solve the problem. It provides no answer to the first objection, since it would still require us to behave barbarically in our treatment of those who are guilty of barbaric crimes. Even if we do not reproduce their actions exactly, any action which caused equal suffering would itself be barbaric. Second, in trying to produce equal amounts of suffering, we run into many problems. Just how much suffering is produced by an airline hijacker or a spy? And how do we apply this principle to prostitutes or drug users, who may not produce any suffering at all? We have rough ideas about how serious various crimes are, but this may not correlate with any clear sense of just how much harm is done.

Furthermore, the same problem arises in determining how much suffering a particular punishment would produce for a particular criminal. People vary in their tolerance of pain and in the amount of unhappiness that a fine or a jail sentence would cause them. Recluses will be less disturbed by banishment than extroverts. Nature lovers will suffer more in prison than people who are indifferent to natural beauty. A literal application of the principle would require that we tailor punishments to individual sensitivities, yet this is at best impractical. To a large extent, the legal system must work with standardized and rather crude estimates of the negative impact that punishments have on people.

The move from calling for a punishment that is identical to the crime to favoring one that is equal in the harm done is no help to us or to the defense of the principle. "An eye for an eye" tells us neither what people deserve nor how we should treat them when they have done wrong.

Proportional Retributivism

The view we have been considering can be called "equality retributivism," since it proposes that we repay criminals with punishments equal to their crimes. In the light of problems like those I have cited, some people have proposed a variation on this view, calling not for equal punishments but rather for punishments which are *proportional* to the crime. In defending such a view as a guide for setting criminal punishments, Andrew von Hirsch writes:

> If one asks how severely a wrongdoer deserves to be punished, a familiar principle comes to mind: Severity of punishment should be commensurate with the seriousness of the wrong. Only grave wrongs merit

severe penalties; minor misdeeds deserve lenient punishments. Disproportionate penalties are undeserved—severe sanctions for minor wrongs or vice versa. This principle has variously been called a principle of "proportionality" or "just deserts"; we prefer to call it commensurate deserts.[2]

Like Kant, von Hirsch makes the punishment which a person deserves depend on that person's actions, but he departs from Kant in substituting proportionality for equality as the criterion for setting the amount of punishment.

In implementing a punishment system based on the proportionality view, one would first make a list of crimes, ranking them in order of seriousness. At one end would be quite trivial offenses like parking meter violations, while very serious crimes such as murder would occupy the other. In between, other crimes would be ranked according to their relative gravity. Then a corresponding scale of punishments would be constructed, and the two would be correlated. Punishments would be proportionate to crimes so long as we could say that the more serious the crime was, the higher on the punishment scale was the punishment administered.

This system does not have the defects of equality retributivism. It does not require that we treat those guilty of barbaric crimes barbarically. This is because we can set the upper limit of the punishment scale so as to exclude truly barbaric punishments. Second, unlike the equality principle, the proportionality view is genuinely general, providing a way of handling all crimes. Finally, it does justice to our ordinary belief that certain punishments are unjust because they are too severe or too lenient for the crime committed.

The proportionality principle does, I think, play a legitimate role in our thinking about punishments. Nonetheless, it is no help to death penalty advocates, because it does not require that murderers be executed. All that it requires is that if murder is the most serious crime, then murder should be punished by the most severe punishment on the scale. The principle does not tell us what this punishment should be, however, and it is quite compatible with the view that the most severe punishment should be a long prison term.

---

2. *Doing Justice* (New York: Hill & Wang, 1976), p. 66; reprinted in *Sentencing*, edited by H. Gross and A. von Hirsch (Oxford University Press, 1981), p. 243. For a more recent discussion and further defense by von Hirsch, see his *Past or Future Crimes* (New Brunswick, N.J.: Rutgers University Press, 1985).

This failure of the theory to provide a basis for supporting the death penalty reveals an important gap in proportional retributivism. It shows that while the theory is general in scope, it does not yield any *specific* recommendations regarding punishment. It tells us, for example, that armed robbery should be punished more severely than embezzling and less severely than murder, but it does not tell us how much to punish any of these. This weakness is, in effect, conceded by von Hirsch, who admits that if we want to implement the "commensurate deserts" principle, we must supplement it with information about what level of punishment is needed to deter crimes.[3] In a later discussion of how to "anchor" the punishment system, he deals with this problem in more depth, but the factors he cites as relevant to making specific judgments (such as available prison space) have nothing to do with what people deserve. He also seems to suggest that a range of punishments may be appropriate for a particular crime. This runs counter to the death penalty supporter's sense that death alone is appropriate for some murderers.[4]

Neither of these retributive views, then, provides support for the death penalty. The equality principle fails because it is not in general true that the appropriate punishment for a crime is to do to the criminal what he has done to others. In some cases this is immoral, while in others it is impossible. The proportionality principle may be correct, but by itself it cannot determine specific punishments for specific crimes. Because of its flexibility and open-endedness, it is compatible with a great range of different punishments for murder.[5] . . .

The Symbolism of Abolishing the Death Penalty

What is the symbolic message that we would convey by deciding to renounce the death penalty and to abolish its use?

---

3. Von Hirsch, *Doing Justice*, pp. 93–94. My criticisms of proportional retributivism are not novel. For helpful discussions of the view, see Hugo Bedau, "Concessions to Retribution in Punishment," in *Justice and Punishment*, edited by J. Cederblom and W. Blizek (Cambridge, Mass.: Ballinger, 1977), and M. Golding, *Philosophy of Law* (Englewood Cliffs, N.J.: Prentice Hall, 1975), pp. 98–99.

4. See von Hirsch, *Past or Future Crimes*, ch. 8.

5. For more positive assessments of these theories, see Jeffrey Reiman, "Justice, Civilization, and the Death Penalty," *Philosophy and Public Affairs* 14 (1985): 115–148; and Michael Davis, "How to Make the Punishment Fit the Crime," *Ethics* 93 (1983).

I think that there are two primary messages. The first is the most frequently emphasized and is usually expressed in terms of the sanctity of human life, although I think we could better express it in terms of respect for human dignity. One way we express our respect for the dignity of human beings is by abstaining from depriving them of their lives, even if they have done terrible deeds. In defense of human well-being, we may punish people for their crimes, but we ought not to deprive them of everything, which is what the death penalty does.

If we take the life of a criminal, we convey the idea that by his deeds he has made himself worthless and totally without human value. I do not believe that we are in a position to affirm that of anyone. We may hate such a person and feel the deepest anger against him, but when he no longer poses a threat to anyone, we ought not to take his life.

But, one might ask, hasn't the murderer forfeited whatever rights he might have had to our respect? Hasn't he, by his deeds, given up any rights that he had to decent treatment? Aren't we morally free to kill him if we wish?

These questions express important doubts about the obligation to accord any respect to those who have acted so deplorably, but I do not think that they prove that any such forfeiture has occurred. Certainly, when people murder or commit other crimes, they do forfeit some of the rights that are possessed by the law-abiding. They lose a certain right to be left alone. It becomes permissible to bring them to trial and, if they are convicted, to impose an appropriate—even a dreadful—punishment on them.

Nonetheless, they do not forfeit all their rights. It does not follow from the vileness of their actions that we can do anything whatsoever to them. This is part of the moral meaning of the constitutional ban on cruel and unusual punishments. No matter how terrible a person's deeds, we may not punish him in a cruel and unusual way. We may not torture him, for example. His right not to be tortured has not been forfeited. Why do these limits hold? Because this person remains a human being, and we think that there is something in him that we must continue to respect in spite of his terrible acts.

One way of seeing why those who murder still deserve some consideration and respect is by reflecting again on the idea of what it is to *deserve* something. In most contexts, we think that what people deserve depends on what they have done, intended, or tried to do. It depends on features that are qualities of individuals. The best person for the job deserves to be hired. The person who worked especially hard deserves our gratitude. We can call the concept that applies in these cases *personal* desert.

There is another kind of desert, however, that belongs to people by virtue of their humanity itself and does not depend on their individual efforts or achievements. I will call this impersonal kind of desert *human* desert. We appeal to this concept when we think that everyone deserves a certain level of treatment no matter what their individual qualities are. When the signers of the Declaration of Independence affirmed that people had inalienable rights to "life, liberty, and the pursuit of happiness," they were appealing to such an idea. These rights do not have to be earned by people. They are possessed "naturally," and everyone is bound to respect them.

According to the view that I am defending, people do not lose all of their rights when they commit terrible crimes. They still deserve some level of decent treatment simply because they remain living, functioning human beings. This level of moral desert need not be earned, and it cannot be forfeited. This view may sound controversial, but in fact everyone who believes that cruel and unusual punishment should be forbidden implicitly agrees with it. That is, they agree that even after someone has committed a terrible crime, we do not have the right to do anything whatsoever to him.

What I am suggesting is that by renouncing the use of death as a punishment, we express and reaffirm our belief in the inalienable, unforfeitable core of human dignity.

Why is this a worthwhile message to convey? It is worth conveying because this belief is both important and precarious. Throughout history, people have found innumerable reasons to degrade the humanity of one another. They have found qualities in others that they hated or feared, and even when they were not threatened by these people, they have sought to harm them, deprive them of their liberty, or take their lives from them. They have often felt that they had good reasons to do these things, and they have invoked divine commands, racial purity, and state security to support their deeds.

These actions and attitudes are not relics of the past. They remain an awful feature of the contemporary world. By renouncing the death penalty, we show our determination to accord at least minimal respect even to those whom we believe to be personally vile or morally vicious. This is, perhaps, why we speak of the *sanctity* of human life rather than its value or worth. That which is sacred remains, in some sense, untouchable, and its value is not dependent on its worth or usefulness to us. Kant expressed this ideal of respect in the famous second version of the Categorical Imperative: "So act as to treat humanity, whether in thine own person or in that of any other, in every case as an end withal, never as a means only." . . .

When the state has a murderer in its power and could execute him but does not, this conveys the idea that even though this person has done wrong and even though we may be angry, outraged, and indignant with him, we will nonetheless control ourselves in a way that he did not. We will not kill him, even though we could do so and even though we are angry and indignant. We will exercise restraint, sanctioning killing only when it serves a protective function.

Why should we do this? Partly out of a respect for human dignity. But also because we want the state to set an example of proper behavior. We do not want to encourage people to resort to violence to settle conflicts when there are other ways available. We want to avoid the cycle of violence that can come from retaliation and counter-retaliation. Violence is a contagion that arouses hatred and anger, and if unchecked, it simply leads to still more violence. The state can convey the message that the contagion must be stopped, and the most effective principle for stopping it is the idea that only defensive violence is justifiable. Since the death penalty is not an instance of defensive violence, it ought to be renounced.

We show our respect for life best by restraining ourselves and allowing murderers to live, rather than by following a policy of a life for a life. Respect for life and restraint of violence are aspects of the same ideal. The renunciation of the death penalty would symbolize our support of that ideal.

Stephen Nathanson: An Eye for an Eye?

1. Nathanson rejects the principle of *lex talionis*, according to which we ought to treat criminals as they have treated others. What reasons does he give for rejecting this principle? Do you find his reasons convincing?

2. Nathanson considers the following modification of the principle of *lex talionis*: "a punishment [should] produce an amount of suffering in the criminal which is equal to the amount suffered by the victim." Do you think this is a plausible principle? What objections does Nathanson offer to the principle?

3. What is the principle of proportional retributivism? Why doesn't Nathanson think that this principle supports the death penalty? Do you agree with him?

4. What symbolic message does Nathanson think that abolishing the death penalty would convey? Is this a good reason to abolish the death penalty?

5. Are there any reasons for supporting the death penalty that Nathanson does not consider? If so, are these reasons ever strong enough to justify sentencing someone to death?

36

========= ❧ =========

Why Gun 'Control' Is Not Enough

Jeff McMahan

··

Jeff McMahan argues for a near-complete ban on gun ownership. Well-trained police and military officials are the only ones who ought to be allowed to own a gun. For all others—that is, for all private citizens—guns are not to be controlled, but banned.

McMahan's case is both positive and negative. The positive argument is that private gun ownership creates a much more dangerous environment for everyone; the more private citizens who have guns, the more the power of the police declines. And when police power declines, people become more vulnerable and so have greater incentive to get a gun to protect themselves. But when most people have guns, everyone becomes less secure compared to a situation in which no one but police officers have guns.

The negative element of McMahan's case amounts to a critique of the two major reasons that gun advocates have offered on behalf of private gun ownership. The first is that guns provide a lot of recreational value, in the form of target shooting and hunting. While McMahan is open to the idea of allowing hunters to own single-chamber shotguns for hunting purposes, he denies that the value of target shooting justifies gun ownership, since enthusiasts could rent guns whose use is restricted to licensed shooting ranges. The second reason gun advocates have offered is that gun ownership is the best means of self-defense, and our right to self-defense justifies a right to own a gun.

New York Times *Opinionator* blog, December 19, 2012, http://opinionator.blogs.nytimes.com/2012/12/19/why-gun-control-is-not-enough/?_r=0

McMahan counters that the need for guns to defend oneself arises primarily because we allow people to have guns in the first place—if we banned all private gun ownership, then we would all live in much safer environments, and so have less need for a gun for self-defense.

McMahan concludes by rebutting a few familiar pro-gun arguments. The first is that a gun ban is impractical, because of existing political opposition. But McMahan argues that gun advocates cannot press this argument in good faith, since it is only their opposition that stands in the way of such a ban. The second argument is that a ban on gun ownership is impractical in that it will not end gun violence. He agrees that such a ban will not be wholly effective but argues that this is hardly a compelling reason not to enforce the ban. After all, we have laws against murder, though we know in advance that having such a law will not prevent all murders. A third argument is that prohibiting private gun ownership is no different from drug or alcohol prohibition, which have been gross failures. McMahan believes, however, that there is a relevant difference, since millions of people need or crave drugs and alcohol and will engage in such consumption regardless of a legal prohibition, whereas the desire for a gun is primarily driven by a desire for self-defense, and, as already indicated, there would be far less need for a gun for self-defense purposes if private citizens were prohibited from having guns in the first place.

....

Americans are finally beginning to have a serious discussion about guns. One argument we're hearing is the central pillar of the case for private gun ownership: that we are all safer when more individuals have guns because armed citizens deter crime and can defend themselves and others against it when deterrence fails. Those who don't have guns, it's said, are free riders on those who do, as the criminally disposed are less likely to engage in crime the more likely it is that their victim will be armed.

There's some sense to this argument, for even criminals don't like being shot. But the logic is faulty, and a close look at it leads to the conclusion that the United States should ban private gun ownership entirely, or almost entirely.

One would think that if widespread gun ownership had the robust deterrent effects that gun advocates claim it has, our country would be freer of crime than other developed societies. But it's not. When most citizens are armed, as they were in the Wild West, crime doesn't cease. Instead, criminals work to be better armed, more efficient in their use of guns ("quicker on the draw"), and readier to use them. When this happens, those who get guns may be safer than they would be without them, but those without them become progressively more vulnerable.

Gun advocates have a solution to this: the unarmed must arm themselves. But when more citizens get guns, further problems arise: people who would once have got in a fistfight instead shoot the person who provoked them; people are shot by mistake or by accident.

And with guns so plentiful, any lunatic or criminally disposed person who has a sudden and perhaps only temporary urge to kill people can simply help himself to the contents of Mom's gun cabinet. Perhaps most important, the more people there are who have guns, the less effective the police become. The power of the citizens and that of the police approach parity. The police cease to have even a near-monopoly on the use of force.

To many devotees of the Second Amendment, this is precisely the point. As former Congressman Jay Dickey, Republican of Arkansas, said in January 2011, "We have a right to bear arms because of the threat of government taking over the freedoms we have." The more people there are with guns, the less able the government is to control them. But if arming the citizenry limits the power of the government, it does so by limiting the power of its agents, such as the police. Domestic defense becomes more a matter of private self-help and vigilantism and less a matter of democratically controlled, public law enforcement. Domestic security becomes increasingly "privatized."

There is, of course, a large element of fantasy in Dickey's claim. Individuals with handguns are no match for a modern army. It's also a delusion to suppose that the government in a liberal democracy such as the United States could become so tyrannical that armed insurrection, rather than democratic procedures, would be the best means of constraining it. This is not Syria; nor will it ever be. Shortly after Dickey made his comment, people in Egypt rose against a government that had suppressed their freedom in ways far more serious than requiring them to pay for health care. Although a tiny minority of Egyptians do own guns, the protesters would not have succeeded if those guns had been brought to Tahrir Square. If the assembled citizens had been brandishing Glocks in accordance with the script favored by Second Amendment fantasists, the old regime would almost certainly still be in power and many Egyptians who're now alive would be dead.

For the police to remain effective in a society in which most of those they must confront or arrest are armed, they must, like criminals, become better armed, more numerous, and readier to fire. But if they do that, guns won't have produced a net reduction in the power of the government but will only have generated enormous private and public expenditures, leaving the balance of power between armed citizens and the state as it was before, the unarmed conspicuously worse off, and everyone poorer except the gun industry. The alternative to maintaining the balance of power is to allow it to shift in favor of the armed citizenry and away from the police, again making unarmed citizens—including those who refuse on principle to contribute to the erosion of collective security by getting a gun—the greatest losers overall.

The logic is inexorable: as more private individuals acquire guns, the power of the police declines, personal security becomes more a matter of self-help, and the unarmed have an increasing incentive to get guns, until everyone is armed. When most citizens then have the ability to kill anyone in their vicinity in an instant, everyone is less secure than they would be if no one had guns other than the members of a democratically accountable police force.

The logic of private gun possession is thus similar to that of the nuclear arms race. When only one state gets nuclear weapons, it enhances its own security but reduces that of others, which have become more vulnerable. The other states then have an incentive to get nuclear weapons to try to restore their security. As more states get them, the incentives for others increase. If eventually all get them, the potential for catastrophe—whether through irrationality, misperception, or accident—is great. Each state's security is then much lower than it would be if none had nuclear weapons.

Gun advocates and criminals are allies in demanding that guns remain in private hands. They differ in how they want them distributed. Criminals want guns for themselves but not for their potential victims. Others want them for themselves but not for criminals. But while gun control can do a little to restrict access to guns by potential criminals, it can't do much when guns are to be found in every other household. Either criminals and non-criminals will have them or neither will. Gun advocates prefer for both rather than neither to have them.

But, as with nuclear weapons, we would all be safer if no one had guns—or, rather, no one other than trained and legally constrained police officers. Domestic defense would then be conducted the way we conduct national defense. We no longer accept, as the authors of the now obsolete Second Amendment did, that "a well-regulated militia" is "necessary to the security of a free state." Rather than leaving national defense to citizens' militias, we now, for a variety of compelling reasons, cede the right of national defense to certain state-authorized professional institutions: the Army, Navy, and so on. We rightly trust these forces to protect us from external threats and not to become instruments of domestic repression. We could have the same trust in a police force designed to protect us from domestic threats.

A prohibition of private ownership would not mean that no one could shoot guns. Guns for target shooting could be rented under security arrangements at the range. And there's perhaps scope for debate about private possession of single chamber shotguns for hunting.

Gun advocates will object that a prohibition of private gun ownership is an impossibility in the United States. But this is not an objection they can press in good faith, for the only reason that a legal prohibition could be impossible in a democratic state is that a majority oppose it. If gun advocates ceased to oppose it, a prohibition would be possible.

They will next argue that even if there were a legal prohibition, it could not be enforced with anything approaching complete effectiveness. This is true. As long as some people somewhere have guns, some people here can get them. Similarly, the legal prohibition of murder cannot eliminate murder. But the prohibition of murder is more effective than a policy of "murder control" would be.

Guns are not like alcohol and drugs, both of which we have tried unsuccessfully to prohibit. Many people have an intense desire for alcohol or drugs that is independent of what other people may do. But the need for a gun for self-defense depends on whether other people have them and how effective the protection and deterrence provided by the state are. Thus, in other Western countries in which there are fewer guns, there are correspondingly fewer instances in which people need guns for effective self-defense.

Gun advocates sometimes argue that a prohibition would violate individuals' rights of self-defense. Imposing a ban on guns, they argue, would be tantamount to taking a person's gun from her just as someone is about to kill her. But this is a defective analogy. Although a prohibition would deprive people of one effective means of self-defense, it would also ensure that there would be far fewer occasions on which a gun would be necessary or even useful for self-defense. For guns would be forbidden not just to those who would use them for defense but also to those who would use them for aggression. Guns are only one means of self-defense and self-defense is only one means of achieving security against attack. It is the right to security against attack that is fundamental. A policy that unavoidably deprives a person of one means of self-defense but on balance substantially reduces her vulnerability to attack is therefore respectful of the more fundamental right from which the right of self-defense is derived.

In other Western countries, per capita homicide rates, as well as rates of violent crime involving guns, are a fraction of what they are in the United States. The possible explanations of this are limited. Gun advocates claim it has nothing to do with our permissive gun laws or our customs and practices involving guns. If they are right, should we conclude that Americans are simply inherently more violent, more disposed to mental derangement, and less moral than people in other Western countries? If you resist that conclusion, you have little choice but to accept that our easy access to all manner of firearms is a large part of the explanation of why we kill each at a much higher rate than our counterparts elsewhere. Gun advocates must search their consciences to determine whether they really want to share responsibility for the perpetuation of policies that make our country the homicide capital of the developed world.

Jeff McMahan: Why Gun 'Control' Is Not Enough

1. Given the political climate in the United States, many think that a gun ban is impractical, and hence unjustified. Present McMahan's reply to this concern and assess its merits.
2. Suppose that a gun-free society is much safer than a gun-filled society. This by itself does not suffice to show that societies should institute a ban on guns. What further assumptions are required in order to get from the initial supposition to the conclusion that a society ought to institute a ban on private gun ownership?
3. McMahan claims that the logic of private gun ownership is "inexorable." Can you clearly state just what this logic is, and why McMahan is concerned about it?
4. How (if at all) do the arguments McMahan offers apply to the question of whether we should allow people to own hunting rifles?
5. Consider McMahan's discussion of the analogy between drug and alcohol prohibition and the prohibition of private gun ownership. Do you find his discussion persuasive? Why or why not?

====== 🖤 ======

37

Is There a Right to Own a Gun?

Michael Huemer

....

Michael Huemer argues that individuals have a powerful right to own a gun and that gun control laws that seek to prevent law-abiding citizens from owning a gun are immoral. Huemer allows that gun rights might sometimes be overridden—i.e., they are not *absolute*—though this is a very small concession, as he believes that no right is absolute. He claims that we have a powerful right to own guns that derives from our fundamental right to liberty: we have a moral right to do whatever we want, so long as we do not violate the rights of others. So we have a moral right to own a gun, so long as we do not use it to violate the rights of others.

According to Huemer, the right to own a gun is significant for two reasons. First, guns are the source of a great deal of recreational value, through target shooting, hunting, etc. Second, and more importantly, guns can be vital means of self-defense. This last consideration leads Huemer to review the statistics on gun crime and crime prevention and to argue that since the right to self-defense is an important right, and since a firearms prohibition would be a significant violation of that right, such a prohibition amounts to a serious rights violation.

Since Huemer allows that any right might possibly be overridden, he then considers whether the right to own a gun might be overridden by the harms caused by guns. To do this he reviews some oft-cited statistical arguments against gun ownership and finds that they are more problematic than people have recognized. He then discusses the

Social Theory and Practice vol. 29 (2003). This selection has been abridged and its notes have been edited and renumbered.

benefits, which lie primarily in the use of guns to prevent crime. Finally, he argues that because the right to own a gun is so morally important, the costs of gun ownership would have to be much greater than the benefits in order to justify a firearms prohibition. Though he admits that calculation of costs and benefits is difficult, he argues that the benefits probably outweigh the costs, and so the right to own a gun—at least on the part of law-abiding citizens—is not in fact outweighed.

....

1. Introduction

Gun control supporters often assume that the acceptability of gun control laws turns on whether they increase or decrease crime rates. The notion that such laws might violate rights, independently of whether they decrease crime rates, is rarely entertained. Nor are the interests of gun owners in keeping and using guns typically given great weight. . . .

I believe these attitudes are misguided. I contend that individuals have a prima facie right to own firearms, that this right is weighty and protects important interests, and that it is not overridden by utilitarian considerations. In support of the last point, I shall argue that the harms of private gun ownership are probably less than the benefits, and that in any case, these harms would have to be many times greater than the benefits in order for the right to own a gun to be overridden. . . .

2. Preliminary Remarks about Rights

2.2. What Sort of Right Is the Right to Own a Gun?

First, I distinguish between *fundamental* and *derivative* rights. A right is derivative when it derives at least some of its weight from its relationship to another, independent right. A right is fundamental when it has some force that is independent of other rights. On these definitions, it is possible for a right to be both fundamental and derivative. Derivative rights are usually related to fundamental rights as means to the protection or enforcement of the latter, though this need not be the only way in which a right may be derivative. I claim that the right to own a gun is both fundamental and derivative; however, it is in its *derivative* aspect—as derived from the right of self-defense—that it is most important.

Second, I distinguish between *absolute* and *prima facie* rights. An absolute right is one with overriding importance, such that no considerations can justify violating it. A prima facie right is one that must be given some weight in moral deliberation but that can be overridden by sufficiently important countervailing considerations. Thus, if it would be permissible to steal for sufficiently important reasons—say, to save someone's life—then property rights are not absolute but at most prima facie. It is doubtful whether any rights are absolute. At any rate, I do not propose any absolute rights; I argue only that there is a strong prima facie right to own a gun. . . .

3. Is There a Prima Facie Right to Own a Gun?

Given the presumption in favor of liberty, there is at least a prima facie right to own a gun, unless there are positive grounds . . . for denying such a right. Are there such grounds?

(i) Begin with the principle that one lacks a right to do things that harm others, treat others as mere means, or use others without their consent. It is difficult to see how owning a gun could itself be said to do any of those things, even though owning a gun makes it easier for one to do those things if one chooses to. But we do not normally prohibit activities that merely *make it easier* for one to perform a wrong but require a separate decision to perform the wrongful act.

(ii) Consider the principle that one lacks a right to do things that impose unacceptable, though unintended, risks on others. Since life is replete with risks, to be plausible, the principle must use some notion of *excessive* risks. But the risks associated with normal ownership and recreational use of firearms are minimal. While approximately 77 million Americans now own guns,[1] the accidental death rate for firearms has fallen dramatically during the last century, and is now about .3 per 100,000 population. For comparison, the average citizen is nineteen times more likely to die as a result of an accidental fall, and fifty times more likely to die in an automobile accident, than to die as a result of a firearms accident.[2]

---

1. Surveys indicate that about half of American men and a quarter of women own guns. See Harry Henderson, *Gun Control* (New York: Facts on File, 2000), p. 231; John Lott, *More Guns, Less Crime*, 2nd ed. (Chicago: University of Chicago Press, 2000), pp. 37, 41.

2. National Safety Council, *Injury Facts, 1999 Edition* (Itasca, Ill.: National Safety Council, 1999), pp. 8–9.

(iii) Some may think that the firearms accident statistics miss the point: the real risk that gun ownership imposes on others is the risk that the gun owner or someone else will "lose control" during an argument and decide to shoot his opponent. Nicholas Dixon argues: "In 1990, 34.5% of all murders resulted from domestic or other kinds of argument. Since we are all capable of heated arguments, we are all, in the wrong circumstances, capable of losing control and killing our opponent."[3] In response, we should first note the invalidity of Dixon's argument. Suppose that 34.5% of people who run a 4-minute mile have black hair, and that I have black hair. It does not follow that I am capable of running a 4-minute mile. It seems likely that only very atypical individuals would respond to heated arguments by killing their opponents. Second, Dixon's . . . claims are refuted by the empirical evidence. In the largest seventy-five counties in the United States in 1988, over 89% of adult murderers had prior criminal records as adults.[4] This reinforces the common sense view that normal people are extremely unlikely to commit a murder, even if they have the means available. So gun ownership does not typically impose excessive risks on others.

(iv) Consider the idea that individuals lack a right to engage in activities that reasonably appear to evince an intention to harm or impose unacceptable risks on others. This principle does not apply here, as it is acknowledged on all sides that only a tiny fraction of America's 77 million gun owners plan to commit crimes with guns.

(v) It might be argued that the *total social cost* of private gun ownership is significant, that the state is unable to identify in advance those persons who are going to misuse their weapons, and that the state's only viable method of significantly reducing that social cost is therefore to prevent even noncriminal citizens from owning guns. But this is not an argument against the existence of a *prima facie* right to own a gun. It is just an argument for overriding any such right. In general, the fact that restricting an activity has beneficial consequences does not show that no weight at all should be assigned to the freedom to engage in it; it simply shows that there are competing reasons against allowing the activity. (Compare:

---

3. Dixon, "Why We Should Ban Handguns," p. 266. Similarly, Jeff McMahan (unpublished comments on this paper, 7 January 2002) writes that "most [murders] occur when a perfectly ordinary person is pushed over a certain emotional threshold by an unusual concatenation of events."
4. Lott, *More Guns*, p. 8.

suppose that taking my car from me and giving it to you increases total social welfare. It would not follow that I have no claim at all on my car.)

It is difficult to deny the existence of at least a *prima facie* right to own a gun. But this says nothing about the *strength* of this right, nor about the grounds there may be for overriding it. Most gun control advocates would claim, not that there is not even a prima facie right to own a gun, but that the right is a minor one, and that the harms of private gun ownership, in comparison, are very large.

4. Is the Right to Own a Gun Significant?

I shall confine my consideration of gun control to the proposal to ban all private firearms ownership. This would violate the prima facie right to own a gun. I contend that the rights violation would be very serious, owing both to the importance of gun ownership in the lives of firearms enthusiasts, and to the relationship between the right to own a gun and the right of self-defense.

4.1. The Recreational Value of Guns

The recreational uses of guns include target shooting, various sorts of shooting competitions, and hunting. In debates over gun control, participants almost never attach any weight to this recreational value—perhaps because that value initially appears minor compared with the deaths caused or prevented by guns. The insistence that individuals have a right to engage in their chosen forms of recreation may seem frivolous in this context. But it is not. . . .

One might claim that the value of the lives that could be saved by anti-gun laws is simply *much greater* than the recreational value of firearms. It is not obvious that this is correct, *even if* gun control would significantly reduce annual gun-related deaths. Many gun owners appear to derive enormous satisfaction from the recreational use of firearms, and it is no exaggeration to say that for many, recreational shooting is a way of life. Furthermore, there are a great many gun owners. At a rough estimate, the number of gun owners is two thousand times greater than the number of annual firearms-related deaths.[5] Even if we assume optimistically that a

---

5. Annual firearms deaths in America, including suicides, are close to 35,000 (Henderson, *Gun Control*, p. 225). Approximately 77 million Americans own guns (ibid., p. 231; Lott, *More Guns*, pp. 37, 41), though most are probably not enthusiasts. This gives a 2200:1 ratio. 46% of gunowners surveyed report hunting or recreation as their main reason for keeping a gun (Henderson, *Gun Control*, p. 234).

substantial proportion of recreational gun users could and would substitute other forms of recreation, we should conclude that the net utility of gun control legislation is greatly overestimated by those who discount the recreational value of guns. For obvious reasons, the utility resulting from recreational use of firearms is not easy to quantify, nor to compare with the value of the lives lost to firearms violence. Yet this is no reason for ignoring the former, as partisans in the gun control debate often do.

But our present concern is not chiefly utilitarian. The argument here is that gun enthusiasts' prima facie right to own guns is significant in virtue of the central place that such ownership plays in their chosen lifestyle. A prohibition on firearms ownership would constitute a major interference in their plans for their own lives. . . . [T]his suffices to show that such a prohibition would be a serious rights violation.

4.2. The Right of Self-Defense

The main argument on the gun rights side goes like this:

1. The right of self-defense is an important right.
2. A firearms prohibition would be a significant violation of the right of self-defense.
3. Therefore, a firearms prohibition would be a serious rights violation.

The strength of the conclusion depends upon the strength of the premises: the more important the right of self-defense is, and the more serious gun control is as a violation of that right, the more serious a rights violation gun control is.

I begin by arguing that the right of self-defense is extremely weighty. Consider this scenario:

Example 1: A killer breaks into a house, where two people—"the victim" and "the accomplice"—are staying. (The "accomplice" need have no prior interaction with the killer.) As the killer enters the bedroom where the victim is hiding, the accomplice enters through another door and proceeds, for some reason, to hold the victim down while the killer stabs him to death.

In this scenario, the killer commits what may be the most serious kind of rights violation possible. What about the accomplice who holds the victim down? Most would agree that his crime is, if not equivalent to murder, something close to murder in degree of wrongness, even though he neither kills nor injures the victim. Considered merely as the act of holding someone down for a few moments, the accomplice's action seems a minor rights violation. What makes it so wrong is that it prevents the victim from either defending himself or fleeing from the killer—that is, it violates the right of self-defense. (To intentionally and forcibly prevent a person from exercising a right is to violate that right.) We may also say that the accomplice's crime was that of assisting in the commission of a murder—this is not, in my view, a competing explanation of the wrongness of his action, but rather an elaboration on the first explanation. Since the right of self-defense is a derivative right, serving to protect the right to life among other rights, violations of the right of self-defense will often cause or enable violations of the right to life.

It is common to distinguish *killing* from *letting die*. In this example, we see a third category of action: *preventing the prevention of a death*. This is distinct from killing, but it is not merely letting die, because it requires positive action. The example suggests that preventing the prevention of a death is about as serious a wrong as killing. In any case, the fact that serious violations of the right of self-defense are morally comparable to murder serves to show that the right of self-defense must be a very weighty right.

· · · ·

We turn to premise 2, that gun prohibition is serious as a violation of the right of self-defense. Consider:

Example 2: As in example 1, except that the victim has a gun by the bed, which he would, if able, use to defend himself from the killer. As the killer enters the bedroom, the victim reaches for the gun. The accomplice grabs the gun and runs away, with the result that the killer then stabs his victim to death.

The accomplice's action in this case seems morally comparable to his action in example 1. Again, he has intentionally prevented the victim from defending himself, thereby in effect assisting in the murder. The arguments from the criteria for the seriousness of rights violations are the same.

The analogy between the accomplice's action in this case and a general firearms prohibition should be clear. A firearms ban would require confiscating the weapons that many individuals keep for self-defense purposes, with the result that some of those individuals would be murdered, robbed, raped, or seriously injured. If the accomplice's action in example 2 is a major violation of the right of self-defense, then gun prohibition seems to be about equally serious as a violation of the right of self-defense.

Consider some objections to this analogy. First, it might be said that in the case of a gun ban, the government would have strong reasons for confiscating the guns, in order to save the lives of others, which (we presume) is not true of the accomplice in example 2. This, I think, would amount to arguing that the self-defense rights of noncriminal gun owners are overridden by the state's need to protect society from criminal gun owners. I deal with this suggestion in §5 below.

Second, it might be argued that example 2 differs from a gun ban in that the murder is *imminent* at the time the accomplice takes the gun away. But this seems to be morally irrelevant. For suppose that the accomplice, knowing that someone is coming to kill the victim tomorrow (while the victim does not know this), decides to take the victim's gun away from him today, again resulting in his death. This would not make the accomplice's action more morally defensible than it is in example 2.

A third difference might be that, whereas we assume that in example 2 the accomplice knows that the victim is going to be killed or seriously injured, the state does not know that its anti-gun policy will result in murders and injuries to former gun owners. This, however, is surely not true. Although the state may claim that the lives saved by a gun ban would *outnumber* the lives cost, one cannot argue that no lives will be cost at all, unless one claims implausibly that guns are never used in self-defense against life-threatening attacks. Some will think the former claim is all that is needed to justify a gun ban; this would return us to the first objection.

Fourth, it may be observed that in example 2, there is a specific, identifiable victim: the accomplice knows who is going to die as a result of his gun confiscation. In contrast, a gun-banning government cannot identify any specific individuals who are going to be killed as a result of its gun ban, even though it can predict that *some* people will be. But this seems morally irrelevant. Consider:

Example 3: An "accomplice" ties up a family of five somewhere in the wilderness where he knows that wolves roam. He has good reason to believe that a pack of wolves will happen by and eat one or two of the family members (after which they will be satiated), but he doesn't know which ones will be eaten. He leaves them for an hour, during which time the mother of the family is eaten by the wolves.

In this case, the fact that the accomplice did not know who would die as a result of his action does not mitigate his guilt. Likewise, it is unclear how the state's inability to predict who will become the victims of its anti-gun policy would mitigate the state's responsibility for their deaths or injury.

Fifth, the victims of a gun ban would presumably have sufficient forewarning of the coming ban to take alternative measures to protect themselves, unlike the victim in example 2. Unfortunately, statistics from the National Crime Victimization Survey indicate that such alternative means of self-protection would be relatively ineffective—individuals who defend themselves with a gun are less likely to be injured and far less likely to have the crime completed against them than are persons who take any other measures.[6] Consequently, though the present consideration seems to mitigate the state's culpability, it does not remove it. The situation is analogous to one in which the accomplice, rather than taking away the victim's only means of defending himself against the killer, merely takes away the victim's most effective means of self-defense, with the result that the victim is killed. Here, the accomplice's action is less wrong than in example 2, but it is still very wrong.

Since gun prohibition is a significant violation of an extremely weighty right, we must conclude that it is a very serious rights violation. The above examples initially suggest that it is on a par with the commission of (multiple) murders, robberies, rapes, and assaults—although the consideration of the preceding paragraph may show that it is somewhat less wrong than that. The point here is not that would-be gun banners are as blameworthy as murderers and other violent criminals (since the former do not *know* that their proposals are morally comparable to murder and have different motives from typical murderers). The point is just to assess the strength of the reasons against taking the course of action that they propose.

5. Are Gun Rights Overridden?

I have argued that there is a strong prima facie right to own a gun. Nevertheless, firearms prohibition might be justified, if the reasons for prohibition were strong enough to override that right. To determine whether this is the case, we consider three questions: First, how great are the harms of private gun ownership? Second, how great are the benefits? Third, what must the cost/benefit ratio be like, for the right to own a gun to be

---

6. Gary Kleck, *Targeting Guns: Firearms and Their Control* (New York: Aldine de Gruyter, 1997), pp. 170–174, 190; Lawrence Southwick, "Self-Defense with Guns: The Consequences," *Journal of Criminal Justice* 28 (2000): 351–370.

overridden? I shall argue, first, that the harms of private gun ownership have been greatly exaggerated; second, that the benefits of private gun ownership are large and in fact greater than the harms; and third, that the harms would have to be many times greater than the benefits in order to override the right to own a gun. . . .

5.1. The Case Against Guns

5.1.1. The 43-to-1 Statistic

One prominent argument claims that a gun kept in the home is 43 times more likely to be used in a suicide, criminal homicide, or accidental death than it is to kill an intruder in self-defense.[7] This statistic is commonly repeated with various modifications; for instance, LaFollette mischaracterizes the statistic as follows:

> For every case where someone in a gun-owning household uses a gun *to successfully stop a life-threatening attack*, nearly forty-three people in similar households will die from a gunshot.[8]

The problem with LaFollette's characterization, which evinces the statistic's tendency to mislead, is that Kellerman and Reay made no estimate of the frequency with which guns are used to stop attacks, life-threatening or otherwise; they only considered cases in which someone was *killed*. Survey data indicate that only a tiny minority of defensive gun uses involve shooting, let alone killing, the criminal; normally, threatening a criminal with a gun is sufficient. To assess the benefits of guns, one would have to examine the frequency with which guns prevent crimes, rather than the frequency with which they kill criminals.

A second problem is that 37 of Kellerman and Reay's 43 deaths were suicides. Available evidence is unclear on whether reduced availability of guns would reduce the suicide rate or whether it would only result in substitution into different methods. In addition, philosophically, it is doubtful that the restriction of gun ownership for the purpose of preventing suicides would fall within the prerogatives of a liberal state, even if such a policy would be effective. One cause for doubt is that such policies infringe upon the rights of gun owners (both the suicidal ones and the nonsuicidal

---

7. Arthur Kellerman and Donald Reay, "Protection or Peril? An Analysis of Firearm-Related Deaths in the Home," *New England Journal of Medicine* 314 (1986): 1557–1560.
8. Hugh LaFollette, "Gun Control," *Ethics* 110 (2000): 263–281, p. 276 (emphasis added).

majority) without protecting anyone else's rights. Another cause for doubt, from a utilitarian perspective, is that one cannot assume that individuals who decide to kill themselves have overall happy or pleasant lives; therefore, one should not assume that the prevention of suicide, through means other than improving would-be victims' level of happiness, increases utility, rather than decreasing it. For these reasons, the suicides should be omitted from the figures. . . .

5.1.2. *International Comparisons*

A second type of argument often used by gun-control proponents relies on comparisons of homicide rates between the United States and other industrialized democracies, such as Canada, Great Britain, Sweden, and Australia. The United States is found to have vastly higher homicide rates, and it is argued that this is due largely to the high gun-ownership rates in the U.S.

Skeptics suggest that the United States has a number of unique cultural factors that influence the murder rate and that invalidate such cross-country comparisons. Some find this claim more plausible than do others. Fortunately, we need not rely on intuitions. Instead, we can test the claim empirically, by examining data within the United States, across jurisdictions with varying gun laws and gun ownership rates and over time periods with changing gun laws and gun ownership rates—this would effectively control for the cultural factors allegedly affecting the murder rate. When we do this, we find that (i) jurisdictions with stricter gun laws tend to have higher crime rates, (ii) shifts to more permissive gun laws tend to be followed by drops in crime rates, (iii) areas with higher gun ownership rates have lower crime rates, and (iv) historically, crime rates have fluctuated with no discernible pattern as the civilian gun stock has increased drastically.[9]

I do not claim to have *proved* that gun laws cause increased crime or that civilian gun ownership fails to do so. Nor do I deny that there is any evidence on the gun control advocates' side. What I am claiming at this point is that the evidence presented by gun control advocates fails to make

---

9. On (i) and (ii), see §5.2.1 below and Kopel, "Peril or Protection?" p. 308. On (iii), see Lott, *More Guns*, p. 114. Lott's figures for the correlation between gun ownership and crime rates include controls for arrest rates, income, population density, and other variables. On (iv), see Don Kates, Henry Schaffer, John Lattimer, George Murray, and Edwin Cassem, "Guns and Public Health: Epidemic of Violence or Pandemic of Propaganda?" *Tennessee Law Review* 62 (1995): 513–596, pp. 571–574.

a very convincing case for the net harmfulness of private gun ownership. The casual comparisons between countries discussed here typically use only a handful of data points, exclude many countries from consideration, and make no attempt to control statistically for any other factors that might affect crime rates. In contrast, far more rigorous studies are available to the other side, as we shall see presently. Thus, at a minimum, one cannot claim justified belief that gun prohibition would be beneficial overall.

5.2. The Benefits of Guns

5.2.1. Frequency of Defensive Gun Uses

Guns are used surprisingly often by private citizens in the United States for self-defense purposes.... Probably among the more reliable [surveys] is Kleck and Gertz's 1993 national survey, which obtained an estimate of 2.5 million annual defensive gun uses, excluding military and police uses and excluding uses against animals. Gun users in 400,000 of these cases believe that the gun certainly or almost certainly saved a life.[10] While survey respondents almost certainly overestimated their danger, if even one tenth of them were correct, the number of lives saved by guns each year would exceed the number of gun homicides and suicides. For the purposes of Kleck and Gertz's study, a "defensive gun use" requires respondents to have actually seen a person (as opposed, for example, to merely hearing a suspicious noise in the yard) whom they believed was committing or attempting to commit a crime against them, and to have at a minimum threatened the person with a gun, but not necessarily to have fired the gun. Kleck's statistics imply that defensive gun uses outnumber crimes committed with guns by a ratio of about 3:1....

5.3. Why a Gun Ban Must Have Much Greater Benefits than Harms to Be Justified

In order to be justified as a case of the overriding of prima facie rights, gun prohibition would have to save many times as many lives as it cost, for:

1. It is wrong to murder a person, even to prevent several other killings. (premise)
2. A violation of a person or group's right of self-defense, predictably resulting in the death of one of the victims, is morally comparable to murder. (premise)

---

10. Gary Kleck and Marc Gertz, "Armed Resistance to Crime: The Prevalence and Nature of Self-Defense with a Gun," *Journal of Criminal Law and Criminology* 86 (1995): 150–187.

3. If it is wrong to commit a murder to prevent several killings, then it is wrong to commit a rights violation comparable to murder to prevent several killings. (premise)

4. Therefore, it is wrong to violate a person or group's right of self-defense, predictably resulting in the death of one of the victims, even to prevent several killings. (from 1, 2, 3)

5. Therefore, it is wrong to violate a group of people's right of self-defense, predictably resulting in the deaths of many of the victims, even to prevent several times as many killings. (from 4)

6. Gun prohibition would violate a group of people's right of self-defense, predictably resulting in the deaths of many of the victims. (premise)

7. Therefore, gun prohibition is wrong, even if it would prevent several times as many killings as it contributed to. (from 5, 6)

Similar arguments can be made concerning other rights—including, for example, the right to engage in one's chosen form of recreation—the general point of which would be that the overriding of a right for consequentialist reasons requires a benefit not merely greater, but *very much* greater than the harm to the rights-bearer. For simplicity, however, I focus only on how the argument works with the right of self-defense.

Consequentialists reject premise (1). But virtually all who accept the notion of rights would accept (1). Consider this well-worn example:[11]

Example 4: You are a judge in a legal system in which judges render verdicts of guilt or innocence. You have a defendant on trial for a crime that has caused considerable public outrage. During the course of the trial, it becomes clear to you that the defendant is innocent. However, the public overwhelmingly believes him guilty. As a result, you believe that if the defendant is acquitted, there will be riots, during which several people will be (unjustly) killed and many others injured. Assume that the crime in question carries a mandatory death sentence. Should you convict the defendant?

Most people, including virtually all who believe in rights, say the answer is no. If this is the correct answer, then we must conclude that it is wrong to violate one person's rights (in particular, his right to life) even if doing so would prevent several rights violations of comparable seriousness. This is

---

11. H. J. McCloskey, "An Examination of Restricted Utilitarianism," *Philosophical Review* 66 (1957): 466–485, pp. 468–469. I have slightly modified the example.

because rights function as *agent-centered constraints*: each individual is enjoined from violating rights, himself, rather than being enjoined to cause a reduction in the total number of rights violations in the world. Something like premise (1) is essential for distinguishing a rights-based moral theory from a consequentialist theory.

Premise (2) was supported by the argument of §4.2.

Premise (3) is supported by the idea that the requirements for overriding a prima facie right are proportional to the seriousness of the rights violation that would be involved. Even if this assumption does not hold in general, it is plausible that it applies to this case, that is, that *if* it is unjustified to kill a person in order to save several lives, and *if* a particular violation of the right of self-defense is morally on a par with killing a person, then it is also wrong to commit that violation of the right of self-defense in order to save several lives. It is difficult to see why the right of self-defense should work differently, by way of being much easier to override, from the right to life.

Step (5) is a reasonable inference from (4). Suppose that the judge in example 4 opts for conviction, acting wrongly. Suppose he is faced with similar situations four more times throughout his career, each time acting in the same wrongful manner. Presumably, the whole *series* of actions, consisting in sum of his killing *five* people unjustly in order to save several times that many people, is also wrong. Now consider one more modification: suppose that instead of coming at different times throughout his career, the same five innocent defendants had all come to him in a single, collective trial, that he gave a collective verdict convicting all of them, and that this action saved the same number of other people. Presumably the judge's action is still wrong. It is for this sort of reason that we should accept the inference from (4) to (5).

Premise (6) is supported by the arguments of §5.2.

Finally, (7) follows from (5) and (6). Given the extremely serious nature of gun prohibition as a rights violation, very severe strictures apply to any attempt to justify it morally—strictures similar to those that would apply to justifying a policy that killed many innocent people to achieve some social goal. . . .

Michael Huemer: Is There a Right to Own a Gun?

1. Huemer believes that there is a prima facie right to own a gun. What does this mean? He thinks it fairly easy to establish the existence of this right—how does he do this?

2. Supporters of firearms prohibitions often claim that the presence of guns leads to greater harm—more crimes are committed, and many

of those that are committed impose more harm than there would be if guns were not on the scene. What is the best reply to this worry that Huemer might offer? How successful is it?

3. Huemer believes that utilitarian considerations are of only minor importance in determining the permissibility of firearms prohibitions. Do you find this claim plausible? If so, why? If not, why not?

4. Consider the various analogies that Huemer uses when claiming that considerations of self-defense provide the central argument for gun rights. Assess whether these analogies provide the support that Huemer believes they do.

5. Imagine a largely gun-free society and one, like the United States, where guns are prevalent. What is gained and lost in each? Can this thought experiment justify any claims about what the law governing gun ownership ought to be in actual societies?

38

Letter from Birmingham City Jail
Martin Luther King, Jr.

....

In this now-classic piece, written while in jail for having violated a court injunction against participating in a demonstration, Martin Luther King, Jr., replies to criticisms from his fellow clergymen. These criticisms target the actions undertaken by King and other civil rights activists in the 1950s and 1960s. The criticisms are largely variations of a single theme: King advocated that laws be broken in order to pursue his goals, and his fellow clergymen disapprove of the means he is taking to try to achieve them.

King has several replies. One of them emphasizes that law-breaking should be used only a last resort response to grave injustice. But he and his fellow protesters had exhausted all efforts to engage in good-faith negotiations with the civic leaders who were committed to maintaining segregation within their communities. A second reply highlights two features of the civil disobedience practiced by King and his followers: first, that it was non-violent, and second, that those who engaged in protest were doing so openly, and thereby willing to accept the punishments that they received. These features enable King to offer a third reply, namely, that such open and non-violent protest actually expresses a respect for law, rather than a disregard for its authority. Finally, he also invokes St. Augustine's claim that "an unjust law is no law at all." Since the segregationist laws were deeply unjust, it would follow that they are no law at all, and so do not need to be followed.

King's remarks are punctuated by his disappointment with his fellow clergymen, and by a steady commitment to a moderate response to injustice. At one extreme are those who have accommodated themselves to the status quo. At the other extreme are those who are so upset by failure to change it that they support violence to change the system. King advocates for a middle path—that of non-violent, persistent protest—as the most principled and effective way to further the cause of justice.

....

16 April 1963

My Dear Fellow Clergymen:

While confined here in the Birmingham city jail, I came across your recent statement calling my present activities "unwise and untimely." Seldom do I pause to answer criticism of my work and ideas. If I sought to answer all the criticisms that cross my desk, my secretaries would have little time for anything other than such correspondence in the course of the day, and I would have no time for constructive work. But since I feel that you are men of genuine good will and that your criticisms are sincerely set forth, I want to try to answer your statement in what I hope will be patient and reasonable terms.

I think I should indicate why I am here in Birmingham, since you have been influenced by the view which argues against "outsiders coming in." I have the honor of serving as president of the Southern Christian Leadership Conference, an organization operating in every southern state, with headquarters in Atlanta, Georgia. We have some eighty-five affiliated organizations across the South, and one of them is the Alabama Christian Movement for Human Rights. Frequently we share staff, educational and financial resources with our affiliates. Several months ago the affiliate here in Birmingham asked us to be on call to engage in a nonviolent direct action program if such were deemed necessary. We readily consented, and when the hour came we lived up to our promise. So I, along with several members of my staff, am here because I was invited here. I am here because I have organizational ties here.

But more basically, I am in Birmingham because injustice is here. Just as the prophets of the eighth century B.C. left their villages and carried their "thus saith the Lord" far beyond the boundaries of their home towns, and just as the Apostle Paul left his village of Tarsus and carried the gospel of Jesus Christ to the far corners of the Greco Roman world, so am I compelled to carry the gospel of freedom beyond my own home town. Like Paul, I must constantly respond to the Macedonian call for aid.

Moreover, I am cognizant of the interrelatedness of all communities and states. I cannot sit idly by in Atlanta and not be concerned about what happens in Birmingham. Injustice anywhere is a threat to justice everywhere. We are caught in an inescapable network of mutuality, tied in a single garment of destiny. Whatever affects one directly, affects all indirectly. Never again can we afford to live with the narrow, provincial "outside agitator" idea. Anyone who lives inside the United States can never be considered an outsider anywhere within its bounds.

You deplore the demonstrations taking place in Birmingham. But your statement, I am sorry to say, fails to express a similar concern for the conditions that brought about the demonstrations. I am sure that none of you would want to rest content with the superficial kind of social analysis that deals merely with effects and does not grapple with underlying causes. It is unfortunate that demonstrations are taking place in Birmingham, but it is even more unfortunate that the city's white power structure left the Negro community with no alternative.

In any nonviolent campaign there are four basic steps: collection of the facts to determine whether injustices exist; negotiation; self-purification; and direct action. We have gone through all these steps in Birmingham. There can be no gainsaying the fact that racial injustice engulfs this community. Birmingham is probably the most thoroughly segregated city in the United States. Its ugly record of brutality is widely known. Negroes have experienced grossly unjust treatment in the courts. There have been more unsolved bombings of Negro homes and churches in Birmingham than in any other city in the nation. These are the hard, brutal facts of the case. On the basis of these conditions, Negro leaders sought to negotiate with the city fathers. But the latter consistently refused to engage in good faith negotiation. . . .

You may well ask: "Why direct action? Why sit ins, marches and so forth? Isn't negotiation a better path?" You are quite right in calling for negotiation. Indeed, this is the very purpose of direct action. Nonviolent direct action seeks to create such a crisis and foster such a tension that a community which has constantly refused to negotiate is forced to confront the issue. It seeks so to dramatize the issue that it can no longer be ignored. My citing the creation of tension as part of the work of the nonviolent resister may sound rather shocking. But I must confess that I am not afraid of the word "tension." I have earnestly opposed violent tension, but there is a type of constructive, nonviolent tension which is necessary for growth. Just as Socrates felt that it was necessary to create a tension in the mind so that individuals could rise from the bondage of myths and half-truths to the unfettered realm of creative analysis and objective appraisal, so must we see the need for nonviolent gadflies to create the kind of tension in society that will help men rise from the dark depths of prejudice and racism to the majestic heights of understanding and brotherhood. The purpose of our direct action program is to create a situation so crisis packed that it will inevitably open the door to negotiation. I therefore concur with you in your call for negotiation. Too long has our beloved Southland been bogged down in a tragic effort to live in monologue rather than dialogue.

One of the basic points in your statement is that the action that I and my associates have taken in Birmingham is untimely. Some have asked: "Why didn't you give the new city administration time to act?" The only answer that I can give to this query is that the new Birmingham administration must be prodded about as much as the outgoing one, before it will act. We are sadly mistaken if we feel that the election of Albert Boutwell as mayor will bring the millennium to Birmingham. While Mr. Boutwell is a much more gentle person than Mr. Connor, they are both segregationists, dedicated to maintenance of the status quo. I have hope that Mr. Boutwell will be reasonable enough to see the futility of massive resistance to desegregation. But he will not see this without pressure from devotees of civil rights. My friends, I must say to you that we have not made a single gain in civil rights without determined legal and nonviolent pressure. Lamentably, it is an historical fact that privileged groups seldom give up their privileges voluntarily. Individuals may see the moral light and voluntarily give up their unjust posture; but, as Reinhold Niebuhr has reminded us, groups tend to be more immoral than individuals.

We know through painful experience that freedom is never voluntarily given by the oppressor; it must be demanded by the oppressed. Frankly, I have yet to engage in a direct action campaign that was "well timed" in the view of those who have not suffered unduly from the disease of segregation. For years now I have heard the word "Wait!" It rings in the ear of every Negro with piercing familiarity. This "Wait" has almost always meant "Never." We must come to see, with one of our distinguished jurists, that "justice too long delayed is justice denied."

We have waited for more than 340 years for our constitutional and God given rights. The nations of Asia and Africa are moving with jetlike speed toward gaining political independence, but we still creep at horse and buggy pace toward gaining a cup of coffee at a lunch counter. Perhaps it is easy for those who have never felt the stinging darts of segregation to say, "Wait." But when you have seen vicious mobs lynch your mothers and fathers at will and drown your sisters and brothers at whim; when you have seen hate filled policemen curse, kick and even kill your black brothers and sisters; when you see the vast majority of your twenty million Negro brothers smothering in an airtight cage of poverty in the midst of an affluent society; when you suddenly find your tongue twisted and your speech stammering as you seek to explain to your six year old daughter why she can't go to the public amusement park that has just been advertised on television, and see tears welling up in her eyes when she is told that Funtown is closed to colored children, and see ominous clouds of inferiority beginning to form in her little mental sky, and see her beginning to distort her personality by developing an unconscious bitterness toward white people; when you have to concoct an answer for a five year old son who is asking: "Daddy, why do white people treat colored people so mean?"; when you take a cross county drive and find it necessary to sleep night after night in the uncomfortable corners of your automobile because no motel will accept you; when you are humiliated day in and day out by nagging signs reading "white" and "colored"; when your first name becomes "nigger," your middle name becomes "boy" (however old you are) and your last name becomes "John," and your wife and mother are never given the respected title "Mrs."; when you are harried by day and haunted by night by the fact that you are a Negro, living constantly at tip-toe stance, never quite knowing what to expect next, and are plagued with inner fears and outer resentments; when you are forever fighting a degenerating sense of "nobodiness"—then you will understand why we find it difficult to wait. There comes a time when the cup of endurance runs over, and men are no longer willing to be plunged into the abyss of despair. I hope, sirs, you can understand our legitimate and unavoidable impatience. You express a great deal of anxiety over our willingness to break laws. This is certainly a legitimate concern. Since we so diligently urge people to obey the Supreme Court's decision of 1954 outlawing segregation in the public schools, at first glance it may seem rather paradoxical for us consciously to break laws. One may well ask: "How can you advocate breaking some laws and obeying others?" The answer lies in the fact that there are two types of laws:

just and unjust. I would be the first to advocate obeying just laws. One has not only a legal but a moral responsibility to obey just laws. Conversely, one has a moral responsibility to disobey unjust laws. I would agree with St. Augustine that "an unjust law is no law at all."

Now, what is the difference between the two? How does one determine whether a law is just or unjust? A just law is a man-made code that squares with the moral law or the law of God. An unjust law is a code that is out of harmony with the moral law. To put it in the terms of St. Thomas Aquinas: An unjust law is a human law that is not rooted in eternal law and natural law. Any law that uplifts human personality is just. Any law that degrades human personality is unjust. All segregation statutes are unjust because segregation distorts the soul and damages the personality. It gives the segregator a false sense of superiority and the segregated a false sense of inferiority. Segregation, to use the terminology of the Jewish philosopher Martin Buber, substitutes an "I-it" relationship for an "I-thou" relationship and ends up relegating persons to the status of things. Hence segregation is not only politically, economically and sociologically unsound, it is morally wrong and sinful. Paul Tillich has said that sin is separation. Is not segregation an existential expression of man's tragic separation, his awful estrangement, his terrible sinfulness? Thus it is that I can urge men to obey the 1954 decision of the Supreme Court, for it is morally right; and I can urge them to disobey segregation ordinances, for they are morally wrong.

Let us consider a more concrete example of just and unjust laws. An unjust law is a code that a numerical or power majority group compels a minority group to obey but does not make binding on itself. This is difference made legal. By the same token, a just law is a code that a majority compels a minority to follow and that it is willing to follow itself. This is sameness made legal. Let me give another explanation. A law is unjust if it is inflicted on a minority that, as a result of being denied the right to vote, had no part in enacting or devising the law. Who can say that the legislature of Alabama which set up that state's segregation laws was democratically elected? Throughout Alabama all sorts of devious methods are used to prevent Negroes from becoming registered voters, and there are some counties in which, even though Negroes constitute a majority of the population, not a single Negro is registered. Can any law enacted under such circumstances be considered democratically structured?

Sometimes a law is just on its face and unjust in its application. For instance, I have been arrested on a charge of parading without a permit.

Now, there is nothing wrong in having an ordinance which requires a permit for a parade. But such an ordinance becomes unjust when it is used to maintain segregation and to deny citizens the First-Amendment privilege of peaceful assembly and protest.

I hope you are able to see the distinction I am trying to point out. In no sense do I advocate evading or defying the law, as would the rabid segregationist. That would lead to anarchy. One who breaks an unjust law must do so openly, lovingly, and with a willingness to accept the penalty. I submit that an individual who breaks a law that conscience tells him is unjust, and who willingly accepts the penalty of imprisonment in order to arouse the conscience of the community over its injustice, is in reality expressing the highest respect for law. . . .

We should never forget that everything Adolf Hitler did in Germany was "legal" and everything the Hungarian freedom fighters did in Hungary was "illegal." It was "illegal" to aid and comfort a Jew in Hitler's Germany. Even so, I am sure that, had I lived in Germany at the time, I would have aided and comforted my Jewish brothers. If today I lived in a Communist country where certain principles dear to the Christian faith are suppressed, I would openly advocate disobeying that country's antireligious laws.

I must make two honest confessions to you, my Christian and Jewish brothers. First, I must confess that over the past few years I have been gravely disappointed with the white moderate. I have almost reached the regrettable conclusion that the Negro's great stumbling block in his stride toward freedom is not the White Citizen's Counciler or the Ku Klux Klanner, but the white moderate, who is more devoted to "order" than to justice; who prefers a negative peace which is the absence of tension to a positive peace which is the presence of justice; who constantly says: "I agree with you in the goal you seek, but I cannot agree with your methods of direct action"; who paternalistically believes he can set the timetable for another man's freedom; who lives by a mythical concept of time and who constantly advises the Negro to wait for a "more convenient season." Shallow understanding from people of good will is more frustrating than absolute misunderstanding from people of ill will. Lukewarm acceptance is much more bewildering than outright rejection. . . .

In your statement you assert that our actions, even though peaceful, must be condemned because they precipitate violence. But is this a logical assertion? Isn't this like condemning a robbed man because his possession of money precipitated the evil act of robbery? Isn't this like condemning Socrates because his unswerving commitment to truth and his philosophical inquiries precipitated the act by the misguided populace in which they made him drink hemlock? Isn't this like condemning Jesus because his unique God consciousness and never ceasing devotion to God's will precipitated the evil act of crucifixion? We must come to see that, as the federal courts have consistently affirmed, it is wrong to urge an individual to cease his efforts to gain his basic constitutional rights because the quest may precipitate violence. Society must protect the robbed and punish the robber.

I had also hoped that the white moderate would reject the myth concerning time in relation to the struggle for freedom. I have just received a letter from a white brother in Texas. He writes: "All Christians know that the colored people will receive equal rights eventually, but it is possible that you are in too great a religious hurry. It has taken Christianity almost two thousand years to accomplish what it has. The teachings of Christ take time to come to earth." Such an attitude stems from a tragic misconception of time, from the strangely irrational notion that there is something in the very flow of time that will inevitably cure all ills. Actually, time itself is neutral; it can be used either destructively or constructively. More and more I feel that the people of ill will have used time much more effectively than have the people of good will. We will have to repent in this generation not merely for the hateful words and actions of the bad people but for the appalling silence of the good people. Human progress never rolls in on wheels of inevitability; it comes through the tireless efforts of men willing to be co-workers with God, and without this hard work, time itself becomes an ally of the forces of social stagnation. . . .

Oppressed people cannot remain oppressed forever. . . . The Negro has many pent up resentments and latent frustrations, and he must release them. So let him march; let him make prayer pilgrimages to the city hall; let him go on freedom rides—and try to understand why he must do so. If his repressed emotions are not released in nonviolent ways, they will seek expression through violence; this is not a threat but a fact of history. So I have not said to my people: "Get rid of your discontent." Rather, I have tried to say that this normal and healthy discontent can be channeled into the creative outlet of nonviolent direct action. And now this approach is being termed extremist.

But though I was initially disappointed at being categorized as an extremist, as I continued to think about the matter I gradually gained a measure of satisfaction from the label. Was not Jesus an extremist for love: "Love your enemies, bless them that curse you, do good to them that hate you, and pray for them which despitefully use you, and persecute you." Was not Amos an extremist for justice: "Let justice roll down like waters and righteousness like an ever flowing stream." Was not Paul an extremist for the Christian gospel: "I bear in my body the marks of the Lord Jesus." Was not Martin Luther an extremist: "Here I stand; I cannot do otherwise, so help me God." And John Bunyan: "I will stay in jail to the end of my days before I make a butchery of my conscience." And Abraham Lincoln: "This nation cannot survive half slave and half free." And Thomas Jefferson: "We hold these truths to be self-evident, that all men are created equal . . ." So the question is not whether we will be extremists, but what kind of extremists we will be. Will we be extremists for hate or for love? Will we be extremists for the preservation of injustice or for the extension of justice? In that dramatic scene on Calvary's hill three men were crucified. We must never forget that all three were crucified for the same crime—the crime of extremism. Two were extremists for immorality, and thus fell below their environment. The other, Jesus Christ, was an extremist for love, truth and goodness, and thereby rose above his environment. Perhaps the South, the nation and the world are in dire need of creative extremists.

I had hoped that the white moderate would see this need. Perhaps I was too optimistic; perhaps I expected too much. I suppose I should have realized that few members of the oppressor race can understand the deep groans and passionate yearnings of the oppressed race, and still fewer have the vision to see that injustice must be rooted out by strong, persistent and determined action. I am thankful, however, that some of our white brothers in the South have grasped the meaning of this social revolution and committed themselves to it. Unlike so many of their moderate brothers and sisters, they have recognized the urgency of the moment and sensed the need for powerful "action" antidotes to combat the disease of segregation. . . .

Perhaps I have once again been too optimistic. Is organized religion too inextricably bound to the status quo to save our nation and the world? Perhaps I must turn my faith to the inner spiritual church, the church within the church, as the true ekklesia and the hope of the world. But again I am thankful to God that some noble souls from the ranks of organized religion have broken loose from the paralyzing chains of conformity and joined us as active partners in the struggle for freedom. They have left their secure congregations and walked the streets of Albany, Georgia, with us. They have gone down the highways of the South on tortuous rides for freedom. Yes, they have gone to jail with us.

Some have been dismissed from their churches, have lost the support of their bishops and fellow min- isters. But they have acted in the faith that right defeated is stronger than evil triumphant. Their witness has been the spiritual salt that has preserved the true meaning of the gospel in these troubled times. They have carved a tunnel of hope through the dark mountain of disappointment.

I hope the church as a whole will meet the challenge of this decisive hour. But even if the church does not come to the aid of justice, I have no despair about the future. I have no fear about the outcome of our struggle in Birmingham, even if our motives are at present misunderstood. We will reach the goal of freedom in Birmingham and all over the nation, because the goal of America is freedom. Abused and scorned though we may be, our destiny is tied up with America's destiny. Before the pilgrims landed at Plymouth, we were here. Before the pen of Jefferson etched the majestic words of the Declaration of Independence across the pages of history, we were here. For more than two centuries our forebears labored in this country without wages; they made cotton king; they built the homes of their masters while suffering gross injustice and shameful humiliation—and yet out of a bottomless vitality they continued to thrive and develop. If the inexpressible cruelties of slavery could not stop us, the opposition we now face will surely fail. We will win our freedom because the sacred heritage of our nation and the eternal will of God are embodied in our echoing demands.

Before closing I feel impelled to mention one other point in your statement that has troubled me profoundly. You warmly commended the Birmingham police force for keeping "order" and "preventing violence." I doubt that you would have so warmly commended the police force if you had seen its dogs sinking their teeth into unarmed, nonviolent Negroes. I doubt that you would so quickly commend the policemen if you were to observe their ugly and inhumane treatment of Negroes here in the city jail; if you were to watch them push and curse old Negro women and young Negro girls; if you were to see them slap and kick old Negro men and young boys; if you were to observe them, as they did on two occasions, refuse to give us food because we wanted to sing our grace together. I cannot join you in your praise of the Birmingham police department. . . .

I wish you had commended the Negro sit inners and demonstrators of Birmingham for their sublime courage, their willingness to suffer and their amazing discipline in the midst of great provocation. One day the

South will recognize its real heroes. They will be the James Merediths, with the noble sense of purpose that enables them to face jeering and hostile mobs, and with the agonizing loneliness that characterizes the life of the pioneer. They will be old, oppressed, battered Negro women, symbolized in a seventy-two-year-old woman in Montgomery, Alabama, who rose up with a sense of dignity and with her people decided not to ride segregated buses, and who responded with ungrammatical profundity to one who inquired about her weariness: "My feets is tired, but my soul is at rest." They will be the young high school and college students, the young ministers of the gospel and a host of their elders, courageously and nonviolently sitting in at lunch counters and willingly going to jail for conscience' sake. One day the South will know that when these disinherited children of God sat down at lunch counters, they were in reality standing up for what is best in the American dream and for the most sacred values in our Judaeo Christian heritage, thereby bringing our nation back to those great wells of democracy which were dug deep by the founding fathers in their formulation of the Constitution and the Declaration of Independence.

Never before have I written so long a letter. I'm afraid it is much too long to take your precious time. I can assure you that it would have been much shorter if I had been writing from a comfortable desk, but what else can one do when he is alone in a narrow jail cell, other than write long letters, think long thoughts and pray long prayers?

If I have said anything in this letter that overstates the truth and indicates an unreasonable impatience, I beg you to forgive me. If I have said anything that understates the truth and indicates my having a patience that allows me to settle for anything less than brotherhood, I beg God to forgive me.

I hope this letter finds you strong in the faith. I also hope that circumstances will soon make it possible for me to meet each of you, not as an integrationist or a civil-rights leader but as a fellow clergyman and a Christian brother. Let us all hope that the dark clouds of racial prejudice will soon pass away and the deep fog of misunderstanding will be lifted from our fear drenched communities, and in some not too distant tomorrow the radiant stars of love and brotherhood will shine over our great nation with all their scintillating beauty.

Yours for the cause of Peace and Brotherhood,
Martin Luther King, Jr.

Martin Luther King, Jr.: Letter from Birmingham City Jail

1. King endorses St. Augustine's view that "an unjust law is no law at all." Do you agree? Why or why not?
2. King supports a policy of non-violent resistance to injustice. Do you think that violent resistance is ever morally justifiable? If not, why not? If so, under what conditions?
3. King also endorses the need of his followers to openly break the law. Why does he say this, and are his reasons plausible ones?
4. Can you express respect for the rule of law while also openly breaking the law? Why or why not?
5. King says that "there is a type of constructive, nonviolent tension which is necessary for growth." What does he mean by this, and is his thought plausible?

═══ ❧ ═══

39

Affirmative Action: Bad Arguments and Some Good Ones

Daniel M. Hausman

∙∙

In this paper, Daniel Hausman sets himself two goals. First, he wants to reveal the flaws of some popular arguments for and against policies of preferential hiring and admissions (PHA). Second, he offers an argument in favor of PHA that he believes is successful in showing that the practice can be justified.

Many people favor or oppose PHA on the basis of their view of its results. But, as Hausman notes, the actual results of PHA programs are difficult to determine and are highly disputed. Hausman does not take a stand, for instance, on whether PHA has actually improved or damaged the self-esteem of minorities, reduced or increased prejudice, etc. The evidence, he thinks, is inconclusive. But we can still assess the merits of arguments for and against PHA even in the absence of such evidence.

One classic argument opposing PHA claims that it is "racism in reverse." Hausman rejects this line of reasoning, pointing out that PHA is not grounded in assumptions of racial inferiority or racial hatred, and that it is not designed to oppress, humiliate, and exclude. Hausman also rejects arguments against PHA that assume that it is morally wrong in hiring or admissions to take into account anything other than the applicant's qualifications.

On the other side, defenders of PHA often rely on arguments from rectification or reparation to make their case. Many defenders think that harms should be rectified (remedied); racist acts are harmful; so they must be rectified, and PHA will do a good job of that. Hausman agrees that harms should be remedied, but by those who have actually done the harm. The harms of slavery, for instance, can no longer be rectified by those who perpetrated them, so this is a poor basis on which to justify PHA.

Arguments from reparations fare no better. Reparations are compensation owed by the government for wrongs that it has done or permitted. Hausman agrees that the U.S. and state governments were indeed responsible for many racist harms. But he offers a variety of reasons for thinking that PHA is not a good way of correcting for those harms.

Hausman concludes with an argument in favor of PHA. Ensuring equality of opportunity is a fundamental government responsibility. Hausman argues that PHA will help to advance this important goal. PHA won't by itself solve all of the problems that our long legacy of racism has created. But it will to some degree level a playing field that unjustly favors white males.

··

Affirmative action has many aspects. Some, such as requiring that job openings be advertised so that minorities can learn of them, are not controversial. Other aspects, such as preferential hiring and admissions (PHA), with which this essay is concerned, are hotly disputed. PHA takes minority status to increase an applicant's chance of getting a job or getting admitted to a university. Though the policy favors applicants with minority status, it does not imply that minority status should determine hiring or admission all by itself. (Nobody is proposing hiring blind bus drivers because they are minorities.) The idea is to favor otherwise qualified applicants who belong to disadvantaged groups. Because the pool of qualified minority applicants is often small, the direct benefits of PHA are also rather small. To limit the discussion, I shall focus in this essay largely on preferential hiring and admissions of African Americans, because they have a special history of slavery and oppression—even though the greatest beneficiaries of PHA have in fact been women.

There are many arguments defending preferential hiring and admissions and many criticizing it. Many of these arguments depend crucially on facts about the consequences. So, for example, critics have argued that PHA harms those it intends to benefit by undermining their self-confidence or by putting them in positions beyond their abilities in which they are bound to fail. Critics have also argued that those favored by PHA are often incompetent, and PHA thus undermines the credentials of beneficiaries, incites racism, and diminishes economic efficiency. Defenders argue that PHA has changed the American population's conception of what minorities and women can aspire to and that PHA has lessened racial disparities. These arguments would be powerful if their factual premises were true. But it is hard to know what the effects of PHA have been, and there is little evidence supporting any of these claims about the consequences of PHA. Heartwarming tales of successes of recipients of PHA and horror stories of harms and abuses are not serious evidence.[1]

The most prominent arguments do not rely on controversial factual premises. Critics argue that PHA is racism in reverse: discrimination is wrong, regardless of whether it is directed against or for African Americans. Defenders argue that PHA helps to rectify past injustices committed against African Americans. These are the arguments one most often hears. But they are not good arguments. Defenders and critics should stop making them.

"Racism in Reverse"

If it was morally impermissible to exclude African Americans from universities and jobs on the basis of their race, how can it be morally permissible to exclude white people on the basis of their race? Lisa Newton, a philosopher at Fairfield University, enunciates this criticism as follows: "The quota system, as employed by the University of California's medical school at Davis or any similar institution, is unjust, for all the same reasons that the discrimination it attempts to reverse is unjust."[2] Louis Pojman writes in this volume that PHA is a racist policy.

Let us formulate this argument precisely. The word "discrimination" causes confusion, because it has both a neutral and a negative sense. In the neutral sense, discrimination is simply drawing distinctions, which may be a good or a bad thing to do. An admissions office does nothing wrong when it discriminates (in this sense) among candidates on the basis of factors such as test scores and high school grade averages. In the negative

---

1. There have been serious investigations of the effects, which I cannot summarize here. In my view, the results have been inconclusive.
2. *National Forum* 58.1 (Winter 1978), pp. 22–23.

sense, discrimination consists in drawing distinctions unjustly. In the neutral sense, PHA obviously involves discriminating among candidates. Does it also discriminate in the negative sense—that is, unjustly? To avoid confusing the two meanings, it is best to avoid the word "discrimination" altogether, and ask instead whether the distinctions PHA draws among candidates are unjust.

Why might it be unjust to allow an applicant's race to influence hiring or admissions? Perhaps injustice lies simply in allowing race to influence choices. But it not always wrong to take race into account. A director making a movie of the life of Martin Luther King commits no injustice in refusing to consider white actors for the lead role. Refusing to hire a white short-order cook is, on the other hand, harder to justify. What's the difference? The answer seems to be that race is relevant to playing Martin Luther King, while it is not relevant to frying eggs.

One way to capture the racism in reverse argument is as follows:

1. It is wrong in hiring or admissions to take into account anything other than the applicant's qualifications.
2. PHA takes the applicant's race into account.
3. Race is almost always not a qualification.
4. Thus, PHA is almost always wrong.

I hope the reader agrees that this is a good way to formulate the racism in reverse argument, because I am trying to get at the truth rather than to win points in a political debate by misrepresenting the critic's position.

Crucial to this argument is the notion of a "qualification." A qualification is any fact about an applicant that is relevant to how successfully the applicant can promote the legitimate goals of the organization to which the applicant is applying. For example, high school class rank and ACT scores are qualifications, because they are correlated with academic performance in college. Running the 100-meter dash in under ten seconds is also a qualification for admission if the success of its athletic teams is among the legitimate goals of a university. For universities without sports teams, like those in Europe, it is not a qualification. The race of applicants would be relevant to a university devoted to white racial supremacy, but the promotion of racial supremacy is not a legitimate goal. Since, as the Martin Luther King movie example illustrates, race is sometimes a qualification, this argument does not conclude that PHA is always wrong, just that it is almost always wrong. On the view that this argument makes precise, what was wrong with the exclusion and special hurdles faced by African Americans during the Jim Crow era was that their prospects were not determined exclusively by their qualifications.

The argument formulated above is a valid argument. The conclusion follows logically from the premises. To assert all three of the premises and at the same time deny the conclusion is to contradict oneself. Constructing valid arguments can be very helpful. If those whom you are trying to persuade grant the premises, then, on pain of contradiction, they must accept the conclusion. Alternatively, if those you are attempting to persuade reject the conclusion, then they must reject at least one of the premises.

Let us examine whether the argument is also sound—that is, whether as well as being valid, all its premises are true. Premise 2 is obviously true: preferential hiring and admission of African Americans takes race into account. Premise 3 in contrast is debatable, because diversity among students and employees arguably serves legitimate goals of universities and some firms. Among the objectives of universities is to train business and political leaders who can interact with and understand people from many different backgrounds. Diversity within the student body serves this purpose.

More can be said about premise 3 and the importance of diversity, but let us focus on premise 1, which says that hiring and admissions should depend exclusively on qualifications. Premise 1 may seem plausible. It apparently explains why the racist exclusion of African Americans from schools, unions, and many professions was wrong: those exclusions were not based on qualifications. But premise 1 is false, and it does not correctly identify what was wrong with racist exclusions of African Americans. Consider three examples of hiring or admissions that depend on more than just qualifications:

- Case 1: Veterans are given preferences on civil service examinations and in college admissions.
- Case 2: An owner of a small grocery store hires his teenage daughter (rather than a more responsible teenager) to deliver groceries after school because he wants to keep an eye on her.
- Case 3: My father, who owned his own small company, often hired ex-convicts rather than applicants without criminal records because he thought that people who had served their time deserved a second chance. He did not hire ex-convicts because he had any illusions that they would be better workers.

Are the hiring or admissions policies in these three examples wrong?

Before answering, it is important to set aside unrelated reasons why the conduct may be wrong. Suppose, for example, that instead of owning his own company, my father was the personnel officer in a corporation, and he was instructed to hire the most qualified employees. If he then hired less qualified ex-cons because of his concern about their plight, he would be failing in his duties to the company that pays his salary. His actions would be wrong, because they violated company policy, whether or not it is permissible to take factors other than qualifications into account. If instead he had instructions to give preferences to ex-cons and refused to follow them, he would be equally at fault. Second, if the grocery store owner were to put out a sign saying "Help wanted. I shall hire whoever is most qualified," and he then hired his daughter even though he knew there were more qualified applicants, he would be acting wrongly. The wrong consists in deceiving the applicants, not in taking into account his personal relationship to his daughter.

There is no defensible general principle that requires hiring and admissions to depend only on qualifications. It is not automatically wrong to take into account a veteran's past service to the nation when providing education or hiring, even when having patrolled the streets of Baghdad or losing a limb is not a qualification. I'm proud of my father's hiring, even though it was not based only on qualifications. If PHA is wrong, it is not because it takes into account factors other than qualifications.

If it is sometimes acceptable to take factors other than qualifications into account, does that mean that it was okay to exclude Black Americans from universities, from unions, from neighborhoods, swimming pools, even bathrooms? Of course not! Those policies were despicable, but what explains those wrongs is not that they took factors other than qualifications into account. Consider segregated bathrooms, which are of no economic importance and superficially appear to treat the races equally. (I was with my father almost sixty years ago, when he was thrown out of a "whites only" bathroom in Florida.) What's wrong with having separate bathrooms for different races? Is it only that the bathrooms for white people were nicer? If the bathrooms had been equally nice and the restrictions had been symmetrical, with white people not allowed into the "colored only" bathrooms as Black people were not allowed into the "whites only" bathroom, how could the policy be unjust or harmful to Black people?

Social context is crucial. In a racist Black nation where there was a widespread view that contact with white people was defiling, segregated bathrooms would be a racist insult to white people. In the U.S., segregated bathrooms, hotels, train cars, and so forth were a humiliating insult to Black people, not to white people. In 1941, when Marian Anderson, the great African-American contralto, gave a concert at Lawrence University, she could not spend the night in Appleton, Wisconsin, where I used to live. In the 1940s, Appleton did not allow African Americans to reside within city limits. Fortunately, Anderson could stay in a hotel in a nearby town. The inconvenience was not enormous, but the insult was. Think about how it feels to be treated as if you were "unclean"—as if mere contact was defiling.

As these examples suggest, the mistreatment of African Americans that constituted Jim Crow consisted in their systematic denigration by white society, which resulted in their poverty, oppression, and exclusion. It relied on intimidation, beatings, humiliation, and murder. It was deeply wrong because of how it treated African Americans, not because it picked its victims by their race. If those mistreated were chosen not because of their skin color but via lottery and then marked as inferior, perhaps with a tattoo on their foreheads, the mistreatment would be no less repugnant and unjust.

In contrast, preferential hiring and admissions policies—whatever their virtues or vices—are not grounded in hatred of white people. PHA does not denigrate or oppress white people, or exclude them from the mainstream of American life. The admissions offices at universities are not full of white-hating racists out to keep white people from soiling their universities. Lisa Newton is wrong: PHA is not unjust "for all the same reasons that the discrimination it attempts to reverse is unjust." If PHA is unjust, it is not for any of the reasons that racial discrimination against Black people is unjust.

The failure of this common criticism of preferential hiring and admissions does not mean that PHA is fair or advisable. There may be other and better criticisms. But there is no moral prohibition on taking factors other than qualification into account in hiring and admissions, and in any case race is sometimes a qualification. PHA is not reverse racism.

Rectification, Reparations, and PHA

The main argument in defense of PHA fares no better. It maintains that PHA is a good way of rectifying past injustices perpetrated against African Americans. Rectification is a familiar idea. If my neighbor, Henry, were to steal my bicycle, justice would require that Henry give it back to me and compensate me for the inconvenience. When rights have been violated, justice requires that, as far as possible, the injustice be "rectified"—that the world be restored to how it would have been if there had been no injustice. African Americans have over the past centuries been the victims of incalculable injustices. They were enslaved, kidnapped, beaten, raped, tortured, and murdered and, after the Civil War brought slavery to an end, African Americans suffered more than a century of lynching, peonage, and relegation to the status of second-class citizens. Though racism persists, things are obviously better now. But these past injustices have not been rectified. Accordingly, many argue that PHA is justified as a form of rectification.

One might state the core of their argument as follows:

1. Those who commit injustices owe their victims damages.
2. Massive injustices have been perpetrated against African Americans.
3. Thus, those who committed these injustices owe damages to their African-American victims.

If intended to justify PHA, this argument has three problems. First, to rectify past injustice, one needs to identify the perpetrators of injustices and the victims of injustices and to determine the magnitude of the damages the perpetrators should pay to the victims. With respect to slavery, both perpetrators and victims are long dead. Descendants of victims of crimes may have claims to particular goods stolen from parents or grandparents, but their claims are limited. Children are not responsible for their parents' and grandparents' crimes, and members of a race are not responsible for injustices committed by other members of their race. How could PHA constitute the compensation that perpetrators of past injustices owe to their victims?

Second, rectification of an injustice is designed to restore people and their circumstances to that condition that would have obtained if no injustice had been done. Rectification in this sense for the wrongs of slavery is impossible. There is no way to know how the world would have been if there had been no slavery. Life in this country would have been utterly different. Few of our parents or more distant ancestors would have met, and consequently only a small portion of contemporary Americans would have existed in a hypothetical world without slavery. How can we possibly envision how things would have been under circumstances so different that they do not even contain the same people?

Third, identifying those who should pay compensation and those to whom compensation is owed would lead to a divisive inquiry into the virtues and vices of our ancestors, when they came to the United States, whether they conserved or squandered ill-gotten gains, and so forth. This is not a road that those who hope to improve race relations should want to follow.

Although widely misunderstood, invoking reparations rather than rectification solves the problem of identifying the responsible party. Reparations are a form of compensation provided by the government (and hence ultimately taxpayers) to acknowledge and partly to rectify past injustices perpetrated or permitted by the government. For example, the U.S. government provided $20,000 in reparations to Japanese-Americans who were interned during World War II, or to their immediate descendants. The funds were raised through taxation of all Americans, including Japanese-Americans. There was no distinction between those people who may have profited from the internment and the great majority who did not benefit from it, because reparations are a civic responsibility for a civic wrong, rather than a personal responsibility for personal wrongs. Because government at all levels perpetrated injustices toward African Americans and acquiesced in many other injustices that could and should have been prevented, it bears a great responsibility for past injustices toward African Americans.

Conceptualizing PHA as the paying of reparations rather than as rectifying individual injustices should thus in principle avoid divisive inquiries into the vices of our ancestors. But public discussion tramples subtle distinctions, and, unfortunately, proponents and critics misunderstand reparations and turn discussion of the issue into acrimonious finger pointing concerning the intergenerational transmission of personal guilt. A few years ago David Horowitz placed advertisements criticizing reparations in a number of college newspapers. These advertisements led to violent protests by those concerned about the disadvantages that African Americans must deal with. Among Horowitz's ten reasons to oppose reparations were: (1) we cannot identify the descendants of the perpetrators of the crimes of slavery; (2) few Americans owned slaves, and (3) most Americans have no clear connection to slavery. Since reparations are a civic responsibility for the wrongs government caused or permitted, these claims are irrelevant, but neither Horowitz nor most of his readers appear to have understood that. Supporters of reparations are just as confused. For example, in an op-ed piece in the New York Times (April 23, 2010), Henry Lewis Gates takes the most vexing problem of reparations to be "how to parcel out blame to those directly involved in the capture and sale of human beings for immense economic gain," and he believes that historical research now makes it possible "to publicly attribute responsibility and culpability where they truly belong, to white people and black people."

Even if reparations did not cause such confusions, other problems with rectification apply equally to reparations. How much should be paid? To whom should reparations be paid? Though there are powerful reasons to diminish the huge racial disparities that divide our nation, those policies should not be regarded as reparations. The risks of misunderstanding, the problems in identifying the recipients, and the problems in determining how much should be paid are reasons not to invoke reparations to justify policies that diminish racial disparities.

Furthermore, even if reparations could be ascertained without provoking confused racial animosity, preferential hiring and admissions policies are not a defensible way of paying reparations. PHA does not focus on those who have been most harmed by past injustices, and it does not distribute the costs of paying reparations in a justifiable way. It unfairly imposes the cost of reparations—a civic responsibility—entirely on non-minority college applicants and job seekers, who bear no more responsibility for past injustices than anyone else. These costs, like the benefits PHA provide, are generally small, but it is still unjust both to make one group in society pay all the costs and arbitrarily to benefit just one group. If PHA were only one of a set of programs whose costs were distributed throughout the population, this objection would not be cogent. But apart from PHA, public policy does little to address racial disparities.

I am not arguing that Americans should forget past injustices. Without understanding the past, how could we understand the present and know what to do about it? Moreover, the fact that the problems of the present arose through past injustices creates a special obligation to address them. But it is impossible to undo the past or rectify old and large-scale injustices. We have no idea what would constitute rectification, and could not carry it out if we did. Although we need to look to the past for understanding, our moral concern should focus on the future. How can we free it of racism and of the disparities that racism has caused?

Preferential Admissions and Equal Opportunity

The other major arguments that do not depend on factual knowledge of details of the consequences of PHA invoke the value of equal opportunity. Critics maintain that equal opportunity condemns PHA. Defenders maintain that PHA promotes equal opportunity. Obviously, both cannot be right.

Consider an analogy. Suppose that in the local elementary school there are two first-grade and two second-grade classes. One of the first-grade teachers is excellent, and one is terrible. One of the second-grade teachers is also excellent, and one is terrible. The socioeconomic status of the families in this community is uniform, and the children have had similar preschool experiences. The school board assigns students to first-grade teachers by lottery on the grounds that the fairest policy gives every student an equal chance at a good first-grade experience.

There is disagreement, however, about how to assign children to the second-grade teachers. Some school board members argue that every child should have one good and one bad teacher. Those children who had the good first-grade teacher should get the bad second-grade teacher and vice versa. These board members say, "If every child has both a good teacher and a bad teacher, then the children's schooling and overall future opportunities will be as close to equal as we can make them." Other school board members argue for a second lottery. They say, "Why should students be punished for having had a good teacher in first grade? Equal opportunity demands that every child should have an equal chance of having a good second-grade teacher."

This analogy is helpful in several regards. First, it explains why it can appear that PHA both promotes and impedes equal opportunity. If one is thinking narrowly about the chance of getting a good second-grade teacher, then a second lottery equalizes opportunity, just as (if there were no racism) the absence of PHA would equalize the chances of being hired or admitted of otherwise equally qualified applicants of different races. On the other hand, if one is concerned with opportunities over a lifetime, insuring that every child has one good teacher and one bad one promotes equality of opportunity, just as PHA does (on the assumption that the opportunities and resources available previously to Black applicants have, on average, been worse than those available to white applicants). Those concerned with equal opportunity should be concerned with lifetime opportunities, not opportunities to acquire one or another immediate benefit or burden. Because of past inequalities and continued racism, PHA lessens inequalities in opportunity.

The school analogy also makes clear that PHA does not punish white applicants, just as assigning children who had the good first-grade teacher to the bad second-grade teacher does not punish them. These kids have done nothing wrong. Indeed, it may be that nobody has done anything wrong. The policy of making sure that each student has one good and one bad teacher is not a way of rectifying in second grade an injustice done in first grade, because no injustice has been done. The justification for the second-grade teacher assignments is to provide children with similar overall opportunities, not to restore children to where they would have been if they had not previously been treated unjustly. In the case of PHA, unlike the elementary school analogy, some of the past inequalities in opportunity have been the result of injustices, but the point is to diminish inequality rather than to rectify injustice.

It is important to distinguish between compensation as rectifying injustice and compensation as equalizing opportunity. The former does not justify PHA, because, as I argued earlier, it is unfair to impose the costs of reparations or rectification on white applicants, since reparations are a social responsibility, and rectification is the responsibility of individual wrongdoers. By contrast, equalizing opportunity can justify PHA, because it is not unjust to diminish the chances of applicants whose prospects have on average been inflated by previous inequalities. The relevant question for a rejected white applicant is not "With my qualifications, would I have been admitted or hired if there were no PHA policy?" Nor is it "With my qualifications, would I have been admitted or hired if I were Black?" The relevant question is "If the qualifications of all the applicants (including me) had not been skewed by past inequalities in opportunity and if there were no continuing racism, would I have been admitted or hired?"

Given previous inequalities and continuing discrimination, PHA brings us on average closer to equal opportunity.[3] Like the children who had the good first-grade teacher, white applicants on average have had

---

3. For example, in one study mailed applications with common African-American names were only half as likely to get callbacks as applications with names that are not associated with African Americans. See "Are Emily and Greg More Employable than Lakisha and Jamal? A Field Experiment on Labor Market Discrimination" by Marianne Bertrand and Sendhil Mullainathan (2004). (https://scholar.harvard.edu/files/sendhil/files/are_emily_and_greg_more_employable_than_lakisha_and_jamal.pdf).

previous advantages. PHA diminishes these inequalities and counteracts some of the continued racist discrimination in hiring.

This argument assumes that the opportunities for Black applicants have been in fact on average worse than the opportunities for white applicants. But there can be no serious doubt about its truth. According to the Pew Research Center, the median wealth of African Americans in 2009 was one-twentieth that of white people. There is no plausible explanation of inequalities in outcomes that are this enormous other than unequal opportunities, and such large inequalities in outcomes obviously translate into inequalities in opportunity. A far higher percentage of Black children live in poverty and in single-parent homes. On average the parents of African-American children are likely to have had less education, and the schools African-American children attend typically have worse facilities, lower-paid teachers, and larger class sizes. Some Black applicants are highly privileged and many white applicants have grown up in dire circumstances, but on average, Black applicants have had to cope with greater poverty, more difficult environments, and worse schooling. Their opportunities have been on average considerably worse, and they face the additional burden of continued discrimination.[4] PHA does a little to lessen these inequalities in opportunity. Valuing equal opportunity (not equal results) is a reason to support it, not to oppose it.

Conclusions

This essay has focused on the most popular arguments concerning PHA. Their popularity does not reflect well on the subtlety of public discourse, because they are not good arguments. PHA is not racism in reverse. It is not racist. It does not aim to denigrate, exclude, oppress, or punish white people. The main argument in defense of PHA is just as weak. PHA is not justified as a form of rectification or of reparations. Reparations and rectification are impractical, racially divisive, and incapable of justifying a policy that imposes costs arbitrarily on only one segment of the population.

As we have seen, there are good arguments to be made in defense of PHA as promoting diversity and equal opportunity, but it could turn out that other consequences of PHA are so harmful that there is good reason

---

4. This conclusion does not rest on the silly view that all differences in outcomes among members of different social groups result from differences in opportunities.

to abandon the policies. If we knew the effects of PHA on racial animosity, on the self-conception and status of the minorities it aims to benefit, and on the extent to which they and others are successful, we would be in a better position to reach a definite conclusion concerning whether PHA is beneficial. But we do not know its effects well enough.

One other consideration should be mentioned. Preferential hiring and admissions policies are more or less the only social policies in the United States that acknowledge the special handicaps disadvantaged minorities face and, in a small way, concretely aim to lessen them. Disadvantaged minorities would inevitably see the abandonment of PHA, without putting something substantial in its place, as white America turns its back on a disgracefully unjust situation. The deck is stacked, and white America gets to shuffle the cards. Will it do anything about the poor hands that minorities have been dealt?

Daniel M. Hausman: Affirmative Action: Bad Arguments and Some Good Ones

1. Why isn't it racist for schools to offer preferential admissions to Blacks and Hispanics? What's the difference between not admitting someone because they are Black or Hispanic and not admitting someone because they are white?
2. If what was wrong with slavery and "Jim Crow" laws was not their racial basis, then what was wrong with them?
3. Suppose that the United States government were to pay reparations to the descendants of slaves. Why should people who are not descended from slave holders (such as recent immigrants) have to pay taxes to support paying these reparations?
4. What is the point of the parable of the two first-grade and two second-grade classes? Is it a good analogy to the circumstances in which preferential hiring or admissions might be called for?
5. What other arguments can you think of supporting or criticizing preferential hiring and admissions? Can you provide logically valid formulations of these arguments?

40

White Privilege: Unpacking the Invisible Knapsack

Peggy McIntosh

In this brief article from the late 1980s, Peggy McIntosh introduces the notion of white privilege and offers many examples of this phenomenon. She stresses how white privilege works in many of the same ways that male privilege does. A central theme of her essay is that some such privileges are perfectly ok to enjoy—indeed, they should be enjoyed by all members of a just society. Other privileges, though, work to the disadvantage of members of oppressed groups. Such privileges cement relations of domination and are forms of unearned, unfair advantage. McIntosh argues that most white people fail to recognize their privilege, but instead take it for granted. Nor is this an accident—the social systems that reinforce oppression are designed in such a way as to mask the unfair advantages that members of dominant groups enjoy. While McIntosh encourages individuals from dominant groups to reflect on their unearned advantages, she does not believe that these advantages can be fully erased through individual action. Instead, she argues, what is needed is a revamping of the entire social structure that fosters oppression.

Peggy McIntosh, "White Privilege: Unpacking the Invisible Knapsack," in *Peace and Freedom Magazine*, July/August, 1989, pp. 10-12, a publication of the Women's International League for Peace and Freedom, Philadelphia, PA.

Through work to bring materials from Women's Studies into the rest of the curriculum, I have often noticed men's unwillingness to grant that they are over-privileged, even though they may grant that women are disadvantaged. They may say that they will work to improve women's status, in the society, the university, or the curriculum, but they can't or won't support the idea of lessening men's. Denials which amount to taboos surround the subject of advantages which men gain from women's disadvantages. These denials protect male privilege from being fully acknowledged, lessened or ended.

Thinking through unacknowledged male privilege as a phenomenon, I realized that since hierarchies in our society are interlocking, there was most likely a phenomenon of white privilege which was similarly denied and protected. As a white person, I realized I had been taught about racism as something which puts others at a disadvantage, but had been taught not to see one of its corollary aspects, white privilege, which puts me at an advantage.

I think whites are carefully taught not to recognize white privilege, as males are taught not to recognize male privilege. So I have begun in an un-tutored way to ask what it is like to have white privilege. I have come to see white privilege as an invisible package of unearned assets which I can count on cashing in each day, but about which I was 'meant' to remain oblivious. White privilege is like an invisible weightless knapsack of special provisions, maps, passports, codebooks, visas, clothes, tools and blank checks.

Describing white privilege makes one newly accountable. As we in Women's Studies work to reveal male privilege and ask men to give up some of their power, so one who writes about having white privilege must ask, "Having described it, what will I do to lessen or end it?"

After I realized the extent to which men work from a base of unacknowledged privilege, I understood that much of their oppressiveness was unconscious. Then I remembered the frequent charges from women of color that white women whom they encounter are oppressive. I began to understand why we are justly seen as oppressive, even when we don't see ourselves that way. I began to count the ways in which I enjoy unearned skin privilege and have been conditioned into oblivion about its existence.

My schooling gave me no training in seeing myself as an oppressor, as an unfairly advantaged person, or as a participant in a damaged culture. I was taught to see myself as an individual whose moral state depended on her individual moral will. My schooling followed the pattern my colleague Elizabeth Minnich has pointed out: whites are taught to think of their lives as morally neutral, normative, and average, and also ideal, so that when we work to benefit others, this is seen as work which will allow "them" to be more like "us."

I decided to try to work on myself at least by identifying some of the daily effects of white privilege in my life. I have chosen those conditions which I think in my case *attach somewhat more to skin-color privilege* than to class, religion, ethnic status, or geographical location, though of course all these other factors are intricately intertwined. As far as I can see, my African American co-workers, friends and acquaintances with whom I come into daily or frequent contact in this particular time, place, and line of work cannot count on most of these conditions.

1. I can if I wish arrange to be in the company of people of my race most of the time.
2. If I should need to move, I can be pretty sure of renting or purchasing housing in an area which I can afford and in which I want to live.
3. I can be pretty sure that my neighbors in such a location will be neutral or pleasant to me.
4. I can go shopping alone most of the time, pretty well assured that I will not be followed or harassed.
5. I can turn on the television or open to the front page of the paper and see people of my race widely represented.
6. When I am told about our national heritage or about "civilization," I am shown that people of my color made it what it is.
7. I can be sure that my children will be given curricular materials that testify to the existence of their race.
8. If I want to, I can be pretty sure of finding a publisher for this piece on white privilege.
9. I can go into a music shop and count on finding the music of my race represented, into a supermarket and find the staple foods which fit with my cultural traditions, into a hairdresser's shop and find someone who can cut my hair.
10. Whether I use checks, credit cards, or cash, I can count on my skin color not to work against the appearance of financial reliability.
11. I can arrange to protect my children most of the time from people who might not like them.

12. I can swear, or dress in second-hand clothes, or not answer letters, without having people attribute these choices to the bad morals, the poverty, or the illiteracy of my race.
13. I can speak in public to a powerful male group without putting my race on trial.
14. I can do well in a challenging situation without being called a credit to my race.
15. I am never asked to speak for all the people of my racial group.
16. I can remain oblivious of the language and customs of persons of color who constitute the world's majority without feeling in my culture any penalty for such oblivion.
17. I can criticize our government and talk about how much I fear its policies and behavior without being seen as a cultural outsider.
18. I can be pretty sure that if I ask to talk to "the person in charge," I will be facing a person of my race.
19. If a traffic cop pulls me over or if the IRS audits my tax return, I can be sure I haven't been singled out because of my race.
20. I can easily buy posters, postcards, picture books, greeting cards, dolls, toys, and children's magazines featuring people of my race.
21. I can go home from most meetings of organizations I belong to feeling somewhat tied in, rather than isolated, out-of-place, out-numbered, unheard, held at a distance, or feared.
22. I can take a job with an affirmative action employer without having coworkers on the job suspect that I got it because of race.
23. I can choose public accommodation without fearing that people of my race cannot get in or will be mistreated in the places I have chosen.
24. I can be sure that if I need legal or medical help, my race will not work against me.
25. If my day, week, or year is going badly, I need not ask of each negative episode or situation whether it has racial overtones.
26. I can choose blemish cover or bandages in "flesh" color and have them more or less match my skin.

I repeatedly forgot each of the realizations on this list until I wrote it down. For me white privilege has turned out to be an elusive and fugitive subject. The pressure to avoid it is great, for in facing it I must give up the myth of meritocracy. If these things are true, this is not such a free country; one's life is not what one makes it; many doors open for certain people through no virtues of their own.

In unpacking this invisible knapsack of white privilege, I have listed conditions of daily experience which I once took for granted. Nor did I think of any of these prerequisites as bad for the holder. I now think that we need a more finely differentiated taxonomy of privilege, for some of these varieties are only what one would want for everyone in a just society, and others give license to be ignorant, oblivious, arrogant and destructive.

I see a pattern running through the matrix of white privilege, a pattern of assumptions which were passed on to me as a white person. There was one main piece of cultural turf; it was my own turf, and I was among those who could control the turf. *My skin color was an asset for any move I was educated to want to make.* I could think of myself as belonging in major ways, and of making social systems work for me. I could freely disparage, fear, neglect, or be oblivious to anything outside of the dominant cultural forms. Being of the main culture, I could also criticize it fairly freely.

In proportion as my racial group was being made confident, comfortable, and oblivious, other groups were likely being made unconfident, uncomfortable, and alienated. Whiteness protected me from many kinds of hostility, distress and violence, which I was being subtly trained to visit in turn upon people of color.

For this reason, the word "privilege" now seems to me misleading. We usually think of privilege as being a favored state, whether earned or conferred by birth or luck. Yet some of the conditions I have described here work to systematically over-empower certain groups. Such privilege simply *confers dominance* because of one's race or sex.

I want, then, to distinguish between earned strength and unearned power conferred systemically. Power from unearned privilege can look like strength when it is in fact permission to escape or to dominate. But not all of the privileges on my list are inevitably damaging. Some, like the expectation that neighbors will be decent to you, or that your race will not count against you in court, should be the norm in a just society. Others, like the privilege to ignore less powerful people, distort the humanity of the holders as well as the ignored groups.

We might at least start by distinguishing between positive advantages which we can work to spread, and negative types of advantages which unless rejected will always reinforce our present hierarchies. For example, the feeling that one belongs within the human circle, as Native Americans say, should not be seen as privilege for a few. Ideally it is an *unearned entitlement*. At present, since only a few have it, it is an *unearned advantage* for them. This paper results from a process of coming to see that some of the power which I originally saw as attendant on being a human being in the U.S. consisted in *unearned advantage* and *conferred dominance*.

I have met very few men who are truly distressed about systemic, unearned male advantage and conferred dominance. And so one question for me and others like me is whether we will get truly distressed, even outraged about unearned race advantage and conferred dominance and if so, what we will do to lessen them. In any case, we need to do more work in identifying how they actually affect our daily lives. Many, perhaps most, of our white students in the U.S. think that racism doesn't affect them because they are not people of color; they do not see "whiteness" as a racial identity. In addition, since race and sex are not the only advantaging systems at work, we need similarly to examine the daily experience of having age advantage, or ethnic advantage, or physical ability, or advantage related to nationality, religion, or sexual orientation.

Difficulties and dangers surrounding the task of finding parallels are many. Since racism, sexism, and heterosexism are not the same, the advantaging associated with them should not be seen as the same. In addition, it is hard to disentangle aspects of unearned advantage which rest more on social class, economic class, race, religion, sex and ethnic identity than on other factors. Still, all of the oppressions are interlocking, as the Combahee River Collective Statement of 1977 continues to remind us eloquently.

One factor seems clear about all of the interlocking oppressions. They take both active forms which we can see and embedded forms which as a member of the dominant group one is taught not to see. In my class and place, I did not see myself as a racist because I was taught to recognize racism only in individual acts of meanness by members of my group, never in invisible systems conferring unsought racial dominance on my group from birth.

Disapproving of the systems won't be enough to change them. I was taught to think that racism could end if white individuals changed their attitudes. [But] a "white" skin in the United States opens many doors for whites whether or not we approve of the way dominance has been conferred on us. Individual acts can palliate, but cannot end, these problems.

To redesign social systems we need first to acknowledge their colossal unseen dimensions. The silences and denials surrounding privilege are the key political tool here. They keep the thinking about equality or equity incomplete, protecting unearned advantage and conferred dominance by making these taboo subjects. Most talk by whites about equal opportunity seems to me now to be about equal opportunity to try to get into a position of dominance while denying that *systems* of dominance exist.

It seems to me that obliviousness about white advantage, like obliviousness about male advantage, is kept strongly inculturated in the United States so as to maintain the myth of meritocracy, the myth that all democratic choice is equally available to all. Keeping most people unaware that freedom of confident action is there for just a small number of people props up those in power, and serves to keep power in the hands of the same groups that have most of it already.

Though systematic change takes many decades, there are pressing questions for me and I imagine for some others like me if we raise our daily consciousness on the perquisites of being light-skinned. What will we do with such knowledge? As we know from watching men, it is an open question whether we will choose to use unearned advantage to weaken hidden systems of advantage, and whether we will use any of our arbitrarily awarded power to try to reconstruct power systems on a broader base.

Peggy McIntosh: White Privilege: Unpacking the Invisible Knapsack

1. McIntosh describes white privilege as "an invisible package of unearned assets which I can count on cashing in each day, but about which I was 'meant' to be oblivious." What do you think she means by this?
2. Early in her article, McIntosh seems to suggest that elevating the status of women and Black people requires lessening the status of white men. Do you think that this is her suggestion, and if so, do agree with it? Why or why not?
3. McIntosh alludes to "the myth of meritocracy." What is this myth, and in what ways is it damaging?
4. McIntosh distinguishes between two forms of privilege. One should be possessed by all members of a just society. What is the other form of privilege? Which items on her list belong to the former group, and which to the latter?
5. Are there any items on McIntosh's list that you think should be omitted? Which items (if any) do you think should be added to her list of privileges that white people enjoy by virtue of their skin color?

41

Who? Whom? Reparations and the Problem of Agency

Chandran Kukathas

....

The word "reparations" comes from the word "repair." In the standard case, reparations are owed when one party (an individual or group) has wronged another; reparations are designed to repair the relationship between wrongdoer and victim, usually by providing compensation for the harm imposed on the victim. Apologies can also play a key role in the process of repair.

In this paper, Chandran Kukathas argues that clear cases of justified reparations share three common elements: an identifiable wrongdoer, a known victim, and a clear harm that can serve as the basis of compensation. When these three are in place, morality requires the wrongdoer to compensate the victim he's wronged. However, when it comes to historic injustices, it can be extremely difficult to determine whether all of these elements are present.

According to Kukathas, when we are talking about reparations for historic injustices, such as chattel slavery in the U.S. or the slaughter of the Maori in New Zealand, the problem of identifying the victims who are today owed compensation becomes very difficult. The victims of those terrible harms are long dead. So the question becomes whether the descendants of those victims are eligible for compensation. Kukathas argues that it can in many cases be very difficult to identify

Chandran Kukathas, "Who? Whom? Reparations and the Problem of Agency," in *Journal of Social Philosophy*, Vol. 37 No. 3, Fall 2006, 330–339.

those descendants. Alternatively, it may be too easy—for nearly every living person, for instance, it is plausible that their mothers, grand-mothers, or great-grandmothers suffered various injustices owing to sexism. Presumably, though, we do not want to identify nearly every living person as the intended recipient of claim to reparations.

Further difficulties arise when trying to identify those who today owe reparations for past injustices. The standard case has the wrong-doer himself owing a duty of repair. But that's not possible when it comes to historic injustices. It seems unfair to hold contemporary indi-viduals liable for injustices that they did not themselves commit. Kukathas considers whether we might instead hold certain groups, such as governments or corporations, liable for past wrongs. He does believe that governments can be held liable for past wrongs that previ-ous administrations perpetrated or allowed, but believes that compli-cations arise when it comes to most other groups, such as churches and corporations.

....

If a person is wronged, whether by a physical violation of his person or by having his property unjustly taken, or even by the besmirching of his reputation, he is, most people agree, entitled to some form of compensation or restitution from the person or persons responsible for the wrong. What form the reparation should take, and how great it should be, are sometimes difficult problems, but this does not change the fact that something is owed and someone must be held to account. If a restaurant goes bust because a supplier fails to fulfill his commitments and a newspaper publishes false reports of the restaurant's allegedly unethical practices, the business owner can seek compensation from those responsible for the harm he has suffered. The fact that apportion-ing responsibility will not be easy makes no difference: the law must try to find an answer that rectifies the injustice. Similarly, it can be argued, the harm suffered by the descendants of victims of unredressed injustices of the past cries out no less urgently for attention. Many people today suffer as a consequence of wrongs committed in the past, and they too, some say, are entitled to some form of restitution. The fact that matters are complex is no reason for them to give up their claims, or for others to give up on the task of finding answers to the question of who owes what to whom.

It seems fair to say that the complexity of the problem of apportioning responsibility, and of settling the nature and extent of compensation owed, should not deter us from trying to do justice. We seek only as much precision as we can plausibly hope for, and make compromises to ensure that some justice is done, imperfect justice being better than no justice at all. Yet matters are importantly different when the problem is not so much determining the form of restitution but establishing who the relevant parties are in the case. In cases of past injustice, the problem of identifying the parties often turns out to be especially troublesome. Indeed, the more remote the original wrong, the more difficult it is to establish who has cause for complaint and who can rightly be held responsible.

In this paper, I argue that the pursuit of justice by making reparation for past wrongs, and particularly for wrongs done more than a generation ago, is not morally justifiable except in some special cases. For the paying of reparations to be defensible, it must be possible to identify two kinds of agent: the victim of injustice, to whom reparation is owed, and the perpetrator or beneficiary of injustice who can be held accountable for the wrong or liable for the cost of restitution. If both agents cannot be identified, there cannot be a case for reparation. It may be possible to justify, say, the return of some lands to people who have been dispossessed, if we can identify the dispossessed and also those who can be held accountable; but it is not possible to justify, say, compensation for the descendants of slavery generally. Some persons can be held responsible for some of the wrongs of the past, but one generation cannot be asked to atone for the sins of earlier ones.

The paper is organized as follows. Section I considers why it is necessary that we be able to identify the agents who are the victims of past injustice and those who are to be held responsible for rectifying them. It is not sufficient merely to establish that injustices did occur, and that there do exist modern-day descendants of the victims of injustice, and modern-day descendants of perpetrators of injustice. Section II argues that it is difficult, if not impossible, accurately to identify the individual agents who can rightly be held responsible for historical injustices, or the agents who are owed reparation. Section III takes up the question of whether responsibility might be understood not as a relationship between individuals but rather as one between groups. In particular, it considers the question of whether the state might be understood as a moral agent with responsibility for rectifying the injustices of the past. It concludes that there is a limit to the extent to which responsibility can be laid at the door of the state.

I

Many people and communities that are the descendants of victims of injustice in the past live disadvantaged lives. The descendants of American slaves are on average worse-off than are the rest of the population of the United States; the descendants of Australian Aborigines are generally worse-off than the non-Aboriginal population; and the Maori of New Zealand do less well than their pakeha counterparts on most measures of well-being, from life expectancy to rates of incarceration. There are many reasons why a political community might want to acknowledge the wrongs of the past. For one thing, it seems likely that the events of the past have had a significant bearing on who fares well and who fares poorly: the probability of one's life going well is affected substantially by the community into which one is born. For another thing, the fact that people are suffering itself gives us some reason to attend to them, and when that suffering has a long history, that very history may need to be acknowledged.

If, however, we wish to do justice to specific individuals or groups, we need to do more than take note of history's injustices. We need to identify with some precision who is a victim of injustice, and who can rightly be held responsible—or liable. But why do we need to be precise if we know that there has been injustice in the past and that there are people who are suffering in the present? One reason is that this is, at least implicitly, what those who see themselves as victims of past injustice demand. Their claim is not that their condition should be remedied because they have simply done badly out of history. It is that they should be compensated in some way because they have been treated unjustly. Their claim is different from that which might be made by the poor more generally: that the background institutions under which they have remained poor are unfair or systematically biased in favor of others or not conducive to equality. Their claim is, rather, that particular wrongs were committed and that it is the further injustices that were consequent upon them that need to be rectified. If this is indeed their contention, then their claims can only be addressed by identifying the agents who deserve restitution and those who are liable for providing it. For them, it will not do simply to lump them in with the poor more generally, for their claim is of a very specific nature.

The next question then is, who are the relevant agents when justice in rectification is at issue? There are three kinds of agent who can make, or be asked to fulfill, moral claims: individuals and two kinds of group agents including collective entities and corporate entities. An individual is an agent insofar as he or she is an actor who is capable of making decisions and can be held to account—or held responsible—for those decisions. A group is an agent when it is capable of making decisions and can be held responsible for them. A group is not an agent when it is merely a category or class of persons, such as the set of all platinum blondes; nor is it an agent when it is simply a collection of people, such as a crowd, or even a neighborhood, since it lacks any locus of decision making, or any structure or organization that establishes an authority capable of taking a decision on its behalf, and that is recognized as such. Group agents include partnerships, families, clubs, churches, companies, and private and public associations of various kinds such as charities and universities. They also include governments of all kinds: local, provincial, and national, as well as international organizations. Tribes can also be regarded as group agents.

When the issue of how to redress historical injustice arises, the problem is to work out who has a claim upon whom for compensation for past wrongs. This means working out which agents have claims against which other agents for actions taken in the past that have damaged some and benefited others. Claims might be made by individuals against other individuals, individuals against groups, groups against groups, and groups against individuals. The validity of any claim would depend, among other things, on the proper identification of the agents in question as persons entitled to make claims or persons liable for fulfilling them. The issue is: how readily can this be done?

II

The problem of identifying the relevant agents in trying to establish claims for restitution for past injustice is more difficult than has been recognized. Who is entitled to compensation for a wrong committed, and who is liable to pay is sometimes easy enough to ascertain when victim and perpetrator are both alive, though it can get progressively more difficult to establish the extent of entitlement and responsibility as time goes on. When generations have passed, even identifying the parties to the case is difficult.

To begin with, let us consider the problem of identifying the claimants, before turning to the problem of establishing who is liable for providing restitution to those who are harmed. Some claimants will be individual descendants of the victims of past injustice. One thing that should be noted at the outset is that it is not obvious that the descendant of a victim of injustice is owed anything by anyone. Certainly the law in most countries does not always presume that descendants have such claims. If Nancy in generation one is beaten and killed by Bill Sykes, her surviving daughter, Nancy Junior, cannot, in generation two, make any claim against Bill Sykes Junior (who earns his living as a boxer, using the skills his father, Bill Senior, imparted to him).[1] Nancy Junior may have been orphaned, and now be destitute, and Bill Junior may have become wealthy as a boxer. If Bill Senior had gone to prison and died penniless (and more than likely, any pennies he had would have been returned to the persons from whom he stole), Nancy Junior would have had no redress against him, and it would be hard to argue that she had a claim upon Bill Junior's human capital. But I propose to set this matter to one side for the moment and assume that a case can be made for saying that descendants of victims of injustice are owed something. The question is: who are the individual descendants of the victims of past injustice?

This question may be read in different ways. One way of reading it is by taking it to mean "who should count as a descendant of a victim of past injustice?" If this is the question, the answer in any given society could be a relatively small or a worryingly large number. It would be a very large number if we considered anyone a descendant of a victim if he or she could identify any ancestor who had suffered injustice. If we confined our analysis to a single society, like the United States, we would get a collection of individuals that included at least the following: the descendants of African slaves, the descendants of Native Americans, the descendants of people who were the victims of war, the descendants of conscripts and neglected war veterans, the descendants of people unjustly incarcerated (including but not only the Japanese imprisoned during World War II), the descendants of anyone who was cheated, swindled, or taken unfair advantage of by governments, businesses, unions, criminal organizations, or individuals. Depending on how broadly injustice was defined, that number could easily encompass the majority of the population. If, for example, we took severe punishment for possessing and selling drugs to be unjust, then many people have been the victims of injustice; but if we took severe punishment in this instance to be warranted, many people are in fact the descendants of the victims of justice. We could also stipulate how broadly or narrowly we wish to construe injustice by determining a strong or weak minimum standard by which we deem whether an injustice has been

---

1. In this example, Nancy Junior and Bill Junior are not siblings.

committed. If being verbally abused by a policeman is sufficient for someone to claim victimhood, the number of victims could be impossibly large. Finally, if we took the victims of injustice to include women who had been treated unjustly in the workplace, in the home, or by laws limiting their right to work or to receive equal pay, the descendants of the victims of past injustice might include everyone.

The point here, of course, is not to suggest that no one could be distinguished as a descendant of a victim of past injustice because everyone is a descendant. It is, rather, to say that identifying the set of people to be recognized as the descendants of victims is a complex and contentious matter. It requires determining not only who to include but who to exclude from consideration.

Another way of reading the question is by taking it to mean "how do we tell if someone is a descendant of a victim of past injustice?" In some cases, this may be relatively straightforward: the child of a slave or former slave is clearly in this category. But what of the children, and grandchildren, of mixed descent? Does a person with one black grandparent or one black great-grandparent count as black or white? Even if we assume that the world is divided conveniently into victims and perpetrators or beneficiaries of injustice, it is not obvious how we should categorize those with ancestors on both sides of the divide—leaving to one side the issue of whether descent should be understood purely biologically or to include relationship through adoption.

A further complexity arises when we consider whether the category of descendants of victims of past injustice should be extended to include people beyond the borders of the political community. Many people around the world are the descendants of refugees who fled persecution, often leaving behind both the experience of violent treatment and their personal wealth or livelihoods. Intermarriage over the generations has created many people who are the descendants of people who have suffered great injustice. Sometimes it is difficult to identify these people. On other occasions it is not: if we take the case of Liberia for example, a country founded by the forcible repatriation of black Americans to African soil, we might say that almost everyone there is the descendant of victims of injustice, although many people there may have only one American ancestor.

The general problem in distinguishing the descendants of victims of past injustice is that it is too easy to reach the point at which a very large proportion of the population can be identified as descendants. If that happens, the moral force of the claims made by some people will be diminished to the extent that many others in the society might simply respond that they too have injustice in their histories. Is there a better way of separating out the descendants of injustice who have strong claims from those who do not?

An obvious alternative is to identify not individuals but groups that are the descendants of victims of past injustice. This might have the immediate advantage of giving us an entity that is easier to isolate and distinguish from other potential claimants because it has persisted over a greater length of time and because tracing an ancestry will not be a problem. Moreover, the most serious injustices of the past, which cry out for rectification, were committed against groups or people as members of groups. The two issues that have to be settled, however, are which groups to count, and whom to include within them. This may be difficult, and we should consider why.

To begin with the matter of which groups to count, it may seem plain that certain groups are almost self-evidently candidates. The descendants of African slaves in modern America, and the indigenous peoples dispossessed of their lands in many parts of the world come to mind. It would be impossible to deny that slaves and dispossessed people were the victims of injustice many generations ago, or that the injustice the people of these groups continued to suffer was injustice in succeeding generations. The main point of contention is not whether such groups are plausible candidates for restitution but whether excluding the descendants of other victims of past injustice is warranted. The question is not just "why these groups and not others?" but also "why not people who don't fall into notable groups, but are the descendants of victims of serious injustice all the same?" One powerful reason for picking out particular groups but not others may be that the injustices suffered by these groups have had a particularly significant impact on the life of the society as a whole—perhaps so much so that it would make a difference to the quality of life in that society if these particular grievances were addressed. While this is an important reason, and one that may well justify attempting to offer restitution to the descendants of some groups, it is not, in the end, a reason that invokes the importance of doing justice for its own sake. (I will return to this point at the conclusion of this paper.)

The issue of who is to be included within a group being recognized as descending from victims of past injustice raises different problems. Most of these problems stem from the fact that groups are made up of individuals, and subgroups of individuals, with different histories, and often quite complex identities. Morally speaking, those histories them-selves can be quite mixed. Consider, for example, the case of the Semi-nole Indians. The Seminoles were bands of Creek Indians who separated from the tribe and settled in northern Florida in the seventeenth cen-tury. They practiced slavery, not only of other Indians captured in battle, but also of Africans whom they purchased or were given as gifts by the British. By the nineteenth century, however, the black Seminole popula-tion had grown and established a strong, independent community, which actually joined with the Seminoles to resist the attempt of Americans to annex Florida. They fought against General Andrew Jackson in the First Seminole War (1817–18), and later in the Second Seminole War (1835–42), and gained a measure of independence. But they were then forced to face the Creek Indians, who were intent on enslaving them, and reintegrating the Seminole Indians into Creek society. Many fled to Mexico to escape Creek slave-hunters, though a good number returned after the Civil War to work as Indian Scouts. They claim that they were promised their own land in Texas in return, but in the end the War Department denied that they had land to offer, and the Bureau of Indian Affairs refused to give them land on the grounds that they were not really Indians.

How should these groups be understood if the issue is the rectification of past injustice? The Seminoles and Creeks were certainly victims of injustice, since theirs is a history of dispossession; but they were also per-petrators of some serious injustices against each other and against Africans, in collaboration with Americans. The black Seminoles appear to have a less ambiguous history, but even they returned to work as scouts in an American army intent on clearing the Southwest of Comanches and Apaches to make room for white settlements. Even they were complicit in serious injustices.

The question is whether the complexity of history and identity should be assumed away in order to focus on the larger story of injustice, in this case the story of African slavery and the dispossession of indigenous peo-ples. If the detail is obliterated in the moral accounting, however, it is not clear that what would be guiding the decision to rectify past injustice are the injustices themselves but other ethical considerations.

More generally, there is a problem in determining whom to include in groups that might be candidates for restitution to the extent that individu-als may be of mixed descent, having ancestors who were both victims and perpetrators of injustice. Others might be descended from a mix of immigrants and ancestors who suffered injustice. This problem may be compounded by the fact that some groups refuse to recognize some individuals or subgroups as members of their communities. At present, for example, the existence of black members of the Seminole Indians is a contentious issue because the sums paid to the Seminoles in compensation for dispossession would have to be further divided if Indians of African descent were included.

None of this is to suggest that identifying the agents who are the descendants of victims of past injustice is impossible. There may well be cases where the identity of the groups in question, and their membership, can readily be settled. My point is only that there are serious obstacles in the way of making a ready determination in many cases.

Yet even if the identities of the descendants of victims of past injustice can be settled, there remains the problem of establishing who should be held liable for restitution. This problem is more serious because even if it is true that injustices were committed in the past and the descendants of victims have suffered as a consequence, this may not be sufficient reason to hold many—or indeed, any—people today responsible for rectifying the situation.

A number of difficulties stand in the way of establishing responsibility for past injustice. One set of difficulties stems from the problem of determining who was responsible for the original injustices that might now generate claims on the part of descendants of victims. If one takes the case of African slavery, the perpetrators of injustice certainly include slave owners, slave traders, and those who supported the institution of slavery, whether by backing governments who upheld it or serving as officials who enforced the law protecting it. But this means some responsibility for the original injustice must be borne by people from other countries who captured and sold slaves. Equally, it is difficult to hold responsible for the injustice of slavery those who had no part in it, or who disapproved of it, or who worked to eliminate it.

It might be argued that all who benefited from slavery can be held responsible to some degree, and one might conclude from this that no one in the United States was free from the taint of this particular injustice. But those who benefited from slavery included not only those whites who lived in the United States but others as well. American assets, including slave enterprises, were held by people in Europe who invested their money abroad; the products of slave labor were sold all around the world; and even some Africans and American Indians took advantage of the slave trade to enrich themselves. White Americans may bear the heaviest burden of responsibility for slavery, as they might also for the dispossession of indigenous peoples, but they do not bear it alone. If that is so, the case for holding their descendants peculiarly responsible for these injustices of the past would be weakened.

The argument for holding these descendants responsible is weakened further by the fact that, with the passing of generations, many countries such as Australia and the United States have admitted immigrants who have had no part in the injustices of the past insofar as they have no ancestors who were even indirectly implicated in wrongs committed in their new country. This view is rejected by Bernard Boxill, who argues that even "white immigrants who arrived in the U.S. after the abolition of slavery" are liable to pay reparations to the descendants of slaves.

They came to take advantage of opportunities, funded by assets to which the slaves had titles, or to take natural assets including land to which the slaves also had titles. The fact that they competed for these opportunities and worked hard misses the point. They have a right to their own earnings, but it does not follow that they own the opportunities that enabled them to make the earnings.[2]

The problem with this argument, however, is that if immigrants can become inculpated in wrongdoing by taking advantage of opportunities that arise out of injustice, it would seem that anyone who so profits can also be inculpated. Investors who never set foot in the United States, but who have traded with a society in which an unpaid debt is owed, would also be liable. There is no reason why residence or membership of a society should make a difference. The number of people who can be held liable could well be more numerous outside the United States than within. But if this is the conclusion to which this principle leads, that is reason to doubt the plausibility of the principle.

Finally, the argument for holding the descendants of the perpetrators or beneficiaries of injustice liable for making restitution is weakened

---

2. Bernard Boxill, "A Lockean Argument for Black Reparations," *The Journal of Ethics* 7 (2003): 63–91, at 77.

by intermarriage and the fact that people's identities are complex mixtures of different inheritances. If responsibility for rectifying past injustice is to be sheeted home to anyone, it would have to be to a different kind of agent.

One possibility here is that we might hold liable not individual persons but certain kinds of group agents. There are a number of candidates, including companies, private organizations such as churches, and governments, from the local to state and national. Such entities might be held responsible for restitution for past injustice because, at least in some cases, they might be not so much the descendants of perpetrators of injustice in the past as entities whose complicity in past injustice is real because they are the same agents as those that originated in the past. Coca-Cola today is the same entity as the Coca-Cola of fifty years ago, and the Catholic Church of today is the same entity as the church of a millennium ago. Companies and churches can be held accountable for the injustices of the past if they themselves committed them. The same might hold for governments, which do not change with each new administration but remain continuous for as long as the polity remains stable and the personnel change without affecting the regime.

This solution might have some merit, but a couple of difficulties ought to be recognized nonetheless. First, there are relatively few companies that have operated for long enough, and continue to exist, which might be found responsible and so held liable for compensating the descendants of their own injustice. There have been many companies in history that were guilty of committing serious injustices in pursuit of profit: the British and Dutch East India Companies are obvious examples. But the number of such corporations that can be identified today as having been responsible for wrongs in the past may be small, if only because corporations are often taken over, or decline and disappear.

Second, if we consider churches to be possible candidates for being held liable for past injustice, we need to ask whether and how far a charitable organization can be held responsible for wrongs committed by those under its authority, and how this should be balanced against the contributions it has made to ameliorating the condition of the poor and the destitute.

In the light of these considerations, perhaps the only entities that can properly be held responsible for rectifying past injustice are the political ones. In part, this is because there may be an argument for holding governments responsible for the wrongs committed in the societies they rule. But more generally, governments could be charged with the task of remedying precisely those wrongs for which it is difficult to identify the real culprits.

III

Governments can clearly be held responsible for rectifying past injustices when they themselves have committed them. If governments can be sued or required to compensate people for taking their property, then they can surely be required to restore people who have been harmed by injustices the government committed a long time ago.

But should governments, or more particularly, the state, be considered a kind of moral agent that can be charged with the duty of acting as a kind of rectifier of last resort of the injustices that societies have been unable to remedy? It is often difficult to establish clear lines of responsibility for many of the wrongs we see in society. This paper has focused on only one kind of difficulty: the problem of identifying the agents involved in issues of historical injustice. Yet it seems evident that some injustices of the past have an enduring legacy, and it surely will not do to let them go unaddressed because clean lines of responsibility cannot readily be drawn. Perhaps it is a part of the role of the state to address precisely these problems: to do justice by considering the relations between different groups and communities that comprise it, and that have shaped the larger political society.

Tempting though this thought may be, it should be resisted. Particularly if the state in question is a liberal democratic state, accountable to its citizens, it is, in the end, obliged to do only what it can justify to those citizens. If there is no plausible justification for holding one part of society responsible for compensating another for injustices committed in the past, there is no warrant for calling upon the state to take any particular action. Or at least, any action it takes in the name of rectifying past injustice could only be seen as having a symbolic quality. In order to repair, not the wrongs done to people in the past, but the fabric of a society that has been torn by serious injustices in its history, it might move to compensate the descendants of victims of past injustice. Its move here would, however, be primarily of symbolic importance. And it could not go too far without raising among the citizenry the question of whether its actions are what justice really demands.

Chandran Kukathas: Who? Whom? Reparations and the Problem of Agency

1. Kukathas uses the example of Nancy and Bill Sykes (borrowed from Dickens's *Oliver Twist*) to show that the child of a perpetrator does not inherit the duty to repair his parent's wrong. Do you agree with Kukathas's analysis? Why or why not?

2. Consider this argument:

   > If you are descended from someone who has suffered a serious injustice, then you are currently owed reparations; nearly everyone has at least one ancestor who has suffered a serious injustice; therefore, nearly everyone has a claim to reparations.

   Do you believe that this argument is sound? Why or why not?

3. What are some of the difficulties that Kukathas presents for trying to identify the legitimate individual recipients of historic injustices? Do you believe that these difficulties can be overcome? Why or why not?

4. What are some of the difficulties that Kukathas presents for trying to identify the legitimate group recipients of historic injustices? Do you believe that these difficulties can be overcome? Why or why not?

5. Reparation requires repair. Can historic injustices be repaired? If so, how so? If not, why not?

42

≡ ❧ ≡

In Favor of Drug Decriminalization
Douglas Husak

Douglas Husak has three primary aims in this selection. First, he seeks to offer some needed clarification of the relevant terms in debates about drug policy. Second, he introduces three argument strategies that are each designed to defend the view that drug use should not be criminalized. Third, he focuses on how debates about drug policy are importantly different from those surrounding other hot-button issues, such as abortion.

Husak first makes clear what he means by "decriminalization," namely, the removal of all criminal prohibitions. He is concerned in this article entirely with the question of whether to decriminalize recreational and medical drug *use*, as opposed to drug possession, manufacture, or sales. He offers an affirmative answer. In his view, since criminalizing some activity brings with it the possibility of punishment, and since no one should be punished just for their recreational or medical use of drugs, we should decriminalize such drug use.

Husak next sketches three types of argument for his thesis. The first is utilitarian or consequentialist. Such arguments claim that drug prohibitions fail to effectively prevent harms from drug use, and in fact cause great harms. The second is a rights-based argument that claims that criminalizing drug use violates our moral rights (e.g., to use our body as we please, or to control our own thought processes). The third strategy, the one he prefers, begins by insisting that any criminal prohibition

---

In Christopher Heath Wellman and Andrew Cohen, eds., *Contemporary Debates in Applied Ethics*, 2nd ed. (Wiley-Blackwell, 2014), pp. 335–344.

be very well justified, since those who violate it are going to be seriously harmed through punishment. He then claims that there has been no good justification offered for criminal prohibitions of drug use.

Husak concludes by drawing our attention to the fact that debates about drug criminalization rarely focus on the *morality* of drug use. And yet most thinkers (Husak included) believe that behavior can rightly be criminalized only if it is immoral. He raises a number of questions about what it would take to show that drug use is immoral, and concludes that in the absence of a compelling case for the immorality of drug use, there can be no good case for criminalizing it.

···

The Meaning of Decriminalization

Philosophers are at their best in clarifying issues. We cannot hope to answer a question unless we understand exactly what it asks. First, one might think we need to identify what *drugs* are. In fact, no accepted definition allows us to categorize whether or not a given substance is a drug. Without an adequate account, how can we be expected to decide whether drugs should be decriminalized? Surely the debate would be improved if a satisfactory definition were available. Despite the problems caused by the absence of a definition, however, I believe we can make progress on questions of criminalization or decriminalization. We can neglect borderline cases and move directly to a discussion of paradigm cases, that is, substances that no reasonable person would fail to categorize as a drug. Should we decriminalize the use of any (currently illicit) drug such as marijuana? Cocaine? The opiates? And should we criminalize the use of any (currently licit) drug such as alcohol? Tobacco? Caffeine? Indeed, sensible discussions of whether criminal punishments are justified must proceed drug by drug; the case in favor of criminalization is far more plausible for some substances than for others. Despite the fact that a detailed analysis would examine one drug at a time, in what follows I will discuss those considerations I believe are applicable to *all* substances we agree to be drugs.

Whether or not we understand exactly what drugs are, it may be surprising that there also is no consensus about the meaning of such terms as *legalization* or *decriminalization*. This lack of consensus is more serious and is bound to compound our confusion. I make little effort to canvass what other commentators take these terms to mean. What *I* mean by proposals to "decriminalize" the use of a given drug is simple—deceptively so. I mean that the *use* of that drug would not be a criminal offense. I take it to be a conceptual truth that criminal laws are those laws that subject persons to state punishment. . . . If persons no longer are eligible for punishment for using a drug, the use of that drug has been decriminalized.

I now want to mention five reasons why I contend that this definition of decriminalization is deceptively simple. First, there is little punishment for mere *use* today. Of course, use is and ought to be punished in situations in which it is especially risky—as when driving or hunting, for example. Still, in most (but not all) jurisdictions throughout the United States, what is punished is *possession* rather than use. Technically, then, drug use per se is not criminalized in most places. But I take the fact that laws punish possession rather than use to be relatively unimportant. Possession is punished rather than use mostly because it is so much easier to prove. Thus I will ignore this technicality in what follows, and will continue to suppose that drug decriminalization pertains to use.

Second, I have indicated that the question to be debated is whether or not drugs should be decriminalized. But expressing the issue in this general way is misleading. Arguably, we cannot decide whether to criminalize or decriminalize drug use without specifying the *purpose* for which that drug is used. If so, our topic is not really about drug use per se, but rather about a particular *kind* of drug use—that is, a particular reason for using drugs. We might well decide that one and the same drug—cocaine, morphine, or Prozac, for example—should be criminalized for some purposes, but decriminalized for others. Presumably, the use of these drugs should not be a criminal offense when people have a medical reason to take them. But public attitudes and state policy often are entirely different when that same drug is used for a non-medical purpose. Although drugs can be used for several different kinds of non-medical purposes, one such purpose is especially significant. This use is *recreational*. It is hard to be precise in characterizing when use is recreational. Roughly, people engage in recreational activities—whether or not these activities involve a drug—in order to seek pleasure, euphoria, satisfaction, or some other positive psychological state. When a drug is used in order to attain a positive psychological state—a drug *high*—I will call that use recreational. Under our present policy, a recreational user of a given drug may face severe punishment, but none at all if his use of that same drug is medical. . . .

Third, decriminalization of a drug means that persons are not subject to punishment simply for using it, but there is no agreement about what kinds of state response amount to punishments. Many reformers argue that drug users should be fined rather than imprisoned. Others argue that drug users should be made to undergo treatment. Still others believe the state should be allowed to seize any illicit drugs persons possess but no additional action should be taken. Each of these ideas has been described as a form of decriminalization. Whether these proposals are compatible with what I mean by decriminalization depends on whether fines, coerced treatment, or seizure of drugs are modes of punishment, rather than alternatives to punishment. I tend to think that these state responses *are* modes of punishment. Even though these modes of punishment almost certainly are preferable to what we now do to drug users, these responses are ruled out by decriminalization as I construe it. . . .

Fourth, decriminalization as I define it has no implications for what should be done to persons who *produce* or *sell* drugs. Therefore, it is not really a comprehensive drug policy that can rival the status quo. As Peter de Marneffe (2013) argues, the considerations that count in favor of decriminalizing use are different from those that pertain to the decriminalization of manufacture and exchange. Thus I recommend that we put production and sale aside. . . .

Fifth and finally, I admit that there is something odd about my understanding of decriminalization. What I call decriminalization in the context of drugs is comparable to what was called *prohibition* in the context of alcohol from 1920 to 1933. In that notorious era, production and sale were banned, but not use or possession. If we replicated the approach of alcohol prohibition in our drug policy, I would call it decriminalization. The oddity of this description underscores the fact that our response to illicit drug users today is far more punitive than anything our country ever did to drinkers of alcohol.

Three Approaches to Decriminalization

At least three different approaches are available to anyone who argues that drug use should be decriminalized. Some of these strategies are more persuasive than others, and each has its strengths and weaknesses. I will briefly summarize two of these approaches before identifying the particular strategy I believe should be especially attractive to a philosopher. Of course, these approaches can be combined to form a stronger case for drug decriminalization than any single rationale. . . .

The first argument in favor of drug decriminalization might be called *utilitarian* or *consequentialist*. The basic idea is that no law should be enacted unless it works. A law works, this argument continues, when it reduces the prevalence of the type of conduct it prohibits without causing unintended effects that are worse than the proscribed conduct itself. More specifically, a criminal law against the use of drugs does not work if it is ineffective or counterproductive.

Critics of criminalization have argued for decades that our drug laws do not work. In the first place, they have done little to reduce the incidence of drug use itself. Despite billions of dollars invested, and millions of persons arrested and convicted, rates of drug use remain high. Even when the use of a given drug falls dramatically in the span of a generation—as with cocaine and LSD—it is hard to believe that criminal punishments account for these patterns. Drug trends are difficult to explain, but punitive state action is only a small part of the story. To some extent, new drugs have replaced the old. Non-medical use of prescription drugs currently exceeds the use of cocaine, opiates, and LSD combined. The threat of punishment is not an especially effective deterrent because illegal drug use is so difficult to detect. Individual users are not foolish to believe they are unlikely to get caught and punished.

An even more worrisome allegation made by utilitarians is that drug laws are counterproductive, causing more harm than good. Drug prohibitions have several pernicious side effects; I will mention only five, but the list could be expanded. First, the enforcement of drug laws has eroded privacy and civil liberties. Second, the health of users is unnecessarily damaged because buyers do not know the strength or purity of the substances they consume. Third, efforts to slow production where drugs are produced have caused unbelievable violence and corruption, especially south of the US border. Fourth, arrests and punishments cost billions of dollars of tax resources that could be put to better purposes.

A fifth counterproductive effect of drug prohibitions is especially worrisome to philosophers who care about social justice. When the state cannot possibly punish *all* of the people who commit a crime, it can only punish *some*. Inevitably, those who get arrested, prosecuted and sentenced are the least powerful. Drug criminalization would have vanished long ago if whites had been sent to prison for drug offenses at the same rate as blacks and Hispanics. Although minorities are no more likely than whites to use illicit drugs, they are far more likely to be arrested, prosecuted, and punished when they do.[1] The enforcement of drug prohibitions has been

---

1. For some useful information on minorities, drugs, and criminal justice, see Erik Kain (2011).

especially devastating to minority communities. And enforcement will remain selective, since not every offender can possibly be punished.

But decriminalization arguments need not be utilitarian or consequentialist. A second argument for decriminalization maintains that drug prohibitions violate moral and legal rights. The enforcement of these laws has always raised concerns about privacy. According to some philosophers—whom we might call *libertarians*—drug prohibitions themselves also violate the right to do whatever you want with your own body unless you harm others. Of course, the existence of this right is controversial. Arguably, whether a person has a right to do something to his own body depends on what happens when he does it. But additional rights might be violated by drug prohibitions. These rights become easier to identify if we return to the issue of exactly what it is that drug laws are designed to prevent. As I have indicated, use per se is rarely prohibited. Instead, the use of most drugs is prohibited only for a given purpose—to produce a drug "high." In case there is any doubt, let me cite the California criminal statute governing nitrous oxide. This statute makes it a crime for "any person [to possess] nitrous oxide . . . with the intent to breathe [or] inhale . . . for purposes of causing a condition of intoxication, elation, euphoria, dizziness, stupefaction, or dulling of the senses or for the purpose of, in any manner, changing . . . mental processes" (California Penal Code, 2012, §381(b)). The ultimate objective of this statute is to prevent a person from breathing something in order to change her mental state. It is hard to see how this objective is legitimate in a country committed to freedom of thought.

Although utilitarian and rights-based arguments for decriminalization are powerful, I prefer a third strategy. Again, we must begin by asking the right question. In my judgment, the most fundamental issue is not whether to *de*criminalize the use of any or all drugs, but whether to *criminalize* the use of any or all drugs. We should not presuppose that the status quo is just; it must be defended. If I have posed the right question to ask, I believe its answer is as follows. The best reason *not* to criminalize drug use is that no argument *in favor* of criminalizing drug use is any good—not nearly good enough to justify the punishment of drug users. Admittedly, this argument is necessarily inconclusive, placing those who favor decriminalization in the unenviable position of trying to prove a negative. How can anyone hope to show that no argument *in favor* of criminalizing drug use is very good? Until an argument has been put on the table, there is nothing to which one can respond. All that can be done is to respond to the best arguments that have been given.

Three arguments are heard most frequently in favor of punishing drug users. First, drugs are bad for the development and maturation of children and adolescents. Any debate about decriminalization is certain to turn to the effects of drugs on our nation's youth. Second, drugs are unhealthy both physically and psychologically. Advocates of decriminalization can expect to be reminded of a study purporting to show that drugs kill brain cells, destroy memory, or drain motivation. Third, drugs are correlated with violent behavior and criminal activity. Many persons arrested for serious crimes test positive for drugs. A vast literature explores these three arguments, each of which must be examined carefully. Although I do not argue the point here, none of these arguments can withstand close scrutiny in my judgment. Alone or in combination, they do not show the state is justified in prohibiting drugs and punishing persons who use them.

A fourth argument is sometimes produced. Many people oppose decriminalization because they predict it would cause a huge increase in drug consumption. The specter of greater drug use is the trump card my opponents play when supporting our existing policy. I am very skeptical of the accuracy of these predictions; they should be taken with a grain of salt. Recall the meaning of decriminalization. The only change that this policy requires is that the state would not *punish* anyone simply for using a drug. The state may adopt any number of devices to discourage drug use, as long as these devices are not punitive. Even more importantly, institutions other than the state can and do play a significant role in discouraging drug use. After decriminalization, some of these institutions might exert even more influence. Private businesses, schools, insurance companies, and universities, to cite just a few examples, might adopt policies to deter drug use. Suppose that employers fired or denied promotions to workers who use cocaine. Suppose that schools barred students who drink alcohol from participating in extracurricular activities. Suppose that insurance companies charged higher premiums to policy holders who smoke tobacco. Suppose that colleges denied loans and grants to undergraduates who use marijuana. I do not endorse any of these ideas; many seem unwise and destined to backfire. I simply point out that these institutions could continue to do a great deal to decrease drug consumption even if use were decriminalized.

But an even more important point is that these predictions may not be relevant to the topic at hand. Philosophers should search for a respectable reason to criminalize drug use. Predictions about how decriminalization will cause an increase in drug consumption simply do not provide such a reason. Indeed, this reason could be given against repealing virtually *any* law, however unjustified it may be. Let me illustrate this point by providing an example of an imaginary crime that I assume everyone would agree to be unjustified. Imagine the state sought to curb obesity by enacting a statute criminalizing the eating of pizza. Suppose a group of philosophers were convened to debate whether we should *change* this law and *decrimi-nalize* the consumption of pizza. Someone would be bound to protest that repealing this offense would cause persons to eat greater amounts of pizza. They would probably be correct. But surely this prediction would not serve to justify retaining this imaginary crime. If we lack a good reason to attack the problem of obesity by punishing pizza eaters in the first place, the effects of repeal on pizza consumption would not provide such a reason. And so with drugs. This prediction does not provide a good reason to continue to impose punishments unless we already *have* such a reason. Of course, whether we have such a reason is precisely the point at issue.

One reason I prefer my third strategy for decriminalization is that it makes minimal assumptions about controversial empirical and normative questions. First, it does not require that we take a stand on whether our regime of drug prohibitions can be tweaked to become more effective and less counterproductive. Moreover, it makes minimal assumptions about justice. Philosophers famously disagree about the content of principles of justice. It seems safe to assume, however, that no one should be punished unless there are excellent reasons for doing so. Punishment, after all, is the worst thing our state is allowed to do to us. The imposition of punishment must satisfy a very demanding standard of justification. Even though principles of justice are enormously controversial, it is hard to believe that anyone rejects the minimal assumption I make here.

We have excellent reasons to punish people who commit theft or rape. These offenses *harm* others by violating their rights. But this rationale cannot explain why drug users should be punished. I do not think there is any sense of harm or any theory of rights that can be invoked to show that I harm someone or violate his rights when I inject heroin or smoke crack. At most, I *risk* harm to myself and/or to others when I use a drug. Should users be punished for creating these risks? Notice the enormous burden any such argument for criminalization would have to bear. Well over 120 million living Americans have used an illicit drug at some point in their lives—about half of our population aged 12 and over. Over 22 million Americans use an illicit drug each month—on literally billions of occasions.[2] Very few of these occasions produced any harm. Longitudinal studies do not indicate that the population of persons who ever have used illicit drugs is very different from the population of lifetime abstainers in any ways that seem relevant to criminalization.[3] Thus an argument for criminalization would have to justify punishing many people whose behavior is innocuous in order to try to prevent a risk that materializes in a very tiny percentage of cases.

. . . Although some drugs are worse than others, I have yet to hear a persuasive case for punishing people merely for using *any* existing drug. But no single argument for decriminalization can hope to respond to each argument for criminalization. We must respond argument by argument and, I think, drug by drug. I do not know anyone who proposes to punish persons who use caffeine, for example. Surely this consensus exists because of empirical facts about caffeine—about how it affects those who use it as well as how it affects society generally. Despite the problems caused by tobacco and alcohol, no prominent figure advocates that we punish persons simply for smoking or drinking. These facts about licit substances are important in the present context. If neither tobacco nor alcohol *should* be punished, we must ask how the drugs we think should be punished differ. If no morally relevant differences between these substances can be identified, we should treat them similarly for legal purposes.

If there is a good reason to criminalize the use of any drug that actually exists, we have yet to find it. We need a better reason to criminalize something other than predictions about how its frequency would increase if punishments were not imposed. These predictions are dubious both normatively and (in this case) empirically. Despite my uncertainty about the future, there is *one* prediction about which we can be absolutely confident. After decriminalization, those who use illicit drugs will not face arrest and prosecution. The lives of drug users would not be devastated by a state that subjects them to punishment. The single prediction we can safely make about decriminalization is that it will not devastate the lives of the hundreds of thousands of people who otherwise would be punished for the crime of using drugs.

---

2. An excellent source of drug use data can be found at DrugWarFacts.org
3. Many longitudinal studies of drug users have been conducted. The most famous is Shedler and Block (1990).

How Debates about Drug Decriminalization Differ from Other Decriminalization Debates

No state should punish persons for engaging in conduct that is morally permissible. Imagine that someone asks *why* he is punished, what he is punished *for*, or what he has done wrong to deserve his punishment. No one who punishes him would respond that he has not done anything wrong, but his punishment is justified nonetheless. This response would be nearly unintelligible. If I am correct about the close connection between wrongfulness and justified punishment, it is crucial to determine the moral status of anything we propose to criminalize. Despite the obvious importance of this issue, advocates of drug decriminalization have treated it in a peculiar way. In other contexts, live controversies about criminalization begin with direct efforts to assess the morality of the conduct in question. Consider the recent history of the debate about the criminalization of homosexual relations, for example. No philosopher opposed the criminalization of this conduct on the ground that the prohibition was ineffective and/or counterproductive. Instead, they tended to argue that criminalization is misguided because homosexual relations are morally permissible. Of course, they were obligated to respond to the (weak) arguments in favor of the contrary position. Still, criminalization is objectionable in principle if the underlying conduct is morally permissible. Thus they had little need to assess the contingent and uncertain empirical considerations involving the enforcement of prohibitions of gay sex.

It is noteworthy that the debate about drug decriminalization has proceeded differently. Commentators rarely purport to address the moral status of drug use itself. In fact, philosophically sophisticated arguments about the morality of drug use are difficult to find anywhere. Opponents of decriminalization frequently assert that drug use is wrongful, but make almost no effort to substantiate their charge. . . .

What *should* philosophers think about the moral status of drug use? To underscore the novelty of this question, I place it in a specific context. Suppose you are a professor of moral philosophy and a student enters your office and announces his intention to use a given drug: crack or heroin, let us suppose. His friends report this drug to be exhilarating, and he wants to experience the sensation himself. He claims to be motivated by the same curiosity that has led him to hang-glide and scuba-dive. The student is not at all interested in his legal obligations or worried about the risks of being caught and arrested. Suppose further that you set aside the possible consequences for your job or professional reputation should your advice become public and brought to the attention of the dean or department chair. The student seeks advice solely from a moral perspective, and that is the perspective from which you purport to advise him. To the best of my knowledge, this basic issue is almost completely untouched in the relevant commentary produced by moral philosophers who debate drug decriminalization. Most professors would have an easier time counseling students who seek advice about obtaining an abortion.

It would be impossible to offer sensible advice to this student without identifying the possible benefits of drug use. Even minimal risks are foolish in the absence of good reasons to take them. It is easy to recommend literature that recites the harms of drug experimentation, but credible commentary on the benefits of drug use is much more difficult to find. As long as drug use is thought to produce all harms and no benefits, its moral status is easy to specify. Presumably, however, most people consume drugs largely because they regard their effects as pleasurable and euphoric. Is pleasure itself a good? If so, is the pleasure caused by drug use any different? Is it good to satisfy curiosity about how something feels? And how are these goods (if they exist at all) to be balanced against the risks drug use imposes? Should this calculus include other advantages frequently alleged on behalf of drug use: spiritual enlightenment, artistic creativity, consciousness expansion, and the like? Even those academic philosophers who regard psychological hedonic states as intrinsic goods—or even as the *only* intrinsic good—have precious little to say about drugs. But even if we would refuse to be connected to a "pleasure machine" that guaranteed we would have more positive psychological sensations than we experience in our existing reality, the possible use of drugs to supplement a good life must be taken seriously.

These largely untouched questions become more vexing as we move from real to imaginary drugs—even though intuitions about thought experiments are a staple of moral and legal philosophy on a wide range of other topics. Consider, by way of contrast, how philosophical reflection on the permissibility of torture is driven by intuitions about "ticking bomb" scenarios—whether or not such scenarios have ever been actualized in the real world. A comparable use of thought-experiments is conspicuously absent in questions about drugs and drug policy. Advocates of decriminalization should be asked whether any drugs can be imagined that it would be *im*permissible to use. What are the properties of these drugs that render their use impermissible, and how confident should we be that these properties are absent in the drugs we propose to allow? Prohibitionists should be asked a parallel question. Can they imagine drugs that it would be permissible to use? What are the properties of these drugs that render their use permissible, and how confident should we be that the drugs to be proscribed lack these properties? These sorts of questions are familiar to moral and legal theorists in other contexts. By focusing on imaginary cases, we have some chance of making progress on moral questions about drug use without the need to take a stand on contested empirical issues.

I think it is easy to imagine a drug that people should be punished for using. Some such drugs are vividly portrayed in great works of fiction. Consider the substance that transformed Dr Jekyll into Mr Hyde. If a drug literally turns users into homicidal monsters, we would have excellent reasons to prohibit its consumption. Fortunately, no such drug actually exists. Are there good reasons to criminalize the use of any real drug? Those who answer affirmatively have the burden of showing why the state is *justified* in doing so—in punishing persons who merely use that drug.

Conclusion

We need to be clear about the meaning of terms such as criminalization and decriminalization in order to have any reasonable chance of deciding whether users of any or all drugs should be punished. I have contended that a drug is decriminalized when persons who use it are no longer subject to state punishment. If I am correct, the most basic question in the entire debate is not whether or why given drugs should be *de*criminalized, but whether or why given drugs should be *criminalized*. Finally, I have suggested that a sensible position on this debate should not evade the issue of whether and under what circumstances the use of a given drug is morally permissible.

References

California Penal Code (2012) §381(b). http://codes.lp.findlaw.com/cacode/PEN/3/1/10/s381b (last accessed 6/17/13).

deMarneffe, P. (2013) Vice laws and self-sovereignty. *Criminal Law and Philosophy* 7(1): 29–41.

Kain, E. (2011) The war on drugs is a war on minorities and the poor. *Forbes*, June 28. http://www.forbes.com/sites/erikkain/2011/06/28/the-war-on-drugs-is-a-war-on-minorities-and-the-poor/(last accessed 6/17/13).

Shedler, J. and Block, J. (1990) Adolescent drug use and psychological health. *American Psychologist* 612. https://druglibrary.org/schaffer/kids/Adolescent_Drug_Use_ALL.htm (last accessed 6/17/13).

Douglas Husak: In Favor of Decriminalization

1. Husak claims, but does not try to show, that there is no good argument for criminalizing drug use. Can you think of such a good argument? If so, present it.
2. Why does Husak think that pointing to the results of drug use is largely irrelevant for establishing the legitimacy of drug prohibitions?
3. If drug use should be legal, should drug manufacture be legal? Why or why not?
4. Do you believe that either a utilitarian or a rights-based argument for decriminalization works? If so, present and defend that argument. If not, give reasons to support your verdict.
5. What is the moral status of recreational drug use? Is it always morally acceptable, always morally forbidden, or sometimes one and sometimes the other? State the reasons in support of your view.

43

America's Unjust Drug War

Michael Huemer

....

Michael Huemer argues that the recreational use of drugs, including cocaine and heroin, ought to be legal, and that the long-standing U.S. policy of criminalizing their possession and sale is morally unjustified. He presents, and then seeks to rebut, what he regards as the two most prominent arguments for their criminalization.

These arguments are, first, that drugs are very harmful to those who use them, and the prevention of such harm justifies the state in criminalizing drug use. The second argument is that drug use reliably causes harm to third parties, and since the state's mission is to prevent such harm, the state is again justified in outlawing drug use. Huemer agrees that there are some cases in which drug use does threaten others (such as when one drives while under the influence), and agrees that such activity ought to be prohibited. But, he argues, this represents a small minority of cases—in all other situations, drug use ought to be legally permitted.

Huemer then turns from criticizing prohibitionist arguments, and offers a positive argument for decriminalization. This argument claims that we have a natural moral right—i.e., one that exists independently of its recognition by society—to use our bodies as we please, so long as we do not violate the rights of others in doing so. Unusual exceptions aside, we do not violate another's rights when we use drugs. Therefore we have a moral right use drugs. Huemer thinks that the government thus violates our moral rights when it prohibits most drug use.

....

Michael Huemer, "America's Unjust Drug War," in Bill Masters, ed., *The New Prohibition* (Accurate Press 2004), pp. 133–144.

Should the recreational use of drugs such as marijuana, cocaine, heroin, and LSD be prohibited by law? *Prohibitionists* answer yes. They usually argue that drug use is extremely harmful both to drug users and to society in general, and possibly even immoral, and they believe that these facts provide sufficient reasons for prohibition. *Legalizers* answer no. They usually give one or more of three arguments: First, some argue that drug use is not as harmful as prohibitionists believe, and even that it is sometimes beneficial. Second, some argue that drug prohibition "does not work," in other words, it is not very successful in preventing drug use and/or has a number of very bad consequences. Lastly, some argue that drug prohibition is unjust or violates rights.

I won't attempt to discuss all these arguments here. Instead, I will focus on what seem to me the three most prominent arguments in the drug legalization debate: first, the argument that drugs should be outlawed because of the harm they cause to drug users; second, the argument that they should be outlawed because they harm people other than the user; and third, the argument that drugs should be legalized because drug prohibition violates rights. I shall focus on the moral/philosophical issues that these arguments raise, rather than medical or sociological issues. I shall show that the two arguments for prohibition fail, while the third argument, for legalization, succeeds.

I. Drugs and Harm to Users

The first major argument for prohibition holds that drugs should be prohibited because drug use is extremely harmful to the users themselves, and prohibition decreases the rate of drug abuse. This argument assumes that the proper function of government includes preventing people from harming themselves. Thus, the argument is something like this:

1. Drug use is very harmful to users.
2. The government should prohibit people from doing things that harm themselves.
3. Therefore, the government should prohibit drug use.

Obviously, the second premise is essential to the argument; if I believed that drug use was very harmful, but I did *not* think that the government should prohibit people from harming themselves, then I would not take this as a reason for prohibiting drug use. But premise (2), if taken without qualification, is extremely implausible. Consider some examples of things people do that are harmful (or entail a risk of harm) to themselves: smoking tobacco, drinking alcohol, eating too much, riding motorcycles, having unprotected or promiscuous sex, maintaining relationships with inconsiderate or abusive boyfriends and girlfriends, maxing out their credit cards, working in dead-end jobs, dropping out of college, moving to New Jersey, and being rude to their bosses. Should the government prohibit all of these things?[1] Most of us would agree that the government should not prohibit *any* of these things, let alone all of them. And this is not merely for logistical or practical reasons; rather, we think that controlling those activities is not the business of government.

Perhaps the prohibitionist will argue, not that the government should prohibit *all* activities that are harmful to oneself, but that it should prohibit activities that harm oneself in a certain way, or to a certain degree, or that also have some other characteristic. It would then be up to the prohibitionist to explain how the self-inflicted harm of drug use differs from the self-inflicted harms of the other activities mentioned above. Let us consider three possibilities.

(1) One suggestion would be that drug use also harms people other than the user; we will discuss this harm to others in section II below. If, as I will contend, neither the harm to drug users nor the harm to others justifies prohibition, then there will be little plausibility in the suggestion that the combination of harms justifies prohibition. Of course, one could hold that a certain threshold level of total harm must be reached before prohibition of an activity is justified, and that the combination of the harm of drugs to users and their harm to others passes that threshold even though neither kind of harm does so by itself. But if, as I will contend, the "harm to users" and "harm to others" arguments both fail because it is not the government's business to apply criminal sanctions to prevent the kinds of harms in question, *then* the combination of the two harms will not make a convincing case for prohibition.

(2) A second suggestion is that drug use is generally *more* harmful than the other activities listed above. But there seems to be no reason to believe this. As one (admittedly limited) measure of harmfulness, consider the mortality statistics. In the year 2000, illicit drug use directly or indirectly caused an estimated 17,000 deaths in the United States.[2] By contrast,

---

1. Douglas Husak (*Legalize This! The Case for Decriminalizing Drugs*, London: Verso, 2002, pages 7, 101–103) makes this sort of argument. I have added my own examples of harmful activities to his list.

2. Ali Mokdad, James Marks, Donna Stroup, and Julie Gerberding, "Actual Causes of Death in the United States, 2000," *Journal of the American Medical Association* 291, no. 10, 2004: 1238–1245, page 1242. The statistic includes estimated contributions of drug use to such causes of death as suicide, homicide, motor vehicle accidents, and HIV infection.

tobacco caused an estimated 435,000 deaths.[3] Of course, more people use tobacco than use illegal drugs,[4] so let us divide by the number of users: tobacco kills 4.5 people per 1000 at-risk persons per year; illegal drugs kill 0.66 people per 1000 at-risk persons per year.[5] Yet almost no one favors outlawing tobacco and putting smokers in prison. On a similar note, obesity caused an estimated 112,000 deaths in the same year (due to increased incidence of heart disease, strokes, and so on), or 1.8 per 1000 at-risk persons.[6] Health professionals have warned about the pandemic of obesity, but no one has yet called for imprisoning obese people.

There are less tangible harms of drug use—harms to one's general quality of life. These are difficult to quantify. But compare the magnitude

---

3. Mokdad et al., page 1239; the statistic includes estimated effects of secondhand smoke. The Centers for Disease Control provides an estimate of 440,000 ("Annual Smoking-Attributable Mortality, Years of Potential Life Lost, and Economic Costs—United States, 1995-1999," *Morbidity and Mortality Weekly Report* 51, 2002: 300–303, http://www.cdc.gov/mmwr/PDF/wk/mm5114.pdf, page 300).

4. James Inciardi ("Against Legalization of Drugs" in Arnold Trebach and James Inciardi, *Legalize It? Debating American Drug Policy*, Washington, D.C.: American University Press, 1993, pages 161, 165) makes this point, accusing drug legalizers of "sophism." He does not go on to calculate the number of deaths per user, however.

5. I include both current and former smokers among "at risk persons." The calculation for tobacco is based on Mokdad et al.'s report (page 1239) that 22.2% of the adult population were smokers and 24.4% were former smokers in 2000, and the U.S. Census Bureau's estimate of an adult population of 209 million in the year 2000 ("Table 2: Annual Estimates of the Population by Sex and Selected Age Groups for the United States: April 1, 2000 to July 1, 2007 [NC-EST2007-02]," release date May 1, 2008, http://www.census.gov/popest/national/asrh/NC-EST2007/NC-EST2007-02.xls). The calculation for illicit drugs is based on the report of the Office of National Drug Control Policy (hereafter, ONDCP) that, in the year 2000, 11% of persons aged 12 and older had used illegal drugs in the previous year ("Drug Use Trends," October 2002, http://www.whitehousedrugpolicy.gov/publications/factsht/druguse/), and the U.S. Census Bureau's report of a population of about 233 million Americans aged 12 and over in 2000 ("Table 1: Annual Estimates of the Population by Sex and Five-Year Age Groups for the United States: April 1, 2000 to July 1, 2007 [NC-EST2007-01]," release date May 1, 2008, http://www.census.gov/popest/national/asrh/NC-EST2007/NC-EST2007-02.xls). Interpolation was applied to the Census Bureau's "10 to 14" age category to estimate the number of persons aged 12 to 14. In the case of drugs, if "at risk persons" are considered to include only those who admit to having used illegal drugs in the past month, then the death rate is 1.2 per 1000 at-risk persons.

6. Based on 112,000 premature deaths caused by obesity in 2000 (Katherine Flegal, Barry Graubard, David Williamson, and Mitchell Gail, "Excess Deaths Associated With Underweight, Overweight, and Obesity," *Journal of the American Medical Association* 293, no. 15, 2005: 1861-7), a 30.5% obesity rate among U.S. adults in 2000 (Allison Hedley, Cynthia Ogden, Clifford Johnson, Margaret Carroll, Lester Curtin, and Katherine Flegal, "Prevalence of Overweight and Obesity Among U.S. Children, Adolescents, and Adults, 1999-2002," *Journal of the American Medical Association* 291, no. 23, 2004: 2847–2850) and a U.S. adult population of 209 million in 2000 (U.S. Census Bureau, "Table 2," *op. cit.*).

of the harm to one's quality of life that one can bring about by, say, dropping out of high school, working in a dead-end job for several years, or marrying a jerk—these things can cause extreme and lasting detriment to one's well-being. And yet no one proposes jailing those who drop out, work in bad jobs, or make poor marriage decisions. The idea of doing so would seem ridiculous, clearly beyond the state's prerogatives.

(3) Another suggestion is that drug use harms users *in a different way* than the other listed activities. What sorts of harms do drugs cause? First, illicit drugs may worsen users' health and, in some cases, entail a risk of death. But many other activities—including the consumption of alcohol, tobacco, and fatty foods; sex; and (on a broad construal of "health") automobiles—entail health risks, and yet almost no one believes those activities should be criminalized.

Second, drugs may damage users' relationships with others—particularly family, friends, and lovers—and prevent one from developing more satisfying personal relationships.[7] Being rude to others can also have this effect, yet no one believes you should be put in jail for being rude. Moreover, it is very implausible to suppose that people should be subject to criminal sanctions for ruining their personal relationships. I have no general theory of what sort of things people should be punished for, but consider the following example: suppose that I decide to break up with my girlfriend, stop calling my family, and push away all my friends. I do this for no good reason—I just feel like it. This would damage my personal relationships as much as anything could. Should the police now arrest me and put me in jail? If not, then why should they arrest me for doing something that only has a *chance* of indirectly bringing about a similar result? The following seems like a reasonable political principle: If it would be wrong (because not part of the government's legitimate functions) to punish people for *directly bringing about* some result, then it would also be wrong to punish people for doing some other action on the grounds that the action has a *chance* of bringing about that result indirectly. If the state may not prohibit me from *directly cutting off* my relationships with others, then the fact that my drug use *might have the result* of damaging those relationships does not provide a good reason to prohibit me from using drugs.

Third, drugs may harm users' financial lives, costing them money, causing them to lose their jobs or not find jobs, and preventing them from

---

7. Inciardi, pages 167, 172.

getting promotions. The same principle applies here: if it would be an abuse of government power to prohibit me from directly bringing about those sorts of negative financial consequences, then surely the fact that drug use might indirectly bring them about is not a good reason to prohibit drug use. Suppose that I decide to quit my job and throw all my money out the window, for no reason. Should the police arrest me and put me in prison?

Fourth and finally, drugs may damage users' moral character, as James Q. Wilson believes:

> [I]f we believe—as I do—that dependency on certain mind-altering drugs *is* a moral issue and that their illegality rests in part on their immorality, then legalizing them undercuts, if it does not eliminate altogether, the moral message. That message is at the root of the distinction between nicotine and cocaine. Both are highly addictive; both have harmful physical effects. But we treat the two drugs differently not simply because nicotine is so widely used as to be beyond the reach of effective prohibition, but because its use does not destroy the user's essential humanity. Tobacco shortens one's life, cocaine debases it. Nicotine alters one's habits, cocaine alters one's soul. The heavy use of crack, unlike the heavy use of tobacco, corrodes those natural sentiments of sympathy and duty that constitute our human nature and make possible our social life.[8]

In this passage, Wilson claims that the use of cocaine (a) is immoral, (b) destroys one's humanity, (c) alters one's soul, and (d) corrodes one's sense of sympathy and duty. One problem with Wilson's argument is the lack of evidence supporting claims (a)-(d). Before we put people in prison for corrupting their souls, we should require some objective evidence that their souls are in fact being corrupted. Before we put people in prison for being immoral, we should require some argument showing that their actions are in fact immoral. Perhaps Wilson's charges of immorality and corruption all come down to the charge that drug users lose their sense of sympathy and duty—that is, claims (a)-(c) all rest upon claim (d). It is plausible that *heavy* drug users experience a decreased sense of sympathy with others and a decreased sense of duty and responsibility. Does this provide a good reason to prohibit drug use?

Again, it seems that one should not prohibit an activity on the grounds that it may indirectly cause some result, unless it would be appropriate to

---

8. James Q. Wilson, "Against the Legalization of Drugs," *Commentary* 89, 1990: 21–28, page 26.

prohibit the direct bringing about of that result. Would it be appropriate, and within the legitimate functions of the state, to punish people for being unsympathetic and undutiful, or for behaving in an unsympathetic and undutiful way? Suppose that Howard—though not a drug user—doesn't sympathize with others. When people try to tell Howard their problems, he just tells them to quit whining. Friends and coworkers who ask Howard for favors are rudely rebuffed. Furthermore—though he does not harm others in ways that would be against our current laws—Howard has a poor sense of duty. He doesn't bother to show up for work on time, nor does he take any pride in his work; he doesn't donate to charity; he doesn't try to improve his community. All around, Howard is an ignoble and unpleasant individual. Should he be put in jail?

If not, then why should someone be put in jail merely for doing something that would have a *chance* of causing them to become like Howard? If it would be an abuse of governmental power to punish people for being jerks, then the fact that drug use may cause one to become a jerk is not a good reason to prohibit drug use.

II. Drugs and Harm to Others

Some argue that drug use must be outlawed because drug use harms the user's family, friends, and coworkers, and/or society in general. A report produced by the Office of National Drug Control Policy states:

> Democracies can flourish only when their citizens value their freedom and embrace personal responsibility. Drug use erodes the individual's capacity to pursue both ideals. It diminishes the individual's capacity to operate effectively in many of life's spheres—as a student, a parent, a spouse, an employee—even as a coworker or fellow motorist. And, while some claim it represents an expression of individual autonomy, drug use is in fact inimical to personal freedom, producing a reduced capacity to participate in the life of the community and the promise of America.[9]

At least one of these alleged harms—dangerous driving—*is* clearly the business of the state. For this reason, I entirely agree that people should be prohibited from driving while under the influence of drugs. But what about the rest of the alleged harms?

Return to our hypothetical citizen Howard. Imagine that Howard—again, for reasons having nothing to do with drugs—does not value

---

9. ONDCP, *National Drug Control Strategy 2002*, Washington, D.C.: Government Printing Office, http://www.whitehousedrugpolicy.gov/publications/policy/03ndcs/, pages 1–2.

freedom, nor does he embrace personal responsibility. It is unclear exactly what this means, but, for good measure, let us suppose that Howard embraces a totalitarian political ideology and denies the existence of free will. He constantly blames other people for his problems and tries to avoid making decisions. Howard is a college student with a part-time job. However, he is a terrible student and worker. He hardly ever studies and frequently misses assignments, as a result of which he gets poor grades. As mentioned earlier, Howard comes to work late and takes no pride in his work. Though he does nothing against our current laws, he is an inattentive and inconsiderate spouse and parent. Nor does he make any effort to participate in the life of his community, or the promise of America. He would rather lie around the house, watching television and cursing the rest of the world for his problems. In short, Howard does all the bad things to his family, friends, coworkers, and society that the ONDCP says *may* result from drug use. And most of this is voluntary.

Should Congress pass laws against what Howard is doing? Should the police then arrest him, and the district attorney prosecute him, for being a loser?

Once again, it seems absurd to suppose that we would arrest and jail someone for behaving in these ways, undesirable as they may be. Since drug use only has a *chance* of causing one to behave in each of these ways, it is even more absurd to suppose that we should arrest and jail people for drug use on the grounds that drug use has these potential effects.

III. The Injustice of Drug Prohibition

Philosopher Douglas Husak has characterized drug prohibition as the greatest injustice perpetrated in the United States since slavery.[10] This is no hyperbole. If the drug laws are unjust, then America has over half a million people unjustly imprisoned.[11]

---

10. Husak, *Legalize This!*, page 2.
11. In 2006, there were approximately 553,000 people in American prisons and jails whose most serious offense was a drug offense. This included 93,751 federal inmates (U.S. Department of Justice, "Prisoners in 2006," December 2007, http://www.ojp.usdoj.gov/bjs/pub/pdf/p06.pdf, page 9). State prisons held another 269,596 drug inmates, based on the 2006 state prison population of 1,377,815 ("Prisoners in 2006," page 2) and the 2004 rate of 19.57% of state prisoners held on drug charges ("Prisoners in 2006," page 24). Local jails held another 189,204 drug inmates, based on the 2006 local jail population of 766,010 ("Prisoners in 2006," page 3) and the 2002 rate of 24.7% of local inmates held on drug charges (U.S. Department of Justice, "Profile of Jail Inmates 2002," published July 2004, revised October 12, 2004, http://www.ojp.usdoj.gov/bjs/pub/pdf/pji02.pdf, page 1). In all cases, I have used the latest statistics available as of this writing.

Why think the drug laws are *unjust*? Husak's argument invokes a principle with which few could disagree: it is unjust for the state to punish people without having a good reason for doing so.[12] We have seen the failure of the most common proposed rationales for drug prohibition. If nothing better is forthcoming, then we must conclude that prohibitionists have no rational justification for punishing drug users. We have deprived hundreds of thousands of people of basic liberties and subjected them to severe hardship conditions, for no good reason.

This is bad enough. But I want to say something stronger: it is not merely that we are punishing people for no good reason. We are punishing people for exercising their natural rights. Individuals have a right to use drugs. This right is neither absolute nor exceptionless; suppose, for example, that there existed a drug which, once ingested, caused a significant proportion of users, without any further free choices on their part, to attack other people without provocation. I would think that stopping the use of this drug would be the business of the government. But no existing drug satisfies this description. Indeed, though I cannot take time to delve into the matter here, I think it is clear that the drug *laws* cause far more crime than drugs themselves do.

The idea of a right to use drugs derives from the idea that individuals own their own bodies. That is, a person has the right to exercise control over his own body—including the right to decide how it should be used, and to exclude others from using it—in a manner similar to the way one may exercise control over one's (other) property. This statement is somewhat vague; nevertheless, we can see the general idea embodied in common sense morality. Indeed, it seems that if there is *anything* one would have rights to, it would be one's own body. This explains why we think others may not physically attack you or kidnap you. It explains why we do not accept the use of unwilling human subjects for medical experiments, even if the experiments are beneficial to society—the rest of society may not decide to use your body for its own purposes without your permission. It explains why some believe that women have a right to an abortion—and why some others do not. The former believe that a woman has the right to do what she wants with her own body; the latter believe that the fetus is a distinct person, and a woman does not have the right to harm *its* body.

---

12. Husak, *Legalize This!*, page 15. See his chapter 2 for an extended discussion of various proposed rationales for drug prohibition, including many issues that I lack space to discuss here.

Virtually no one disputes that, *if* a fetus is merely a part of the woman's body, *then* a woman has a right to choose whether to have an abortion; just as virtually no one disputes that, *if* a fetus is a distinct person, then a woman lacks the right to destroy it. Almost no one disputes that persons have rights over their own bodies but not over others' bodies.

The right to control one's body cannot be interpreted as implying a right to use one's body in *every* conceivable way, any more than we have the right to use our property in every conceivable way. Most importantly, we may not use our bodies to harm others in certain ways, just as we may not use our property to harm others. But drug use seems to be a paradigm case of a legitimate exercise of the right to control one's own body. Drug consumption takes place in and immediately around the user's own body; the salient effects occur *inside* the user's body. If we consider drug use merely as altering the user's own body and mind, it is hard to see how anyone who believes in rights at all could deny that it is protected by a right, for: (a) it is hard to see how anyone who believes in rights could deny that individuals have rights over their own bodies and minds, and (b) it is hard to see how anyone who believes in such rights could deny that drug use, considered merely as altering the user's body and mind, is an example of the exercise of one's rights over one's own body and mind.

Consider two ways a prohibitionist might object to this argument. First, a prohibitionist might argue that drug use does not *merely* alter the user's own body and mind, but also harms the user's family, friends, co-workers, and society. I responded to this sort of argument in section II. Not just *any* way in which an action might be said to "harm" other people makes the action worthy of criminal sanctions. Here we need not try to state a general criterion for what sorts of harms make an action worthy of criminalization; it is enough to note that there are some kinds of "harms" that virtually no one would take to warrant criminal sanctions, and that these include the "harms" I cause to others by being a poor student, an incompetent worker, or an apathetic citizen.[13] That said, I agree with the prohibitionists at least this far: no one should be permitted to drive or operate heavy machinery while under the influence of drugs that impair their ability to do those things; nor should pregnant mothers be permitted

---

13. Husak (*Drugs and Rights*, Cambridge University Press, 1992, pages 166–168), similarly, argues that no one has a *right* that I be a good neighbor, proficient student, and so on, and that only harms that violate rights can justify criminal sanctions.

to ingest drugs, if it can be proven that those drugs cause substantial risks to their babies (I leave open the question of what the threshold level of risk should be, as well as the empirical questions concerning the actual level of risk created by illegal drugs). But, in the great majority of cases, drug use does not harm anyone in any *relevant* ways—that is, ways that we normally take to merit criminal penalties—and should not be outlawed.

Second, a prohibitionist might argue that drug use fails to qualify as an exercise of the user's rights over his own body, because the individual is not truly acting freely in deciding to use drugs. Perhaps individuals only use drugs because they have fallen prey to some sort of psychological compulsion, because drugs exercise a siren-like allure that distorts users' perceptions, because users don't realize how bad drugs are, or something of that sort. The exact form of this objection doesn't matter; in any case, the prohibitionist faces a dilemma. If users do not freely choose to use drugs, then it is unjust to *punish* them for using drugs. For if users do not choose freely, then they are not morally responsible for their decision, and it is unjust to punish a person for something he is not responsible for. But if users *do* choose freely in deciding to use drugs, then this choice is an exercise of their rights over their own bodies.

I have tried to think of the best arguments prohibitionists could give, but in fact prohibitionists have remained puzzlingly silent on this issue. When a country goes to war, it tends to focus on how to win, sparing little thought for the rights of the victims in the enemy country. Similarly, one effect of America's declaring "war" on drug users seems to have been that prohibitionists have given almost no thought to the rights of drug users. Most either ignore the issue or mention it briefly only to dismiss it without argument.[14] In an effort to discredit legalizers, the Office of National Drug Control Policy produced the following caricature—

> The easy cynicism that has grown up around the drug issue is no accident. Sowing it has been the deliberate aim of a decades-long campaign by proponents of legalization, critics whose mantra is "nothing works," and whose central insight appears to be that they can avoid having to propose the unmentionable—a world where drugs are

---

14. See Inciardi for an instance of ignoring and Daniel Lungren ("Legalization Would Be a Mistake" in Timothy Lynch, ed., *After Prohibition*, Washington, D.C.: Cato Institute, 2000, page 180) for an instance of unargued dismissal. Wilson (page 24) addresses the issue, if at all, only by arguing that drug use makes users worse parents, spouses, employers, and co-workers. This fails to refute the contention that individuals have a right to use drugs.

ubiquitous and where use and addiction would skyrocket—if they can hide behind the bland management critique that drug control efforts are "unworkable."[15]

—apparently denying the existence of the central issues I have discussed in this essay. It seems reasonable to assume that an account of the state's right to forcibly interfere with individuals' decisions regarding their own bodies is not forthcoming from these prohibitionists.

IV. Conclusion

Undoubtedly, the drug war has been disastrous in many ways that others can more ably describe—in terms of its effects on crime, on police corruption, and on other civil liberties, to name a few. But more than that, the drug war is morally outrageous in its very conception. If we are to call ours a free society, we cannot deploy force to deprive people of their liberty and property for whimsical reasons. The exercise of such coercion requires a powerful and clearly stated rationale. Most of the reasons that have been proposed in the case of drug prohibition would be considered feeble if advanced in other contexts. Few would take seriously the suggestion that people should be imprisoned for harming their own health, being poor students, or failing to share in the American dream. It is still less credible that we should imprison people for an activity that only *may* lead to those consequences. Yet these and other, similarly weak arguments form the core of prohibition's defense.

Prohibitionists are likewise unable to answer the argument that individuals have a right to use drugs. Any such answer would have to deny either that persons have rights of control over their own bodies, or that consuming drugs constituted an exercise of those rights. We have seen that the sort of harms drug use allegedly causes to society do not make a case against its being an exercise of the user's rights over his own body. And the claim that drug users can't control their behavior or don't know what they are doing renders it even more mysterious why one would believe drug users deserve to be punished for what they are doing.

I will close by responding to a query posed by prohibition-advocate James Inciardi:

> The government of the United States is not going to legalize drugs anytime soon, if ever, and certainly not in this [the 20th] century. So why

---

15. ONDCP, *National Drug Control Strategy 2002*, page 3.

spend so much time, expense, and intellectual and emotional effort on a quixotic undertaking? . . . [W]e should know by now that neither politicians nor the polity respond positively to abrupt and drastic strategy alterations.[16]

The United States presently has 553,000 people unjustly imprisoned. Inciardi may—tragically—be correct that our government has no intention of stopping its flagrant violations of the rights of its people any time soon. Nevertheless, it remains the duty of citizens and of political and social theorists to identify the injustice, and not to tacitly assent to it. Imagine a slavery advocate, decades before the Civil War, arguing that abolitionists were wasting their breath and should move on to more productive activities, such as arguing for incremental changes in the way slaves are treated, since the southern states had no intention of ending slavery any time soon. The institution of slavery is a black mark on our nation's history, but our history would be even more shameful if no one at the time had spoken against the injustice.

Is this comparison overdrawn? I don't think so. The harm of being unjustly imprisoned is qualitatively comparable (though it usually ends sooner) to the harm of being enslaved. The increasingly popular scapegoating and stereotyping of drug users and sellers on the part of our nation's leaders is comparable to the racial prejudices of previous generations. Yet very few seem willing to speak on behalf of drug users. Perhaps the unwillingness of those in public life to defend drug users' rights stems from the negative image we have of drug users and the fear of being associated with them. Yet these attitudes remain baffling. I have used illegal drugs myself. I know of many decent and successful individuals who have used illegal drugs. Nearly half of all Americans over the age of 11 have used illegal drugs—including at least two United States Presidents, one Vice-President, one Speaker of the House, and one Supreme Court Justice.[17] But now leave aside the absurdity of recommending criminal

---

16. Inciardi, page 205.

17. In 2006, 45% of Americans aged 12 and over reported having used at least one illegal drug (U.S. Department of Health and Human Services, "National Survey on Drug Use and Health," 2006, Table 1.1B, http://www.oas.samhsa.gov/NSDUH/2k6NSDUH/tabs/Sect1peTabs1to46. htm). Bill Clinton, Al Gore, Newt Gingrich and Clarence Thomas have all acknowledged past drug use (reported by David Phinney, "Dodging the Drug Question," ABC News, August 19, 1999, http://abcnews.go.com/sections/politics/DailyNews/prez_questions990819.html). George W. Bush has refused to state whether he has ever used illegal drugs. Barack Obama has admitted to cocaine and marijuana use (*Dreams from My Father*, New York: Random House, 2004, p. 93).

sanctions for all these people. My point is this: if we are convinced of the injustice of drug prohibition, then—even if our protests should fall on deaf ears—we can not remain silent in the face of such a large-scale injustice in our own country. And, fortunately, radical social reforms *have* occurred, more than once in our history, in response to moral arguments.

Michael Huemer: America's Unjust Drug War

1. Huemer admits that using drugs can be harmful to the user, but points out that alcohol, tobacco, unhealthy food, and unsafe sex can also be harmful. Is there any morally relevant difference between the harms caused by drugs and the harms caused by these other activities?
2. Huemer invokes the following principle: "if it would be wrong to punish people for *directly bringing about* some result, then it would also be wrong to punish people for doing some other action on the grounds that the action has a *chance* of bringing about that result indirectly." Do you find this principle plausible? Why or why not?
3. Consider Huemer's case involving Howard. Should Howard be punished for acting the way he does? If not, does it follow that we should not punish drug users?
4. Do individuals have a right to use drugs? What is Huemer's argument for thinking that they do? Do you find it convincing?
5. Suppose that we accept Huemer's contention that we ought to legalize recreational drug use. Does it follow that all of those currently in prison for drug-related offenses have been unjustly imprisoned?

Against the Legalization of Drugs
Peter de Marneffe

∙∙∙

Peter de Marneffe argues for a moderate position on the sale and use of drugs. On the one hand, he believes that drug *use* ought to be decriminalized. According to de Marneffe, people have a moral right to self-sovereignty—a right to do as they please, so long as their actions do not harm or wrong others—that entitles them to put into their bodies anything they like, so long as this does not involve violating the rights of others. The right to self-sovereignty implies that people have a moral right to use drugs, so long as such use is not likely to lead to drug users violating the rights of others. And if they have a moral right to use drugs, then it is wrong of the government to criminalize such use.

On the other hand, the government does have the moral authority to criminalize the manufacture and sale of substantial amounts of drugs. And, according to de Marneffe, the government is fully justified in using that authority to criminalize such behavior. The argument against drug legalization is simple: if the sale and manufacture of drugs is legalized, then many more people will abuse drugs, or abuse them more often than they currently do. Such abuse has terrible consequences. Governments should do what they can to reduce the terrible consequences that beset their citizens. So governments should make the manufacture and sale of drugs illegal.

De Marneffe devotes the bulk of his article to presenting and then replying to a variety of objections to his proposal. These include the

From Andrew I. Cohen and Christopher Heath Wellman, eds., *Contemporary Debates in Applied Ethics*, 2nd ed. (Blackwell, 2013), pp. 346–357.

objection that such governmental prohibitions are ineffective; that they are objectionably paternalistic; that they violate the rights of drug users; that they have led to the many problems of the so-called War on Drugs; that they have immoral effects on imprisoned youth; that they lead to and reinforce racial discrimination; that they only increase the amount of violence in society; that they foster the corruption of government officials in the foreign countries where drugs are manufactured; that it is inconsistent to legally allow the sale and manufacture of cigarettes and alcohol while prohibiting the sale and manufacture of other drugs; that if drugs ought to be illegal then so too should the sale and manufacture of unhealthy foods; and, finally, that there is no scientific proof that drug abuse would increase with the legalization of drugs.

Introduction

By the *legalization of drugs* I mean the removal of criminal penalties for the manufacture, sale, and possession of large quantities of recreational drugs, such as marijuana, cocaine, heroin, and methamphetamine. In this chapter, I present an argument against drug legalization in this sense. But I do not argue against *drug decriminalization*, by which I mean the removal of criminal penalties for recreational drug use and the possession of small quantities of recreational drugs. Although I am against drug legalization, I am for drug decriminalization. So one of my goals here is to explain why this position makes sense as a matter of principle.

The argument against drug legalization is simple. If drugs are legalized, they will be less expensive and more available. If drugs are less expensive and more available, drug use will increase, and with it, proportionately, drug abuse. So if drugs are legalized, there will be more drug abuse. By drug abuse I mean drug use that is likely to cause harm.

Ineffectiveness Objection

A common objection is that drug laws do not work. The imagined proof is that people still use drugs even though they are illegal. But this is a bad argument. People are still murdered even though murder is illegal, and we do not conclude that murder laws do not work or that they ought to be repealed. This is because we think these laws work well enough in reducing murder rates to justify the various costs of enforcing them. So even if drug laws do not eliminate drug abuse, they might likewise reduce it by enough to justify their costs.

Why should we think that drug laws reduce drug abuse? For one thing, our general knowledge of human psychology and economic behavior provides a good basis for predicting that drug use will increase if drugs are legalized. People use drugs because they enjoy them. If it is easier and less expensive to do something enjoyable, more people will do it and those who do it already will do it more often. Laws against the manufacture and sale of drugs make drugs less available, because they prohibit their sale in convenient locations, such as the local drug or liquor or grocery store, and more expensive, because the retail price of illegal drugs reflects the risk to manufacturers and sellers of being arrested and having their goods confiscated. So if drugs are legalized, the price will fall and they will be easier to get. "Hey honey, feel like some heroin tonight?" "Sure, why not stop at Walgreens on the way home from picking up the kids?"

The claim that drug laws reduce drug abuse is also supported by the available empirical evidence. During Prohibition it was illegal to manufacture, sell, and transport "intoxicating liquors" (but not illegal to drink alcoholic beverages or to make them at home for one's own use). During this same period, deaths from cirrhosis of the liver and admissions to state hospitals for alcoholic psychosis declined dramatically compared to the previous decade (Warburton, 1932, pp. 86, 89). Because cirrhosis and alcoholic psychosis are highly correlated with heavy drinking, this is good evidence that Prohibition reduced heavy drinking substantially. Recent studies of alcohol consumption also conclude that heavy drinking declines with increases in price and decreases in availability (Edwards et al., 1994; Cook, 2007). Further evidence that drug use is correlated with availability is that the use of controlled psychoac- tive drugs is significantly higher among physicians and other health care professionals (who have much greater access to these drugs) than it is among the general population (Goode, 2012, pp. 454–455), and that veterans who reported using heroin in Vietnam, where it was legal, reported not using it on returning to the USA, where it was illegal (Robins et al., 1974).

For all these reasons it is a safe bet that drug abuse would increase if drugs were legalized, and it is hard to find an expert on drug policy who denies this. This alone, however, does not settle whether laws against drugs are a good policy because we do not know by how much drug abuse would increase if drugs were legalized and we do not know how much harm would result from this increase in drug abuse. It is important to recognize, too, that drug laws also cause harm by creating a black market, which fosters violence and government corruption, and by sending people to prison. It is possible that the harms created by drug laws outweigh their benefits in reducing drug abuse. I will say more about this possibility below, but first I address some philosophical objections to drug laws.

Paternalism Objection

One objection is that drug laws are paternalistic: they limit people's liberty for their own good. A related objection is that drug laws are moralistic: they impose the view that drug use is wrong on everyone, including those who think it is good. It is true that drug use can be harmful, but most people who use drugs do not use them in a way that harms some-one or that creates a significant risk of harm. This is true even of so-called "hard drugs" such as heroin and cocaine. Is it not wrong for the government to prohibit us from doing something we enjoy if it causes no harm?

To oppose drug legalization, however, is to oppose the removal of penalties for the *commercial manufacture* and *sale* and *possession* of *large quantities* of drugs; it is not to support criminal penalties for the use or possession of small quantities of drugs. To oppose drug legalization is therefore not to hold that anyone should be prohibited from doing something they enjoy for their own good, or that the government should impose the controversial view that drug use is wrong on everyone.

Violation of Rights Objection

A more fundamental objection to drug laws is that they violate our rights. I believe there is some truth to this. So I want to explain why it makes sense to oppose drug legalization even though some drug laws do violate our rights.

Each of us has a right of self-sovereignty: a moral right to control our own minds and bodies. Laws that prohibit people from using drugs or from possessing small quantities of them violate this right because the choice to use drugs involves an important form of control over our minds and bodies, and recreational drug use does not usually harm anyone or pose a serious risk of harm. The choice to use drugs involves an important form of control over our minds partly because recreational drug use is a form of mood control, which is an important aspect of controlling our minds.

There are also perceptual experiences that we can have only as the result of using certain drugs, such as LSD, and certain kinds of euphoria that we can experience only as the result of using certain drugs, such as heroin. The choice to put a drug into one's body—to snort it, smoke it, inject it, or ingest it—is also an important form of control over one's body. Because we have a right to control our own minds and bodies, the government is justified in prohibiting us from using a drug only if the choice to use this drug is likely to harm someone, which is not true of most recreational drug use. Laws that prohibit us from using recreational drugs therefore violate our right of self-sovereignty and for this reason should be repealed.

The choice to manufacture or sell drugs, in contrast, does not involve an important form of control over one's own mind or body—no more than the choice to manufacture or sell any commercial product does. These are choices to engage in a commercial enterprise for profit, and may therefore be regulated or restricted for reasons of public welfare, just as any other commercial enterprise may be. One might think that there is something "hypocritical" or "inconsistent" about prohibiting the manufacture and sale of drugs and not prohibiting their possession and use, but this is confused. If one opposes drug legalization on the ground that the government should do whatever it can to reduce drug abuse, regardless of whether it violates anyone's rights, then it would be inconsistent to oppose drug criminalization. But it is not inconsistent to oppose drug criminalization if one opposes drug legalization on the ground that the government should do whatever it can to reduce drug abuse consistent with respect for individual rights. This is because it makes sense to hold that whereas drug criminalization violates the right of self-sovereignty, non-legalization does not (de Marneffe, 2013).

Some might argue that non-legalization violates the right of self-sovereignty too, because it is not possible to use drugs if no one is legally permitted to sell them. But this is obviously false because people still use drugs even though selling them is illegal. Although this fact is sometimes cited to demonstrate the futility of drug control, ironically it makes drug control easier to justify. If drug non-legalization really did make it impossible to use drugs, and so to have the unique experiences they provide, this policy would arguably violate the right of self-sovereignty on this ground. But drug control laws do not make drug use impossible; they only increase the price and reduce the availability of drugs. This is no more a violation of self-sovereignty than a decision by the local supermarket not to carry a certain food or to double its price.

High Costs of the Drug War Objection

Laws against the manufacture and sale of drugs might of course still be a bad policy even if they do not violate the right of self-sovereignty. This is because these laws have costs, and these costs might outweigh the benefits of these laws in reducing drug abuse. Laws against the manufacture and sale of drugs create a black market, which fosters violence, because when disputes arise in an illegal trade the disputants cannot go to the legal system for resolution. The black market also fosters government corruption, because those in an illegal trade must pay government officials for protection from arrest and confiscation. Drug laws also cost money to enforce, which might be better spent in other ways. Finally, drug laws result in some people being arrested and imprisoned and being left with criminal records. It is certainly possible that these costs outweigh the benefits of drug control in reducing drug abuse.

It is important to understand, though, that drug control policy need not be as costly as the so-called War on Drugs, which is current US policy. So even if the War on Drugs is too costly, as critics maintain, it does not follow that drugs should be legalized. The case against drug legalization rests on the assumption that the benefits of drug control in reducing drug abuse are sufficient to justify the costs of drug control *once these costs are reduced as much as possible consistent with effective drug control*. By *effective* drug control, I mean a policy that reduces drug abuse substantially compared to the amount of drug abuse that would exist if drugs were legalized. I do not mean a policy that eliminates drug abuse altogether. It is no more possible to eliminate drug abuse than it is to eliminate crime. But just as effective crime control is still possible, effective drug control is possible too. And if it is possible to have effective drug control without the high costs of the War on Drugs, then the benefits of prohibiting the manufacture and sale of drugs are more likely to justify the costs.

One compelling objection to the War on Drugs is to the sentencing rules for drug law violations, which require judges to impose long prison terms for drug trafficking offenses. Critics rightly argue that mandatory sentences and long prison terms for selling drugs are morally indefensible. These are not, however, necessary features of effective drug control policy. They are not features of European drug control policy, for example. So it makes sense to oppose harsh mandatory penalties while also opposing drug legalization.

Drug control works primarily by increasing price and reducing availability, which can be accomplished by reliably enforcing laws against the manufacture and sale of drugs with moderate penalties. Where it is illegal to manufacture and sell drugs, most business persons avoid the drug trade because they do not want to be arrested and have their goods confiscated. This reduces supply, which increases price. Where it is illegal to sell drugs, stores that aim to retain their licenses also do not sell them, which reduces availability. Heavy penalties no doubt drive the price up even higher and decrease availability even more by increasing the risks of drug trafficking— but the biggest increases in price and the biggest reductions in availability come simply from the illegality of the trade itself together with reliable enforcement of laws against manufacture and sale (Kleiman et al., 2011, pp. 48–50). If effective drug control does not require harsh mandatory penalties, then the fact that such penalties are unjustifiable is not a good argument for drug legalization.

Effect on Imprisoned Youths Objection

Another objection to US drug control policy is that it results in many young people being arrested, imprisoned, and left with criminal records, who would otherwise not suffer these misfortunes. Some might retort that if a person chooses to deal drugs illegally, he cannot legitimately complain about the foreseeable consequences of his choice. But this response is inadequate because by making drugs illegal the government creates a hazard that otherwise would not exist. By making the manufacture and sale of drugs illegal, the government creates a lucrative illegal market, and the money-making opportunities that this market creates are attractive, especially to young people who lack a college education or special training, because they can make much more money by dealing drugs than by doing anything else. When the government creates a system of penalties for manufacturing and selling drugs it therefore creates a hazard; it creates a tempting opportunity to make money and then imposes penalties for making money in this way.

In general, the government has an obligation to reduce the risk to individuals of being harmed by the hazards it creates. When the government tests weapons, for example, it must take care that people do not wander into the testing areas. Bright signs are not enough; it must also build fences and monitor against trespass. The government also has an obligation to help young people avoid the worst consequences of their willingness to take unwise risks. It has an obligation to require teenagers to wear helmets when they ride a motorcycle, for example. So when the government creates the hazard of imprisonment by making the manufacture and sale of drugs illegal, it must guard against the likelihood of imprisonment, and it must take special care to reduce this likelihood for young people who commonly lack a proper appreciation of the negative impact that conviction and imprisonment will have on their lives. For all these reasons, the government must structure drug laws so that young people have an adequate opportunity to avoid being imprisoned for drug offenses, and to avoid acquiring a criminal record. This means, among other things, that no one should be arrested for a drug offense prior to receiving an official warning; no penalty for a first conviction should involve prison time; initial jail or prison sentences should be short and subject to judicial discretion; and imprisonment for subsequent convictions should increase in length only gradually and also be subject to judicial discretion.

Racial Discrimination Objection

A related objection to the War on Drugs is that those imprisoned for drug offenses in the USA are disproportionately black inner city males (Alexander, 2012). This objection would be addressed to some degree by the changes in sentencing policy just proposed, but one might predict that any effective drug control policy would result in the same sort of disproportionality, which some might see as an argument for drug legalization. However, it also is important to consider the potential negative impact of drug legalization on inner city communities. Drug legalization will result in a substantial increase in drug abuse. Drug abuse commonly leads parents to neglect their children, and to neglect their own health and jobs, which harms their children indirectly. Drug abuse also distracts teenagers from their schoolwork, interferes with the development of a sense of responsibility, and makes young people less likely to develop the skills necessary for acquiring good jobs as adults. If drugs are legalized, there will therefore be more child neglect as a result and more truancy by teenagers. This is likely to have an even more devastating impact on the life prospects of young people in non-affluent inner city communities than it has on the life prospects of young people in affluent suburbs. I suspect this is the primary reason why many inner city community leaders oppose drug legalization.

It is true that incarcerating large numbers of inner city youths for drug offenses also has a negative impact on inner city communities. A man who is in jail cannot be present as a parent or make money to support his children, and a person with a criminal record has a harder time finding a decent job. These consequences alone would warrant drug legalization if there were no downside. If we assume, however, that drug legalization would result in a substantial increase in child neglect and adolescent truancy, then legalization does not seem like a good way to improve the life prospects of inner city youth overall. It seems better to maintain laws against the manufacture and sale of drugs, and reduce the number of those who are convicted and imprisoned for drug offenses. This would be consistent with effective drug control because the number of dealers in prison could be reduced dramatically without making drugs noticeably cheaper or easier to get (Kleiman et al., 2011, p. 203).

Increase in Violence Objection

Another objection to US drug control policy is that it has increased violence in other countries, particularly Mexico. Americans enjoy using drugs and are willing to pay for them. Because it is illegal to manufacture and sell drugs in the USA, American drug control policy creates opportunities for people south of the border to get rich by making drugs and selling them wholesale to retailers north of the border. Because those in the drug trade use violence to control market share and to intimidate law enforcement, US drug laws result in violence. If drugs were legalized in the USA, the recreational drug market would presumably be taken over by large US drug, liquor, and food companies and it would not be possible for anyone in Mexico to get rich by selling illegal drugs to Americans, which would eliminate the associated violence there.

Drug legalization, however, is not the only way to reduce drug-related violence abroad. Here are some alternative strategies:

- The USA might legalize the private production of marijuana for personal use (the way it was legal during Prohibition to make alcoholic beverages at home). Because much of the Mexican drug trade is in marijuana, this would reduce its profitability, and so presumably the associated violence.
- The USA might also concentrate its drug enforcement efforts in Mexico on the most violent drug trafficking organizations, as opposed to concentrating on the biggest and most profitable organizations, which would create incentives for those in the Mexican drug trade to be less violent.

- The USA might also ease border control at entry points not on the US-Mexico border. The violence in Mexico is created partly by the fact that it is the primary conduit of cocaine from South and Central America to North America. If the USA were to loosen border control in Florida, fewer drugs would travel through Mexico. Because the USA imports so many goods, it is not possible to stop drugs from coming into this country. Some would cite this as proof that drug control is futile, but this conclusion is unwarranted because border controls still raise the retail price of drugs substantially, which results in less drug abuse (Kleiman et al., 2011, pp. 162–163). The suggestion here is that a general policy of border control is consistent with US law enforcement experimenting with different border control policies with an eye to reducing violence abroad (Kleiman et al., 2011, p. 170).

None of these proposals would eliminate drug-related violence in Mexico, but it is unrealistic to think that criminal violence in Mexico would be eliminated by drug legalization in the USA. After all, what will career criminals in Mexico do once they cannot make money via the drug trade? Presumably they will turn to other criminal activities, such as kidnapping, extortion, and human trafficking, which also involve violence.

Corruption of Foreign Governments Objection

Another objection to US drug control policy is that it fosters the corruption of foreign governments. Because those in the foreign drug trade need protection from arrest, prosecution, and confiscation of assets, because they are willing to pay government officials to look the other way, and because some government officials are willing to accept this payment, the drug trade increases government corruption. If drugs were legalized in the USA, this would destroy the illegal market abroad, which would remove an important contributing factor in government corruption.

It is naive, though, to think that US drug control policy is the primary cause of government corruption abroad. Although we associate police corruption with drug trafficking, the latter tends to flourish where government officials are already corrupt (Kleiman et al., 2011, p. 177). [A] foreign police force that is not fully professionalized will be susceptible to financial corruption regardless of whether the USA legalizes drugs.

The Inconsistency Objection

Another argument against drug laws is that it is hypocritical or inconsistent for our government to prohibit the manufacture and sale of heroin, cocaine, and methamphetamine while permitting the manufacture and sale of alcohol and cigarettes. Drinking and smoking cause far more harm than other kinds of recreational drug use. This is partly because there is so much more drinking and smoking, which is partly because the manufacture and sale of alcohol and cigarettes are legal. But drinking and smoking are also inherently more harmful than other forms of drug use. Drinking alcohol is correlated much more highly with violence, property crime, and accidental injury than the use of heroin is, and a regular user of heroin who uses it safely—in moderate doses with clean equipment—does not face any significant health risk as a result, whereas cigarette smoking is known to cause heart and lung disease. So it can seem that if the government is justified in prohibiting the manufacture and sale of heroin, it must also be justified in prohibiting the manufacture and sale of alcohol and cigarettes.

This would be a good objection to drug laws if laws against the manufacture and sale of alcoholic beverages and cigarettes were wrong in principle, but it is hard to see why they would be. After all, drinking and smoking cause a lot of harm and neither policy would violate the right of self-sovereignty discussed above, because a law that prohibits only the manufacture and sale of a drug does not prohibit its possession or make its use impossible. Of course, the suggestion that alcohol prohibition might be justified is commonly dismissed with the incantation that Prohibition was a disastrous failure, but historians agree that Prohibition succeeded in substantially reducing heavy drinking, and it would have been even more effective had its enforcement been adequately funded and had it been administered from the outset by law enforcement professionals instead of by political appointees (Okrent, 2010, pp. 134–145, 254–261). Prohibition did fail politically, but so did Reconstruction and the Equal Rights Amendment. The fact that a policy is rejected or abandoned does not show that it was wrong in principle. Finally, it is worth noting that alcohol prohibition still exists in some parts of this country, on Indian reservations, for example, and that these policies make sense as part of an effort to reduce alcoholism and the harms associated with it.

It is not necessary, though, to advocate alcohol prohibition in order to defend other drug laws, because there are relevant differences between them. For one thing, the institution of alcohol prohibition now is likely not to reduce heavy drinking by as much as drug non-legalization reduces drug abuse. Drinking is widely accepted and a part of normal social rituals, in a way that heroin, cocaine, and methamphetamine use is not. This means that alcohol prohibition now would not work in tandem with a strong social stigma, which would presumably reduce its effectiveness in reducing alcohol abuse. It is possible, too, that in an environment of social acceptance, sharply increasing the excise taxes on alcoholic beverages would achieve almost as much as prohibition in reducing the harms caused by heavy drinking with none of the costs of prohibition (though it is worth noting here that liquor industry lobbying has been more effective in preventing excise tax increases than it was in preventing Prohibition). There are also important ways in which instituting alcohol prohibition now would be more burdensome than continuing with drug non-legalization. Many people have built their lives around the alcoholic beverage industry. If alcohol were now prohibited, many of these people would lose their jobs, and many companies, restaurants and bars would go out of business, which would be a serious hardship for owners and employees. In contrast, people who go into the drug trade do so knowing that it is illegal. So the burden on them of maintaining drug laws is not as great as the burden that alcohol prohibition would impose on those who have built their lives around the liquor trade on the assumption that the manufacture and sale of alcohol will remain legal. Ironically, it is drug *legalization* that would burden those in the illegal drug trade, in much the same way as Prohibition burdened those in the legal liquor trade: by depriving them of their livelihood.

There are also important differences between illicit drugs and cigarettes. Drug legalization, I assume, would result in a substantial increase in drug abuse, which, I assume, would also result in a substantial increase in child neglect and adolescent truancy, which would have a substantial negative impact on the life prospects of many young people. Cigarette smoking, in contrast, does not make someone a worse parent or a worse student or employee. Furthermore, because heavy smoking typically has a negative impact on a person's life only toward the end when he or she is older, smoking as a young person is less likely than adolescent drug abuse to have a negative impact on the *kind* of life a person has. Finally, although psychologically challenging, it is quite possible to quit smoking as an adult and so to reduce the long-term health consequences of starting to smoke as a teenager—much easier than it is to reverse the long-term negative consequences of having had inadequate parenting or having failed out of high school as the result of drug abuse. Given these differences between the consequences of smoking and drug abuse, one can consistently oppose the legalization of drugs for the reasons I have given here without advocating prohibiting the manufacture and sale of cigarettes.

In explaining above how one might consistently oppose the legalization of drugs without advocating alcohol prohibition, I observed that drinking is so widespread and socially accepted that alcohol prohibition is likely to reduce heavy drinking by less than drug abuse is reduced by laws against the manufacture and sale of illicit drugs. This same point might now be given as an argument for legalizing marijuana: marijuana use is so widespread and socially accepted that laws against the manufacture and sale of marijuana do not do very much to reduce it. It might also be argued that legalizing marijuana would not result in a dramatic increase in drug abuse because marijuana is less subject to abuse than other drugs (including alcohol). Finally, legalizing marijuana in the USA would dramatically reduce the drug trade in Mexico, which would result in a corresponding reduction in violence and government corruption there. Should not marijuana be legalized, then, even if other drugs should not be?

In this chapter I am arguing against the view that the manufacture and sale of *all* drugs should be legalized; I am not arguing that there is *no* drug that should be legalized. Suppose that marijuana legalization would not result in a substantial increase in drug abuse. Suppose that most of those who would use marijuana if it were legalized are already using it and using it almost as much as they want to. Or suppose that marijuana use itself is harmless and does not lead to the use of more harmful drugs. If either of these things is true, then marijuana should be legalized. It is also possible, though, that, as a result of legalization, many more young people would use marijuana than do now, and that a sizable fraction of them would use it in ways that interfere with their education or employment, and that a sizable fraction of them would go on to abuse more harmful drugs who would otherwise never have tried them. Because I am not sure that these things would not happen, I do not support legalizing marijuana. With more information, though, I might change my mind. So it is important to make clear that whether a drug should be legalized depends on the consequences of legalizing it, and not on whether any *other* drug should be legalized. Hence, even if marijuana should be legalized, it would not follow that heroin, cocaine, and methamphetamine should be legalized too.

Unhealthy Foods Objection

Another argument against drug laws is that if the government is justified in prohibiting us from putting a drug into our bodies for our own good, then it is also justified in prohibiting us from putting unhealthy foods into our bodies for our own good. The suggestion that the government is entitled to control what we eat strikes many of us as outrageous. Why is it not likewise outrageous for the government to prohibit us from using recreational drugs?

For the reasons given above, I think it is. Laws that prohibit us from using drugs—or drinking alcohol or smoking cigarettes—violate our right of self-sovereignty in the same way that laws that prohibit us from eating high fat or high sugar foods would. However, just as laws that prohibit the manufacture and sale of drugs do not violate our self-sovereignty, laws that regulate the sale of fatty or sugary foods do not either. So if the government prohibits fast food restaurants from selling humongous hamburgers, or prohibits convenience stores from selling sugary soda in giant cups, or prohibits vending machines in schools from stocking items with high fat or sugar content, no one's right of self-sovereignty is violated. Whether these policies are a good idea is a separate question, but if they are a bad idea, it is not because they violate anyone's rights.

No Scientific Proof Objection

In arguing against drug legalization, I assume that drug abuse would increase substantially if drugs were legalized. Some might now object that there is no proof of this, and this is true, but there is also no proof that murder rates will rise if murder is decriminalized. That is, this assumption is not warranted by any set of controlled laboratory experiments or randomized field trials. Should murder therefore be decriminalized? Obviously not. Some might say that the freedom to murder is not a very important liberty, so the standard of proof need not be so high. But most of us also support on the basis of assumptions for which there is no scientific proof policies that do impinge on important liberties. For example, many of us support restrictions on campaign contributions on the assumption that unrestricted contributions would result in more political corruption. But there is no scientific proof of this, and restrictions on campaign contributions impinge on the important freedom of political speech.

Many of us also support immigration laws on the assumption that unrestricted immigration would lower our quality of life. But there is also no scientific proof of this, and freedom of movement is also an important liberty. Should we withdraw our support for these policies just because we support them on the basis of scientifically unproven assumptions? I think not. In general we are justified in supporting a legal restriction for a reason if two conditions are met: (a) this reason would justify this restriction if it was based on true assumptions, and (b) we are warranted by the available evidence in believing that the relevant assumptions are true. So if we are warranted by the available evidence in believing that drug abuse will increase if drugs are legalized, then we are justified in making this assumption for the purpose of evaluating drug control policy. And we are warranted in making this assumption—by what we know about patterns of alcohol and drug consumption and more generally about human psychology and economic behavior.

Conclusion

If drug abuse would increase substantially if drugs were legalized, and laws that prohibit the manufacture and sale of drugs do not violate our right of self-sovereignty, and effective drug control requires only moderate penalties reliably and conscientiously enforced, then it makes sense to oppose drug legalization. This, in essence, is the argument I have made here. In evaluating drug policy, it is important, too, to consider how public policy would be shaped if drugs were legalized. Beer, liquor, and cigarette companies already do as much as they can to prevent the government from adopting policies that would reduce drinking and smoking and so their associated harms. They do as much as they can to prevent increases in excise taxes, which increase the price of alcohol and cigarettes, and so reduce their sales, and so smoking and drinking. They do as much as they can to prevent restrictions on the hours and locations of the sale of alcohol and cigarettes. They do as much as they can to prevent licensing and rationing policies, which would reduce the amount of alcohol consumed by problem drinkers. And they do as much as they can to make their products attractive through advertising, particularly to young people. We should expect that if drugs are legalized, drug companies will behave in the same way: that they will do everything they can to prevent the enactment of laws that restrict the marketing and sale of heroin, cocaine, and methamphetamine, and that they will do everything they can to market these drugs successfully, particularly to young people, who will be their most profitable market. Because drug use is currently stigmatized, drug companies are unlikely to be as successful as liquor companies in preventing sound public policy, at least initially. But if we envision a world in which legal drug companies are legally trying to persuade consumers to buy recreational drugs from legal vendors and legally trying to prevent any socially responsible legislation that reduces their legal sales, it is hard to envision a world that does not have much more drug abuse.

References

Alexander, M. (2012) *The New Jim Crow: Mass Incarceration in the Age of Color-blindness*. New York: New Press.

Cook, P. J. (2007) *Paying the Tab: The Economics of Alcohol Policy*. Princeton, NJ: Princeton University Press.

de Marneffe, P. (2013) Vice laws and self-sovereignty. *Criminal Law and Philosophy* 7: 29–41.

Edwards, G., Anderson, P., Babor, T. F., et al. (1994) *Alcohol Policy and the Public Good*. New York: Oxford University Press.

Goode, E. (2012) *Drugs in American Society*, 8th ed. New York: McGraw-Hill.

Kleiman, M. A. R., et al. (2011) *Drugs and Drug Policy: What Everyone Needs to Know*. New York: Oxford University Press.

Okrent, D. (2010) *Last Call: The Rise and Fall of Prohibition*. New York: Scribner.

Robins, L. N., et al. (1974) Drug use by U.S. army in Vietnam: a follow-up on their return home. *American Journal of Epidemiology* 99: 235–249.

Warburton, C. (1932) *The Economic Results of Prohibition*. New York: Columbia University Press.

Peter de Marneffe: Against the Legalization of Drugs

1. Is it consistent to favor drug decriminalization while also urging that the sale and manufacture of drugs be illegal? Why or why not?
2. Reconstruct the argument from self-sovereignty in support of drug decriminalization. Is that argument sound?
3. Is there another objection to the criminalization of the sale and manufacture of drugs that de Marneffe has failed to consider and that you find compelling? If so, what is it?
4. De Marneffe has considered eleven objections to his argument. Are any of these objections stronger than he supposes? If so, which ones?

45

The Case Against Perfection
Michael J. Sandel

Michael Sandel argues against genetic enhancement and engineering by asking us to focus on what he calls "the gifted character of human powers and achievements." By this he means that our talents and our abilities are not entirely a product of our efforts. And this, he argues, is a very good thing. That much of what is important in a life is effectively outside of our control should encourage in us a degree of humility about our accomplishments. Genetic enhancement and engineering is an effort to control the key elements of our appearance, fitness, and personality in a way that supports pride and arrogance rather than humility. Further, we expand our human sympathies and sense of social solidarity if we recognize that the problems and difficulties confronted by others are not always of their own making.

Sandel draws a parallel between genetic engineering and the kind of "hyperparenting" in which parents obsessively attend to every detail of their children's lives. In both cases, a quest for perfection "represents the anxious excess of mastery and dominion that misses the sense of life as a gift." Recognizing a child's limitations and vulnerabilities helps a parent not only to develop important moral virtues such as compassion, sympathy and empathy, but also provides an opportunity to appreciate the frailty and imperfections that come in every life.

Another worry about genetic engineering is that it is really no different from the eugenics programs of old. Those state-run programs

"The Case Against Perfection," *Atlantic Monthly* (April 2004), pp. 56-62.

forcibly sterilized, or compelled abortions of, members of unpopular minority groups, in the name of creating a finer "race" of human beings. Although the state coercion at the heart of such programs is certainly morally troubling, Sandel argues that the impulse to genetically engineer a more perfect next generation is still morally problematic, even if we imagine that such engineering is done without any coercion at all.

....

It is commonly said that genetic enhancements undermine our humanity by threatening our capacity to act freely, to succeed by our own efforts, and to consider ourselves responsible—worthy of praise or blame—for the things we do and for the way we are. It is one thing to hit seventy home runs as the result of disciplined training and effort, and something else, something less, to hit them with the help of steroids or genetically enhanced muscles. Of course, the roles of effort and enhancement will be a matter of degree. But as the role of enhancement increases, our admiration for the achievement fades—or, rather, our admiration for the achievement shifts from the player to his pharmacist. This suggests that our moral response to enhancement is a response to the diminished agency of the person whose achievement is enhanced.

Though there is much to be said for this argument, I do not think the main problem with enhancement and genetic engineering is that they undermine effort and erode human agency. The deeper danger is that they represent a kind of hyperagency—a Promethean aspiration to remake nature, including human nature, to serve our purposes and satisfy our desires. The problem is not the drift to mechanism but the drive to mastery. And what the drive to mastery misses and may even destroy is an appreciation of the gifted character of human powers and achievements.

To acknowledge the giftedness of life is to recognize that our talents and powers are not wholly our own doing, despite the effort we expend to develop and to exercise them. It is also to recognize that not everything in the world is open to whatever use we may desire or devise. Appreciating the gifted quality of life constrains the Promethean project and conduces to a certain humility. It is in part a religious sensibility. But its resonance reaches beyond religion.

It is difficult to account for what we admire about human activity and achievement without drawing upon some version of this idea. Consider two types of athletic achievement. We appreciate players like Pete Rose, who are not blessed with great natural gifts but who manage, through striving, grit, and determination, to excel in their sport. But we also admire players like Joe DiMaggio, who display natural gifts with grace and effortlessness. Now, suppose we learned that both players took performance-enhancing drugs. Whose turn to drugs would we find more deeply disillusioning? Which aspect of the athletic ideal—effort or gift—would be more deeply offended?

Some might say effort: the problem with drugs is that they provide a shortcut, a way to win without striving. But striving is not the point of sports; excellence is. And excellence consists at least partly in the display of natural talents and gifts that are no doing of the athlete who possesses them. This is an uncomfortable fact for democratic societies. We want to believe that success, in sports and in life, is something we earn, not something we inherit. Natural gifts, and the admiration they inspire, embarrass the meritocratic faith; they cast doubt on the conviction that praise and rewards flow from effort alone. In the face of this embarrassment we inflate the moral significance of striving, and depreciate giftedness. This distortion can be seen, for example, in network-television coverage of the Olympics, which focuses less on the feats the athletes perform than on heartrending stories of the hardships they have overcome and the struggles they have waged to triumph over an injury or a difficult upbringing or political turmoil in their native land.

But effort isn't everything. No one believes that a mediocre basketball player who works and trains even harder than Michael Jordan deserves greater acclaim or a bigger contract. The real problem with genetically altered athletes is that they corrupt athletic competition as a human activity that honors the cultivation and display of natural talents. From this standpoint, enhancement can be seen as the ultimate expression of the ethic of effort and willfulness—a kind of high-tech striving. The ethic of willfulness and the biotechnological powers it now enlists are arrayed against the claims of giftedness.

The ethic of giftedness, under siege in sports, persists in the practice of parenting. But here, too, bioengineering and genetic enhancement threaten to dislodge it. To appreciate children as gifts is to accept them as they come, not as objects of our design or products of our will or instruments of our ambition. Parental love is not contingent on the talents and attributes a child happens to have. We choose our friends and spouses at least partly on the basis of qualities we find attractive. But we do not choose our children. Their qualities are unpredictable, and even the most conscientious parents cannot be held wholly responsible for the kind of children they have. That is why parenthood, more than other human relationships, teaches what the theologian William F. May calls an "openness to the unbidden."

May's resonant phrase helps us see that the deepest moral objection to enhancement lies less in the perfection it seeks than in the human disposition it expresses and promotes. The problem is not that parents usurp the autonomy of a child they design. The problem lies in the hubris of the designing parents, in their drive to master the mystery of birth. Even if this disposition did not make parents tyrants to their children, it would disfigure the relation between parent and child, and deprive the parent of the humility and enlarged human sympathies that an openness to the unbidden can cultivate.

To appreciate children as gifts or blessings is not, of course, to be passive in the face of illness or disease. Medical intervention to cure or prevent illness or restore the injured to health does not desecrate nature but honors it. Healing sickness or injury does not override a child's natural capacities but permits them to flourish.

Nor does the sense of life as a gift mean that parents must shrink from shaping and directing the development of their child. Just as athletes and artists have an obligation to cultivate their talents, so parents have an obligation to cultivate their children, to help them discover and develop their talents and gifts. As May points out, parents give their children two kinds of love: accepting love and transforming love. Accepting love affirms the being of the child, whereas transforming love seeks the well-being of the child. Each aspect corrects the excesses of the other, he writes: "Attachment becomes too quietistic if it slackens into mere acceptance of the child as he is." Parents have a duty to promote their children's excellence.

These days, however, overly ambitious parents are prone to get carried away with transforming love—promoting and demanding all manner of accomplishments from their children, seeking perfection. "Parents find it difficult to maintain an equilibrium between the two sides of love," May observes. "Accepting love, without transforming love, slides into indulgence and finally neglect. Transforming love, without accepting love, badgers and finally rejects." May finds in these competing impulses a parallel with modern science: it, too, engages us in beholding the given world, studying and savoring it, and also in molding the world, transforming and perfecting it.

The mandate to mold our children, to cultivate and improve them, complicates the case against enhancement. We usually admire parents who seek the best for their children, who spare no effort to help them achieve happiness and success. Some parents confer advantages on their children by enrolling them in expensive schools, hiring private tutors, sending them to tennis camp, providing them with piano lessons, ballet lessons, swimming lessons, SAT-prep courses, and so on. If it is permissible and even admirable for parents to help their children in these ways, why isn't it equally admirable for parents to use whatever genetic technologies may emerge (provided they are safe) to enhance their children's intelligence, musical ability, or athletic prowess?

The defenders of enhancement are right to this extent: improving children through genetic engineering is similar in spirit to the heavily managed, high-pressure child-rearing that is now common. But this similarity does not vindicate genetic enhancement. On the contrary, it highlights a problem with the trend toward hyperparenting. One conspicuous example of this trend is sports-crazed parents bent on making champions of their children. Another is the frenzied drive of overbearing parents to mold and manage their children's academic careers.

As the pressure for performance increases, so does the need to help distractible children concentrate on the task at hand. This may be why diagnoses of attention deficit and hyperactivity disorder have increased so sharply. Lawrence Diller, a pediatrician and the author of *Running on Ritalin*, estimates that five to six percent of American children under eighteen (a total of four to five million kids) are currently prescribed Ritalin, Adderall, and other stimulants, the treatment of choice for ADHD. (Stimulants counteract hyperactivity by making it easier to focus and sustain attention.) The number of Ritalin prescriptions for children and adolescents has tripled over the past decade, but not all users suffer from attention disorders or hyperactivity. High school and college students have learned that prescription stimulants improve concentration for those with normal attention spans, and some buy or borrow their classmates' drugs to enhance their performance on the SAT or other exams. Since stimulants work for both medical and nonmedical purposes, they raise the same moral questions posed by other technologies of enhancement.

However those questions are resolved, the debate reveals the cultural distance we have traveled since the debate over marijuana, LSD, and other drugs a generation ago. Unlike the drugs of the 1960s and 1970s, Ritalin and Adderall are not for checking out but for buckling down, not for beholding the world and taking it in but for molding the world and fitting in. We used to speak of nonmedical drug use as "recreational." That term no longer applies. The steroids and stimulants that figure in the enhancement debate are not a source of recreation but a bid for compliance—a way of answering a competitive society's demand to improve our performance and perfect our nature. This demand for performance and perfection animates the impulse to rail against the given. It is the deepest source of the moral trouble with enhancement.

Some see a clear line between genetic enhancement and other ways that people seek improvement in their children and themselves. Genetic manipulation seems somehow worse—more intrusive, more sinister—than other ways of enhancing performance and seeking success. But morally speaking, the difference is less significant than it seems. Bioengineering gives us reason to question the low-tech, high-pressure child-rearing practices we commonly accept. The hyperparenting familiar in our time represents an anxious excess of mastery and dominion that misses the sense of life as a gift. This draws it disturbingly close to eugenics.

The shadow of eugenics hangs over today's debates about genetic engineering and enhancement. Critics of genetic engineering argue that human cloning, enhancement, and the quest for designer children are nothing more than "privatized" or "free-market" eugenics. Defenders of enhancement reply that genetic choices freely made are not really eugenic—at least not in the pejorative sense. To remove the coercion, they argue, is to remove the very thing that makes eugenic policies repugnant.

Sorting out the lesson of eugenics is another way of wrestling with the ethics of enhancement. The Nazis gave eugenics a bad name. But what, precisely, was wrong with it? Was the old eugenics objectionable only insofar as it was coercive? Or is there something inherently wrong with the resolve to deliberately design our progeny's traits?

James Watson, the biologist who, with Francis Crick, discovered the structure of DNA, sees nothing wrong with genetic engineering and enhancement, provided they are freely chosen rather than state-imposed. And yet Watson's language contains more than a whiff of the old eugenic sensibility. "If you really are stupid, I would call that a disease," he recently told *The Times* of London. "The lower 10 percent who really have difficulty, even in elementary school, what's the cause of it? A lot of people would like to say, 'Well, poverty, things like that.' It probably isn't. So I'd like to get rid of that, to help the lower 10 percent." A few years ago Watson stirred controversy by saying that if a gene for homosexuality were discovered, a woman should be free to abort a fetus that carried it. When his remark provoked an uproar, he replied that he was not singling out gays but asserting a principle: women should be free to abort fetuses for any reason of genetic preference—for example, if the child would be dyslexic, or lacking musical talent, or too short to play basketball.

Watson's scenarios are clearly objectionable to those for whom all abortion is an unspeakable crime. But for those who do not subscribe to the pro-life position, these scenarios raise a hard question: If it is morally troubling to contemplate abortion to avoid a gay child or a dyslexic one, doesn't this suggest that something is wrong with acting on any eugenic preference, even when no state coercion is involved?

Consider the market in eggs and sperm. The advent of artificial insemination allows prospective parents to shop for gametes with the genetic traits they desire in their offspring. It is a less predictable way to design children than cloning or pre-implantation genetic screening, but it offers a good example of a procreative practice in which the old eugenics meets the new consumerism. A few years ago some Ivy League newspapers ran an ad seeking an egg from a woman who was at least five feet ten inches tall and athletic, had no major family medical problems, and had a combined SAT score of 1400 or above. The ad offered $50,000 for an egg from a donor with these traits. More recently a Web site was launched claiming to auction eggs from fashion models whose photos appeared on the site, at starting bids of $15,000 to $150,000.

On what grounds, if any, is the egg market morally objectionable? Since no one is forced to buy or sell, it cannot be wrong for reasons of coercion. Some might worry that hefty prices would exploit poor women by presenting them with an offer they couldn't refuse. But the designer eggs that fetch the highest prices are likely to be sought from the privileged, not the poor. If the market for premium eggs gives us moral qualms, this, too, shows that concerns about eugenics are not put to rest by freedom of choice.

A tale of two sperm banks helps explain why. The Repository for Germinal Choice, one of America's first sperm banks, was not a commercial enterprise. It was opened in 1980 by Robert Graham, a philanthropist dedicated to improving the world's "germ plasm" and counteracting the rise of "retrograde humans." His plan was to collect the sperm of Nobel Prize-winning scientists and make it available to women of high intelligence, in hopes of breeding supersmart babies. But Graham had trouble persuading Nobel laureates to donate their sperm for his bizarre scheme, and so settled for sperm from young scientists of high promise. His sperm bank closed in 1999.

In contrast, California Cryobank, one of the world's leading sperm banks, is a for-profit company with no overt eugenic mission. Cappy

Rothman, M.D., a co-founder of the firm, has nothing but disdain for Graham's eugenics, although the standards Cryobank imposes on the sperm it recruits are exacting. Cryobank has offices in Cambridge, Massachusetts, between Harvard and MIT, and in Palo Alto, California, near Stanford. It advertises for donors in campus newspapers (compensation up to $900 a month), and accepts less than five percent of the men who apply. Cryobank's marketing materials play up the prestigious source of its sperm. Its catalogue provides detailed information about the physical characteristics of each donor, along with his ethnic origin and college major. For an extra fee prospective customers can buy the results of a test that assesses the donor's temperament and character type. Rothman reports that Cryobank's ideal sperm donor is six feet tall, with brown eyes, blond hair, and dimples, and has a college degree—not because the company wants to propagate those traits, but because those are the traits his customers want: "If our customers wanted high school dropouts, we would give them high school dropouts."

Not everyone objects to marketing sperm. But anyone who is troubled by the eugenic aspect of the Nobel Prize sperm bank should be equally troubled by Cryobank, consumer-driven though it be. What, after all, is the moral difference between designing children according to an explicit eugenic purpose and designing children according to the dictates of the market? Whether the aim is to improve humanity's "germ plasm" or to cater to consumer preferences, both practices are eugenic insofar as both make children into products of deliberate design.

A number of political philosophers call for a new "liberal eugenics." They argue that a moral distinction can be drawn between the old eugenic policies and genetic enhancements that do not restrict the autonomy of the child. "While old-fashioned authoritarian eugenicists sought to produce citizens out of a single centrally designed mould," writes Nicholas Agar, "the distinguishing mark of the new liberal eugenics is state neutrality." Government may not tell parents what sort of children to design, and parents may engineer in their children only those traits that improve their capacities without biasing their choice of life plans. A recent text on genetics and justice, written by the bioethicists Allen Buchanan, Dan W. Brock, Norman Daniels, and Daniel Wikler, offers a similar view. The "bad reputation of eugenics," they write, is due to practices that "might be avoidable in a future eugenic program." The problem with the old eugenics was that its burdens fell disproportionately on the weak and the poor, who were unjustly sterilized and segregated. But provided that the benefits and burdens of genetic improvement are fairly distributed, these bioethicists argue, eugenic measures are unobjectionable and may even be morally required.

The libertarian philosopher Robert Nozick proposed a "genetic supermarket" that would enable parents to order children by design without imposing a single design on the society as a whole: "This supermarket system has the great virtue that it involves no centralized decision fixing the future human type(s)."

Even the leading philosopher of American liberalism, John Rawls, in his classic *A Theory of Justice* (1971), offered a brief endorsement of noncoercive eugenics. Even in a society that agrees to share the benefits and burdens of the genetic lottery, it is "in the interest of each to have greater natural assets," Rawls wrote. "This enables him to pursue a preferred plan of life." The parties to the social contract "want to insure for their descendants the best genetic endowment (assuming their own to be fixed)." Eugenic policies are therefore not only permissible but required as a matter of justice. "Thus over time a society is to take steps at least to preserve the general level of natural abilities and to prevent the diffusion of serious defects."

But removing the coercion does not vindicate eugenics. The problem with eugenics and genetic engineering is that they represent the one-sided triumph of willfulness over giftedness, of dominion over reverence, of molding over beholding. Why, we may wonder, should we worry about this triumph? Why not shake off our unease about genetic enhancement as so much superstition? What would be lost if biotechnology dissolved our sense of giftedness?

From a religious standpoint the answer is clear: To believe that our talents and powers are wholly our own doing is to misunderstand our place in creation, to confuse our role with God's. Religion is not the only source of reasons to care about giftedness, however. The moral stakes can also be described in secular terms. If bioengineering made the myth of the "self-made man" come true, it would be difficult to view our talents as gifts for which we are indebted, rather than as achievements for which we are responsible. This would transform three key features of our moral landscape: humility, responsibility, and solidarity.

In a social world that prizes mastery and control, parenthood is a school for humility. That we care deeply about our children and yet cannot choose the kind we want teaches parents to be open to the unbidden. Such openness is a disposition worth affirming, not only within families but in the wider world as well. It invites us to abide the unexpected, to live with dissonance, to rein in the impulse to control. A *Gattaca*-like world in which parents became accustomed to specifying the sex and genetic traits of their children would be a world inhospitable to the unbidden, a gated community writ large. The awareness that our talents and abilities are not wholly our own doing restrains our tendency toward hubris.

Though some maintain that genetic enhancement erodes human agency by overriding effort, the real problem is the explosion, not the erosion, of responsibility. As humility gives way, responsibility expands to daunting proportions. We attribute less to chance and more to choice. Parents become responsible for choosing, or failing to choose, the right traits for their children. Athletes become responsible for acquiring, or failing to acquire, the talents that will help their teams win.

One of the blessings of seeing ourselves as creatures of nature, God, or fortune is that we are not wholly responsible for the way we are. The more we become masters of our genetic endowments, the greater the burden we bear for the talents we have and the way we perform. Today when a basketball player misses a rebound, his coach can blame him for being out of position. Tomorrow the coach may blame him for being too short. Even now the use of performance-enhancing drugs in professional sports is subtly transforming the expectations players have for one another; on some teams players who take the field free from amphetamines or other stimulants are criticized for "playing naked."

The more alive we are to the chanced nature of our lot, the more reason we have to share our fate with others. Consider insurance. Since people do not know whether or when various ills will befall them, they pool their risk by buying health insurance and life insurance. As life plays itself out, the healthy wind up subsidizing the unhealthy, and those who live to a ripe old age wind up subsidizing the families of those who die before their time. Even without a sense of mutual obligation, people pool their risks and resources and share one another's fate.

But insurance markets mimic solidarity only insofar as people do not know or control their own risk factors. Suppose genetic testing advanced to the point where it could reliably predict each person's medical future and life expectancy. Those confident of good health and long life would opt out of the pool, causing other people's premiums to skyrocket. The solidarity of insurance would disappear as those with good genes fled the actuarial company of those with bad ones.

The fear that insurance companies would use genetic data to assess risks and set premiums recently led the Senate to vote to prohibit genetic discrimination in health insurance. But the bigger danger, admittedly more speculative, is that genetic enhancement, if routinely practiced, would make it harder to foster the moral sentiments that social solidarity requires.

Why, after all, do the successful owe anything to the least-advantaged members of society? The best answer to this question leans heavily on the notion of giftedness. The natural talents that enable the successful to flourish are not their own doing but, rather, their good fortune—a result of the genetic lottery. If our genetic endowments are gifts, rather than achievements for which we can claim credit, it is a mistake and a conceit to assume that we are entitled to the full measure of the bounty they reap in a market economy. We therefore have an obligation to share this bounty with those who, through no fault of their own, lack comparable gifts.

A lively sense of the contingency of our gifts—a consciousness that none of us is wholly responsible for his or her success—saves a meritocratic society from sliding into the smug assumption that the rich are rich because they are more deserving than the poor. Without this, the successful would become even more likely than they are now to view themselves as self-made and self-sufficient, and hence wholly responsible for their success. Those at the bottom of society would be viewed not as disadvantaged, and thus worthy of a measure of compensation, but as simply unfit, and thus worthy of eugenic repair. The meritocracy, less chastened by chance, would become harder, less forgiving. As perfect genetic knowledge would end the simulacrum of solidarity in insurance markets, so perfect genetic control would erode the actual solidarity that arises when men and women reflect on the contingency of their talents and fortunes.

Thirty-five years ago Robert L. Sinsheimer, a molecular biologist at the California Institute of Technology, glimpsed the shape of things to come. In an article titled "The Prospect of Designed Genetic Change" he argued that freedom of choice would vindicate the new genetics, and set it apart from the discredited eugenics of old.

> To implement the older eugenics . . . would have required a massive social programme carried out over many generations. Such a programme could not have been initiated without the consent and co-operation of a major fraction of the population, and would have been continuously subject to social control. In contrast, the new eugenics could, at least in principle, be implemented on a quite individual basis, in one generation, and subject to no existing restrictions.

According to Sinsheimer, the new eugenics would be voluntary rather than coerced, and also more humane. Rather than segregating and eliminating the unfit, it would improve them. "The old eugenics would have required a continual selection for breeding of the fit, and a culling of the unfit," he wrote. "The new eugenics would permit in principle the conversion of all the unfit to the highest genetic level."

Sinsheimer's paean to genetic engineering caught the heady, Promethean self-image of the age. He wrote hopefully of rescuing "the losers in that chromosomal lottery that so firmly channels our human destinies," including not only those born with genetic defects but also "the 50,000,000 'normal' Americans with an IQ of less than 90." But he also saw that something bigger than improving on nature's "mindless, age-old throw of dice" was at stake. Implicit in technologies of genetic intervention was a more exalted place for human beings in the cosmos. "As we enlarge man's freedom, we diminish his constraints and that which he must accept as given," he wrote. Copernicus and Darwin had "demoted man from his bright glory at the focal point of the universe," but the new biology would restore his central role. In the mirror of our genetic knowledge we would see ourselves as more than a link in the chain of evolution: "We can be the agent of transition to a whole new pitch of evolution. This is a cosmic event."

There is something appealing, even intoxicating, about a vision of human freedom unfettered by the given. It may even be the case that the allure of that vision played a part in summoning the genomic age into being. It is often assumed that the powers of enhancement we now possess arose as an inadvertent by-product of biomedical progress—the genetic revolution came, so to speak, to cure disease, and stayed to tempt us with the prospect of enhancing our performance, designing our children, and perfecting our nature. That may have the story backwards. It is more plausible to view genetic engineering as the ultimate expression of our resolve to see ourselves astride the world, the masters of our nature. But that promise of mastery is flawed. It threatens to banish our appreciation of life as a gift, and to leave us with nothing to affirm or behold outside our own will.

Michael J. Sandel: The Case against Perfection

1. Explain the difference between "accepting love" and "transforming love." To illustrate, give an example of each. Why does Sandel think both are important and how does he think they should be balanced?

According to Sandel, what implications does this have for how parents should treat their children? Do you agree? Why or why not?

2. Explain how "liberal eugenics" differs from "old-fashioned authoritarian eugenics." Under what conditions do the proponents of "liberal eugenics" think that genetic engineering is morally permissible? Do you think that these conditions could ever be met? If they could be met, do you agree that in such circumstances genetic engineering would be morally permissible? Why or why not?

3. What does Sandel think the point of sports is? Explain the distinction between talent and striving, and how each contributes to our assessments of athletes and athletic performances. How do these considerations mirror those relevant to the moral permissibility of human enhancement? What lesson does Sandel draw from his consideration of athletics?

4. Sandel thinks that the practice of bioengineering will "[dissolve] our sense of giftedness," which in turn will "transform three key features of our moral landscape." Identify these three features and explain how Sandel thinks bioengineering would transform them. Do you agree with his assessment? Do you think the likely effects of bioengineering are a good reason to reject it? Defend your answer.

5. What does Sandel mean by "the ethic of giftedness"? What obligations does it impose upon us? What kind of obligations do we have that conflict with giftedness? According to Sandel, what implications does the ethic of giftedness have for the moral permissibility of human enhancement? Do you agree with this assessment? Why or why not?

46

Genetic Interventions and the Ethics of Enhancement of Human Beings

Julian Savulescu

....

Julian Savulescu offers three arguments in defense of the genetic enhancement of human beings.

First, suppose that parents could greatly improve their child's intelligence by altering the child's diet. They are lazy and fail to do this. We would condemn the parents for their laziness. Things are no different when it comes to genetic enhancements. If parents have the opportunity to greatly benefit their children, but deliberately or negligently fail to do so, then they have acted wrongly. It doesn't matter whether the benefit is conferred by enhanced diet or by introducing genetic changes.

Second, consistency requires that we treat "environmental" and biological enhancements in the same way. We train our children to be cooperative, intelligent and well behaved. Such parental "interventions" alter a child's brain structure in irreversible but highly beneficial ways. This is exactly what many genetic interventions do. Instilling useful and enjoyable traits in one's child is morally required. Genetic enhancement helps parents to meet this requirement.

Third, if we accept the treatment and prevention of disease as an important goal, then we should accept genetic interventions. Diseases

---

Julian Savulescu, "Genetic Engineering and the Ethics of Enhancement of Human Beings," in Bonnie Steinbock, ed., *The Oxford Handbook of Bioethics* (Oxford University Press, 2007), pp. 520–532.

undermine health, which in turn undermines a person's well-being and quality of life. Failure to prevent diseases by the use of genetic intervention is just as bad as failure to prevent them by the use of available drugs or surgeries.

Savulescu then replies to various objections that have been leveled against genetic enhancement. (1) Such practices amount to "playing God." Reply: we rightly make life or death decisions all the time, and many are permissible. (2) Genetic interventions will have discriminatory results. Reply: many people are born with serious biological handicaps, and genetic intervention can level the playing field and thus erase much existing disparity between those who were favored in the "natural lottery" and those who weren't. (3) Genetic engineering will lead to a single model of a desired child, and a sterile world where the surprise and mystery of life would disappear. Reply: manipulating genes will never erase differences among people and will still leave huge elements of our lives subject to chance. (4) Genetic enhancement is contrary to human nature. Reply: our nature as human beings is to be rational, and that requires us to use our reason to determine how best to improve our lives. Genetic engineering will do just that. (5) Genetic enhancement is self-defeating; its goal of making some people superior—more beautiful, intelligent, hard-working than others—will fail if everyone is genetically enhanced. Reply: critics have mistaken the goal of such enhancement: it is not to create or reinforce social divisions, but rather to improve people's lives.

....

Should we use science and medical technology not just to prevent or treat disease, but to intervene at the most basic biological levels to improve biology and enhance people's lives? By 'enhance', I mean help them to live a longer and/or better life than normal. There are various ways in which we can enhance people but I want to focus on biological enhancement, especially genetic enhancement.

The Ethics of Enhancement

We want to be happy people, not just healthy people.

I will now give three arguments in favour of enhancement and then consider several objections.

First Argument for Enhancement: Choosing Not to Enhance Is Wrong

Consider the case of the Neglectful Parents. The Neglectful Parents give birth to a child with a special condition. The child has a stunning intellect but requires a simple, readily available, cheap dietary supplement to sustain his intellect. But they neglect the diet of this child and this results in a child with a stunning intellect becoming normal. This is clearly wrong.

But now consider the case of the Lazy Parents. They have a child who has a normal intellect but if they introduced the same dietary supplement, the child's intellect would rise to the same level as the child of the Neglectful Parent. They can't be bothered with improving the child's diet so the child remains with a normal intellect. Failure to institute dietary supplementation means a normal child fails to achieve a stunning intellect. The inaction of the Lazy Parents is as wrong as the inaction of the Neglectful Parents. It has exactly the same consequence: a child exists who could have had a stunning intellect but is instead normal.

Some argue that it is not wrong to fail to bring about the best state of affairs. This may or may not be the case. But in these kinds of case, when there are no other relevant moral considerations, the failure to introduce a diet that sustains a more desirable state is as wrong as the failure to introduce a diet that brings about a more desirable state. The costs of inaction are the same, as are the parental obligations.

If we substitute 'biological intervention' for 'diet', we see that in order not to wrong our children, we should enhance them. Unless there is something special and optimal about our children's physical, psychological, or cognitive abilities, or something different about other biological interventions, it would be wrong not to enhance them.

Second Argument: Consistency

Some will object that, while we do have an obligation to institute better diets, biological interventions like genetic interventions are different from dietary supplementation. I will argue that there is no difference between these interventions.

In general, we accept environmental interventions to improve our children. Education, diet, and training are all used to make our children better people and increase their opportunities in life. We train children to be well behaved, cooperative, and intelligent. Indeed, researchers are looking at ways to make the environment more stimulating for young children to maximize their intellectual development. But in the study of the rat model of Huntington's Chorea, the stimulating environment acted to change the brain structure of the rats. The drug Prozac acted in just the same way. These environmental manipulations do not act mysteriously. They alter our biology.

The most striking example of this is a study of rats that were extensively mothered and rats that were not mothered. The mothered rats showed genetic changes (changes in the methylation of the DNA) that were passed on to the next generation. ... More generally, environmental manipulations can profoundly affect biology. Maternal care and stress have been associated with abnormal brain (hippocampal) development, involving altered nerve growth factors and cognitive, psychological, and immune deficits later in life.

Some argue that genetic manipulations are different because they are irreversible. But environmental interventions can equally be irreversible. Child neglect or abuse can scar a person for life. It may be impossible to unlearn the skill of playing the piano or riding a bike, once learnt. One may be wobbly, but one is a novice only once. Just as the example of mothering of rats shows that environmental interventions can cause biological changes that are passed onto the next generation, so too can environmental interventions be irreversible, or very difficult to reverse, within one generation.

Why should we allow environmental manipulations that alter our biology but not direct biological manipulations? What is the moral difference between producing a smarter child by immersing that child in a stimulating environment, giving the child a drug, or directly altering the child's brain or genes?

One example of a drug that alters brain chemistry is Prozac, which is a serotonin reuptake inhibitor. Early in life it acts as a nerve growth factor, but it may also alter the brain early in life to make it more prone to stress and anxiety later in life by altering receptor development. . . . Drugs like Prozac and maternal deprivation may have the same biological effects.

If the outcome is the same, why treat biological manipulation differently from environmental manipulation? Not only may a favourable environment improve a child's biology and increase a child's opportunities, so too may direct biological interventions. Couples should maximize the genetic opportunity of their children to lead a good life and a productive, cooperative social existence. There is no relevant moral difference between environmental and genetic intervention.

Third Argument: No Difference from Treating Disease

If we accept the treatment and prevention of disease, we should accept enhancement. The goodness of health is what drives a moral obligation to treat or prevent disease. But health is not what ultimately matters—health enables us to live well; disease prevents us from doing what we want and what is good. Health is instrumentally valuable—valuable as a resource that allows us to do what really matters, that is, lead a good life.

What constitutes a good life is a deep philosophical question. According to hedonistic theories, what is good is having pleasant experiences and being happy. According to desire fulfilment theories, and economics, what matters is having our preferences satisfied. According to objective theories, certain activities are good for people: developing deep personal relationships, developing talents, understanding oneself and the world, gaining knowledge, being a part of a family, and so on. We need not decide on which of these theories is correct in order to understand what is bad about ill health. Disease is important because it causes pain, is not what we want, and stops us engaging in those activities that give meaning to life. Sometimes people trade health for well-being: mountain climbers take on risk to achieve, smokers sometimes believe that the pleasures outweigh the risks of smoking, and so on. Life is about managing risk to health and life to promote well-being.

Beneficence—the moral obligation to benefit people—provides a strong reason to enhance people in so far as the biological enhancement increases their chance of having a better life. But can biological enhancements increase people's opportunities for well-being? There are reasons to believe that they might.

Many of our biological and psychological characteristics profoundly affect how well our lives go. In the 1960s Walter Mischel conducted impulse control experiments in which 4-year-old children were left in a room with one marshmallow, after being told that if they did not eat the marshmallow, they could later have two. Some children would eat it as soon as the researcher left; others would use a variety of strategies to help control their behaviour and ignore the temptation of the single marshmallow. A decade later they reinterviewed the children and found that those who were better at delaying gratification had more friends, better academic performance, and more motivation to succeed. Whether the child had grabbed for the marshmallow had a much stronger bearing on their SAT scores than did their IQ (Mischel et al. 1988).

Impulse control has also been linked to socio-economic control and avoiding conflict with the law. The problems of a hot and uncontrollable temper can be profound.

Shyness too can greatly restrict a life. I remember one newspaper story about a woman who blushed violet every time she went into a social situation. This led her to a hermitic, miserable existence. She eventually had the autonomic nerves to her face surgically cut. This revolutionized her life and had a greater effect on her well-being than the treatment of many diseases.

Buchanan and colleagues have discussed the value of 'all purpose goods' (Buchanan et al. 2000). These are traits that are valuable regardless of the kind of life a person chooses to live. They give us greater all-round capacities to live a vast array of lives. Examples include intelligence, memory, self-discipline, patience, empathy, a sense of humour, optimism, and just having a sunny temperament. All of these characteristics—sometimes described as virtues—may have some biological and psychological basis capable of manipulation using technology.

Technology might even be used to improve our moral character. We certainly seek through good instruction and example, discipline, and other methods to make better children. It may be possible to alter biology to make people predisposed to be more moral by promoting empathy, imagination, sympathy, fairness, honesty, etc.

In so far as these characteristics have some genetic basis, genetic manipulation could benefit us. There is reason to believe that complex virtues like fair-mindedness may have a biological basis. In one famous experiment a monkey was trained to perform a task and rewarded with either a grape or a piece of cucumber. He preferred the grape. On one occasion he performed the task successfully and was given a piece of cucumber. He watched as another monkey who had not performed the task was given a grape and he became very angry. This shows that even monkeys have a sense of fairness and desert—or at least self-interest!

At the other end, there are characteristics that we believe do not make for a good and happy life. One Dutch family illustrates the extreme end of the spectrum. For over thirty years this family recognized that there were a disproportionate number of male family members who exhibited aggressive and criminal behaviour (Morell 1993). This was characterized by aggressive outbursts resulting in arson, attempted rape, and exhibitionism. When a family tree was constructed, the pattern of inheritance was clearly X-linked recessive. This means, roughly, that women can carry the gene without being affected; 50 per cent of men at risk of inheriting the gene get the gene and are affected by the disease.

Genetic analysis suggested that the likely defective gene was a part of the X chromosome known as the monoamine oxidase region. This region codes for two enzymes that assist in the breakdown of neurotransmitters. Neurotransmitters are substances that play a key role in the conduction of nerve impulses in our brain. Enzymes like the monoamine oxidases are required to degrade the neurotransmitters after they have performed their desired task. It was suggested that the monoamine oxidase activity might be disturbed in the affected individuals. Urine analysis showed a higher than normal amount of neurotransmitters being excreted in the urine of affected males (Morell 1993). These results were consistent with a reduction in the functioning of one of the enzymes (monoamine oxidase A).

How can such a mutation result in violent and antisocial behaviour? A deficiency of the enzyme results in a build-up of neurotransmitters. These abnormal levels of neurotransmitters result in excessive, and even violent, reactions to stress. This hypothesis was further supported by the finding that genetically modified mice that lack this enzyme are more aggressive.

This family is an extreme example of how genes can influence behaviour: it is the only family in which this mutation has been isolated. Most genetic contributions to behaviour will be weaker predispositions, but there may be some association between genes and behaviour that results in criminal and other antisocial behaviour.

How could information such as this be used? Some criminals have attempted a 'genetic defence' in the United States, stating that their genes caused them to commit the crime, but this has never succeeded. However, it is clear that couples should be allowed to test to select offspring who do not have the mutation that predisposes them to act in this way, and if interventions were available, it might be rational to correct it since children without the mutation have a better chance of a good life.

"Genes, Not Men, May Hold the Key to Female Pleasure" ran the title of one recent newspaper article (*The Age* 2005), which reported the results of a large study of female identical twins in Britain and Australia. It found that "genes accounted for 31 per cent of the chance of having an orgasm during intercourse and 51 per cent during masturbation." It concluded that the "ability to gain sexual satisfaction is largely inherited" and went on to speculate that "The genes involved could be linked to physical differences in sex organs and hormone levels or factors such as mood and anxiety."

Our biology profoundly affects how our lives go. If we can increase sexual satisfaction by modifying biology, we should. Indeed, vast numbers of men attempt to do this already through the use of Viagra.

Summary: The Case for Enhancement

What matters is human well-being, not just treatment and prevention of disease. Our biology affects our opportunities to live well. The biological route to improvement is no different from the environmental. Biological manipulation to increase opportunity is ethical. If we have an obligation to treat and prevent disease, we have an obligation to try to manipulate these characteristics to give an individual the best opportunity of the best life.

How Do We Decide?

If we are to enhance certain qualities, how should we decide which to choose? Eugenics was the movement early in the last century that aimed to use selective breeding to prevent degeneration of the gene pool by weeding out criminals, those with mental illness, and the poor, on the false belief that these conditions were simple genetic disorders. The eugenics movement had its inglorious peak when the Nazis moved beyond sterilization to extermination of the genetically unfit.

What was objectionable about the eugenics movement, besides its shoddy scientific basis, was that it involved the imposition of a state vision for a healthy population and aimed to achieve this through coercion. The movement was aimed not at what was good for individuals, but rather at what benefited society. Modern eugenics in the form of testing for disorders, such as Down syndrome, occurs very commonly but is acceptable because it is voluntary, gives couples a choice of what kind of child to have, and enables them to have a child with the greatest opportunity for a good life.

There are four possible ways in which our genes and biology will be decided:

1. nature or God;
2. 'experts' (philosophers, bioethicists, psychologists, scientists);
3. 'authorities' (government, doctors);
4. people themselves: liberty and autonomy.

It is a basic principle of liberal states like the United Kingdom that the state be 'neutral' to different conceptions of the good life. This means that we allow individuals to lead the life that they believe is best for themselves, implying respect for their personal autonomy or capacity for self-rule. The sole ground for interference is when that individual choice may harm others. Advice, persuasion, information, dialogue are permissible. But coercion and infringement of liberty are impermissible.

There are limits to what a liberal state should provide:

1. safety: the intervention should be reasonably safe;
2. harm to others: the intervention (like some manipulation that increases uncontrollable aggressiveness) should not result in harm. Such harm should not be direct or indirect, for example, by causing some unfair competitive advantage;
3. distributive justice: the interventions should be distributed according to principles of justice.

The situation is more complex with young children, embryos, and fetuses, who are incompetent. These human beings are not autonomous and cannot make choices themselves about whether a putative enhancement is a benefit or a harm. If a proposed intervention can be delayed until that human reaches maturity and can decide for himself or herself, then the intervention should be delayed. However, many genetic interventions will have to be performed very early in life if they are to have an effect. Decisions about such interventions should be left to parents, according to a principle of procreative liberty and autonomy. This states that parents have the freedom to choose when to have children, how many children to have, and arguably what kind of children to have.

Just as parents have wide scope to decide on the conditions of the upbringing of their children, including schooling and religious education, they should have similar freedom over their children's genes. Procreative autonomy or liberty should be extended to enhancement for two reasons. First, reproduction: bearing and raising children is a very private matter. Parents must bear much of the burden of having children, and they have a legitimate stake in the nature of the child they must invest so much of their lives raising.

But there is a second reason. John Stuart Mill argued that when our actions only affect ourselves, we should be free to construct and act on our own conception of what is the best life for us. Mill was not a libertarian. He did not believe that such freedom is valuable solely for its own sake. He believed that freedom is important in order for people to discover for themselves what kind of life is best for themselves. It is only through 'experiments in living' that people discover what works for them and others come to see the richness and variety of lives that can be good. Mill strongly praised 'originality' and variety in choice as being essential to discovering which lives are best for human beings.

Importantly, Mill believed that some lives are worse than others. Famously, he said that it is better to be Socrates dissatisfied than a fool satisfied. He distinguished between 'higher pleasures' of 'feelings and imagination' and 'lower pleasures' of 'mere sensation' (Mill 1910: 7). He criticized 'ape-like imitation', subjugation of oneself to custom and fashion, indifference to individuality, and lack of originality (1910: 119–20, 123). Nonetheless, he was the champion of people's right to live their lives as they choose.

> I have said that it is important to give the freest scope possible to uncustomary things, in order that it may appear in time which of these are fit to be converted into customs. But independence of action, and disregard of custom, are not solely deserving of encouragement for the chance they afford that better modes of action, and customs more worthy of general adoption, may be struck out; nor is it only persons of decided mental superiority who have a just claim to carry on their lives in their own way. There is no reason that all human existence should be constructed on some one or small number of patterns. If a person possesses any tolerable amount of common sense and experience, his own mode of laying out his existence is the best, not because it is the best in itself, but because it is his own mode. (Mill 1910: 125)

I believe that reproduction should be about having children with the best prospects. But to discover what are the best prospects, we must give individual couples the freedom to act on their own value judgement of what constitutes a life with good prospects. 'Experiments in reproduction' are as important as 'experiments in living' (as long as they don't harm the children who are produced). For this reason, procreative freedom is important.

There is one important limit to procreative autonomy that is different from the limits to personal autonomy. The limits to procreative autonomy should be:

1. safety;
2. harm to others;
3. distributive justice;
4. such that the parent's choices are based on a plausible conception of well-being and a better life for the child;
5. consistent with development of autonomy in the child and a reasonable range of future life plans.

These last two limits are important. It makes for a higher standard of 'proof' that an intervention will be an enhancement because the parents are making choices for their child, not themselves. The critical question to ask in considering whether to alter some gene related to complex behaviour is: Would the change be better for the individual? Is it better for the individual to have a tendency to be lazy or hardworking, monogamous or polygamous? These questions are difficult to answer. While we might let adults choose to be monogamous or polygamous, we would not let parents decide on their child's predispositions unless we were reasonably clear that some trait was better for the child.

There will be cases where some intervention is plausibly in a child's interests: increased empathy with other people, better capacity to understand oneself and the world around, or improved memory. One quality is especially associated with socio-economic success and staying out of prison: impulse control. If it were possible to correct poor impulse control, we should correct it. Whether we should remove impulsiveness altogether is another question.

Joel Feinberg has described a child's right to an open future (Feinberg 1980). An open future is one in which a child has a reasonable range of possible lives to choose from and an opportunity to choose what kind of person to be; that is, to develop autonomy. Some critics of enhancement have argued that genetic interventions are inconsistent with a child's right to an open future (Davis 1997). Far from restricting a child's future, however, some biological interventions may increase the possible futures or at least their quality. It is hard to see how improved memory or empathy would restrict a child's future. Many worthwhile possibilities would be open. But it is true that parental choice should not restrict the development of autonomy or reasonable range of possible futures open to a child. In general, fewer enhancements will be permitted in children than in adults. Some interventions, however, may still be clearly enhancements for our children, and so just like vaccinations or other preventative health care.

Objections

Playing God or Against Nature

This objection has various forms. Some people in society believe that children are a gift, of God or of nature, and that we should not interfere in human nature. Most people implicitly reject this view: we screen embryos and fetuses for diseases, even mild correctable diseases. We interfere in nature or God's will when we vaccinate, provide pain relief to women in labour (despite objections of some earlier Christians that these practices thwarted God's will), and treat cancer. No one would object to the treatment of disability in a child if it were possible. Why, then, not treat the embryo with genetic therapy if that intervention is safe? This is no more thwarting God's will than giving antibiotics.

Another variant of this objection is that we are arrogant if we assume we could have sufficient knowledge to meddle with human nature. Some people object that we cannot know the complexity of the human system, which is like an unknowable magnificent symphony. To attempt to enhance one characteristic may have other unknown, unforeseen effects elsewhere in the system. We should not play God since, unlike God, we are not omnipotent or omniscient. We should be humble and recognize the limitations of our knowledge.

A related objection is that genes are pleiotropic—which means they have different effects in different environments. The gene or genes that predispose to manic depression may also be responsible for heightened creativity and productivity.

One response to both of these objections is to limit intervention, until our knowledge grows, to selecting between different embryos, and not intervening to enhance particular embryos or people. Since we would be choosing between complete systems on the basis of their type, we would not be interfering with the internal machinery. In this way, selection is less risky than enhancement.

But such a precaution could also be misplaced when considering biological interventions. When benefits are on offer, such objections remind us to refrain from hubris and over-confidence. We must do adequate research before intervening. And because the benefits may be fewer than when we treat or prevent disease, we may require the standards of safety to be higher than for medical interventions. But we must weigh the risks against the benefits. If confidence is justifiably high, and benefits outweigh harms, we should enhance.

Once technology affords us the power to enhance our own and our children's lives, to fail to do so would be to be responsible for the consequences. To fail to treat our children's diseases is to wrong them. To fail to prevent them from getting depression is to wrong them. To fail to improve their physical, musical, psychological, and other capacities is to wrong them, just as it would be to harm them if we gave them a toxic substance that stunted or reduced these capacities.

Another variant of the 'Playing God' objection is that there is a special value in the balance and diversity that natural variation affords, and enhancement will reduce this. But in so far as we are products of evolution, we are merely random chance variations of genetic traits selected for our capacity to survive long enough to reproduce. There is no design to evolution. Evolution selects genes, according to environment, that confer the greatest chance of survival and reproduction. Evolution would select a tribe that was highly fertile but suffered great pain the whole of their lives over another tribe that was less fertile but suffered less pain. Medicine has changed evolution: we can now select individuals who experience less pain and disease. The next stage of human evolution will be rational evolution, according to which we select children who not only have the greatest chance of surviving, reproducing, and being free of disease, but who have the greatest opportunities to have the best lives in their likely environment. Evolution was indifferent to how well our lives went; we are not. We want to retire, play golf, read, and watch our grandchildren have children.

'Enhancement' is a misnomer. It suggests luxury. But enhancement is no luxury. In so far as it promotes well-being, it is the very essence of what is necessary for a good human life. There is no moral reason to preserve some traits—such as uncontrollable aggressiveness, a sociopathic personality, or extreme deviousness. Tell the victim of rape and murder that we must preserve diversity and the natural balance.

Genetic Discrimination

Some people fear the creation of a two-tier society of the enhanced and the unenhanced, where the inferior, unenhanced are discriminated against and disadvantaged all through life.

We must remember that nature allots advantage and disadvantage with no gesture to fairness. Some are born horribly disadvantaged, destined to die after short and miserable lives. Some suffer great genetic disadvantage while others are born gifted, physically, musically, or intellectually. There is no secret that there are 'gifted' children naturally. Allowing choice to change our biology will, if anything, be more egalitarian, allowing the ungifted to approach the gifted. There is nothing fair about the natural lottery: allowing enhancement may be fairer.

But more importantly, how well the lives of those who are disadvantaged go depends not on whether enhancement is permitted, but on the social institutions we have in place to protect the least well off and provide everyone with a fair chance. People have disease and disability: egalitarian social institutions and laws against discrimination are designed to make sure everyone, regardless of natural inequality, has a decent chance of a decent life. This would be no different if enhancement were permitted.

There is no necessary connection between enhancement and discrimination, just as there is no necessary connection between curing disability and discrimination against people with disability.

The Perfect Child, Sterility, and Loss of the Mystery of Life

If we engineered perfect children, this objection goes, the world would be a sterile, monotonous place where everyone was the same, and the mystery and surprise of life would be gone.

It is impossible to create perfect children. We can only attempt to create children with better opportunities of a better life. There will necessarily be difference. Even in the case of screening for disability, like Down syndrome, 10 per cent of people choose not to abort a pregnancy known to be affected by Down syndrome. People value different things. There will never be complete convergence. Moreover, there will remain massive challenges for individuals to meet in their personal relationships and in the hurdles our unpredictable environment presents. There will remain much mystery and challenge—we will just be better able to deal with these. We will still have to work to achieve, but our achievements may have greater value.

Against Human Nature

One of the major objections to enhancement is that it is against human nature. Common alternative phrasings are that enhancement is tampering with our nature or an affront to human dignity. I believe that what separates us from other animals is our rationality, our capacity to make normative judgements and act on the basis of reasons. When we make decisions to improve our lives by biological and other manipulations, we express our rationality and express what is fundamentally important about our nature. And if those manipulations improve our capacity to make rational and normative judgements, they further improve what is fundamentally human. Far from being against the human spirit, such improvements express the human spirit. To be human is to be better.

Enhancements Are Self-Defeating

Another familiar objection to enhancement is that enhancements will have self-defeating or other adverse social effects. A typical example is increase in height. If height is socially desired, then everyone will try to enhance the height of their children at great cost to themselves and the environment (as taller people consume more resources), with no advantage in the end since there will be no relative gain.

If a purported manipulation does not improve well-being or opportunity, there is no argument in favour of it. In this case, the manipulation is not an enhancement. In other cases, such as enhancement of intelligence, the enhancement of one individual may increase that individual's opportunities only at the expense of another. So-called positional goods are goods only in a relative sense.

But many enhancements will have both positional and non-positional qualities. Intelligence is good not just because it allows an individual to be more competitive for complex jobs, but because it allows an individual to process information more rapidly in her own life, and to develop greater understanding of herself and others. These non-positional effects should not be ignored. Moreover, even in the case of so-called purely positional goods, such as height, there may be important non-positional values. It is better to be taller if you are a basketball player, but being tall is a disadvantage in balance sports such as gymnastics, skiing, and surfing.

Nonetheless, if there are significant social consequences of enhancement, this is of course a valid objection. But it is not particular to enhancement: there is an old question about how far individuals in society can pursue their own self-interest at a cost to others. It applies to education, health care, and virtually all areas of life.

Not all enhancements will be ethical. The critical issue is that the intervention is expected to bring about more benefits than harms to the individual. It must be safe and there must be a reasonable expectation of improvement. Some of the other features of ethical enhancements are summarized below.

What Is an Ethical Enhancement?

An ethical enhancement:

1. is in the person's interests;
2. is reasonably safe;
3. increases the opportunity to have the best life;
4. promotes or does not unreasonably restrict the range of possible lives open to that person;
5. does not unreasonably harm others directly through excessive costs in making it freely available;

6. does not place that individual at an unfair competitive advantage with respect to others, e.g. mind-reading;

7. is such that the person retains significant control or responsibility for her achievements and self that cannot be wholly or directly attributed to the enhancement;

8. does not unreasonably reinforce or increase unjust inequality and discrimination—economic inequality, racism.

What Is an Ethical Enhancement for a Child or Incompetent Human Being?

Such an ethical enhancement is all the above, but in addition:

1. the intervention cannot be delayed until the child can make its own decision;

2. the intervention is plausibly in the child's interests;

3. the intervention is compatible with the development of autonomy.

Conclusion

Enhancement is already occurring. In sport, human erythropoietin boosts red blood cells. Steroids and growth hormone improve muscle strength. Many people seek cognitive enhancement through nicotine, Ritalin, Modavigil, or caffeine. Prozac, recreational drugs, and alcohol all enhance mood. Viagra is used to improve sexual performance.

And of course mobile phones and aeroplanes are examples of external enhancing technologies. In the future, genetic technology, nanotechnology, and artificial intelligence may profoundly affect our capacities.

Will the future be better or just disease-free? We need to shift our frame of reference from health to life enhancement. What matters is how we live. Technology can now improve that. We have two options:

1. Intervention:
   - treating disease;
   - preventing disease;
   - supra-prevention of disease—preventing disease in a radically unprecedented way;
   - protection of well-being;
   - enhancement of well-being.

2. No intervention, and to remain in a state of nature—no treatment or prevention of disease, no technological enhancement.

I believe that to be human is to be better. Or, at least, to strive to be better. We should be here for a good time, not just a long time. Enhancement, far from being merely permissible, is something we should aspire to achieve.

References

Buchanan, A., Brock, D., Daniels, N., and Wikler, D. (2000), *From Chance to Choice* (Cambridge: Cambridge University Press).

Davis, D. (1997), "Genetic Dilemmas and the Child's Right to an Open Future," *Hastings Center Report*, 27/2 (Mar.–Apr.), 7–15.

Feinberg, J. (1980), "The Child's Right to an Open Future," in W. Aiken and H. LaFollette (eds.), *Whose Child? Parental Rights, Parental Authority and State Power* (Totowa, NJ: Rowman and Littlefield), 124–153.

Mill, J. S. (1910), *On Liberty* (London: J. M. Dent).

Mischel, W., Shoda, Y., and Peake, P. K. (1988), "The Nature of Adolescent Competencies Predicted by Preschool Delay of Gratification," *Journal of Personality and Social Psychology*, 54/4:687–696.

Morell, V. (1993), "Evidence Found for a Possible 'Aggression Gene,'" *Science*, 260: 1722–1723.

Julian Savulescu: Genetic Interventions and the Ethics of Enhancement of Human Beings

1. What limits does Savulescu place on procreative autonomy over and above the limits placed on personal autonomy? Why does he think these limits are important? Do you think these limits are enough to protect the rights of children? Explain and defend your answer.

2. Explain Savulescu's consistency argument. What do you think the most powerful objection to this argument is? How do you think Savulescu would respond? Do you think this objection is ultimately successful? Why or why not?

3. Explain why eugenics might pose a problem for Savulescu's view. According to Savulescu, who should decide when and how to enhance certain qualities? Do you think his account is enough to neutralize the eugenics worry? Defend your response.

4. Savulescu considers a number of objections to his account. Reconstruct one of the objections as a valid argument. Then, explain how Savulescu responds to this argument by saying which premise he rejects and why. Do you think his response is successful? Why or why not?

5. Savulescu defends genetic enhancement by arguing that it is analogous to treating disease. Explain this argument. Then discuss the potential differences between treating disease and genetic enhancement. Is Savulescu right to say that there is no morally relevant difference between the two? Defend your response.
6. Explain the principle of procreative liberty and autonomy. Then, explain the two reasons Savulescu cites for applying this principle to human enhancement. Do you think that this is enough to show that parents should have some freedom in determining their children's genes? Why or why not?

47

═══ ❧ ═══

Don't Let the Doctor Do This to Your Newborn

Christin Scarlett Milloy

....

Christin Scarlett Milloy opens her brief piece with an arresting thought experiment, designed to raise a pointed question: should parents of newborns allow medical professionals to impose a small risk of great harm on those infants, for the sake of enforcing traditional gender roles? The risk is imposed by the practice of gender assignment at birth. Such a practice isn't medically necessary. It confers benefits on most children who grow up cis-gendered (i.e., such as to conform to conventional gender roles). But the practice can and does cause substantial harm to children who are transgendered. Milloy likens the practice to playing Russian roulette with your infant's well-being, and recommends that we abolish the practice, replacing it with one that allows children (typically at age two or three) to choose for themselves which gender (if any) to adopt.

....

Imagine you are in recovery from labor, lying in bed, holding your infant. In your arms you cradle a stunningly beautiful, perfect little being. Completely innocent and totally vulnerable, your baby is entirely dependent on you to make all the choices that will define their life for

Christin Scarlett Milloy, "Don't Let the Doctor Do This to Your Newborn," *Slate*, June 26, 2014. https://slate.com/human-interest/2014/06/infant-gender-assignment-unnecessary-and-potentially-harmful.html many years to come. They are wholly unaware (at least, for now) that you would do anything and everything in your power to protect them from harm and keep them safe. You are calm, at peace.

Suddenly, the doctor comes in. He looks at you sternly, gloved hands reaching for your baby insistently. "It's time for your child's treatment," he explains from beneath a white breathing mask, shattering your calm. Clutching your baby protectively, you eye the doctor with suspicion.

You ask him what it's for.

"Oh, just standard practice. It will help him or her be recognized and get along more easily with others who've already received the same treatment. The chance of side effects is extremely small." This raises the hairs on the back of your neck, and your protective instinct kicks your alarm response up a notch.

"Side effects?"

The doctor waves his hand dismissively. "Oh, in 1 or 2 percent of cases, we see long-term negative reactions to this," he says with a hint of distaste. "It leads to depression, social ostracism, difficulty finding or keeping a job. Those with negative reactions often become subject to intense discrimination in society. Suicide is not uncommon." At your look of alarm, he smiles again, reassuringly. "But as I said, this happens in very few cases. The overwhelming likelihood," he says as he cracks his knuckles, "is that this will make life simpler and more comfortable for your child to interact with others." He tries to assuage your concerns, but cold equations, percentage points, and population counts dance in your mind.

"Is it really necessary? If we don't take the treatment, will my baby get sick?"

The doctor flashes a paternalistic smile. "No, no . . . but your child would lose the social advantage this treatment offers. If you choose not to take it, others who have may not accept your child as easily. Virtually every child receives it, so it would be very unusual not to," he says matter-of-factly. "This is a standard practice. People just wouldn't understand why you didn't go along with it," he says, casting a judgmental glance.

Would you consent to this treatment for your child? A good chance for improved social privilege, with a comparatively tiny risk of negative (albeit potentially catastrophic) consequences? Or would the stakes be too high: Russian roulette with your baby's life?

It's a strange hypothetical scenario to imagine. Pressure to accept a medical treatment, no tangible proof of its necessity, its only benefits conferred by the fact that everyone else already has it, and coming at a terrible expense to those 1 or 2 percent who have a bad reaction. It seems unlikely that doctors, hospitals, parents, or society in general would tolerate a standard practice like this.

Except they already do. The imaginary treatment I described above is real. Obstetricians, doctors, and midwives commit this procedure on infants every single day, in every single country. In reality, this treatment is performed almost universally *without even asking for the parents' consent*, making this practice all the more insidious. It's called infant gender assignment: When the doctor holds your child up to the harsh light of the delivery room, looks between its legs, and declares his opinion: It's a boy or a girl, based on nothing more than a cursory assessment of your offspring's genitals.

We tell our children, "You can be anything you want to be." We say, "A girl can be a doctor, a boy can be a nurse," but why in the first place must *this person* be a boy and *that person* be a girl? Your infant is an *infant*. Your baby knows nothing of dresses and ties, of makeup and aftershave, of the contemporary social implications of pink and blue. As a newborn, your child's potential is limitless. The world is full of possibilities that every person deserves to be able to explore freely, receiving equal respect and human dignity while maximizing happiness through individual expression.

With infant gender assignment, in a single moment your baby's life is instantly and brutally reduced from such infinite potentials down to one concrete set of expectations and stereotypes, and any behavioral deviation from that will be severely punished—both intentionally through bigotry, and unintentionally through ignorance. That doctor (and the power structure behind him) plays a pivotal role in imposing those limits on helpless infants, without their consent, and without your informed consent as a parent. This issue deserves serious consideration by every parent, because no matter what gender identity your child ultimately adopts, infant gender assignment has effects that will last through their whole life.

We see more and more high-profile stories about transgender people in the news. The shame and the mysticism surrounding them is fading at an exponential rate, as public consciousness matures from the depths of exploiting puerile stereotypes and bigoted joke depictions of the trans experience into a more complex awareness of, and sensitivity to, the humanity and emotions of non-cis people. Every parent today knows there is a chance their child might be transgender. A small chance, perhaps, but a chance higher than zero.

If a child of any minority status (be it sexual, racial, ability, religious, etc.) is subjected to slurs or physical harassment at school, we do not view the emotional and physical injuries as the unfortunate but inevitable result of that child's minority status. Rather, we correctly lay the blame where it belongs, on the *wrong actions* of hateful bullies whose *willful decisions* were responsible for causing the pain.

Only a cruel parent would punish their son by making him wear a dress in public, or punish their daughter by shaving her head. That's psychological abuse. But for gender nonconforming kids, that's the everyday reality of their lives. We know transgender people are far more likely to be depressed, with a heartbreaking 41 percent rate of suicide attempts, nearly nine times the social average. That's not evidence of mental illness, it's evidence of trauma and distress. They're not miserable *because* they're transgender, they're miserable as the result of *being assigned the wrong gender at birth*.

Infant gender assignment is a willful decision, and as a maturing society we need to judge whether it might be a wrong action. Why must we force this on kids at birth? What is achieved, besides reinforcing tradition? What could be the harm in letting a child wait to declare for themselves who they are, once they're old enough (which is generally believed to happen around age 2 or 3)? Clearly, most children will still turn out like we'd expect, but it's unlikely the extra freedom would harm them. On the other hand, we *do know* the massive harm caused to *some* children by the removal of that freedom.

As a parent or potential parent, would you love your children less if they are transgender? Would you love them more if they aren't? If you answered those questions with the decency and compassion that go hand-in-hand with unconditional parental love, then I ask you to please take that thought process one step further and consider the intense psychological harm it might cause your child before you allow the doctor to decide for both of you whether your baby will be a boy or a girl. Sure, it usually works out for the best—but sometimes, it goes horribly wrong. Just because an infant may survive being left alone in a car on a hot day, while the parent runs to the store, doesn't mean that parent made the right decision—in fact, they made a dangerous decision and just got lucky with the outcome.

Is it better to play the odds, or play it safe? Think carefully. Infant gender assignment might just be Russian roulette with your baby's life.

Christin Scarlett Milloy: Don't Let the Doctor Do This to Your Newborn

1. What are the benefits of the practice of infant gender assignment?
2. What are the drawbacks of that practice?
3. Milloy likens the practice to Russian roulette. Do you find the analogy apt? Why or why not?
4. How attractive is the idea of allowing very young children to determine their own gender identity?
5. Some argue that certain elements of one's identity—ethnic or racial affiliation, for example—are not a matter of individual choice. Is that view plausible? If not, why not? If so, do the same considerations support the idea that gender identity is also not a matter of individual choice?

═══ ❧ ═══

48

Ignoring Differences between Men and Women Is the Wrong Way to Address Gender Dysphoria

Kathleen Stock

In this wide-ranging article, Kathleen Stock explores the phenomenon of gender dysphoria: the feeling of strong discomfort at the sexed aspects of one's physical appearance, even to the point of feeling "born into the wrong body." As is now common, Stock talks of sex as a biological category, and focuses on gender to refer to the social norms and stereotypes governing a particular sex category.

Gender dysphoria is especially prevalent among those who think of themselves as transgender, or as gender non-binary. How should society seek to relieve this sort of distress? Stock considers two approaches. The first is what she calls sex eliminationism, which calls on us to abandon the categories of biological sex. In doing so, we should remove any social practice that differentiates trans people from those who are born into the sex category they identify with. The ideal here would be the integration of trans women into all female social and legal categories, and trans men into corresponding male categories. The second approach, which Stock calls gender eliminationism, argues that we should retain our

Kathleen Stock, "Ignoring Differences between Men and Women Is the Wrong Way to Address Gender Dysphoria," *Quillette* April 11, 2019. https://quillette.com/2019/04/11/ignoring-differences-between-men-and-women-is-the-wrong-way-to-address-gender-dysphoria/

notions of biological sex categories, and instead get rid of gender, as understood above. The ideal social situation, under this approach, would eliminate all of the harmful norms and stereotypes associated with masculinity and femininity, while maintaining that the population, as always, consists almost entirely of biological boys and men, on the one hand, and biological girls and women, on the other. The underlying idea here is that gender dysphoria would be greatly reduced among the trans population if there were no stereotypical gendered expectations imposed on those of one biological category or the other.

After discussing the major motivations for sex eliminationism, Stock argues that it suffers from an important failing—namely, that abandoning the categories of biological sex makes it harder to describe and combat the effects of sexism and misogyny. She then discusses the pros and cons of gender eliminationism. In a concluding section, she outlines a third approach, called fictionalizing, in which we act in many contexts as if trans people really are members of the biological sex they identify with. Though Stock indicates her attraction to gender eliminationism, she offers the fictionalizing option as one that may be more practical, as well as more conciliatory to the interests and preferences of trans people.

⋯⋯

A mong the many divisive topics animating people these days, sex and gender are perhaps the most incendiary. This is in large part because not one but two groups feel that their political identities are at stake.

On one hand, many women feel blindsided by the argument that trans women should be considered *literal* women, and question the effect of the trans movement on female sex-based rights and protections, as they have come to define them. On the other, many trans people are aghast at what they feel are attempts to block their political advancement toward equal social and legal status. Whether the arenas of dispute are bathrooms, schools, sport, women's organizations, or parades, the emotions are intense and the arguments apparently intractable.

To understand what's at stake, it's helpful to delineate two argumentative positions at play: (1) *sex eliminationism*, which argues for the abolition of the recognition of biological sex as a meaningful category; and (2) *gender eliminationism*, which argues for the abolition of gender. As a feminist and philosopher who finds herself stuck between these two positions and their passionate advocates, I see it as a defining challenge of our complicated modern times to carve out some pragmatic middle ground: to find a narrative and set of policies protective of both the rights of trans people in a gender-conforming society, and those of females in a misogynist society. In attempting this, we should recognize that many on both sides of the dispute share at least some common ground. Specifically, they both share a deep discomfort with the sociocultural norms and stereotypes associated with being a woman or a man. I believe that this common ground may provide some basis for rapprochement.

Since a lot of skirmishes in the gender wars involve people talking past each other, we first need to pause to clarify certain terminology. We should remember that "sex" here primarily refers to a biological category and has nothing to do with sexuality (or not directly, anyway). We also need to note that "gender" has several common meanings. Often, "gender" is used, perfectly correctly, as an ordinary synonym for "sex." Equally, the terms "woman" and "man" have traditionally been treated as straightforward synonyms for "female" and "male," and all four terms have referred to sex category. But in the 1970s, as Pepperdine University philosopher Tomas Bogardus recently noted in *Quillette*, "gender" also came to refer to the social and cultural norms and stereotypes governing a particular sex category, in relation to behavior, role, mental characteristics and appearance.

There is also a third use of "gender," which is particularly prevalent in academic circles, though not more widely. This is the idea, perceptively explored by Bogardus, that "gender" should stand not only for the sociocultural norms associated with biological sex, but also that we should define the terms "woman" and "man" in terms of the sociocultural roles associated with those norms. This is a step that goes well beyond previously staked claims, which left our sex-based definitions of the terms "woman" and "man" as they were. In contrast, this move, as Bogardus makes clear, defines the very notions of womanhood and manhood, not in terms of the biological, but the sociocultural.

Some feminist philosophers use "gender," "woman" and "man" in this way. A particular riff on this move, grounded in the prior work of Andrea Dworkin and Catharine MacKinnon, is the argument that we should take a pattern of specifically *oppressive* sociocultural relations, associated with femaleness and maleness respectively, as definitive of what counts as womanhood and manhood. It seems to follow that, to be truly progressive, we should aim to eliminate womanhood and manhood altogether as meaningful categories.

Later on, I shall have mostly negative things to say about such "social-role" views of gender, as Bogardus calls them—but not yet. In the meantime, I'll use "sex" to refer to biological sex, and "gender" only to refer to the sociocultural norms and stereotypes governing biological sex. Since I disagree with the idea that the terms "woman" and "man" either do, or should, refer only to distinctive sociocultural roles, I will continue to use these two terms with their original, still-perfectly-respectable meanings, as denoting females and males, in the biological sense, respectively.

* * *

A somewhat odd aspect of this dispute is that both sides nominally tend to have at least one core belief in common. This is the thought that gender, in the sense of sociocultural norms, can be a source of harm. It harms women, who are endlessly confronted with objectifying images purporting to represent them. It harms men who feel like failures for being unable to provide for their families. It harms children who find themselves read against type, teased as "scaredy-cat" boys or "bossy" girls. It makes older women seem less authoritative and older men more so. It teaches girls to be sexually submissive, and boys to be sexually aggressive, against the better interests of both. It's a likely contributory factor to the prevalence of self-harm and anorexia in females, and of depression and suicide in males. At every turn, by way of external or internal pressures, gender can limit one's life—including in ways that go unnoticed.

No doubt, many readers disagree with a lot of this. They might argue that what I am treating here as sociocultural norms are in fact biologically produced differences. They might say that at least some gender norms conform to expectations that arise from the different forms of genetically encoded, evolutionarily developed programming contained in men and women. In either case, there's less likely to be talk about *harm*.

Even so, it's possible to coherently combine a view that some behavioral and mental characteristics are endogenously sexed and unalterable, with the view that many others are functions of environment and culture. So any differences on this score should not prevent us from joining to lament the harms caused by at least some sociocultural norms in regard to maleness and femaleness.

One group that apparently is particularly harmed by gender comprises those whose alienation from prescribed norms contributes to their feeling radically at odds with their bodies. The words we use for this distress is "gender dysphoria": strong discomfort at the sexed aspects of physiognomy, even to the point of feeling "born into the wrong body." It seems likely that gender-dysphoric people have been around for as long as gendered societies have existed. Indeed, it's tempting to speculate about a causal link between the two. In social worlds with rigid physical and mental stereotypes governing males and females, it is predictable that some people, having unconsciously internalized those stereotypes as the "right" way for males and females to be, will then look at their particular, non-stereotypical bodies or minds, and self-diagnose as internally discordant, with radicalized feelings to match. Feelings of wrongness can, in certain cases, tip over into a narrative of an outside that doesn't fully fit one's insides.

Though it's hard to pin down the reasons, the expression of gender dysphoria is on the increase. The UK Gender Identity Service, a National Health Service provider, has in the last few years seen a big rise in referrals among children, from ninety-seven in 2009–2010 to 2,519 in 2017–2018. One, though not the only, recognized therapeutic response to feelings of gender dysphoria is social transition: living as a different sex. Most trans women, trans men and so-called non-binary people have, in response to feelings of dysphoria, made the decision to live as the opposite sex, or in the case of some non-binary people, as no sex at all. Some of these people go on to procure a legal sex change. Yet neither social nor legal transition can change facts about individual sex determination and differentiation at a biological level. No surgery or hormone treatment can achieve this, either. Nevertheless, by social (or sometimes socio-legal) means—such as by adopting gendered behaviors, clothing and sometimes surgically-constructed or drug-altered appearances, culturally indicative of a particular sex (or, in the case of nonbinary people, indicative of androgyny)—these individuals can attempt to reduce the distressing mismatch they feel between how they wish to be perceived and how they are perceived, both by themselves and others.

Transition may be effective for many. And it is commonly claimed that it reduces overall suicide risk in dysphoric individuals. But it can also have severe personal costs. Where stark differences are promoted between the sexes, those perceived to sit uncomfortably between gendered worlds are vulnerable to projected ridicule, harassment or even disgust. All trans people recognized as such—whether through self-declaration or because they don't "pass"—are vulnerable in this regard. Arguably, then, gender can *doubly* harm trans people: by helping to induce their dysphoria in the first place, then punishing them for their survival strategy.

What kind of society, then, should we attempt to build, to help gender-dysphoric people? In contemporary public discussion and practice, two competing approaches can be discerned, each with different social consequences. (In what follows, I deliberately articulate extreme versions of both; in reality, of course, many on each side endorse only certain aspects and reject others, but it remains true that a significant number of people would, in each case, endorse the extreme version.)

The first approach—what I'm calling sex eliminationism—says we should remove any social practice whatsoever that would serve to differentiate trans people from those who are born into (or, if you prefer, "assigned at birth" into) their preferred (i.e., self-identified) sex category. The ideal, under this strategy, would be the seamless integration of trans women into all female social and legal categories, and trans men into corresponding male categories, without any unsought reference to either's sex category. An underlying assumption of sex eliminationism is that if we built a society that didn't recognize biological sex, the social problems faced by trans people would be minimized.

The second approach—which I call gender eliminationism—argues that we should instead get rid of gender, as that word is understood to encompass sociocultural norms and stereotypes. The ideal, under this strategy, is a world of males and females, recognized biologically as such, but with none of the prevalent stereotypes associated with those categories. This strategy, as it intersects with the issue of gender dysphoria, seeks to counter the narrative that there is a particular right or "normal" way for males and females to be, in the hope that those suffering from dysphoria will no longer feel so ill-at-ease.

Though activist groups do not, to my knowledge, use the term "sex eliminationism," this has in effect become the preferred approach of all mainstream LGBT charities and lobbying groups in western countries. Within a limited but influential sphere, the strategy has had considerable political success. Under Barack Obama in 2016, reference to "sex" as a characteristic protected under Title IX of the Education Amendments Act of 1972 was officially interpreted as a reference to "gender identity." When the UK Equalities Minister Penny Mordaunt told reporters in 2018 that "trans women are women," she was echoing the stance of the British LGBT charity Stonewall: Trans women, such groups tell us, are women in every literal sense, and anyone who disagrees should "get over it." Many public organizations in the UK have followed states such as California by making the sex one "identifies as having"—not the sex one has by birth, or even at law—the determinant of whether they may permissibly enter women-only spaces, with or without a legal sex change. This policy is known internationally as "self-ID." From prisons to youth hostels to colleges to changing rooms to swimming pools to shared train sleeper carriages to hospital wards, self-ID has become the de facto criterion of entry.

The UK government recently has come under significant pressure to use self-ID as the sole criterion required for a legal sex change—without any confirmation of surgery, medical diagnosis of dysphoria, or other substantive constraints. A vast and fractious public government consultation took place about this last year, the results of which have yet to be published. Countries that already have made self-ID a largely sufficient basis for sex change-eligibility include Canada, Ireland, Denmark, Norway and Sweden, as have New York State, California and Nevada. According to many sex eliminationists, we should make a universal practice of referring to "gender identity" instead of sex, and encode this practice in law and policy. And gender identity, in turn, means the sex with which one feels strongly aligned.

To buttress the claim that sex is not a useful category, sex eliminationists tend to emphasize the existence of differences in sexual development ("DSDs"), which characterize the relatively small group of people sometimes also known as "intersex." The appearance of DSDs is consistent with the view of many philosophers, including me, that there is no hard and fast "essence" to biological sex, at least in our everyday sense: no set of characteristics a male or female *must* have, to count as such. But competent nonessentialists don't think it follows from this that there are no real constraints on what counts as sex (or biological kinds, for that matter). Rather, as the philosopher Alison Stone has argued, the concept of biological sex is what philosophers call a "cluster concept." That is, it's determined by possession of most or all of a cluster of particular designated properties—chromosomal, gametic, hormonal and morphological—produced via endogenous biological processes. The vast majority of us have all of the designated properties for a given sex; a smaller number have most; a tiny number—much smaller than typically reported—have some of both. Perhaps this entails that sex is not a binary, or that there are more than two sexes—or perhaps not. Either way, there's no good reason to think we can coherently go from facts about proliferating material sex categories to a conclusion about the nonexistence of material sex.

A further source of support for sex eliminationism comes from poststructuralist philosophy. Biological sex, we are told by enthusiastic readers of Judith Butler, is socially constructed. This isn't just the claim that sex has social meaning, or that sex isn't a binary. It's the much more radical claim that sex is socially produced all the way down: There are no material, non-social facts underpinning our habitual division into male and female. It's easy to see how this otherwise startling claim fits nicely into a sex-eliminationist case—for if there's no such thing as material facts about sex, then all that we're left with is gender identity.

This is not a widely endorsed view—in part because, as I have just noted, there is an entirely respectable (and far less radical) alternative to this conclusion, which is that sex categories are effectively clusters of (non-social) material properties. And even if this were wrong, and it were true that sex is thoroughly socially constructed, this wouldn't support the idea that the collective social fact of sex should be ignored, politically, in favor of a subjective inner feeling of gender identity. A social fact is no less a fact for being social in character.

A final source of argumentative support for sex eliminationism is allegedly embedded in the social-role view of womanhood and manhood, as described by Bogardus, and sketched out in my introduction above. This says that—whether or not material facts about femaleness and maleness exist or not—the terms "woman" and "man" don't actually refer to those facts, but rather refer to sociocultural roles. One of the main draws of this sort of view has been its apparently "inclusive" nature: If womanhood is no longer shackled to femaleness, transwomen can be women too, at least in this sense. As Bogardus writes: "Adopting this view of sex and gender allowed the acceptance of transgender people as individuals who genuinely are the gender they take themselves to be—with, one hopes, a consequent reduction in oppression, bullying and medical pathologizing."

There are, however, several problems with the social-role view. I agree with Bogardus that, as a supposed reconstruction of our existing public concepts of *woman* and *man*, the social-role view is alien to the ordinary, non-academic manner by which people discuss and classify human beings. Some philosophers acknowledge this, explicitly arguing instead for a revisionary or "ameliorative" approach. They argue that "woman" and "man" *ideally* should refer to two social roles, as an improvement on ordinary usage, even if the ordinary terms don't do so now.

But advocates of this proposal fail to properly consider the likely negative effects of any such revision that would appear alongside any expected benefits. For many women, to have such a fundamental category as womanhood so closely tied, via definition, to a socially disadvantaged position, is offensively reductive, not to mention demoralizing. (This is especially so in relation to the version of a social-role view that explicitly identifies womanhood in terms of oppression and objectification.) This isn't, of course, to deny that oppressive social roles exist for women; it's to argue that womanhood shouldn't be defined in those terms. Moreover, social-role views arguably are just as divisive as they are inclusive, since they apparently suggest that females who don't occupy whatever social role is supposed to be normative for womanhood aren't real women.

Social-role views also fail on the narrow goal of being "inclusive" to trans people. If we are to take the concept of social role seriously, we must acknowledge that it entails complex processes of formation, starting in childhood development, and manifesting in many different facets of behavior, self-conception and one's treatment by others. They certainly cannot be easily shifted or cast off by a relatively "surface" change such as changing one's appearance or getting drugs or surgery. Many trans men retain their pre-transition social role, post-transition, as do many trans women. This is often noted wryly by old-school feminists, but is equally noted by trans activists, unhappy at the still-chafing restrictions this apparently puts upon who may count as a woman or man, and who may not.

For this reason, as Bogardus relates, some philosophers in tune with the zeitgeist recently have rejected social-role views of womanhood, and moved to accounts more firmly rooted in a subjective feeling of gender identity. As Bogardus describes, one variant of the latter makes womanhood a matter of self-identification directly; another makes womanhood a matter of feeling that the norms of womanhood apply to oneself. I share Bogardus's reservations about both of these variants. But either way, the argument here is that feelings maketh the woman; and, as with the social-role view, biological sex is firmly out of the picture as irrelevant.

The main public, non-academic driver of sex eliminationism isn't biology or philosophy. It's a political project rooted in the commendably empathic desire to make things right for vulnerable people in psychological distress; to shield them from harassment; and to provide them with an environment in which gender dysphoria is minimized. Yet a growing number of voices are pointing out that sex eliminationism is detrimental to the interests of another group, also with historical claims to vulnerability.

* * *

The main problem with sex eliminationism is that, in a nutshell, it leaves us with no adequate language to describe a politically important feature of material reality. For a range of purposes, academics and statisticians need to track actual facts about sex, as it operates across various social groups, practices and discourses. The elimination of talk of sex hampers that. To take a concrete example: current proposals to base data about the numbers of males and females in the Scottish 2021 Census directly on the basis of the individual self-identification of respondents, and even to introduce a third "non-binary" option, risk corrupting what is normally a major source of research data for academics and policy-makers about sex and related matters.

Categorizing sex is particularly important if you want to describe the effects of sexism and misogyny. Most participants in this dispute recognize, at least on paper, that sexism and misogyny exist. A major source of opposition to sex eliminationism has come from second-wave-inspired feminists, concerned about inequality predicated on sex-category membership. These feminists—of which I am one—assume that, alongside inequality based on race, class and other markers, there is a distinctive form of inequality directed at females as such, by virtue of their belonging to the category of people associated with the burden of reproduction, as well as, on average, their being the physically weaker sex. These two facts, so the story goes (a story I happen to believe), have led to the historical exploitation and oppression of females. Indeed, many harmful gender stereotypes are thought to stem indirectly from these facts.

We can see the negative effects on sex eliminationism upon data about sex, and so upon data about harm to females in a misogynist society, if we look at new practices regarding the statistical tracking of crime. Guidance offered by the UK Crown Prosecution Service, and apparently currently followed by UK police and the court system, advises that "all relevant papers regarding prosecutions involving victims . . . or defendants make reference to the correct presented gender status." Lobbying organizations such as GLAAD advise the U.S. media to report crimes by trans people in a manner consonant with the criminals' and victims' preferred self-identification. This practice thwarts the reasonable aim of getting a clear statistical picture of certain types of crime according to sex category, both in terms of perpetrators and victims. In a society where sexual assaults on females by males is apparently endemic, this aim is especially pressing.

Removing references to sex, and replacing them with self-ID, also means undermining the capacity to combat sexism, since the practice undermines special measures originally introduced to create equality of opportunity in a sexist world. To take just one example, the UK Labour Party's decision in 2018 to admit trans women as eligible for the role of Constituency Party Women's Officer—a role naturally understood as designed to facilitate equality of opportunity for females in a male-dominated organization—has resulted in at least two cases of trans women successfully obtaining the role in their respective constituencies.

There are also issues for females in relation to a policy of self-ID in certain public spaces. Sex-separated spaces are an imperfect but useful form of protection for females in places where they are vulnerable to sexual aggression and invasions of privacy, such as bathrooms, changing rooms, dormitories, refuges and prisons. Recent Freedom of Information requests reveal that in the UK, two-thirds of sexual assaults in public pools and leisure centers took place in mixed-sex or "unisex" facilities. A pre-operative trans woman prisoner, Karen White, sexually assaulted two female inmates recently whilst on remand in a British women's prison. Critics argue from such evidence that making self-ID the legitimate means of accessing women-only spaces puts females in those spaces at risk—occasionally from trans women, but also from predatory males who are not trans, but who now cannot be confidently challenged in such spaces. The inclusive language of "gender-neutrality" tends to obscure the fact that a policy of self-ID effectively makes spaces mixed-sex by stealth.

Though defenders of self-ID eagerly point to studies apparently dismissing such worries as unfounded, plenty of time is needed to see the real impact. And those with expertise in safeguarding would prefer a cautious attitude in the meantime. We also shouldn't forget that, alarmingly, it's unclear how authorities would even know about the extent of any problems, given the approach to crime recording just described.

In considering this difficult issue, we need to be aware of the fact, often glossed over or treated as heresy if mentioned, that a substantial number of trans women are pre-operative and retain natal genitalia, and that many are sexually attracted to females. The public stereotype of a trans woman as a post-operative transsexual, attracted only to males, has yet to catch up with the reality of the so-called "trans umbrella."

With respect to the point about female-attraction, critics tend to cry: "But what about lesbians in woman-only spaces"? But crucially, there's no analogous pattern of lesbian aggression here that is even remotely equivalent to background facts regarding statistical male violence patterns, generally; not to mention the average strength differentials between biological men and biological women. (Even if there were, there would be no practically available conventional means of keeping lesbians out of female-only spaces, as we already have, more or less, for males in the case of single-sex provision.)

Another important though neglected aspect of sex eliminationism is its far-reaching implications for how we categorize, and then politically protect, sexual orientation, including lesbianism. Orientation categories—heterosexuality, homosexuality and bisexuality—are normally defined in terms of: (1) the sex of the subject; and (2) the sex (or sexes) to which the subject is attracted. In the new sex-eliminationist paradigm, however, each orientation is now supposed to be defined in terms of: (1) the gender identity of the subject; and (2) the gender identity (or identities) to which the subject is attracted. Hence female-attracted trans women, and trans woman–attracted females, can be "lesbians." Male-attracted trans men, and trans man–attracted males, can be "gay men." This apparently leaves us with no linguistic resources to talk about that form of sexual orientation that continues to arouse the distinctive kind of bigotry known as homophobia. This won't cease to exist just because it's no longer talked about.

There's also a significant worry about the effect on vulnerable emerging sexualities of gay children and teens, when told by peers and lobbying organizations that trans people of the opposite sex are "lesbians" and "gay men" just like them. In most other settings, progressives would be quick to denounce the peer-pressuring of gay young people to renounce their fundamental orientation; in queer circles, matters now do not seem so clear-cut.

* * *

We now move to gender eliminationists, in whose idealized world there would be candid and unproblematic talk of sex, but there would be no gender—no behaviors stereotypically associated with being male or female at all. Gender eliminationists therefore reject the quasi-mystical notion of "gender identity." They see it as contributing to the promulgation of gender hang-ups, assuming that gender identity is in fact determined by whichever gendered stereotypes one feels fit one best. We are told of trans teenager Jazz Jennings that, "growing up, Jazz's bedroom was filled with girly things—pink bed linen, a closet filled with dresses and an ample collection of stuffed animals." We are told of British trans celebrity Munroe Bergdorf that "as a child, she would regularly steal her mum's lip gloss and wear it to school." There's nothing remotely harmful about these activities *for males*, gender eliminationists argue. What *is* harmful, however, is society agreeing that such activities are a part of what it means to be a woman or girl.

For gender eliminationists, then, a fundamental problem with sex eliminationism is its inherent conservativism. And indeed, some draw attention to the fact that many of the supposedly tell-tale signs of gender dysphoria among trans-identified children seem like stereotypes plucked out of ladies' home-furnishing magazines from the early Cold War era. Sex eliminationism appears to calcify gender, imprisoning both trans and non-trans people alike in its restrictive grip. The application of the category "cis" is thought to contribute to this phenomenon. Sex eliminationists often use the term "cis" to designate, within the otherwise supposedly unified classes of women and men, those members who don't feel challenged by the gender norms applicable to them, and therefore are not trans. Yet this seems inadequately simplistic, since many people who aren't trans still feel strong unease at the gendered constraints imposed upon them.

Gender eliminationists prefer to focus on protecting existing sex-based protections and resources, while simultaneously inhibiting the further entrenchment of gender. They protest the stratification of societies into pink and blue. They defend and celebrate gender non-conformity, whether in career or fashion choice: stay-at-home dads and men in dresses, female engineers and women in tuxes. And many of them refuse to use the preferred pronouns or category-nouns of trans people. Though this practice is widely criticized, most don't do it to be insulting. Rather, they do so as an expression of their allegiance to a philosophical position: one in which shifting one's use of pronouns and other descriptors to fit a person's gender identity, rather than their sex, contributes inadvertently to the further conservation of harmful gender norms.

The pursuit of gender eliminationism comes at an obvious cost: namely, distress caused to trans people. If successful integration is a therapeutic goal for trans people, the insistent use of sex-based pronouns, and other constant reminders of the sex they wish to forget, may seriously undermine well-being. When trans people describe themselves as living in fear, it's rarely hyperbole. These are facts to which some gender eliminationists seem either oblivious or indifferent—inexplicably, since the threat to trans people for their nonconformity is another terrible by-product of the rigidly gendered social environment that gender eliminationists decry.

The point is most starkly made in relation to policy decisions about how best to accommodate trans women in public spaces where they, too, can be vulnerable. Hardliners insist that trans women should be in male bathrooms, male hostels, male dormitories and prisons; that what happens to them there is of no concern to females, since females won't be the direct perpetrators of any subsequent harm.

A different and more general critique of gender eliminationism is whether the strategic objective of eliminating gender makes coherent sense in the light of knowledge about cognition. Increasingly, cognitive scientists are emphasizing that our brains are essentially predictive: constantly modelling on the basis of past experience, and updating the model only when incoming data doesn't match the prediction. From vision to emotion to action choices, the role of unconscious, reflexive prediction is increasingly thought to be critical to cognitive processes. This potentially includes implicit stereotypes, such as gender stereotypes. Some cognitive scientists propose that brains use stereotypes unavoidably, as part of their ordinary working, as a kind of energy-saving fast heuristic.

If this is correct, then it seems that we cannot eliminate gender completely—since there will always be some social stereotypes about the sexes that remain programmed in our minds, if only because they correspond to statistically recurrent empirical truths about biological men and women. Instead of being gender eliminationists, the most we can reasonably be, perhaps, is "gender critical": consciously critical of the particularly damaging social stereotypes we collectively uphold, aiming to replace them over time with better and more socially useful ones.

* * *

And so we are left with two factions, feeling united only by resentment. Members of each camp delight in taking the most radicalized possible example of the opposition as representative. Each thinks the other more powerful. Both are right, in a sense. Sex eliminationism as a strategy has had extraordinary success in a small but influential circle, though it remains mostly incomprehensible to the population as a whole. (Thus, those who insist on the point that trans women are biologically male are left in the surreal position of being accused of heresy in the faculty lounge and banality in the pub.) Many on both sides, meanwhile, feel scared. Females, especially survivors of sexual assault, are frightened of losing places they can go without aggressive biological males being present. Trans women feel frightened for roughly the same reason, and worry that they won't feel welcome in *any* space. Both feel as though they are losing their political identity.

Social media doesn't help, siphoning users into paranoid, angry silos. Critics of sex eliminationism are reduced by their opponents to the status of "TERF," a pejorative that stands for "trans exclusive radical feminist," whose use is habitually accompanied by sneering and sometimes threats of violence. For their part, gender eliminationists are also capable of dehumanizing and insulting language: referring to trans women as "trannies," "men in frocks," and so on. . . .

To return to my premise: It's worth remembering that both sides of this dispute are strongly uncomfortable with aspects of gender, though each has a different strategic response to the discomfort. Sex elimination-ists want to help individual people "identify out" of a particular set of gen-dered norms, by eliminating talk of sex; gender eliminationists want to get rid of the norms that cause discomfort in the first place, for everyone. Pragmatists should try to draw upon this limited common ground, constructively.

I confess that I skew to the gender-eliminationist side of the debate—or, at least, that I reject sex eliminationism as a workable or desirable strat-egy. And the proposal I offer below reflects this. But I also ask whether it is possible simultaneously to, on the one hand, act compassionately and respectfully toward trans people in a way that fits their desired self-image, and doesn't expose them to harm; while, on the other hand, avoid entrench-ing the gendered norms that harm people generally, especially females, and that may well partly cause dysphoria in the first place.

I think one important first step is to talk about an aspect of the debate that most people—especially trans advocates—would prefer to ignore, because it feels impolite. But we cannot dance around the issue if we hope to make progress.

Legally, we are where we are: People have built the fabric of their lives around the possibility of legal transition, and that legal option shouldn't be ripped away. However, in my view, we have to remain clear-eyed that legal transition is, and always was, fictional, not actual. The existence of a legal category of trans people implicitly asks people to inhabit a fiction in which trans people are actually members of another sex, even if many don't actu-ally believe these equivalences to be real (the term I use later on is "fiction-alizing"). Indeed, one of the reasons the debate over this issue seems so raw and divisive is that even the most passionate trans advocates know, on some level, that they can't get what they truly want (and never will)—which is the widespread and total acceptance, at the individual psychologi-cal level, of all trans women as full-on women and all trans men as full-on men. There are limits to what policy and language can achieve. The human brain remains a reality-based organ.

We're generally very familiar with the social practice of acting: con-sciously inhabiting a role for a limited amount of time, and living "as if" something were true. When we watch a tragedy, we might laugh, cry, and cower in fear, but we don't run onto the stage to save the protagonist. Away from the arts, knowingly engaging with and generating fictions are often a crucial part of sensitive social interaction, and of sparing the feelings of others. Reality often hurts, after all. But equally, there are contexts where reference to reality is still needed. To help her recovery, I may act as if a loved one isn't ill; but not when the doctor visits.

My critics will no doubt leap to the point that trans women, in particular, have been presented throughout history as—in philosopher Talia Mae Bettcher's words—"evil deceivers and make believers," and that my position here taps into that trope, egregiously. But that would be to miss my point. "Make-believe" has connotations of playfulness and unseriousness that fictionalizing need not share. Fictionalizing, as I've just emphasized, can be a serious and socially valuable exercise: life-saving, even. Meanwhile, as I've also stressed, a practice of fictionalizing that is known to be such, exercised within circumscribed limits, and which is compatible with truth-telling in other contexts, is by definition not deceitful, nor (obviously) is it evil.

On one reading, current attempts to suppress talk of material facts about sex by progressive institutions and academics can be read as a sympathetic attempt to bolster the fiction of actual transition: to preserve an illusion that sex-change is literally possible. In the background seems to be the assumption that to fictionalize about something successfully, you also need to fictionalize that you aren't *fictionalizing*. But that would only be true if the goal of fictionalizing was getting people to actually and permanently believe something was real. In contrast, much social fictionalizing is non-deceptive: it doesn't attempt to fully disguise its own nature. This is the kind of thing I'm suggesting we should aim for.

How should this all work in terms of policy? We should continue to grant those suffering from severe dysphoria the option of a legal sex-change in order to help them, assuming the evidence continues to show that it does indeed help. But equally, we must not detach that option from careful medical oversight and diagnosis, and proof of strong commitment from the applicants, for fear of the obvious dangers for females that such detachment would pose. Self-ID as a route to a legal sex change continues to be a terrible idea. Nor, more generally, should we lose track of the fact that sex isn't literally changed. In some cases, it is good manners to pretend that a person really has changed their sex. But this act of politeness should not be encoded in law.

As individuals and institutions, we should sympathetically encourage the voluntary use of preferred pronouns in interpersonal contexts for trans people, as a therapeutic device. But in the services of retaining a much-needed grip on reality, we must not enforce this practice, and nor should we banish reference to sex from those many discourses where we still absolutely need to discuss it. As a society, we should put resources into dedicated "third" spaces for trans people, wherever they risk harm: bathrooms, refuges, hostels, prisons. But sex-based legal protections, resources, and spaces should also be robustly maintained, wherever they are the best solution to sex-based harms. (Ironically, to date the public conversation has operated in strikingly binary fashion: *either* sex-based spaces and resources *or* trans-accommodating spaces and resources; yet we could have both).

I realize that stating things so baldly will inevitably be shocking for those whose only goal seems to be to preserve illusions in this area, both for themselves and others. Sometimes you just have to step out of the fiction for a while, and say how things really are. Too much is at stake not to. I also know that my proposal is unlikely to satisfy those at either pole of the dispute. Sex eliminationists will argue that trans people don't want others to insultingly *pretend*. Gender eliminationists will object that fictions are inherently unstable things, constantly tempting us to take them more seriously than we should. The latter point doesn't seem true; most of us can draw a clear line between fiction and reality, as long as we know it's fiction we're dealing with in the first place. Meanwhile, to the former we should say: in a case of genuinely competing interests, as this undoubtedly is, it's unreasonable to think that everyone will get exactly what they want.

One might also ask the two sides what their objection is, precisely, to engaging with fictions: not least because each side seems to be doing a good deal of rather more deceptive fictionalizing already. Effectively, many sex eliminationists pretend that sex-based harm doesn't exist; and many gender eliminationists pretend that trans-directed discrimination doesn't exist. Yet the fact is that both do. We therefore need a sensible collective approach that doesn't leave us stuck, between a damaging tendency toward reality-denial on one side, and a brutal realism destructive of good social relations on the other.

Kathleen Stock: Ignoring Differences between Men and Women Is the Wrong Way to Address Gender Dysphoria

1. What are the merits of sex eliminationism? What are its potential drawbacks?
2. What are the merits of gender eliminationism? What are its drawbacks?
3. Stock writes that "[f]or gender eliminationists, then, a fundamental problem with sex eliminationism is its inherent conservativism." What does she mean by this? Do you find her critique plausible? Why or why not?

4. Stock argues for a fictionalist approach as the best practical solution to gender dysphoria. What are the key elements of this approach? Which (if any) are most appealing? Which (if any) are least appealing?

5. Many advocates for transgender people argue that the choices of each individual as to their gender identity are decisive, in the following sense: sincerely identifying as a man makes you a man; sincerely identifying as a woman makes you a woman; identifying as neither a man nor a woman makes you gender non-binary. Do you think that such self-identification is decisive in this way? Why or why not?

49

How (Not) to Talk about, and to, Trans Women

Sophie-Grace Chappell

....

In writing about her experience as a trans woman, philosopher Sophie-Grace Chappell addresses the claim that those who were born as boys and later transition are not really women at all. Whether that claim is true depends on what one takes a woman to be. If being a woman is essentially a matter of which sex organs, hormones, and genes one has, then trans women are not fully women. If instead being a woman is primarily a matter of the gender roles one is socialized into, then it depends on how one lives. On this view, some trans women indeed qualify as women. But Chappell suggests that we instead recognize a third category, alongside cisgender men and women—that of trans women. This category, being relatively new, has not inherited the oppressive social roles that accompany the standard male/female dichotomy. Chappell thinks that viewing people like her through the lens of a non-oppressive identity might serve as a model for how to retain gender identities but shed them of their long associations with oppression.

Chappell next considers the issue of whether, by sincerely announcing that one is a woman, one thereby becomes one. Many trans advocates believe that self-identifying as a woman is sufficient for being one. Not Chappell. She argues that identifying oneself as a member of a

Sophie-Grace Chappell, "How (Not) to Talk about, and to, Trans Women," in Bob Fischer, ed., *College Ethics* 2e (Oxford University Press, 2021), pp. 238-245.

given gender (or ethnicity or citizenship) does not make you such a member; your feeling of belonging is not so powerful as to change your identity in that way.

Chappell then introduces an analogy that structures the remainder of the essay: trans women are to women as adoptive parents are to parents. The analogy isn't perfect, as Chappell admits. But she argues that it is instructive nonetheless. Though in both cases biology stands in the way of satisfying a cherished desire, we can provide social and legal recognition of adoptive parents that enable them to meaningfully fulfill the desire to raise children of their own; the same holds for trans women when it comes to their desire to live as a woman in the world.

....

How Not to Talk about Trans Women

Some people perhaps think—and certainly some people say—that "Trans women are deluded, mentally ill." Really? So what is our delusion? What is the falsehood that we irrationally believe? I don't believe falsely that I was born with a female-shaped body, or that I have one now; I am perfectly well aware that, alas, I wasn't, and alas, I don't. That's the whole point about being transgender, at least as I experience it: it's a longing to be a certain way that essentially depends for its force and tone on your own awareness that at any rate to the naked eye you *aren't* that way, and (/or) weren't born that way.

Certainly it's all rather *strange*. Trans women are not like most people, and the way they are can seem both peculiar and unfortunate to people who aren't trans. To me, frankly, it's neither. It's not peculiar, it's just my reality. And it's not unfortunate—it can be frustrating, sure, but it can also be, to reference Greta Thunberg, a kind of super-power.

But to an outside eye it can in particular seem odd, and a rather cruel stroke of luck, that trans women characteristically long desperately for what natural-born women have and take for granted, while trans men characteristically long desperately for what natural-born men have and take for granted. Apart from dressing up as a girl whenever I could get away with it, one thing I did as a small child was go round waking up moths during the daytime. After all, I reasoned, they were attracted by light. So why did they go to sleep whenever the sun came up—when what they want is light, and the sun is the biggest *light* there is? Their behavior seemed odd and kind of perverse to me. So might the wishes of trans people—always wanting, as someone might see it, to be "something other than they are."

We're odd then, we trans women. Yes. But what does that prove? It certainly doesn't prove delusion. In fact, it might prove the opposite. Because I am a trans woman, there are lots of aspects of living as a woman that I absolutely delight in (being called "Darlin'" on Dundee buses for instance, and having people assume—correctly in my case—that I'm totally, hopelessly, jaw-droppingly rubbish at DIY) that so far as I know give natural-born women no particular pleasure at all, and perhaps just rather annoy them. Maybe they're missing something. Maybe it *is* delightful to live as a woman, and I register it while they miss it. Likewise, maybe there are delights in living as a man. And perhaps not all of them were lost, when I lived that way, even on me.

Here we meet a second thing you often hear said or implied, that "Trans women are men really." What should we say about that? Some trans women want to double down, as it's now called, on the insistence that trans women are women; some people unsympathetic to or uncomprehending of trans women want to double down on the insistence that trans women are men. But why insist on the extremes? Why not take a softer and more accommodating line?

Here's what I think we should say: what Aristotle in the *Metaphysics* (and elsewhere) so often, and usually so wisely, says: "Yes in some respects; but no in others." Or as he might also say, "men" is "said numerous ways"— the term is ambiguous. That is, if by "men" you mean what are more accurately called males—i.e., humans with masculine anatomy, hormones, and genes, then certainly some trans women are males—though the ones who've had gender-reassignment surgery aren't males in two of these senses: they have feminine anatomy and hormones. But if by "men" you mean what Sally Haslanger means, namely humans who are socialized into our society's masculine gender role, then it depends how trans women live.[1] The more time a trans woman spends living in our society as a woman, the more she will be socialized as a woman, not as a man—at any rate, that's what will happen if she "passes"—i.e., if she looks enough like a natural-born woman to be unquestioningly identified as a woman by the society around her.

---

1. Sally Haslanger, "Gender and Race," *Nous* 2000, 31–55.

Of course, society might also identify her, not as a woman, nor yet as a man, but as a member of a third category: as a trans woman. That I think is what mostly happens to me; I'd love to pass, but I very rarely do. The solution to this, in my view, is just to accept it, and live in society in the gender role of trans woman. I think that's pretty much how I live. And given that this isn't Saudi Arabia, it's fine—so far.

The point about the gender role of a trans woman is that it isn't the same as either cis gender role: and so far as I can see it doesn't inherently involve oppression. The development of a trans woman gender role might even be a way of pointing forward to a state of things where we have gender roles, but *none* of them are oppressive. And to have something like such roles but without oppression, if that were possible: that would be a very good thing.

But this is probably also the place for me to push back against a view that seems quite common among trans women which I think is clearly mistaken. I call this the mistake-at-the-hospital view of transgender persons. Some trans women seem to think that they've been oppressed because when they were born the doctors in the hospital assigned them to the male gender, and that that was a clear mistake (how could it then have been a clear mistake?), which was clearly the cause of all their later woes. I don't wish to dismiss anyone's experience, but I struggle to see how this could be anyone's actual experience, as opposed to a report of their experience that they give because they think it's the report that they're expected to give because they've heard other trans women give it. (In a nice distinction from Bernard Williams, I can see how it could be what they think they think; but not how it could be what they think.[2])

Even if I speak only for myself in saying this, I'm sure that when I was born there was no mistake at the hospital: they correctly identified mine as a newborn male's body. And since that was the only question that concerned them—they weren't trying to see into the strange phantasmagorical landscape that I am pleased to call my mind—they didn't miss anything. It later on turns out (not very much later actually, but later) that I have a profound sense that my body's shape is not the one I want or feel at home in or comfortable with: I want a female body, which is not the body I was born with. That's what it is, I think, to be a trans woman: it's

---

2. Bernard Williams, *Shame and Necessity*. Berkeley, California: University of California Press, 1993, pp. 7, 91.

body dysmorphia of a profound kind. But as I say, they didn't miss this at the hospital because they weren't looking for it. To put it roughly, they were looking for sex, not for gender; and they got the sex bit entirely right.

Another thing trans women and others sometimes say: "I *identify* as transgender," or "I identify as a woman." I am puzzled by this form of words. It seems that a lot of people invest a lot of rhetorical and emotional energy in statements of identity like this one, but I have to confess that I don't always see how they are supposed to work. In normal discourse I say things like "I identify as a Lancastrian" or "I identify as a Scot" or "I identify as European" meaning that I have that identity, I am in that category, anyway, no matter what I think of it as a category—and what I'm saying by talking about identifying as it, is that this identity that I have anyway is one that matters to me. So when I say "I identify as transgender" or "I identify as a woman," perhaps I'm doing something similar: just picking out one of the categorizations that already fit me, and saying that that's one that matters. Fine so far; but now people seem to want to use such remarks as announcements, as political moves: as if making such an identification statement was self-fulfilling—as if you become (officially, publicly, politically?) transgender by saying this; and as if such a statement were the key thing that *makes* you transgender.

It's this last bit that puzzles me most. For as far as I can see, "I identify as a woman" is not a performative, like "I declare this supermarket open." Unlike the supermarket declaration, saying "I identify as a woman" (even in the right context, etc.) doesn't make it true that you *are* a woman. You may get the public status of being recognized as a woman just by saying this, but you don't get to be a woman just by saying it. On the contrary: unless you are already (in some sense) a woman, you can't say this at all. It does seem to me that there are some confusions in the recent debate in this sort of vicinity.

One other thing that people can mean by "Trans women are men really" is that trans women are *disguised* men, men *pretending* to be women. The charge of sexual predatoriness is not far away here (see below). Also close to hand is a reaction to trans women that frequently leads to violence against them. Some men find it threatening that trans women are people who present as female but have, or often have, male anatomy. Why so? Possibly because those men are insecure in their own masculinity. Either they're afraid for some reason that if they don't react violently to trans women, they'll find that they want to dress up as girls themselves. Or they're worried for some reason about the possibility that they might be sexually attracted to trans women. (To both these worries, I have to say, I'm strongly tempted to reply "What's so scary? Why not try it and see?") Or they take exception to what they see as an attempt to deceive them—the thinking is that trans women want their sexual attentions, and are trying to con them into bestowing them. I don't need to say anything to bring out what Neolithic responses these all are. Still, maybe it is better to understand these reactions, given that they regularly result in trans women's deaths.

How to Talk about Trans Women

So are trans women *really* men? Maybe we should stop thinking that there is just one answer to this that uniquely fits the contours of metaphysical reality. Maybe we should think about the contours of social reality too. Maybe we should look at it like this: Trans women/men are to women/men as adoptive parents are to parents. There are disanalogies of course, and the morality of adoption is a large issue in itself which I can't do full justice to here. Still, the analogies are, I think, important and instructive.

An adoptive parent is someone who desperately wants to be a parent but can't be one in the normal biological sense. (At any rate, usually—there are families with a mix of biological and adopted children. But here I'll focus on the commoner and simpler case.) So society has found a way for them to live the role of a parent, and to be recognized socially and legally as a parent, which kind of gets round the biological obstacle.

"Kind of": plenty of adoptive parents report an abiding regret that they aren't biological parents, and there can be problems on either side of the adoptive relationship. It is clear that the existence of adoptive relationships creates psychological difficulties, both for the parents and for the children, that would not otherwise exist. But these problems are not big enough to make adoption a net bad thing.

One reason why not is that adoptive parents are, in the nature of the case, deeply committed to parenting. Unlike some biological parents, they aren't parents by accident. (Like trans women, they treasure things that their biological counterparts often don't even notice.) And by and large—though unfortunately adoptive parents do suffer some sorts of discrimination—society recognizes and values their commitment, and accepts them for many purposes as parents like any others, though of course there are contexts (blood transfusion, organ donation, testing for inherited illness) where the fact that they're adoptive parents makes a difference.

How to Talk to Trans Women

Nobody sensible thinks that it's alright, when you find out that someone is an adoptive parent, to get in her face and shout "Biology! Science! You're running away from the facts! You're delusional! You're not a real parent!" As well as being incredibly rude and insensitive, that would be importantly false: there is a perfectly good sense in which an adoptive parent most certainly is a real parent. Yet since this aggressive accusation is also, alas, only too intelligible to the parent who is subjected to it, it would also be stamping up and down in the crassest and cruellest way on what anyone can see at once is likely to be a sore point for her. (Here I speak, I'm sorry to say, from personal experience of analogous shoutings.)

Nobody sensible thinks that it's an infraction of Jordan Peterson's or Germaine Greer's human rights, or rights of free speech, to impose on them a social, ethical, and sometimes even legal requirement that they call adoptive parents parents. (Notice how I put that: crossing this line shouldn't *always* be treated as a crime. Sometimes it's a crime, but sometimes it's just gratuitously offensive: just bad manners. And nobody sensible thinks that being rude should or even could always be a crime.)

Nobody sensible thinks that, if you refer to an adoptive parent as a non-parent, then you don't owe it to that parent, as a matter of basic courtesy, to retract, correct, and apologize.

Nobody sensible thinks that the existence of adoptive parents undermines our understanding of what it is to be a parent. On the contrary, it extends it.

Nobody sensible thinks that adoptive parents are, typically and as such, a threat to other parents. Or that they only went in for adoptive parenting as a way to get their hands on vulnerable children or vulnerable parents. Of course it's not impossible that someone who is an adoptive parent might be bad or dangerous in either or both of these ways, and of course it would then be right to protect ourselves and other potential victims from that person. But if that happened, it wouldn't throw any shade on adoptive parenthood itself, as such. (This is one of those points in discourse where we are reminded how bad humans are at risk assessment. When we just go by instinct and intuition, we consistently overestimate the probability of *sensational* risks, like nuclear disasters, and underestimate the probability of *boring* risks, like getting run over by a car.)

Nobody sensible thinks that there's automatically a problem about having adoptive parents in parents-only spaces. There might be some special spaces that should indeed be reserved for biological parents only—pre- and post-natal groups, for instance, or a group like the one that helped my wife and me when we had a still-born child in 1995.[3] We should be prepared to listen carefully and sympathetically to the case that might be made sometimes for biological-parents-only spaces. But in general, adoptive parents have similar enough concerns and interests to biological parents for it to be, in most cases, both natural and useful to include them in such spaces.

Nobody sensible thinks that adoptive parents are necessarily buying into an oppressive ideological agenda of parenthood, and, by their choice to be parents, imposing that agenda on other parents. There are oppressive ideological agendas about parenthood; of course there are. But to be an adoptive parent is not necessarily to buy into them. It might even be a way of subverting them.

Nobody sensible thinks that there's just one right way to be a good adoptive parent, any more than there is a unique right way to be a good parent in general. Though there are some things that have to be in common between all good parents, there are lots of different ways of being a good parent. The broad schema of what parenthood is, adoptive or not, is set by biology and sociology. But sociology can certainly be challenged and often should be (fighting back is called *politics*), and even biology is not always just to be accepted (fighting back is called *medicine*). Within the general role of "a good parent," there is all sorts of room and scope for creativity, self-expression, and imaginative invention and reinvention.

We don't always know, on meeting some parent, whether she is an adoptive parent or a biological parent. Often there are visible clues and giveaways, or at least we can see things that make us strongly suspect an

---

3. https://www.sands.org.uk

adoptive relationship. But in most contexts it would be rude and intrusive to ask. The implicit social convention is loud and clear: you don't ask, you wait to be told. But when we know all the facts about any parent, we know which they are, biological or adoptive, without any difficulty.

This implicit social convention is, of course, one that ramifies. It's first about adoptive parent–child relations. But secondarily it is about other things too. As Cora Diamond writes to me in a private communication, commenting on an earlier version of this essay:

> One thing that I hope you mention some time is (in addition to adoptive parenthood) adoptive brothers/sisters. My two step-grandchildren are adopted. I would be aghast if anyone asked whether they are "really brothers." There may indeed be contexts in which someone is concerned with their health, and in which the fact that they are not biologically akin is relevant. The case is somewhat different from the case you discuss, of adoptive parents. The boys never decided to be brothers, in the way adoptive parents have decided to be parents, have taken on being parents. But they may well be subjected to intrusive forms of scepticism on the part of others, in the light (for example) of their lack of resemblance.

In our society, the role of adoptive parent is almost completely uncontested. (Almost, though there can be some resistance, and it can be unreasonably hard to get into the role in the first place.) If you're an adoptive parent, you're a parent—for most purposes—and no one sensible scratches their head or clutches their brow over that, or decrees that you can't sit on school parents' councils, or sees it as somehow dangerous or threatening or undermining of "real parents" or dishonest or deceptive or delusional or a symptom of mental illness or a piece of embarrassing and pathetic public make-believe. On the contrary, people just accept you as a parent, and value your commitment to parenthood as an important contribution to the well-being of our society that you could not have made if you didn't have the psychological set-up that you do.

We can imagine adoptive parents, when talking among themselves, needing and finding a phrase for parents who aren't adoptive parents. You can see why the phrase they'd choose might not be "real parents"; that would be doing themselves down. (And you can see how that phrase might be weaponized against adoptive parents, by unkind other parents.)

Anyway, these adoptive parents might choose, for this purpose, a phrase like "biological parents." Then language use being what it is, maybe they shorten it to "bio-parents." Now in this scenario that I'm imagining—for all I know there are subcultures where it is real—two extreme stances strike me as overdone and unreasonable. One is for the adoptive parents to insist that all biological parents always call themselves bio-parents. The other is for bio-parents to take offence at ever being called bio-parents. Yet apparently both these stances are actually taken in discussions of "cis" and "trans." Here what I want to say is: Maybe we should all calm down a bit?

* * *

Maybe we could follow the philosopher Derek Parfit and say that "once we know all the facts," the further question "Are they really women/men?" is an "empty question"—akin to "How big does a hill have to be to count as a mountain?"[4] Or maybe we can say what I actually want to say, which is related to Parfit's move, but different. I want to say that the question is not *empty* at all, but it has different substantive answers for different substantive purposes. The right answer in the workplace may not be the right one in the doctor's office, which may not be the right one on Tinder. And that, provided we keep the score carefully in our language game(s), there's no reason at all why anyone should be confused about any of the semantic-logical ins and outs of "trans woman/man" any more than they are with "adoptive parent."

Sophie-Grace Chappell: How (Not) to Talk about, and to, Trans Women

1. Chappell claims that to be a trans woman is to experience "body dysmorphia of a profound kind." Explain and assess her claim here.
2. Some theorists argue that whether one qualifies as a woman depends entirely on one's biology. Others argue that it depends entirely on whether one is socialized into certain oppressive social roles. Do you find either of these views compelling? Why or why not?

---

4. See his *Reasons & Persons* (New York: Oxford University Press, 1984), circa p. 262.

3. Chappell suggests that we introduce a third gender category—that of being a trans woman—in addition to being cisgender male or cisgender female. Do you find this suggestion attractive? Why or why not?
4. Chappell argues that self-identifying as a woman is not enough to qualify one as a woman. What reasons does she offer for this view? Do you agree with her? Why or why not?
5. What do you think of the analogy that Chappell draws between being an adoptive parent and a trans woman? In what ways (if any) is it appealing? In what ways (if any) does it break down?